Keys to Successful Writing

Unlocking the Writer Within

FOURTH EDITION

Marilyn Anderson

El Camino College

PEARSON

Longman

New York • San Francisco • Boston
London • Toronto • Sydney • Tokyo • Singapore • Madrid
Mexico City • Munich • Paris • Cape Town • Hong Kong • Montreal

Acquisitions Editor: Melanie Craig
Senior Supplements Editor: Donna Campion
Media Supplements Editor: Jenna Egan
Marketing Manager: Thomas DeMarco
Production Manager: Eric Jorgensen
Project Coordination, Text Design and Electronic Page Makeup: Pre-Press Company, Inc.
Cover Design Manager: Wendy Ann Fredericks
Cover Designer: Joseph DePinho
Cover Art: Nanette Hooslag/Getty Images
Photo Researcher: Clare Maxwell
Senior Manufacturing Buyer: Alfred C. Dorsey
Printer and Binder: Courier Corporation, Westford
Cover Printer: The Lehigh Press

Please visit us at **www.ablongman.com**

ISBN 0-205-51941-5
ISBN 13 9780205519415

1 2 3 4 5 6 7 8 9 1 0—CRW—10 09 08 07

The act of writing is the act of discovering what you believe.

—David Hare

With gratitude and love I dedicate this book to the Manhattan Beach
Community Church; Daniel F. Kelly, M.D.; the UCLA Brain Injury Research
Center; El Camino College students, colleagues, and dean; dear friends; Guy
and Michelle, Lisa and Bill, Michael, Emily, Samantha, Billy;

And forever and always, Austin

Brief Contents

PART ONE

Exploring the Realm of College Reading and Writing   1

PART TWO

Exploring Development Options:
Choosing Patterns to Fit Purpose   183

PART THREE

Exploring Other Options: A Writer's Toolkit   305

PART FOUR

Exploring Other Writers: A Collection of Readings   333

PART FIVE

Editing Essays: A Concise Handbook   403

Detailed Contents

(Note: For a full list of reading selections included by subject, see Thematic Contents.)

PART ONE
Exploring the Realm of College Reading and Writing   1

PART FIVE
Editing Essays: A Concise Handbook   403

Rhetorical Contents

(Note: Some selections appear under more than one heading.)

Thematic Contents

Preface for Instructors

What led me to write this text? Observation of students in my classroom, frustration with existing texts, and discussions with colleagues who shared similar concerns gave me the desire to write a text that would meet students' complex needs. This new textbook, I decided, would:

- Entice students to participate in the community of college readers and writers;

- Familiarize students with the essay writing process, offering them plenty of practice in the skills and strategies necessary to build competency and confidence;

- Empower students to communicate clearly in written and electronic modes, both on the job and in their civic and personal lives.

The first, second, and third editions of *Keys to Successful Writing* have helped meet all these diverse needs while using a friendly and assuring tone. *Keys* addresses students not as individuals lacking in certain skills but as writers about to embark on an odyssey of self-discovery. *Keys* also provides flexibility and support to the instructor through many excellent student models and professional readings on a variety of thought-provoking topics, computer activities adaptable to the ever-changing technology on campus, and a rubric—the five "keys"—allowing relevant and clear evaluation of student writings.

Keys unlocks the composing process for students by offering practical, class-tested solutions to their problems. It also makes clear the connection between classroom assignments and workplace writing.

NEW TO THIS EDITION

Every chapter in Parts One and Two now features cross-references to applicable handbook activities, which taken in sequence permit students to complete numerous grammar and mechanics practice exercises, including paragraph and essay editing.

Throughout this edition, the coverage of audience has been expanded in relation to the "five keys" and the writing process. Each chapter includes expanded writing options, including those labeled "Film and Literature" and "Service Learning." In addition, the writing options for Part Two chapters covering two methods of essay organization feature "Challenge Options," encouraging students to use multiple rhetorical strategies in these assignments.

Expanded in Chapter 4 is the coverage of thesis statements; "Evaluating Thesis Statements" presents students with several alternative theses, explaining the strengths and weaknesses of each.

New to Chapter 5 are presentation and practice in avoiding unclear use of the pronouns "this" and "it." The chapter explains primary and secondary support, and students examine a paragraph with these support levels clearly mapped. A blank paragraph map allows students to diagram their own body paragraph based on levels of sentence specificity.

Throughout this edition, the Using the Computer sections have been updated and expanded.

Chapter 7 now features a comma rules chart that encourages students to use an acronym to memorize correct comma usage. This chapter has also been expanded to include tips and practice in eliminating wordiness. Chapter 8's new section "Use 'the Sandwich' with Quotes" offers explanation and practice in avoiding a dropped quotation and achieving smooth integration of quoted material with student essays. This chapter also features expanded coverage of paraphrase, summary, and avoidance of plagiarism, ending with a new MLA-formatted student research essay.

Chapter 13 contains a new section on logical fallacies and how to avoid them.

Part Three now features Writing about Film and Literature, which introduces students to key terms and offers questions for analyzing film, prose, and poetry. A brief fiction reading, a poem, and a student essay model are included.

Part Four readings have been updated—over one quarter of these are new to this edition. Each reading is followed by several questions on content and strategy to ensure that students understand a reading's content as well as think about why the writer uses particular tactics in his or her essay development.

FEATURES

Like the first three editions, this text continues to be practical and pedagogically sound, yet innovative. I hope that instructors and students will appreciate the traditional organization of *Keys* and the support it lends to the following dynamic features:

A Strong Process-plus-skills Orientation, in a 3-in-1 Format

Keys describes the recursive process of essay writing, offering writing instruction, a wide range of readings, and a concise handbook, all in one package.

An Appreciation of the Real-world Goals of Student Writers

Today's students face many challenges and opportunities in their course work, their career planning, and their personal lives. *Keys* is deeply concerned with making the work of the writing classroom relevant to all that today's students do. Each chapter includes photographs and profiles of students who share their essays, journals, and goals to help make the link.

Toolkit of Practical Applications

Part 3 offers specific strategies for using the five "keys" in special writing situations, from timed classroom writing to writing about film and literature to public speaking.

A Distinctive Five "Keys" Heuristic to Ease Learning and Retention

The text offers a system for teaching writing (and becoming a writer) that is easily grasped through repetition and reinforcement. The following five "keys" are defined and consistently applied to the formal elements of the writing process:

PURPOSE: The writer's primary goal in writing.

FOCUS: The writer's choice of subject and the main point the writer makes about the subject.

MATERIAL: The writer's content, including details, facts, and supporting evidence.

STRUCTURE: The writer's organization or arrangement of material to support the main point clearly and completely.

STYLE: The writer's sentence structure, sentence variety, word choice, and placement of words within sentences to present a unique piece of writing.

This class-tested set of principles helps students become better readers as well as develop their writing skills. Reviewers and instructors who have used *Keys* have responded enthusiastically to the structure and consistent application of the "keys" throughout the text, noting that the five "keys" lead to greater student writing success and ease in essay evaluation. Students affirm that the "keys" are easy to grasp and applicable to a variety of college and real-world writing situations.

An Emphasis on Using Computers

"Using the Computer" activities in each chapter show students how the computer can enhance their writing process, help them do research, and find a job. This fourth edition of *Keys* offers computer activities that go beyond enhanced typing—encouraging students to join online communities, to research areas of personal and professional interest, to report back to the class on their findings, and ultimately to use the vast resources of the Web to achieve their goals. All activities use straightforward, nontechnical language, and many are designed to be fun as well as practical.

A Wide Variety of Engaging Writing Assignments

The writing opportunities in *Keys* are geared to student sensibilities and popular culture, using interesting contemporary content as the prompt for journal writing, collaboration, critical reading, and analysis. Within each chapter, there are numerous and varied assignments that can be used to complete in-class writing, as well as complex or reflective prompts that could lead to longer essays. Each chapter has three kinds of assignments:

Options for Writing: Innovative, thoughtful, and absorbing prompts for writing compositions. These essay choices, newly expanded, build on the chapter's discussion of an aspect of the writing process or a specific pattern of development. One writing option focusing on the use of film and literature and another option using service learning are included in all of the chapters.

Some writing options ask students to respond to one of the student models or professional readings as a point of reference, some challenge students to consult an outside source or conduct an interview, and others suggest personal experience and/or the experiences of others in the class as material. All prompts have been classroom-tested. Many are collaborative.

Journal Writing: These prompts include advice on working with a journal, as well as exercises for journal writing. Both reflective and suggestive, these prompts are casual enough to allow for a wide range of student response, yet close enough to chapter content to be useful as the starting point for essay drafts.

Responding to Writing: Students learn to become critical readers as they reflect upon and write in response to a wide range of texts, from the work of other students to the essays of professional writers. Many prompts can be used for either individual or collaborative work. In the "Responding" section of each chapter, students see the "keys" at work in the writings of others, and then they are asked to apply the strategies and principles in these models to their own drafts or to the drafts of their peers.

Solid, Provocative, and Varied Readings

Keys features student and professional models of writing on issues of both contemporary and enduring interest, ranging from career planning, AIDS awareness, 9/11, and social justice to pets, roommates, and car repair. A rhetorical table of contents allows students and instructors to find readings that use specific patterns of development.

Opportunities for Critical Thinking and Collaboration

Critical thinking and reading are given extensive attention throughout *Keys*. Chapter 1, "Reading, Thinking, and Writing for College," affirms the reading/ writing connection that continues to be emphasized throughout the text. Six strategies for active reading—including previewing and annotating texts—are introduced in Chapter 1 and are stressed consistently throughout the text in examining readings, student models, and peer drafts.

Critical Thinking in Connecting Texts activities at the end of each chapter challenge students to synthesize reading from student and professional models. In this collaborative brainstorming activity, students are asked to make connections in themes, points of view, and subjects presented within each chapter and occasionally between different chapters. Critical thinking and collaborative activities are the goals here.

Collaborative Work and Peer Editing also appear frequently in the "Options for Writing" section as well as in several "Responding to Writing" sections with the inclusion of peer editing strategies and helpful peer editing worksheets.

ORGANIZATION

Recognizing the diversity of departmental and individual approaches to developmental writing, the structure of *Keys* allows for a variety of classroom, lab, and writing conference uses. Instructors can easily adapt chapters and chapter sections to course schedules, instructional emphases, and programs that vary from 10 to 18 weeks in length. In addition, instructors will appreciate the quick assessment of student in-text response and the general comprehension the book offers.

- Part 1 focuses on the reading-writing connection, the parts of the essay, and the stages of the composing process.

- Part 2 builds on this knowledge by introducing specific patterns of essay development and encouraging writers to explore these patterns in their reading and writing.

- Part 3 provides a toolkit of models and strategies for future academic and professional writing: timed in-class writing, writing about film and literature, and public speaking/public writing.

- Part 4 features a thematically organized collection of 22 readings, each accompanied by questions on content and strategy.

- Part 5, the handbook, begins with a diagnostic test, followed by an overview of basic grammar and usage. The handbook then focuses on helping students to pinpoint and solve habitual errors in grammar, usage, sentence boundaries, punctuation, mechanics, and format. Numbered practice items as well as student-generated practice paragraphs and essays for editing help students reinforce their skills.

Keys is easy to use and teach from. A **predictable organizational structure** increases familiarity from chapter to chapter. Each chapter's opening "Preview" concisely presents the strategies and content to be covered in the chapter. Following the "Characteristics" and "Guidelines" sections, each chapter's "Strategies" section applies the five "keys" to the particular structure or process under discussion. The student models early in each chapter provide a starting-off point to teach the writing process and build toward the writing assignments. A format that allows each chapter and section to stand alone enhances flexibility, and the great variety of reading and exercise options in each chapter provides instructors with multiple choices of how to adapt the text to their particular classroom needs. A glossary further assists students and instructors in locating specific content and concepts for classroom discussion and individual study. Most important, this is a text that has been written *for* the student, in language that is refreshingly accessible, honest, engaging, and clear. *Keys* takes a friendly approach toward writing and academic work, emphasizing explanation and reassurance over prescriptive formulas.

TEXT SPECIFIC SUPPLEMENTS

Instructor's Manual. The instructor's manual (0-321-49603-5) includes teaching tips, sample syllabi, and suggested answers.

THE LONGMAN DEVELOPMENTAL ENGLISH PACKAGE

Longman is pleased to offer a variety of support materials to help make teaching developmental English easier on teachers and to help students excel in their coursework. Many of our student supplements are available free or at a greatly reduced price when packaged with Keys to Successful Writing, 4e. Contact your local Longman sales representative for more information on pricing and how to create a package.

Additional Support Materials For Writing Instructors

Printed Test Bank for Developmental Writing (Instructor / 0-321-08486-1). Features more than 5,000 questions in all areas of writing, from grammar to paragraphing through essay writing, research, and documentation.

Electronic Test Bank for Developmental Writing (Instructor / CD 0-321-08117-X).   Features more than 5,000 questions in all areas of writing, from grammar to paragraphing through essay writing, research, and documentation. Instructors simply choose questions from the electronic test bank, then print out the completed test for distribution OR offer the test online.

Diagnostic and Editing Tests, 6/e (Instructor / Print ISBN 0-321-19647-3/CD ISBN: 0-321-19645-7).   This collection of diagnostic tests helps instructors assess students' competence in standard written English to determine placement or to gauge progress.

The Longman Guide to Classroom Management (Instructor / 0-321-09246-5). This guide is designed as a helpful resource for instructors who have classroom management problems. It includes helpful strategies for dealing with disruptive students in the classroom and the "do's and don'ts" of discipline.

The Longman Instructor's Planner (Instructor / 0-321-09247-3).   This planner includes weekly and monthly calendars, student attendance and grading rosters, space for contact information, Web references, an almanac, and blank pages for notes.

For Writing Students

The Longman Writer's Portfolio and Student Planner (0-321-29609-5).   This unique supplement provides students with a space to plan, think about, and present their work. In addition to the yearly planner, this portfolio includes an assessing/organizing area (including a grammar diagnostic test, a spelling quiz, and project planning worksheets), a before and during writing area (including peer review sheets, editing checklists, writing self-evaluations, and a personal editing profile), and an after-writing area (including a progress chart, a final table of contents, and a final assessment), as well as a daily planner for students including daily, weekly, and monthly calendars.

Longman English Tutor Center Access Card (VP: 0-201-71049-8 or Stand Alone: 0-201-72170-8).   Unique service offering students access to an in-house writing tutor via phone and/or email. Tutor available from 5pm-12am Sun-Thurs.

The Longman Writer's Journal, by Mimi Markus (Student / 0-321-08639-2). Provides students with their own personal space for writing and contains helpful journal writing strategies, sample journal entries by other students, and many writing prompts and topics to get students writing.

ESL Worksheets, 3/e (Student / 0-321-07765-2).   These worksheets provide ESL students with extra practice in areas they find the most troublesome. Diagnostic tests, suggested writing topics, and an answer key are included.

Peer Evaluation Manual, 7/e (Student / 0-321-01948-2).   Offers students forms for peer critiques, general guidelines, and specific forms for different stages in the writing process and for various types of papers.

Learning Together (Student / 0-673-46848-8).   This brief guide to the fundamentals of collaborative learning teaches students how to work effectively in groups.

Longman Editing Exercises (Student / 0-205-31792-8).   54 pages of paragraph editing exercises give students extra practice using grammar skills in the context of longer passages.

100 Things to Write About (Student / 0-673-98239-4).   This brief book contains over 100 individual writing assignments, on a variety of topics and in a wide range of formats, from expressive to analytical writing.

Research Navigator Guide for English, H. Eric Branscomb & Doug Gotthoffer (Student/ 0-321-20277-5).   Designed to teach students how to conduct high-quality online research and to document it properly, Research Navigator guides provide discipline-specific academic resources; in addition to helpful tips on the writing process, online research, and finding and citing valid sources. Research Navigator guides include an access code to Research Navigator™-providing access to thousands of academic journals and periodicals, the NY Times Search by Subject Archive, Link Library, Library Guides, and more.

Penguin Discount Novel Program.   In cooperation with Penguin Putnam, Inc., Longman is proud to offer a variety of Penguin paperbacks at a significant discount when packaged with any Longman title. Excellent additions to any English course, Penguin titles give students the opportunity to explore contemporary and classical fiction and drama. To review the complete list of titles available, visit the Longman-Penguin-Putnam website: http://www.ablongman.com/penguin.

The New American Webster Handy College Dictionary (Student / 0-451-18166-2).   A paperback reference text with more than 100,000 entries.

Oxford American College Dictionary (Student / 0399144153).   Drawing on Oxford's unparalleled language resources, including a 200-million-word database, this college dictionary contains more than 175,000 entries and more than 1000 illustrations, including line drawings, photographs and maps. *Available at a significant discount when packaged with a Longman textbook.*

The Oxford American Desk Dictionary and Thesaurus, 2/e (ISBN 0-425-18068-9).   From the Oxford University Press and Berkley Publishing Group comes this one-of-a-kind reference book that combines both of the essential language tools—dictionary and thesaurus—in a single, integrated A-to-Z volume. The 1,024 page book offers more than 150,000 entries, definitions, and synonyms so you can find the right word every time, as well as appendices of valuable quick-reference information including: signs and symbols, weights and measures, presidents of the U.S., U.S. states and capitals, and more.

Multimedia Offerings

Interested in incorporating online materials into your course? Longman is happy to help. Our regional technology specialists provide training on all of our multimedia offerings.

MyWritingLab (www.mywritinglab.com)

This complete online learning system is the first that will truly help students become successful writers-and therefore, successful in college and beyond.

- **A Comprehensive Writing Program:** MyWritingLab includes over 9,000 exercises in grammar, writing process, paragraph development, essay development, and research.

- **A Customized Study Plan:** Based on their text in use, students are automatically provided with a customized learning path that complements their textbook table of contents and extends textbook learning.

- **Diagnostic Testing:** MyWritingLab includes a comprehensive diagnostic test that thoroughly assesses students' skills in grammar. Based on the diagnostic test results, the students' study plan will reflect the areas where they need help the most and those areas that they have mastered.

- *Recall, Apply, and Write Exercises*: The heart of MyWritingLab is this progression of exercises within each module of the learning path. In completing the *Recall, Apply* and *Write* exercises, students move from literal (*Recall*) to critical comprehension (*Apply*) to demonstrating concepts to their own writing (*Write*).

- **Progress Tracker:** All student work in MyWritingLab is captured in the site's Progress Tracker. Students can track their own progress and instructors can track the progress of their entire class in this flexible and easy-to-use tool.

- Other resources for students in MyWritingLab: access to an interactive **Study Skills website,** access to **Research Navigator,** and a complimentary subscription to our **English Tutor Center,** which is staffed by live, college instructors.

For more information and to view a demo, go to **www.mywritinglab.com**!

STATE SPECIFIC SUPPLEMENTS

For Florida Adopters

Thinking Through the Test: A Study Guide for the Florida College Basic Skills Exit Test, by D.J. Henry (FOR FLORIDA ADOPTIONS ONLY. This workbook helps students strengthen their reading skills in preparation for the

Florida College Basic Skills Exit Test. It features both diagnostic tests to help assess areas that may need improvement and exit tests to help test skill mastery. Detailed explanatory answers have been provided for almost all of the questions. *Package item only—not available for sale.*

Available Versions:

Thinking Through the Test A Study Guide for the Florida College Basic Skills Exit Tests: Reading and Writing, with Answer Key, 3/e	0-321-38739-2
Thinking Through the Test A Study Guide for the Florida College Basic Skills Exit Tests: Reading and Writing (without Answer Key), 3/e	0-321-38740-6
Thinking Through the Test A Study Guide for the Florida College Basic Skills Exit Tests: Writing, with Answer Key, 3/e	0-321-38741-4
Thinking Through the Test A Study Guide for the Florida College Basic Skills Exit Tests: Writing (without Answer Key) 3/e	0-321-38934-4

Writing Skills Summary for the Florida State Exit Exam, by D. J. Henry (Student / 0-321-08477-2).   FOR FLORIDA ADOPTIONS ONLY. An excellent study tool for students preparing to take Florida College Basic Skills Exit Test for Writing, this laminated writing grid summarizes all the skills tested on the Exit Exam. *Package item only—not available for sale.*

CLAST Test Package, 4/e (Instructor/Print ISBN 0-321-01950-4).   These two, 40-item objective tests evaluate students' readiness for the Florida CLAST exams. Strategies for teaching CLAST preparedness are included.

For Texas Adopters

The Longman THEA Study Guide, by Jeannette Harris (Student / 0-321-27240-0).   Created specifically for students in Texas, this study guide includes straightforward explanations and numerous practice exercises to help students prepare for the reading and writing sections of THEA Test. *Package item only—not available for sale.*

TASP Test Package, 3/e (Instructor / Print ISBN 0-321-01959-8).   These 12 practice pre-tests and post-tests assess the same reading and writing skills covered in the Texas TASP examination

For New York/CUNY Adopters

Preparing for the CUNY-ACT Reading and Writing Test, edited by Patricia Licklider (Student/ 0-321-19608-2).   This booklet, prepared by reading and writing faculty from across the CUNY system, is designed to help students prepare for the CUNY-ACT exit test. It includes test-taking tips, reading passages, typical exam questions, and sample writing prompts to help students become familiar with each portion of the test.

Preface for Students

"All good writing is swimming under water and holding your breath."

—F. Scott Fitzgerald, author of *The Great Gatsby* and other novels

PERSONAL INVENTORY

If you were to answer truthfully, what would you say in response to the following set of questions:

1. Do you believe good writers are born, not made?

2. Do you enjoy personal writing?

3. Do you worry about your ability to succeed in a college writing class?

4. How long has it been since you've been in a classroom situation?

5. Was your last classroom writing experience positive, negative, or a little of both? (Explain briefly.)

6. What are two specific things you'd like to learn from this course?

HOW THIS TEXT CAN HELP YOU

No matter how you have answered these questions—regardless of your concerns, hopes, expectations, or fears upon beginning this course—rest assured that you can use *Keys to Successful Writing: Unlocking the Writer Within* to improve your skills and confidence. Just as metal keys are instruments for unlocking and opening doors, the five "keys" presented in this text will offer you access into the realm of effective college, workplace, and everyday writing. Please consider this preface your personal invitation to embark on an exciting journey of self-discovery through reading, writing, and thinking.

You may have less than pleasant memories of past classes involving writing, or you may worry that you've been "away" from classrooms or from writing assignments too long to succeed in college. Although you might not feel confident about your writing now at the beginning of your course, your careful reading and interaction with this book, its clear explanations, and its engaging writing options will enable you to succeed in this writing course.

As you watch your writing abilities increase, you will undoubtedly find that, even though you may already enjoy writing in some circumstances, you will take even more pleasure from being able to write clearly and effectively in many writing situations. As you progress in your reading and application of

Keys, you'll be gratified that the skills you've learned through study of this text will lead directly to your increased success in other college courses and on the job. Regardless of your college major or future career plans, clear writing is crucial. You'll be able to transfer the guidelines and rules from *Keys* to almost all writing situations because although every writing circumstance is unique, almost all real-world writing situations ask you to read actively, think critically, and write clearly. Your understanding of the five "keys" and your knowledge of how the composing process really works will enable you to do just that.

MARILYN ANDERSON

ACKNOWLEDGMENTS

Keys to Successful Writing: Unlocking the Writer Within would not exist without the talent and work of a large number of dedicated people. Although I'll never be able to thank them adequately, I want to acknowledge their invaluable contribution to the creation of this text.

Heartfelt thanks to all the reviewers of the first edition of this book: Kelly Belanger, Youngstown State University; Bob Brannan, Johnson County Community College; Kathleen Britton, Florence-Darlington Technical College; Alice Cleveland, College of Marin; Sally Crisp, University of Arkansas; Norma Cruz-Gonzales, San Antonio College; Scott Douglass, Chattanooga State Technical Community College; Eileen Eliot, Broward Community College; Doug Fossek, Santa Barbara City College; Joe Fulton, Dalton College; Clifford Gardiner, Augusta College; Timothy Giles, Georgia Southern University; Rima Gulshan, University of Maryland; Mary Hart, Laramie County Community College; Christine Hubbard, Tarrant County Junior College, Southeast Campus; Judy Hubbard, De Anza Community College; Lee Brewer Jones, DeKalb College; Laurie Knox, Kennesaw State College; Patricia J. McAlexander, University of Georgia; Michael McKay, Community College of Denver; Patricia Malinowski, Finger Lakes Community College; Marilyn Martin, Quinsigamond Community College; Elizabeth Meehan, San Diego City College; Tim Miank, Lansing Community College; Elizabeth Ott, El Camino College; Sylvia Pack, Weber State University; Richard Rawnsley, College of the Desert; Julie Segedy, Chabot College; Karen Standridge, Pike's Peak Community College; David Steinhart, Community College of Allegheny County; Dreama Stringer, Marshall Community College; Elaine Sundberg, Sonoma State University; Bill Sweet, Lane Community College; Carolyn Varvel, Red Rocks Community College; Martha Vertreace, Kennedy-King College; Michael Warren, Maple Woods Community College; Richard W. White, Edison Community College; and Sam Zahran, Fayetteville Technical Community College.

In addition, I am indebted to Karen Standridge not only for her review, but for her enthusiasm, her helpful comments, suggestions, and the kind sharing of her own strategies and assignments in the "Using the Computer" sections of this text.

For the second edition, I am grateful to the following reviewers: Roger Bailey, San Antonio College; Jessica Carroll, Miami-Dade Community College,

Wolfson Campus; Frank Cronin, Austin Community College; Patricia Dungan, Austin Community College; Julia Ferganchick, University of Arkansas, Little Rock; Nadine Gandia, Miami-Dade Community College, InterAmerican Campus; Susanmarie Harrington, Indiana University, Purdue University, Indianapolis; James E. Hodges, Thomas University; John Hubanks, University of Arkansas, Little Rock; Suzanne M. Kaylor, Craven Community College; Sara McKinnon, Pueblo Community College; Catherine Schaff-Stump, Kirkwood Community College; Kathryn Sheffield, Phoenix College; Patricia Wangler, University of La Verne; and Kenneth E. Wilson, Cuyahoga Community College.

For this fourth edition, I want to express appreciation to the following reviewers: Isabel Baca, El Paso Community College; Margaret Johnson, Idaho State University; Ted E. Johnston, El Paso Community College; Gregory Palmerino, Mitchell College; and Sandy Vogel, Utah Valley State College.

I am forever grateful for the privilege of working with and learning from such wonderful students. Some are still on my campus and they drop by to say "hello." Some are now studying in other colleges and universities, while still others are out in the workforce pursuing careers in various fields. These student writers had the faith in me and in this project to share their writing, their photographs, and their informal comments on writing, college, career, and personal goals. I thank them and wish them success in all their future endeavors: Robert Amerson, Sherie Amos, Emily Anderson, Jorge Arellano, Laura Ballesteros, Dawn Beverly, Rafiekki Boykin, Leilani Bryant, Bryant Burns, Ginell Cabanilla, Darlene Cabrales, Victoria Castaneda, Matt Cirillo, Dylan Covert, Patty Crippen, Douglas Cwiak, Olasumbo Davis, Carlos De Jesus, Ravinder Degun, Jinnie Delacruz, Cyrus Doherty, Letictia Elder, Desirea Espinoza, David Estrada, Margarita Figueroa, Leah Ford, Russell Fullerton, Jose Garcia, Candi German, Rachel Gibson, Yen Glassman, Brenda Grant, Shelly Grieve, Nicoll Grijalva, Preston Hollister, Daniel Hollywood, Tommy Honjo, Peter Huang, Elias Kary, Frederick Kessee, Charles Kim, Edwin Ksiezopolski, Sandra Lee, Joel Lopez, Jessica Madrid, Cenovio Maeda, Lucy Mardirossian, Cinthya Martinez, Shawn Marzulli, Deanna McAmis, Greg McMillan, Dax Mears, Brent Monicello, Brian Morton, Rebecca Obidi, Chuks Ofoegbu, Taiwo Olukunle, Grethel Peralta, Swarupa Reddy, David Redmond, Greg Reilly, Corona Reynolds, Laura Rezende, Courtney Risdon, Vanessa Rivas, Sam Roham, Keith Seigman, Cindy Sharp, Charles Singson, Jeremy Smith, In Sung Song, Erika Staggers, Carmen Tull, Tori Ueda, Janet Vidaurre, Brian Villapudua, Mitchell Wexler, Monifa Winston, and Azucena Zepeda.

My foremost note of gratitude goes to Wendy Wright who designed the splendid diagram for the composing process that appears in Chapter 2. Thanks to Elizabeth Ott, another office mate, who bravely volunteered to use the manuscript in her classroom and offered excellent feedback in the form of a daily journal.

My gratitude also goes to Alice Grigsby, El Camino College reference librarian, who put on her supersleuth hat and tracked down several sources for me.

I want to thank the tutors I continue to work with in many English A classes while various editions of the book are being tested. These people—talented teachers and writers—have been through trial-and-error with me to discover what works and what does not in the classroom and in the writing conference scenario. They deserve a round of applause: Martin Addleman, Lynn Johnson, Susan Mrazek, Sean Patrick, Kim Runkle, Beth Shibata, Mark Sundeen, and Judy Sunderland.

A special note of gratitude goes to Barbara Budrovich, Writing Center Coordinator, for lending me textbooks on several occasions, for having such wonderful support staff, and for the terrific resource and backup support the Writing Center offers to students on our campus. Thanks go also to the Special Resource Center and to the Learning Resource Center.

My gratitude to Dean Tom Lew, who over the years has continued to inspire me with his calm intelligence, his dedication, and his love of the humanities.

I don't really know if many textbook authors establish such a solid e-mail relationship with their editors, but everyone I have worked with at Longman has put up with my many e-mail queries and comments. Looking back, I have been graced with what I am sure many textbook writers envy: people who share my vision and want to see it unfold clearly. I thank everyone at Longman for unlocking the writer within me.

MARILYN ANDERSON

PART ONE

Exploring the Realm of College Reading and Writing

Chapter 1

Reading, Thinking, and Writing for College

Like writers, readers plan by determining their purposes for reading a text, assessing what they know about the topic, focusing their goals and topics, and questioning themselves.

—Robert Tiemey and P. David Pearson, "Toward a Composing Model of Reading"

Preview

In this chapter you will learn

- Why we read
- What is meant by a writer's audience
- How to recognize the five "keys"—PURPOSE, FOCUS, MATERIAL, STRUCTURE, and STYLE
- How to use the five keys in active reading, critical thinking, and effective writing
- How to take notes in the classroom
- How to keep a reading log
- The advantages of computer use for college reading and writing

After reading this chapter and completing its practice activities, you will be equipped to tackle college texts and respond to their ideas in your writing.

THE READING/WRITING CONNECTION

The news is out—national studies as well as countless experiences in classrooms prove beyond all doubt that active readers are better writers. When you read well and often, you absorb new ideas, information, and vocabulary. In addition, you think about these ideas, questioning and challenging them with ideas and information of your own. Thanks to active reading, you end up with a wealth of material for writing.

Still, many college students lack confidence in their reading and writing. Even professional writers lack this confidence. Jane Smiley, Pulitzer Prize winner for her novel *A Thousand Acres*, confides, "I am not a good reader. I am slow and not very determined. I never make myself read a book to the end if I get bored in the middle." Clues to our attitudes about reading and writing may be related to *why* we read and how.

Why We Read

Think back to what you have read most eagerly and easily—chances are that your interest in the material motivated you to continue reading. And because no two people have identical interests, this motivation varies tremendously. One student reports that she reads her friend's letters because they "make me feel good about myself"; another student confides that he finished an entire article at a grocery checkout stand because "this mega rap star and I come from similar backgrounds and have faced the same obstacles as young inner-city African-American males." Your purpose in reading may be one or more of the following:

- **To be emotionally moved**
  A student asserts, "I enjoy reading mysteries because they make my imagination run wild. I imagine myself putting on a long black coat and hat and turning into a sly detective."

- **To be informed**
  Another student reports, "I like to read *Time* and *Popular Mechanics* because these magazines have short articles informing me of science innovations."

- **To be persuaded**
  According to this student, "Reading *Chicken Soup for the Soul* persuades me that I can do anything I put my mind to."

Practice 1.1   Take a moment to think about what you have read in the past few weeks. Don't exclude any type of printed or electronic material. On a piece of paper, record the last work you remember reading, and then try to explain in a few words why you were motivated to continue reading. ❏

CHARACTERISTICS OF SUCCESSFUL COLLEGE WRITERS AND READERS

Although you probably enjoy reading about subjects of personal interest, you may not feel the same about your college textbooks. They may be more demanding, and as a result, you may not be as willing, eager, or alert an audience. In the world of reading and writing, an **audience** refers to the people who read a writer's words on paper or on a computer screen. For one thing, the sheer size of many college texts may be intimidating. In addition, college texts often require greater concentration and effort on your part because of the complex material, technical terms, unfamiliar words, and new concepts they contain. You may be motivated not by personal interest but by a different motive instead: The text is required reading. If, however, you examine the habits of successful college writers, you can identify three strategies they use in making the reading/writing connection: (1) they read actively, (2) they think critically, and (3) they employ helpful keys in both reading and writing.

To see how a writer uses these three strategies, read the following essay.

LET'S TELL THE STORY OF ALL AMERICA'S CULTURES

Ji-Yeon Mary Yufill

1   I grew up hearing, seeing and almost believing that America was white—albeit with a little black tinge here and there—and that white was best.

2   The white people were everywhere in my 1970s Chicago childhood: Founding Fathers, Lewis and Clark, Lincoln, Daniel Boone, Carnegie, presidents, explorers and industrialists galore. The only black people were slaves. The only Indians were scalpers.

3   I never heard one word about how Benjamin Franklin was so impressed by the Iroquois federation of nations that he adapted that model into our system of state and federal government. Or that the Indian tribes were systematically betrayed and massacred by a greedy young nation that stole their land and called it the United States.

4   I never heard one word about how Asian immigrants were among the first to turn California's desert into fields of plenty. Or about Chinese immigrant Ah Bing, who bred the cherry now on sale in groceries across the nation. Or that plantation owners in Hawaii imported labor from China, Japan, Korea and the Philippines to work the sugar cane fields. I never learned that Asian immigrants were the only immigrants denied U.S. citizenship, even though they served honorably in World War I. All the immigrants in my textbook were white.

5   I never learned about Frederick Douglass, the runaway slave who became a leading abolitionist and statesman, or about black scholar W. E. B. Du Bois. I never learned that black people rose up in arms against slavery. Nat Turner wasn't one of the heroes in my childhood history class.

6   I never learned that the American Southwest and California were already settled by Mexicans when they were annexed after the Mexican-American War. I never learned that Mexico once had a problem keeping land-hungry white men on the U.S. side of the border.

7   So when other children called me a slant-eyed chink and told me to go back where I came from, I was ready to believe that I wasn't really an American because I wasn't white.

8   America's bittersweet legacy of struggling and failing and getting another step closer to democratic ideals of liberty and equality and justice for all wasn't for the likes of me, an immigrant child from Korea. The history books said so.

9   Well, the history books were wrong.

10   Educators around the country are finally realizing what I realized as a teenager in the library, looking up the history I wasn't getting in school. America is a multicultural nation, composed of many people with varying histories and varying traditions who have little in common except their humanity, a belief in democracy and a desire for freedom.

11   America changed them, but they changed America too.

12   A committee of scholars and teachers gathered by the New York State Department of Education recognizes this in their recent report, "One Nation, Many Peoples: A Declaration of Cultural Interdependence."

13   They recommend that public schools provide a "multicultural education, anchored to the shared principles of a liberal democracy."

14   What that means, according to the report, is recognizing that America was shaped and continues to be shaped by people of diverse backgrounds. It calls for students to be taught that history is an ongoing process of discovery and interpretation of the past, and that there is more than one way of viewing the world.

15   Thus, the westward migration of white Americans is not just a heroic settling of an untamed wild, but also the conquest of indigenous peoples. Immigrants were not just white, but Asian as well. Blacks were not merely passive slaves freed by northern whites, but active fighters for their own liberation.

16   In particular, according to the report, the curriculum should help children "to assess critically the reasons for the inconsistencies between the ideals of the U.S. and social realities. It should provide information and intellectual tools that can permit them to contribute to bringing reality closer to the ideals."

17   In other words, show children the good with the bad, and give them the skills to help improve their country. What could be more patriotic?

18   Several dissenting members of the New York committee publicly worry that America will splinter into ethnic fragments if this multicultural curriculum is adopted. They argue that the committee's report puts the focus on ethnicity at the expense of national unity.

19   But downplaying ethnicity will not bolster national unity. The history of America is the story of how and why people from all over the world came to the United States, and how in struggling to make a better life for themselves, they changed each other, they changed the country, and they all came to call themselves Americans.

20   *E pluribus unum.* Out of many, one.

21   This is why I, with my Korean background, and my childhood tormentors, with their lost-in-the-mist-of-time European backgrounds, are all Americans.

22   It is the unique beauty of this country. It is high time we let all our children gaze upon it.

Notice that Yufill connects her reading to her writing by using the following strategies:

- **Active reading**
  Paragraphs 1 through 6 reveal that in reading her textbooks, Yufill remained alert and involved with her subjects, for she offers specific examples, including Lincoln, Lewis and Clark, Benjamin Franklin, and Carnegie. Yufill began to question certain statements that she read: "the only black people were slaves," "the only Indians were scalpers," and "all the immigrants . . . were white."

- **Critical thinking**
  Yufill analyzed what she had read in her history books. After a time of acceptance, as a teenager she evaluated her reading and its sources, and she concluded that "the history books were wrong." This evaluative step in her critical thinking led Yufill to read further, to look up "the history I wasn't getting in school." Later in her essay, in paragraphs 12 through 18, Yufill demonstrates her critical thinking skills again: after reading the

New York State Department of Education report, Yufill analyzed, summarized, and evaluated it for herself and, later, for her reading audience.

- **Tools to connect reading and writing**
Only after engaging in active reading and critical thinking did Yufill begin to think of writing an essay. When she did write, she used a set of tools, or "keys," to help her evaluate and develop her own writing.

You can first identify and then employ guidelines for active reading, critical thinking, and effective writing.

GUIDELINES FOR BEING AN ACTIVE READING AUDIENCE

When you engage in **active reading,** you respond in much the same way you might react while sitting in a movie theater, a concert hall, or a sports stadium: You react to everything you see. You are constantly questioning and responding to what you're reading. To be an active reader, you need to ask yourself periodically how you feel or think about what you're reading. "Aha," you say. "But how do I remain connected to material that might not interest me? What if I'm confused from the beginning about what's on the page?" The following are six strategies for becoming a participatory member of an active reading audience.

Strategies for Active Reading

- Preview the reading.

- Use a dictionary and contextual definitions.

- Annotate your text.

- Summarize what you have read.

- Respond in a journal.

- Use critical thinking to evaluate what you have read.

Preview the Reading

To **preview** a reading, look at the chapter titles and section headings printed in larger lettering or in bold type. These will give you a good idea of all the topics to be discussed in the chapter. (You will notice that this book contains a "Preview" section at the beginning of every chapter.) Then, for a reading assigned within a chapter, examine any background information on the author, look closely at the title, and flip the pages quickly to the end to get an idea of the length and complexity of the reading. Previewing the entire reading by skimming it quickly will give you a better idea of how challenging your reading assignment will be. For example, if you see that the article has long paragraphs, statistics, or charts, you might schedule more time for your reading. If, on the other hand, your previewing reveals that the article has short paragraphs and few technical terms, you can plan to spend less time and perhaps less effort on active reading.

In addition to giving you an edge on your reading assignment, previewing may help you discover important clues about a writer's subject and **point of view,** or attitude, regarding the subject. These clues will help you in active reading, giving you added insight into whether a particular writer is qualified to address the issue or if the writer is biased.

Practice 1.2   To test the value of previewing, take a look at the following background information and titles and see if you can figure out the author's point of view toward the subject. The first example has been done for you.

Point of View about Subject

1. "Sex, Lies, and Advertising"   *advertising is deceitful*

2. "The Woes of a Waitress"

3. Author is an environmentalist and the subject is our national parklands.

4. "Crime Is the Basic Problem, Not Guns"

(For additional information on point of view, see page 191 in Chapter 9 and page 241 in Chapter 11.) ❏

Use Dictionary Definitions and Contextual Definitions

To increase your understanding of the material you are reading, keep a good college-level dictionary close at hand and use it to look up words that you don't know. You'll be amazed at your increasing retention of information and also at your growing vocabulary.

If you don't have a dictionary handy or you don't have time to look up all unknown words, try to determine the meaning of a word from the **context** of the passage. Look at the words and sentences both before and after the unfamiliar word to reach a contextual definition.

Practice 1.3   Return to the essay "Let's Tell the Story of All America's Cultures" (pp. 4–5). Find the words *tinge* in paragraph 1 and *galore* in paragraph 2. See if you can come up with a contextual definition for both words. Circle the words and then write your definitions in the margins of the essay. ❏

Annotate

When you **annotate,** you mark up or highlight the reading, and you make notes in the margins of your text. You can annotate in a number of ways: You can ask questions, underline important points, insert definitions, or indicate with notes your agreement or disagreement with the author. Here is a student's annotated copy of a college text used in a physics course:

When scientists are trying to understand a particular set of ⟨phenomena⟩ they often make use of a **model**. A model, in the scientist's sense, is a kind of ⟨analogy⟩ or mental image of the phenomena in terms of something we are familiar with. One example is the wave model of light. We cannot see waves of light as we can water waves; but it is valuable to think of light as if it were made up of waves because experiments indicate that light behaves in many respects as water waves do.

like from everyday life?

having peaks? how?

PHENOMENA events that can be described

ANALOGY similarity

—Giancoli, Douglas C. From *Physics: Principles W/Applications* 4/E by Giancoli © 1995
Reprinted by permission of Prentice-Hall, Inc. Upper Saddle River, N.J.

Practice 1.4 To test your annotation skills, try to annotate the following paragraphs, which come immediately after the sample you just read.

The purpose of a model is to give us a mental or visual picture—something to hold onto—when we cannot see what actually is happening. Models often give us a deeper understanding: The analogy to a known system (for instance, water waves in the above example) can suggest new experiments to perform and can provide ideas about what other related phenomena might occur.

No model is ever perfect, and scientists are constantly trying to refine their models or to think up new ones when the old ones do not seem adequate. The atomic model of matter has gone through many refinements. At one time or another, atoms were imagined to be tiny spheres with hooks on them (to explain chemical bonding), or tiny billiard balls continually bouncing against each other. More recently, "the planetary model" of the atom visualized the atom as a nucleus with electrons revolving around it, just as the planets revolve about the Sun. Yet this model too is oversimplified and fails crucial tests.   ❏

Summarize

Summarizing what you read is another way to read actively. A **summary** is a statement of the main points or the most important ideas of the text. When you write a summary, you use your own words to create a much more condensed version of the original. Here's an illustration: Before you arrive on campus each day, you complete any number of chores and activities; if you were asked to recount these in detail, you might write from one to several pages. However, you could summarize by omitting all details and grouping information into two or three broad categories to give your reader the general idea: "Today, I dressed, ate breakfast, gathered my supplies together, and left for school." Notice that the example omits information on the kind of cereal eaten for breakfast and the exact content of "supplies."

Summaries are good tests of whether you understand what you are reading. If you cannot easily write a summary, you need to go back, reread more carefully, and possibly engage in more annotating. To examine summary writing more closely, look back at the first paragraph from the physics text in the previous section. As you read the following summary of this paragraph, notice that the summary is written in the writer's own words, using no passages from the original text. It is substantially more condensed than the original, and it omits details, presenting instead only the most important ideas.

Models help scientists to understand events because models compare scientific events to happenings we do understand already.

Practice 1.5   Review the second and third paragraphs from the same physics text (in Practice 1.4, page 8) and write a summary on a separate sheet of paper.   ❑

Respond in a Journal

Responding to your reading in a journal, or **journal writing,** is an excellent way to form a personal connection to what you have read. This active reading strategy will help you focus your thoughts and can furnish you with lots of information for future writing assignments. In fact, journal writing is so important that every chapter in this book contains a section on journals. To get started, find a notebook to suit your personal tastes (unless your instructor specifies a certain type of notebook). Consider what you write in your journal as a personal and informal record of your ideas about and reactions to what you have read. You may also want to use your journal to complain about, to question, or to ponder anything you read. No matter what format for journal writing your instructor may ask you to follow, keeping a journal can help you generate ideas for the writing assignments in this text.

To illustrate, look at this journal entry from a student who was asked by her instructor to respond in her journal to an essay about a young mother trying to attend college for the first time:

> I liked what she had to say about the problems she had. It reminded me of what I am going through. I'm learning to juggle my time between my sons and school. My eight-year-old thinks he is getting away with things. So I have to take time out to help him with his schoolwork. My three-year-old isn't hiding his feelings, and since he is still a little boy, he needs his own time and attention from me. Like the author, I may not think there is enough time in a day, but there is, and it can be done.
>
> —Erika Staggers, *student*

Practice 1.6   To get your journal started, write for five minutes about one obstacle or difficulty you have encountered while attending college.   ❑

Think Critically

You engage in **critical thinking** when you carefully probe or inspect what you read. The word *critical* used with *thinking* doesn't refer to negative thinking or finding fault with something, as when someone is *critical* of the way you look or act. Instead, critical thinking refers to thinking beyond what is obvious—to reading "between the lines." You probably do this kind of thinking every day. For example, suppose you have just finished interviewing for a job and the interviewer gestures to the exit door with the words, "We'll be getting back to you, but I want you to know that the competition for this job is tremendous." You read between the lines that your chances of getting that job are probably less than if the interviewer personally escorts you to the door with these slightly different words: "We'll be getting back to you, but I want to tell you how impressed I am with your resume."

If you think about it, every time you hear someone speak, you're taking in not only the words but also the speaker's tone and body language. To become a successful college student, you need to transfer these critical thinking skills to your reading of college textbooks. And because you can't see the writer when you are reading, you need to examine closely every new thought, phrase, and word on the page. To be a critical thinker, follow these steps:

1. **Analyze a reading by breaking it down into smaller parts.**
   To illustrate, if you're asked to read a ten-page article for psychology class, try to break it into logical sections or idea chunks. Then take each chunk and consider it separately.

2. **Summarize the main point—the most important idea—of the reading.**
   Now that you've had a chance to practice summarizing, continue to ask yourself after every reading, "How would I state the main point in one sentence?"

3. **Evaluate the reading based on your analysis.**
   When you evaluate, ask yourself, "How do I feel about what I've read? Do I agree or disagree?" Think of the last movie you saw or book you read. Did you like it? Did you ask yourself "why" or "why not"? Did you share your reaction with a friend? Were you surprised to find that your friend's reaction was different?

In order to think critically about what you are reading, you need to go beyond understanding the main points and summarizing. You need to read between the lines so that you can then decide if you agree or disagree with what you have read.

To get a better idea of the critical thinking process, take a third look at the paragraphs from the physics text (p. 8). You previously analyzed the writer's content by examining each paragraph separately. You completed the second step in critical thinking when you summarized the writing. Now, after rereading the text excerpts and the student summary, ask yourself, "What does the writer want the reader to think?" Take the last critical thinking step by asking yourself, "Do I agree with the paragraphs? Why or why not?"

Practice 1.7   Write a brief evaluation of the paragraphs from the physics text (p. 8).   ❏

If you continue to work on the steps involved in active reading and critical thinking, you'll be rewarded with a better understanding rather than being confused by what you read. Finally, mastering the process of critical thinking will allow you to participate thoughtfully in writings, discussions, and public forums in your college, career, and community life.

GUIDELINES FOR NOTE-TAKING IN THE CLASSROOM

In this class, as well as all of your other college classes, you will want to listen to your instructor carefully and learn to take notes on what is being said as well as written on the board or shown on the overhead projector. These notes can be a roadmap back to important facts, topics, and concepts covered in your courses. The following strategies will help you develop your note-taking skills:

Strategies for Effective Note-taking

- Use a notebook that holds three-holed paper—this will let you more easily insert handouts and also rearrange and reread your notes over the course of the semester.
- Try to sit near the front and center of the class so that you can see the board easily and remain connected with your instructor.
- Be sure to include a date and subject heading for all your notes.
- Try to attend all your classes—you'll be amazed at how much material you can learn just from being there, listening carefully, and jotting down important points.
- Read the assigned material in your text so this background information will allow you to understand the lecture or discussion more clearly.
- Don't try to write down absolutely everything your professor says—this would take so much time as to be almost impossible. Instead, listen for what is important.
- Learn to recognize what's important enough to note by listening for the following clues: Your teacher tells you it's important, pauses before or after a statement, speaks more slowly or more loudly, repeats an idea or point, writes on the board, spends a certain period of time going over a particular idea, and uses key words such as "importantly," "especially," "notably," or "significantly."
- Use abbreviations.
- Translate ideas into your own words whenever possible; you will remember your words more easily.
- Don't worry about grammar and spelling since these notes are for your eyes only.
- Try to keep your notes legible; remember that you want to be able to read them again later.

For useful abbreviations in your note-taking, see http://www.arc.sbc.edu/notes.html or http://sas.calpoly.edu/asc/ssl/notetaking.systems.html.

GUIDELINES FOR CONNECTING READING AND WRITING

So far in this chapter, the focus has been on reading, thinking, listening, and the **private writing** you engage in to be an active reader. Private writing includes annotating, summarizing, and responding in a journal; it is not meant to be shared with a reading audience and is for your own use only, unless your instructor asks to see it. But your success as a writer in college and in your career will depend on your ability to compose **public writing**—the college essays, memos, reports, business letters, and other kinds of writing meant to be read by a specific audience. (For more information on public writing as well as additional public writing options, see Unit 3, pp. 328–330.)

To help you connect your reading and thinking about the writings of others with the public writing you'll be doing, this text offers you a set of principles called *keys*—the tools you can use to examine and evaluate what you read, and later what you write. Much as a carpenter uses a hammer, saw, and nails to build a sturdy house, you will be using the following five keys to build your confidence and ability as a college reader, critical thinker, and writer: PURPOSE, FOCUS, MATERIAL, STRUCTURE, and STYLE. This chapter introduces and briefly defines these keys, but in future chapters you'll be examining them in greater detail. In the same way you check your pockets or purse to make sure you have your house keys or car keys, get in the habit of mentally reviewing these five keys whenever you read the writings of others or engage in public writing.

Purpose

Your reading **audience** is composed of people who will respond to your (printed or electronic) words in much the same way that an audience sits in a darkened movie theater or concert hall and responds to the performance (see the figure below).

Know Your Audience and Purpose

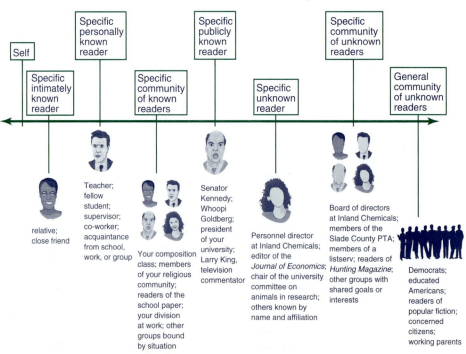

The primary goal is a writer's **purpose.** As a writer, you will want to address a specific audience and do one or more of the following:

- Express

- Inform

- Persuade

Although a writer often has more than one purpose, only one should stand out as primary, or most important, for any piece of writing.

If you're writing a letter to complain about faulty merchandise you've purchased, you're certainly expressing yourself (and your irritation, perhaps!); you're informing your audience (in this case the company that sold you the product); but above all, you want to persuade this audience to offer you a refund.

Practice 1.8   Reread Yufill's essay beginning on page 4. Identify the writer's primary purpose. Who do you think her intended audience was? Support your answer by stating why. ❑

Focus

Focus refers to a writer's choice of a subject and the main point the writer is making about that subject. Let's take that same complaint letter. Your subject is a household appliance you recently bought, and the controlling idea is your opinion that the appliance did not perform as you expected.

Practice 1.9   Review Yufill's essay again, this time searching the writing for its subject and main point. State Yufill's focus in your own words. ❑

Material

Material refers to the content of a piece of writing and may include details, facts, and supporting evidence. A writer can draw material from a variety of sources: personal experience, observation, imagination, interviews, outside readings, or research. For instance, your letter of complaint should mention every detail and fact that will persuade your audience: the date you bought the appliance, the nature of your conversation with the salesperson, how many times you've used the merchandise, and any other information that will convince your audience that you should get a refund.

Practice 1.10   Scan Yufill's essay, this time noting three or more examples of the material that this writer uses. ❑

Structure

The **structure** of a text is the writer's arrangement of the material to support the main point clearly and completely. For instance, when you sit down to put all your evidence about your kitchen appliance in your letter, you will decide which details to put first, second, third, and so forth. At some point you'll come up with a logical way of ordering all the information clearly so that your audience is never confused.

Practice 1.11   Return to Yufill's essay, this time focusing on the writer's "ordering" of material. Make a brief list of this order.   ❑

Style

The **style** involves three separate parts:

- First, style refers to the way a writer puts words together to form sentences and then groups of sentences to form longer passages. Your style communicates your own unique signature. For example, once you've sketched out the information you want to include in your letter and you have an idea of the organization you want to use, you need to think about those specific words and phrases that would be most effective in getting your point across.

- Second, style refers to the "correctness" of a piece of writing. To illustrate, before you mail your complaint letter, you'll want to **proofread,** or check to see that you've used complete sentences as well as grammatically correct constructions, punctuation, and spelling. For help with proofreading for correctness, consult the handbook section of this text (pp. 403–480).

- Third, style involves conforming to format, or the proper appearance of a piece of finished writing. For instance, in the case of your letter, you should check for appropriate margins, tabs, and spacing.

Grammar Key

Editing Essays: Handbook Practice

Give yourself the Diagnostic Test beginning on page 405. After your instructor has shared with you the correct answers, complete the "Diagnostic Test Error Analysis Chart" on pages 417–418.

Practice 1.12   Reread Yufill's essay, focusing this time on her sentence structure, variety, and word choice. Write down one or two memorable phrases or sentences and try to explain briefly why you chose them.   ❑

To observe how all five "keys" come together to connect writer with reader, examine the following complaint letter—a letter written about a frustrating experience with faulty merchandise. Like many college students faced with writing assignments, you might say to yourself, "I know what I want to say. I just have trouble making my reader understand." However, if you were to use the five "keys" to unlock a method for getting these ideas on paper and communicating them clearly to your intended audience, the following letter might result.

MODEL WITH KEY QUESTIONS

When Matt Cirillo and Cindy Sharp purchased a coffeemaker that proved defective, they called the store. The customer service representative asked them to write a complaint letter and send it to the store's office.

A LETTER OF COMPLAINT

Matt Cirillo and Cindy Sharp

Matt Cirillo and Cindy Sharp are roommates who wanted to voice their disappointment with a product they had recently purchased. They found that getting their ideas on paper was easier than they had thought it would be and that collaborating on their writing was fun. Matt has plans to become a computer animator, and Cindy hopes to become a teacher for the deaf.

January 29, 2006

Dear Customer Service Representative:

1   We believe we are valued customers of yours. Both of us have purchased items from your department store in the past. We want to tell you about some faulty merchandise we recently bought from you in the hope that you will grant us a refund of our money or a cash credit.

2   Two weeks ago, January 15, we purchased from Rick, a salesperson on your staff, a Wilson coffeemaker, Model XJ. When we told Rick that we were searching for a fairly inexpensive yet dependable coffeemaker, he suggested several possible brands and models, describing the features of each. We decided on the Wilson coffeemaker even though it was a little more expensive—we really liked the automatic timer feature since this would allow us to "program" our coffeemaker the night before to brew at a particular time early the next morning. We paid with a credit card and happily took our new kitchen appliance home.

3   We were quite excited to test out our new coffeemaker, so that same evening we set the automatic timer, carefully following the instructions in the manual. Unfortunately, this feature did not work. When we came into the kitchen early the following morning, there was no fresh brewed coffee but instead an empty glass coffeepot. Not giving up, we made the coffee without the automatic timer, and the machine worked well.

4   Since that first day, we have each reread the manual several times, checking to make sure we were following directions. The results have been the same: We have never been able to get the automatic timer feature to work for us. Although the coffeemaker works fine otherwise, we had looked forward to this feature and had been willing to spend more to get it. Because the automatic timer does not seem to work with this particular machine, we'd rather have a cheaper model.

5   We would appreciate it if you would consider our request for a refund or credit. To expedite this process, we're enclosing in this letter the credit card receipt and our home and work phone numbers.

Sincerely,

Matt Cirillo
Cindy Sharp   ○

Now take a look at the following set of "key" questions to go with the letter you've just read. These are similar to questions you'll encounter throughout this text after each student writing sample. The "key" questions challenge you to analyze and evaluate what you've read by examining the five "keys"—PURPOSE, FOCUS, MATERIAL, STRUCTURE, and STYLE—to decide whether the writers have effectively communicated with their audience. In the course of your close examination of all student and professional writings in this text, use the "keys" to discover what strategies writers use for particular situations. In the process of reading the writing of others, you'll discover what does and doesn't work for writers. Then when you turn to your own writing assignments, you'll have practice and confidence in using the "keys" as your tools for successful writing.

Key Questions

1. **Purpose**   Where in the letter do the writers state the primary goal or aim of the writing? Who is Cirillo and Sharp's audience?
2. **Focus**   Can you state in your own words the subject and main point about that subject the writers are making?
3. **Material**   What kinds of information or detail do the writers offer?
4. **Structure**   Can you explain how the letter is organized?
5. **Style**   Write down any words or phrases that stand out as especially effective in getting the writers' primary goal across.

As you work through the reading and writing assignments in this text, remember that every writer presented here faced a blank page at one time. These writers had to decide on their primary purpose, and determine how to focus on a subject and stay focused. They also had to decide what details, facts, and other material to use, and how to organize this material effectively. Finally, they had to decide which specific language and format would get their point and purpose across most successfully. Also remember the reading/writing connection—as a college student embarking on many semesters of challenging classes, the more essays you read, analyze, discuss, and think about using the "keys," the better equipped you'll be as a thinker and a writer.

JOURNAL WRITING: THE READING LOG

Journal writing, one of the tips for active reading mentioned earlier, allows you to reflect and respond by writing about what you have read. Because journal writing is "for your eyes only" unless your instructor tells you otherwise, it can free you from worrying about your writing as a finished product.

While a journal may take many forms, creating a **reading log** will help you pinpoint meaningful passages from a reading and then question and evaluate these passages. Students who consistently keep reading logs in their journals find that they have more detailed information to share and a better understanding of the material when they are asked to complete a written assignment. In addition, these students learn more and perform at a higher level academically because their reading logs lead them to greater understanding of their textbooks and classroom lectures and activities.

1. To set up your reading log, simply make two columns by drawing a line down the middle of your paper. In the left column, record brief **direct quotes,** passages from the text copied word for word that you want to explore further, along with their page numbers. In the right column, write your reaction to the specific quote in the left column. Include here summaries, feelings, connections, evaluations, opinions, and especially, questions—any comments in your own words that will help you to "re-see" part or all of the reading. To see how a reading log might look, examine a portion of the student log shown here for a college textbook excerpt entitled "American Health, Then and Now" (pp. 372).

TEXT	REACTION
1. "Your habits matter" (30)	1. What habits do I have that could be harmful to my health?
2. "Introduction of wonder drugs" (27)	2. Ask instructor if the wonder drugs are those listed on figure 1 - insulin, sulfa, penicillin, anti-TB - or if there are others.
3. "For several years, life expectancy rates no longer improved" (27)	3. This is surprising - why not, especially with open-heart surgery, etc.?!
4. "Less fat in the diet, more exercise, and reduction in tobacco use" (27)	4. Wonder which one has the greatest impact on decline in death rates - I guess less fat, but not sure.

Read this excerpt and respond to it in your reading log. Or, if you prefer, choose a reading from one of your own college textbooks for your first reading log entry.

2. In another journal entry, explore where, how, and when you like to read and write. Do you have a special place or scheduled time? A particularly comfortable chair for reading or a favorite pen or paper for writing? Writer Louise Erdrich, well known for her novel *Love Medicine*, reports that she used to write with her free hand while holding a child in her other arm. Truman Capote, who wrote *Breakfast at Tiffany's* and *In Cold Blood*, confided that he was a "completely horizontal author," who must be lying down in order to think and write. How about you?

Using the Computer for College Reading and Writing

1. Looking for a word? Want to impress your friends with a really obscure new term? Many publishing companies and search engines have online dictionary sites that go beyond providing definitions. Some provide a "word of the day" or snippets of language history. Does your search engine have a dictionary? Use it to look up a word. Or go to **http://www.m-w.com**, the Merriam-Webster dictionary site. You can subscribe for free and receive a "word of the day" to expand your vocabulary at the following sites:

   http://dictionary.reference.com/wordoftheday/list/index.html
   http://www.oed.com/cgi/displaywotd
   http://www.wordsmith.org/awad/index.html

2. After reading this chapter's interview with Annie Dillard (pp. 20–21), find out more about this Pulitzer Prize–winning author of *Pilgrim at Tinker Creek* and other books by logging on to the following Web site:

   http://www.eartglight.org/earthsaint24.html

3. For more information on how to read and schedule your college assignments, visit this Web site:

   http://www.csuohio.edu/writingcenter/frmHandouts.html

OPTIONS FOR WRITING

Many of the following writing assignments ask you to reflect on your reading habits and write about them. As with all of the "Options for Writing" in this text, your instructor may direct you to respond to a particular one, or you may be able to choose the option that most appeals to you. When you have made your decision, take a moment to read the interview with author and writing instructor Annie Dillard (p. 20–21) to explore the way one writer gathers her material and sets about preparing to write. Notice that for Dillard, the process of writing involves active reading and critical thinking. Her writing does not happen all at once but rather is broken down into separate steps. To help you get started, the "Options for Writing" will always include a few brief tips, but don't forget that your instructor and your fellow students can be excellent sources for additional help.

1. Write a personal reading history. Some people love to read while others avoid it. How about you? You may belong to a family or culture that emphasizes oral storytelling rather than the printed text. Maybe you remember being read to as a child, or listening to stories, poems, or songs on cassette. Perhaps you now read to your own children. List on paper as many different examples of your activities relating to reading, writing, and language as you can remember. Include reading materials in your home and work environment, in both your native and nonnative

languages. One student reports, "I found out that although I dislike reading, I read every day on the job because as a doorman at a club, I have to check people's IDs." Also take notes on your attitude and that of other family members toward reading and writing. When you feel you have enough material on paper, try to arrange this information to introduce yourself and your reading history to another student or to your instructor. Use specific book and story titles that you remember.

2. Write about a particular experience with reading. Many of us can remember becoming so consumed with a particular novel, magazine article, or letter from a friend or loved one that we almost forgot time and place. Think back to such a time and then make some notes, getting down as much detail as you can remember about the event. Where were you sitting? Was anyone else in the room during this time? What was the reading material that so involved you? Do you remember the color of the book cover or the pages themselves? If it was a letter, what did the stationery look like? When you feel that you have enough detail to communicate this, arrange the details in a clear order.

3. In "Let's Tell the Story of All America's Cultures" (p. 4), Yufill mentions certain leaders she read about and others she learned about through her own research: Lewis and Clark, Abraham Lincoln, Daniel Boone, Andrew Carnegie, Benjamin Frankin, Ah Bing, Frederick Douglass, W.E.B. Du Bois, and Nat Turner. Look up any one of these leaders in an encyclopedia. Read about your subject using active reading strategies and then write a summary of what you read.

4. Read "American Health, Then and Now" (pp. 372). Imagine that your audience is a group of classmates in a health class, and write a summary of this reading to share with your class.

5. Amazon, an Internet bookseller, can be located by logging on to **http://www.amazon.com**. This site offers readers a wealth of information on books, tapes, CDs, and other materials. Log on to Amazon's Website and follow the directions for locating a favorite book of yours or a book that you've heard about. Next, read the reviewers' comments about the book. Send an e-mail message to Amazon in which you ask several questions about the book, or, if you have already read it, write a customer's review of the book and submit it to Amazon, following the site's easy directions.

6. Write about your personal reading plan. Now that you are a college student, you may notice that your textbooks are full of fairly complicated information. Complete the first journal activity on page 9. Take notes about how college has affected your reading. Ask yourself how your textbooks differ from books that you're used to reading, what information you're expected to retain from what you've read, what schedule you've made for yourself to make sure you have time to read, how you handle distractions, and which tips for active reading you currently follow and which you intend to try. When you feel you have enough information to explain your plan for successful college reading, organize this information in a logical way.

7. After taking group notes for the activity on page 22, write an essay explaining three or more misconceptions, false statements, or questionable comments that your group discussed.

8. After reviewing the letter written by Matt Cirillo and Cindy Sharp, think of a product that disappointed you or malfunctioned after you bought it. Write a complaint letter to the manufacturer or company detailing your reasons for purchasing the product, the sales transaction itself, subsequent problems, and your current expectations from the company.

9. *(Film and Literature)* Read Daphne Du Maurier's short story "The Birds" and then watch Alfred Hitchcock's scary film by the same name. Write a film review in which you explain to your audience how Hitchcock and Du Maurier develop the conflict of humans with nature (the birds).

10. *(Service Learning)* In her essay "Let's Tell the Story of All America's Cultures" (pp. 4–5), Yufill tells her audience that she did not learn about the real multicultural history of the United States in her classrooms, but rather in her local library. Make an appointment with the principal of a public intermediate or high school nearby or telephone the administrative office of this school. Ask to see the history textbooks used at the school. Examine these textbooks carefully (glancing at the table of contents may help you to evaluate the book's content) and then write a report of your findings to share with classmates. Did you find that the school's history books presented the multicultural aspect of American history?

RESPONDING TO WRITING: USING ACTIVE READING STRATEGIES

Becoming an active reader involves responding to what you are reading. Throughout this course, you will be reacting to your own writing, writings of other students, and the work of professional writers. For some practice in responding, read the following interview and then respond to it by using the "Guidelines for Being an Active Reading Audience" (p. 6). Test the validity of Dillard's comments by trying her strategy for yourself. In this interview Dillard talks with Elizabeth Cowan, a college English instructor. (The names of both interview participants have been abbreviated.)

EC: How did the book [*Pilgrim at Tinker Creek*] come about?

AD: I read a lot. After I got out of college, I settled down to educate myself. I read books and read books. Then I started keeping notes on my reading, because like any normal human being I can't remember what I read. So I started taking notes on my reading in little spiral notebooks.

EC: What exactly would you put in those notebooks from the books?

AD: Well, I would put interesting facts. I would put down quotations I liked. And I would also put my own observations down in writing. . . .

EC: So, this reading was the first stage of your writing *Pilgrim at Tinker Creek*?

AD: . . . What I was doing was gathering facts; when you gather enough facts, you will start to have ideas about those facts. When you have material, you will automatically shape. The facts in this case were just like the potter's clay. They were material. You can't do art without material. It turns out that when you have a lot of material, you just automatically sort of organize it. . . . I copied all the information from the journals which I thought would be pertinent—which was just about everything. . . . I copied all these on four-by-six index cards. . . .

EC: What did you do with these cards?

AD: Then I put them into piles—which anyone can do. You know, if you think about writing a book, you think it is overwhelming. But actually you break it down into tiny tasks that any moron could do. A pile of index cards divides itself into categories. . . .

EC: And then . . .

AD: The question was how in the hell to write about it! I went back to the good nature books that I had read. And I analyzed them. I wrote outlines of whole books—outlines of chapters—so that I could see their structure. And I copied down their transitional sentences or their main sentences or their closing sentences or their lead sentences. I especially paid attention to how these writers made transitions between paragraphs and scenes. . . .

EC: And after analyzing these books?

AD: Then I put all these index cards into a filing cabinet, arranged by chapter, and started writing. . . . And, of course, I would immediately get carried away. The chapter would just develop itself. In fact, the stuff on the index cards actually occupied only about a quarter of the material of the chapter. But the cards anchored, gave me something to start with, a direction to go in. I had an outline. . . . And almost instantly [I would] depart from the outline. "Oh, shoot, I have departed from the outline once again!" . . . You are always going back and forth between the outline and the writing, bringing them closer together, or just throwing out the outline and making a new one.

Now that you have read this interview, in which Dillard clearly connects her reading with her writing activities, answer the following questions, reviewing this chapter's main points if necessary.

1. Name one fact you learned about Dillard from the background information you previewed.

2. Write a contextual definition of *pertinent*. Now look up the meaning of the word *pertinent* in a dictionary. Write the meaning in your own words.

3. Write a contextual definition of *transitional*.

4. Annotate the interview.

5. Summarize Dillard's most important ideas in no more than three sentences.

6. Respond in your journal.

7. To evaluate Dillard's strategies, test them by choosing an "Option for Writing" for this chapter. Do the following as you work through the writing assignment:

   • Take some notes in your journal to "gather facts," as Dillard recommends, to serve as your material for the writing assignment.

   • Organize this material by sorting similar ideas and points and putting these together. Refer to this sorted list as you are writing your first version of the assignment.

   • Examine your writing in light of the five "keys" (p. 16) and implement any changes you feel will improve what you've written.

CRITICAL THINKING

In Connecting Texts

You've seen how reading shaped the perceptions and the writing of Yufill in her essay (pp. 4–5). Yufill began to question and evaluate her early textbooks and she discovered misrepresentation and omission of certain truths. Annie Dillard reports in her interview (pp. 20–21) that she "settled down to educate myself" by engaging in active reading.

With a partner or in a small group, work together to draw up a list of misconceptions, false statements, or questionable comments that you or others in your group have read. Consider your past reading in newspapers, magazines, books, posters, advertisements, and other printed material as well as electronic material. If time permits, share your findings with the rest of the class. Take notes and keep them; they might serve as material for a future essay.

Chapter 2

Defining the Essay and the Composing Process

Essay: A short literary composition dealing with its subject . . . and, usually, expressive of the author's outlook and personality.

—Webster's New World Dictionary

Preview

In this chapter you will learn

- To identify the parts of the college essay—introduction, thesis, body paragraphs, and conclusion
- To recognize the stages of the composing process: discovering, drafting, revising, polishing, and responding
- To relate the five "keys"—PURPOSE, FOCUS, MATERIAL, STRUCTURE, and STYLE—to the essay's parts and to the composing process

After reading this chapter and completing its practice activities, you will be familiar with the essay's parts and ready to use the stages of the composing process in your writing.

How do the types of writing mentioned in Chapter 1—annotating, note taking, summarizing, and journal writing—differ from the type of writing found in a college essay? The types of writings discussed in Chapter 1 are private responses designed not for communication with other readers, but as activities to help you with active reading. The essay, in contrast, is designed as a public writing, meant to be shared with an audience of readers. If you think about it, you're already experienced in public writing. Every time you write a note or memo, register a complaint, dash off an e-mail, or send out an invitation, you're writing for an audience. Just as each of these public writings has specific characteristics, so has the essay.

CHARACTERISTICS OF THE ESSAY

An **essay** is made up of a number of paragraphs that develop and support a single idea, impression, or point. Although the term *essay* may be used to refer in general to writing that explores a topic or presents factual information, in the context of most college writing, *essay* refers to a composition that is carefully structured and contains particular parts that work together to communicate the writer's main ideas. Because readers want to see material in manageable portions, writers use **paragraphs,** or several sentences that together develop one thought. The essay can be divided into parts based on the function of its paragraphs.

To observe an essay and its parts, take a look at the following essay by the late Arthur Ashe, keeping in mind that no two essays are exactly alike. Ashe, an American tennis champion, became famous as the first African-American male to win both Wimbledon and the U.S. Open tournaments.

A BLACK ATHLETE LOOKS AT EDUCATION

Arthur Ashe

Thesis

Introduction

1   Since my sophomore year at UCLA, I have become convinced that we blacks spend too much time on the playing fields and too little time in the libraries. Consider these facts: for the major professional sports of hockey, football, basketball, baseball, golf, tennis, and boxing, there are roughly only 3170 major league positions available (attributing 200 positions to golf, 200 to tennis and 100 to boxing). And the annual turnover is small.

2   There must be some way to assure that those who try but don't make it to pro sports won't wind up on street corners or in unemployment lines. Unfortunately, our most widely recognized role models are athletes or entertainers—"runnin'" and "jumpin'" and "singin'" and "dancin'."

3   Our greatest heroes of the century have been athletes—Jack Johnson, Joe Louis, Muhammad Ali. Racial and economic discrimination forced us to channel our energies into athletics and entertainment. These were the ways out of the ghetto, the ways to get that Cadillac, those regular shoes, that cashmere sport coat.

Body Paragraphs

4   Somehow, parents must instill a desire for learning alongside the desire to be Walt Frazier. Why not start by sending black professional athletes into high schools to explain the facts of life?

5   I have often addressed high school audiences and my message is always the same: "For every hour you spend on the athletic field, spend two in the library. Even if you make it as a pro athlete, your career will be over by the time you are 35. You will need that diploma."

6   Have these pro athletes explain what happens if you break a leg, get a sore arm, have one bad year or don't make the cut for five or six tournaments. Explain to them the star system, wherein for every star earning millions there are six or seven others making $15,000 or $20,000 or $30,000. Invite a bench-warmer or a guy who didn't make it. Ask him if he sleeps every night. Ask him whether he was graduated. Ask him what he would do if he became disabled tomorrow. Ask him where his old high school athletic buddies are.

7   We have been on the same roads—sports and entertainment—too long. We need to pull over, fill up at the library and speed away to Congress and the Supreme Court, the unions and the business world.

Conclusion

8   I'll never forget how proud my grandmother was when I graduated from UCLA. Never mind the Davis Cup. Never mind the Wimbledon title. To this day, she still doesn't know what those names mean. What mattered to her was that of her more than thirty children and grandchildren, I was the first to be graduated from college, and a famous college at that. Somehow, that made up for all those floors she scrubbed all those years. ○

Notice that Ashe's essay contains the following parts:

- **Thesis**

  This statement, usually one sentence, is often found within the essay's first paragraph and contains the main point, idea, or opinion the writer wants to convey to a particular audience about a subject, along with his or her attitude toward the subject.

  Ashe jumps right into his thesis with his first sentence. The main idea of his essay is that "we blacks spend too much time on the playing fields and too little time in the libraries."

- **Introduction**

  This beginning part of the essay approaches the subject and captures the interest of the audience.

  When Ashe states, "I have become convinced . . ." in paragraph 1 of his essay, he is presenting a signal to his readers about his purpose: to convince his audience of his main point.

- **Body paragraphs**

  These paragraphs form the middle of the essay and develop the writer's thesis through the use of details, examples, and evidence from a variety of sources.

  Ashe's body paragraphs include information he recalls from his past as athlete, student, and later, pro tennis player and guest speaker. In addition, his body paragraphs contain details and facts that he has researched. Every piece of information in Ashe's body paragraphs relates clearly to his thesis.

- **Conclusion**

  At the end of the essay, this closing paragraph (or paragraphs) serves to emphasize the author's thesis, offer closure, and tie the contents of the essay together.

  In a moving and persuasive closing, Ashe emphasizes his thesis and his overall purpose by telling the audience about his own background. The information he shares in the conclusion serves as evidence that his college degree mattered more to him and to his grandmother than a much-sought-after tennis championship. Ashe's final image of his grandmother scrubbing floors is a powerful one with which to conclude the essay.

Even though essays can vary tremendously in length and content, they will always share the following parts: introduction, thesis, body paragraphs, and conclusion. Now that you are familiar with the basic essay format, read the following student model and see if you can identify the parts of a college essay.

MODEL WITH KEY QUESTIONS

Douglas Cwiak wrote the following essay for his college English class; a few months later, he submitted the essay to a local newspaper. "Matilda" was subsequently published in *The Beach Reporter*, a California newspaper with a readership of approximately 61,000 people.

MATILDA

Douglas W. Cwiak

In a conference with his instructor on the first day of his writing class, Douglas Cwiak revealed his fear of writing and of failing in the class. Doug confided that after being diagnosed with dyslexia, he had given up on school for several years. At the end of the semester, he shared his new outlook on the composing process this way: "I have fallen in love with writing and I write every day now." Doug has now graduated from film school, been accepted in a graduate film program, and hopes to work in the film industry as a writer or cinematographer.

1   Many people have owned a dog at sometime in their lives. I have owned many: Labradors, Irish setters and a German shepherd. All my dogs have been what I consider normal. At least, that was until Matilda entered my life. Matilda is a one-year-old female pug. What sets her apart from other dogs are her unconventional personality traits. She is simply not a normal dog.

2   Her dining habits go far beyond anything that I have seen. A meal begins with Matilda standing in the corner of the room like a child who has just been punished. Then as her food bowl is placed in its proper place, she begins a ritual dance. It commences with one or two steps toward the bowl. Then comes a pause. What follows can only be described as pure chaos: a mad dash to the bedroom followed by two perfectly executed laps around the dining room table. Finally she performs a slide across the kitchen floor that would make any baseball player envious, right up to her bowl. She then calmly eats her meal.

3   For Matilda, playing is not just for fun. It is the reason for her existence. A simple game of tug of war becomes an epic battle of wits. She with one end of the rope in her mouth and I with the other end in my hand, both maneuver to gain the advantage. Her tactics range from violently shaking her head back and forth, attempting to tear the rope from my hands, to a simple whimper for sympathy. Then when she has won the battle, she ceremoniously parades through the house with the rope dangling from her mouth and head held high. Needless to say, she has never lost a game of tug of war.

4   After the food has been served and the battles won, sleep is Matilda's last activity of the day. She struggles to keep her eyes open as she patiently waits for me to shuffle off to bed. As she makes the brief journey to the bedroom, she stops to retrieve her most treasured toy—a yellow and purple stuffed dinosaur. Once in bed she performs a fifteen-minute search for the most comfortable spot. This spot is always in the same place, under the covers with her head just peering out. As she slips into a deep trance-like sleep, something happens that can only be appreciated through personal experience. From this little dog comes an earth-shattering

snore. This snore, which sometimes awakens neighbors, is continuous throughout the night.

5   Most dogs lead their lives quietly performing their daily tasks and always wishing for more. Matilda, on the other hand, lives her life with an excitement and quest that few dogs, let alone humans, could ever hope to achieve. For her, simple mundane tasks become wild new adventures while bedtime becomes a nap under a star-filled sky. What seems to me like strange and unusual behavior is really an extreme love of life and I believe, in the end, a much more natural behavior than my own. ○

Key Questions

1. **Purpose**   What is the writer's purpose in this essay (to express, inform, or persuade)? Who do you think his audience is?

2. **Focus**   What main point is the writer making about his dog? Annotate the essay by finding and labeling Cwiak's thesis.

3. **Material**   Where does the writer get his material?

4. **Structure**   How has the writer ordered or arranged the material?

5. **Style**   What makes this animal essay different from other essays about pets? Why does Cwiak end with the words, "a much more natural behavior than my own"?

GUIDELINES FOR WRITING THE ESSAY

By taking a second look at each part of the essay and applying the five "keys"—PURPOSE, FOCUS, MATERIAL, STRUCTURE, and STYLE—introduced in Chapter 1, you can begin to establish some useful guidelines for writing essays.

Purpose

Use your essay's introduction to make your purpose in writing clear to your audience—do you want to inform, express, or persuade? The introduction is in one sense a promise or pledge to discuss a particular topic from your point of view. For example, Ashe's point of view in his essay (pp. 24–25) is evident in the straightforward attitude he takes in the first three words of his second sentence: "Consider these facts." Then in the second paragraph, Ashe keeps his audience and purpose firmly in mind. He begins with a problem his audience is already familiar with: unemployment lines.

In your introduction, you can also briefly preview what is to come later in the essay, but first you need to grab your audience's attention. Think for a few minutes about how you begin reading a magazine or newspaper. What attracts your attention to an article and makes you keep reading? What qualities sometimes cause you to flip the page or to put aside the article? Chances are, like many readers, you look to the opening sentences or paragraphs. The introductory paragraph of your essay is your audience's first impression of your writing and your point of view. Readers of an essay often decide in the first paragraph whether they want to read further.

Practice 2.1 Think about an article, book, essay, poem, note or e-mail from a friend, or any other type of writing that you have read recently. Note what it is that you remember reading and then, considering the audience, describe the writer's purpose. ❑

Focus

In writing your thesis, focus on the main point you wish to make in the essay. Remember that this thesis is the seed from which your entire essay will grow as you give detailed support and elaboration in your body paragraphs. This focus usually begins near the end of the introductory paragraph (the first paragraph in many cases). Notice that Cwiak places the thesis in his essay (p. 26) near the end of the first paragraph, but Ashe places his thesis in the first sentence (p. 24). Wherever you decide to place your thesis, make sure your main point is clear. To get helpful feedback, you might try comparing your thesis with others as a class or in groups, rephrasing and refocusing as necessary.

In your essay's conclusion, you'll want to relate your comments clearly to your thesis; try to reinforce or emphasize the thesis in your concluding remarks. Notice that both Ashe and Cwiak connect their final comments with their original purpose and thesis. Ashe concludes by contrasting the insignificance of the Davis Cup and Wimbledon compared with the importance of a college degree, thus restating his idea that athletes need to spend more time studying and less time worrying about their sport. Cwiak concludes by stating that "what seems to me like strange and unusual behavior is really an extreme love of life." The writer hearkens back to his thesis that Matilda is "not a normal dog" to conclude that she really possesses a "much more natural behavior than my own."

Practice 2.2 For practice in identifying an essay's thesis, choose any essay in Part 4, "Exploring Other Writers: A Collection of Readings" (pp. 333–401). Read the essay carefully, and then write down its thesis. Remember that although a writer's thesis is often found in the first or second paragraph, it can come anywhere in the essay. ❑

Material

In developing body paragraphs, make sure you have enough material to convince your audience of your main point. You should evaluate all material to make sure that it effectively supports your main point. For example, Ashe has chosen specific examples as the material for paragraph 3. Many of us are familiar with at least some of these famous athletes, and the images of a "Cadillac" and a "cashmere sport coat" further support Ashe's main point. In paragraph 5, Ashe's material establishes his authority on the subject: He has had personal experiences in these high schools, speaking before these students. To evaluate material for effectiveness, check each detail, example, or piece of evidence in your body paragraphs to make certain this material will convince your audience of your thesis. Your material must be sufficient and clearly related to your thesis. Your essay, like Ashe's and Cwiak's, should state your opinion or point of view in the thesis and then use the material in the body paragraphs to explain why you feel this way.

Practice 2.3   To gain more experience spotting material that is used to develop a thesis, reread either Ashe's or Cwiak's essay, underlining all pieces of information you find. Look for any content—facts, examples, statistics, illustrations, and comments from experts—that helps develop the writer's thesis. ❏

Structure

As you arrange the material for your body paragraphs, determine the best structure for communicating your main point. Experiment with different ways of arranging your details. Ashe's first or second draft of this final published essay probably ordered paragraphs and ideas differently. In the final version of his essay, you can see that Ashe has chosen a particular structure. For example, in his first two body paragraphs, he mentions first the unemployed, failed athletes. Then in the following body paragraphs, he mentions the athletes who became heroes. What if Ashe had reversed this order? The impact on his audience would not have been the same. Try out different arrangements for your body paragraphs to learn what structure works best for your essay.

Practice 2.4   Reread Cwiak's essay (p. 26), thinking about the order of the material. In the following space, list the writer's three main points in the order that they appear.

1. _____

2. _____

3. _____

❏

Style

Examine your entire essay for considerations of style. For you as well as other student writers like Cwiak and professional writers like Ashe, checking for style involves three separate components:

- First, you'll want to look at the *way* you've written the essay rather than *what* you've written in it. To do this, examine your choice of specific words, phrases, and sentences, including how the sentences work together in a paragraph. Ask yourself what it is about your writing style, just like your speaking or clothing style, that makes it distinctive—that establishes your own signature or flair. For instance, Ashe's writing style is effective in making his point in paragraph 2 of his essay. The phrase "on street corners" works because it creates a powerful image for the reader. A distinctive style is at work again in paragraph 6, where Ashe uses repetition effectively to drive home a point. Ashe chooses to begin four sentences with the same two words—"Ask him . . ."—showing how a simple phrase can be used to reinforce a point. In paragraph 7, Ashe chooses images related to roads with the phrases "fill up at the library" and "speed away to Congress"—to make a point about career paths.

- Second, examine the grammar, spelling, punctuation, and word usage in your essay. This process includes **proofreading**—reading over every sentence and making corrections before presenting the essay to its intended audience.

Grammar Key

Editing Essays: Handbook Practice

Review the parts of speech discussed on pages 419. Complete Exercise 1.

- Finally, make sure that your essay conforms to the accepted **manuscript format,** the layout of the essay with title, margins, and page numbers specified by your instructor.

These finishing touches will give you confidence that your essay presents your main point effectively and clearly, and that it presents you as a thoughtful and careful writer.

Practice 2.5   Reread Cwiak's essay, this time looking only at the writing style. Note in particular Cwiak's choice of words and phrases: In paragraph 2, he refers to Matilda's "dining habits," her "perfectly executed laps," and her "slide . . . that would make any baseball player envious." In paragraph 3, Cwiak uses the term "epic battle," and in paragraph 5 he refers to Matilda's "quest." Explain how you think these words work to communicate Cwiak's main point about Matilda to his audience.

How can you create your own effective college essay? Just as Ashe could not have learned to play championship tennis without many hours logged on the courts, essays as good as Ashe's or Cwiak's are not usually the result of sudden, last-minute inspiration. Nor are they the products of a single effort. No doubt both Ashe and Cwiak wrote multiple drafts before arriving at the polished drafts you just read. They probably also shared their drafts with an editor, and perhaps with friends, for suggestions and ideas.

Just as there is no magical formula for athletic skill or musical ability, there is no secret trick to creating a memorable essay. However, many successful writers who began by struggling with writer's block have found that they can relax and enjoy writing if they accept it as a process with several stages. ❏

AN OVERVIEW OF THE COMPOSING PROCESS

The **composing process** comprises stages in which you take an idea from its beginning to its final presentation, in writing, to a reading audience. The four broad stages in this process are *discovering, drafting, revising,* and *polishing,* in addition to a recurring stage, *writer/audience response.* This section briefly discusses each stage; later chapters go into greater detail. To examine one student's writing process in each of his four stages, consult "One Essay's Trip through the Composing Process" at the end of this chapter (pp. 41–47).

Writers and researchers agree that these are the stages most writers work through. The diagram shown in Figure 2.1 presents the stages of the composing process in visual terms. Notice that the diagram emphasizes writing as being **recursive**—having certain stages and activities that can be returned to or repeated. In other words, as you move forward in the composing process, you can also look back, which enables you to revisit a particular stage to strengthen your drafts.

You can see from this diagram that writing does not necessarily proceed in neat, straightforward, or predictable steps. During the course of a writing assignment, for example, you may collect and sort your initial ideas, draft a section of the paper, return to an earlier stage to gather additional material, revise a part of the draft, and adjust your organization before moving on.

When you view writing in this flexible way, you need not feel trapped by the anxiety that sometimes comes when you face the blank screen or page: you don't have to worry if the words that finally come aren't "just right" the first time. By experimenting with and practicing the various stages of the composing

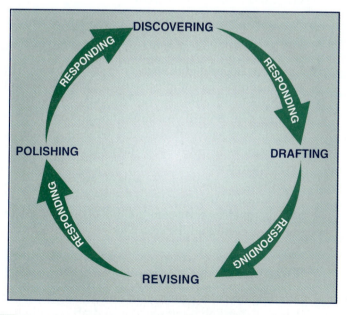

FIGURE 2-1   The Composing Process *Devised by Wendy Wright, El Camino College*

process, you will come to realize that beginnings are just that—beginnings—which you can alter, improve, and refine.

Keep in mind that these stages represent a model only. No two writers will follow exactly the same routines in working; the way you began your last writing project may not be the way you proceed with the next. Nor will you always perform the same activities in a particular order.

Practice 2.6   Close your eyes and visualize in your "mind's eye" the last time you took pen to paper or turned on the computer to write. Try to remember what it was that you were attempting to write, who your reading audience was, and how you began and then continued the process right through to a final draft. Write as many details as you can remember about that process. If you have a chance to share your responses with other class members, you'll quickly discover the unique nature of each writer's process. ❏

Knowing the *kinds* of activities that occur during the composing process and having a ready supply of techniques and strategies for dealing with them will help you to feel more in control when you write. You will be able to progress confidently through the many writing opportunities you will encounter.

To observe what writers do during each of the four stages of the composing process, and how they respond to their writing, consider the following stages of composing. Cwiak experienced each of them in creating his essay (p. 26).

Discovering

Discovering, also referred to as **prewriting,** includes everything you do in relation to a writing assignment or task that leads to your first draft. The discovering stage has two main parts:

1. Exploring and gathering ideas and information

2. Selecting ideas and grouping and organizing the material

Once Cwiak decided to write an essay focusing on his pet, he gathered as much information as he could by recalling Matilda's habits. Sometimes, too, discovering can involve things you "don't do." For instance, you might refrain from writing a draft until you have allowed time for thought. In Cwiak's case, his period of reflection allowed him to realize that he needed to extend his discovery tactics to include observation. He decided to watch his dog and take notes on her activities.

Giving yourself time to reflect—to consider, explore, inquire, and analyze your ideas—is important to the discovering stage. The organizing that occurs as you group ideas and begin to think of ordering them in an understandable way for a prospective audience can move you confidently toward the first draft.

Drafting

Drafting refers to "getting your thoughts on paper" in the form of sequenced sentences, paragraphs, and sections. A **draft** is a rough sketch or early version of an essay; a **working draft** is a draft-in-progress. This second term also hints at what drafting involves: work! When you draft, you take all the ideas and information you've gathered in discovering and then choose those you want to use in your first draft. Next, you attempt to put these ideas in some logical order to develop the main point you want to make in your essay. Focusing on a main point and then sorting and arranging material are your goals when you draft. Drafting can be an exciting stage once you feel that you are beginning to communicate with your audience, making your thoughts and ideas available through the pages of a written text. For Cwiak, drafting began after he gathered information and reflected. He had learned from a prior hastily composed and poorly received essay not to wait until the night before the assignment was due.

Keep in mind that drafting involves shaping, shifting, and rethinking your writing. It is rarely a neat or easy process. Cwiak experienced this reality when a student in his class who read his first draft for "Matilda" reported that she was confused by his organization. Cwiak found the feedback of his peer editor helpful rather than threatening. Because he had drafted on a computer, Cwiak returned to the keyboard to begin revising.

Revising

Revising, which means "looking back" or "seeing again," is the third stage of the composing process. In this stage, you are not so much concerned with correcting your draft sentence by sentence as with reflecting on it and reseeing it. This involves reexamining the effectiveness of the whole paper in terms of the ideas presented and the ordering of those ideas.

After a conference with his instructor, Cwiak reflected on his essay. During the conference, he defended his paragraph ordering, which took Matilda from playtime to bedtime to mealtime. Later, he felt that to avoid reader confusion, he should use a chronological order to take Matilda from the beginning to the end of her typical day. When you are revising, think in terms of adding, deleting, and rearranging ideas if necessary. Be sure to allow yourself sufficient time to think about your revisions rather than rushing through the steps of revising.

Polishing

Polishing, the fourth stage of the composing process, involves refining language for effect, proofreading for correctness, and checking the manuscript format. In the polishing stage, examine your writing for effective and precise words, sentences that have variety—that do not begin and end the same way—and fresh, specific images that activate the senses. During polishing, you can take the time to find that "just-right" word, to create the unexpected phrase or sentence, and to add the details that will bring your subject vividly to life.

When Cwiak was notified that a local newspaper was going to publish "Matilda," he began the process of reviewing his essay. He noticed that there were vague word choices as well as errors in sentence structure that his instructor had circled in her evaluation of his essay. In paragraph 2, he replaced the word *strangeness* with *chaos*; in paragraph 3, he substituted the word *maneuver* for *try*. He wanted to stress the contrast between Matilda and most dogs, so he added the phrase "on the other hand" in paragraph 5. Finally, he corrected a sentence that was actually an incomplete thought: He had originally written, in paragraph 4, "Always in the same place, under the covers with her head just peering out."

Polishing is best addressed after you have made larger adjustments to content and organization in the drafting and revising stages. The handbook section of this text (pp. 403–480) will help you in proofreading for correctness.

Writer/Audience Response

Writer/audience response is a crucial part of the entire composing process. As you can see in "The Composing Process" diagram (Figure 2-1, p. 31), writer/audience response involves reacting to and interacting with what you've written during and after *each* stage of the process. Responding can also be a shared activity, as you consider the questions, comments, or suggestions from peer readers, a collaborator, an instructor, or whoever comprises your audience. In order to respond thoughtfully and make the necessary adjustments, set aside time to reflect on and review your writing. Ask yourself if you have achieved your goals and met the expectations of your original assignment and of your audience.

The following three steps for responding to an essay will help you take more control of your own writing, and offer constructive feedback if you are the reading audience:

1. Recognize strengths as well as troublesome areas in the writing.

2. Identify needed improvements by testing the writing against the five "keys"—PURPOSE, FOCUS, MATERIAL, STRUCTURE, and STYLE.

3. If you are the reader, suggest appropriate changes to improve the writing, and if you are the writer, make the appropriate changes.

Responding can have a range of results. You might discover your real concerns beneath the surface of a first draft, launch a search for new material, or mark places in the margin where you stumble over sentences as you reread.

Practice 2.7   Identify the appropriate stage in the composing process for each of the following statements. Review the stages (pp. 31–34) if necessary.

> *Example: You receive your assignment and begin to gather material.*
> *Discovering*

1. You have gathered sufficient material, you have a thesis or main point to focus on, and you have an idea of how to structure the material. You begin writing your first version of the essay.

2. Your essay is almost ready, and the deadline is approaching, but there are a few words and sentences that are not as effective as you would like them to be. You have not yet proofread your essay for spelling errors and typos.

3. After sharing a draft of your essay with your peers, you're now reflecting on their comments before attacking the essay once more.

4. You've written a couple of drafts of your essay, but after responding to reader feedback, you decide the structure needs adjusting and your focus in the thesis needs to be sharper. ❏

The five "keys" and your composing process are closely related. If you think about it, the composing process involves putting purpose, focus, material, structure, and style "into action" as you write. While you work through any of the "Options for Writing" in this chapter (pp. 37–39), refer to the strategies in the ensuing sections to see how you can use the keys during the stages of your composing process.

Strategies for Writers

1. **Purpose**   During the discovering stage, determine if your purpose in writing the essay is to express, to inform, or to persuade your audience. Identify the specific audience you want to address in your essay. In revising, check to see that your introduction engages your audience and advances your purpose. Check to ensure that your conclusion offers closure and connnects the essay with your purpose.

2. **Focus**   Early in the composing process, try to form a "working" thesis that you can revise and refine as you continue to focus your essay. In gathering information and in drafting, make certain that each piece of information relates clearly to your working thesis.

3. **Material**   During the discovering stage, gather as much information as you can from a variety of sources, if possible.

4. **Structure**   In preparation for drafting, try to arrange your material logically. Decide, at least for now, which material you will include first, second, third, and so forth. As you draft and revise, question this order, get feedback on your draft, and experiment with the order to come up with the best organization for your essay.

5. **Style**   In polishing, make sure that you're using the most effective words and that you're varying your sentences to keep your audience interested in your subject. Proofread your essay to eliminate any distracting errors or typos. Check your manuscript to be sure that it conforms to your instructor's directions for format.

JOURNAL WRITING: EXAMINING YOUR COMPOSING PROCESS

As you learned in Chapter 1, journal writing is a valuable way to reflect on your reading. Your journal is also a useful place to reflect on your writing. After answering the following questions for the first two activities in your journal, you will have a better idea of how the stages of the composing process have worked for you in the past and how you might use them in the future to become a more relaxed and efficient writer. The second journal activity, focusing on the writers featured in this chapter, will provide useful ideas and material for an essay.

1. Think about your own composing process. How do you usually go about a writing assignment, business or personal letter, or workplace report? In a journal entry, describe your composing process. Answering some of the following questions will help you recall various aspects of how you write:

   - How much time do you spend thinking before beginning to write?

   - What activities help you to generate ideas? Do you make notes, discuss your ideas with others, or read?

   - How and when do you organize your material?

   - How do you get started on a draft?

   - How long does it take you to produce a page? A first draft?

   - How many drafts do you usually work through?

   - How do you decide what changes to make or what needs work?

2. Answer the following questions in another short piece of journal writing to consider some ways in which you could become a better, more efficient writer:

   - What are your strengths as a writer?

   - Which aspects of writing do you enjoy or find easy?

   - What are the difficult parts of writing for you?

   - At what stage or stages in the process do you meet obstacles or have trouble continuing?

3. In a journal entry, write your ideas about and reactions to any of the three essays in this chapter: "A Black Athlete Looks at Education" (p. 24), "Matilda" (p. 26), and "What I Have Lived For" (p. 39).

   - What did you like about the essay?

   - What questions or comments would you address to this writer?

   - What connections can you make to your own personal experiences and attitudes?

   - If writing about "Matilda," you might ask yourself if there are any "Matildas" in your life. That is, do you have some special person, animal, object, or place that has not only impressed you as unique but may have led you to reconsider some of your own attitudes and behaviors?

- If writing about "A Black Athlete Looks at Education," think about the last time you were in a library. Why were you there, and how long did you stay?

- Do you agree with Ashe that libraries are important to college students? Why?

- If writing about "What I Have Lived For," think about the author's statement that love "relieves loneliness." Do you agree with the author's vision of love? If not, how is your vision of love different?

Using the Computer: Opening a Planning File

1. To help you in the discovery stage of your essay writing, try creating a **planning file**, in which you record and save your plans for a particular essay. You can create this file either on disk or on your hard drive. After you have created and named your file, type the following planning questions, leaving enough space to insert your answers. You can answer each question later when you begin prewriting.

   a. Who is my audience?

   b. What is my purpose in writing to them? (To express, inform, or persuade?)

   c. What main point am I trying to make about my subject?

   d. Where should I look for material to support my main point? What specific example or piece of evidence would help me prove my main point?

   Because this is a planning file, you might want to continue adding ideas to it as you draft your essay. But try not to delete any text from this planning file—not even the ideas you think you won't use. (*Hint:* If you want to move text directly from your planning file into your essay draft, use the Copy function instead of Cut.)

2. If you would like to review the essay's parts in greater detail, visit this Web site:

   http://lrs.ed.uiuc.edu/students/fwalters/essaybasic.html

OPTIONS FOR WRITING

For this assignment, you will be integrating the five "keys"—PURPOSE, FOCUS, MATERIAL, STRUCTURE, and STYLE—into your composing process. Whatever option you choose, consider your prospective audience carefully, gather as much material as you can in your discovery stage, and then work on focusing and structuring the material in the drafting stage.

1. Bertrand Russell's essay "What I Have Lived For" (p. 39) develops "three passions" for which the writer has lived: love, knowledge, and pity. In an essay, discuss three passions for which you live. Your passions might include, for example, a family member, a loved one, a particular

job, a hobby or sports activity, a certain musical group or type of music, a specific place or locale, or a certain kind of food.

2. Write an essay supporting one of the following theses:

   - In my life, I have the ambition to accomplish three goals. (You can also mention obstacles to be overcome.)

   - Ambitious people are sometimes downright obnoxious and ruthless.

   - Having lofty ambitions allows us to dream, plan, and overcome obstacles.

   - Having lofty ambitions often leads to disappointment.

3. In "Matilda," Cwiak gives readers a close look at his dog. Write an essay about a subject you are familiar with: a person, animal, or specific place. Gather as much material as you can from memory, observation, or photos.

4. In "What I Have Lived For," Russell mentions the objects of pity in his life: "children in famine, victims tortured by their oppressors, helpless old people a hated burden to their sons." Find a newspaper or magazine article that discusses an object of pity in our current world. After reading the article, write an essay explaining the situation and possibly offering some solutions.

5. In "A Black Athlete Looks at Education," Ashe mentions role models. If you have had an important role model or mentor in the form of a relative, teacher, coworker, or friend, explain the nature of your relationship and describe the impact this person has had on your ambitions and achievements.

6. After completing the "Critical Thinking in Connecting Texts" activity (p. 40), explore in your group whether different cultures have radically different values. Be careful not to stereotype or generalize. Write an essay discussing your findings.

7. Many of us have learned from a mentor, teacher, relative, or friend how to do or make something. Explain the process you learned. Assume that your audience is a group interested in learning about the process you are detailing. How old were you when you learned how to complete this task? What was your relationship to the person who explained the process to you? What problems did you encounter? How did you feel about the process you learned?

8. Imagine a scene in which Ashe, Cwiak, and Russell carry on a conversation. Based on your knowledge of their interests, writing styles, and personalities, what might they say about each other? Compose an essay analyzing your three characters: Ashe, Russell, and Cwiak. Mention characteristics that you find similar as well as those that only one of the characters possesses.

9. *(Film and Literature)* View the 1995 version of William Shakespeare's *Romeo and Juliet* and then view the Academy Award–winning 1961 musical *West*

Side Story. Write an essay in which you use specific examples from both films to illustrate one theme (main idea) the two films share.

10. *(Service Learning)* Contact a child abuse or family violence hotline or center in your area, arrange an interview with an employee, and write an informative essay increasing public awareness. You may want to team up with one or more partners and collaborate on your essay.

RESPONDING TO WRITING: ANNOTATION

Practice in recognizing the five "keys"—PURPOSE, FOCUS, MATERIAL, STRUCTURE, and STYLE—and how they function in essays will allow you to become more confident in responding to your own essays and those of others. In the following short essay, Bertrand Russell, a British philosopher, mathematician, and political activist who worked for individual freedoms, shares the three overriding passions of his life. As you read, notice how clearly the essay exhibits the characteristics and guidelines presented in this chapter.

WHAT I HAVE LIVED FOR

Bertrand Russell

1   Three passions, simple but overwhelmingly strong, have governed my life: the longing for love, the search for knowledge, and unbearable pity for the suffering of mankind. These passions, like great winds, have blown me hither and thither, in a wayward course, over a deep ocean of anguish, reaching to the very verge of despair.

2   I have sought love, first, because it brings ecstasy—ecstasy so great that I would often have sacrificed all the rest of life for a few hours of this joy. I have sought it, next, because it relieves loneliness—that terrible loneliness in which one shivering consciousness looks over the rim of the world into the cold unfathomable lifeless abyss. I have sought it, finally, because in the union of love I have seen, in a mystic miniature, the prefiguring vision of the heaven that saints and poets have imagined. This is what I sought, and though it might seem too good for human life, this is what—at last—I have found.

3   With equal passion I have sought knowledge. I have wished to understand the hearts of men. I have wished to know why the stars shine. And I have tried to apprehend the Pythagorean power by which number holds sway above the flux. A little of this, but not much, I have achieved.

4   Love and knowledge, so far as they were possible, led upward toward the heavens. But always pity brought me back to earth. Echoes of cries of pain reverberate in my heart. Children in famine, victims tortured by oppressors, helpless old people a hated burden to their sons, and the whole world of loneliness, poverty, and pain make a mockery of what human life should be. I long to alleviate the evil, but I cannot, and I too suffer.

5   This has been my life. I have found it worth living, and would gladly live it again if the chance were offered me. ○

Now reread the essay, annotating it (as explained in Chapter 1), making notes in your text. Follow the instructions below for annotating, but feel free to include additional comments of your own.

1. Label the introduction, the body paragraphs, and the conclusion.

2. Underline and label the thesis in this essay. Remember that to be effective, a thesis statement should focus an essay by making a point about the topic.

3. Each of the body paragraphs also has a particular focus. Underline and label the words or sentences that state the focus of each body paragraph.

4. Each paragraph supports the thesis with material—reasons, details, and examples. A paragraph is well developed when it contains enough material to support the main idea and to allow the reader to "see" and understand an author's subject. Note several instances of specific details or examples that name and show the writer's material rather than simply telling about it.

5. The writer has structured his material very clearly. Note any words or groups of words that help you follow his structure easily.

6. An author's style includes effective use of language, the author's word choice, the length and variety of sentences, and the author's voice that we can "hear" as we read. Choose a few specific words, groups of words, or sentences that make this essay effective or memorable for you. Label these for later discussion.

7. Reexamine the title of the essay. Decide whether Russell's primary purpose is to express, inform, or persuade. Write the purpose next to the title.

Now that you are familiar with annotating an essay, use this technique to examine your own writing as soon as you have a first draft. If you find this practice helpful, repeat the process with later drafts.

CRITICAL THINKING

In Connecting Texts

Although the authors of the three essays in this chapter differ in their choice of subject matter—Ashe focuses on education, Cwiak describes a pet, and Russell talks of passions—they all touch on the issue of *values*, those qualities we consider important in our lives. Get together with a partner or group and take another look at each of these essays. See if you can come up with a phrase or sentence for each author that sums up what he seems to value most. Now examine your response to see if the three writers share any values. At this point, you might want to brainstorm with your group, taking notes about the values that each of you holds dear. Are they the same as the shared values of the authors? Keep your notes; you might use them as material for an essay on the subject of values.

ONE ESSAY'S TRIP THROUGH THE COMPOSING PROCESS

Discovering
Assignment: Explore the issue of censorship of music lyrics—does this censorship violate First Amendment rights or is some censorship necessary to protect minors from harmful influences?

Cyrus Doherty's prewriting for the essay assignment:

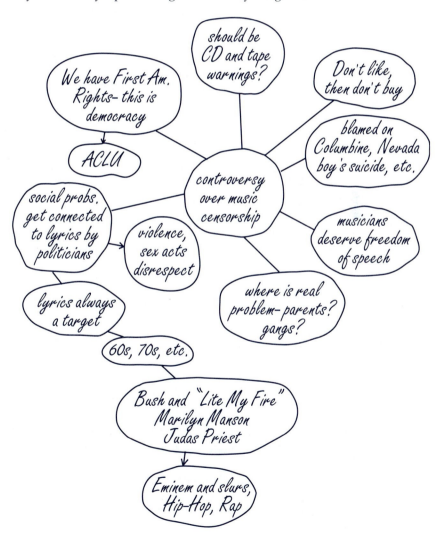

Drafting
Doherty's rough draft of the essay with instructor's response:

CONTROVERSY OVER MUSIC

Cyrus Doherty

or a more focused title?

1   A major difference between America and the rest of the world is that we have the First Amendment. Through history, it seems that musicians have been targeted because of their controversial sounds or their controversial lirics. Over and over again there have been efforts *repeated?* to keep musicians from saying what they want

focus on lyrics only?

is all of society doing this?

what social problems?

to say in their music. Why? Maybe since it's easy for society to blame its social problems on performers. But how realistic is that? If our politicians are looking for why we have all our social problems, they should not try to use these tactics of saying that bad crimes happen because of graffic lirics. Our politicians have to know that trying to put restrictions on music is only an open attack on our free speech rights in this country.

who?

2   How funny that this year at the Bush inauguration, they played Jim Morrison's "Light My Fire." Our politicians never are able to remember their own youth. In the sixties, musicians were the center of controversy like they are today.

such as? Give some examples?

Their eyes seem to be closed to these obvious facts. This is ironic since they are playing those same tunes at Bush's inauguration that were once thought to be outrageous and evil.

write a topic sentence, not question.

3   And how about the eighties? Politicians make such a fuss over the words of Marilyn Manson's songs, when two decades before, it was the lirics of Judas

make this less conversational, more academic in tone

Priest that were considered the same type of dark evil. What about those politicians who blames Judas Priest's lirics for the suicide of a boy in Nevada? Funny, how two decades later, these people want to point the finger at Marilyn Manson. *for what?*

Maybe they act this way since it's easier for them to blame music than to actually find out how these tragedies happen. What needs to be understood is that children are not driven by songs. Banning them won't stop the tragedies in our society. We should realize that with freedom of speech comes responsibility. Okay, there may be a handful of cases of tragedy that somebody says was caused by music lirics, but what about most of the people who listen to the same words in music and take them for what they are?

make this less conversational, more academic in tone

Use a topic sentence that forecasts the subject of the paragraph

avoid pov shift

4   This assault on lirics has been an ongoing pattern of injustice. One controversial artist whose lirics were assaulted was Eminem. You would think that college educated, grown adults might have adjusted to the fact that musicians' lirics are not the cause of young people's rebellion. We should not have to justify Eminems' lirics as acceptable to all parts of society. The reason Eminem can say cruel, demeaning, homophobic slurs is the same reason gays and lesbians can be openly homosexual, thus making the U.S. different from other countries. America was build on freedom of speech, and no one should try to change that politician or activist.

sp

wrong word

phrasing— make more clear?

verb form

5   The American Civil Liberties Union (ACLU) issued its position on free speech and censorship by stating, "The First Amendment exists precisely to protect the most offensive and controversial speech from government suppression. The best way to counter obnoxious speech is with more speech. Persuasion, not coercion, is the solution." We must agree with this quote. If we don't, we will be threatening all forms of speech.

don't refer to the comment as a "quote"

Cyrus—great draft with lots of info. on a really volatile topic—revisit to revise this potentially effective essay!

Revising
Doherty's revised draft of the essay with peer editor's response:

FREEDOM OF SPEECH AND MUSIC IN AMERICA

Cyrus Doherty

*You could
try for
a more
attention-
getting
intro—
maybe get
a quote
on the
subject?*

1   A major difference between America and the rest of the world is that we have the First Amendment. Since the 1960s, it seems that musicians have been targeted because of their controversial lyrics. There have repeatedly been efforts to keep musicians from saying what they want to say in their music. It is easy for Americans to blame our social problems on musicians. But how realistic is that? If our politicians are looking for the cause of all our social problems, they should not try

*"not try to
convince us
that"?*

to use tactics of saying that bad crimes happen because of graphic lyrics. Our politicians have to know that attempts to restrict music lyrics are an open attack on our free speech rights in this country.

2   Our politicians do not find it easy to remember their own youth when they criticize contemporary musicians. The irony of this is that the same songs that were considered outrageous and evil are now played at the President's inauguration. This year at George Bush's inauguration, his staff played Jim Morrison's "Light My Fire." Yet in the sixties, musicians like Jim Morrison, Jimmy Hendrix, and Janis Joplin were the center of controversy. Politicians cannot remember how they felt as youth when other politicians badgered them about listening to music they had chosen.

3   In the eighties and nineties, controversy over music lyrics continued to haunt musicians. Politicians in the nineties made such a fuss over the words of Marilyn Manson's songs, when in the eighties, it was the lyrics of Judas Priest that were considered the same type of dark evil. Politicians do not want to recall when they blamed Judas Priest's lyrics for the suicide of a boy in Nevada. It should be no sur-

that

prise some time later, politicians wanted to point the finger at Marilyn Manson.

what way? 4   Perhaps our lawmakers act this way because it is easier for them to blame mu-

sic lyrics than actually to find out how these tragedies happen. We need to under-

stand that children are not driven by words in songs. Banning certain words from

where?   songs will not stop the tragedies in our society. We should realize that with freedom

of speech comes responsibility. Yes, there may be one or two cases of tragedy that

just might be caused by music lyrics, but what about the overwhelming majority of

people who listen to the same words in music and take them for what they are?

5   The most recent assault on a controversial artist is the assault on Eminem, also

*find a
different
word here?*   known as Marshall Mathers. One would think that in our twenty-first century,

college educated, grown adults might have adjusted to the fact that musicians'

*all adults
aren't
college
educated*   lyrics are not the cause of young people's rebellion. Mathers should not have to

justify his lyrics as acceptable to all parts of society. The reason Eminem can make

cruel, demeaning, homophobic slurs is the same reason gays and lesbians can be

openly homosexual, in both cases making the U.S. different from other countries.

America was built on freedom of speech, and no one—politician, activist,

parent—should be allowed to take that freedom away.

6   The American Civil Liberties Union (ACLU) issued its position on free speech

and censorship by stating, "The First Amendment exists precisely to protect the

most offensive and controversial speech from government suppression. The best

way to counter obnoxious speech is with more speech. Persuasion, not coercion,

is the solution." We must agree with this comment; if we do not, we will be threat-

ening all forms of speech, whether spoken or sung. ○

Polishing
Doherty's final draft after polishing:

AMERICAN MUSICIANS AND AMENDMENT RIGHTS

Cyrus Doherty

Cyrus Doherty felt strongly about freedom of speech as this right connects with popular music. This final draft won first place in El Camino College's "Our Voices" contest.

1   In 1950, Harry S. Truman said, "There is no more fundamental axiom of American freedom than the familiar statement: 'In a free country we punish men for crimes they commit but never for the opinions they have.'" The First Amendment is what separates America from the rest of the world. Since the 1960s, it seems that musicians have been targeted because of their controversial lyrics. There have repeatedly been efforts to keep musicians from saying what they want to say in their music. It is easy for Americans to blame our social problems on musicians. But how realistic is that? If our politicians are looking for the cause of all our social problems, they should not try to convince us that bad crimes happen because of graphic lyrics. Our politicians have to know that attempts to restrict music lyrics are an open attack on our free speech rights in this country.

2   Our politicians do not find it easy to remember their own youth when they criticize contemporary musicians. The irony of this is that the same songs that were considered outrageous and evil are now played at the President's inauguration. This year at George Bush's inauguration, his staff played Jim Morrison's "Light My Fire." Yet in the sixties, musicians like Jim Morrison, Jimmy Hendrix, and Janis Joplin were the center of controversy. Politicians cannot remember how they felt as youth when other politicians badgered them about listening to music they had chosen.

3   In the eighties and nineties, controversy over music lyrics continued to haunt musicians. Politicians in the nineties made such a fuss over the words of Marilyn

Manson's songs, when in the eighties, it was the lyrics of Judas Priest that were considered the same type of dark evil. Politicians do not want to recall when they blamed Judas Priest's lyrics for the suicide of a boy in Nevada. It should be no surprise that some time later, politicians wanted to point the finger at Marilyn Manson.

4   Perhaps our lawmakers find it easier to blame music lyrics than actually to find out how these tragedies happen. We need to understand that children are not driven by words in songs. Banning certain words from songs, books, or magazines will not stop the tragedies in America. We should realize that with freedom of speech comes responsibility. Yes, there may be one or two cases of tragedy that might be caused by music lyrics, but what about the overwhelming majority of people who listen to the same words in music and take them for what they are—only words?

5   The most recent assault on a controversial artist is the attack on Eminem, also known as Marshall Mathers. One would think that in our twenty-first century, college-educated lawmakers might have adjusted to the fact that musicians' lyrics are not the cause of young people's rebellion. Mathers should not have to justify his lyrics as acceptable to all parts of society. The reason Eminem can make cruel, demeaning, homophobic slurs is the same reason gays and lesbians can be openly homosexual, in both cases making the United States different from other countries. America was built on freedom of speech, and no one—politician, activist, parent—should be allowed to take that freedom away.

6   The American Civil Liberties Union (ACLU) issued its position on free speech and censorship by stating, "The First Amendment exists precisely to protect the most offensive and controversial speech from government suppression. The best way to counter obnoxious speech is with more speech. Persuasion, not coercion, is the solution." We must agree with this comment; if we do not, we will be threatening all forms of speech, whether spoken or sung. ○

Chapter 3

Discovering Through Prewriting

Writing is easy; all you do is sit staring at a blank sheet of paper until the drops of blood form on your forehead.

—Gene Fowler, *journalist, scriptwriter, biographer*

Preview

In this chapter you will learn

- How to gather material in prewriting
- How to identify and use prewriting strategies: freewriting, brainstorming, listing, questioning, clustering, mapping
- How to respond to prewriting using the "keys"

After reading this chapter and completing its practice activities, you will feel confident in collecting and recording material for an essay draft.

CHARACTERISTICS OF PREWRITING

Have you had the unpleasant experience Fowler mentions of staring endlessly at a blank sheet of paper? Once you've received a writing assignment, do you agonize over how to begin? Or do the words sometimes seem to flow effortlessly onto the page or the computer screen? Some writers have no trouble finding those first words to put on paper, but for many others, actually getting started can be the most challenging aspect of writing. As you read about and test several strategies for prewriting in this chapter, remember that no two writing situations are exactly alike. Oftentimes a strategy that works well for one essay may not be the one you want to use for the next. Experimenting and practicing will allow you to feel comfortable with different prewriting strategies. You'll learn which techniques work best for you in a given writing situation.

MODEL WITH KEY QUESTIONS

Student Olasumbo Davis was asked to write an essay about a particular character trait occurring among residents of Los Angeles. Davis began with prewriting, and when she felt she had enough information, she went back, reconsidered her assignment, and came up with a second prewriting list. She then drafted, revised, and polished this essay—three stages we'll cover in greater detail later in this text.

PUBLIC PARKING AND ROAD WAR

Olasumbo Davis

Although Davis's original home was Nigeria, Africa, she found it easy to prewrite about what she has noticed regarding residents of Los Angeles. One of this writer's most difficult tasks has been to spell certain words in the American and not the British forms. Davis plans to transfer to USC, where she would like to obtain a bachelor's degree in education.

1   The other day, my friend came back from Lucky's market with a busted lip. No, he didn't walk blindly into a grocery shelf. What he got was the worst end of an argument over who should get to park in a coveted spot in the store's ample parking lot. Another time and somewhere else, another friend had the headlight of her car smashed as a result of a parking war. It's safe to guess that by now everyone in Los Angeles must have participated in or witnessed the daily meaningless battle that is waged in many of our city's parking lots and on countless numbers of roads in our county.

2   What this battle is all about is who gets to park a car as close as he or she can to whatever public place's entrance. God help the driver who harbors the desire for the coveted space because that driver is doomed to an encounter that might rival a battle of gladiators. As crazy as the analogy may seem, it really is an asphalt arena. As in all wars, it may be difficult to put a figure on the costs: the lost tempers, the charged emotions, the frayed nerves, not to mention the punches thrown daily by the combatants.

3   One need only listen to the expletives that accompany every driver's defeat and victory to know the extent of the combat.

4   The people and the automobile have quite a peculiar relationship—a real love/hate relationship that encompasses much of the daily lives of those who live in this area. There must be something about the automobile that sparks off the worst in Angelenos. Put any supposedly normal, reasonable, peaceful person behind the wheel of a car and the person immediately becomes cantankerous, irrational, and combative. He or she suddenly turns into a one-person army. If a he, he is Schwarzenegger and Stallone combined. If a she, she morphs into Wonder Woman or Princess Leia. The automobile becomes a weapon and all other drivers are enemies who must be conquered by any available means.

5   Someone from some faraway planet, say Tallahassee or Spartenburg or St. Louis or some other benign environment, may be perplexed about the stupidity of this war. But they don't understand: this is Los Angeles, not their saner world. We Angelenos take as much pride in our road wars as we do in our palm trees

and sunshine! Do not ask why the healthy-looking, tanned, and physically fit men and women we see in these parking lots would rather lose their sanity and temper than walk some hundred yards from the back of the lot. We will get no answer because they themselves do not know.

6   It is a sight to see the reconnaisance, the defense, the maneuver, and the attack employed in an L.A. parking lot. Say Driver A is about to vacate one of the cherished spots. During peak hours, there may be as many as five other drivers gunning for the same spot. There is Driver B, who might have been patrolling the lot the past twenty minutes for a choice spot—never mind that there are some empty slots in the backlot half a block away. B sees A preparing to move and B swoops. But there is also, lurking in the wings, Driver C who has the same ambition. As often happens, Drivers B and C converge on the spot before A leaves. Chaos reigns. Expletives are exchanged, and sometimes blows are struck.

7   Just as my friends did, somebody may end up with a busted lip or a smashed headlight. So what is the solution? It is doubtful that more parking spaces are the answer since the problem has never been about the shortage of spots. And since it is not possible to build all parking spaces as near as possible to the main entrances of public places, an end to the parking war can only come from a change in attitude on the part of parking lot users. What is needed is greater civility among road users, and a universal willingness to walk those hundred yards from the backlot, if necessary. Then can we truly call Los Angeles the "City of Angels"?   ○

Key Questions

1. **Purpose**   Identify the writer's audience—who would want to read this essay, and what might be the extent of the reader's knowledge on the subject?

2. **Focus**   State the writer's thesis in your own words.

3. **Material**   In which body paragraph does the writer give the audience the clearest sense of the essay's subject matter? Which is the weakest body paragraph in this respect? Be sure to state your reasons for your answers.

4. **Structure**   How is the information organized—in other words, how does Davis break down the information into sections of material and establish a sequence for her essay?

5. **Style**   What sentence or phrase leaves you with the most vivid impression of the writer's subject?

Grammar Key

Handbook Practice: Fragments

Read the explanation of sentence fragments on page 426. Complete Exercise 3 and the paragraph following the exercise.

GUIDELINES FOR PREWRITING

As you remember from the discussion of the composing process in Chapter 2, discovering through **prewriting** is the first of four stages. In this stage, you explore and gather ideas and information, reflect on the material you have gathered, and then begin to select and group this material into a workable structure for an essay. Prewriting is not a "finished writing"; it is a way to get ideas on paper. Before you can decide which prewriting strategy for gathering material you'd like to try, you need to consider why and for whom you're writing the essay.

Consider Your Audience

Your essay assignment might describe a specific audience you should write for. Even if a specific audience is not part of the assignment, it will help you focus your essay if you consider audience and purpose. Of course, you can choose to write for your classmates and your instructor—people like you who are part of the college community and represent a variety of different backgrounds, interests, and general knowledge. Addressing the following questions about your intended audience will help you develop appropriate material for your essay:

Audience Assessment Questions

- Which group of readers would be most interested in your proposed subject?

- What might this group want to learn about your subject?

- What might they already know about your subject?

- How can you help this particular audience understand your information? Are there terms you need to define? Background information you should mention? Misconceptions you should clear up?

Practice 3.1 For practice in considering audience, turn to "Options for Writing" (p. 60) and answer these audience questions for the first writing option.   ❏

Allow Prewriting Free Rein

The goal of any prewriting strategy is to try to get down as much information as you can without stopping to evaluate it. This is not the time for censorship; later you can decide what information to keep and what to scrap. In the discovering stage of your writing, have fun, be playful, experiment with ideas, and develop unexpected connections.

Freewriting

One strategy for prewriting is **freewriting**—when you freewrite, you write nonstop on a subject for a fixed length of time, perhaps 15 minutes. While you're freewriting, don't stop to correct spelling, punctuation, or inappropriate words. Just try to get on paper or computer the things that pop into your mind when you think of the subject. Include the mental connections and leaps in thought you make to any other aspects of the subject.

To illustrate, examine this freewriting by student writer and mother April Buell:

Over and over again hearing everybody say you won't amount to anything— teen mom and having to raise my child on my own I had to prove that they were wrong. Put downs and staying up late, diapers and schoolbooks and no support still with 2 yrs of high school left. Then got a job at U.S. Customs, became independent it felt so good not to have to ask my parents for money. I learned to be prompt, made 8 dollars an hr. Graduated with a 4 point GPA and now am a full-time college student I have to do this for me and for my son, incl. washing clothes, cleaning house, studying without enough sleep, taking him to the doctor and trying to juggle classes and work, on and on, it never ends, I deserve recognition for all that I have achieved in spite of negative comments—my goals are still set high I won't quit.

Practice 3.2 Choose an "Option for Writing" from this chapter (pp. 60–62) that interests you. Write on the subject for 15 minutes without stopping.   ❑

Brainstorming
Another strategy for prewriting is **brainstorming,** a group prewriting activity in which participants call out ideas and comments on a subject while one person records them. Brainstorming generates lots of material because two or more heads are often better than one for coming up with information.

Here are the results from three students who brainstormed about drug legalization:

PROS	CONS
Quality Control	Effects on certain foreign economics?
Eliminate motive for smuggling	Many trained staff members needed
Monitoring users	Additional costs to taxpayers for staff
Regulate dosage	Still those who want more illegally??
Supervise activities of users?	Condoning a bad activity
Driving	Hospitals for observation?
Drug testing?	Cheating by staff members?
Reduction in drug-related deaths (sellers, go-betweens, etc.)	Cost to taxpayers for the drugs themselves

Practice 3.3 With a partner or small group, organize a brainstorming session. Choose a subject, appoint a recorder for your group, and start collecting information on your subject.   ❑

Listing

Listing is yet another prewriting technique you can use to generate ideas for essays. You simply make a random list, perhaps similar to a shopping or "to-do" list, including everything you can think of related to your subject. Later you can examine your list and find large groups of ideas in which to divide the material.

Davis used the following two lists to gather material for her essay (p. 49). After a brief review, you'll see that in her second list, Davis found four large groups of ideas into which to divide her material.

Practice 3.4 Choose another "Option for Writing" from this chapter and draw up a list of information on your subject. For your first list, don't worry about grouping your information. Just keep your pen moving and get down as much information as you can. ❑

Questioning

Reporters have an effective way of gathering information for a story—they ask, then answer, a set of standard questions about their subject: *who? what? when? where? how?* and *why?* You can use these **journalists' questions** as a prewriting technique, eliminating any of the questions that don't seem to apply to your subject. If your subject is a person, for example, you might ask yourself the following questions:

Whom am I writing about?
What is my relationship with this person? What is it that makes this person unique? What do I want to say about this person to my audience?
When did we meet? When did particular aspects of the person that are unique appear?
Where did the person exhibit the qualities I find unique?
How can I communicate this person's special quality to readers?
Why am I writing about this person? Why do I find him or her special?

Practice 3.5 Choose a subject to write about for "Options for Writing" (pp. 60–62), and then answer the six journalists' questions on a separate sheet of paper. ❑

Clustering

Clustering is a prewriting technique for randomly discovering information in a purely visual format. For some writers, clustering is less threatening than trying to fill up a blank page. To create a clustering diagram, write your subject in the middle of a blank page and then circle it. Then draw lines to connect that subject to more specific details or examples related to your subject. You can keep adding clusters to whatever ideas seem to lead you to more details. Note that your clusters can be in the form of single words, phrases, or questions. The following diagram illustrates student Elias Kary's clustering on the subject of reading.

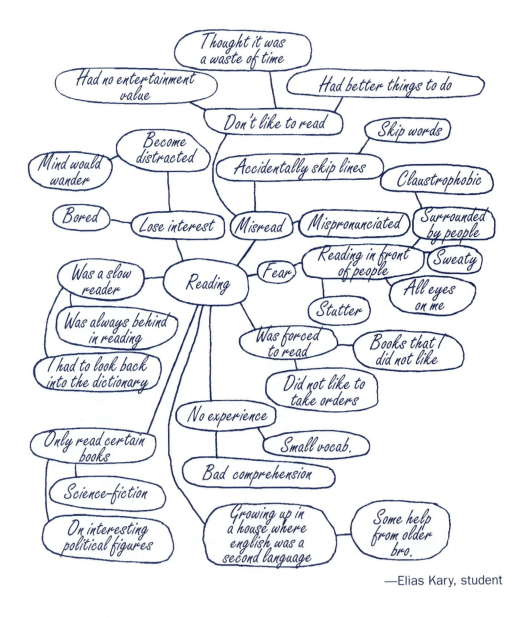

—Elias Kary, student

Practice 3.6   Choose an "Option for Writing" (pp. 60–62) you haven't worked with, and complete the clustering diagram provided. You can add more clusters if necessary. ❑

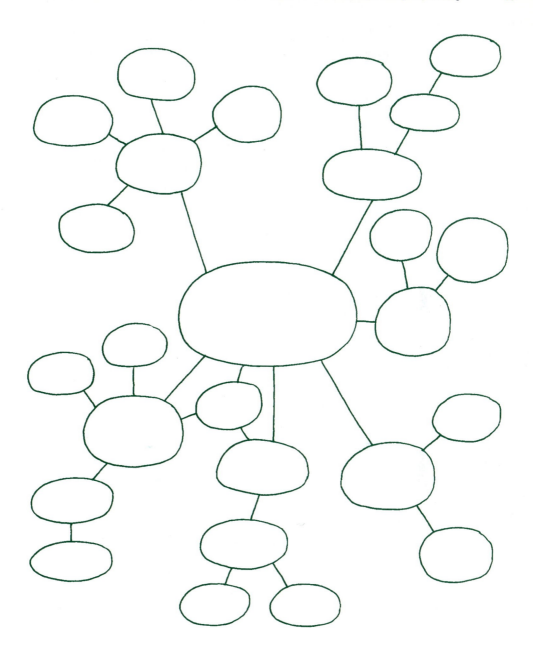

Mapping an Essay

Once you have in mind a few points you'd like to use in your essay, mapping can give you a visual picture of your organization and content. Examine the following essay map as an example:

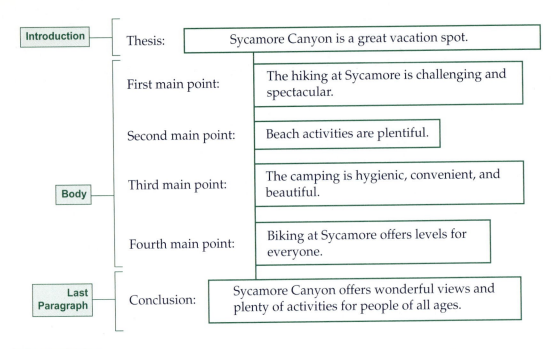

| Introduction | Thesis: | Sycamore Canyon is a great vacation spot. |

	First main point:	The hiking at Sycamore is challenging and spectacular.
	Second main point:	Beach activities are plentiful.
Body	Third main point:	The camping is hygienic, convenient, and beautiful.
	Fourth main point:	Biking at Sycamore offers levels for everyone.

| Last Paragraph | Conclusion: | Sycamore Canyon offers wonderful views and plenty of activities for people of all ages. |

Practice 3.7 To see how mapping an essay can help organize your material, create an essay map for the clustering you created in Practice 3.6. ❏

Thesis:

First main point:

Second main point:

Third main point:

Fourth main point:

Conclusion:

Strategies for Prewriting

1. **Purpose**   When you have a subject for your essay, ask yourself why you want to write about it. Think of any information you might want to collect to ease the readers' understanding of the subject.

2. **Focus**   Once you have completed one prewriting activity, examine your information carefully to discover which pieces of information you want to concentrate on. If helpful, repeat the same prewriting activity or use a different one to gather more information on your more focused subject.

3. **Material**   Experiment with different prewriting strategies to discover which one allows you to collect the most information for a particular assignment. Write down every idea that comes to you without censoring. In prewriting, too much material is better than not enough.

4. **Structure**   Once you've gathered all the prewriting information you can, reread what you have written, identify large groups of ideas in which to divide the material, and then delete any information that does not relate clearly to these groups.

5. **Style**   Get a peer or instructor to respond to your prewriting by indicating effective details and clear examples as well as confusing or vague information.

JOURNAL WRITING: DISCOVERING ENTRY

The "Journal Writing" in Chapter 1 introduced you to the reading log, a reading and writing strategy that you can now use to respond to an article written for the *New York Times* by a well-known American fiction writer who discusses an interesting prewriting strategy. Joyce Carol Oates contributes short stories and novels that often deal with pop culture and its influence on the dreams and aspirations of young adults. The following article is one of several in a series entitled "Writers on Writing," in which writers discuss with readers their individual writing processes.

1. Because of Oates's extensive vocabulary, it will help to look up the following words and note their definitions before reading the article. The essay paragraphs in which the words can be found are noted in parentheses, allowing you to annotate your text.

   efflorescence (1)

   analogue (2)

   atavistic (3)

   atoned (7)

   inextricably (8)

cisterns (9)

assuaging (12)

wraiths (13)

neurophysiology (18)

2. Respond in your reading log by following the instructions on page 16. In the left column, try to include phrases from the article that relate to gathering and developing material for writing. Remember to use the left column for passages from the article and the right column for your responses.

3. Oates asserts that for her, both writing and running are highly addictive activities. Do you have any two addictions or interests that, in a similar way, seem to go hand in hand? In another journal entry, write about these.

4. Reread the article, annotating phrases that reveal Oates's writing process. How is her writing process different from yours? Similar to yours?

To Invigorate Literary Mind, Start Moving Literary Feet

Joyce Carol Oates

1   Running! If there's any activity happier, more exhilarating, more nourishing to the imagination, I can't think what it might be. In running the mind flies with the body; the mysterious efflorescence of language seems to pulse in the brain, in rhythm with our feet and the swinging of our arms. Ideally, the runner who's a writer is running through the land- and city-scapes of her fiction, like a ghost in a real setting.

2   There must be some analogue between running and dreaming. The dreaming mind is usually bodiless, has peculiar powers of locomotion and, in my experience at least, often runs or glides or "flies" along the ground or in the air. (Leaving aside the blunt, deflating theory that dreams are merely compensatory: you fly in sleep because in life you crawl, barely; you're soaring above others in sleep because in life others soar above you.)

3   Possibly these fairy-tale feats of locomotion are atavistic remnants, the hallucinatory memory of a distant ancestor for whom the physical being, charged with adrenaline in emergency situations, was indistinguishable from the spiritual or intellectual. In running, "spirit" seems to pervade the body; as musicians experience the uncanny phenomenon of tissue memory in their fingertips, so the runner seems to experience in feet, lungs, quickened heartbeat, an extension of the imagining self.

4   The structural problems I set for myself in writing, in a long, snarled, frustrating and sometimes despairing morning of work, for instance, I can usually unsnarl by running in the afternoon.

5   On days when I can't run, I don't feel "myself"; and whoever the "self" is I feel, I don't like nearly so much as the other. And the writing remains snarled in endless revisions.

6   Writers and poets are famous for loving to be in motion. If not running, hiking; if not hiking, walking. (Walking, even fast, is a poor second to running, as all runners know, what we'll resort to when our knees go. But at least it's an option.)

7   The English Romantic poets were clearly inspired by their long walks, in all weather: Wordsworth and Coleridge in the idyllic Lake District, for instance; Shelley ("I always go until I am stopped and I never am stopped") in his four intense years in Italy. The New England Transcendentalists, most famously Henry David Thoreau, were ceaseless walkers; Thoreau boasted of having "traveled much in Concord," and he had to spend more than four hours out of doors daily, in motion; otherwise he felt "as if I had some sin to be atoned for."

8   Both running and writing are highly addictive activities; both are, for me, inextricably bound up with consciousness. I can't recall a time when I wasn't running, and I can't recall a time when I wasn't writing.

9   My earliest outdoor memories have to do with the special solitude of running or hiking in our pear and apple orchards, through fields of wind-rustling corn towering over my head, along farmers' lanes and on bluffs above the Tonawanda Creek. Through childhood I hiked, roamed, tirelessly explored the countryside: neighboring farms, a treasure trove of old barns, abandoned houses and forbidden properties of all kinds, some of them presumably dangerous, like cisterns and wells covered with loose boards.

10   These activities are intimately bound up with storytelling, for always there's a ghost-self, a "fictitious" self, in such settings.

11   Beyond the lines of printed words in my books are the settings in which the books were imagined and without which the books could not exist. Sometime in 1985, for instance, running along the Delaware River south of Yardley, Pa., I glanced up and saw the ruins of a railroad bridge and experienced in a flash such a vivid, visceral memory of crossing a footbridge beside a similar railroad trestle high above the Erie Canal in Lockport, N.Y., when I was 12 to 14 years old, that I saw the possibility of a novel. This would become "You Must Remember This," set in a mythical upstate New York city very like the original.

12   Yet often the reverse occurs: I find myself running in a place so intriguing to me, amid houses, or the backs of houses, so mysterious, I'm fated to write about these sights, to bring them to life (as it's said) in fiction. I'm a writer absolutely mesmerized by places: much of my writing is a way of assuaging homesickness, and the settings my characters inhabit are as crucial to me as the characters themselves. I couldn't write even a very short story without vividly "seeing" what its characters see.

13   Stories come to us as wraiths requiring precise embodiments. Running seems to allow me, ideally, an expanded consciousness in which I can envision what I'm writing as a film or a dream. I rarely invent at the typewriter but recall what I have experienced. I don't use a word processor but write in longhand, at considerable length. (Again, I know: writers are crazy.)

14   By the time I come to type out my writing formally, I've envisioned it repeatedly. I've never thought of writing as the mere arrangement of words on the page but as the attempted embodiment of a vision: a complex of emotions, raw experience.

15   The effort of memorable art is to evoke in the reader or spectator emotions appropriate to that effort. Running is a mediation; more practically it allows me to scroll through, in my mind's eye, the pages I've just written, proofreading for errors and improvements.

16   My method is one of continuous revision. While writing a long novel, every day I loop back to earlier sections to rewrite, in order to maintain a consistent, fluid voice. When I write the final two or three chapters of a novel, I write them simultaneously with the rewriting of the opening, so that, ideally at least, the novel is like a river uniformly flowing, each passage concurrent with all the others.

17   My most recent novel is 1,200 finished manuscript pages, which means many more typed-out pages, and how many miles of running, I dare not guess!

18   Dreams may be temporary flights into madness that, by some law of neurophysiology unclear to us, keep us from actual madness. So, too, the twin activities of running and writing keep the writer reasonably sane and with the hope, however illusory and temporary, of control.   ○

Using the Computer: Organizing Prewriting

1. Many of the prewriting strategies described in this chapter can be enhanced by using a word-processing program. For example, a *columns* or *table* feature can make it easier to cluster similar ideas, helping you to see patterns in your thoughts that might lead to an essay after you have brainstormed on paper.

    This is what student Elias Kary's clustering (p. 54) might look like if it were sorted using columns:

Feelings about books	Feelings about reading	Feelings about family reading
Liked books on political figures	Was a slow reader	English was second language in my house
Liked science fiction books	Stuttered over words	Older brother helped me read
	Disliked reading out loud	
	Got sweaty	

    Find a cluster or another kind of prewriting you've generated. Use your word-processing program's columns or tables feature to organize your prewriting into similar ideas. Be sure to *name* and *save* this work.

2. If you would like to examine another type of prewriting called *looping*, consult the following Website:

    www.writing.ku.edu/students/docs/prewriting.shtml

    To examine a list of prewriting questions for book, movie, or play reviews, go to this Website:

    http://leo.stcloudstate.edu/acadwrite/bookrevpre.html

OPTIONS FOR WRITING

You're now familiar with the characteristics of the college essay (discussed in Chapter 2) and the many promising ways of discovering material for essays through the prewriting techniques discussed in this chapter. Choose one of the options listed. Keeping your audience and purpose in mind, gather information using one or more prewriting strategies. After you have worked through the discovering stage of the composing process, give yourself time and distance, and possibly get some feedback from your instructor or peers. You can then evaluate your prewriting, making adjustments before proceeding to the next stage in your composing process. Write an essay developing your subject with an introduction, thesis, body paragraphs, and conclusion.

1. Discuss one or more major problems with your college or university. This could be something connected to facilities—classrooms, parking, cafeteria food or service, for example. Or the problem could have to do with class size, attendance policies, or course requirements. You may want to interview faculty members, administrators, other college personnel, or your classmates. Detail the problem as you see it and then try to put forth one or more solutions.

2. Write an essay about something you've learned on the job. Share your newfound knowledge and how you came to it.

3. Search newsstands or your college or local library for an article dealing with gender differences. You might also track down some information by interviewing class members, friends, and relatives. You might want to read the student essay "Men Are Makita, Women Are Marigolds" (p. 261). Write an essay exploring your views on gender differences.

4. Write about an area of your life in which you would like to achieve recognition. Student April Buell writes in her freewriting assignment (p. 52) that she would like recognition as a single mother, worker, and struggling college student. Have you accomplished something for which you feel you should be recognized?

5. Write about your favorite movie genre: scary movie, detective film, romantic comedy, historical drama, or other. Try to define the particular type of film you really enjoy, and then illustrate with examples based on your past film experiences.

6. Explain in an essay how to break a bad habit—think of a habit such as smoking, gambling, overeating, procrastination, or other. Inform your audience using your own personal experience or the experience of someone you know quite well to show how this habit can be broken.

7. Write an essay exploring a radical change in your appearance. Tell your audience what you looked like before, what experiences or process you underwent to effect the change, and how you feel about your altered appearance.

8. Describe a time when you experienced racism. The racism could have been directed at you or someone else. What in the situation do you feel prompted the racism? How did the parties involved react to the racism? What do you think of this incident now, looking back to that day?

9. *(Film and Literature)* Watch the 2001 film *O* and then read William Shakespeare's play *Othello*. Write an essay in which you discuss which version you think is better—support your claim with specific evidence.

10. *(Service Learning)* Find out if there is an office that coordinates service learning or volunteer efforts at your college. If so, contact instructors who offer service learning courses and ask them about the kinds of projects they have worked on.

RESPONDING TO WRITING: DISCOVERING KEYS FOR PREWRITING

For this activity, read the following student's freewriting and answer the key questions. You can then offer peer suggestions to help the student writer evaluate the success of her prewriting.

Prejudiced — what most people think they're not. Ha! Most people think they're so open-minded and accepting and different from their parents and ancestors in that respect but what about what happens to them when they come face to face with an HIV victim? These same people who think they're so free of prejudice are afraid they'll catch the deadly virus just by touching him, so they avoid him and shun him for no reason other than prejudice. And the obese teenage girl who is made fun of and sits alone eating in the school cafeteria because her peers are too cool to sit by her or even say hi to her, what is she if not another victim of PREJUDICE! What has she done to deserve this hurt of being ignored or shunned except if we believe being overweight is a sin, but people are still so smug saying oh no, I'm not prejudiced. Let's see, oh, I can think of lots of examples it just makes me mad all this hypocrisy, oh yeah, how about the factory worker whose boss drives an expensive car to work and wears an Armani suit and then gets the hate look from the worker just because the man is rich and the factory worker is poor, it's not the fault of the rich man, again what did he DO to deserve this prejudice? Nothing, not a thing. And what about the prostitute who has to make her living that way because she had a rotten childhood and doesn't have another skill and she really wants to turn her life around but she can't find a decent place to live or get a normal date because the minute people find out she's a prostitute they don't want a person like this as a neighbor or even a friend, they just shun her meanwhile saying to themselves that they are open-minded and have no prejudices.

—Corona Reynolds, *student*

Key Questions

1. **Purpose**   If the writer were to decide to develop this freewriting into an essay, state what purpose she might have in writing on this subject.

    In a phrase or sentence, identify the audience that would be most interested in the subject.

    What might this group of readers already know about the subject?

2. **Focus**   What is the word or phrase that forms the focal point of Reynolds's freewriting?

    Based on this freewriting, write a possible working thesis Reynolds might consider.

3. **Material**   Do you think the writer has enough material here for an essay, or should she continue to gather more material with this or another form of prewriting? (Support your answer with specific statements referring to Reynolds's prewriting.)

4. **Structure**   Could you suggest a way Reynolds might want to break up her information into smaller sections developing similar ideas?

5. **Style**   Note one phrase that was powerful for you, and then explain why you reacted to it strongly.

CRITICAL THINKING

In Connecting Texts

In this chapter you've heard from writers who share a search for and discovery of material. Joyce Carol Oates explores the parallel "in-flight" activities of running and writing. In her discussion of the discovery of material, Oates uses a **metaphor**—a direct comparison of one thing with another. Oates discusses the feeling that being in motion gives writers and poets: a "spirit seems to pervade the body." Work with a partner or small group and come up with your own metaphor for the discovering stage of the writing process. It may help to think of some totally unrelated but physical activity. Once you have an effective and powerful metaphor, see if you can develop it with details. Share your metaphor with the rest of the class if time permits. If you would like more information on the use of metaphors in writing, see "Responding to Writing: Comparisons" in Chapter 10 (p. 230).

Chapter 4

Finding a Thesis and Drafting

The first essential is to choose a subject which is clear and precise in your mind and which interests you personally. . . . The next thing is to devise a form for your essay.

—Gilbert Highet, *writer and educator*

My first draft usually has only a few elements worth keeping. I have to find out what those are and build from them and throw out what doesn't work, or what simply is not alive.

—Susan Sontag, *playwright, novelist, and critic*

Preview

In this chapter you will learn

- How to identify and create the parts of an effective thesis: subject, controlling idea, specific language, appropriate tone
- How to use an outline to focus and organize your draft
- How to draft an essay with the "keys" in mind
- How to participate in peer editing

After reading this chapter and completing all of its practice activities, you will be able to write a working draft of an essay that develops a clearly phrased thesis.

Now that you are familiar with prewriting strategies, you're ready to narrow your subject and organize and shape the essay. Although each writer's composing process is unique, the narrowing, organizing, and shaping of an essay often take place in the drafting stage of the process. As you focus on a particular aspect of your subject, you will want to develop an effective thesis—the foundation of your essay. Your essay will develop as you give detailed support to your thesis in your body paragraphs. Do you remember playing with blocks as a child? You needed to create your base first, and that base had to be sound or the blocks you stacked on it would come tumbling down. In a similar way, your thesis forms the foundation or spine of your entire essay.

CHARACTERISTICS OF A THESIS STATEMENT

You'll recall that a thesis, one of the parts of the essay introduced in Chapter 2, contains the main point, idea, or opinion the writer wants to convey about a subject. It also enables the audience to identify what a writer is going to focus on, usually before the end of the first paragraph of the essay. An effective thesis has four characteristics:

- It states the subject of the essay clearly.

- It includes a controlling idea about the subject.

- It uses specific language rather than vague words.

- It establishes a tone that is appropriate for the subject and the intended audience.

If any one of these four qualities is missing, the thesis will not provide the needed focus and the essay will not have a strong foundation. In addition, the thesis *may* include a plan of development.

To see how these characteristics work together to strengthen the foundation of your essay, read the following sample thesis:

> Living in a large city has become increasingly challenging due to higher costs of housing, more crowded roads and freeways, and increasing crime rates.
>
> —Greg Smith, *student*

If you want to find Smith's **subject**, ask yourself, "What is he writing about?"

If you want to find the **controlling idea**, or the writer's opinion about the subject, ask yourself, "What is Smith's feeling about his subject?"

To identify **specific language**, ask yourself, "Which word or group of words in this thesis paints the strongest 'word picture' by using precise words?"

When you're analyzing the thesis for **tone**, look for hints about the writer's attitude and whether or not this attitude is appropriate for the subject and audience. In identifying Smith's tone, you could ask, "Does he seem rational in his approach to the subject, or does he appear to rant and rave offensively? Is he humorous or serious?"

You'll notice that Smith includes a **plan of development**—a group of words that breaks his subject into separate parts. Although a plan of development is not a characteristic of all thesis statements, sometimes it is helpful as a kind of road map for the writer, and later, the audience. In his drafting, Smith decided to focus his discussion of the challenges of big-city living on three specific problems. Review Smith's thesis and note his plan of development.

Practice 4.1   For practice in recognizing the characteristics of a thesis, read the following thesis statements and then identify the characteristics you find in each: subject, controlling idea, example of specific language, tone, and plan of development. You may want to refer to the sample thesis and accompanying questions.

1. Love is an illness, and it has its own set of obsessive thoughts.

    —Richard Selzer, from "Love Sick"

    Subject:

    Controlling idea:

    Example of specific language:

    Tone:

    Plan of development?

2. The life support systems of this almost impossibly beautiful planet are being violated and degraded, causing often irreparable damage, yet only a small proportion of humans have focused on this crisis.

    —Charlene Spretnak, from *Reweaving the World: The Emergence of Ecofeminism*

    Subject:

    Controlling idea:

    Example of specific language:

    Tone:

    Plan of development?

3. The Arab-Israeli conflict and the oil crisis of the 1970s have exacerbated an atmosphere of hostility toward Arabs who have chosen to make their home in the U.S.

    —Mustafa Nabil, from "The Arab's Image"

    Subject:

    Controlling idea:

    Example of specific language:

    Tone:

    Plan of development?

4. The most important day I remember in all my life is the one on which my teacher, Anne Mansfield Sullivan, came to me. I am filled with wonder when I consider the immeasurable contrast between the two lives which it connects.

    —Helen Keller, from "The Day Language Came into My Life"

    Subject:

    Controlling idea:

    Example of specific language:

    Tone:

    Plan of development?

5. I had cybersex the other night, and, boy, am I sorry.

—Sandra Tsing Loh, from "Cybersex Gal"

Subject:

Controlling idea:

Example of specific language:

Tone:

Plan of development?   ❑

Did you notice a lot of variety in these thesis statements? Although each author makes unique choices, each of these thesis statements has a clear and interesting subject, a controlling idea, specific language, and a tone appropriate for the intended audience. When you are trying to create an effective thesis for your own essay, how can you be sure that your thesis also contains these characteristics? Using the following guidelines and considering the five "keys" will help. Also, remember that you should experiment with and then periodically evaluate your thesis statement as you develop your essay. This trial-and-error process will help you discover if you have omitted any of the four characteristics of an effective thesis. You can then make the necessary changes and adjustments.

GUIDELINES FOR WRITING THESIS STATEMENTS

Consider Audience in Selecting a Subject

Once you have chosen or have been assigned a particular writing option, you'll want to consider subjects that will be interesting and suitable. Although a gifted writer may be able to write a fascinating essay on almost any subject, it's a good idea to avoid subjects about which readers are either experts or completely uninterested. For instance, if you are asked to write about friends and friendships, you might bore an audience with a thesis such as this:

In my life I have had three different types of friends—the best friend, the good friend, and the acquaintance.

Although this thesis has a helpful plan of development, most readers are already familiar with these categories of friends; you really wouldn't be sharing any new information. Instead, if you want to explore the subject of friends, and if the assignment permits personal experience as material, you might consider a thesis like this:

I have a distinct relationship and I take on a different persona with each of the following: my friends at work, my friends at college, and my longtime friends from childhood.

In your selection process, avoid a subject that is so broad you can discuss it only in general terms without offering your audience in-depth information or insight. It is much wiser to focus on a particular aspect of a broader subject that interests you rather than trying to cover, say, the causes of the Persian Gulf War or the impact of environmental pollution. If one of these topics excites you, you could choose to explore the effects of a particular battle in the Persian Gulf War or the fight to save pelicans that have been affected by a recent oil spill.

Practice 4.2   For practice in identifying appropriate and interesting subjects for a thesis, examine the following sentences, considering what an audience of college students, for example, might already know versus what they might like to find out. If you think the sentence is suitable for a thesis, explain why. If not, revise the sentence to create an effective thesis for an essay.

1. Colors are interesting.

2. Many couples choose to adopt children.

3. Belief in God varies throughout the world.

4. The Supreme Court justices are appointed for life.

5. Although compact discs cost more than cassette tapes, discs have better sound quality. ❏

Check for a Controlling Idea

A quick way to determine the quality of your thesis is the "So what?" test. If your thesis statement might prompt a reader to respond, "So what?" you know you need to do some reworking of the thesis, possibly to clarify your controlling idea. Look at the following thesis statement:

> Parks are places where a lot of people gather every weekend.

This thesis is too general; it states the information but has no focus on the writer's opinion. It does not pass the "So what?" test. Perhaps this was the writer's first thesis in prewriting or even early drafting. After more consideration, the writer might come up with the following revised version of a working thesis:

> Parks in my neighborhood have become a place where people of all ages enjoy individual pursuits and interact with one another.

Notice that the subject, parks, has been narrowed, and that the writer now has an evident controlling idea: Parks have become a positive force in the neighborhood. The reader can now determine the writer's opinion about the subject.

Practice 4.3   You can test your ability to narrow a subject by including a controlling idea for the following subjects. Once you've added a controlling idea, try to create a working thesis for each subject. Remember that a working thesis is not "written in stone," but is one that you feel you can work with as you write and revise the essay. The first thesis has been done for you.

Subject	Controlling Idea	Working Thesis
1. Pro sports stars	*Outrageous salaries*	*The outrageous salaries of many pro sports stars lead to unrealistic expectations on the part of hopeful teen athletes.*
2. Part-time jobs		
3. Single-parent families		
4. Violence		
5. Television ❏		

Avoid an Announcement

Although you want to be as specific as possible, some writers make the mistake of "announcing" their thesis. They refer to their process and thus distract the reader from the subject by writing phrases such as "In this essay, I will attempt to show," or "I believe that this statement is true," or "This essay will now describe. . . ." You want to avoid the announcement approach.

Practice 4.4   In the following thesis statements, identify those that are announcements and then rewrite them so that they refer to the subject, not the process.

1. I'm going to discuss the pros and cons of body piercing.

2. The Internet offers us an opportunity to research a subject in the privacy and comfort of our homes.

3. I will argue that freshman composition should not be a required course.

4. I will describe my sister for you so that you can see how different we are.

5. My sister and I, although twins, couldn't look more alike or be more different in our tastes, interests, and friends.   ❏

Use Specific Language

If you've ever talked with someone who says "kinda" or "sorta" or "all that stuff," you'll grasp the importance of using specific language in a thesis. Although specific word choice is desirable throughout your essay, it is perhaps most essential to your thesis. After all, the thesis is often in your introductory paragraph—the one that tells the reader what the essay will focus on. If your word choices are vague, confusing, dull, or misleading, your thesis statement is not going to achieve its desired effect: It cannot successfully establish the foundation of your essay. How can you tell if what is crystal clear to you is also being communicated to your audience? Specific word choice in a thesis statement faces a subject head-on, rather than "straddling the fence." For example, the following thesis statement is confusing:

Many people say that capital punishment is cruel and unusual punishment, and in certain respects this is definitely and undeniably true.

The reader is confused here most of all by the vague phrase "in certain respects this is true" because "in certain respects" does not explain the writer's distinct opinion of the cruelty of capital punishment. Here is a more specific version:

> Theologians and medical experts alike argue that capital punishment is cruel because the victim suffers extreme psychological and physical effects.

There is a world of difference between these two thesis statements. In the second version, readers know without question where the writer will go for the bulk of evidence, and also what specific effects the writer will detail.

At other times, although the subject and the controlling idea are clear, the word choices lack the clarity to allow the reader to focus fully on the impact of the thesis statement. Consider the following example:

> Many innovations and technical advances in the last few years in our society have given us a lot more options, but these have cost us something too in the way in which we relate to one another.

After rethinking and working on more specific language, the writer might revise this thesis as follows:

> Computers have given us new research and communication capabilities, but they have also depersonalized our daily lives and circumvented human interaction.

While in the first version the writer may have been thinking specifically of computers, readers were unable to picture anything specific with the term *technical advances*. Also, instead of merely indicating vaguely that there are negative as well as positive consequences associated with computers, the writer's second version of the thesis makes the focus clear: the depersonalizing effects of computers.

Practice 4.5   See if you can hone your use of specific language by revising the following thesis statements. Replace any vague words or terms you find.

1. College can be a strange place for a new student.
2. Our current political system is in need of a big change.
3. Owning a pet can be rewarding.
4. Choosing the right career is really important.
5. Homeless people should not be looked down upon. ❏

Establish an Appropriate Tone

If someone were to snarl at you, "Don't speak to me in that tone of voice!" you would know immediately that you had been offensive. In the same way, your attitude comes through not just in *what you say* but also in *how you say it* in your thesis. And this tone can encourage your reader either to give you the benefit of the doubt, or to decide before reading any further that you're not to be trusted. Consider this thesis:

> Television commercials are worse than worthless—they are the most despicable examples of blatant, deceptive, sexist, hard-sell tactics in the advertising world today.

Although the thesis has an interesting subject, a controlling idea, and specific language, the writer might want to reconsider both the purpose and the audience. It is possible that some, perhaps many, readers enjoy television commercials on occasion; some readers might be advertising executives or work in some related way in the television commercial industry. It is commendable that the writer has found a subject he or she feels strongly about, but perhaps a more reasonable tone would help the thesis. Examine this revised version and ask yourself which version promises a more rational, thoughtful writer:

> Although television commercials are often entertaining and sometimes informative, they seldom tell the whole truth but instead lure the viewer with false claims.

Perhaps you responded to this second version more readily because the writer's tone is reasonable and straightforward. Because tone is so important to an effective thesis, you want to make sure that your tone is:

- Appropriate for your audience

- Helpful for your purpose

While your journal entries, e-mail, and letter writing to close friends will be informal, the college essay requires a more formal tone; you don't share the same level of familiarity with your reading audience that you do with a close friend. In addition, particular writing situations call for differing levels of formality, although all require you to use reasonable, nonconfrontational language in order to gain your reader's trust.

Practice 4.6   Read about the following essay-writing situations. Then, in a few words, describe the most appropriate tone for the reader to take in each situation. The first activity has been done for you.

Audience	Situation	Tone
1. Highly educated professionals	Inform of dangers of secondhand smoke	*Fairly formal, serious*
2. Fellow college students	Make fun of procrastinators	
3. The President of the United States	Persuade to increase spending for education	
4. Junior high students	Inform of dangers of secondhand smoke	
5. Subscribers of community newspaper	Express disapproval of city council action	

Test and Reverse

If you have drafted several versions of your working thesis, how do you decide which one will provide the strongest foundation for your essay? A good strategy for determining the effectiveness of your thesis is *reverse testing*—a process in which you test your thesis statement by reversing your position on your subject and determining what the opposing viewpoint might be. You can try this with all versions of your thesis to see which one works best. To take a look at reverse testing in action, recall student Greg Smith's thesis presented at the beginning of this chapter:

> Living in a large city has become increasingly challenging due to higher costs of housing, more crowded roads and freeways, and increasing crime rates.

If Smith were to reverse test, he would think about the opposing viewpoint and come up with something like this:

> Living in a large city has become more desirable due to increased job opportunities, greater number of cultural activities, and efficient and economical public transportation.

This reverse thesis would clue Smith in to an opposing opinion. He might choose to alter his thesis to anticipate counterarguments, as in the following thesis:

> Although living in a large city has become more desirable for several reasons, it has also become increasingly challenging due to higher costs of housing, more crowded roads and freeways, and increasing crime rates.

You can see that reverse testing helps you predict the opposing viewpoint. You can then determine if your own thesis will stand up to that opposition.

Practice 4.7   Write an opposing version of the following thesis statements in order to test the thesis.

1. All college students should be required to take a basic psychology course in order to have an elementary understanding of human behavior.

2. Lack of handgun control has led to increased crime, injury, and murder across the United States.

3. Giving college athletes special help and privileges in college courses creates an atmosphere of injustice among college students and faculty. ❏

Practice 4.8   Write a thesis that would be appropriate for the material covered in the following supporting points in an essay.

1. Many vacationers flood freeways, campsites, and hotels during this time. Because many college as well as high school students are out of school, resorts can be crowded with visitors. Airlines and hotels charge more during the holiday season.

2. Cutting shown on caffeine will reduce insomnia at right. Salt reduction in one's diet will reduce water retention. Eating plenty of fruits and

vegetables will provide antioxidants reported to stave off cancer. Limiting cholesterol will help guard against stroke and other debilitating illness.

3. A computer allows one to store material on disk, taking up much less space than paper files. Computers offer easy access to various merchandise online. Computers permit users to correspond instantly and easily with friends and relatives. Computers allow users to see photographs of people that could be on the other side of the world.   ❑

Evaluating Thesis Statements

Based on the guidelines just discussed, examine the following thesis statements to take note of their strengths and weaknesses.

Weak: Musical comedies of the 1930s are interesting. (Readers do not know what the write means by the subjective term "interesting.")
Stronger: Musical comedies of the 1930s are famous for stars that could sing, dance, and act with excellence. (This thesis tells readers the three specific aspects of these musical comedies that will be discussed.)

Weak: Advertising can be deceptive to consumers. (Readers already know this fact; this thesis falls into the "so what?" category.)
Stronger: Deceptive advertising often causes consumers to spend money needlessly and to expect unrealistic results from products. (Readers expect the essay to cover two specific effects deceptive advertising has on consumers.)

Weak: *Romeo and Juliet* is a play about love. (This thesis leads readers to expect that the writer will cover an incredibly broad area, love, in relation to the play. This thesis is too general to offer any direction for readers.)
Stronger: *Romeo and Juliet* becomes William Shakespeare's treatise against feuding clans. (This thesis makes clear that the writer will be arguing against warring groups who fail to trust each other.)

Weak: We need to pay attention to the environment. (Again, because readers know this to be true, this thesis falls into the "so what?" category.)
Stronger: Congress should encourage rebates for those who purchase hybrid vehicles. (Rather than attempting to talk about every aspect of our environment, this thesis tells readers that the writer will focus on fuel-efficient vehicles and how they are environment-friendly.)

Weak: In the novel *Passage to India,* Dr. Aziz is flighty and emotional, but at the same tine he is loyal and likeable. (This thesis confuses readers by pulling in two opposing directions.)
Stronger: In the novel *Passage to India,* Dr. Aziz is a likeable character who nevertheless can be flighty and overly emotional. (This thesis tells readers that two traits can be illustrated in the actions and comments of Dr. Aziz.)

Weak: We will examine the problems many first-generation college students face. (This thesis uses an "announcement" in the first three words.)

Stronger: Many first-generation college students face problems with finances, nonsupportive family, and peers. (The thesis informs readers of the three areas to be discussed.)

Weak: Siblings can be as different as night and day. (Readers know that siblings have differences—what about them?)

Stronger: Chronological placement in the family may be responsible for some personality differences among siblings. (This thesis informs readers that the writer will focus on age and ranking differences as a determining factor in siblings' personalities.)

Weak: Parking on our college campus is really horrendous. (This thesis does not have a controlling idea about the subject that is specifically phrased.)

Stronger: Parking lots on our campus could be greatly improved if they were closer to classrooms, more plentiful, and safer at night. (This thesis forecasts three main areas of concern about campus parking.)

Weak: Part-time jobs for high school students are not a good idea. (Lack of specific focus makes it hard for readers to know what the writer feels about these jobs.)

Stronger: Part-time jobs for high school students can cause lower performance in classes and less involvement in extra-curricular activities at school. (Readers know that the essay will discus two effects of students working part-time.)

Weak: Some Americans think there is too much freedom of speech, and others feel there is not enough. (This thesis confuses readers by pulling in two opposing directions.)

Stronger: Although our First Amendment guarantees freedom of speech, we need at least a few limitations on this freedom. (This thesis tells readers that the writer will discuss our First Amendment rights and argue that limitations should be made.)

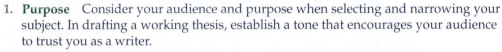

Strategies for Writing Thesis Statements

1. **Purpose**   Consider your audience and purpose when selecting and narrowing your subject. In drafting a working thesis, establish a tone that encourages your audience to trust you as a writer.

2. **Focus**   Limit your subject by including a controlling idea in your thesis statement.

3. **Material**   Delete any material that makes your thesis sound like an announcement. Reverse test to determine the opposing point of view and get peer feedback. Make necessary adjustments.

4. **Structure**   Experiment with the arrangement of the subject and controlling idea in your thesis statement. If breaking your subject into parts will allow readers to follow your ideas more easily, include a plan of development.

5. **Style**   Check to see that your thesis uses specific language to convey a clear word picture to your audience.

When you have written a working thesis, be sure to pull back from the thesis and evaluate it carefully to determine whether it needs additional rephrasing. You may still be adjusting and narrowing your subject to shape a thesis as you enter the second stage of the composing process: drafting.

CHARACTERISTICS OF DRAFTING

After you have experimented with one or more prewriting techniques, determined your audience and purpose, gathered material, and responded to your prewriting, it is time to begin drafting your essay. Remember from Chapter 2 that a draft is a rough preliminary version of a piece of writing. A first draft, or **preliminary draft**, is only one of what will probably be many drafts before you produce the **final draft**, which you will present to your audience. Peter Drucker, a well-known business author, referred to his first draft as "the zero draft"—after that he would start counting! And writer and teacher Anne Lamott tells her writing students jokingly that the first draft is the "down" draft—you just get it down on paper, while the subsequent drafts are the "up" drafts—you work on fixing them up.

If you approach drafting as an opportunity to put your planning into action and experiment with various ways of getting your ideas across to your reader, *knowing that you can revise the draft later,* you'll feel more comfortable about this stage of the writing process. To get a better idea of what a first draft might look like, let's examine one student's preliminary draft. (The instructor's comments on this draft, a later revised draft, peer response on this draft, and the student's final draft, are included in Chapter 7.)

MODEL (FIRST DRAFT) WITH KEY QUESTIONS

Margarita Figueroa's assignment involved reading an essay about dishonesty in America, agreeing or disagreeing with the author's thesis, and then writing an essay that supported her position with specific examples. Once Figueroa had completed prewriting and developed a working thesis, she decided she had enough material to begin drafting. As she wrote this first draft, Figueroa kept her working thesis and the informal outline on page 79 next to her computer keyboard. Figueroa noted when she finished the draft that although she had not communicated all of her ideas as clearly as she had hoped, she was exhilarated to have transformed all the information from her prewriting into a first draft. Figueroa experienced that tremendous sense of accomplishment that many writers have when they get their first drafts on paper.

Dishonesty

Margarita Figueroa

Margarita Figueroa decided in the first weeks of her writing class that learning to write clearly would be crucial to her future profession, nursing. Throughout the semester, she worked hard not only on getting first drafts on paper but also on revising and polishing them. Margarita confides that right now she has little free time, but when she does have a few hours, she enjoys reading mysteries.

1   I was reading an essay written by Marya Mannes called "The Thin Grey Line." It was a very interesting article, separating honesty from dishonesty. It made me really think about if people are dishonest or honest. I feel that dishonesty is more characteristic of our society than honesty.

2   Well, first there is the fake car accident that results in getting money out of auto insurance companies. For instance, I had friends that would get together and collaborate with one another and would report to the insurance company about an accident that they were involved in, but it wasn't a real accident. It was a fraudolent claim. They even had a friend who was a lawyer that would help them set everything up as if it was a legitimate accident. They used their own cars, license plate numbers, and insurance companies, and each person received an out-of-court settlement of five hundred dollars. Another reason for dishonesty is when an opportunity arises for an individual to become dishonest.

3   The circumstance that occurs and causes an indivual to become dishonest. For example, my sister told me about an incident that happened to her at Burger King. My sister had ordered burgers, fries, and drinks for her family. After she placed her order, the woman who works at Burger King rang the order up, but meanwhile my sister and the woman were having a conversation about kids. Then, my sister saw the total amount due, which was $14.83, so she gave the woman a twenty dollar bill and the woman gave my sister her order and then gave her the change due to her. This is when the woman made a mistake and gave her back the total amount due, which was $14.83, instead of $5.17, which was the change due. My sister noticed the mistake the woman made, but she didn't say anything. She walked out of Burger King, got in her car, and went home.

4   Dishonesty can also occur between two people in a relationship. It can result in blaming others for mistakes made by someone else. I have a friend that lives in the apartment complex where I stay. Her husband one day was backing up his car into his stall underneath the carport, when all of a sudden he hit one of the wooden poles that holds up the carport and moved it out of place. Then he called the owner of the building and explained to him about the incident that occurred, but instead of taking the blame for hitting the pole, he put the blame on his wife. Every time someone asked him what happened to the pole next to his car, he would reply, "Oh, my wife hit the pole when she was parking the car."

5   Finally, I do agree with the article "The Thin Grey Line" and Marya Mannes' opinion separating honesty from dishonesty because if we really take a close look at different situations, we would probably find a little dishonesty here and there. I feel that everyone has had some sort of dishonesty once in their lives, whether it

was a little white lie or not, but dishonesty is a way of life for some people. We need to be more responsible for our dishonest decisions and behaviors, but most of all, we need to strengthen our moral beliefs because dishonesty can have a major effect on everyone involved. ○

Key Questions

1. **Purpose**   What seems to be the writer's purpose in this draft? What kind of audience does she appear to be addressing?

2. **Focus**   Find and underline Figueroa's thesis. Does it have the four characteristics discussed earlier in this chapter for an effective thesis? Which ones are missing or could be improved?

3. **Material**   Where does the writer get her material? Could she use more examples or different ones? In which paragraphs could additional or different material help?

4. **Structure**   How has Figueroa ordered or arranged the material?

5. **Style**   Which phrase seems most effective in getting across the writer's thesis?

Grammar Key

Handbook Practice: Run-ons and Comma Splices

Read pages 427–428 and complete Exercise 4, correct the paragraph following Exercise 4, and then edit Jorge Arellano's essay "A Safer Driver" on pages 430–431.

GUIDELINES FOR DRAFTING

In writing drafts of essays for previous assignments, Figueroa had stared at a blank computer screen for what seemed like an eternity. Because she did not want to be plagued again with writer's block, she decided to try some of the following suggestions for drafting.

Assess Material

After completing one or more prewriting activities, spread out all the material you have gathered in front of you. If your prewriting was completed on computer, print out all your notes—it's easier to assess material on a printed page. Make sure you have enough paper and pens or pencils. Keeping all supplies and notes within easy reach will allow you greater concentration and fewer interruptions.

Practice 4.9   To determine a strategy for beginning a draft, find in the text the two supplies Figueroa used when drafting. Now list all the supplies, outlines, and so forth you recall using when you drafted your last essay. Which items were most useful? What items or resources will you add to this list? ❏

When you have all of your notes in front of you, assess the information to decide what to use in this first draft. Evaluate your material with your purpose and audience in mind. Ask yourself which details, facts, and examples most effectively support your working thesis for your audience. Make a tentative selection, setting aside (for now) any material that you won't use right away.

Order Material

Each writer needs to discover what works best for him or her—especially during the drafting stage. Your preliminary draft will probably include a working thesis, some support for that thesis, and a tentative method for organizing this support. Some writers begin to draft by jumping right in and writing an introduction that includes their thesis statement. Beginning with an introduction, no matter how rough, may give you a strong sense of having formally begun to write.

Other writers find it more useful to begin drafting in what will become the middle of their essay. Using their working thesis as a guide, they begin to develop and organize the examples, details, and other supporting materials that will provide the body of the essay and support their working thesis.

Begin in the Middle

Although some writers like to begin with the introduction, others prefer to begin with the body paragraphs, saving the introduction and the conclusion until later. If you discover that this approach works for you, you should know that you're in good company. Richard Wright had almost finished drafting his powerful novel *Native Son* when he discovered, through development of the novel's characters, exactly what to write in his introductory pages.

The following are common ways of organizing material:

- Chronological order

- Spatial order

- Logical order

When you arrange your material in **chronological order**, you're choosing to proceed based on the time order in which events occur. For example, if you're writing an essay describing an event or observing someone or something over a progression of time, chronological order would be a good choice. You would be telling the events or situations in the order in which they occurred.

If, on the other hand, the subject of your essay is physical—for example, a computer setup and operation, or the layout of an efficient office, you might prefer **spatial order**, in which you would proceed from left to right, top to bottom, or front to back. Finally, if your essay deals with ideas and concepts rather than with time or space, you might choose **logical order**. Examples of logical order include **exemplification**, or explanation through the use of examples, cause and effect, comparing and contrasting, proceeding from a general statement to a particular one, or from a minor detail to the whole picture.

For more information and for practice in identifying and choosing an order for your draft, see the section in Chapter 5 on organizing your support.

Outline

Once you have an idea of how your essay should be organized, you may want to develop an **outline,** a structural plan that uses headings and subdivisions to present the main points and subpoints of an essay. An outline can serve as an easy-to-read checklist and visual guide, and it can be as formal or as informal as you like. Think of your outline as a blueprint; you will refer to it frequently as you draft your essay to remind you what to do next.

The Informal Outline

The **informal outline** is meant for your use only and can be simply a list of the main ideas you want to develop. This type of outline should be easy to create based on your notes and prewriting, and it can help you decide what should come first, second, and third in the development of your material. To see an example of an informal outline, examine the one that Figueroa used in preparation for drafting "Dishonesty":

> Thesis: I feel that dishonesty is more characteristic
>   of our society than honesty.
> Dishonesty in groups
>   friends and fake car accident
> Dishonesty in individuals
>   Burger King incident
> Dishonesty in not accepting responsibility
>   man who shifted blame to his wife

The Formal Outline

Later in the semester, Figueroa's instructor assigned a research-based essay. With her instructor's permission, Figueroa decided to explore more thoroughly the concept of dishonesty. She was asked by her instructor to create a **formal outline** for the research-based essay. The formal outline is one that conforms to certain rules for numbering, lettering, and general format. A formal outline can help you examine the organization of a longer essay or research-based writing to determine if your essay will be logical and complete. Figueroa created the formal outline below. Notice its format.

Thesis: The thin line separating honest from dishonest behavior in America is becoming blurred because families, schools, and public as well as private institutions are neglecting responsibilities and accepting corruption as natural.

I. Families fail to enforce appropriate values.
    A. Mothers and fathers allow children instant gratification, denying them nothing.
        1. Parents give in to all material desires of their offspring.
        2. Children are not expected to work for what they want.
    B. Parents do not model honest behavior for their children.
        1. Many adults engage in dishonest behavior by cheating on taxes or bribing officials.
        2. Other adults refuse to take responsibility and be a "hero" when they witness corrupt behavior in others.

II. Schools either try to teach values and fail or refuse to recognize responsibility.

    A. Programs designed to teach values have been instigated.

        1. These programs have cost taxpayers lots of money and teachers much classroom time.

        2. The programs have accomplished little or nothing in the way of changing the behavior of students.

    B. Many school districts have refused to participate in the programs to teach values.

        1. These districts cite the meager success rate of the programs.

        2. They also stress the high cost of the programs.

        3. They feel it is not the responsibility of educators, but of parents, to teach values.

III. American institutions are rife with dishonesty and corruption.

    A. People who work in public institutions exhibit dishonest behavior.

        1. Politicians, law enforcement officers, and city officials engage in corrupt activities.

        2. Lower-ranking officials in institutions may be guilty of small deceptions.

    B. People who work for private institutions also engage in dishonesty on the job.

        1. Many businesspersons pad their expense accounts and take extra long lunch breaks and frivolous "business trips."

        2. Office staff and temporary or part-time office staff are also guilty of corrupt behavior.

You can see that the formal outline follows this format:

- It begins with a thesis.

- It indicates the main points with uppercase Roman numerals (I, II, III, IV).

- It identifies subcategories of topics with uppercase letters (A, B, C, D).

- It distinguishes support or evidence related to these subcategories with Arabic numbers (1, 2, 3, 4).

- It would indicate, if the writer wished to include additional information, specific details with lowercase letters (a, b, c, d).

Figueroa found that using a formal outline for a longer, more complex essay helps to organize material and maintain focus during drafting.

Practice 4.10   Turn to "Responding to Writing: Practice in Outlining" (p. 85) and complete the activities, or find an essay draft that you prepared for another assignment. Create either a formal or an informal outline of the main points and support as evidence in your draft.   ❑

Draft in Sections

If, like Wright, you find yourself staring at a blank page or screen during the drafting process, and you feel hesitant or confused about the introduction, jump right in and proceed with your thesis and supporting material. You can always come back to the introduction later.

You'll have a much greater feeling of accomplishment if you work through your draft in sections rather than try to complete the entire essay in a short period of time. Try drafting a paragraph or two and then taking a short break. This will allow you to get a little distance. You'll be able to see what you've written with "new eyes" when you come back and review your writing before moving on.

Define All Terms

Regardless of the subject matter of your essay, part of keeping your audience and purpose in mind as you're drafting requires that you define any unfamiliar or possibly confusing terms that you use. If you're telling your reader how to install "woofers" in a sound system or make reference to the "operatory" where the patient is reclining, the average reader is going to be confused unless you briefly but clearly define these terms. (For more information on definitions, see Chapter 10.)

Draft Multiple Versions

When you do come to a section of your draft that poses a problem or that you're unsure about, try drafting at least two different versions of the section. Later, when you review your draft, you can judge which version seems to work better. For example, Figueroa decided to check her working thesis by reverse testing. She experimented by switching the original order of paragraphs 2 and 3.

Reserve Technical Considerations

Don't let spelling, grammar, or punctuation errors slow you down in your drafting stage—you will address these concerns in good time in the revising and polishing stages. Instead, focus all your energies on getting your ideas on paper. This may be especially difficult advice to follow, for you may want to write "the perfect essay." Just remember that this is a draft. Your goal is to get ideas down on paper—later on you'll fix them up. If you are distracted at this stage by things like spelling and commas, you'll get sidetracked from what you're trying to communicate to your audience.

Share Drafts with Peers

Although many of us get butterflies in the stomach at the thought of someone else reading our writing, the feedback that we get from instructors, tutors, and peers can be very helpful. **Peer response**, also called **peer editing**, involves sharing your draft (this could be a first, second, or almost final draft) with another class member or within a small group. Your instructor may have a particular system for peer editing, or you may want to initiate a peer editing session yourself by suggesting it to another student. Although all feedback is helpful, you will want to evaluate carefully the quality of feedback from student editors.

Strategies for Drafting

1. **Purpose**   As you draft, don't worry about spelling, grammar, or other technical considerations. Do consider what your audience already knows about the subject, and define all unfamiliar terms. Draft multiple versions of troublesome sections to determine which version best suits your purpose.

2. **Focus**   Begin drafting based on a working thesis that includes a subject, controlling idea, specific language, and appropriate tone. Glance back often at your thesis to make sure that what you are writing relates clearly to it.

3. **Material**   Before starting to draft, assess your material from prewriting and make sure you can access all notes easily.

4. **Structure**   Work from an outline, either formal or informal, to give your draft a logical structure. Experiment with various drafting strategies, such as breaking the draft into smaller chunks or beginning in the middle.

5. **Style**   Seek out peer or instructor response to gauge the effectiveness of your draft.

Practice 4.11   To get a better idea of how peer feedback can help you in drafting, locate a preliminary draft of an essay that you are working on or one that you've kept from a past assignment. Exchange essays with another student in your class. Turn to the peer editing activity in Chapter 7 (p. 132). Answer all "key" questions on a separate sheet of paper.   ❏

JOURNAL WRITING: FROM IDEA TO ESSAY

The following activities will help you to focus on your own drafting process. You'll also practice the process of moving from the shaping of ideas to the framing of a clear thesis.

1. If you have been keeping a reading log as suggested in Chapter 1, return to your log and review what you've written. Choose one journal entry and reread your notes. Can you zero in on what seems to be the most interesting note on the reading? Pick the one direct quote from the left-hand side and your response to it on the right-hand side. For example, let's suppose you've read and kept a reading log for "Stuttering Time" (p. 86). After looking at your log, you find that you've noted the following passage on the left-hand side of your journal: "feels like the canary that miners used to carry into a mine." On the right-hand side of your journal, you've written these words: "Remember reading that these birds were used to see if miners were safe or if they would die. Does author Edward Hoagland mean that his stuttering friend is a test case for the rest of us?" Once you've found a particular response of yours that you'd like to experiment with, write a working thesis based

on the response that you could support in an essay. In the previous example, here's what might result:

> The stutterer in Hoagland's essay "Stuttering Time" serves to warn us of the dangers of an increasing detachment that is a scary result of our new technology.

As you use your journal notes to create a thesis, refer back to the guidelines (p. 67).

2. For this exercise, examine your drafting process. Thinking about the last essay you wrote, respond to the following questions in your journal:

- What did you do to get ready to draft?

- How did you go about assessing your material?

- Did you work from an outline? Did it help? Even if you didn't work from an outline this time, should you try it with the next essay?

- Did you "begin in the middle" or did you write the introduction first? How did this technique work for you in drafting?

- Did you try to tackle small sections at a time, or did you write from the beginning of the essay to the end?

- Did you attempt to draft multiple versions of difficult sections to see which versions seemed to work best? How did this strategy for drafting work for you?

- Did you save technical concerns for later, or did you find yourself getting bogged down with spelling, grammar, and punctuation problems while drafting?

Using the Computer:
Outlining Your Paper and Visiting Websites

1. After you have chosen one of the "Options for Writing" in the section that follows, type up and then print out an informal outline. Evaluate this first version, then mark any changes you want to make on the hard copy and use the editing functions (*Cut, Copy, Paste*) to make the changes on-screen. If your word-processing program offers an *Outline* function, open a new file with a blank outline. Move the information from your informal outline file into the computer's version of a formal outline. Did you have to rearrange anything in your informal outline to make it fit in the computer's formal outline? Which version do you prefer?

2. For additional examples of effective thesis statements, visit this Web site: **http://www.hamilton.edu/academics/resource/wc/Intro_Thesis.html**

To find out how to use outlines to help you organize an essay, visit this Web site: **http://www.amherst.edu/~writing/writingbetter/chapter1.html#traditional**

- Did you share your draft with peers, your instructor, or a tutor? How did you feel about having somebody else comment on your writing? Did you agree with the feedback you received? What points did you disagree with?

OPTIONS FOR WRITING

Once you've chosen a writing option or have been assigned one by your instructor, begin by using a discovery strategy (p. 32) to generate material. When you have a working thesis and feel ready to begin drafting, review the strategies for drafting (p. 82). Think about how you want to structure your essay. You might create an informal outline. While you're drafting, the outline will help you get your ideas on paper and stay on track with your organization; you can also create a different outline and "audition" an alternate structure for your main points.

1. After rereading the essay "Dishonesty," decide whether you agree or disagree with Figueroa's working thesis. Although Figueroa explores everyday dishonesties, you might want to write about dishonesty in high places or unlikely places. If you've had experience in another community or environment, you could compare that level of dishonesty with what you've witnessed in your current situation. You can gather more material by polling your friends, relatives, and fellow -students. Do you think there are circumstances when it is better—perhaps kinder—to lie? If so, you might want to write an essay in defense of dishonesty. Develop your opinion in an essay containing an effective thesis.

2. Do you feel that your generation has been wrongfully labeled? Does your age group carry with it certain stereotypes or preconceived notions? Do these stereotypes lead to snap judgments or misunderstanding of your generation by others? Discuss the traits or stereotypes associated with your age group in an essay.

3. In the essay "Dishonesty" (p. 76), writer Figueroa uses an element of American popular culture—a Burger King fast-food restaurant—as an example to support one of her main points. In an essay, identify one or more elements of American popular culture and explore the impact that this element has on you or on your acquaintances.

4. In "Stuttering Time" (p. 86), Hoagland asserts that technology has lessened society's tolerance for certain handicaps. However, others assert that technological advances, particularly in the areas of medical and computer technology, have greatly increased the quality of life for many people with physical and other handicaps. Do you know of anyone personally who has been helped or hindered by technological breakthroughs? Are there students on your campus who use a computer for physically challenged individuals? Students who benefit from motorized wheelchairs or telephone communications systems for the hearing-impaired? Write an essay in which you agree or disagree with Hoagland. If possible, interview one or more people on your campus.

5. In "Stuttering Time," Hoagland mentions a friend who stutters and the intolerance he encounters because of his handicap. His friend feels with advancing technology, the intolerance may well become worse. He knows that he will have to figure out new ways to cope with his handicap. Perhaps you have a physical obstacle or know someone who does. Think about how you or this other person "rose to the occasion" and turned a seemingly hopeless situation into a positive one. In an essay, discuss and give examples of this turnaround.

6. The issue of academic cheating has received much attention by the press. According to recent polls, this form of dishonesty has become more acceptable and, according to some, more necessary in American schools than ever before. Write an essay in which you explore several potential causes of academic cheating. Propose some potential solutions.

7. Think about one opinion you held before coming to college and explore whether that opinion has changed or stayed the same. Write an essay discussing your point of view on the subject.

8. Discuss the issue of whether controversial organizations like the Ku Klux Klan should be allowed to speak on campuses.

9. *(Film and Literature)* After reading "Stuttering Time" (p. 86), view the film *My Left Foot,* which deals with the life of Christy Brown, an artist and writer with cerebral palsy. Then write an essay in which you discuss whether living in a more technologically advanced society would have benefited Brown. Would there be disadvantages to greater technology? If so, also discuss these.

10. *(Service Learning)* Contact the Center for Campus Organizing online at **http://www.cco.org** or write or call Box 748, Cambridge, MA 02412, (617) 354-9363. This resource promotes the creation of alternative newspapers and student-initiated social justice efforts through its Website and national magazine, *Infusion.* Write an essay clearly detailing the information you discovered through your research.

RESPONDING TO WRITING: PRACTICE IN OUTLINING

Practice in outlining will enable you to understand how other writers organize their material in support of a thesis. This understanding will permit you to organize material in your own drafts more effectively. Read the following essay by Edward Hoagland, an American writer well known for his essays, fiction, and travel books. Notice that Hoagland begins with a clear thesis: He asserts that technology may lead to decreased tolerance for disabled individuals. Hoagland supports this thesis by describing the ways that technology might lead to intolerance for any individual differences. After you have read Hoagland's essay, complete the outline that has been started for you.

STUTTERING TIME

Edward Hoagland

1   We have a friend who stutters; and while he notices no increase in rudeness or sarcasm from people in person, he does hear more impatience from telephone operators, secretaries, businessmen, switchboard personnel, and other strangers whom he must deal with over the phone. As he stands at a phone booth or holds on to the devilish device at home, the time allotted to him to spit out the words seems to have markedly shrunk; perhaps it has been halved in the past half-dozen years. This alarms him because at the same time the importance of the telephone in daily transactions has zoomed. Indeed, many people use answering machines to consolidate their calls, and soon voiceprinting may become a commonplace method of identification. Imagine, he suggests, stuttering into a voiceprinting machine.

2   [Telephone] operators, who used to be the most patient people he encountered, now often seem entirely unfamiliar with his handicap. They either hang up or switch him to their supervisors as a "problem call" after listening for only a few seconds, interrupting a couple of times to demand that he "speak clearly, please." They seem automated themselves, as if rigged to a stop clock that regulates how long they will listen to anything out of the ordinary, though twenty years ago, he says, they practiced their trade with a fine humanity.

3   But it is not just individuals in individual occupations who have changed. The division between personal life and business life has deepened, and the brusqueness of business gets worse all the time. At the bank, one can no longer choose one's teller but must stand in a single line. (The tellers seem to work more slowly, having less responsibility individually for the length of the line.) And inevitably, as we all become known more and more by account numbers, doing business will become still more impersonal, and any voice that doesn't speak as plainly as digits entering a computer will cause problems.

4   We have no solutions to offer. We have brought up the subject only because our friend sometimes feels like the canary that miners used to carry into a mine. He believes his increasing discomfort foretells a worsening shortness of breath in other people—even those who started out with no handicaps at all. ○

Thesis: Technology and an increasingly depersonalized society have resulted in less humanity and tolerance.

I. A stutterer has noticed more curt and rude responses in telephone transactions.

   A. He is allowed less time to try to frame his words.

      1. He notices this in phone booths.

      2. He notices this also when making calls from his home.

   B. He is alarmed because the telephone grows ever more important in daily life.

      1. More people use answering machines to make their calling more efficient.

      2. Voiceprinting may soon become the norm (indeed, since this article was written it has become very common).

      3. A person who stutters feels at a disadvantage with such technology.

II.

    A.

        1.

        2.

    B.

III.

    A.

        1.

        2.

    B.

IV.

    A.

    B.

You have seen how to use outlining in your writing to organize support for your thesis during the drafting stage. Outlining is also a useful study strategy. Making an outline of an essay you have read can help your understanding of a writer's main points and organizational plan.

CRITICAL THINKING

In Connecting Texts

In "Stuttering Time" (p. 86) Hoagland warns that telephone operators and voiceprinting machines display decreasing tolerance for people who stutter or have other speech differences. Is our modern society becoming less or more tolerant of differences? With a small group of students, discuss people's treatment of groups perceived as "different" because of their race, age, physical or mental challenges, or ability to communicate in English. You might examine other kinds of differences as well. In your group, discuss the impact that the media has on our levels of tolerance and understanding. Do television, films, magazines, and newspapers serve to increase or decrease our tolerance for differences? See if you can reach some form of agreement within your group. Then, if time permits, collaborate in creating a thesis and informal outline for an essay developing these ideas.

Chapter 5

Using Body Paragraphs to Develop Essays

[A paragraph is] a collection of sentences with unity of purpose.

—Alexander Bain, from *English Composition and Rhetoric*

Preview

In this chapter you will learn

- To recognize the characteristics of effective body paragraphs: topic sentence, sufficient support, clear order, precise language
- To determine when to paragraph
- To compose body paragraphs with topic sentences and adequate detail using chronological, spatial, or logical order
- To use a paragraph map to create primary and secondary support
- To recognize and avoid the unclear "this" and "it"
- To use repetition and parallel structure in body paragraphs
- To use cue words within body paragraphs and from one body paragraph to the next
- To identify ground rules for peer editing and to peer edit body paragraphs

After reading this chapter and completing all practice activities, you will have the necessary skills for writing effective body paragraphs.

Just as the paragraph is a "collection of sentences," each body paragraph, individually and in connection with other body paragraphs, supports and develops the thesis of the college essay. This chapter focuses on the essential paragraphs that are found between the introduction and the conclusion of essays. Body paragraphs include a writer's main points and most of the details and information to support these main points. Although certainly there is information in an essay's introduction and conclusion, body paragraphs form the bulk of the college essay. Put another way, if the essay's thesis is its spine, as we saw in Chapter 4, the body paragraphs are the real muscles of the essay.

CHARACTERISTICS OF BODY PARAGRAPHS

Body paragraphs vary tremendously in purpose, length, style, and subject matter, but almost every effective body paragraph contains the following characteristics:

- It makes one main point.
- It contains sufficient support, using from one to many kinds of evidence to develop its main point.
- It proceeds according to a clear organizational plan.
- It contains no material that does not relate to its point.
- It employs precise language.

In addition, the separate body paragraphs work effectively together within an essay if they possess the following traits:

- Each moves clearly and smoothly from one main point to the next.
- Each makes use of the organizational plan that suits the writer's purpose, logically follows the previous paragraph, and clearly leads to the next paragraph.

Grammar Key

Handbook Practice: Verbs

Read pages 432–436. Complete Exercises 6 and 7. Then edit the paragraphs following these exercises and the essay "A Blessing in Disguise" (440–441).

MODEL WITH KEY QUESTIONS

Student Jeremy Smith was eager to share his interpretation of a particular word with readers. As you read his essay, see how many of the characteristics of body paragraphs you can identify in paragraphs 2 through 6 of Smith's essay.

RELATIVITY

Jeremy Smith

Jeremy Smith wanted to be creative in his essays and "express my perspective on ideas or events that I feel passionately about." Sometimes Jeremy found that phrases and whole sections of essay drafts that were clear to him would not be clear to another reader. Peer editing and instructor conferences helped him to "resee" his earlier drafts. Jeremy reports that he loves children and is working part-time at a day care center now.

1   Is New York far from California? Is China far from America? Many people today think of the word *far* in terms of distance from point A to point B. And while the word does have that meaning ("to, at, or from a considerable distance" according to Webster), a considerable distance today stretches much farther outward both physically and symbolically than when the word was first used. As times have changed, so has the meaning of this term *far.*

2   The term *far* used to refer to geographical distances we now consider the opposite—*close*. In 1492 when Columbus sailed to the Americas, he was said to have traveled very far, embarking on a journey that was to take him and his crew many months to complete. The approximate distance of his travels was over six thousand miles, an unheard-of distance during Columbus' time. In contrast, to-day we can travel this same distance in well under a day; we can make the trip in little over a half-day. Modern technology has transformed far into close.

3   On July 20, 1969, a man named Neil Armstrong set foot on the moon—a desti-nation that we in the twenty-first century still consider far. However, even though the moon is some 300,000 miles away from the earth, I fully expect my grand-children to be making a lunar or other planetary voyage during their lifetimes. In the future, I predict that distances we now still consider far will be regarded as close.

4   In the same way that we have pushed the envelope for the term *far* as it relates to geographical distances, we have also expanded our vision of far to refer to the advances a person makes in his or her life. We have perhaps heard the expression, "You will go far in life." In the time of Columbus, not everyone received an edu-cation. Those not born to noble parentage had to struggle just to make ends meet. For this person, "You will go far" might have meant, "you will be fortunate enough to feed and clothe your children—you may even have a little nest egg put aside." However, today, at least in America, this same forecast may be uttered about anyone, regardless of race, creed, or sex. Furthermore, in our day, "You will go far" might foreshadow financial success, political or artistic fame, celebrity sta-tus in sports or entertainment, or many other possibilities.

5   Contrary to what we currently mean by the expression "You will go far," in some distant future this expression might be directed not to the way the outside world regards any given individual, but instead to the way the individual regards himself or herself. It is possible that civilization will know a time when a shep-herd on a hill, living a pure life of self-sacrifice, meditation, and moderation, but living this life dressed in rags and living in a humble cottage, will be regarded by his contemporaries as "having gone far."

6   Finally, computer technology has served to change my personal definition of the term *far*, and I believe that this technology will continue to have an impact on the next generation. If I want to call my friends overseas, I have always been able to pick up the phone. But if I wanted to correspond with them, in the past, I have waited up to three or four weeks for my letter to get to them and then for them to return my mail. By the time I received their letter, in many cases the information that they shared was no longer current. In contrast, with the advances offered by e-mail, I can send off a detailed explanation of what has been happening with me and pretty well expect to get a response the same day—sometimes within a few minutes or hours. Perhaps this is why some experts say that the "global village" has arrived; no place on earth is remote or far.

7   *Far* is a word that will continue to change, I'm positive. Although I feel inade-quate to predict the extent of these changes, I know one thing that I can predict:

mankind will go far with time—we're well on our way and the distance is no longer considerable.   ○

Key Questions

1. **Purpose**   What is Smith's purpose in this essay?

2. **Focus**   What is the thesis of the essay?
    Annotate the essay by finding and underlining the sentence in each body paragraph that states the main point for that paragraph.

3. **Material**   What are two examples of specific support in two different body paragraphs?

4. **Structure**   Are the body paragraphs clearly organized? Choose any body paragraph (2 through 6) and explain how the writer organized the material.

5. **Style**   Reread the essay. Find one or more words that take the reader from one idea to the next. Are there important words that the writer repeats?

GUIDELINES FOR BODY PARAGRAPHS

Determine the Paragraph's Purpose

Before you begin working on your separate body paragraphs, consider how each body paragraph relates to your broader purpose in writing the essay. For example, if you take another look at Smith's essay, you can see that the writer's purpose in paragraph 2 is to persuade his audience that the meaning of the term *far* has changed over the centuries. His purpose in paragraph 3 is to convince readers that the term will change yet again in the future.

Practice 5.1   Reread paragraphs 4, 5, and 6 of Smith's essay. In the margin of the essay, write what you think the writer wants his audience to think, feel, or do as a result of reading these body paragraphs.   ❏

Use Topic Sentences

Just as your essay needs a thesis that states the main point of the essay, each body paragraph requires a **topic sentence.** This sentence states the overall idea or point you're trying to make in the paragraph. Each topic sentence should clearly relate to your essay's thesis.

Make sure that your topic sentence for each of your body paragraphs does the following:

- It names the main point of the paragraph.

- It contains a **controlling idea**.

- The controlling idea reveals your attitude—what you, the writer, think about your main point—or it limits the main point by telling what particular aspect of the point you will discuss in the paragraph.

For example, look again at the topic sentence for paragraph 2 in Smith's essay:

> The term *far* used to refer to geographical distances we now consider the opposite—*close*.

Smith's sentence tells his audience that the main point in this first body paragraph is geographical distances. His controlling idea—the limitation Smith puts on this main point—is how these distances have changed over time.

Practice 5.2   Examine the following topic sentences. Annotate each one, circling the main point and underlining the controlling idea. If the sentence does not contain both, put a check by it to indicate that it needs to be rewritten. On a separate sheet of paper, revise those topic sentences in need of more work.

1. Last fall I went on a vacation to the East Coast.

2. College students who work part- or full-time must organize their time efficiently.

3. Buying some basketry supplies can be the beginning of a fun and lucrative hobby.

4. The college library is available for all students.

5. There are many different kinds of friends.   ❏

Body paragraphs usually begin with a topic sentence, giving the audience the chance to absorb the writer's main point and controlling idea before getting the detailed information to support this main point. If you look again at Smith's essay, you'll see that the writer has placed his topic sentence for paragraph 2 at the beginning of his body paragraph. Sometimes, however, you may prefer to use a different type of organization by withholding the subject and controlling idea until your audience has absorbed the details. This type of organization can give your body paragraph dramatic impact.

The writer of the following body paragraph decided to place her topic sentence at the end of the paragraph. What is the effect of this strategy?

> First, the parking lot was far away from the court building and I had to take a shuttle to the building. The bus driver would not let me in unless I had a juror's badge, which I had forgotten. After I showed him my summons and he let me on the bus, he dropped all of us off at the criminal court building. I didn't know where to go, so I followed the crowd that was on the bus to the entrance. I then realized that I would have to go through the metal detector, and I was detained and asked to empty my purse. Then I took the elevator to the seventh floor, and I saw huge crowds of people standing around. These people looked confused, just like me. It turns out that they had all been summoned. All in all, appearing for jury duty was not at all what I had expected.
>
> —Leah Ford, *student*

Implied Topic Sentences: Proceed with Caution
Instead of stating the main point of the paragraph outright, a writer may decide to hint at the main idea of the paragraph. This hint is referred to as an **implied topic sentence**. In these cases, all the details in a body paragraph relate clearly enough to one obviously understood subject, as is the case with the following paragraph:

> She had on a kind of dirty-pink—beige maybe, I don't know—bathing suit with a little nubble all over it and, what got me, the straps were down. They were off her shoulders looped loose around the cool tops of her arms, and I guess as a result the suit had slipped a little on her, so all around the top of the cloth there was this shining rim. If it hadn't been there you wouldn't have known there could have been anything whiter than those shoulders. With the straps pushed off, there was nothing between the top of the suit and the top of her head except just *her*, this clean bare plane of the top of her chest down from the shoulder bones like a dented sheet of metal tilted in the light. I mean, it was more than pretty.
>
> —John Updike, *from* "A and P"

Updike's implied topic sentence in this paragraph could be stated as something like the following:

> The shoulders of the girl in the bathing suit (main point) were captivating (controlling idea).

If you do want to try an implied topic sentence, make certain that your audience will understand your hints. Every sentence must clearly develop your unstated main point. Otherwise, you may find yourself with a paragraph that makes perfect sense to you but will appear to your reader to have no main point.

Practice 5.3   Read author Barbara Ehrenreich's "Zipped Lips" (p. 351). Underline the topic sentence in each body paragraph. If you encounter a paragraph that appears to have no topic sentence, ask yourself if the topic sentence could be implied and then annotate the paragraph by writing the implied topic sentence in the margin.   ❑

Practice 5.4   Develop each of the following subjects into a topic sentence for a body paragraph. Be sure that each topic sentence includes both a main point and a controlling idea.

1. A local park or monument:
2. Final exams:
3. Cigarette advertisements:
4. Plastic surgery:
5. Family bonding:
6. Interracial dating:
7. School shootings:

8. Freedom of speech:

9. Live performers in concert:

10. Clothing styles: ❑

Develop Supporting Details

The supporting material for your body paragraphs can come in a variety of forms and from many different sources—your memory, personal interviews, observations, readings, outside research, even your imagination if appropriate for the essay assignment. Even though the type of support may vary tremendously from body paragraph to body paragraph and from essay to essay, the material you use should possess the following characteristics:

- It should relate clearly to your topic sentence. This means that you should omit any information, no matter how exciting or valid, that veers off the subject of the body paragraph.

- It should be stated as clearly as possible. This means using precise rather than vague words. It may also mean defining any unfamiliar terms for your audience.

- It should be reliable. You want to use details that come from firsthand knowledge or the knowledge of trustworthy sources rather than hearsay. You also want to use information that is current rather than dated unless your subject is one for which dates have no importance.

- It should be sufficient. You need enough information to convince your audience of the main point you are making in the body paragraph.

Underdeveloped body paragraphs are perhaps the most common weakness of many college writers. To make sure you have enough information, try to gather *more* than enough, and then you can be selective later with what you decide to use.

The following body paragraph includes sketchy, underdeveloped support material:

> Saturday night's party at Tom's house became so crowded that disaster soon followed. Everybody was packed together. The noise was really deafening and the smells were intense. Later some furniture got hurt and the floors were ruined.
>
> —Mitch Wexler, *student*

Although Wexler has a good topic sentence for the paragraph, he doesn't really paint a clear picture of the disaster, as his topic sentence promises. We don't have too much specific information about the noise or the smells; we don't know what furniture gets hurt, or even what "hurt" means—did something break or did it tear? Or did someone spill something on it? Finally, we're left unsatisfied about how the floors were ruined. Here's how Wexler revised his underdeveloped body paragraph after receiving helpful comments from his instructor and a peer editor:

> Saturday night's party at Tom's house became so crowded that disaster soon followed. People were pressed body to body from the walls to the center of the rooms, and they had to scream at each other to be heard over the pulsating, drum-heavy beat of the band. In spite of the open windows, through which people now climbed because the front door had been locked, the place reeked. The hardwood floors were slick and sticky from drinks and pizza spills; around nine o'clock, there was a cracking sound like a baseball when it makes contact with a bat as a kitchen chair snapped and its two occupants scrambled to avoid hitting the floor.

Practice 5.5 Annotate both the earlier and later versions of Wexler's paragraphs by underlining the main point and the controlling idea in each. In the second paragraph, circle all words or phrases that create a clear picture of his main point. ❑

Practice 5.6 To gain experience in developing clear, reliable, and sufficient support in your body paragraphs, choose one of the ten topics that you expanded into topic sentences in Practice 5.4. After writing the topic sentence, use any prewriting strategy to come up with enough material for an effective body paragraph. ❑

Stay on Topic

Remember that every piece of information and every detail in a body paragraph needs to relate to and develop the topic sentence. It's easy to get **off-topic** without realizing it. You are off-topic when your supporting details no longer clearly relate to your topic sentence. For instance, when Wexler began to revise his underdeveloped paragraph, he found he could add many details that would allow his audience to envision the wild party scene. In his enthusiasm, Wexler included information about the actual songs being played by the band—their specific titles, the names of the original performers for each song, and those songs that were his personal favorites. After rereading his paragraph, Wexler decided to delete these details about the songs because they did not develop the main point in his topic sentence.

In revising your essay, make sure that each detail in the paragraph clearly supports the paragraph's main point.

Practice 5.7 Read the following paragraph and underline the main point and the controlling idea in the topic sentence. Next, reread the paragraph, crossing out any sentences or phrases that do not support the topic sentence.

> Location is critical for a successful garage sale. Just getting to the sale must be made as difficult as possible to enhance consumer excitement. If the directions the consumers receive send them in circles, they will feel that this garage sale must have some hidden treasures and anticipation will build! Signs are an important ingredient. Make sure the signs are made from sturdy and dependable cardboard, tough enough to withhold the strains of rainy or windy weather. Another hot tip is flyers. Drive over to a copy shop and make about a thousand flyers to hand out at a local

mall. My favorite copy shops are the ones that stay open twenty-four hours. Some of these offer discounts on weekends. While you're handing out the flyers at the mall, be sure to eat lunch because you won't be able to take a break during your garage sale.

—Brian Morton, *student*   ❏

Use Precise Words

Make sure that each detail in your body paragraphs is as precisely stated as possible. Some essay writers may get several sentences about a subject down on paper, but they don't take the time to make sure that they're not repeating themselves or being vague or "fuzzy" in their writing. In your revising stage, give yourself the time—and if possible, the help of another editor—to ensure that each body paragraph contains the vivid, specific, and effective words that develop your subject by painting as clear a verbal picture as possible.

Practice 5.8   To recognize vague development, read the following early draft of a body para-graph. Work with a partner to revise the underlined vague expressions.

Certain athletes become obsessive and really take sports <u>too far</u>. For example, some football players really get competitive <u>out there</u>. The guys on the team are always trying to show their strength and be better than the player next to them, but when a player will do anything to be better than the other teammates, there is a <u>problem</u>. Also, certain weight trainers and track stars obsess on their sport so much and their success in their sport that they resort to <u>bad practices</u>. They may take <u>some drugs</u> to make them stronger or faster, but these drugs may be illegal and unhealthy. Finally, there are even some examples of competitive athletes cheating in their events. A track person took a shortcut in a big race and she ended up disqualified because of her actions.

—Nicoll Grijalva, *student*   ❏

Organize Your Support

Once you have your topic sentence for body paragraph and have decided which details will support that topic sentence, think about what might be the most effective organizational plan for that material. It isn't enough to scat-ter the material randomly among your body paragraphs. In developing your body paragraphs into an essay, you might want to work from an informal outline as discussed in Chapter 4 and again to use the three options for arrang-ing the order of your material: chronological, spatial, and logical. In addition, you can apply the many patterns of essay development covered in Part 2 of this book to the development of individual body paragraphs as well as entire essays.

Chronological Order to Show Time Progression

If the supporting details in your body paragraph unfolded over a period of time, you might do well to arrange your support in **chronological order**. To illustrate, notice that the writer of the following paragraph has organized his material according to time progression. He begins with the first event that relates to the topic sentence:

> I felt that the most scary part of the date was about to happen and things were now out of my control. Once inside the house, I went through the official handshakes and greetings with the parents. Immediately after I introduced myself, a creepy silence fell upon the room. I began to feel sweaty and uncomfortable. I didn't know what to say, but I could feel the parents eyeballing me from head to toe, just looking for the slightest flaw. Then my nightmare came true. The father started to interrogate me. He asked me questions like, "So, do you work?" and "So, where exactly are you two going tonight?" and finally, "So, what time are you planning on bringing her home?" At this point, I was willing to accept any curfew the parents were willing to give us as long as I got out before I turned to Jell-O.
>
> —Keith Siegman, *student*

Practice 5.9   Reread and then annotate the above paragraph by numbering events in the order in which they occurred. To recognize instances in which you might use chronological order in developing a body paragraph, return to the list of topic sentences you created in Practice 5.4. Put a "C" by any of these topics that could be developed in this manner.   ❑

Spatial Order to Show Physical Properties

If the main point of your body paragraph concerns a person, place, or object that has physical properties, use **spatial order,** in which the supporting details can be arranged in a visual pattern, such as from left to right, top to bottom, or front to back.

Practice 5.10   To get a better idea of how to use spatial order to organize material, read the following body paragraph:

> As my mother and I enter the lobby of the movie theatre, we are always struck by familiar sights and sounds. The quick and efficient ticket-takers are at the front doors to take our tickets. About twenty feet away and to the right are the food counters, with three smiling uniformed helpers standing in front of brightly lit popcorn in glass cages, popping and giving off a buttery aroma. My eyes are caught by the shiny, colorful candy wrappers displayed in these glass counters: Snickers, KitKat, and Reese's beckon me. At the far left edge of the counter are little brown baskets for people to place trash. Many are filled with gum and old receipts. On the right end of the counter are ketchup, relishes, and other condiments for hot dogs.
>
> —Desirea Espinoza, *student*   ❑

Work with a partner after rereading the paragraph and draw a quick map of the space Espinoza describes. To identify situations in which to use spatial order in body paragraphs, look again at your list of topic sentences in Practice 5.4 and mark an "S" by those topic sentences that could be developed with spatial organization.

Logical Order to Show Examples

Some main points do not exist as physical objects or take place over a period of time. To develop this kind of topic sentence, you might want to consider **logical order**—organizing the details of your paragraph in the most sensible and reasonable manner possible. The logical order you determine will depend on your main point in the paragraph:

- If you're writing about a situation, you might want to start with causes and proceed to effects.

- If you're comparing two subjects, you might want to progress from similarities to differences or vice versa.

- If you're using examples, you might want to begin with your weakest example and save your most powerful one for the end.

As you read the following illustration of logical order in a body paragraph using examples, note that the writer has chosen to save her most powerful examples for last:

> Many of our city parks today are unsafe and could be hazardous to the health of our children. Some parks have potholes on the ground or cracks in the pavement that are dangerous for a child to run on. Others have unsanitary restrooms where toilets don't flush, walls are covered with graffiti, and the smell is disgusting. Even more potentially hazardous to young children is the poor condition of the park equipment: Dirty swings, rusty monkey bars, and old slides invite disaster. Trash, cigarette butts, and dog droppings are also common sights in these parks. Finally, because many of our city's parks are frequented by gangs, children must contend with drive-by shootings and fights among gang members. Because parks are important for the development of children, we should think more seriously about how we can make them safer, more inviting places.
>
> —Grethel Peralta, *student*

Although Peralta's topic sentence mentions a place, she decided to use logical rather than spatial order because she did not want to discuss the physical details of any one park. Instead, she wanted to make the point that many parks are unsafe. Notice that after offering her final detail, this writer repeats her topic sentence as a wrap-up at the end of her paragraph. Because the paragraph offers quite a few examples, Peralta felt she wanted to reinforce her main idea by repeating it at the conclusion of the body paragraph.

Use a Map to Understand Levels of Support

How much support do you need? In writing the college essay, you must have enough support to convince your reader of your main point. While one or two pieces of evidence might not be enough to establish your credibility in a body paragraph, three or more good strong supports will. And for each of these **primary supports** (reasons, steps, stages, causes, effects, and so forth) you will need two or more **secondary supports** (incidents, examples, anecdotes, facts, statistics). If you were to "map out" one of your body paragraphs, it might look something like this:

Body Paragraph Map

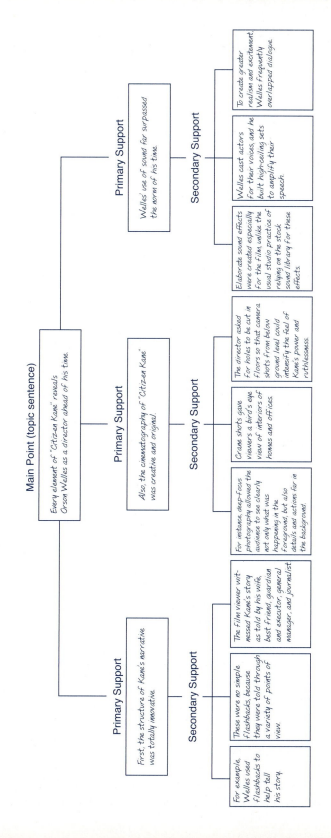

Main Point (topic sentence)

Every element of "Citizen Kane" reveals Orson Welles as a director ahead of his time.

Primary Support

First, the structure of Kane's narrative was totally innovative.

Secondary Support

For example, Welles used flashbacks to help tell his story.

These were no simple flashbacks, because they were told through a variety of points of view.

The film viewer witnessed Kane's story as told by his wife, best friend, guardian and executor, general manager, and journalist.

Primary Support

Also, the cinematography of "Citizen Kane" was creative and original.

Secondary Support

For instance, deep-focus photography allowed the audience to see clearly not only what was happening in the foreground, but also details and actions far in the background.

Crane shots gave viewers a bird's eye view of interiors of homes and offices.

The director asked for holes to be cut in floors so that camera shots from below ground level could intensify the feel of Kane's power and ruthlessness.

Primary Support

Welles' use of sound far surpassed the norm of his time.

Secondary Support

Elaborate sound effects were created especially for the film, unlike the usual studio practice of relying on the stock sound library for these effects.

Welles cast actors for their voices, and he built high-ceiling sets to amplify their speech.

To create greater realism and excitement, Welles frequently overlapped dialogue.

Now that you are familiar with this paragraph structure, use the blank practice paragraph map on page 101 to sketch in one of your body paragraphs.

Know When to Paragraph: Some General Rules

If you remember that each body paragraph focuses on one main point, you should not have a problem knowing when to begin a new paragraph. As a rule, each new point or subject needs to have its own paragraph. As you are drafting, you may notice that not all of your paragraphs are the same length. Don't let the difference in length bother you, as long as each paragraph includes enough support for its topic sentence. The difference in length may occur for several reasons. Some main points are more complicated than others, or some main points may require the writer to define unfamiliar terms. There are, however, a few generally acknowledged rules for paragraph length.

Overlengthy Paragraphs

As a courtesy to readers, try to avoid paragraphs that go beyond three-quarters of a typed, double-spaced page, and never write a paragraph that goes beyond a full typed page. Because you do not want to delete valuable material to make the paragraph shorter, one solution is to break your subject into two clear parts, thus dividing one body paragraph into two. Even if this revision calls for you to write an additional topic sentence and perhaps to rearrange your material, by all means do it. You will be allowing your audience to follow the development of your ideas much more easily.

Practice 5.11 Read the following two body paragraphs, which have been typed incorrectly to make them appear as one. Place a mark in the spot where you think the paragraph break should logically go and then write the missing topic sentence for the second paragraph.

> Keeping long work hours will affect grades of high schoolers and may cause them to stop going to school altogether. A friend named James worked for a fast-food franchise—his hours were 11 in the morning to 9 in the evening on the weekends, and from 5 to 9 on weekdays. When Monday rolled around, he just didn't have the energy for school work most Mondays. From the time he got his job, his grades started to drop and he didn't graduate from high school. Instead, when he discovered that he was failing his classes, he gave up going to school and dropped out. I have another friend who works for a different fast-food franchise, and he is learning only how to set a timer for French fries, how to heat up burgers already cooked by somebody else, and how to collect money from customers. He says that none of these skills will mean anything on his resume and that he has not learned anything he can transfer to any job other than fast food. He even says that if he got another fast-food job, he would probably have to learn these same skills differently, because each franchise has its own food preparation methods.
>
> —Peter Huang, *student*

Missing topic sentence:

❏

Just as you want to break up paragraphs that are more than a page long, you also want to expand short body paragraphs if they are underdeveloped, as

Body Paragraph Map

Main Point (topic sentence)

Primary Support

Primary Support

Primary Support

Secondary Support

Secondary Support

Secondary Support

Additional Support?

Additional Support?

Additional Support?

mentioned earlier. The only exceptions are body paragraphs that are short because they are transition paragraphs—they actually move the readers from one main point to the next instead of offering a discussion of a new subject.

Topic Sentence in Wrong Paragraph

When drafting your paragraphs, be careful not to place a topic sentence for your next body paragraph in the body paragraph that you're just wrapping up. Although it might seem like a good idea to "preview coming attractions," this only confuses your readers. To see an example of a misplaced topic sentence, read the following two paragraphs:

> Dishonest behavior on our city streets is on the rise. On the freeways, there are more and more cars traveling above the speed limit. And people feel picked on when they do get a ticket rather than feeling guilty about being dishonest in breaking a law. Also, many drivers speed through yellow lights rather than slow down and stop. Instead of regarding the yellow light as a warning to slow down, many people take this as a signal to go faster and they step on the gas even harder. Other examples of dishonest behavior on streets include illegal U-turns, illegal parking, and lane changes without signaling. However, it's not just on our city streets that we witness dishonest behavior. Deceptive behavior is also becoming more and more common in the workplace.
>
> People "borrow" supplies from the company without telling anyone—this is sometimes just pens, pencils, little items, but oftentimes more expensive equipment, such as typewriters or video cameras are "borrowed." Many workers think nothing of calling in "sick" when they really just want a vacation day. And countless people on the job take extended lunches and coffee breaks, often to run personal errands on company time. Another deceptive behavior involves the use of the company telephone for personal calls, sometimes even costing the company lost business because the clients can't get through or are ignored by the office staff.
>
> —In Sung Song, *student*

Practice 5.12   Find the topic sentence in Song's first paragraph that relates to the material in the second paragraph. Underline the sentence and draw an arrow where you think the sentence best fits in the second paragraph. ❏

Signal Shifts in Thought

Cue words or **transitions** are words or phrases that allow readers to anticipate what's to come in the body paragraphs of an essay. If you use cue words effectively, your audience will follow your thought process more easily from one detail or main point to the next. Cue words are thus useful not only within body paragraphs but throughout the entire essay. Additional details are discussed in Chapter 7, where you will find an extensive list of cue words to help you signal to your reader that you are moving from one detail or main point to the next.

Practice 5.13   Improve the following paragraph, which has no transitions, by inserting any cue words from the list in Chapter 7 (p. 141) that might help the reader follow the writer's ideas.

I have several good reasons for missing class today. My car was totaled in an accident yesterday afternoon, and I have no way of getting to school. My dog ate my homework, and my instructors will never believe that this really happened. My favorite soap opera is featuring a guest star this week whom I absolutely adore and cannot miss, and the VCR is on the blink so I can't tape the show for later viewing. I have no doubt that all of my instructors will understand my situation and take pity on me. ❑

Avoid the Unclear "This" and "It"

Remember that even though we use the word *this* to substitute for a noun, using this pronoun by itself often leads to reader confusion. Try to use *this* with a noun to show clearly what you mean.

Problem: The man looked behind him stealthily and tiptoed out of the room. *This* aroused the police officer's suspicions. (The reader does not know for sure whether the writer means that the man was suspect because he looked behind him, because he tiptoed out of the room, or both.)

Solution: The man looked behind him stealthily and tiptoed out of the room. *These actions* aroused the police officer's suspicions.

Problem: Television has been accused of destroying family ritual. *This* may be true, but TV is not the only culprit.

Solution: Television has been accused of destroying family ritual. *This destruction* may be partially due to TV, but TV is not the only culprit.

Similarly, the frequent use of unexplained *it* can leave a reader confused. Get into the habit of rereading any sentence in which you have used the word *it* to make sure your reader knows for what noun this pronoun substitutes. This may involve adding a noun or rephrasing your sentence.

Problem: She placed her notebook on the desk. *It* toppled to the ground moments later.

Solution: She placed her notebook on the desk. Her *notebook* toppled to the ground moments later.

Problem: We took John's brand new car to the film's opening ceremony. *It* was an amazing experience.

Solution: We took John's brand new car to the film's opening ceremony. The *film's opening* was an amazing experience.

Repeat Important Words

You can keep your body paragraphs focused on the main point by using appropriate repetition of important words and phrases. To avoid becoming monotonous in your writing and to make your repetitions more interesting, use **synonyms**—substitute words that have the same or almost the same meaning as the original word.

Practice 5.14   To examine repetition of important words in a body paragraph, read the following example, in which repeated words have been underlined.

Secondhand smoke is another possible cause of Sudden Infant Death Syndrome. Smoking during pregnancy and smoking around the baby after it is born increase the risk of SIDS compared to infants not exposed to cigarette smoke. Studies show that "infants exposed to 1 to 10 cigarettes a day were 2.4 times as likely to die of SIDS as unexposed infants, while those exposed to 11 to 20 cigarettes a day were 3.6 times as likely to die" (Maugh A-1). The more smoke infants inhale and are exposed to, the higher the risk of their dying from SIDS. Parents should lessen the risk by not smoking at all before pregnancy and after. Those who cannot quit should cut down on the amount and try to smoke away from the infant, so the child won't be affected.

—Letictia Elder, *student*

What is one synonym that you found?   ❏

Practice 5.15   Return to student Jeremy Smith's essay "Relativity" (p. 89). See if you can identify at least two important words used several times throughout the essay.   ❏

Use Parallel Sentence Structures

Similar ideas can be effectively, and sometimes quite dramatically, linked by using **parallel sentence structures.** Parallel sentence structures repeat a sentence pattern for dramatic effect.

To see how parallel sentence structure works in body paragraphs, read the following example. The repeated sentence structures have been underlined:

A woman who has had a tough childhood ends up on the streets, working as a prostitute, and she becomes the victim of prejudice. She desperately wants to turn her life around. She wants to go to school; she wants to get a job. But she can't, for when people find out she is a prostitute, no one is interested in hiring her. She wants a decent place to live; she wants to go out on a regular date; she wants to go to church. But she can't find a neighborhood, a date, or a church that will accept her. Why? Because no one wants to live next to an ex-prostitute, no one wants to go out with someone with her reputation, and no one wants to sit next to a woman like that in church. And these are all people who say, "I'm not prejudiced."

—Corona Reynolds, *student*

Practice 5.16   Underline all repeated sentence structures you find in the following paragraph:

But although I was initially disappointed at being categorized as an extremist, as I continued to think about the matter I gradually gained a measure of satisfaction from the label. Was not Jesus an extremist for love: "Love your enemies, bless them that curse you, do good to them that hate you, and pray for them which despitefully use you, and persecute you." Was not Amos an extremist for justice? "Let justice roll down like waters and righteousness like an ever-flowing stream." Was not Paul an extremist for the Christian gospel: "I bear in my body the marks of the Lord Jesus." Was not Martin Luther an extremist: "Here I stand; I cannot do otherwise, so help me God." And John Bunyan: "I will stay in jail to the end of my days before I make a butchery of my conscience." And Abraham Lincoln: "This nation cannot survive half slave and half free." And Thomas Jefferson: "We hold these truths to be self-evident, that all men are created equal. . . ." So the question is not whether we will be extremists, but what kind of extremists we will be.

—Martin Luther King, Jr., from "Letter from Birmingham Jail"   ❏

Strategies for Body Paragraphs

1. **Purpose**   Know what you want to accomplish in each of your body paragraphs as well as the broader purpose of each paragraph in relation to your entire essay. When revising, check to see that each body paragraph has achieved its individual purpose and also works with the other body paragraphs to support the essay's thesis.

2. **Focus**   Use a topic sentence (or an implied topic sentence) to focus on a main point and connect all details in each body paragraph. Make sure your topic sentence names the main point and has a controlling idea. In your support material for each body paragraph, omit or revise any information that does not clearly relate to the topic sentence, or rephrase the topic sentence so that it relates to the support material you have presented.

3. **Material**   Check your draft to make sure that each body paragraph has clearly stated, reliable, and adequate support for the topic sentence. Revise any vague or underdeveloped paragraphs.

4. **Structure**   Use an organizational plan for each body paragraph that seems to work best for your material—chronological, spatial, or logical order. Create a new paragraph when you move on to a new main point. Insert cue words to signal a change in direction or level of detail, both within each body paragraph and from one body paragraph to the next.

5. **Style**   Reread, respond, and revise all body paragraphs so that they use the most precise words possible. Make sure you repeat important words and use parallel sentence structures.

JOURNAL WRITING: FROM IDEA TO PARAGRAPH

This activity will help you identify topic sentences in nonacademic writing—writing that can be described as informal or casual. This activity will also allow you to explore some topics of current public interest, generating material that could be useful in the body paragraphs of an essay.

1. Find and read an article in a current newspaper, popular magazine, or Website. (You can check out the editorial page of the newspaper for more in-depth articles.) Choose any paragraph and identify its topic sentence. (Note that newspaper, magazine, and Website body paragraphs tend to be shorter than the body paragraphs in college essays. However, even short paragraphs have topic sentences—and these may be found at the beginnings as well as the ends of paragraphs, or they may be implied.) In a journal entry, copy the topic sentence you've chosen, and then write your evaluation of it. Is it a good topic sentence for the paragraph? Does it state the main point and controlling idea?

Finally, write your reaction to the entire body paragraph, explaining whether it is adequately supported.

2. If this part of the journal entry prompts you to write more about the subject, continue to write about your reaction. If not, locate another topic sentence in another body paragraph of the same article or a different one and begin another journal entry.

Using the Computer: Moving from Prewriting to Paragraphing and Editing

1. For additional practice writing body paragraphs, visit the following Web site: **http://www.lcc.gatech.edu/regents/body_paragraphs/html**

   After reading the explanation of developmental paragraphs and the samples, go to "Practice Exercise: Body Paragraphs" in this site.

2. Drafting on a computer makes it easy to experiment with different ways of ordering paragraphs. Open a prewriting file that you've saved on disk or hard drive and print it out. Next, referring back to the guidelines and strategies for body paragraphs in this chapter, open a new file and type in two or more body paragraphs of an essay based on the prewriting. (Don't worry about your introductory or concluding paragraphs for now.) Identify the topic sentence for each body paragraph and highlight it by changing the type to either *bold* or *italic*. Next, experiment with the most effective placement for this topic sentence by using the *Copy*, *Cut*, and *Paste* edit functions to move this sentence to other places or even to take it out of the paragraph entirely. Print each different version and compare them. Which is the most effective?

3. Precise, well-chosen words can help convey a feeling or idea to an audience. A *thesaurus*, available on almost all word-processing programs, offers one quick way to discover various word choices. Open your essay draft file and locate a word that doesn't seem as interesting, precise, or unusual as it could be. Highlight this word and then click on your program's *Thesaurus* option. The program will suggest alternative words to you. If your word-processing program doesn't have a thesaurus option, or you'd just like to see more possibilities for substitute words, you can visit an interactive thesaurus at **http://www.thesaurus.com**

OPTIONS FOR WRITING

As you work through any of the following writing options, focus on developing effective body paragraphs, each with a topic sentence and sufficient supporting details clearly related to the main point. Have a plan for organizing your material. In responding to your draft and revising, consult the "Strategies for Body Paragraphs" (p. 105).

1. Choose one of the ten topics listed in Practice 5.4 and develop your ideas on the subject into an essay.

2. Prewrite to discover three activities you like to engage in to relax, relieve stress, or refresh yourself. In an essay, explain each of these activities and their effect on you.

3. As a college student, you probably have many tips for how to survive the first semester or at least the first few weeks of college life. Share these survival strategies with an audience of new college students.

4. In Jeremy Smith's essay (p. 89), the writer discusses a term whose meaning has substantially changed over time. Write an essay focusing on another term, word, or expression that used to mean one thing and now means something quite different.

5. Read Barbara Ehrenreich's essay "Zipped Lips" (p. 351). Agree or disagree that democracy is at risk when employers have free speech rights but employees don't. In your thesis, take a clear position on the issue of free speech in the workplace. In your body paragraphs, support your stand by developing separate main points. You could use examples based on your own work experience or the experience of people you know. (*Caution:* Dress codes in the workplace become a free speech issue *only* if the clothing item in question contains a slogan or phrase.)

6. In his paragraph (p. 109), student Carlos De Jesus reports that female police officers find "lewd comments made to them" on the job examples of sexual harassment. Interview your college's dean of students or talk with a few faculty members to discover the content of the college's sexual harassment policy. In an essay, summarize the official position of the college on sexual harassment. Discuss any limitations on the freedom of speech of students, faculty, and other college personnel.

7. Interview several classmates on the issue of lab testing of animals. Be sure to take notes on your classmates' responses. Write an essay focusing on the pros and cons of the issue, based on other students' statements.

8. After using the Internet to explore the affirmative action issue, write an essay supporting or opposing affirmative action in the workplace. Consult two or more of the following Web sites, taking notes as you read:

   http://plato.stanford.edu/entries/affirmative-action/
   http://www.ncfm.org/afiract.html
   http://www.uri.edu/affirmative_action

9. (*Film and Literature*) View the following Academy Award–winning films: *Ordinary People* and *Good Will Hunting*. In an essay, describe the plots of the two films, emphasizing any similarities in story lines. Do you agree with some critics that part of the plot of *Good Will Hunting* was stolen from *Ordinary People*? Why or why not?

10. (*Service Learning*) Call your local Chamber of Commerce and ask about particular community service opportunities. Get as much information on each of these activities as you can. Write an essay detailing all available community service activities to your classmates.

RESPONDING TO WRITING: PEER EDITING BODY PARAGRAPHS

Body paragraphs from three student essays appear below. You will be asked to edit each paragraph. Review the previous strategies before reading the paragraphs, and refer back to them when needed to complete these or future peer-responding activities.

Strategies for Peer Editing

If you are responding to another student's draft:

- Respond with seriousness, even though the draft may have many errors or not be the kind or quality of draft that you would write.
- Withhold both your judgment and your comments until you have read the entire draft.
- Make all comments specific; avoid general remarks that will not help the writer in revising.
- Resist the urge to fix sentence errors, rewrite sentences, or correct punctuation. Instead, just circle or underline problematic areas so the writer will be sure to notice them.

If you are sharing your draft with a peer editor:

- Find someone who will not hesitate to give you honest feedback about your essay; close friends may not be the best peer editors.
- Give your peer editor a clean, legible copy of your draft, typewritten if possible; use double or triple spacing so the peer editor will have room to write comments.
- Give your peer editor a fairly complete rather than a partial draft of the assignment.
- Give yourself time to reflect upon your peer editor's comments before revising. If you are confused by the comments, ask for an explanation or consult your instructor or another peer editor for a second opinion.

After you have read the following body paragraphs, respond to each one by answering the peer-editing questions that follow.

This restaurant in Gardena is an enjoyable place where I can relax. I go by myself or with my friends. I always look forward to going there. Every time I walk through the door, I feel so comfortable there. The room is very dimly lit, and it's filled with the aroma of heavenly garlic. The walls are a light color. I also like the old-fashioned paintings on the walls. Booths surround the dining area. Four tables placed straight down the middle fill the room. The center tables have very large chairs. The carpet is worn, but colorful.

—Laura Rezende, *student*

I could tell by looking at the room that a grandmother lived there. Even before I had turned on the ancient hurricane lamp, the scent of potpourri sachets caught my attention. Directly beyond the lamp is a very delicate looking Victorian style, wing-backed chair. It appears to be the kind of chair in which children (or anyone else for that matter) are never allowed to sit. Continuing around the room in a counter-clockwise manner, we next come to a collection of antique dolls, looking very much their age. Some of them have only hairline cracks in their yellowed porcelain faces; others with noses and fingers either missing or showing obvious attempts at repair with new age-darkened glue and the odd loose thread hanging out. Above and to the left of here, we find a window sill covered with glass bottles and jars turning green from both time and the sun. Still more to the left, in the corner farthest from the door, is the china cabinet. This cabinet is filled with painstakingly detailed, hand painted bone china. But perhaps the most telling sign of the room's ownership are that the two remaining walls seem to be completely covered with photographs. There were pictures of toddlers taking their first steps, young couples in wedding garb, and finally, older folks from this and a previous century, mostly in their finest attire. Even with no other people in the room, it had a warm loving feeling that only the coldest of people could fail to sense.

—Greg McMillan, *student*

Numerous women who are sexually harassed at work are now for the first time taking action against their harassers. For example, last month the Los Angeles County Metropolitan Transportation Authority reported that at least a third of the women officers have filed sexual harassment complaints in a short period of time. These women are reporting being bumped or groped in hallways, having lewd comments made to them, being humiliated at staff meetings, and being confronted by embarrassing photographs. Then, early this week, a Pasadena Police Department cadet reported that she was "repeatedly raped" by a superior while on the job. This young woman told authorities that the rapes took place in various parts of the department building and in police cars. Increasingly, women are being commended for speaking out so that those who are guilty of sexual misconduct in the workplace receive proper punishment.

—Carlos De Jesus, *student*

Key Questions

1. **Purpose**   What appears to be the purpose of this body paragraph? Does the writer accomplish the purpose? If not, what changes might help?

2. **Focus**   Can you find a topic sentence for the paragraph? Does that sentence contain a clear main point and controlling idea? If it does not, what is missing? Does all the information in the paragraph relate to and support the topic sentence? If it does not, what should be deleted or changed?

3. **Material**   Is the support for the main point sufficient or is the paragraph underdeveloped? Is the support reliable and clear? If it is not, what are the weak spots that need to be strengthened?

4. **Structure**   Can you find an organizational plan? What type of organization has the writer used for the paragraph? Are any cue words used? What are they? What changes would you suggest in the use of cue words?

5. **Style**   Search the paragraph for instances of precise word choice, repetition of important words, and use of parallel sentence structure. Find an example of effective use of one or more of these items. Which of these concerns of style, if any, do you feel could be strengthened? What are your suggestions?

Choose any body paragraph you completed for the "Options for Writing" section. Complete a draft and ask a peer editor to respond to the editing questions for your body paragraph. You can use these questions when you share your drafts in the future.

CRITICAL THINKING
In Connecting Texts

In "Relativity" (p. 89), student Jeremy Smith explores the concept of distance. Smith notes that e-mail, for example, has changed notions of distance by allowing us to communicate quickly with people all over the world. However, some critics favor limitations on freedom of speech in cyberspace. Working with a partner or small group, decide where we should draw the line. Should employers have the right to restrict employees' speech? Should chat groups and other Internet communications be monitored or censored? What about the rights of professors in the classroom? Should college students or faculty be permitted to use "hate speech" or racist speech in the name of the First Amendment? Should advertisers be allowed to deceive or mislead consumers in print and on television? Should a film or television producer be required to restrict offensive language? Should music lyrics be censored? If time permits, share your findings with the rest of the class.

Chapter 6

Creating Effective Introductions and Conclusions

Great is the art of beginning, but greater the art is of ending.

—Henry Wadsworth Longfellow, from "Elegiac Verse"

Preview

In this chapter you will learn

- How to recognize and evaluate introductory strategies
- How to identify voice and tone in introductory paragraphs
- How to write a compelling introduction
- How to identify and evaluate concluding strategies
- How to write a memorable conclusion

After reading this chapter and completing its practice activities, you will have increased confidence in grabbing your audience's attention in introductory paragraphs and offering effective closure in final paragraphs of essays.

Think of the introduction to an essay as a tantalizing appetizer—whetting the audience's appetite for the main course—and the conclusion as the dessert—satisfying, flavorful, and essential to a complete essay meal. This chapter offers helpful pointers on beginning and ending essays. As you read the information on introductory and concluding paragraphs, keep in mind that *when* you write these two important parts of your essay is a matter of personal preference. Some writers complete the introduction and conclusion when revising, while others prefer to sketch out these two parts with the preliminary draft, knowing that they will revise later. You'll discover which composing process works best for you.

CHARACTERISTICS OF INTRODUCTIONS

First impressions count! Employers decide whether to hire in the first few seconds of job interviews; readers decide just as quickly whether to read on or put the page down. A catchy introduction is crucial if you want to have a successful essay. Although introductions to college essays vary in length from one to several paragraphs, an effective introduction contains the following characteristics:

- It captures the attention of the reading audience through the use of a particular strategy.
- It guides the audience smoothly into the subject.
- It sets the tone for the entire essay.
- It either states or moves toward the thesis.

MODEL WITH KEY QUESTIONS

Tommy Honjo wanted to explain a simple task that he felt could save car owners money and result in better road performance. Honjo worried about how to capture the reader's interest in a mechanical procedure that the average person might not understand. As you read his introduction, see which characteristics of effective introductions you can identify. After you've read the brief summary of Honjo's body paragraphs and his conclusion, evaluate the success of the introductory paragraph in leading the reader smoothly into the subject.

DON'T BE AFRAID TO POP THE HOOD

Tommy Honjo

A logical thinker, Tommy Honjo consistently wrote well-organized essays. He confided that he enjoyed writing to explain mechanical processes and technical procedures. Throughout the semester, Tommy worked on solving problems with verbs. Tommy's future plans include a four-year degree, but currently he is an undeclared major, leaving his options open.

1   Have you ever been stuck on the side of the road because your car has broken down? Supposing you could save between twenty and thirty dollars and decrease the likelihood that you'd have car trouble in the future by learning a simple, easily grasped procedure—would you try it? If you're like most people who own cars, once or twice a year, provided you remember, you take your car to a shop that does a quick oil change. You hand over your money, and your car is filled with recycled oil or possibly incorrect oil for your car, which could damage your engine. However, even though you know little about cars and have never popped the hood, you can easily learn to change your car's oil yourself, save money, and have better automotive performance. To complete this important tune-up procedure, you simply need to track down a few tools and follow several steps.

[Four body paragraphs discuss the necessary parts for the procedure and the items useful in preparation for the oil change, followed by a step-by-step explanation of the procedure and several precautions and recommendations.]

2   Now you may be saying to yourself, "Hold it! This is more complicated than I thought!" But actually the entire oil change should take only an hour or less, and once you have purchased the wrenches, your only expense is the oil and filter. The next time you see a motorist stranded by the side of the road, remember that it's more than likely this person did not change the oil in his or her own car. In the long run, if you're willing to pop the hood and learn to change your car's oil, you might be saving a lot more than the twenty or thirty dollars—you might be saving yourself a substantial tow and car repair bill. ○

Key Questions

1. **Purpose**   What sentence or phrase in the introductory paragraph first indicates Honjo's purpose for his audience?

2. **Focus**   Locate Honjo's thesis and underline it.

3. **Material**   What kind of material does Honjo use in the introductory paragraph to capture the attention of his audience?

4. **Structure**   Describe in a few words the organization of the introductory paragraph. After Honjo opens with a general question, how does he move his readers smoothly toward his thesis?

5. **Style**   How does the concluding paragraph "frame" the essay? That is, how does it tie back to the introductory paragraph and offer a satisfying closure for the reader?

Grammar Key

Handbook Practice: Pronouns

Read pages 441–444. Complete Exercise 8 (p. 444).

GUIDELINES FOR INTRODUCTIONS

Hook Your Audience

The first sentence of your introductory paragraph should hook your audience—it should seize their attention and pull them into the subject. You need to give readers a reason to read more of your essay, and there are many introductory strategies you can use to hook your audience. Seven of these introductory strategies follow with sample introductory paragraphs. The strategies are set off from the rest of the introductory paragraphs with italics.

Background Information

Many subjects for college essays benefit from a brief historical overview or some concise background information on the situation to be discussed. The strategy here is to explain background circumstances so that the reader's appetite is whetted to learn more about the subject. Here is an example of this type of introductory technique:

> Up until the 1960s, African-Americans, Latinos, and other people of color as well as women were blatantly discriminated against in the American workplace and college admissions for no other reason than their gender or the color of their skin. When affirmative action was implemented, it was designed to help minorities and women gain greater representation in jobs, promotions, college admissions, and business contracts. Today, however, because affirmative action has resulted in misunderstanding, bitterness, and verbal warfare, the program should be reviewed and revised.
>
> —Cenovio Maeda, *student*

Question

Another introductory strategy involves asking your readers a provocative question or series of questions. Look again at "Don't Be Afraid to Pop the Hood" (p. 112), and you will see that Honjo asks the readers two questions that serve to involve them actively with the subject. Here is another example of this introductory strategy:

> Are you one of many people who dream of becoming a recording artist? Are you stymied because you have the talent but not the first idea of how to get started in the recording business? If so, get out that music and practice those scales, because you're going to learn how to record your own demo tape. Making a demonstration tape and sending it off to record companies could be the first steps in making your dream of vocal stardom come true.
>
> —Anonymous, *student*

Story or Incident

This strategy involves opening the essay with a story or anecdote that directly illustrates the main idea. If you use this strategy, be sure that you keep the length of the story under control—remember that your purpose is to heighten the audience's interest and curiosity in your subject, not to digress into a lengthy narration. The following example uses a story as an introductory strategy:

> I was eight years old when my parents moved to a new apartment located in Bourj-Hamoud, Lebanon, a beautiful city that used to be called "Little Paris." When I first saw this big building, I thought we were going to live on a boat, so much did the building resemble a boat. What I remember most was our two-hundred–foot-long balcony, wrapping all around our apartment. The first few days after we moved in, I was afraid to venture out on this balcony because it was so large. As the days passed by, the balcony became the place where I spent all my time and where I learned about the outside world.
>
> —Lucy Mardirossian, *student*

Statistic, Fact, or Statement

Oftentimes you can command your readers' interest by beginning with a startling statistic or fact. Notice that the writer of the following introductory paragraph uses a specific amount of money to appeal to his audience's regard for wise spending:

> *Last year over half of the nation's computer users spent 50 dollars or more on phone calls and books for technical support related to problems installing or running computer programs.* This money could have been saved if computer users had a better knowledge of how to install a program. And program installation is not as complicated as many people believe. Most programs require three fairly simple steps, each accompanied by a few precautions.
>
> —Peter Huang, *student*

Quotation

You may decide to use a quotation to open your essay. Every chapter of this text begins with a brief quotation that introduces the subject to be explored in the chapter. If you use this introductory technique, you need to identify the source unless the quote is a generally known proverb or saying. Libraries have books of quotations listed by subjects, so you might try looking up your subject to see if you can find a thoughtful quotation. If you are writing an essay about a particular book, story, or article, you may choose to begin your introductory paragraph with a quotation from the source you're discussing, just as the following student does in this example:

> *"A stranger blocked her path, but she passed him blindly. He had to touch her arm before she would look up."* The woman was Mrs. Ardavi, arriving from Iran, and the stranger was Hassan, her son, whom she had not seen in over ten years. Both Ardavi and Hassan are characters in the short story "Your Place Is Empty" by Anne Tyler. Both Mrs. Ardavi and her son Hassan must come to terms with differences in culture, personality, religion, and age.
>
> —Cinthya R. Martinez, *student*

Definition

If your essay focuses on a subject that your audience might not readily understand, you may want to ease the readers into the topic by first defining any confusing terms. If you do choose this strategy as your hook, avoid the overused "according to Webster's" or "the dictionary defines" phrasing. The following example of definition as an introductory device was chosen because the writer's subject—artificial bait—is relatively obscure for the average reader. Notice that this author tries to introduce his audience to his subject gently and whet their curiosity at the same time:

> If you enjoy prime fishing, you should know that the northern states have excellent fishing lakes. And if you do plan a visit, it will help you to be familiar with Rapalas and their use in game fishing. *What exactly is a Rapala? It is an artificial bait that is tied to the end of a fishing line in place of a basic fishing hook. It is handcrafted of either cedar or balsa wood with two sets of hooks attached to its cigar-shaped body.* If you want to take home a freezer-full of the best largemouth bass, northern pike, walleye, or the highly valued muskellunge, you should learn how and when to use Rapalas.
>
> —Robert Amerson, *student*

Examples or Details

You may want to arouse audience interest and introduce your subject by giving a series of examples or details associated with the subject. The following introductory paragraph uses this strategy:

> *Unless you have felt like an outsider, been singled out by resident advisors, stayed up for hours studying for finals, been denied financial loans, failed a test, sat in the wrong class by mistake, read the wrong pages for homework, become sick from cafeteria food on campus, experienced writer's block, paid over three hundred dollars for books, bought the wrong books and could not return them*—unless you have experienced at least some of these situations, you have not known the "joys" of being a college student. But though college may be one big pain and one of the greatest challenges you'll ever face, without a college education you are dead.
>
> —Monifa Winston, *student*

Practice 6.1   For practice in identifying introductory strategies, work alone or with a partner and examine introductory paragraphs from any of the essays in this textbook, either within the chapters or in "Exploring Other Writers: A Collection of Readings" (p. 333–401). Write the name of the essay, the page on which you found it, and then the strategy used by the writer to hook the interest of the audience. Do this for four separate essays. ❏

Introduce the Subject

In addition to capturing the interest of the reader, the essay's introduction should also introduce the subject. Return to the introductory paragraphs used as examples earlier and you will notice that each also introduces the subject.

Practice 6.2   Reread each of the four introductory paragraphs you have chosen for Practice 6.1. Annotate them by circling the first indication of the writer's subject in each essay. ❏

Establish a Voice and Tone

Every effective introductory paragraph sets up the voice and tone for the remainder of the essay. **Voice** refers to the writer's personality and the way this personality comes through in the essay. **Tone** refers to the writer's attitude toward a subject and to the writer's perception of an audience and relationship with them. If you reread Honjo's introductory paragraph, you'll notice that the writer's voice is informal: He uses conversational phrases such as "stuck on the side of the road," "hand over your money," and "pop the hood." Honjo's tone is helpful—he communicates to his readers his wish to help them learn a money-saving procedure. A strong, easily recognizable tone in your introduction establishes a firm relationship with your reader and helps you maintain consistency throughout the body and conclusion of your essay.

Examine the following introductory paragraphs to get an idea of differences in voice and tone.

Rape is an outrage that cannot be tolerated in civilized society. Yet feminism, which has waged a crusade for rape to be taken more seriously, has put young women in danger by hiding the truth about sex from them.

—Camille Paglia, from "Rape and Modern Sex War"

Notice that the author's voice is fairly formal—she does not use "I" or address the reader directly by using "you." This voice reveals that she prefers her writing personality to be somewhat removed from her reader. In addition, her tone is serious, as indicated by such word choices as "outrage," "crusade," and reference to putting women "in danger by hiding the truth." Paglia's introductory paragraph establishes a tone of warning that she uses throughout the essay.

Now take a look at another introductory paragraph dealing with the same subject:

I thought that the old "blue balls" defense—you remember, that's the one where backseat Romeos claimed they couldn't halt their sexual advances because their aching gonads imperiously demanded relief—went out with air raid shelters and doo wop. But now there are those like Camille Paglia who are bringing back blue balls with a vengeance. According to Paglia and her cohorts, men really *can't* control their urges. Rape for men is just doin' what comes naturally. And gals, don't bother fighting it—just get used to it again.

—Helen Cordes, from "The Blue Balls Bluff"

Notice this writer's more informal voice—she addresses the audience with "you remember," and she uses the conversational "doin' what comes naturally." This voice establishes a more direct, personal relationship with the writer's audience. Cordes's sarcasm in the phrase "men really *can't* control their urges" helps to signal the reader that the tone of the essay will be mocking.

Practice 6.3   To gain some practice in identifying voice and tone, return to the introductory paragraphs used as examples (p. 114–116). Annotate them by writing a word or two about the writer's voice and tone in the margin.   ❏

State the Thesis

After capturing the attention of your audience and indicating the subject, your introduction should either state the thesis for the essay or move toward a more focused subject. The thesis is most often found within the introductory paragraph, as is the case with each of the previous introductory paragraphs.

Practice 6.4   Reread the paragraphs starting on page 114, and annotate each paragraph by underlining and labeling the thesis in each one.   ❏

Avoid Truisms or Generalized Questions

Hastily composed introductory paragraphs often result in **truisms**—statements that, while true, are all too obvious or general. For instance, on a first draft the opening line, "Love is important to everyone," might seem like a great beginning for an essay on neglected children. However, a second, more critical glance at this opening line should alert you that the average reader might respond with a yawn, putting the essay down without another glance. Don't use the introduction to tell your audience anything they already know. By the same token, don't base your introduction on generalized questions that are meaningless, for which the answers are all too obvious, or questions that are total "setups" as leads into the subject. For instance, scrap anything like the following: "Have you ever wondered what the world would be like if there were no disagreements?" or "Do you know the difference between a successful college student and a floundering one?" or "Have you ever experienced discrimination?" When thinking about opening sentences for your introductory paragraph, you should take the time to experiment with different strategies to see which leads most smoothly into your subject.

Practice 6.5   Read the following essay assignments and first lines for an essay. Working with a partner, come up with a better introductory sentence for the subject.

1. (*Assignment:* Focus on the inappropriate disciplining of teenagers by overly strict parents.) Introductory sentence: "Parents are annoying at times."

2. (*Assignment:* Discuss lifestyle differences between college graduates and high school dropouts.) Introductory sentence: "Have you ever wondered what a big difference a college education will make in your life?"

3. (*Assignment:* Explore some negative effects of television for teenagers and children.) Introductory sentence: "Have you ever thought that television might be bad for children and teenagers?"

4. (*Assignment:* Take a stand on the issue of illegal immigration.) Introductory sentence: "Immigration is a controversial issue today." ❏

Strategies for Introductions

1. **Purpose**   Make sure that your introduction hooks your audience, indicates your purpose, and establishes a voice and tone appropriate for your audience and subject.

2. **Focus**   Move smoothly from your introductory strategy to a clear thesis.

3. **Material**   Regardless of which introductory strategy you choose, use specific and interesting information rather than truisms or generalized questions or statements.

4. **Structure**   Organize the material in your introduction so that you heighten reader interest and convey all necessary background information.

5. **Style**   Use words and compose phrases and sentences carefully to lead the audience from indication of subject to clear statement of thesis.

Grammar Key

Handbook Practice: read pages 446–448. Complete Exercise 9 and the paragraph that follows this exercise (pages 448–449).

CHARACTERISTICS OF CONCLUSIONS

While the introduction to an essay is important because it determines whether the reader will read further, the conclusion forms the last impression—the final and most lingering memory—of your writing. If you return to Honjo's essay (p. 112), you'll see that the final paragraph has the following characteristics of an effective conclusion:

- **It conveys a feeling of completion.**
  Notice that rather than bringing up any new steps in the process of changing oil, Honjo comments on the ease of the entire process, signaling the reader that he has communicated all necessary information.

- **It "frames" the essay by tying all the main points together and wrapping up any loose ends for the reader.**
  Honjo repeats (from his introductory paragraph) that the procedure will save the reader money and improve the car's performance. He also makes a prediction, an effective concluding strategy: "You might be saving yourself a substantial tow and car repair bill."

GUIDELINES FOR CONCLUSIONS

Offer Closure

If you've ever been disconnected during a phone conversation, then you know the frustration that accompanies an abrupt and untimely ending. In the same way, your essay should not end with your last main point or with a detail related to a main point. Conclude instead with a few sentences that signal the reader that the essay is ending.

Practice 6.6   Turn to any student essay in this text and read the entire essay, except for the last paragraph. Record your impressions on a separate sheet of paper. Go back to the essay and read the concluding paragraph. What words or phrases signal that the writer is drawing to a close?   ❏

Frame the Essay

Much as a frame forms a finite border for a painting, an effective conclusion brings together the contents of an essay for the audience. Successful framing makes use of any of a number of concluding strategies. You can use the introductory strategies mentioned earlier in this chapter to create effective conclusions. The following five concluding techniques could also be helpful:

Summary

This common strategy works best for essays that are longer than three type-written pages. Summarizing a shorter essay is unnecessary—in fact, your audience may be insulted that you doubt their ability to remember this amount of material. On the other hand, if your essay deals with complex or technical material, or if the essay is, say, a ten-page research paper, your audience might appreciate a recap of the information.

To illustrate, the following conclusion summarizes the information from the entire essay:

> Overall, although having a part-time job can crowd a teen's schedule and limit study time, this job may be exactly what the teen may need. Learning to meet responsibilities on the job, growing to respect and get along with employers and coworkers, and developing the maturity to budget money are three skills that more teens should acquire.
>
> —Patricia Crippen, *student*

Recommendation

One effective way to end an essay is to make a recommendation to your audience. To see the impact a recommendation might have on an audience, read the following example:

> So now that you've been behind the scenes to see what a waitress has to cope with and juggle during every working hour, perhaps the next time you visit a restaurant or coffee shop, you'll view your waitress with different eyes. As she approaches your table smiling with composure and good humor, try to respond with the same courtesy to this person who does much more for you than just serve up the food.
>
> —Deanna McAmis, *student*

Prediction or Warning

Using a prediction or issuing a warning can be a dramatic and memorable way to end your essay. For a better idea of how this concluding strategy works, read the following final paragraph:

> If parents continue to ignore the suggestive sitcoms, films, and music videos their children watch, and if they fail to monitor their children's viewing, there will be more irresponsible sex and mindless violence in our society. Now more than ever, parents need to teach their children right from wrong. If parents leave this teaching to the media, our society will become even more toxic to young people.
>
> —Carmen Tull, *student*

Call to Action

The call to action as a concluding strategy challenges the audience to become involved by doing something about a situation or problem. Notice that Tull's concluding paragraph in the previous example hints at an action: increased involvement of parents and the monitoring of television programs.

The following is an example of a concluding paragraph with an even more obvious plea for action:

> These many examples of unclear wording in our college's sexual harassment policy point out the need for a policy review. Every student on this campus, every faculty member and every staff member—all of us should write, call, or visit the board of trustees and urge them to revise the current sexual harassment policy so that the language is clear, easily understood, and fair to all parties involved.
>
> —Edwin Ksiezopolski, *student*

Reference to Introductory Strategy

An interesting and satisfying concluding strategy involves referring back to the introductory example, story, statistic, quote, or other device and elaborating or connecting the information, tying the end to the beginning of the essay. The following introductory and concluding paragraphs demonstrate this strategy.

> I can remember a time when I could play in my own backyard without fear of harm. Today, however, my children do not feel safe in our yard, not because they live in a different community, but because they are growing up in a different time. After reading "A Child's Tragedy Is a Grown-Up's Failure" by Robin Abcarian and "Get It If You Can" by Roy Rivenburg, I agree with the authors that we live in a toxic society.
>
> [Body paragraphs develop three main points with examples relating to a toxic society.]
>
> Although I'm glad I don't have to be a child growing up in this society, I worry and fear for my children. I also wonder if there isn't more that parents, educators, and lawmakers can do to help my children and the children of others feel safe from harm in their own backyards.
>
> —Swarupa Reddy, *student*

Practice 6.7 Look again at each of the following essays from various chapters in this text. Working with a partner, identify which of the five concluding strategies each writer uses in these essays. Then rank the effectiveness of each conclusion, assigning the number 1 to the strongest and 3 to the weakest.

> "Zipped Lips" (p. 351)
>
> "McDonald's Is Not Our Kind of Place" (p. 358)
>
> "We're Lying: Safe Sex and White Lies in the Time of AIDS" (p. 344) ❏

Avoid Pitfalls

Whatever concluding strategy you decide on, you'll want to avoid the following three potential pitfalls:

New Material

Resist the urge to introduce new material, such as another main point or another detail, in your conclusion. Remember that this is the time to wrap up what you have said and to bring together all your main points into a coherent closing statement.

Apology

Never weaken your position by apologizing—even in your concluding paragraph. For example, your audience will be confused and possibly offended if you conclude with something like the following: "Although I don't know everything about this problem . . ." or "I may not be one hundred percent right, but I think . . ."

Moralizing

Avoid preaching in your concluding paragraph. Although some students have the mistaken idea that essays should end with a moral or lesson learned, this is not a good strategy to use. Leave the lesson or moral for the reader to decipher—your essay will be much more memorable if you hint or suggest a lesson rather than forcing one upon your audience.

For example, the following writer might decide in a revised draft to delete the italicized last sentence of this paragraph:

> Today everyone in our family is working. We can now buy ourselves the things we need to get by. There are no more money problems and everyone is happy. Learning to pull together has taught all of us a lesson. Without communicating and helping each other, we wouldn't be able to get by. Everybody appreciates one another for all their hard work. We managed to get closer to one another. Responsibility counted a lot but we've all learned to deal with it. *Times are tough but not impossible if you learn to work together.*
>
> —Ginell Cabanilla, *student*

Strategies for Conclusions

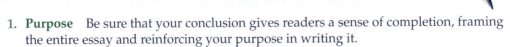

1. **Purpose**   Be sure that your conclusion gives readers a sense of completion, framing the entire essay and reinforcing your purpose in writing it.
2. **Focus**   Choose a concluding strategy that works well with the rest of the essay.
3. **Material**   Avoid introducing any new material in the form of main points or supporting details. Do expand material to include a warning, specific recommendation, prediction, or call to action if appropriate.
4. **Structure**   Organize the concluding paragraph so that your most memorable or arresting statement comes at the end of the conclusion.
5. **Style**   Revise your conclusion if your tone sounds apologetic or preachy.

JOURNAL WRITING: EXPERIMENTING WITH VOICE AND TONE

For this journal entry you will need to locate any essay you've written—this can be an essay in progress or one you've already completed.

1. Read the essay over carefully, paying special attention to the first and last paragraphs. After reviewing the information on voice and tone earlier in this chapter, focus on the voice and tone you used in your essay and then complete the following activities:

   • Imagine a completely different purpose for your essay. Then, choosing a new voice and tone but keeping the same subject matter, rewrite your introductory paragraph in a journal entry. For example, if you were Tommy Honjo, writer of the essay "Don't Be Afraid to Pop the Hood," you might decide to address a friend and adopt a flippant, offhand voice and use a lighthearted, confidential tone. Or you could use a much more formal voice and employ a distant, reserved tone.

   • In a second journal entry, rewrite the concluding paragraph of the same essay. Use the same voice and tone that you employed for your first rewritten introduction.

2. After you've completed the journal writing, compare the introductory and concluding paragraphs of your essay with the new versions you've just written in your journal. Think about the appropriateness of each for academic writing, and ponder when you might want to use a different voice and tone in your writing. Notice that once you establish a particular voice and tone in your introduction, your reading audience has a right to expect this voice and tone to be used throughout the essay.

Using the Computer: Crafting Conclusions and Online Research

1. What was the last blockbuster movie that you saw? Did it have an especially scary, dramatic, or romantic ending? Chances are that ending wasn't in the original script. Many big movie studios these days show multiple endings of movies to test audiences to see which will be the most popular—and make the most money. You might not be writing for big box-office dollars, but you can try the following exercise on your word processor to "test" the effectiveness of different kinds of conclusions on your essays.

   Open a file that contains an essay draft or an essay that you have already completed. Make a copy of this file, and *close* the original. If you already have a conclusion to this essay draft, evaluate it. What kind of concluding strategy did you use?

(Review "Frame the Essay," p. 119.) Was it effective? Now, split the screen, and open a new file. In this new file, use any of four strategies—summary, recommendation, prediction or warning, or call to action—to write at least two alternative conclusions to your essay. Would these alternative conclusions be more effective or less effective for your essay? Do any of these strategies seem wrong for your audience and purpose?

2. Journalist Meghan Daum in her essay "We're Lying: Safe Sex and White Lies in the Time of AIDS" (p. 344) describes what it's like to be a young person in the age of AIDS. She contrasts the messages she hears from public health officials and school counselors about "safe sex" with the actual behavior and attitudes of people her age. However you feel about Daum's experiences, AIDS has had a powerful impact both internationally and within your own community. There are many excellent sites on the Web to find more information about AIDS. Two resources are the following:

   a. *The Body: A Multimedia AIDS and HIV Information Resource* (**http://www.thebody. com**): This site includes discussions and stories from people worldwide living with or affected by the HIV virus. Log on to read their stories, follow their arguments, and share your own opinions and experiences. You can also explore the site's resources to find out more about AIDS education and prevention.

   b. *AIDS Education Global Information System* (**http://www.aegis.com**): This site provides a wealth of information, both accessible and more technical, about AIDS education, treatment, and prevention. Visit one or both of these Web sites, and in your journal record information or summarize postings that you think people in your community need to know. Report back to the class with your findings.

3. To understand how to participate in the U.S. political process, log on to the following Web sites that offer guidance on writing letters to officials and newspaper editors:

   For the Democratic National Committee, Take Action:

   http://www.democrats.org/takeaction/index.html

   For the Republican National Committee, Reaching Out:

   http://www.rnc.org/directory/contact.html

OPTIONS FOR WRITING

In your drafting and then revising of an "Option for Writing," pay particular attention to your introductory and concluding paragraphs. Use the guidelines offered in this chapter to hook your audience with an effective introductory strategy and later, to frame your essay with a satisfying and memorable conclusion.

1. Write an essay about a beginning or ending in your life—perhaps related to a relationship or a job, your education, where you live, or how you live your life. You might want to contrast the way you viewed yourself before and the way you see yourself or the world now. For your introductory paragraph, search a book of quotations or find a quote by a favorite author to use as a dramatic opening quote related to your experience.

2. In "Don't Be Afraid to Pop the Hood" (p. 112), Honjo explains how to perform a procedure that saves money and promotes better automotive maintenance. Write an essay explaining how to do or complete a project, task, hobby, or chore. Choose something that the average person might not know how to do. In your introduction, be sure to convince the reader of the value of the activity.

3. Write an essay detailing a lie you told or someone told you. Explain why or what happened to cause the lie, or what happened as a result of the dishonesty. In your concluding paragraph, resist the urge to moralize.

4. Unsafe sex practices that some teenagers and adults engage in have been described as like putting loaded guns to their heads every night. Write an essay exploring the causes for potentially self-destructive, dangerous behavior in our society. Track down a statistic or fact that will hook your audience in your introduction. In addition to unsafe sex, other self-destructive behaviors might include drug abuse, driving and drinking, gambling, eating disorders such as anorexia or bulimia, engaging in extreme sports, and the like.

5. Do the college health-service counselors on your campus give you and other students the straight talk? Pay a visit to the health service on your college campus. Ask for any available information about HIV and other sexually transmitted diseases. If possible, interview a college nurse or health-service employee. Write an essay discussing your findings.

6. Honjo's introduction tells his audience that the writer's purpose is to teach us how to change a car's oil. Have you ever had a car-related mishap? Perhaps your car ran out of gas or became overheated? Explain your particular car incident in an essay: where you were, where you were headed, and what happened. Be sure to grab your audience's attention in your introduction and offer closure in your conclusion.

7. Communicate in an essay the most courageous moment in your life: where you were, who you were with, what happened, how you responded, and how you felt about the incident both then and now in reflection.

8. Write an essay describing the most hilarious incident that you ever witnessed in a public place: this could be a doctor's office, supermarket, school, park, or work establishment, for instance.

9. (Film and Literature) If you believe that no drama dealing with the Holocaust could ever contain comic elements, you might be wrong! View the Academy Award–winning film Life Is Beautiful. The movie is controversial because filmmaker Roberto Benigni uses comedic language to depict the horror of the Holocaust. Write an essay in which you take a stand in favor of or against the use of comedic language in this film— use clear examples to prove your points.

10. (Service Learning) Find out how you can become a volunteer for your state department of conservation. Interview an authority on the subject of recycling. Publish your notes in the form of an essay.

RESPONDING TO WRITING: BEGINNINGS AND ENDINGS

Read the following introductory and concluding paragraphs. For each paragraph, answer the set of questions on page 127.

Introductory Paragraphs
Paragraph A

When you leave your apartment or house, do you begin to feel better? If you leave for a week-long trip, do you find your head clears, your migraine disappears, dizziness stops, your aches and pains subside, depression fades away, and your entire attitude is better? If so, chemical pollution of the atmosphere in your home may be making you ill.

—Marshall Mandell, from "Are You Allergic to Your House?"

Paragraph B

On seeing another child fall and hurt himself, Hope, just nine months old, stared, tears welling up in her eyes, and crawled to her mother to be comforted—as though she had been hurt, not her friend. When 15-month-old Michael saw his friend Paul crying, Michael fetched his own teddy bear and offered it to Paul; when that didn't stop Paul's tears, Michael brought Paul's security blanket from another room. Such small acts of sympathy and caring, observed in scientific studies, are leading researchers to trace the roots of empathy—the ability to share another's emotions—to infancy, contradicting a long-standing assumption that infants and toddlers were incapable of these feelings.

—Daniel Goleman, from "Researchers Trace Empathy's Roots to Infancy"

Paragraph C
[This introduction by Margaret Atwood and paragraph F belong to the same essay.]

The noses of a great many Canadians resemble Porky Pig's. This comes from spending so much time pressing them against the longest undefended one-way mirror in the world. The Canadians looking through this mirror behave the way people on the hidden side of such mirrors usually do: They observe, analyze, ponder, snoop, and wonder what all that activity on the other side means in decipherable human terms.

—Margaret Atwood, from "Through the One-Way Mirror"

Concluding Paragraphs
Paragraph D

Periodically my pilot and I climb into our aircraft and head out over the Minnesota wilderness, following a succession of electronic beeps that lead to some of the last remaining wolves in the lower 48 states. We hope that the data we collect will provide a better understanding of the wolf. We especially hope that our work will help guide authorities into a management program that will insure the perpetuation of the species in the last stages of its former range.

—L. David Mech, from "Where Can the Wolves Survive?"

Paragraph E

I who am blind can give one hint to those who can see—one admonition to those who would make full use of the gift of sight: Use your eyes as if tomorrow you would be stricken blind. And the same method can be applied to the other senses. Hear the music of voices, the song of the bird, the mighty strains of an orchestra, as if you would be stricken deaf tomorrow. Touch each object you want to touch as if tomorrow your tactile sense would fail. Smell the perfume of flowers, taste with relish each morsel, as if tomorrow you could never smell and taste again. Make the most of every sense; glory in all facets of pleasure and beauty which the world reveals to you through the several means of contact which Nature provides. But of all the senses, I am sure that sight must be the most delightful.

—Helen Keller, from "Three Days to See"

Paragraph F

Americans don't have Porky Pig noses. Instead they have Mr. Magoo eyes, with which they see the rest of the world. That would not be a problem if the United States were not so powerful. But it is, so it is.

—Margaret Atwood, from "Through the One-Way Mirror"

Questions on Introductions and Conclusions

1. What introductory or concluding strategy does the writer use?
2. What appears to be the subject of the essay?
3. Describe the writer's tone.
4. Note the most memorable word or phrase.
5. With reference to the five "keys," evaluate the introductory or concluding paragraph by commenting briefly on its effect on an audience.

You can use these same questions in responding to your own or a peer's introductory and concluding paragraphs. Identify strengths and respond to weaknesses in your beginnings and endings of essays by making the necessary changes.

CRITICAL THINKING
In Connecting Texts

In "We're Lying: Safe Sex and White Lies in the Time of AIDS" (p. 344), Meghan Daum asserts that advertisers have been less than completely honest about the AIDS problem. In "A Black Athlete Looks at Education" (p. 24), Arthur Ashe claims that the media advance the false image of athletes as overnight successes and proper role models for youngsters. Working in a small group, draw up a list of other areas of public concern— for instance, how do advertisers and television spokespersons handle alcohol consumption? What about ethnic stereotypes? Environmental concerns? Once you have a list of issues, choose one and come up with a plan for reform—a plan for more responsible, honest handling of the issue by the media. If time permits, share your findings with the rest of the class.

Chapter 7

Revising and Polishing the Essay

What makes me happy is rewriting. . . . It's like cleaning house, getting rid of all the junk, getting things in the right order, tightening things up.

—Ellen Goodman, *syndicated newspaper columnist*

Preview

In this chapter you will learn

- How to revise a preliminary draft—responding to peer and instructor comments by rethinking the draft and then adding, cutting, substituting, or rearranging information
- How to polish a revised draft—rereading to trim and clarify, eliminating wordiness, inserting cue words, creating a title, proofreading, and using correct manuscript format
- How to work through revisions with the "keys" in mind
- How to identify weak spots and design personal revision strategies
- How to be an effective peer editor and how to use peer editing to strengthen your own essays

After reading this chapter and completing its practice activities, you will understand specific strategies for revising and then polishing your essay drafts.

Have you ever reached a snap decision, slept on it, and changed your mind the next morning? Do you recall dropping a letter in the mailbox, leaving a voice-mail message, or dashing off an e-mail, only to wish you could reclaim your words later, once you had a chance to cool down and reflect on your actions? If you've experienced any of these scenarios, then you know something about the importance of *revision* (literally, *seeing again*) for the writer. The composing process does not end with drafting—it continues with revising and polishing. In the revising stage of the composing process, you reevaluate your essay draft in order to make both major and minor adjustments. This chapter explores specific strategies for revising and then polishing the final draft of your essay.

CHARACTERISTICS OF REVISING

Many writers revise as they compose. Examine any essay draft that you've worked on, and you'll probably see crossed-out words, arrows moving sentences or phrases around, question marks in the margin, and other notations and changes made while you were in the process of writing. You may actually track changes (such as insertions, deletions, or rearrangement of material) from draft to draft, especially if you have drafted and saved your drafts on the computer and used your word-processing program's editing functions.

But in addition to making changes while you're drafting, revising also involves responding to your draft by standing back and reseeing your essay as a whole—how does it all come together to accomplish your purpose? In the revising stage, you question and evaluate the thesis, structure, and material of your essay. Finally, when you polish your revision, you evaluate issues such as sentence structure, grammar, punctuation, and spelling.

MODEL WITH KEY QUESTIONS

Chapter 4 presented the first draft of an essay by student Margarita Figueroa, who shared that preliminary version with her instructor. The draft was returned to her with several comments. As you reread Figueroa's first draft, now with her instructor's responses, notice that the instructor uses the five "keys"—purpose, focus, material, structure, and style—to evaluate Figueroa's draft. Be on the lookout as you read for places where Figueroa might want to add, cut, substitute, or rearrange her material.

DISHONESTY

Margarita Figueroa

Margarita Figueroa discovered that instructor and peer feedback helped her in the revising and polishing stages of her writing. She continued to work on the draft you may recall reading in Chapter 4 (p. 76), and she was pleased with the result of her efforts. Almost finished with her writing classes at this point in her college career, Margarita asserts that she will continue to use her writing skills when she becomes a nurse.

make your purpose clear in intro

1 I was reading an essay by Marya Mannes called "The Thin Grey Line." It was
What in particular interested you? Focus on subject
a very interesting article, separating honesty from dishonesty. It made me really

think about if people are dishonest or honest. I feel that dishonesty is more char-

acteristic of our society than honesty.

Narrow the focus in thesis - don't forget controlling idea + specific language - should you break down dishonesty?

2

you have lots of material - try to structure your material with a major point first, and then your details?

Well, first there is the fake car accident that results in getting money out of auto insurance companies. For instance, I had friends that would get together and collaborate with one another and would report to the insurance company about an accident that they were involved in, but it wasn't a real accident. It was a fraudolent claim. They even had a friend who was a lawyer that would help them set everything up as if it was a legitimate accident. They used their own cars, license plate numbers, and insurance companies, and each person received an out-of-court settlement of five hundred dollars. Another reason for dishonesty is when an opportunity arises for an individual to become dishonest.

style problem - rephrase so reader can understand statement

3

The circumstance that occurs and causes an individual to become dishonest. For example, my sister told me about an incident that happened to her at Burger King. *Is this material necessary?* My sister had ordered burgers, fries, and drinks for her family. After she placed her order, the woman who works at Burger King rang the order up, but

Again, you have lots of material, but rethink and remember your purpose and specific focus = dishonesty among individuals.

meanwhile my sister and the woman were having a conversation about kids. Then, my sister saw the total amount due, which was $14.83, so she gave the woman a twenty dollar bill and the woman gave my sister her order and then gave her the change due to her. This is when the woman made a mistake and gave her back the total amount due, which was $14.83, instead of $5.17, which was the change due. My sister noticed the mistake the woman made, but she didn't say anything. She walked out of Burger King, got in her car, and went home.

are these exact amounts necessary to make your point?

Your structure is clear - good paragraph breaks

4

Dishonesty can also occur between two people in a relationship. It can result

not clear - rephrase or explain?

in blaming others for mistakes made by someone else. I have a friend that lives in

I might be more convinced if you had other examples rather than so much info on one isolated incident.

the apartment complex where I stay. Her husband one day was backing up his car into his stall underneath the carport, when all of a sudden he hit one of the wooden poles that holds up the carport and moved it out of place. Then he called the owner of the building and explained to him about the incident that occurred, but instead of taking the blame for hitting the pole, he put the blame on his wife.

possibly losing focus?

Every time someone asked him what happened to the pole next to his car, he

would reply, "Oh, my wife hit the pole when she was parking the car."

For a college essay, try omitting "I," "me," "my" throughout?

5   Finally, I do agree with the article "The Thin Grey Line" and Marya Mannes'

check for style - rephrase

opinion separating honesty from dishonesty because if we really take a close look

vague?

at different situations, we would probably find a little dishonesty here and there.

Aha - Good idea to mention possible solutions in conclusion - can you tie this back to your thesis and your overall purpose - are you trying to persuade us to change our behavior? I'm not quite clear.

I feel that everyone has had some sort of dishonesty once in their lives, whether it

be specific

was a little white lie or not, but dishonesty is a way of life for some people. We

need to be more responsible for our dishonest decisions and behaviors, but most

of all, we need to strengthen our moral beliefs because dishonesty can have a ma-

jor effect on everyone involved.   ○

Margarita-
You're headed in the right direction with this draft.
For now,
1 Reread the Mannes essay - this would help you remember what
it was about dishonesty that struck you so strongly.
2 Rethink & narrow your thesis - what's your point of view about
all this dishonesty?
3 Re-examine your structure + the material you've chosen for para-
graphs 2, 3, and 4. Each one of these paragraphs can really
build a strong case for your thesis.
Good job with the first draft.
I look forward to reading your revised draft!

Key Questions

1. **Purpose**   Name one change Figueroa might make in paragraph 1 in response to her instructor's comments.

2. **Focus**   Why has Figueroa's instructor circled the use of exact dollars and cents? What should Figueroa consider doing with these amounts in her revised essay draft?

3. **Material**   What do the instructor's comments indicate about Figueroa's material in paragraph 4?

4. **Structure**   If Figueroa considers her instructor's comments, will she change or maintain her present structure for the essay?

5. **Style**   Rephrase the first sentence in paragraph 3 so that readers can understand the thought more clearly.

Grammar Key

Handbook Practice: Modifier Problems

Read pages 449–450. Complete Exercise 10 and the subsequent paragraph on pages 450–451.

GUIDELINES FOR REVISING

Allow Time for Reflection

After you have completed your preliminary draft, your first thought may be, "At last, I'm finished with that essay." Resist the impulse to accept this version as your final draft, even though to you the first draft may *look* pretty good. This advice is doubly true if you are drafting on a computer because the final, clean look of the typeset letters may fool you into thinking your draft is ready for its intended audience. Instead, allow a day or two, or at least a few hours, in which to reflect on your preliminary draft. As you go about your other activities during this time, allow yourself time to think about your draft, jotting down any ideas that come to mind. This way, when you begin to revise, you'll be more likely to resee your draft with objective eyes. Thoughtful revision involves scheduling enough time to reflect on your writing. Ideally, you could take all the time you need to stand back and evaluate what you've written; realistically, you have deadlines to meet.

Use Audience Response: Peer and Instructor Editing

Peer editing can be a helpful tool in the revising stage of the composing process. Although you may think your ideas are coming across clearly in a draft, there's nothing like the honest reaction of an unbiased reading audience to put you in touch with what is and is not working in your essay draft. Your instructor may have a specific format for peer editing, or you may be free to structure peer evaluations on your own. If the latter is the case, find another student whose feedback you value and ask the student to read and respond to your essay.

Here are a few popular methods of structuring peer response:

- **Readaround or workshopping**
  Students divide into groups of three or four and each student brings an extra copy of a draft to share with the group. During an allotted time, the group members silently read all essays circulating within their group and jot comments on them or on a separate sheet of paper.

- **Read aloud**
  Students divide into small groups, each student reading an essay out loud while others respond on paper with constructive comments for revision.

- **Anonymous peer editing**
  Students turn in drafts to instructor or submit drafts using e-mail with only a student body number (no name) on the draft; instructor distributes

essays at random to class or circulates them via e-mail for evaluation and anonymous comment.

- **Peer response worksheet**
  Instructor distributes to the class specific sets of questions for students to respond to when reading and evaluating another student's essay. To see an example of such a worksheet, turn to page 154.

In revising, you will often have the advantage of your instructor's response to a draft. This can be a helpful complement to self-evaluation and peer editing for three reasons:

- Your instructor is obviously familiar with your assignment—your primary purpose in writing the essay.

- Your instructor has expertise not only in writing but also in objectively commenting on student essays in a way designed to help you in revising.

- Your instructor wants to help you succeed both in this course and in your future college writing.

Rethink the Draft

Once you have additional feedback from a peer or your instructor, you can rethink the draft. This rethinking can take you in a variety of directions in your revising process.

For example, let's say that your instructor, after reading your draft, suggests that your thesis is too broad and that just one of your supporting points could actually be the basis for an entire paper. You think about this comment and decide that you agree that your subject would be more focused if you limited the thesis. You could then include material in support of this thesis that would be much more convincing and specific than the material you now have. This rethinking of your essay results in a shift in your focus. And now as you begin to work on your new thesis, you won't be using some of the material from your first draft. As a result, you may need to return to the discovering stage to gather more material in support of your new thesis.

This example of rethinking involves a significant adjustment on your part. Other adjustments that occur after rethinking the draft also characterize the revising stage. For many writers these adjustments include adding, cutting, substituting, and rearranging.

Add to the Draft

If your instructor or a peer editor feels that you left some vital information out of your draft or that some point needs further clarification or explanation, you will want to add more material to your draft where appropriate.

Cut What Is Not Working

You may find that you need to cut a part of your draft—to delete words, sentences, or even large sections because they don't pertain clearly to your thesis, they don't suit your primary purpose in the essay, or they repeat what has already been stated. Cutting can be hard because you've put so much time and effort into finding the material in the first place. However, cutting repeated, off-topic, or unnecessary information can substantially strengthen an essay.

Make Substitutions

Often after you cut inappropriate material, you find you need to replace what is now missing with new material. This can involve inserting substitutions—words, sentences, whole groups of sentences, or even paragraphs. You may need to return to prewriting to discover more material for your revised draft.

Rearrange Material

Upon rethinking your draft, you may feel—or your peer editor or instructor may have commented—that your material, although supportive of your purpose, should be rearranged. Restructuring your material might result in a more logical flow of ideas. A different way of organizing could also give the essay more dramatic punch.

Practice 7.1   Reread Figueroa's first draft of "Dishonesty" (p. 129), along with her instructor's comments. Annotate the draft by indicating where she might want to add, cut, make substitutions, or rearrange material. ❏

Strategies for Revising

1. **Purpose**   Distance yourself from your draft for a few hours or a day or two, then reread it, asking yourself if it achieves its purpose.
2. **Focus**   Check and, if appropriate, adjust your thesis based on instructor or peer comments.
3. **Material**   Search for places in the draft where additional information would help make your point. Delete any material that doesn't clearly relate to your thesis.
4. **Structure**   Experiment with different ways of arranging material and get feedback from your instructor or peers.
5. **Style**   Be sure that you have an introduction that grabs the interest of your audience and a conclusion that offers closure and ties up loose ends. Check to see that every word and sentence works to communicate your subject clearly to readers. Revise any vague words or phrases.

CHARACTERISTICS OF POLISHING

If you've ever polished a car or a treasured piece of furniture or jewelry, you know the satisfaction that comes from pride of ownership—you've taken something you love and made it even more wonderful. When you polish an essay, you refine it—you check for flaws on its surface, correcting mistakes as well as adding those finishing touches that will make your writing sparkle.

Polishing is the final, crucial stage in the composing process, but students often overlook this stage in their haste to meet an assignment deadline. The polishing stage can make all the difference in the impact your essay has on its audience. While the revising stage of your writing involves the "big picture"—rethinking your draft in terms of what ideas you want to add, delete, and re-arrange—the polishing stage demands that you use a mental magnifying glass to scrutinize every detail of your revised draft, to search out inappropriate or weak words and phrases as well as grammatical, spelling, and punctuation errors. This stage concludes when you present the final draft of your essay in the correct format indicated by your instructor.

MODEL WITH KEY QUESTIONS

Figueroa's preliminary draft appears on page 76. When Figueroa completed her second draft, she brought this revised draft to class, where she received feedback from a peer editor. First, read Figueroa's revised draft of the essay, and then examine her peer's response. Notice that the peer editor wrote directly on Figueroa's draft as well as on the peer-editing sheet. Next, read Figueroa's final draft, retitled "Practicing What We Preach" (p. 137), which incorporates many of the peer editor's suggestions and the fine-tuning Figueroa gave to her essay in polishing it.

DISHONESTY

Margarita Figueroa

1   Lots of people cheat on their taxes and lie to their loved ones, or don't mention an error when they receive change if that means they would get the benefit of extra money. If we read an essay by Marya Mannes called "The Thin Grey Line," we'll be forced to examine the issue of dishonesty in our society. Although it is not a pleasant thought, dishonesty seems to be winning over honesty in our personal lives, when we go to work, and in our dealings with strangers.   *Thesis*

2   Even as we stress the importance of dishonesty, many adults don't "practice *← To whom?* what they preach." For example, one partner in a marriage may be cheating on another by having an affair or playing around on the sly. Or perhaps pride chal- *→ Save face?* lenges a husband or wife to tell a lie. For instance, a neighbor's husband lies when

his car hits a wooden pole holding up a carport. He then calls the owner of the building who lives down the street, putting the blame on his own wife, he even persuades his wife to go along with his lie that "my wife hit the pole when she was parking the car."

You could use a transition here.

3   Deception appears in the workplace also. How many times have we or those we've known "borrowed" supplies from the company we work for? And what

or leaving work early? more examples?

about taking an extra hour for lunch? Possibly the most dangerous form of dishonesty in the workplace occurs when we are asked by an employer to deceive a customer, many of us have been told, "If he calls, just tell him I'm not in." *Add material?*

Not always! Explain when?

4   Finally, dishonesty occurs in our day-to-day encounters with total strangers. For example, there are those who collaborate to report a fake car accident in order to get money from auto insurance companies. Lawyers help with deceptions, urging out-of-court settlements for hundreds of dollars. Also, people confide that when given wrong change at fast food establishments, they deceive the casheer by saying nothing. Instead these people get in their cars and laugh.

Clarify this - why do they laugh? What if the error means they get cheated out of money?

5   Perhaps if we could strengthen our morals and be examples of honesty, our children wouldn't be as likely to be dishonest. ○

Your conclusion needs work. Try to link these remarks somehow with your examples of dishonesty in intro. paragraph??

After taking time to evaluate her peer editor's comments, Figueroa worked through the polishing stage for this essay. She had planned to spend several days on the entire composing process, and she was much happier with her final draft of this essay than she had been with earlier assignments for which she had devoted less time.

As you read Figueroa's final draft, notice in particular that in polishing her essay, she made changes based on her peer editor's comments and her own evaluation of her draft. Figueroa noticed that Tommy Cheng, her editor, found a particular phrase, "practice what they preach" memorable, so she decided to use the phrase in her revised title. She also refined her introduction and conclusion, two weaker areas noted by Cheng. Figueroa wanted the final draft to move more smoothly from one idea to the next, so she inserted cue words where they would be helpful. Finally, Figueroa checked her spelling, repaired some grammatical errors, and improved her word choice in certain paragraphs noted by Cheng as needing a little polishing.

PRACTICING WHAT WE PREACH

Margarita Figueroa

1   How many people cheat on their taxes? Lie to their loved ones? Fail to mention an error in receiving change when the error happens to be in their favor? Reading an essay by Marya Mannes entitled "The Thin Grey Line" forces us to examine the issue of dishonesty in our society. Although it is not a pleasant thought, dishonesty seems to be winning over honesty in our personal lives, our professional lives, and our day-to-day interaction with total strangers.

2   Even as we stress to our children the importance of honesty, many adults don't "practice what they preach." For example, one partner in a marriage may be cheating on another. Or perhaps pride challenges a husband or wife to "save face" by telling a lie. For instance, a neighbor's husband lies when his car hits a wooden pole holding up a carport. He then calls the owner of the building, putting the blame on his own wife and even persuading the wife to go along with his lie that "my wife hit the pole when she was parking the car."

3   Unfortunately, deception doesn't stop with personal relationships—it also appears in our professional lives. How many times have we or those we've known "borrowed" supplies from the company we work for? And aren't we crossing that "thin gray line" every time we leave from work early, come in late, or take an extra hour for lunch? Possibly the most dangerous form of dishonesty in the workplace occurs when we are asked by an employer to deceive a customer. Many of us have been told, "If he calls, just tell him I'm not in," or, "Don't mention a refund if the client doesn't ask."

4   Finally, dishonesty occurs in our day-to-day encounters with total strangers if circumstances or greed motivate us to lie. For example, there are those who collaborate to report a fake car accident in order to get money from auto insurance companies. These fraudulent claims sometimes involve lawyers who help with the deceptions, urging out-of-court settlements for hundreds of dollars. Also, people confide that when given incorrect change at fast-food establishments, they deceive the cashier by saying nothing if an error is made in their favor. Instead, these individuals get in their cars, drive home, and pocket their newfound money.

5   If we really take a closer look at different situations in our personal and professional lives and our daily interactions with strangers, we will find more than a little dishonesty. Why? Perhaps if we could strengthen our morals and be examples of honesty to our children, the next generation wouldn't be as likely to cheat on taxes or lie to their loved ones.   ○

Key Questions

1. **Purpose**   What appears to be the writer's purpose in this final, polished draft of the essay?

2. **Focus**   Explain whether or not Figueroa's revised conclusion focuses more clearly on her thesis.

3. **Material**   What new example has Figueroa added in paragraph 3 as a result of her editor's comments?

4. **Structure**   Which new cue words help Figueroa's audience follow her main points as she develops them?

5. **Style**   Find one example of a new word or phrase that Figueroa uses in her polished, final draft.

Grammar Key

Handbook Practice: Commas

First, examine the Comma Rules below; then read pages 452–454 and complete Exercise 11 and the paragraph on pages 454–455.

Comma Rules Chart

D   <u>D</u>irect address: *Barbara*, will you please give me some advice?
A   <u>A</u>djectives: The Lakers had an *intimidating*, overpowering defense.
D, <u>D</u>ates: Jackie Robinson was born on *January 31, 1919*, in a small hospital.

N   <u>N</u>on-restrictive words, phrases, or clauses: Electronic mail, *which sends messages instantaneously*, is beginning to replace "snail mail."
I   <u>I</u>ntroductory words, phrases, or clauses: *Taking her baby along*, Phyllis joined Shane on a business trip to Orlando.
C   <u>C</u>ompound sentences: You can turn left at the next light, or you can follow the main highway for three blocks.
E   <u>E</u>lements in a series: *Books, newspapers, and magazines* lay on the table.

Q   <u>Q</u>uotations: *"Don't leave any questions blank,"* the instructor said.
U
I   <u>I</u>nterrupters: She knew, *by the way*, that the television didn't work.
P! <u>P</u>lace names: The address is *1600 Broadway, New York, New York 10019*.

GUIDELINES FOR POLISHING

Reread Your Revised Draft

Even after you've revised a first or second draft, resist the temptation to consider your work complete. Instead, read the draft out loud slowly. You'll often be amazed at what you discover. Writer and teacher Eudora Welty read aloud everything she wrote because she believed that "the sound of what falls on the page begins the process of testing it for truth."

You can also try reading your essay backward, not word by word but sentence by sentence. Although your sentences may make little sense in relation to your thesis, you can more easily spot errors in grammar, punctuation, spelling, missing words, and typos by reading backward.

Use Your Tools to Improve Weak Spots

Do you have an "Achilles heel"? (Achilles was a mythological Greek warrior who had one area of vulnerability—his heel—in an otherwise mighty body.) Today, we use the expression to refer to an individual weakness or trouble spot.

Do instructor or peer comments indicate that you have a tendency to misspell words? To use vague words instead of specific ones? To write incomplete sentences? If you have a recognized weakness, you can use this knowledge to your best advantage as a writer. Be on the lookout for this vulnerable area and polish your essay by addressing the problem.

Once you've identified a particular weakness, consult the appropriate section in the handbook in Part 5 of this book and complete the exercises and activities. If you notice or suspect any spelling problems, or if you're not completely sure of the meaning of a word that you're using, remember that your dictionary can help. In addition, a computer's spell checker can certainly help you catch many spelling errors, but you should know that it does not correct misspellings caused by word confusion—for example, misuse of *their* for *there* or *accept* for *except*. For a complete list of similar sounding words and their meanings, see page 473–474 in the handbook.

Practice 7.2 To help you identify troublesome areas in your writing, consult a few assignments you've submitted to your writing instructor. After looking over the evaluations of your assignments along with any markings and comments, identify two trouble spots connected with grammar, spelling, punctuation, word choice, or usage for which you could use some additional help and practice. ❏

Use Peer Editing and Instructor Response

Just as feedback from both your instructor and your peers was an important part of revising your first draft, new feedback on your revised drafts will help you continue to refine your essay in the polishing stage. By all means, share your second and third drafts, and then respond thoughtfully to the comments of your readers.

Trim and Clarify

One important way you can polish your essay involves making certain that every word you use is necessary, specific, and clearly understood by the reader. Go through the essay sentence by sentence and see if you can find any words or phrases you could trim or make more accurate or descriptive.

Practice 7.3 Annotate the following concluding paragraph of an essay draft by trimming or replacing words or word groups where appropriate:

So to make a long story short, trying to find the right mate is like trying to find a needle in a haystack. At this point in time, we can only hope that dating services will grow more efficient at matching guys with chicks according to their true interests and personalities rather than according to some touched-up photos or carefully rehearsed videos. It is a crying shame that some enterprising person hasn't seen the light and established just such a service. Perhaps somewhere out there in the great beyond of cyberspace there is a perfect match for each of us. ❏

Eliminate Wordiness

Wordiness occurs when we pad our writing with lots of unnecessary and sometimes meaningless words or phrases. Although many of us have some wordy sections in rough drafts, reading the draft aloud with a pencil in hand can often help us spot and repair wordy passages by rephrasing to eliminate these fillers. Here are some examples of wordiness followed by corrections:

- **Omit "it is," "there is," and "there are" at the beginnings of sentences.**
  Wordy: It is difficult to understand the role of the lobbyist in Washington, D.C.
  Revised: The role of the lobbyist in Washington D.C. is difficult to understand.

- **Omit "this" from the beginning of a sentence by linking it to the prior sentence with a comma.**
  Wordy: Celebrex has been banned from pharmacies. This has decreased the dangers to those with heart conditions.
  Revised: Celebrex has been banned from pharmacies, decreasing dangers to those with heart conditions.

- **Replace passive verbs (in which the subject of the sentence is being acted upon) with active verbs (in which the subject is the actor).**
  Wordy: The world's weather is being affected by global warming.
  Revised: Global warming is affecting the world's weather.

- **Change "is" or "was" when they occur alone to a strong verb:**
  Wordy: A new library is necessary for the school.
  Revised: The school needs a new library.

- **Replace "is," "are," "was," "were," or "have + an –ing word" to a simple present or past tense verb.**
  Wordy: The community theatre was embarking on a new fundraiser.
  Revised: The community theatre embarked on a new fundraiser.

- **Replace "due to the fact that" with "since" or "because."**
  Wordy: They elected Dilbert due to the fact that he proposed many innovative changes.
  Revised: They elected Dilbert because he proposed many innovative changes.

Practice 7.4   Revise the following paragraph by identifying wordiness and making appropriate changes.

It is in San Francisco that tourists will find many exciting places to visit. When tourists are going to Golden Gate Park, they will get to see buffalo as well as the Japanese Tea Garden. Tourists should also visit the Golden Gate Bridge due to the fact that the view from the bridge is spectacular. Also, it is interesting to visit Chinatown and Fisherman's Wharf. These are wonderful sites where many visitors are eating and drinking. ❏

Insert Cue Words

When you're putting those finishing touches on your essay in the polishing stage, you want to make sure (if you have not considered this in an earlier draft) that your audience can follow the flow of your ideas smoothly and effortlessly. Have you ever careened around the streets with an erratic driver—one who presses hard on the gas pedal and then, seconds later, without warning, slams on the brakes? This kind of car ride is jerky and unpleasant, in much the same way that an essay that jerks the reader roughly and without warning from one point to another may fail to achieve its purpose. It is intimidating to the reader not to know what to expect next.

You can solve this problem with the use of **cue words**, words or phrases that signal the reader that some shift in thought is taking place. Cue words tell the reader you're moving from a main point to a specific detail, from comparison to contrast, from cause to effect, and so on. Refer to the list of cue words, found in the box, when you're searching for just the right cue word for your essay.

Cue Words

- Try using these if you want to signal a change in time:

then	after a while	in the future	afterward
finally	in the past	now	previously
currently	meanwhile	immediately	in the meantime
at last	earlier	soon	simultaneously
formerly	next	until now	eventually
suddenly	before now	at the same time	later
after this	presently	at length	subsequently

- Experiment with these if you want to show some order, progression, or a series of steps (not necessarily time-oriented):

first, second	finally	last	in addition
next	another	furthermore	further
also	moreover	besides	not only . . . but also

- Work with these to cue a contrast or change in what has been said before:

in contrast	on the other hand	regardless	nevertheless
conversely	however	on the contrary	despite, in spite of
but	even though	still	although
yet	instead		

- To show a similarity or comparison with what you have stated before:

similarly	in the same way	just as	in a similar manner
likewise	in comparison	as well as	equally important

- To signal that you are going into more detail or elaboration:

for example	for instance	as an illustration	to illustrate
to explain	in particular	to expand on this	

(continued)

- To signal repetition:

| again | in other words | to repeat | as has been noted |

- To show emphasis or stress:

basically	more important	without question	most important
truly	without a doubt	moreover	undeniably
essentially	above all	indeed	

- To signal some cause/effect relationship:

| because | as a result | since | consequently |
| thus | accordingly | for this reason | therefore |

- To cue the reader that you are concluding:

| finally | in conclusion | on the whole | all things considered |
| in brief | to summarize | in summary | in closing |

Practice 7.5 Read the following paragraph and insert appropriate cue words from the list.

I have several good reasons for missing class today. _____, my car was totaled in an accident yesterday afternoon, and I have no way of getting to school today. _____, my dog ate my homework, and the instructor will never believe this really happened. _____, my favorite soap opera is featuring a guest star this week whom I really want to see, and the VCR is on the blink so I can't tape it for later. _____, I have no doubt that any intelligent instructor would take pity on me and allow me to make up any class work that I have missed. ❏

Create a Captivating Title

Some writers like to have at least a working title right from the moment they begin to draft the essay; others prefer to wait until the final polishing to create a title. Experiment with what works best for you. Keep in mind that a title is important—it is your reader's first impression of your essay and will help you forecast your particular point of view as well as the subject you'll be discussing. Finally, avoid using a complete sentence as a title. Titles cannot function as thesis statements; instead, try to create a title from one to several words long.

Practice 7.6 To see how titles can communicate to a reader, turn back to the table of contents for this text and scan the essay titles. From those essays that you have read, locate a title that you find particularly effective and briefly explain why. ❏

Check for Correct Manuscript Format

Manuscript format refers to the general layout of a final draft, including name and title placement, margins, and page numbers. If your instructor does not specify a particular layout, you can follow the most common format: double-space your essay on 8½- by 11-inch white bond paper, set 1-inch margins on the top, bottom, and sides of the page, indent paragraphs five to eight spaces, center the title, and put your name, section number or class name, and your assignment number or description in the upper-right corner.

Strategies for Polishing

1. **Purpose**   Make certain that every word you use is the best one to support your essay's purpose. As you polish, delete and replace cliches, jargon, undefined terms, wordy expressions, and vague words.

2. **Focus**   Check your thesis to be sure that the wording clearly communicates your subject to your audience.

3. **Material**   Be certain that each main point is supported by clearly phrased, easy-to-read sentences and that paragraphs are of an appropriate length.

4. **Structure**   Find any places within and between paragraphs where cue words would help lead your readers from one idea to the next. Insert appropriate cue words.

5. **Style**   Ask yourself if your title and introduction engage your audience. Be sure your conclusion offers closure and ties up all loose ends. Finally, proofread the essay carefully for spelling, punctuation, grammar mistakes, typos, omitted words, and correct manuscript format. Do not rely solely on a computer's spelling—or grammar—correction functions. Repair all mistakes.

JOURNAL WRITING: A REVISION DIALOGUE

Writing in your journal about your experiences when revising and polishing a draft will allow you to explore your feeling about the various activities in these two stages. Journal writing can furnish you with a record of what did and did not work for you, so that in the future you can repeat effective strategies and avoid ineffective ones.

1. Locate a final draft of one of your essays, along with all prewriting and earlier drafts. Answer at least five of the following questions in a journal entry:

   - How much time did you allow for the revising stage of this essay? Was this enough, too much, or about right?

   - Did you work from an outline? Did your plan for structuring the essay work? Did you experiment with changing the structure?

   - If you received peer or instructor response to a draft, how did you react to the comments?

   - Did your original thesis change?

   - In your drafts, what material did you add? Delete? Substitute?

- Did you keep your original title? Introduction? Conclusion?

- Did you use a checklist in revising? In polishing?

- Did you read your draft out loud to spot mistakes?

- Did you try reading the essay backward, sentence by sentence? Was this helpful?

- Did you use a dictionary and the handbook section of this text when polishing?

- Did you proofread your essay on the computer screen or on hard copy?

2. Examine the essays you've written for this course. Based on your instructor's comments and your own evaluations, write a list of your strengths and weak spots as a writer. Or, if you prefer, create a personal checklist of problems that seem to recur from essay to essay. Then write a plan to deal with these problems in future essays. You might set up a conference with your instructor or with the writing center on your campus to discuss this plan.

If you find these journal entries helpful, return to this page after you've worked through the composing process for your next essay and answer other questions.

Using the Computer: Revising and Polishing

1. Although using a computer can facilitate your revision, studies show that students who revise on hard copy (the printed page) write better essays. Many professional writers and editors also prefer to revise using hard copy. To make revising hard copy easier, print out a triple-spaced version with extra wide margins for a draft you're currently revising. You'll have lots of room to evaluate and experiment with adding, deleting, substituting, and rearranging information. Practice revision strategies on this draft or ask a peer editor to respond to the draft, making suggestions between the lines and in the margins of the draft.

2. Many word-processing programs offer options for annotating and questioning text. Although it is easy to simply change the appearance of words on the screen (as in the previous exercise), you might find it more effective to use *annotating, revising, strikeout/strikethrough, insert, comment,* and other *text editing* commands. First, use your program's *Help* function to see which of these commands are available. Practice using a sample or draft text. In most programs, *annotating* allows you to make comments on the screen that are visible to you on the screen but do not show up when a document is printed. Many peer editors find this function especially useful. *Strikeout/Strikethrough* makes lines through words that you delete, without actually erasing them from the screen. This is a good way to keep track of changes that

you are thinking of making, or that a peer editor has suggested. Try this in your draft.

3. To track down words that you think you may have used too often or incorrectly, use *Search* to locate and change those words. For effective editing, you might be on the lookout for vague words like *thing, very, society,* or *really.* When you find these words, reread the sentence in which they appear. Do you "really" need the word? Is there a more interesting, accurate word you could use instead? The *Search/Replace* function can help you save time in revision. If you notice that you've used the wrong spelling or format throughout your essay—for example, you've typed *effect* where you should have typed *affect*—search/replace will automatically find all the errors and make the correction.

4. Although a *spell checker* can be a terrific help as you polish your essay, it should be your last resort. A spell checker looks at each word individually and pays no attention at all to context. This might not seem like such a big deal, until you realize just how many homonyms (words that sound exactly alike but mean different things) there are in the English language. Incorrect usages of apostrophes and pronouns also tend to glide through a spell checker uncorrected. Here are some sentences that a spell checker would let you get away with—but your instructor would not find so funny:

   - Although their was a report of piece, gorilla warfare continues.
   - The nurse had many patience hear in the hospital.
   - Sam was board with the teacher's lessen.
   - I would like to meat you, but my voice is horse today and I'm afraid I wouldn't be herd.

5. Looking for a word? Want to impress your friends with a really obscure new term? Many publishing companies and search engines have online dictionary sites that go beyond providing definitions. Some provide a "word of the day" or snippets of language history. Does your search engine have a dictionary? Use it to look up a word. Or go to **http://www.m-w.com**, the *Merriam-Webster Dictionary* site.

6. For excellent help in revising and polishing your essay, read the strategies offered at the following Web site:

   http://owl.english.purdue.edu/handouts/general/gl_edit.html

7. After reading the Declaration of Independence (p. 147), visit the following Web site to learn more about Jefferson's drafting process:

   http://www.loc.gov/exhibits/declara/declara3.html

OPTIONS FOR WRITING

The first four options ask you to practice revising and polishing one or more drafts of your earlier essays. Roald Dahl, the creator of *James and the Giant Peach, Charlie and the Chocolate Factory,* and many other children's books, candidly revealed his writing process: "By the time I'm nearing the end of a story, the first part will have been reread and altered and corrected at least 150 times. . . . Good writing is essentially rewriting." You won't have the chance to complete 150 revisions of your essays for this course, but in the following options you will have the opportunity to choose one or more essay drafts that you'd like to revise and polish.

1. After reviewing the "Guidelines for Revising" (p. 132), reread an essay that your instructor has commented on, and then rethink your draft. You may need to readjust your thesis accordingly. After you have worked through a revised draft, use the Peer-Edit Worksheet (p. 154), adding your own questions if you like. Ask another student to read and comment on your revised draft. After you have read that student's peer response, take some time to rethink your draft again and review the "Guidelines for Polishing" (p. 138). Now polish your draft, making necessary changes.

2. Review "Trim and Clarify" (p. 139) and the list of cue words on pages 141–142. Choose a draft of one of your essays and read the draft aloud, underlining or highlighting any vague or ineffective words or phrases and inserting cue words where helpful to guide the reader. Then write a more polished draft of the essay, consulting the "Strategies for Polishing" (p. 143).

3. Select a few of your essays that your instructor has graded or evaluated and analyze them using the checklists for revising and polishing. Write a paragraph focusing on your strengths and weaknesses in writing and your plan for strengthening future essays.

4. Exchange one of your past essays with another student in your class. (If possible, print out a clean copy of essays for each other.) After reading your partner's essay twice, write a letter to each other using the following structure:

   • Paragraph 1: General discussion of the writer's essay topic as you understand it.

   • Paragraph 2: What would you advise changing? Offer specific, clear suggestions.

   • Paragraph 3: Any aspect of the essay you really liked. (Feel free to discuss any elements related to the five keys: PURPOSE, FOCUS, MATERIAL, STRUCTURE, and STYLE.)

5. Write an essay about an incident or experience in your life that helped you discover a new principle to live by. Detail the incident, including what happened, the circumstances, and how you felt about what happened. Communicate the new principle you discovered so that your audience can understand it. Explain how this new principle affected you and changed your views in an important way.

6. Describe an "ideal marriage" in today's terms. Is there such a thing in real life, or only in the reruns of old 1950s television shows or movies?

7. Is it true that many college athletes don't graduate? Interview a coach as well as a college administrator (one who would have figures and

statistics to share with you). Write an essay in which you inform your audience of the numbers of athletes who don't graduate and follow up by speculating on possible reasons as well as solutions.

8. In a small group, explore people and organizations with a concern for ecological catastrophes. Are these people alarmists, or is there great validity in their arguments for action? Think of one widely debated threat: water shortages for urban areas, global warming, runaway population growth in underdeveloped countries, acid rain, or another. Brainstorm for material and arrange the material into a clearly developed essay.

9. *(Film and Literature) Point of view* refers to the author's or filmmaker's attempt to show the world in a certain way. To see how point of view works in film, research the well-known Indian leader Gandhi using encyclopedias, online sources, or articles from magazines. Then view the film *Gandhi* and write an essay detailing how the filmmaker's point of view can be detected in camera work—through whose eyes do we see the ongoing action of the film? Does the point of view change or stay the same throughout the film?

10. *(Service Learning)* Write a letter to your city council in which you call for stricter supervision of, or more official support for, the local police.

RESPONDING TO WRITING: PEER EDITING

As you become more experienced in peer editing the essays of others and in responding to the suggestions of your peers, remember to read peer comments carefully, evaluate them, and rethink your draft, and then revise and polish accordingly.

Peer editing is not limited to college English classes. Many writers in the workplace have other workers or supervisors examine their writing of reports, memos, letters, and other documents in order to offer revision suggestions. Nor is peer editing something new. In drafting the Declaration of Independence, one of the most famous of America's documents, Thomas Jefferson sought and heeded the comments of peer editors Benjamin Franklin and John Adams, along with other members of Congress. As you read the rough draft of this document written in 1776, notice the revisions Jefferson's peers made.

DECLARATION OF INDEPENDENCE

1   When in the course of human events it becomes necessary for a ~~a~~ *one* people to *dissolve the political bands which have connected them with another, and to* ~~advance from that subordination in which they have hitherto remained, & to~~ assume among the powers of the earth the ~~equal & independent~~ *separate and equal* station to which

the laws of nature & of nature's god entitle them, a decent respect to the opinions of mankind requires that they should declare the causes which impel them to *the*

separation
~~change~~.

2   We hold these truths to be ~~sacred & undeniable~~ *self-evident*; that all men are created equal

& ~~independent~~; that ~~from that equal creation they derive in rights~~ *they are endowed by their creator with* ~~equal rights, some of which are~~ *rights; that* inherent &

inalienable *among* ~~which~~ *these* are ~~the preservation of~~ life, & liberty, & the pursuit of

happiness; that to secure these ~~ends~~ *rights*, governments are instituted among men de-

riving their just powers from the consent of the governed; that whenever any

form of government ~~shall~~ becomes destructive of these ends, it is the right of the

people to alter or to abolish it, & to institute new government, laying it's founda-

tion on such principles & organizing it's powers in such form, as to them shall

seem most likely to effect their safety & happiness. prudence indeed will dictate

that governments long established should not be changed for light & transient

causes: and accordingly all experience hath shewn that mankind are more dis-

posed to suffer while evils are sufferable, than to right themselves by abolishing

the forms to which they are accustomed. but when a long train of abuses &

usurpations, begun at a distinguished period, & pursuing invariably the same

object, evinces a design to ~~subject~~ reduce them ~~to arbitrary power~~ **under absolute Despotism*, it is their right,

it is their duty, to throw off such government & to provide new guards of their

future security. such has been the patient sufferance of these colonies; & such is

now the necessity which constrains them to expunge their former systems of

government. the history of ~~his~~ *†the* present ~~majesty~~ *king of Great Britian* is a history of unremitting injuries

and usurpations, among which ~~no one fact stands single or solitary~~ *appears no solitary fact* to contradict

the uniform tenor of the rest, ~~all of which~~ *but all* have in direct object the establishment

of an absolute tyranny over these states. to prove this, let facts be submitted to a

candid world, for the truth of which we pledge faith yet unsullied by falsehood.

3   he has refused his assent to laws the most wholesome and necessary for the

public good:

†Mr. Adams' handwriting
*Dr. Franklin's handwriting

4   he has forbidden his governors to pass laws of immediate & pressing importance,

unless suspended in their operation till his assent should be obtained; and

when so suspended, he has neglected utterly to attend to them.

5   he has refused to pass other laws for the accomodation of large districts of people

in the legislature
unless those people would relinquish the right of representation, a right in-

estimable to them & formidable to tyrants only:

6   *he has called together legislative bodies at places unusual, uncomfortable & distant from*

the depository of their public records for the sole purpose of fatiguing them into

compliance with his measures:

7   he has dissolved, Representative houses repeatedly & continually, for opposing

with manly firmness his invasions on the rights of the people:

†*time after such dissolutions*
8   ~~he has dissolved~~ he has refused for a long ~~space of time~~ to cause others to be elected,

whereby the legislative powers, incapable of annihilation, have returned to the

people at large for their exercise, the state remaining in the meantime exposed

to all the dangers of invasion from without, & convulsions within:

9   he has endeavored to prevent the population of these states; for that purpose ob-

structing the laws for naturalization of foreigners; refusing to pass others to

encourage their migrations hither; & raising the conditions of new appro-

priations of lands:

10   he has suffered the administration of justice totally to cease in some of these

states
~~colonies~~, refusing his assent to laws for establishing judiciary powers:

11   he has made our judges dependent on his will alone, for the tenure of their offices,

**the   and payment*
and amount of their salaries:

12   he has erected a multitude of new offices by a self-assumed power, & sent hither

swarms of officers to harass our people & eat out their substance:

~~without our consent~~   *without ~~our~~ the consent of our legislatures*
13   he has kept among us in times of peace standing armies & ships of wars;

†Mr. Adams' handwriting
*Dr. Franklin's handwriting

14   he has effected to render the military, independent of & superior to the civil

power:

15   he has combined with others to subject us to a jurisdiction foreign to our constitu-

tions and unacknoleged by our laws; giving his assent to their pretended

~~acts of~~ legislation,

16   for quartering large bodies of armed troops among us;

which
for protecting them by a mock-trial from punishment for any murders they

should commit on the inhabitants of these states;

for cutting off our trade with all parts of the world;

for imposing taxes on us without our consent;

for depriving us of the benefits of trial by jury;

for transporting us beyond seas to be tried for pretended offenses;

for abolishing the free system of English laws in a neighboring province, establishing

therein an arbitrary government, and enlarging it's boundaries so as to render it

at once an example & fit instrument for introducing the same absolute rule into

these ~~colonies~~ states;
valuable
*abolishing our most ~~important~~ laws
for taking away our charters, & altering fundamentally the forms of our

governments;

for suspending our own legislatures & declaring themselves invested with

power to legislate for us in all cases whatsoever:

17   he has abdicated government here, withdrawing his governors, & declaring us

out of his allegiance & protection:

18   he has plundered our seas, ravaged our coasts, burnt our towns & destroyed the

lives of our people:

19   he is at this time transporting large armies of foreign mercenaries to compleat the

works of death, desolation & tyranny, already begun with circumstances of

cruelty & perfidy unworthy the head of civilized nation:

*Dr. Franklin's handwriting
†Mr. Adams' handwriting

20   he has endeavored to bring on the inhabitants of our frontiers the merciless Indian

savages, whose known rule of warfare is an undistinguished destruction of

al ages, sexes, & conditions of existence:

21   he has incited treasonable insurrections of our fellow-citizens, with the allure-

ments of forfeiture & confiscation of our property:

22   *he has constrained others* taken captives ~~falling into his hands~~*, on the high seas to bear arms against*

their country ~~& to destroy & be destroyed by the brethren whom they love~~*, to become*

the executioners of their friends & brethren, or to fall themselves by their hands.

23   he has waged cruel war against human nature itself, violating it's most sacred

rights of life & liberty in the persons of a distant people who never offended him,

captivating & carrying them into slavery in another hemisphere, or to incur

miserable death in their transportation thither. this piratical warfare, the oppro-

brium of *infidel* powers, is the warfare of the *Christian* king of Great Britain. *deter-*

mined to keep open a market where MEN should be bought & sold, he has prostituted

his negative for suppressing every legislative attempt to prohibit or to restrain

~~determining to keep open a market where MEN should be bought & sold~~

this execrable commerce and that this assemblage of horrors might want no fact

of distinguished die, he is now exciting those very people to rise in arms among

us, and to purchase that liberty of which *he* has deprived them, by murdering the

people upon whom *he* also obtruded them; thus paying off former crimes com-

mitted against the *liberties* of one people, with crimes which he urges them to

commit against the *lives* of another.

24   in every stage of these oppressions we have petitioned for redress in the most

humble terms; our repeated petitions have been answered *by repeated injury. a
                                                                      *only

prince whose character is thus marked by every act which may define a tyrant, is

unfit to be the ruler of a people who mean to be free. future ages will scarce be-

lieve that the hardiness of one man, adventured within the short compass of

*Dr. Franklin's handwriting

build
to ~~lay~~ a foundation so broad & undisguised for tyranny
twelve years only, ~~on so many acts of tyranny without a mask,~~ over a people
˄
freedom
fostered & fixed in principles of ~~liberty.~~

25   Nor have we been wanting in attentions to our British brethren. we have

warned them from time to time of attempts by their legislature to extend a jurisdic-

tion over these our states. we have reminded them of the circumstances of our emi-

gration & settlement here, no one of which could warrant so strange a pretension:

that these were effected at the expence of our own blood & treasure, unassisted

by the wealth or the strength of Great Britain: that in constituting indeed our sev-

eral forms of government, we had adopted one common king, thereby laying a

foundation for perpetual league & amity with them: but that submission to their

parliament was no part of our constitution, nor ever in idea if history may be

credited: and we appealed to their native justice & magnanimity as well as to the

ties of our common kindred to disavow these usurpations which were likely to in-

connection &
terrupt our correspondence ~~& connection.~~ they too have been deaf to the voice of
˄
justice & of consanguinity, & when occasions have been given them, by the regu-

lar course of their laws, of removing from their councils the disturbers of our har-

mony, they have by their free election re-established them in power. at this very

time too they are permitting their chief magistrate to send over not only soldiers

*destroy us
of our common blood, but Scotch & foreign mercenaries to invade & ~~deluge us in~~
˄
~~blood.~~ these facts have given the last stab to agonizing affection, and manly spirit

bids us to renounce forever these unfeeling brethren. we must endeavor to forget

our former love for them, and to hold them as we hold the rest of mankind,

enemies in war, in peace friends. we might have been a free & a great people

together; but a communication of grandeur & of freedom it seems is below their

& to glory
dignity. be it so, since they will have it: the road to ~~glory &~~ happiness is open to
˄
apart from them
us too; we will climb it ~~in a separately state,~~ and acquiesce in the necessity which
˄
de
pronounces our ~~everlasting adieu!~~ eternal separation!

*Dr. Franklin's handwriting

26   We therefore the representatives of the United States of America in General Congress assembled do, in the name & by authority of the good people of these states, reject and renounce all allegiance & subjection to the kings of Great Britain & all others who may hereafter claim by, through, or under them; we utterly dissolve & break off all political connection which may have heretofore subsisted between us & the people or parliament of Great Britain; and finally we do assert and declare ~~these~~ colonies to be free and independent ~~states~~, and that as *have* free & independent states they shall hereafter have power to levy war, conclude peace, contract alliances, establish commerce, & to do all other acts and things which independent st~~ates may of right~~ do, *full* And for the support of this declaration we mutually pledge to each other our lives, our fortunes, & our sacred honour. ○

Peer editing can help revise and polish your essay. As a writer, you have a right to agree or disagree with how a peer or even an instructor responds to your writing. As your writing course continues, you and your classmates will become more effective peer editors. To practice editing, first reread the Declaration of Independence, and then complete the Peer-Edit Worksheet that follows.

Peer-Edit Worksheet

Your name or student number: _____

Writer's name or student number: _____

1. **Purpose**   Does the introduction grab your attention? _____ Are you clear about this essay's purpose? _____ Is it to express, inform, or persuade? _____ In which sentence does the writer's purpose first become apparent? Write the sentence in the following space: _____

   _____

2. **Focus**   Find the writer's thesis and underline it on the draft. Does this thesis have a suitable subject, controlling idea, specific language, and appropriate tonw? _____ Which of these elements needs more work? _____

   _____

3. **Material**   Is the material in the essay clear and effective in developing the thesis? _____ Where could the writer add more material? Delete material? Substitute material? (Indicate by writing directly on the draft.)

4. **Structure**   Can you follow the development of ideas clearly from sentence to sentence and from one paragraph to he next? _____ What might help? (Indicate on draft by rearranging, adding cue works, etc.)

5. **Style**   Jot down in the following space a word group or word that is especially effective. _____ Find in the essay any examples of vague, inappropriate, or incorrect words and circle these on the draft. Indicate one weak area that this writer might check more carefully in proofreading for mistakes.

   _____

   Does the writer's conclusion effectively close the essay and tie back to the thesis with effective phrasing? _____

Now that you've practiced using an editing sheet, find a draft of one of your own recent essays and exchange it with another student, responding to the same peer editing questions or others that you or your instructor creates. When your draft and the peer-editing sheet are returned to you, read your editor's comments and complete these statements:

1. I agree with the following comments made by my peer editor:

2. I disagree with the following comments:

3. I plan to revise my essay in the following way:

PURPOSE

FOCUS

MATERIAL

STRUCTURE

STYLE

As you become more experienced in peer editing the essays of others and in responding to the suggestions of your peers, remember to read peer comments carefully, evaluate them, rethink your draft, and then revise and polish accordingly.

CRITICAL THINKING
In Connecting Texts

In her essay "Practicing What We Preach" (p. 137), Margarita Figueroa discusses instances of dishonesty within contemporary America. But modern-day Americans are not the only ones guilty of dishonest behavior. Although the writers of the Declaration of Independence showed great courage and initiative in drafting this important American document, Thomas Jefferson and his peer editors misled many into thinking that the Declaration represented the interests of all Americans. In actuality, the writers of this document were all white, free, male, property-owning Protestants—in short, they were certainly not representative of all Americans living then or now. Working in collaboration with a partner or small group, revise the first two paragraphs of the Declaration of Independence so that all Americans are represented, and try to update the language so that it reflects modern thought and usage. After you revise the draft, polish it and then share it with the rest of the class. Vote for the most effective revision.

Chapter 8

Writing with Sources

In your work and in your research there must always be passion.

—Ivan Petrovich Pavlov, *Russian physiologist*

Preview

In this chapter you will learn

- How to write an essay using sources
- How to identify your audience
- How to collect material from interviews, print, and electronic sources
- How to evaluate these sources
- How to take notes: summaries, paraphrases, direct quotes
- How to integrate quotations in your paragraphs
- How to document all sources according to Modern Language Association (MLA) format

After reading this chapter and completing its practice activities, you will feel comfortable researching and writing essays using sources.

When you use outside sources in your writing, you examine a subject further by going beyond what you already know and researching someone else's data and thoughts. You'll be utilizing sources in many settings—in college, on the job, and in your personal life. In addition, source-based essays incorporate many skills of successful essay writing that you've been learning and practicing throughout Part 1 of this book: clear thesis, captivating introduction and conclusion, well-developed body paragraphs, and logical organization of material.

CHARACTERISTICS OF SOURCE-BASED WRITINGS

In the **research** process, you collect information from any or all of the following: people, books, magazines, indexes, newspapers, surveys, and electronic sources. You then sift through this data and organize your findings to come up with a conclusion or recommendation. Quite possibly your instructor has asked you or will ask you to find a newspaper article on a particular subject, track down a book or magazine article related to a subject, or use an Internet browser to learn more about an issue.

Academic research is research completed according to an accepted format for a college audience. One main difference requires that you credit your sources in order to share the exact origin of your information. Essays with sources possess the following characteristics:

- The subject is worthy of and appropriate for research.

- The essay makes use of one or more sources for information.

- The source data are presented in the essay in a variety of ways, including summary, paraphrase, and direct quotes.

- The essay leads to a particular conclusion.

Examine the following source-based essay to identify these characteristics.

MODEL WITH KEY QUESTIONS

BLUE SKY, WHY?

Melissa Lombardi

Melissa Lombardi comments, "As a high school student, I did not recognize the benefits of freewriting and getting my instructor's input on my rough draft. I was never satisfied with the finished product back then! Now, I begin well in advance so that I have time to make every paragraph say what I want it to say." Melissa wants to become a physicist and says that her plans have not changed since she researched this career for her essay. However, she confides, "I'll take it a little more slowly so I can spend time with Caroline, my new baby."

1   A physicist is like a small child. Children wonder why the sky is blue; adults never notice the sky because it has always been there, and they never ponder its color, because it has always been blue. Adults are too jaded, and too familiar with the world around them; they are conditioned by it, and just accept it without question. Like a child, a physicist looks at the world through eyes that are not prejudiced by expectations. A physicist must be objective, rational, honest, and above all, curious. In his description of the work of a physicist, James Gonyea, a career counselor on America Online, states that "physicists explore and identify basic principles governing the structure and behavior of matter and energy." Physicists study the most fundamental aspects of the universe—where it came from, what it is made of, what rules it is governed by, and where it is going.

2   Physics is broken down into countless subfields; two of the most popular of these at the moment are elementary particle physics and astrophysics (Dodge and Mulvey 4). Elementary particle physicists study matter on the smallest scale; their work focuses on fundamental particles such as quarks and leptons, which are the

building blocks of atoms. Astrophysicists, on the other hand, study stars, which are the largest discrete objects in the universe. Within these fields, there are three different types of researchers: experimentalists, theorists, and computational physicists. Experimentalists work in a lab setting, theorists use mathematics, and computational physicists use computer modeling to test their ideas.

3   Physicists generally work in universities or in industry. At a university, a physicist's responsibilities may include researching, publishing papers, teaching, and serving on committees. The research may be pure, meaning that the only goal is knowledge, or applied, meaning that there is a specific, real-world application in mind. In industry, a physicist's primary responsibility is research. Physicists conduct applied research with commercial applications in mind, such as medical applications of lasers.

4   University jobs carry more prestige, but prestige doesn't pay the mortgage. Physicists employed in industry have a median salary of $30,000 higher than physicists employed in universities (Curtin and Chu 1). Dr. Gabriel Lombardi (the author's husband), a physicist at Mission Research Corporation, "chose to work in industry, even though [he] loves teaching, because it just seemed better all the way around. Faculty positions don't pay as well, and there are very few open at any given time." John Dooley, a physics professor at Millersville University in Pennsylvania, acknowledges that the pay isn't very good, but he loves teaching, and has worked in a school setting throughout his career. Ironically, Dr. Lombardi wonders "if an academic career path would have been more satisfying," and Dr. Dooley "always wanted to work in industry."

5   To qualify for work in either a university or in industry, a prospective physicist must go through college, graduate school, and a postdoctoral research position. This can require up to 10 years of training after completion of undergraduate studies, but according to James Gonyea, "persons with only a bachelor's degree in physics or astronomy are not qualified to enter most physicist or astronomer jobs."

6   The level of career satisfaction among physicists is very impressive. Dr. Bill Shackleford, who is now retired, says that after a 30-year career, he has no regrets about his choice to become a physicist, and he feels he worked in the "golden age" of physics. Dr. Dooley recognizes that he gets paid to do something he enjoys, and knows that this is "not a common experience." These satisfied physicists are just two of many curious, childlike individuals who are fascinated by what makes the sky blue, as well as other fundamental questions about our universe.

[Note: you always begin a new page for works cited.]

Works Cited

Curtin, Jean M., and Raymond Y. Chu. *Society Membership Survey: Salaries 2000.* College Park, Maryland: The American Institute of Physics, 2001.

Dodge, Elizabeth, and Patrick J. Mulvey. 2000 *Graduate Student Report* College Park, Maryland: The American Institute of Physics, 2001.

Dooley, John. Interview. 11 Nov. 2002. 23 June 2003 <http://www.aol.com/dooley/physics/employment.html>.

Gonyea, James. Interview. 7 Nov. 2002. 20 June 2003 <www.Jgonyea@ecc.edu>.

Lombardi, Gabriel G. Interview. 10 Nov. 2002. 18 May 2003 <www.pierce.edu/physics/Lombardi>.

Shackleford, William L. "Re: Job query." E-mail to Melissa Lombardi. 15 June 2003.   ○

Key Questions

1. **Purpose**   How is a physicist "like a small child," according to Lombardi, and what might these childlike qualities have to do with the author's purpose in this essay?

2. **Focus**   In the writer's final sentence of paragraph 1, she states that the field of physics has countless subfields. How many of these subfields does Lombardi mention in paragraph 2?

3. **Material**   Examine Lombardi's "Works Cited" section at the end of her research essay. Where does the writer seem to have obtained most of her material for this essay?

4. **Structure**   Examine the contents of the essay carefully. Make a "scratch outline" of Lombardi's main points. Does her organization of material appear clear and logical?

5. **Style**   Lombardi's opening statement comparing a physicist to a small child might seem unexpected and almost bizarre to many readers. Yet by the end of her essay, Lombardi returns to her opening image with the phrase "childlike individuals ... fascinated by what makes the sky blue." Has the writer offered her audience a sense of closure, and if so, how has she achieved this?

Grammar Key

Handbook Practice: Semicolons, Colons, Apostrophes, and Quotation Marks

Read pages 455–461. Complete Exercises 12-16 and all the accompanying paragraphs.

GUIDELINES FOR WRITING ESSAYS WITH SOURCES

Pose a Question to Launch Your Investigation

Begin your investigation by posing a question about a subject that intrigues you. What is it you would be most interested in finding out about the subject? For example, in "Blue Sky, Why?" student writer Melissa Lombardi was curious to find out what a physicist actually does on a day-to-day basis on the job. This question about your subject will serve as a tentative thesis, which is likely to change as you learn more about your topic.

Practice 8.1   Examine the following broad topics and try to pose a question for which you would like to find an answer by exploring one or more outside sources:

1. Sports utility vehicles

2. Ethnic breakdown of universities in the United States

3. Purchase of airline tickets through Internet sources

4. Childcare facilities for working parents with sick children

5. Investment in the stock market   ❏

Identify Your Audience

Once you've posed your question for investigation, you'll need to identify your audience, which in the case of an academic essay is narrowed to a college community of students and professors. Try to target an aspect of your investigative question that your audience would be most interested in.

Practice 8.2   For each of the following investigative questions, identify a specific audience:

1. In the twentieth century, have an increasing number of animal species become extinct or not? If extinctions are on the rise in this century, to what factors can we attribute this increase?

2. Is it possible to control pornography on the Internet? If so, how should pornography be controlled?

3. If a person is physically abused as a child, how likely is it that this same person will become abusive toward other family members?

4. Does the use of capital punishment in the United States serve to deter potential murderers from committing murder?

5. Is it both possible and desirable to allow prayer in public schools during school hours?   ❏

Collect Data from Appropriate Sources

Now that you have posed a question to investigate and have identified your reading audience, you will need to collect enough material to support your particular position relating to your subject of research. Source-based material can be found in interviews, print sources, and electronic sources.

Interviews
The **personal interview,** a prearranged meeting with a person in which particular questions are asked, is a good way to gather firsthand information on a research subject. In "Blue Sky, Why?" Lombardi interviewed several sources. (For interview strategies, see p. 189 in Chapter 9.)

Print Sources
Your college or local library is the best place to find printed sources, which include books, magazine and newspaper articles, articles in scholarly journals, book reviews, pamphlets, encyclopedias, special-interest encyclopedias, and various kinds of dictionaries and reference books. You might want to begin your search by consulting either a general encyclopedia, such as the *Encyclopaedia Britannica,* or a specialized encyclopedia, such as the *Encyclopedia of Science and Technology* or the *Encyclopedia of Psychology.* An encyclopedia may suggest specific subject headings or direct you to other useful sources.

Indexes to periodicals, or lists of articles organized by subject and author, can also help you find information for your research. The *Readers' Guide to Periodical Literature* lists articles from hundreds of popular magazines. Other, more specialized indexes, such as the *Humanities Index* and the *Social Sciences Index,* offer lists of articles in particular fields of study.

You may find that some of the articles you are trying to locate are available in hard copy, while others are kept on **microfilm,** a film on which printed sources are copied in a much smaller size for easier storage. Librarians can help you track down information and use the library's microfilm machines.

Electronic Sources

Many magazine, newspaper, and journal articles can be found in computerized indexes. The *Readers' Guide to Periodical Literature* is available on computer as well as in hard copy in most college and many local libraries. In addition, your college library will probably have at least two other computerized databases that can be helpful if you are looking for information on a subject not covered in general-interest periodicals.

If you have online access at home or college, you can obtain information through the Internet, interview a subject online, or search encyclopedias or other sources on the Web. However, if you use Internet sources or Websites, be sure to evaluate all of your sources especially carefully. While most books from recognized publishers and articles from well-known magazines or scholarly journals are reviewed or overseen in publication, Internet and Web sources many times have not been edited or reviewed by knowledgeable readers. For further help with Internet and Web source evaluation, visit the following Web sites:

http://lib.nmsu.edu/instruction/eval.html
http://www.lib.berkeley.edu/ TeachingLib/Guides/Internet/evaluate.html
http://www.uwec.edu/library/ Guides/tencs.html
http://owl.english.purdue.edu/handouts/research/r_evalsource4.html

Practice 8.3   Based on the information in this section, name the source or sources where you would be most likely to find the following:

1. A source that offers limited general information on your subject as well as suggests a specific subject heading or directs you to other useful sources

2. Recent sources on a subject covered in general-interest periodicals

3. The online version of the *New York Times*

4. An article from a scholarly journal that deals with the works of a particular and outstanding author

5. A person who is a reputable expert in the subject you are researching ❏

Evaluate Your Data

Before you decide to use any source, appraise it by asking yourself the following questions:

- Does the information relate directly to the subject and focus of my research?

- Is the information current? This is of no importance with certain timeless subjects, for example, the origin of a particular myth. However, it is of the utmost importance with those subjects that rely on recent information, such as career opportunities in physics or possible cures for the ebola virus. For many subjects, a source that is ten or more years old is considered out of date.

- Is the source objective or biased? If a source is reputed to voice an opinion on only one side of the issue, this source is possibly biased. Examine the way the source obtained information on the subject. If studies were conducted, were they conducted fairly and did they include a sufficient number of participants to be valid? Make sure you are presenting balanced information. Assure yourself a source has nothing to gain politically or economically from taking a particular stand before including the information in your essay.

- Is the information reliable and error-free? If the source uses an editor to verify all information, then you can feel that the source may be trustworthy. Remember, though, that unlike editors used in most printed sources, a Website can be created by anyone saying anything. If you have questions or doubts about your source, ask your college or local librarian or your instructor about the validity of a source.

- Is the source convincing and detailed enough for an academic audience? While an article from *Good Housekeeping* on the subject of indoor pollutants may have some valid information, an article on the same subject printed in *Scientific American* might offer more detailed and well-supported information.

Practice 8.4   As you read the following sources, decide whether the source listed for each subject would be considered reliable if presented to an audience of college students and professors.

1. Subject: Caring for family members who have suffered a stroke

    a. Article from *UCLA Brain Institute* on caring for those who have experienced a stroke

    b. Article from *Redbook* magazine entitled "Starting Over"

    c. Chapter on the effects of a stroke in an introductory textbook entitled *American Health: Then and Now*

2. Subject: Exploring the effects of marijuana use on teenagers

    a. Newspaper article written by the parents of a marijuana-using teenager

    b. Article from the *American Medical Association* journal on the effects of teenage marijuana use

    c. Pamphlet on teenage drug use written by the National Organization for Marijuana Legalization

3. Subject: Implementing programs to reduce sexual harassment in the workplace

    a. El Camino College's official sexual harassment policy and statement

    b. Website for problems experienced by working women on the West Coast

    c. Article from *Psychology Today* on the after-effects of sexual harassment as experienced by working women   ❏

Record Your Data: Three Kinds of Notes

Before you begin taking notes, record the following information about each printed source:

- Author or editor of the article or book
- Title of the article or book
- Name of the magazine or journal
- Place of publication for a book
- Publisher for a book
- Publication date (and volume number if this is a scholarly journal)
- Exact page or pages where the information is found

For electronic sources, the information you'll want to record is slightly different:

- Author name if available
- Title of the article or work

- Date and location of original publication of material if originally published in print
- Date of electronic publication as well as the date document was accessed
- Page, paragraph, or section numbers, if available
- URL (uniform resource locator) enclosed in angle brackets (< >)

Once you've recorded this basic information for each source, you can proceed with note taking, which usually takes one of three forms: (1) summary, (2) paraphrase, or (3) direct quotes.

Summary

As explained in Chapter 1, a **summary** is a statement *in your own words* of the most important points of a piece of writing. Use a summary note when it's important to get only the main ideas of the source. In "Blue Sky, Why?" (p. 157), Lombardi used summary in her note taking. In the first sentence in paragraph 5 of her essay, Lombardi summarizes information from Gonyea, one of her sources; she condenses several sentences from her source into one sentence of main points, written in her own words. The most effective summary notes are taken after reading the source carefully and annotating by marking the thesis and supportive main points.

While you are taking notes on your sources, try to remember these tips for summary note taking:

- After mentioning the source by title and name of author, in your own words write the author's complete thesis.
- Proceed by writing in your own words the main points in the order in which they are developed in the source. Delete less important ideas or examples.
- Remain objective; do not pass judgment on any of the author's ideas or opinions. A summary is not an evaluation or critique. In a summary you would not want to begin this way: "Johnson asserts that the moon is green. I absolutely disagree."
- Keep the summary short—it should be substantially shorter than the source you are using.
- Do not plagiarize by using the exact words in the source.

Examine an original source and then contrast an unacceptable summary with an acceptable one.

Original source:

Women's liberation has struck India late and hard. In a country where divorce occurs in one out of a million marriages (if that), where virginity is still highly prized in a prospective bride, where the concept of "damaged goods," as far as women are concerned, still plays a determining role in a man's choice, the assertion of female autonomy and independence is both an incidental irritation in male consciousness as well as a real and frightful challenge to the so-called emancipated urban woman.

—Sasthi Brata, *India: Labyrinths in the Lotus Land*

Unacceptable summary:

Sasthi Brata believes that in India, women's liberation has come late. Here, divorce happens in one out of a million marriages and virginity is prized highly in a bride-to-be. Females, even urban women, are not autonomous or independent, as ridiculous and backward as this is.

This summary is unacceptable even though it does attempt to shorten the content of the source. Notice that certain phrases have been lifted from the original rather than put in the author's own words and sentence structure. In addition, this summary includes the writer's interpretation rather than remaining objective.

Acceptable summary:

As Sasthi Brata reports, women's liberation has only recently come to India. Stigmatization of divorced women, traditional views on the importance of a woman's virginity, and a general absence of independence or self-sufficiency for women have hindered the arrival of total liberation for females.

This summary is an objective explanation of main points in the writer's own words.

Practice 8.5   To practice your summary-writing skills, review the first paragraph of Lombardi's essay "Blue Sky, Why?" Write in your own words a one- to two-sentence summary of this paragraph.   ❏

Practice 8.6   Referring to this book's table of contents, choose any article you have not yet read, read it carefully, annotate it, and then summarize it in your own words. Try limiting your writing to one note card.   ❏

Paraphrase

When you **paraphrase,** you take the information from a source and put it in your own words without condensing it. When might you take notes in the form of paraphrasing instead of summarizing? Use this form of note taking when it's important not to condense the information, but instead to communicate all of the data—specific facts and details—to readers. Although you communicate these facts *in your own words*, you must still credit the source of that information. For instance, when Lombardi uses information obtained from Curtin and Chu at the beginning of paragraph 4, she paraphrases this information by putting it in her own words. She also includes the source and the particular page where she found the information. If the source's original writing uses technical terms that have no synonyms, you may quote the original's words, but use this quoting only when absolutely necessary. Do not distort the source's meaning as you put the material in your own words. In paraphrasing, be sure to reproduce the source's sequence of ideas.

Examine the following original source and then contrast an unacceptable paraphrase with an acceptable one.

Original source:

For it is the extraordinary fact that once we have typecast the world, we tend to see people in terms of our standardized pictures. In another demonstration of the power of stereotypes to affect our vision, a number of Columbia and Barnard students were shown thirty photographs of pretty but unidentified girls, and asked to rate each in terms of "general liking," "intelligence," "beauty," and so on. Two months later, the same group were shown the same photographs, this time with fictitious Irish, Italian, Jewish, and "American" names attached to the pictures. Right away the ratings changed. Faces which were now seen as representing a national group went down in looks and still farther down in likability, while the "American" girls suddenly looked decidedly prettier and nicer.

—Robert L. Heilbroner, "Don't Let Stereotypes Warp Your Judgments"

Unacceptable paraphrase:

According to Robert L. Heilbroner, we actually typecast the world, seeing people the way our standardized picture dictates. For instance, several students from Columbia and Barnard colleges looked at thirty photos of unidentified but pretty girls. Then the students were asked to rate the girls in terms of beauty, intelligence, and general liking. When two months later, the same students were shown the same photos, these pictures were accompanied by fabricated names that were Irish, Italian, Jewish, and "American." The same photos seen two months earlier and called pretty, likable, and intelligent were now seen as inferior in every way to "American" names. Supposed "American" young women pictured became prettier and nicer (452).

In this paraphrase, the writer merely changes a few words, keeping much that is in the original material. Therefore, the paraphrase is plagiarized even though the author's name is given.

Acceptable paraphrase:

Robert L. Heilbroner shares evidence proving that we stereotype people based on our expectations. He cites a study of students from Columbia and Barnard colleges who were shown thirty student photos of random pretty girls. Students were asked to rate the girls immediately after viewing the pictures, and then two months later these students were shown the same photos. However, in this second viewing, the girls pictured were identified as Irish, Italian, Jewish, or "American." When these labels were used, the supposed "American" girls became much more attractive in every way, and the other girls were rated less highly in looks and likeability.

This paraphrase is acceptable because it catches the meaning of the original source in the student's own words.

Practice 8.7   To get a better idea of paraphrasing, examine paragraph 2 of Lombardi's essay "Blue Sky, Why?" After reading this paragraph a few times, write your own paraphrase of Lombardi's material.   ❑

Direct Quote

Sometimes the exact words of the source are dramatic, or the language is as important as the source's ideas. In this case, you'll want to use a **direct quote**—

the exact words of a source without omissions, changes, or additions, and set off from the rest of the text by quotation marks or indentation. For instance, in paragraph 1 of "Blue Sky, Why?" the writer introduces her source and then uses his exact words: "physicists explore and identify basic principles governing the structure and behavior of matter and energy."

If you want to omit words because they are irrelevant, you must signal this to your reader with **ellipsis points;** if you add words, you must enclose them in **brackets.** (See pp. 460–466 in the handbook for use of quotation marks, ellipsis points, and brackets.)

Never use a quotation as your thesis statement or as a topic sentence in a body paragraph—these main points should be in your own words.

Examine an original source and then contrast incorrect uses of quotations with correct uses:

Source: Conant, Jennet. "My Grandfather and the Bomb." *Between Worlds: A Reader, Rhetoric, and Handbook.* 5th Ed. New York: Longman, 2007. 18–22.

Original (Conant's exact words):

At the Hiroshima Peace Memorial Museum, erected at ground zero, we sat and watched the horrifyingly graphic documentary made in the aftermath of the attack, showing the black and burning city and the unspeakable suffering of those who survived the blast.

Incorrect use of quotation:

Jennet Conant states, "At the Hiroshima Peace Memorial Museum we sat and watched the documentary" (20).

This direct quote has taken words away from the original without using the required ellipsis points.

Incorrect use of quotation:

According to Jennet Conant, "The black and burning city and the unspeakable suffering of those who survived the blast" (20).

This sentence does not make sense as a complete grammatical unit—there is no verb to complete the thought.

Correct use of quotation:

Jennet Conant, whose grandfather was among those who created the first atomic bomb, recalls, "At the Hiroshima Peace Memorial Museum, erected at ground zero, we sat and watched the horrifyingly graphic documentary made in the aftermath of the attack, showing the black and burning city and the unspeakable suffering of those who survived the blast" (20).

Correct use of quotation with ellipsis:

As Jennet Connant confides, "At the Hiroshima Peace Memorial Museum . . . we sat and watched the horrifyingly graphic documentary . . . showing the black and burning city and the unspeakable suffering of those who survived the blast" (20).

Note that the omitted words in two places are indicated by ellipsis points.

Correct use of quotation with brackets:

Jennet Conant recalls a childhood experience: "At the Hiroshima Peace Memorial Museum, erected at ground zero, we [Connant's family] sat and watched the horrifyingly graphic documentary made of the attack, showing the black and burning city and the unspeakable suffering of those who survived the blast" (20).

Here the writer of the essay wants to share with readers who "we" refer to in this quotation from Conant.

Practice 8.8 Find an interesting article in your local newspaper or in a popular magazine. After reading the article, locate a comment that might be of value in a source-based paper on a related subject. On a piece of paper, introduce the quote by mentioning the author by name and, if available, the author's position or title. Then copy the quote either word for word or omit some words by using ellipsis points. ❏

Use "the Sandwich" with Your Quotes

When you move from note taking to drafting, and you want to incorporate a quotation into the body of your essay, introduce your reader to the quotation by identifying the speaker by name, title, or authority he or she has concerning the subject. Following the quotation, explain or analyze the quoted material in a sentence before proceeding to the next point. Take a look at the following use of "the sandwich":

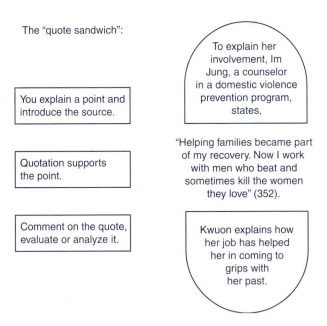

The "quote sandwich":

You explain a point and introduce the source.

Quotation supports the point.

Comment on the quote, evaluate or analyze it.

To explain her involvement, Im Jung, a counselor in a domestic violence prevention program, states,

"Helping families became part of my recovery. Now I work with men who beat and sometimes kill the women they love" (352).

Kwuon explains how her job has helped her in coming to grips with her past.

As Im Jung Kwuon, a counselor in a domestic-violence-prevention program states, "Helping families became part of my recovery. Now I work with men who beat and sometimes kill the women they love" (352). Kwuon explains how her job has helped her in coming to grips with her past.

Using "the sandwich" helps you avoid a dropped or dumped quotation and helps readers to understand why you chose to share the quoted material in the essay.

Practice 8.9   Read the original material from "McDonald's Is Not Our Kind of Place" by Amitai Etzioni on pages 358–360. Then evaluate the passages that show unacceptable uses of quotations. Explain the problems, and then revise each passage, making sure you use "the sandwich" when possible.

Original material:

Although it is true that these workplaces provide income and even some training to such low-skilled youngsters, they also tend to perpetuate their disadvantaged status. Such jobs provide no career incentives and few marketable skills, and they can undermine school attendance and involvement.

The hours are long. Often the stores close late, and after closing workers must tally and clean up. There is no way that such amounts of work will not interfere with schoolwork, especially homework. Fifty-eight percent of the seniors at Walt Whitman High School in Montgomery County, an affluent area in Maryland, acknowledge that their jobs interfere with their schoolwork.

Unacceptable Uses of Quotations

1. Franchised workplaces offer students additional money and a little bit of job experience for beginners. "They tend to perpetuate their disadvantaged status" (Etzioni 359).

2. According to Amitai Etzioni, "Fifty-eight percent of the seniors acknowledge that their jobs interfere with their schoolwork" (359).

3. Because Amitai Etzioni feels that "often the stores close late, and after closing workers must tally and clean up" (359).

4. Amitai Etzioni asserts, "Such jobs provide career incentives and marketable skills" (359). He seems to have these two positive points to make about student jobs in places like McDonald's. ❏

Practice 8.10   To test your ability to differentiate summary, paraphrase, and direct quote, read the following paragraph. Then examine the three individual notes and identify each as summary, paraphrase, or direct quote.

Working his living room like a pumped-up lawyer trying to sway a skeptical jury, J.D. Moss, 17, rattled off the reasons his parents should let him host something he called a "coed sleepover party." "It's the newest thing," J.D. said, explaining how 20 of his closest friends, male and female, would spend the night playing ping-pong, talking and watching movies in the basement until the sun rose. J.D. tried using parental logic. "It's too dangerous for us to be out late at night with all the drunk drivers. Better that we are home," he told his parents. "It's better than us lying about where we are and renting some sleazy motel room." His father relented, saying his son's arguments rang true. And since making that speech, J.D. has hosted not just one but two coed sleepovers, the second one last month after he and his Fairfax

County, VA, high school classmates attended the homecoming dance. Forget the old slumber parties where teenage girls talked about the boys they had crushes on. These days, those boys are sometimes sleeping in the same room.

—"Coed Slumber Parties Are a Test of Parents' Trust" from *Washington Post*

1. The journalist asserts that J.D. Moss is one of several teenagers who are successfully convincing their parents that "coed sleepover parties" are a safer alternative for teens than being "out late at night with all the drunk drivers" or having to find a "sleazy motel room."

2. The journalist reports that teens like J.D. Moss are telling their parents that having coed slumber parties is a better solution than possible alternatives of encountering drunk drivers on the road or trying to find a run-down motel for the night. Evidently, parents are accepting arguments like Moss's for allowing teen coed slumber parties. Today the number of such parties is on the rise.

3. Teens nationwide have been more successful than ever in convincing their parents that coed slumber parties are quite safe and that they should be permitted.   ❏

Avoid Plagiarism

Regardless of whether you summarize, paraphrase, or quote, in an essay using sources you should always credit your source. Giving credit shows your honesty as a writer, lends authority to what you've written, and helps others who might like to follow up on your research by reading your sources. If you fail to give this credit, you commit **plagiarism**—the act of stealing someone else's words, ideas, facts, or visual images without crediting the source.

Many colleges consider plagiarism such a serious offense that they may expel a student for committing it. College instructors are not the only people who react negatively to plagiarism: In the workplace, plagiarism can lead to an employee being fired and interfere with future hiring possibilities; in addition, legal implications come into play when a person uses someone else's intellectual property without permission or credit. The plagiarist could very well land in court with stiff fines to pay and a much damaged reputation to live with.

In college writing assignments, sometimes plagiarism is committed inadvertently when students use one or more outside sources. To guard against this possibility, be sure that as you take notes, you always record the source of every idea you use. In addition to acknowledging your source for any direct quote, you also need to acknowledge your source for any idea, concept, or fact that you mention in your writing *even when you paraphrase, putting these ideas, concepts, or facts into your own words.*

Practice 8.11   To facilitate your understanding of the difference between plagiarism and acceptable use of sources, examine the following excerpt from an article:

Why is "Generation Next" (as Pepsi puts it) downing caffeine at rates never seen before? One likely reason is that most parents are unaware of the health problems associated with caffeine. Solid scientific research has linked caffeine to anxiety, respiratory ailments, possible bone loss, and other health worries—although there has been slight coverage of this. But what turned children on to caffeine in the first place? Kids' desire to get wired didn't simply occur as a mass switch in personal preference. The major caffeine suppliers to kids have been throwing millions into advertising and giveaways. Mountain Dew, for example, has distributed half a million free pagers to kids, who can use them to call friends—but only after they read the Mountain Dew promo that automatically pops up.

—Helen Cordes, from *"Generation Wired"*

Now read the following three paragraphs using Cordes's paragraph as a source. Which paragraph is plagiarism-free? Support your answer with specific reasons.

1. Most parents are not aware of the health problems associated with caffeine. Research has linked caffeine to anxiety, respiratory ailments, possible loss of bones, and lots of other health concerns. What turned children on to caffeine? This has happened mainly because the big caffeine suppliers to kids have been throwing millions of dollars into ads and giveaways. Mountain Dew is an example of a company that has distributed half a million free pagers to kids!

2. In an article entitled "Generation Wired," Helen Cordes tells us that children are drinking more caffeinated beverages than ever before. She attributes this increase in caffeine intake to the probability that many of these children's parents are unaware of caffeine-related health problems. Cordes continues that another reason for the rise in children's caffeine intake is that beverage companies working with ad agencies have been bombarding children with propaganda about these drinks— Mountain Dew has given away hundreds of thousands of free pagers (with their product's promo attached) to kids.

3. What turned children on to caffeine in the first place? Helen Cordes asserts that Mountain Dew has distributed half a million free pagers to kids. These efforts on the part of ad agencies and manufacturers have caused "Generation Next" to down caffeine at rates never seen before. Another likely reason is that most parents are unaware of the health problems associated with caffeine. Scientific research has linked caffeine to possible bone loss, anxiety, respiratory ailments, and other health worries. ❑

To view several examples of unintentional as well as intentional plagiarism, acceptable corrections, and explanatory comments on each example, visit the following helpful Web site: **http://www.depts.drew.edu/composition/ Avoiding_Plagiarism.htm**

Strategies for Using Sources and Avoiding Plagiarism

1. Always check to be sure you have inserted quotation marks around words or phrases that you quote.

2. Never copy or paste into your essay any sentences, terms, or longer passages—later you will not be able to remember where you received the information and which ideas were yours.

3. Cite the source for any ideas that have come from another source even if you put these ideas in your own words.

4. Remember to acknowledge sources even if you have combined multiple sources to arrive at your own conclusion.

5. Never assume that your instructor cannot detect plagiarism—the instructor's familiarity with your writing style combined with most colleges' access to Web sites that electronically check your essay against available material help instructors who might suspect plagiarism.

6. As you are taking notes, write down all the facts you need for documenting each source including page numbers—this will guard against your having to spend needless hours retracing your steps.

7. Get in the habit of summarizing or paraphrasing material before you put it into your notes.

8. Never allow quoted material to comprise more than a fifth of your paper; instead, rely on paraphrase and summary. Most of your source-based essay should be in your own words.

9. Be sure to consult with your instructor if you are not clear on any step in the source-gathering process.

10. The following verbs make your integration of summaries, paraphrases, and quotations more effective:

acknowledges	concedes	discusses
agrees	concludes	analyzes
confirms	argues	asserts
asks	contends	Considers
begins	contrasts	estimates
believes	declares	claims
demonstrates	finds	comments
compares	describes	grants
complains	develops	illuminates
illustrates	says	implies
points out	indicates	shows
informs	insists	speculates
maintains	recognizes	states
notes	remarks	thinks
notices	observes	reports
reveals	writes	recommends

DOCUMENTATION

Citing sources, also called **documentation,** is a writer's indication in an accepted format that he or she has used the words, ideas, or information from a source or sources.

In "Blue Sky, Why?" the sources are cited both in the text (**in-text citations** or **parenthetical citations**), with the authors and page numbers given for summaries, paraphrases, and quotes, and at the end of the essay in the "Works Cited" section (**end-text citations**).

In an English course, for most essays using outside sources you will need to use the Modern Language Association (MLA) format. In contrast, APA format (a style recommended by the American Psychological Association) is used in social sciences. If you are asked to use APA style for your essay, consult the following reference work: American Psychological Association, *Publication Manual of the American Psychological Association*, 5th ed. Washington, DC: APA, 2001. Because source-based essays written for English and other humanities classes require the MLA format, this is the format discussed on the following pages. Please note that model in-text citations are given first, followed by end-text citations:

Book with single author

in-text:

As Anne Lamott tells readers, her father was a writer, and she became a voracious reader as a result of watching her parents read (22).

Or

As the author tells readers, her father was a writer, and she became a voracious reader as a result of watching her parents read (Lamott 22).

end-text:

Lamott, Anne. *Bird by Bird.* New York: Doubleday, 1994.

Book with multiple authors (two or three)

in-text:

According to Nicolas Bentley, Michael Slater, and Nina Burgis, "Dickens was always observant of detail" (82).

Or

According to three critics, "Dickens was always observant of detail" (Bentley, Slater, and Burgis 82).

end-text:

Bentley, Nicolas, Michael Slater, and Nina Burgis. *The Dickens Index.* New York: Oxford UP, 2002.

More than three authors

Use either the first author's last name followed by the term *et al.* (standing in Latin for "and others") or all of the authors' last names:

in-text:

As Jones et al. contend . . . (142).

Or

As several journalists contend . . . (Jones et al. 142).

end-text:

Jones, William et al. *The Psychology of Love.* New York: Penguin, 2003.

Article in a magazine

in-text:

John Ellis conveys to his readers that Franklin was unpredictable (89).

Or

One expert conveys to his readers that Franklin was unpredictable (Ellis 89).

end-text:

Ellis, John. "Franklin's Cop-Out." *Time* 15 June 1997: 89–93.

Unknown author

in-text:

According to the essay "Pros and Cons of Lethal Injection," . . . (58).

Or

According to one source, ... ("Pros and Cons" 58). (For in-text citations at the end of a sentence, you can shorten the title to the first few important words of the title.)

end-text:

"Pros and Cons of Lethal Injection." *Newsweek* 12 January 1999: 54–61.

Work within an anthology

in-text:

As Ernest Gaines asserts, ". . ." (213).

Or

As one famous African-American writer tells us, "_____" (Gaines 213).

end-text:

Gaines, Ernest. "Why I Write." *Gaines, Angelou, and other African-American Writers.* Ed. Charles Winston. San Francisco: Riverdale Press, 1996. 213–23.

Indirect sources

(someone's published account of another person's spoken remarks): If what you quote is itself a quotation, put the short form *qtd. in* (standing for "quoted in") before your citation of the indirect source.

in-text:

According to Reseka (qtd. in Bray 21) ". . .".

Or

According to one controversial leader, ". . ." (Reseka qtd. in Bray 21).

end-text:

Bray, Marcus. "The Global Warming Crisis." Sierra 18 May 2003: 47–58. (Notice that Reseka is not mentioned here because you took his comments from Marcus's account.)

Electronic and nonprint sources

in-text:

As stated in the site "Planning Trips through the Net," major deals can be made if one "logs on early and often."

end-text:

"Planning Trips through the Net." *Los Angeles Times* 23 Apr. 2002. 12 May 2002 <http://www.latimestravel.com>.

E-mail

(give author's name, subject line if available in quotation marks, *e-mail to*, and recipient's name, ending with date of the message):

in-text:

As Doctor Jamison discussed, . . .

Or

As one prominent doctor discussed, "____" (Jamison).

end-text:

Jamison, Dr. Anne. "Answers to Back Pain." E-mail to John Sweetzer. 1 July 2003.

Material from a CD-ROM database

in-text:

Clarissa Netherland admits in "Union Issues" that these problems have been magnified.

end-text:

Netherland, Clarissa. "Union Issues on 23 Campuses." *EPSCO Host.* CD-ROM. Los Angeles: University of California Press, 2003.

Personal interview

in-text:

As Hironi Saigusa indicates, "..."

end-text:

Saigusa, Hironi. Personal interview. 3 February 2003.

Film or video

in-text:

As one can see in the courtroom scene from *Mr. Smith Goes to Washington.* ...

Or

As one can see in the film, "_____" *(Mr. Smith).*

end-text:

Mr. Smith Goes to Washington. Dir. Frank Capra. Perf. James Stewart, Claude Raines. MGM, 1946.

Practice 8.12   Using your knowledge of MLA format, test your skills by creating an in-text as well as an end-text citation for each of the following:

1. A book called Air Conditioning and Repair. The book was published in 2004 by Doubleday in Chicago, Illinois. No author is named.

2. An unsigned article titled Death Takes to the Highways. The article was published in the December 23, 2002 edition of the Sacramento Bee. It appears on page 5 of section F.

3. An essay written by Brent Staples titled Black Men and Public Space. The essay appeared in the fourth edition of a textbook written by Susan Bachmann and Melissa Barth titled Between Worlds, published in 2004 by Longman Press in New York. The essay appears on pages 237–240.

4. A book written by Kate Chopin titled The Awakening. The book was published in 2001 by W. W. Norton and Company in New York.

5. An article written by Nancy Cervetti titled In the Breeches, Petticoats, and Pleasures of Orlando. The article appeared in the Journal of Modern Literature number 20, volume 2, published in 2000. It was found on January 8 2004 at the Web site http://www.indiana.edu/-iupress/journals/mod-art2.html. ❏

Move from Notes to a Plan

Read through your notes on your sources, putting aside those that don't seem to relate clearly to your current thesis. This process should help you focus your thesis question. Next, take the notes that you think you can use to develop your thesis and try to sort them into some logical order. You might find an outline helpful for a source-based essay because you may be pulling information together from one or more sources. (For a review of outlining, see Chapter 4.)

Incorporate Sources in Your Draft

To begin drafting, follow your outline and try to use material from your note taking—summarized information, paraphrases, and direct quotes—applying your best judgment as to which points lend themselves to particular ways of conveying the information.

Strategies for Essays Using Sources

1. **Purpose**   Once you have a topic, pose a question that you would like to answer. Determine the aspect of the topic that would be of primary interest to your audience.

2. **Focus**   Compose a flexible thesis, based on your question. Your thesis may change as you gather information from sources.

3. **Material**   Make sure that all of your sources are reliable and current. Try to collect information from appropriate printed, electronic, and interview sources. In note taking and in drafting, use a mixture of summaries, paraphrases, and direct quotes. Remember to introduce and credit all sources.

4. **Structure**   Work from an outline to make sure you're presenting material in an organized way to your audience.

5. **Style**   In revising and polishing, check to see that you've identified all sources, and that you've employed quotation marks, ellipses, and brackets where appropriate. Reread your draft to find and correct any places where you've paraphrased or summarized information without giving credit to the source.

JOURNAL WRITING: SLEUTHING AROUND

For a source-based assignment, it is extremely important that you be excited by your topic and motivated to learn as much as you can, because you may be working for several days or weeks on investigating, then compiling information, and finally drafting and revising your essay. Writing in your journal can help you discover several topics that you might want to learn more about. To find a topic that will inspire you, think of yourself as a *sleuth*, a word that originally meant a type of dog—a bloodhound—that could follow a trail by scent. More recently, *sleuth* has come to mean a person who acts like a detective to seek out information. Respond in your journal to the following questions:

1. Have you reacted in any strong way lately to a world event or a national, local, or campus event? What was this event, and how did you feel when you first heard of it? Now that a little time has passed, have you found out more information on the subject? Do you find that your reaction is just as strong now as when you first heard of the event? Why or why not? If you could ask a series of questions about the event, what would they

be? To whom would you like to address these questions? Where might you find additional information either in print or electronically?

2. Have you read lately in a magazine, newspaper, or journal article information about an issue or occurrence that you feel strongly about? What additional information would you like to gain about this issue or event? Where would you go for this information?

3. Is there a policy, trend, or position on an issue that you would like to question? In what way would you question it? What official or expert could you contact for further information? Can you think of specific questions that you'd like to ask of the expert?

Using the Computer: Searching the Net and Citing Sources Using MLA and APA Format

Whether you've been assigned a specific topic to investigate or can choose your own topic, the Internet can be a helpful source.

1. Here is a site that can help you budget and program your time effectively; it will show you how to establish a timetable:

   http://www.coun.uvic.ca/personal/stress.html

2. These sites will give you advice on developing your research topics, getting information, and finding and evaluating books, articles, recordings, and Internet sources:

   http://www.library.cornell.edu/okuref/research/tutorial.html

   http://www.library.cornell.edu/okuref/research/skill1.htm

3. This site presents a full workshop on performing electronic research easily:

   http://www.lib.berkeley.edu/TeachingLibGuides/Internet/FindInfo.html

4. You can try these sites for general and specialized encyclopedias online:

   http://www.britannica.com

   http://www.encyclopedia.com

5. These sites are for you if you want information on detecting and avoiding plagiarism:

   http://www.indiana.edu/~istd/

   http://www.web.gc.cuny.edu/provost/pdf/AvoidingPlagiarism.pdf

6. For help with citing according to MLA style, consult one of these sites:

   http://www.columbia.edu/cu/cup/cgos/idx_basic.html

   http://www.mla.org

7. For help with citing using APA style, consult the following site:

   http://www.apa.org

OPTIONS FOR WRITING

1. Think about the particular type of music you really enjoy; perhaps you can zero in on one or two musicians whose tapes or CDs you own and play often. Research either the specific type of music you like or focus on one musician or musical group, discovering as much information as you can about the musicians' beginnings, background, successes, failures, future goals, and any other material that will allow your audience to understand more fully that which is "music to your ears."

2. If you have always wanted to visit a certain place, research how much it would cost you and how you could get to this location; what clothes you would need to take; what language you might want to learn (at least a few key phrases); what special sites, museums, monuments, and antiquities you would want to visit; and the kind of night life and restaurant experience you could expect. In addition to researching books and magazine articles, you might want to interview some travel agents and use travel Web sites.

3. If your campus has a career center, visit this facility to explore information about a career you think you might be interested in pursuing. You will want to share with your reading audience the qualifications you would need to get the job, the kind of work you would be doing, the advantages as well as the disadvantages of being involved in this kind of career, the potential salary range, working conditions, benefits, and humanitarian rewards connected to this career.

4. *Extreme sports* is a relatively new term for exciting but potentially life-threatening sports. For example, climbing Mt. Everest is an extreme sport: It is expensive, dangerous, and both physically and psychologically stressful. You will find information on such sports if you use the specific sport as a keyword in your library computer search; you can also ask your librarian to direct you to information on the particular sport you want to explore.

5. Read Guy Davenport's essay "The Geography of the Imagination" (p. 363). Notice the extent of Davenport's research on various details shown in the painting. Using his essay as a model, choose another painting and write an essay in which you use research to focus on several key elements of the painting: historical, social, or cultural meanings.

6. Find a source or sources on the issue of spending millions of dollars on wiring for "smart" classrooms: updating lecture halls with Internet connections and installing technology that will allow students to view film clips, hear speeches, and share their writing with other students or instructors in a different location. In your research on this subject, be sure that your sources are as current as possible.

7. Research the issue of marketing appeal used by advertisers to sell products. In addition to articles from newspapers, magazines, and scholarly

journals on the subject of misleading advertising, you will also be able to find sample advertisements from magazines or newspapers to use as evidence. Read "Illusions Are Forever" by Jay Chiat (p. 398). Write an essay in which you show how advertising influences our perceptions of truth.

8. Find the weekly schedule for the public radio station in your area. Choose a radio program from this station that you think might interest you. For example, Terry Gross, in her daily program *Fresh Air*, interviews famous writers, musicians, artists, and others. Listen to the program, taking notes on points that strike you as most important. Assemble your notes into an outline and then write an essay in which you summarize the information presented in the program.

9. *(Film and Literature)* Under the keywords *John Fitzgerald Kennedy*, find information on President Kennedy's assassination. Next, view Oliver Stone's film *JFK*. Write an essay explaining what you think really happened. Make your evidence as specific as possible.

10. *(Service Learning)* As a class, discuss a problem of concern to your state or local area. Then, working alone, find one or more sources on the issue and write a source-based letter to the governor of your state or the mayor of your city. Detail the specific problem and urge your audience to search for particular solutions.

RESPONDING TO WRITING: DISSECTING A STUDENT'S SOURCE-BASED PAPER

One helpful activity in preparation for writing your own source-based essay is the examination of another student's essay using outside sources. Student Brent Monacelli read Swarupa Reddy's essay "TV as a Culprit" (pp. 247–248). He researched some of the findings that Reddy had made and wrote a source-based essay questioning some of her assertions.

TV: IS IT A BEAUTIFUL CURSE?

1   In Swarupa Reddy's essay "TV as a Culprit," Reddy talks about the negative effects of TV on different aspects of our society; she claims TV is responsible for a decline in family togetherness, that it affects the performance of students in their schoolwork, and that it promotes sex and violence. As informative as her essay is, Reddy has missed the point in a few respects. Although TV does promote sex, violence, and other inappropriate behavior, this invention is not solely responsible for inevitable changes that, over time, occur in any culture.

2   Reddy fails to make the distinction between TV-induced decline in family bonding and unavoidable changes in family practices. Reddy states, "[families] they actually gathered together and shared ideas, interests, and experiences. Since television, this apparently does not occur in most families" (245). Reddy's ideal

family experience could not be more old-fashioned and wrong. Family together-ness happens in different ways today. In this technological age, family members do not have to gather around the old family table and talk; they communicate in more modern ways. Family members send each other e-mails about events or may even call each other on a cell phone to share an idea with another family member while the idea is still fresh in their mind. Furthermore, Reddy neglects to acknowledge that family bonding takes place in different ways. For example, a family may have a TV show that they all enjoy, and they will come together as a family and watch the show. After the program is over, they may talk about their views of what they had just seen and heard. Also, family members may join to-gether to play a video game and bond in that way. Reddy fails to notice the posi-tive aspects of this shift to a new age.

3   Second, Reddy tries to convince readers that TV creates a decline in perfor-mance of schoolwork by children and teens. She states, "Statistics released reveal that many more elementary, junior high, and high school students watch televi-sion than twenty years ago . . . and teens are watching for more extended periods of time" (245). This may be true, but the IQ of these students is much higher than the IQs of students twenty or more years ago. According to a worldwide study performed by James R. Flynn, a political scientist from New Zealand, people's IQs are rising. As Flynn asserts, "The IQs of American children have been rising even during periods when the time spent in school remained the same. Stimulation by the media, and in particular by television, may be another reason." So how can Reddy think that children are not performing in their studies? In addition, chil-dren now spend a lot of their time on computers. With many Web servers that let students "instant message" each other, or Web pages like "My space," children are on the computer more than they watch TV. A youth can talk to a friend and type or research a paper at the same time through the use of a computer. There-fore, students learn how to multitask more effectively than their parents ever did.

4   However, Reddy correctly claims that TV does have a major effect in one area. She states, "Television actually promotes sex and violence" (245). This assertion is backed by solid evidence. Rebecca Collins, a psychologist, performed a study of the effects different types of TV programs have on children ages 12 to 17. She reports, "Teenagers who watch a lot of television with sexual content are twice as likely to engage in intercourse than those who watch few such programs." Furthermore, many shows today tell children that sex is fine and that violence is just a fact of life. In a popular show with young people, *That 70's Show*, the only goal in the life of the boys is to "get laid," and teenagers are shown sitting in a smoky room in a circle, possibly smoking marijuana. In new "reality" shows, many participants are por-trayed as having sex without the thought of any responsibility. Also, music videos have a strong sexual overtone and seem to objectify women, showing them as noth-ing but sex toys for men. Shows like *The Shield* and *CSI* desensitize young viewers. Shows such as these have become more forensic-centered, showing autopsies and other graphic scenes inappropriate for children. Reddy is correct in stating that TV leads children on a downward spin when it comes to their morality.

5   Quite possibly what we can learn from Swarupa Reddy's essay is that TV can have negative repercussions on children. If parents do not control the time and content of TV for their children, TV may become a beautiful curse.

Works Cited

Flynn, James R., and William T. Dickens. "Heritability Estimates Versus Large Environmental Effects: The IQ Paradox Resolved." *Psychological Review* 2001. Vol. 108. No. 2. Nov. 24, 2005.
http://www.apa.org/journals/features/rev1082346.pdf

Reddy, Swarupa. "TV as a Culprit." *Keys to Successful Writing*. Marilyn Anderson. Third Edition. New York: Pearson, 2005. 245-246.

"Teen Sex Linked to Racy TV Programs." Reuters. Sept. 7, 2004. Nov. 24, 2005. <http://www.msnbc.msn.com/id/5930891/> ○

1. Locate Monacelli's thesis statement and underline it in your text.

2. What outside sources does the writer use? Does this information lend credibility to the subject? If so, how?

3. In what way does Monacelli agree with Swarupa Reddy?

4. In what way does he disagree with Reddy?

5. Who is James R. Flynn and why is he quoted?

6. Is Rebecca Collins a reliable source? Why or why not?

7. Are you familiar with the TV shows that Monacelli mentions in his last body paragraph? If so, do you agree or disagree that these shows are inappropriate for children?

8. Why are no page numbers given for the information from the two Internet sources?

CRITICAL THINKING
In Connecting Texts

At the beginning of this chapter, recall Pavlov's statement, "In your work and research there must always be passion." Perhaps Pavlov makes this remark because research always requires much time, effort, and energy. As you have seen in this chapter, before you can even begin to write a rough draft, you should focus on a topic, find one or more reliable sources, engage in note taking, and come up with a skeletal outline. You may find that your class might enjoy working together on a larger source-based project rather than approaching the assignment individually. If this is the case, discuss with others and your instructor some possibilities for research—for instance, a major problem, such as finding viable solutions to prison overcrowding, reforming the financing of presidential election campaigns, or requiring fast-food chains to use more environmentally friendly packaging. Once you have agreed on one of these larger research topics, engage as a group in some initial research, breaking the problem into smaller projects that each student can present based on his or her interest. When the research project is finished, bind all individual reports into a document for class presentation.

Exploring Development Options: Choosing Patterns to Fit Purpose

Chapter 9

Writing About Events: Narration and Illustration

Time passes and the past becomes the present. . . . These presences of the past are there in the corner of your life today. You thought . . . they had died, but they have just been waiting their chance.

—Carlos Fuentes, *diplomat, essayist, and dramatist*

Preview

In this chapter you will learn

- How to identify the characteristics of narration and illustration—the recounting of an event or the sharing of one or more examples—to serve a particular purpose
- How to use narration within an essay by using chronological order, setting the scene, maintaining a consistent point of view, and incorporating descriptive detail, specific action, and appropriate dialogue
- How to use illustration within a narrative or illustrative essay by using clear, vivid, convincing examples
- How to interview a source to gain narrative material

After reading this chapter and completing its practice exercises, you will be able to use narration and illustration as patterns of development in your essays.

Each of the five chapters in Part 2 introduces different methods you can use to develop an essay. This chapter will focus on narration and illustration. Narration is a strategy that we humans have enjoyed from our earliest existence as cave dwellers to the present day. We are a storytelling species, and as children, no matter what our cultural background, we have begged our parents or loved ones to tell us stories. As we mature, rather than losing this fascination with the telling of events, we seek and find narration in film and television plots, news events reported by journalists, and books of fiction and nonfiction. In fact, every time we recount an event or incident, we're using narration.

Later in the chapter, we will discuss illustration, a way of supporting a topic, explaining a claim, or defending a generalization by using specific situations. If you were asked to write an essay claiming that road rage in America is on the rise, in addition to statistics supporting this view, you might also want to offer specific examples of road rage. Illustration is a pattern of essay development especially useful in making an abstract idea or unfamiliar term clear for your audience.

CHARACTERISTICS OF NARRATION

This exploration of narration focuses not on the fictional stories composed in a creative writing class, but rather on the narration of real-life events to explain or prove a point in an essay. Although you may certainly focus on events that you have experienced firsthand, it may also suit your essay's purpose to narrate events of public, civic, or academic importance. For instance, if your thesis focuses on the problems of working while taking a full load of college classes, you might want to narrate your own experiences or those of friends to prove your point. If you are in a lab and want to explain what happens when two chemicals are mixed together, you would narrate the steps in order to document your experiment. In a workplace report, if you want to persuade your client to build a particular office structure, you could narrate the success of developers with similar structures in the area. Because narration can be such a helpful way of making a point about an abstract idea by tying real-life experiences to this idea, you will want to familiarize yourself with the characteristics of this writing strategy.

When you use **narration** in an essay, you recount an event or series of events, usually in chronological order. The selection of specific details related to the place and people involved is critical in allowing the reader to grasp the importance of the event or experience.

To illustrate narration at work to support a thesis, read the following excerpt. The writer, whose Korean mother spoke little English, focuses on the power of language to distance immigrants as outsiders in an "English-only world":

1   One day was unusually harrowing. We ventured downtown in the new Ford Country Squire my father had bought her [the writer's mother], an enormous station wagon that seemed as long—and deft—as an ocean liner. We were shopping for a special meal for guests visiting that weekend, and my mother had heard that a particular butcher carried fresh oxtails, which she needed for a traditional soup.

2   We'd never been inside the shop, but my mother would pause before its window, which was always lined with whole hams, roasts, and ropes of plump handmade sausages. She greatly esteemed the bounty with her eyes, and my sister and I did also, but despite our desirous cries she'd turn us away and instead buy the packaged links at the Finast supermarket, where she felt comfortable looking them over and could easily spot the price. And, of course, not have to talk.

3   But that day she was resolved. The butcher store was crowded, and as we stepped inside the door jingled a welcome. No one seemed to notice. We waited for some time, and people who entered after us were now being served. Finally, an old woman nudged my mother and waved a little ticket, which we hadn't

taken. We patiently waited again, until one of the beefy men behind the glass display hollered our number.

4   My mother pulled us forward and began searching the cases, but the oxtails were nowhere to be found. The man, his big arms crossed, sharply said, "Come on, lady, whaddya want?" This unnerved her, and she somehow blurted the Korean word for oxtail, *soggori*.

5   The butcher looked as if my mother had put something sour in his mouth, and he glanced back at the lighted board and called the next number.

6   Before I knew it, she had rushed us outside and back in the wagon, which she had double-parked because of the crowd. She was furious, almost vibrating with fear and grief, and I could see she was about to cry.

7   She wanted to go back inside, but now the driver of the car we were blocking wanted to pull out. She was shooing us away. My mother, who had just earned her driver's license, started furiously working the pedals. But in her haste she must have flooded the engine, for it wouldn't turn over. The driver started honking and then another car began honking as well, and soon it seemed the entire street was shrieking at us.

—Chang-rae Lee, from "Mute in an English-Only World"

Notice that Lee's narration contains the following characteristics:

- **A specific event or a series of related events is the focus of the narration and forms the subject of the thesis.**
  Lee's specific event involves his mother's encounter with someone unsympathetic to her limited English.

- **The significance of the event forms the controlling idea in the thesis.**
  Lee tells the reader that the day was "unusually harrowing"—through the unfolding of Lee's narrative we understand why the event was so frustrating, and by the time his audience has finished the narrative, Lee has made clear his unspoken but implied thesis: Intolerance in multilingual communities can lead to frustration and rage.

- **The setting, people, and actions connected to the event are described in accurate detail and specific action words.**
  Lee tells his audience that the store window is "lined with whole hams, crown roasts, and ropes of plump handmade sausages," that "an old woman nudged my mother and waved a little ticket," that the butcher stands "with big arms crossed," and that later he "hollered our number."

- **The structure is chronological.**
  Lee's narration begins with the car trip, proceeds to the store and the encounter with the butcher, and then ends with the family's return to the car.

- **A particular point of view is used throughout the narrative.**
  Notice that Lee confides to the reader, "*we* ventured downtown," and then "*we* patiently waited."

To notice how narration works within a college essay, read the following model and see how many of the characteristics previously discussed you can identify.

MODEL WITH KEY QUESTIONS

In her narrative essay, Tori Ueda wanted to emphasize an event that eventually led her to a more profound understanding of her mother and the cultural and generational gap many American teenagers experience. As you read, notice how the writer sets the scene, keeps the sequence of events in clear order, and begins as well as ends her essay with a discussion of the event's significance.

Model 1   ## "BRADY BUNCH" WANNA-BE

Tori Ueda

In discovering material for her essays, Tori Ueda found clustering and group brainstorming especially helpful. Tori also reported that she was unsure about the value of peer editing in the beginning, but by the end of the semester she felt that the process had helped in the revision of her essays. In evaluating her writing, Tori stated, "My weak essays were due to my inability to overcome my own personal procrastination." Tori plans to go to law school after receiving her undergraduate degree, and eventually she would like to become a probate attorney—one who deals with wills, estates, and guardianships.

1   How does the culture of one's childhood lay a distinctive foundation that survives well into adulthood? After seeing *The Brady Bunch: The Movie* a few weeks ago, I was thinking about my adolescent years. As I was transformed to my childhood, years that were filled with the turmoil of living with a traditional Japanese family, I remembered a particular incident because it changed the way I perceived my relationship with my mother.

2   Like many other children, I grew up watching most of the "all American" shows such as "The Brady Bunch" and "Leave It to Beaver." The themes of these programs dealt with children rebelling against their parents and going through phases. In my family, unlike the families of my peers, Dad dished out the scolding, shaming, ridicule, and severe punishments while Mom practiced a therapeutic technique of talking problems out. Being a curious child, one early afternoon I took it upon myself to find out if some of the things I saw on television would work on my parents. Unfortunately I discovered that my mother was not as understanding as the "Carol Brady" mothers I was used to watching.

3   On this afternoon I found myself sitting in front of the television watching an episode of "The Brady Bunch." In the show, Marsha got angry with her mother and ran to her bedroom, slamming her door. The mother did not get angry with the girl; instead she simply sighed and thought up ways to make her daughter feel better. After the show, I sat on the sofa and thought about how this mother-daughter relationship differed from my own. Then I turned on the radio and began to have the time of my life imagining that I was Madonna—since no one was home, I sang my heart out—I WAS the Material Girl giving a live concert at the Great Western Forum. As the afternoon progressed, I was having so much fun that I totally forgot my responsibility, which was always to clean the house before my mother came home from work.

4   An hour later when my mother did come home, she found the house exactly as she had left it in the morning—dirty dishes from breakfast in the sink, unfolded laundry on the sofa, and toys scattered everywhere. She sternly looked at me for a moment and then started yelling at me, "What have you been doing all afternoon? Why is this house still a mess when you've been home from school for three hours?"

5   When these words rushed out of her mouth, hands on her hips, her body leaning in to me, I wondered where my sweet, understanding mom, the one who would wipe away my tears after Dad handed out the discipline, had gone. I blinked, saying nothing, and next she continued to scold me. I blurted out, "Why don't you just take a chill pill and calm down?" After these words, I stood there, not believing I had disrespected my mother so. I watched a play of emotions roll over her face. When she finally tried to say something, I turned my face away from her. This was the final insult my mother was willing to take from me. She slapped me—she slapped me hard! The slap stung just like the sting of a bee, and moments later I could feel the skin on my face swelling up. I just stood there face-to-face with my mother, thinking to myself, "She actually hit me, and not my father. But if she hit me, then who's going to comfort me and buy me ice cream and tell me everything will be okay?" Tears began to swell under my eyes, my lips were quivering, and my hands were shaking. And my mouth was paralyzed.

6   Now that I look back on this incident, I believe I was crying not because of the pain of the slap, but because I was filled with regret and embarrassed for my actions. I went to my room and basked in self-pity. In the next few minutes I spent in my room, I aged tremendously. I think that this incident made a lasting impression on me because it was the first time my mother had ever physically punished me. I thought to myself, "Why did Marsha get away with yelling at her mother and slamming the door to her room, while I could not stand up for myself in my own house?" That day in my room I was very angry with my mother, and I suspect that my mother felt betrayed—she had somehow raised a daughter to disrespect an elder—a terrible sin in Japanese tradition.

7   When I think about this experience now, I understand what had angered my mother so much and why my tantrum had not worked as well as Marsha's. That slap became the starting point toward a mature relationship with my mother; we had bridged the generation and the culture gap in that encounter. I was never to watch "The Brady Bunch" with such naïve eyes again. My rite of passage prompted me to think of families on television no longer as a symbol for the way all people live. ○

Key Questions

1. **Purpose**   What is Ueda's controlling idea connected to this event?

2. **Focus**   What specific event does Ueda narrate?

3. **Material**   Find examples of dialogue. Name one thing you learn about Ueda or her mother from the dialogue.

4. **Structure**   Find three cue words or phrases the writer uses to signal a transition and to keep the sequence of events clear.

5. **Style**   Find two words or phrases that help you visualize the people or the setting of Ueda's event. Find a phrase that communicates the writer's personal reaction to the event.

GUIDELINES FOR WRITING NARRATION

Determine Your Purpose

Narration is an effective writing choice if your purpose in writing your essay will be strengthened by recounting an event or events. Make sure that while your audience is caught up in the event you're narrating—the setting, details, people involved—they also know *why* you're recounting the event. The event you choose to narrate to support your thesis may have involved you personally. For example, you might want to recount your first driving experiences to persuade young readers that driver training is essential before trying to get a driver's license. You may also use narration to describe events that you have researched but could not have witnessed. For instance, a history assignment might require you to narrate the experiences of Alexander the Great in ancient Greece in order to share information or prove a point.

The event itself need not be dramatic or earthshaking—what is important is why you want to share the event with your audience. What is the meaning of the event in relation to your thesis? Determining your purpose will help you select appropriate details for your narration.

Practice 9.1 To identify writing situations in which narration might be a helpful strategy, work alone or with a partner and examine each of the following subjects. Circle the numbers of those subjects for which narrative development might work. After each, write a sentence focusing on the event. The first sentence has been completed for you.

1. The Columbine murders
   Survivors of the Columbine High School shootings discuss the events that led to their rescue.

2. The physical layout of a local park in your community

3. A refund request for faulty merchandise purchased in a department store

4. The atmosphere of your favorite restaurant

5. Job duties of a payroll clerk

6. Limitations of freedom of speech in the workplace ❑

Interview Sources If Helpful

Interviews with individuals who witnessed or participated in an event can yield a wealth of essay material for narrative essays as well as for essays using other methods of development. To obtain information for your narration, you can conduct an interview, either in person, by telephone, or online.

To gain the most detailed information from an interview, follow these six steps:

1. Contact your interview subject well in advance of any assignment's due date. Identify yourself as a college student, explain the nature of your assignment, and gain permission to conduct the interview. Assure the

person to be interviewed that the information will be used for class-room purposes only.

2. Agree with your interview subject on an appropriate date and time for the interview.

3. Agree on a time limit, possibly 30 minutes. Establishing a limit will allow you adequate time for questioning and note taking, and it will assure your interview subject that the interview will not drag on.

4. Draw up a list of questions connected with the event you wish to narrate. You may want to use the journalists' questions from Chapter 3: *Who? What? Where? When? Why? How?* Send the list of questions to the person to be interviewed early enough to allow the subject sufficient time to think about the questions and responses.

5. During the interview, take notes and ask **follow-up questions**—questions that arise in your mind because of what the interview subject has answered to your original set of questions.

6. As soon as possible after the interview, take some time to review your notes, writing down any additional details that come to mind.

Practice 9.2   Interview a friend or student about life's most embarrassing moment. Follow the six steps for an interview and, if time permits, develop the material from this interview into an essay using narration. ❏

Frame Thesis Around Significance of the Event

If you are writing an entire essay using narration, the event you're recounting serves as your subject, and the impact or significance of the event becomes your controlling idea. To illustrate, return to the topics on page 189. Assume that in the case of the first topic, the survivors of the Columbine shootings, you want to write an essay for your psychology class. You might come up with a thesis such as this:

SUBJECT	CONTROLLING IDEA
The individual reactions of the parents of the Columbine victims	Reveal a curious aspect of human behavior when experiencing the loss of a family member.

Practice 9.3   Examine topics 3 and 6 from the list on page 189. Working with a partner, create a thesis for an essay using narration. ❏

Set the Scene for Your Audience

William Shakespeare's famous line "All the world's a stage" certainly applies to narration. In recounting any event, it is thus helpful to think in terms of "staging" your material for the reader. Any background information that allows your audience to visualize the event will help your narration come alive. In "'Brady Bunch' Wanna-be" (p. 187), the writer creates a vivid scene—"dirty dishes from breakfast in the sink, unfolded laundry on the sofa, and toys scattered everywhere"—in paragraph 4.

Practice 9.4   To identify scene-setting elements, reread "'Brady Bunch' Wanna-be" and find three more details that allow you to visualize the event.   ❑

Choose and Maintain a Consistent Point of View

Decide which point of view you will use, and maintain it throughout your narrative. If you choose the **first person,** you will use the words *I, me, my* or *we, us, our.* First person stresses the writer's involvement in the event; often this point of view is used when it suits a writer's purpose for the audience to connect with the writer's feelings about and reactions to the event. If you choose the **third person,** you will use the words *he, him, his* or *she, her, hers.* This will indicate that the story is being told by someone other than the person involved in the event. It might be more appropriate to use the third-person point of view if, for instance, you're narrating the history of bagel production in America.

Practice 9.5   Examine the following writing situations and then decide whether first person or third person would be more appropriate.

1. An essay for a political science class on the early childhood of George W. Bush.

2. An essay for college admittance on an obstacle or hardship you've overcome.

3. A report detailing how the company you work for has used grant money in the past two years.

4. An essay for a philosophy class on the persecution of Socrates.   ❑

Follow a Clear Order

Narration usually makes use of chronological order—relating events in the order in which they happened or are happening. In a narration, the **past tense** describes actions that have occurred, the **present tense** describes actions that are occurring, and the **future tense** describes events that have not yet occurred. For example, if you were asked on a college or employment application to write an essay about your work experience, you would choose the past tense. If, on the other hand, the application asked you to describe your present volunteer or community service involvement, you would choose the present tense. If you were asked to detail your career plans and goals for the next five years, the future tense would be your choice. Once you've chosen a tense appropriate to your subject and purpose, be consistent throughout your narration.

Practice 9.6   Read "A Hanging" (p. 203), underlining the action words and noting the sequence of events and the tense the writer used.   ❑

Use Cue Words

As you draft your narrative, keep the sequence of events clear for readers by using cue words. Consult the table of cue words (pp. 141–142), noting especially those words signaling a change in time. Try to work these time markers into your narrative where they will help take your reader from one action or detail to the next.

Practice 9.7   Read the following paragraph from a student narrative and insert the appropriate cue words in the blanks, consulting your list if you need to.

> As my dad walked downstairs to say hello to my mother, I began to think this was the best day of my young life. _____ it was not to remain a happy day. About five minutes after sending my father away, I began to hear an argument forming in the downstairs kitchen. _____ piercing words flew from both my parents' mouths. _____ my mother yelled about how my father was always gone, and that he was never there when his family needed him. _____ my father retorted by saying that my mother was making a big deal out of nothing, that she worried and nagged too much. _____ I passed this off as one of their normal fights, in which they stayed mad for a little while and then apologized to each other. _____ I just quietly shut my door and minutes later, I heard a shrill, piercing scream. _____ this was followed by another lower toned scream. I thought that if I played with my new bus real hard and real well that they would stop fighting. _____ it was too late; creaking footsteps soon became audible on the staircase.
>
> —Courtney Risdon, *student*   ❏

Incorporate Descriptive Detail and Specific Action

If you take another look at the narratives in this chapter, you will notice that they all use descriptive detail and specific action words to make the event come alive. We can visualize the "ropes of plump handmade sausages" in the butcher shop Lee describes (p. 185); we feel Ueda's pain when she writes "tears began to swell under my eyes, my lips were quivering, and my hands were shaking" (p. 187).

Practice 9.8   Read the following excerpt and then annotate it by underlining all words or phrases that describe something or show action. Mark all descriptive words with an "n" for noun and an "a" for adjective, and mark action words with a "v" for verb. (For help in recognizing nouns, adjectives, and verbs, refer to the handbook in Part 5 of this book.)

> The ramifications of this biological invention were endless. Plants traveled as they had never traveled before. They got into strange environments heretofore never entered by the old spore plants or stiff pinecone-seed plants. The well-fed, carefully cherished little embryos raised their heads everywhere. Many of the older plants with more primitive reproductive mechanisms began to fade away under this

unequaled contest. They contracted their range into secluded environments. Some, like the giant redwoods, lingered on as relics; many vanished entirely.

—Loren Eiseley, from "How Flowers Changed the World" ❏

Use Dialogue If Appropriate

Dialogue, words or sentences spoken by people and set off from the text by quotation marks or indentation, can often help writers of narratives give readers a sense of "being there." Good dialogue conveys meaningful information about a person as well as details about events. No two people have the same way of talking—the same mannerisms, dialects, and particular sentence patterns.

Practice 9.9   To see how dialogue can help in narrative development, reread "'Brady Bunch' Wanna-be" (p. 187). Annotate the essay by highlighting all of the dialogue. When you have finished this, read only the dialogue, noting who says what. Now write down any information you learned from the dialogue itself. ❏

Practice 9.10   There are many narrative situations in which dialogue would not be appropriate. Although you never want to "insert" dialogue just to include it in your narration, it will help to read through your narrative draft, noting in the margin the places where dialogue might help your audience visualize the scene and the people. For help with punctuating dialogue, refer to the handbook in Part 5. ❏

Strategies for Writing Narration

1. **Purpose**   Determine if narration suits your purpose and audience in the essay.
2. **Focus**   Frame a thesis using an event or events as the subject and the significance or impact of the event as the controlling idea. Maintain a consistent point of view throughout your narrative, and check to see that all details focus on the event and its meaning.
3. **Material**   If you are recounting an event that happened to you, use your memory to gather material in prewriting. Play the scene over again in your mind, taking notes. If you are recounting an event not connected to you personally, be sure you have gathered enough material from sources and interviews to communicate the event. In drafting, include descriptive detail and specific action to help the audience visualize the people and the exact place connected to the event.
4. **Structure**   Check to see that cue words indicate for the reader a clear sequence of events. Make sure that you are proceeding in chronological order.
5. **Style**   In addition to the usual proofreading you do during polishing, examine your narration for any places where dialogue would help the event come alive for your audience. Ask yourself if your introduction sets the appropriate tone for your event. Finally, make sure your conclusion thoughtfully communicates the connection between the event and your purpose in recounting it.

OPTIONS FOR WRITING NARRATION

The following writing options offer you the chance to recount an event and communicate the significance of that event to your audience. Harriet Doerr, a writer who did not discover her talent for narrative until she went back to college in her seventies, confides, "I have everything I need. A square of sky, a piece of stone, and memory raining down on me in sleeves." In working through any of the options, refer to the guidelines and strategies in this chapter as needed.

1. In her essay (p. 187), Ueda refers to her "rite of passage" and a subsequent change in her relationship with her mother. We all have certain rites of passage—events that alter our lives for better or worse. For example, in some cultures, a particular birthday is viewed as significant; in other cultures, certain events such as graduating from high school or getting a driver's license signify a passage to maturity or a move into a new phase. Whatever the event, quite often as a result we experience an altered sense of perception, or an "awakening." Write an essay narrating such an event and explain its significance for you.

2. The word *place* can refer not only to a physical setting or location but also to a position or standing in which we feel comfortable. We are all continually involved in this process of "finding our place." As we grow, we need to move on to new places or positions. Recall a time when you felt different, "out of place," an outsider, or not taken seriously. Write an essay telling about how you found your place or gained acceptance.

3. One of the purposes of narration can be to help the reader visualize or understand an abstract idea. Choose any one of the well-known statements below or find another one that you prefer. Write a narration essay that illustrates the statement.

    • Pride goes before a fall.

    • The more things change, the more they stay the same.

    • Don't judge a book by its cover.

    • The road to hell is paved with good intentions.

    • Hell hath no fury like a woman (or man) scorned.

4. Use narration in an essay in order to make a point about some injustice in the world, perhaps something that you personally experienced or a historical event that happened long before you were born. You can find a good model for this in George Orwell's "A Hanging" (p. 203), in which the writer narrates an event in order to persuade his audience of the inhumanity of capital punishment.

5. Write an essay detailing your wildest fantasy. Offer your audience specific sensory elements so that all readers can visualize your fantasy.

6. Write an essay detailing your worst nightmare. This could be something that actually happened to you or something you are or were afraid of at

one point in your life. Again, make sure that your essay uses enough vivid language to help your audience see your nightmare clearly.

7. Decide on a historical figure of special interest to you. Consult some Internet or printed sources, taking notes as you read the material. Write an essay exploring details related to this historical figure.

8. Think about a writer, playwright, artist, or musician of special interest to you. Consult some Internet or printed sources, taking notes as you read the material. Write an essay exploring details related to this famous person.

9. *(Film and Literature)* If you are a commuter and have lots of driving time on your hands, find the wonderful Books-on-CD version of Dumas's *Count of Monte Cristo*. After listening to this action-packed tale, view the 2002 film adaptation. Write an essay in which you narrate the count's life.

10. *(Service Learning)* Contact a seniors' center near your school or home. Ask the administrator there if you can meet with a senior who might want to share a personal story with you. Set up a schedule that is feasible for both of you, take notes as you interview your subject, and then edit, revise, and polish the senior's story carefully. After you have typed the finished product and inserted the story in a folder or binder, visit the senior and suggest that he or she have a book-signing party for close friends and relatives.

JOURNAL WRITING: THE AUTOBIOGRAPHICAL ENTRY

Although writing in your journal regularly can help you in all of your college reading and writing, journal entries can be of special assistance in collecting material for narrative essays. The following activities will focus on material that is **autobiographical**—having to do with the people, places, and events connected to your own life. Choose one or more of these activities to respond to in a journal entry. Later, some of these autobiographical reflections may serve as the basis for a narrative essay.

1. Track down photographs of yourself from several years ago. In a journal entry, discuss the person you were then—what you liked and disliked, thought about, hoped for, and feared. Narrate an important event that occurred during that time in your life.

2. Recall an incident that changed the way you viewed yourself or some aspect of your life. In a journal entry, write about your perceptions before the incident, then during and after the event. Be sure to mention all specific details connected with the event as you are recounting it.

3. Think about a time that you felt like an outsider—this could have been because you were new to a school or community, spoke a different language or dialect, looked or acted differently than your peers or family members, or felt somehow alienated. In an entry, tell about the events that led to this feeling and how you coped with your situation.

4. Think about writing an **obituary**—a written description of a deceased person's life and accomplishments, usually published in a newspaper. If you were to write your own obituary, what one event would serve to illustrate a time in your life when you "rose to the occasion" and acted in a manner that made you proud? In a journal entry, write all the details connected with this particular event.

CHARACTERISTICS OF ILLUSTRATION

Illustration is a pattern of writing in which you use examples to support your thesis or to make a point. If you think about it, we use illustration every day in our conversations with friends, colleagues, coworkers, and family, among others. "For example," "to illustrate," and "for instance" are all-too-familiar sentence openers in our world. Sometimes when our goal is to explain an abstract quality or term to a listener, a concrete example works beautifully to get our point across. If we want to explain the meaning of *compound interest* to someone, we might illustrate by using an example of how much $50 earning 5 percent interest would appreciate in ten years. If we'd like to explain the expression *American food* to a newly arrived foreigner, we might mention hamburgers, French fries, fried chicken, popcorn, and apple pie. To see how illustration helps to develop an essay, read the following paragraph:

> The human senses detect only a fraction of reality: We can't see the ultraviolet markers that guide a honeybee to nectar; we can't hear most of the noises emitted by a dolphin. In this way, the senses define the boundaries of mental awareness. But the brain also defines the limits of what we perceive. Human beings see, feel, taste, touch, and smell not the world around them but a version of the world, one their brains have concocted. "People imagine that they're seeing what's really there, but they're not," says neuroscientist John Maunsell of Baylor College of Medicine in Houston. The eyes take in the light reflecting off objects around us, but the brain only pays attention to part of the scene. Looking for a pen on a messy desk, for example, you can scan the surface without noticing the papers scattered across it.
>
> —Shannon Brownlee and Traci Watson, "The Senses,"
> *US News & World Report*, 13 January 1997

Notice that Brownlee and Watson's illustration has the following characteristics:

- **The examples provide concrete detail:**
  Because Brownlee and Watson want to make a point having to do with "a fraction," a highly abstract term, the writers use tangible specifics to aid them with reader comprehension of their term: "Ultraviolet markers," "honeybee," "nectar," "dolphin," "pen," and "papers scattered."

- **The examples are selected with care:**
  Notice that because Brownlee and Watson's subject is the human senses, they have chosen examples that deal with both sight (ultraviolet markers and honeybees) and hearing (noises and a dolphin).

- **The organization of examples supports the writer's purpose:**
Because Brownlee and Watson's subject has nothing to do with time sequences, they realize that there is no need for an organizational plan for
detail based on chronological order. However, because the paragraph
makes two separate points, the writers use examples illustrating their
first point—that humans "detect only a fraction of reality"—and then
their second point—that humans imagine a "version of the world,"
rather than the entire world.

MODEL WITH KEY QUESTIONS

Student David Redmond wanted to convey the meaning of the term *customer
service* to his audience. Notice the examples from his work experience that he
uses to clarify the meaning of this term. In drafting this essay, Redmond found
that he could use illustrations to show what customer service is, as well as
what it is not.

Model 2   ### TRICK OF THE TRADE

David Redmond

*David Redmond has worked in a large supermarket in the Los Angeles area for two years. Red-
mond enjoys attending and participating in his college classes a lot more than performing his
often-frustrating job duties. When David is not in class or on the job, he enjoys dirt biking.
Although this writer confides that his two writing weaknesses are tense shifts and off-topic comments, he feels that "now that I'm in college and paying for my own schooling and books, I have
to do well, and that's a great motivator!"*

1   Since I first started working my job at Von's, there's one factor that I have had
to put up with the most: I have to go by the saying, "The customer is always
right." Even if I know that a customer is wrong, even if I'm one hundred percent
sure of this, I'm not allowed to tell this to him or her blatantly. In order to tell the
customer that he or she is wrong about anything, basically I have to beat around
the bush by being polite and courteous, which is pretty hard to do sometimes.

2   If a person were to define "good customer service," an appropriate definition
might be "gracious service given to feisty customers." The first time I had a con-
frontation with a customer, she came up to me screaming in my ear and saying
that she had been overcharged for a boneless beef roast on sale. I looked at her
and said, "Okay, I'll check the price for you, so would you please wait a minute
and I'll be right back?" When I got to the meat department, I noticed right away
that this department was having a sale on bone-in beef roasts. Immediately I suspected that she had misread the sign and had assumed that this sign referred to
"boneless beef roasts." So I walked back to her and politely let her know that she
might have looked at the sale sign and become confused about the beef that was
on sale. At this point, the woman totally "flipped out"! She looked me right in the
eyes and said, "Are you trying to tell me that I can't read?" By now, her face was

as red as a beet. At that moment, I was ready to tell her, "Why can't you accept the fact that you are wrong and I am right?" Instead, I had to grit my teeth and take her to the sign she had misinterpreted.

3   Giving good customer service also means that I can't "lose my cool" with the customers. Even if a customer comes at me with a bad attitude, I can't allow myself to communicate with him or her on the same grouchy level. What I have discovered is that most of the time, if I'm totally polite with the irate customer, I can get a simple smile out of him or her. A trick that serves me well on my job is making even grouchy people laugh simply by spitting out some corny line to ask this customer if he or she needs a hand out to the car. For example, I'll say, "Do you want to take advantage of our complimentary carry-out service, free of charge?" I think this line makes even a grumpy person laugh because it sounds so cheesy.

4   In just about every workplace in the world, good customer service will bring in customers and therefore increase business for a company. Polite, attentive employees make people feel comfortable whether they're shopping or just browsing. As a result, every manager wants to hire people who already know how to be courteous and polite. Although these traits don't always come easily for me in my current job, knowing how to extend good customer service or at least using a few tricks of the trade may help me in my future profession, whatever it may turn out to be. ○

Key Questions

1. **Purpose**   What specific audience of readers might benefit from this essay?

2. **Focus**   Locate Redmond's thesis and underline it in your text.

3. **Material**   In your own words, describe the example Redmond uses in paragraph 2. In paragraph 3, the writer uses a different example. In what sense is the example used in paragraph 2 an example of something one *shouldn't* do while the example in paragraph 3 represents something one *should* do?

4. **Structure**   Is the organizational plan chronological? Would the essay be just as effective if Redmond had reversed the order of paragraphs 2 and 3? Why or why not?

5. **Style**   Find a simile used in the essay. Does it help readers visualize the scene or not?

GUIDELINES FOR WRITING ILLUSTRATION

Consider Audience and Purpose

To a large degree, your reason for writing and your audience determine the number of examples you should use. If you use examples for a research paper or a persuasive essay, for instance, even though examples may add weight to your thesis, you might want to use statistics, expert testimony, and historical background or overview as well. Therefore, the number of examples you use will be limited. On the other hand, if your essay is informative—for instance, you want to explain to your city council the extent of renovation necessary to upgrade a city's parks—your audience would expect several clearly detailed examples.

Practice 9.11 Examine the following list of topics and determine whether you would want to use several or merely one or two examples to develop your essay; remember to think about who might want to read this essay and why you would be writing the essay for this particular audience.

1. Effective parenting

2. Stress reduction activities

3. Major problems in this city

4. The unfairness of a particular boss

5. People who steal from their company ❏

Decide on a Point to Illustrate

Once you have a purpose, audience, and topic in mind, zero in on a specific thesis. Your thesis in this case should be the idea that all your examples help to support.

Practice 9.12 Return to the topics listed in Practice 9.11 and choose one. Shape one of these broad topics into a thesis supportable by one or more examples. ❏

Choose and Evaluate Examples

You'll be able to amass a large number of examples by listing or freewriting on your own or by brainstorming with a classmate or small group. Once you have some examples, you need to evaluate them. Remember to choose those examples that support the point or idea you want to illustrate. For example, if your thesis is that college parking lots are too crowded to allow timely class arrival by students, you would not want to mention a student in your math class who is always late but who arrives by bus. Also try to choose a variety of examples rather than several that deal with the same aspect of your main point. For instance, in an essay arguing that a particular high school's students don't have enough extracurricular activity possibilities, you wouldn't want to illustrate the lack of band and drama activities unless you also illustrated the shortage of art and sports activities available at the same school. Don't forget that in addition to examples, you can also illustrate your essay by using observations, statistics, expert opinion, or quotations. Finally, be careful to be responsible in your use of illustration: Rather than rare or unusual examples, out of regard for your audience use representative examples and typical cases.

Practice 9.13 Working with a partner, examine the following writing assignments and decide which assignment you can discover the most examples for. Evaluate the examples found and agree on which ones you would keep if you were to proceed from brainstorming to the rough draft of an essay using illustration.

1. After agreeing on two or three extremely important traits of a college instructor, discover examples that would demonstrate each trait.

2. Find examples that would support an essay persuading your state government to raise the age of legal driving from 16 to 18.

3. Find examples from your own work experience that reinforce Redmond's thesis in his essay "Trick of the Trade" (p. 197).

4. Discover examples from your own experience with your family that reinforce Ueda's thesis in "'Brady Bunch' Wanna-be" (p. 187).

5. Find examples from your own experience that would support a thesis related to the importance of a mentor in a young person's life. ❏

Organize Examples to Suit Your Purpose

If you are using only one extended example for your illustration, you need not be concerned about which organizational plan to use. However, if you use several examples, you'll need to decide how to organize them. You might choose logical order (see p. 78), and in addition group your examples either from most important to least important or from least important to most important—this decision might be guided by your particular subject and your own preference of presentation. If you have many examples, you can also consider grouping them in categories: For example, if your essay focuses on heroes in English literature, you could group your examples into several for the Middle English period, some for the Elizabethan period, and others for the Victorian period.

Strategies for Writing Illustration

1. **Purpose**   Determine if narration suits your purpose and audience in the essay.
2. **Focus**   Frame a thesis that can be supported through the use of examples.
3. **Material**   After coming up with a comprehensive list of possible examples, evaluate each to make sure it offers concrete detail related to the thesis, helps in developing a variety of examples, and serves as a valid and striking example in relation to the other examples given.
4. **Structure**   Determine whether your organization needs to be chronological or logical. Also experiment with the order of your examples to make sure you have used the most effective and clear structure possible.
5. **Style**   In your word choice, try to make each example vivid and compelling by offering your audience the detail necessary to flesh out a picture in relation to the other examples given. Use quotations, expert testimony, statistics, and observations where helpful.

OPTIONS FOR WRITING ILLUSTRATION

1. Write an essay in which you assert that effective parenting requires three specific traits. Use enough examples explaining each of the traits to support your thesis.

2. Interview the mayor or a city council member of your city or community. Discover one or more problems that your community is now battling. Write an essay persuading your audience of the importance of this problem and its solution by using illustrations.

3. Stealing from one's employer can occur in a variety of ways that don't involve taking cash from the company; employees "borrow" equipment from the work environment or take a two-hour lunch, to name just two examples of cheating. Write an essay persuading your audience that in a former or current job of yours, this occurs on a regular basis, or that this does not occur on a regular basis.

4. Write an essay explaining the three or more traits an ideal teacher must have by using examples from your own experience in college, high school, or other academic communities. If you prefer, write an essay illustrating three or more traits found in an ineffective teacher.

5. After reading "A Hanging" by George Orwell (p. 203), what do you think of the use of capital punishment in America? As a nation, we have a history of punishing those found guilty of murder by giving them the death penalty. In our execution of criminals, we have moved from hanging and the firing squad, to the gas chamber and electrocution, to the latest means—lethal injection. After researching any one of these execution methods, give examples of cases in which the equipment malfunctioned in some way, causing "cruel and unusual punishment" to the person executed—a violation of the Eighth Amendment to our Constitution. Your college library probably has an encyclopedia of capital punishment, an extremely informative book.

6. You may have experienced the traumas of searching for a job. Many people feel that job hunting is more stressful than actually performing a job once you find one. Write an essay illustrating the stresses and difficulties involved with job hunting.

7. Violence in film and on television has become a major issue in America. Choose one side of this issue and write an essay supporting your point of view with pertinent illustrations from television, film, or both.

8. Procrastination may be a college student's worst enemy. In addition, procrastination can also affect the lives of those not connected with college. Write an essay developed by the use of examples of procrastination.

9. *(Film and Literature)* After reading "A Hanging" (p. 203), view the film *Dead Man Walking*, based on Sister Prejean's book by the same name. In an essay, illustrate ways the film changed views you previously held on the issue of capital punishment in America.

10. *(Service Learning)* Contact your local humane society and ask them if you can create a current flyer for campus distribution. In order for your flyer to increase your college's awareness of the services of the humane society, you will need to illustrate your flyer with specific examples past and present of animals in need of help. In addition to informing by use of examples, you might want to include pictures of these animals.

Using the Computer: Devising and Sharing Narratives

1. Once you have an event you want to write about, open a file and list in chronological order all of the details associated with the event. Don't forget to set the scene and describe the people involved as you're narrating, using descriptive and action words when appropriate. Include all material connected with the event, and type these events in the order in which they occurred. After you have completed this list of details and saved this information, use the *Copy* and *Move* functions to change the sequence of details to begin with another point in time, creating a **flashback**—an interruption in the forward chronological movement of a narrative that goes back to some prior time in the sequence of events. Once you have at least two versions, compare them to see which one you prefer.

2. Some online communities provide an opportunity to engage in a fascinating information exchange with others who have narratives to share. Retirees are one such source; you can link up with them to ask them questions or engage in a dialogue about an important event in their lives. You may then choose to narrate this event in an essay. First, go to one of these Web sites:

   • Senior Net (**http://www.seniornet.org**)

   • Blacksburg Electronic Village (**http://www.bev.net/community/seniors/ sol.sol.html**)

   Explain that you are a student who wishes to interview someone about a meaningful event in his or her life as part of a classroom writing assignment. Be sure to leave your e-mail address so interested people can contact you. When you have a response from someone you would like to write about, follow the steps for interviewing (p. 189). You might want to begin by e-mailing your interviewee a list of questions. As you exchange e-mail with your online partner, remember to get enough details about the setting and people to help you and the future readers of your essay visualize the event you will narrate. Be sure to send your online partner a copy of the narration you create from your e-mail correspondence.

   But remember that with this activity, as with other online communication, you should protect yourself by refusing to share any information of a private nature.

RESPONDING TO WRITING: EXAMINING NARRATIVE STRATEGIES

In this activity you'll see how several of the narrative strategies this chapter discusses worked for George Orwell, a famous British writer who served in the British Imperial Police in India. When Orwell wrote "A Hanging" in 1950, he wanted to recount an event so that readers could see firsthand the cruelty of capital punishment. After you read Orwell's narrative, you'll be asked to examine it again to analyze its effectiveness and then to examine one of your own essays using narration.

A HANGING

George Orwell

1   It was in Burma, a sodden morning of the rains. A sickly light, like yellow tinfoil, was slanting over the high walls into the jail yard. We were waiting outside the condemned cells, a row of sheds fronted with double bars, like small animal cages. Each cell measured about ten feet by ten and was quite bare within except for a plank bed and a pot for drinking water. In some of them brown, silent men were squatting at the inner bars, with their blankets draped round them. These were the condemned men, due to be hanged within the next week or two.

2   One prisoner had been brought out of his cell. He was a Hindu, a puny wisp of a man, with a shaven head and vague liquid eyes. He had a thick, sprouting mustache, absurdly too big for his body, rather like the mustache of a comic man on the films. Six tall Indian warders were guarding him and getting him ready for the gallows. Two of them stood by with rifles and fixed bayonets, while the others handcuffed him, passed a chain through his handcuffs and fixed it to their belts, and lashed his arms tight to his sides. They crowded very close about him, with their hands always on him in a careful, caressing grip, as though all the while feeling him to make sure he was there. It was like men handling a fish which is still alive and may jump back into the water. But he stood quite unresisting, yielding his arms limply to the ropes, as though he hardly noticed what was happening.

3   Eight o'clock struck and a bugle call, desolately thin in the wet air, floated from the distant barracks. The superintendent of the jail, who was standing apart from the rest of us, moodily prodding the gravel with his stick, raised his head at the sound. He was an army doctor, with a grey toothbrush mustache and a gruff voice. "For God's sake, hurry up, Francis," he said irritably. "The man ought to have been dead by this time. Aren't you ready yet?"

4   Francis, the head jailer, a fat Dravidian in a white drill suit and gold spectacles, waved his black hand. "Yes sir, yes sir," he bubbled. "All iss satisfactorily prepared. The hangman iss waiting. We shall proceed."

5   "Well, quick march, then. The prisoners can't get their breakfast till this job's over."

6   We set out for the gallows. Two warders marched on either side of the prisoner, with their rifles at the slope; two others marched close against him, gripping him by arm and shoulder, as though at once pushing and supporting him. The rest of us, magistrates and the like, followed behind. Suddenly, when we had

gone ten yards, the procession stopped short without any order or warning. A dreadful thing had happened—a dog, come goodness knows whence, had appeared in the yard. It came bounding among us with a loud volley of barks and leapt around us wagging its whole body, wild with glee at finding so many human beings together. It was a large woolly dog, half Airedale, half pariah. For a moment it pranced around us, and then, before anyone could stop it, it had made a dash for the prisoner, and jumping up tried to lick his face. Everybody stood aghast, too taken aback even to grab the dog.

7   "Who let that bloody brute in here?" said the superintendent angrily. "Catch it, someone!"

8   A warder detached from the escort, charged clumsily after the dog, but it danced and gambolled just out of his reach, taking everything as part of the game. A young Eurasian jailer picked up a handful of gravel and tried to stone the dog away, but it dodged the stones and came after us again. Its yaps echoed from the jail walls. The prisoner, in the grasp of the two warders, looked on incuriously, as though this was another formality of the hanging. It was several minutes before someone managed to catch the dog. Then we put my handkerchief through its collar and moved off once more, with the dog still straining and whimpering.

9   It was about forty yards to the gallows. I watched the bare brown back of the prisoner marching in front of me. He walked clumsily with his bound arms, but quite steadily, with that bobbing gait of the Indian who never straightens his knees. At each step his muscles slid neatly into place, the lock of hair on his scalp danced up and down, his feet printed themselves on the wet gravel. And once, in spite of the men who gripped him by each shoulder, he stepped lightly aside to avoid a puddle on the path.

10   It is curious; but till that moment I had never realized what it means to destroy a healthy, conscious man. When I saw the prisoner step aside to avoid the puddle, I saw the mystery, the unspeakable wrongness, of cutting a life short when it is in full tide. This man was not dying, he was alive just as we are alive. All the organs of his body were working—bowels digesting food, skin renewing itself, nails growing, tissues forming—all toiling away in solemn foolery. His nails would still be growing when he stood on the drop, when he was falling through the air with a tenth-of-a-second to live. His eyes saw the yellow gravel and the grey walls, and his brain still remembered, foresaw, reasoned—even about puddles. He and we were a party of men walking together, seeing, hearing, feeling, understanding the same world; and in two minutes, with a sudden snap, one of us would be gone—one mind less, one world less.

11   The gallows stood in a small yard, separate from the main grounds of the prison, and overgrown with tall prickly weeds. It was a brick erection like three sides of a shed, with planking on top, and above that two beams and a crossbar with the rope dangling. The hangman, a greyhaired convict in the white uniform of the prison, was waiting beside his machine. He greeted us with a servile crouch as we entered. At a word from Francis the two warders, gripping the prisoner more closely than ever, half led, half pushed him to the gallows and helped him clumsily up the ladder. Then the hangman climbed up and fixed the rope around the prisoner's neck.

12   We stood waiting, five yards away. The warders had formed in a rough circle round the gallows. And then, when the noose was fixed, the prisoner began crying out to his god. It was a high, reiterated cry of "Ram! Ram! Ram! Ram!" not urgent and fearful like a prayer or cry for help, but steady, rhythmical, almost like the tolling of a bell. The dog answered the sound with a whine. The hangman, still standing on the gallows, produced a small cotton bag like a flour bag and drew it down over the prisoner's face. But the sound, muffled by the cloth, still persisted, over and over again: "Ram! Ram! Ram! Ram! Ram!"

13 The hangman climbed down and stood ready, holding the lever. Minutes seemed to pass. The steady, muffled crying from the prisoner went on and on, "Ram! Ram! Ram!" never faltering for an instant. The superintendent, his head on his chest, was slowly poking the ground with his stick; perhaps he was counting the cries, allowing the prisoner a fixed number—fifty, perhaps, or a hundred. Everyone had changed colour. The Indians had gone grey like bad coffee, and one or two of the bayonets were wavering. We looked at the lashed, hooded man on the drop, and listened to his cries—each cry another second of life; the same thought was in all our minds; oh, kill him quickly, get it over, stop that abominable noise!

14 Suddenly the superintendent made up his mind. Throwing up his head he made a swift motion with his stick. "Chalo!" he shouted almost fiercely.

15 There was a clanking noise, and then dead silence. The prisoner had vanished, and the rope was twisting on itself. I let go of the dog, and it galloped immediately to the back of the gallows; but when it got there it stopped short, barked, and then retreated into a corner of the yard, where it stood among the weeds, looking timorously out at us. We went round the gallows to inspect the prisoner's body. He was dangling with his toes pointed straight downwards, very slowly revolving, as dead as a stone.

16 The superintendent reached out with his stick and poked the bare brown body; it oscillated slightly. "*He's* all right," said the superintendent. He backed out from under the gallows, and blew out a deep breath. The moody look had gone out of his face quite suddenly. He glanced at his wrist-watch. "Eight minutes past eight. Well, that's all for this morning, thank God."

17 The warders unfixed bayonets and marched away. The dog, sobered and conscious of having misbehaved itself, slipped after them. We walked out of the gallows yard, past the condemned cells with their waiting prisoners, into the big central yard of the prison. The convicts, under the command of warders armed with lathis, were already receiving their breakfast. They squatted in long rows, each man holding a tin pannikin, while two warders with buckets marched around ladling out rice; it seemed quite a homely, jolly scene, after the hanging. An enormous relief had come upon us now that the job was done. One felt an impulse to sing, to break into a run, to snigger. All at once everyone began chattering gaily.

18 The Eurasian boy walking beside me nodded towards the way we had come, with a knowing smile: "Do you know, sir, our friend (he meant the dead man) when he heard his appeal had been dismissed, he pissed on the floor of his cell. From fright. Kindly take one of my cigarettes, sir. Do you not admire my new silver case, sir? From the boxwallah, two rupees eight annas. Classy European style."

19 Several people laughed—at what, nobody seemed certain.

20 Francis was walking by the superintendent, talking garrulously: "Well, sir, all has passed off with the utmost satisfactoriness. It was all finished—flick! Like that. It iss not always so—oah, no! I have known cases where the doctor was obliged to go beneath the gallows and pull the prissoner's legs to ensure decease. Most disagreeable!"

21 "Wriggling about, eh? That's bad," said the superintendent.

22 "Ach, sir, it iss worse when they become refractory! One man, I recall, clung to the bars of hiss cage when we went to take him out. You will scarcely credit, sir, that it took six warders to dislodge him, three pulling at each leg. We reasoned with him, 'My dear fellow,' we said, 'think of all the pain and trouble you are causing to us!' But no, he would not listen! Ach, he wass very troublesome!"

23 I found that I was laughing quite loudly. Everyone was laughing. Even the superintendent grinned in a tolerant way. "You'd better all come out and have a drink," he said quite genially. "I've got a bottle of whisky in the car. We could do with it."

24   We went through the big double gates of the prison into the road. "Pulling at his legs!" exclaimed a Burmese magistrate suddenly, and burst into a loud chuckling. We all began laughing again. At that moment Francis' anecdote seemed extraordinarily funny. We all had a drink together, native and European alike, quite amicably. The dead man was a hundred yards away. ○

RESPONDING TO ORWELL'S NARRATIVE

1. What specific details about the place and the people help you visualize the scene in paragraphs 1 and 2?

2. Orwell uses dialogue in several places. Find and copy the most effective use of dialogue in the narrative and explain why it is effective for you.

3. What tense does Orwell use in his narrative? Find three effective action words.

4. Reread the essay, circling any cue words or phrases that serve as time markers to keep the sequence of events clear.

5. Notice that like Ueda, Lee, and Redmond, Orwell shares his personal reaction to the event on a moment-to-moment basis. In fact, much of the success of Orwell's narration stems from the writer's communication of feelings both during and immediately after the event. Return to the essay and underline all of Orwell's reactions to the situation.

6. In titling his narrative simply "A Hanging" and in recounting this event by sharing his feelings rather than denouncing capital punishment, Orwell makes his point effectively and accomplishes his purpose. In what way does the concluding paragraph reinforce Orwell's point?

7. Does it bother you that Orwell never reveals the man's crime? Explain and support your reaction.

RESPONDING TO YOUR OWN NARRATIVE DRAFT

Once you have a draft of an essay using narration, respond to your draft by completing the following activities:

1. Find and label in your draft all specific details about the place and people connected with the event you're recounting.

2. Find and label any use of dialogue. (Check the handbook to see if this dialogue is correctly punctuated.) If you would like to include dialogue in your draft, experiment by adding a sentence or two of dialogue.

3. Experiment with tense by changing all action words from past to present tense. (Pencil these changes in or keep a copy of your original draft if you are drafting on the computer.) Compare the two versions of your essay to decide which tense is more effective for your particular narration.

4. Search your draft for cue words signaling time order for the reader. Circle these and mark any places where the order of events might not be clear. Add cue words and rearrange details if necessary.

5. Reread your draft, noting places where your moment-to-moment reaction to the event would help your audience feel a part of the action. Mark these spots and then add your reaction where appropriate.

6. Examine your draft's title and conclusion. Will the title capture the reader's interest without giving too much away? Will your conclusion offer closure and communicate the significance of the event to your audience just as Orwell's conclusion does? Evaluate and make appropriate revisions.

7. Is there any material that in rethinking the draft you might prefer to cut? For example, in his preliminary draft, Orwell may have mentioned the man's crime; he might later have decided that this information did not relate to the main point he was trying to develop in his narrative. Make necessary deletions in your own draft.

For more essays using narration, please refer to the following essays in Part 4: "We're Lying: Safe Sex and White Lies in the Time of AIDS," "Delivering the Goods," and "Facing Down Abusers."

For more essays using illustration, please refer to the following essays in Part 4: "The Path of Books and Bootstraps," and "Illusions are Forever."

CRITICAL THINKING
In Connecting Texts

In this chapter, you've read examples of narration and illustration. A writer may use narration, like other methods of development, for an entire essay or for a portion of an essay that uses multiple methods of development. For an example of the latter, turn again to Edward Hoagland's "Stuttering Time" (p. 86). Notice that the writer introduces his essay with a narration—he tells the story of his friend who stutters. Then in paragraph 3 Hoagland uses illustration—to support his point that "brusqueness in business" is getting more pronounced all the time, whereby the writer gives his audience a specific example. Working with a partner, refer to other essays in earlier chapters of this book and see how many examples you can find of essay development by use of narration or illustration. Jot down the titles of the essays as you work together. See if you can also discover the following for each essay you examine:

• How the narrative supports the writer's thesis

• What point of view and tense the writer used

• If the writer used dialogue

If time permits, share your findings with the class.

Chapter **10**

Observing the World: Description and Definition

To see a world in a grain of sand
And a heaven in a wild flower,
Hold infinity in the palm of your hand
And eternity in an hour.

—from "Auguries of Innocence" by William Blake, *eighteenth-century English poet and artist*

Preview

In this chapter you will learn

- To develop your powers of observation and investigation
- To recognize the characteristics of effective description
- To write an essay using descriptive detail
- To identify the characteristics of effective definition
- To write an essay using various strategies and sources of definition: from a dictionary and a thesaurus to books of quotations and encyclopedias
- To differentiate between connotative and denotative words
- To use comparison to strengthen description and definition

After reading this chapter and completing all practice activities, you will be able to use description and definition as patterns of development in your essays.

When was the last time that you took the opportunity to *observe* a flower, as Blake suggests, rather than vaguely glimpse it out of the corner of your eye? The last time you went to the bank or worked your way through the checkout line at the supermarket, did you notice the people around you? In our fast-paced world, there is often little time for the rewarding art of careful observation.

This chapter focuses on description and definition, two patterns of essay development that rely on your ability to observe something within your world—to notice it carefully—and then clearly communicate that observation to an audience. Both of these patterns are invaluable in developing sentences, paragraphs, and entire essays.

CHARACTERISTICS OF DESCRIPTION

Description is a writing strategy that depicts an observable subject with vivid sensory details. If you are describing the rose you observed on the walk to your classroom or office, you might convey its smell, texture, exact coloration, and shape, right down to that drop of dew glistening on one freshly opened outer petal.

To get an idea of how description works to develop material, read the following excerpt:

> He and my father went bowling together, and I was sometimes allowed to tag along. I didn't particularly care for the sport, but I loved Castle's Bowling Alley, a dark, narrow (only four lanes) low-ceilinged basement establishment that smelled of cigar smoke and floor wax. I loved to put my bottle of Nehi grape soda right next to my father's beer bottle on the scorecard holder and to slide my shoes under the bench with my father's when we changed into bowling shoes. I loved the sounds, the heavy clunk of the ball dropped on wood, its rumble down the alley, the clatter of pins, and above it all, men's shouts—"Go, go, gogogo!" "Get *in* there!" "Drop, *drop*!" Then the muttered curses while they waited for the pin boy to reset the pins. When I was in Castle's Alley I felt, no matter how many women or children might also be there, as though I had gained admittance to a men's enclave, as though I had *arrived.*
>
> —Larry Watson, from *Montana 1948*

Notice that Watson's description contains the following characteristics:

- **It focuses on an observable subject.**
  For Watson, the subject is Castle's Bowling Alley. The writer informs the audience of the subject early in the description.

- **It uses sensory detail—specific details related to the senses.**
  For instance, Watson's phrase "dark, narrow . . . low-ceilinged basement establishment" uses visual imagery; "smelled of cigar smoke and floor wax" appeals to the reader's sense of smell; "slide my shoes under the bench" incorporates the sense of touch; the phrases "heavy clunk of the ball dropped on wood, its rumble down the alley, the clatter of pins and above it all, men's shouts" appeal to the reader's sense of hearing.

- **It relates the detail in an order that allows the reader to grasp the subject, using cue words to form transitions from one detail to the next.**
  Watson moves the reader visually from the ceiling to the bowling lanes and benches with such cue words as "next to," "under," and "down."

To see how description works within a college essay, read the following model and see how many of the characteristics just discussed you can identify.

MODEL WITH KEY QUESTIONS

Brenda Grant wanted to describe an object that has special meaning for her—a photograph of her two granddaughters. In drafting her descriptive essay, Grant referred often to this photo, which is shown here.

Model 1   ## DOUBLE A'S, DOUBLE JOYS

Brenda Grant

Brenda Grant retired from the workplace to care for her two grandchildren. Soon she was urged by her adult children to attend college. Quite anxious about her writing skills when she first returned to school, Brenda later asserted, "I've learned that I really can write. Now I rely on my life experiences to help me write my essays." Although Brenda continues to struggle with clear organization of her material in essays, she feels much more confident about her writing. Upon completing community college requirements, Brenda plans to leave retirement to become a child care coordinator.

1   Alexia and Ashley, my granddaughters, are the two joys of my life. Alexia is almost four years old, and Ashley, the baby, is a year and a half. They're both beautiful in their youth and enthusiasm for life. I became a part of their enthusiasm when for a while, I was the grandmother who took care of them. When their mother, Tiffany, was in the army and their father, Moses, drove a school bus, out of necessity I became Alexia and Ashley's baby-sitter, cook, and playmate. Today, although the girls live far away from me, I carry a special picture of Alexia and Ashley in my wallet.

2   Whenever I look at this picture of "my two A's" sitting together with smiles on their faces, I remember picture day at Lock Child Care Center. I dressed both girls alike and took them to school. Upon seeing them, the cameraman said, "We will call this picture two sisters in love." In the picture, Alexia wears a white ribbon in her longer, wavy hair, while Ashley's little bit of much curlier hair is held in place on top of her head with a small yellow plastic barrette. Ashley and Alexia both wear white, short-sleeved shirts with small yellow sunflowers. Their pants are blue-checked with the same sunflower pattern featured in their shirts. They both wear dark blue tennies. The picture background is a giant yellow crayon box on the left and a huge blue crayon with lighter blue background to the right. Across the girls' legs is a red crayon, which both Alexia and Ashley are holding as they sit on a blue carpeted step.

3   In spite of their almost identical clothing, I can see differences in my granddaughters' personalities when I look at their facial expressions in this picture. Alexia, who has a larger smile on her face revealing her teeth, is more outgoing and friendly. She's like a playful pup. Ashley, whose eyebrows are raised as she looks up at the cameraman, can be as timid as a mouse around strangers. Although both girls enjoy playing with their friends, in this picture Ashley has

carefully positioned her hands in a way that reminds me of how much she likes to be the boss when she is playing. In contrast, Alexia's hand positioning is more carefree, and her bandaged finger reveals one of her traits: she often gets hurt in her play.

4   I remember that right after this picture was taken, Ashley looked around at the school and said to Alexia, "I'm a big girl like you and I want to go to school with you, Alexia." Now that the girls' mother is stationed in Atlanta, Georgia, their father and Alexia and Ashley have also moved to Atlanta so they can all be together. I grew so close to my granddaughters because of my responsibilities looking after them, and now I find this picture helps me remember them when I get lonely. ○

Key Questions

1. **Purpose**   Is Grant's purpose to convey factual information or express a dominant impression of her subject?

2. **Focus**   How does Grant limit her subject?

3. **Material**   What kinds of details does Grant use to describe her subject?

4. **Structure**   How would you describe Grant's organization of the material?

5. **Style**   Find one example of precise word choice that helps in communicating Grant's subject to her audience. Why do you find it effective in describing the subject?

GUIDELINES FOR WRITING DESCRIPTION

Consider Audience and Purpose

Whether you use description as a pattern of development for all or merely a part of your essay, you will be describing in order to convey one or both of the following to your audience:

- *Factual information about your subject:* In this case your purpose is **objective**—having to do with facts rather than feelings or impressions about a subject.

- *Dominant impression of your subject:* In this case your purpose is **subjective**—stressing feelings and impressions rather than factual information about your subject.

For example, if you want to describe a particular planet for an astronomy class, you will be relying on factual information. If, however, you want to express to a group of peers the effect that a certain room or book had on you when you were a child, your supporting detail would probably be a mixture of facts and sensory impressions. You state your objective or subjective purpose for a descriptive essay in your thesis. If you are writing a descriptive paragraph, you state this purpose in your topic sentence.

In "Double A's, Double Joys," Grant uses factual detail, such as the colors and patterns of the girls' clothing and the arrangement of their hair. Grant also expresses her feelings about her subject when she states, "Today, although the girls live far away from me, I carry a special picture of Alexia and Ashley in my wallet." While Grant's impressions about her subject are appropriate for an audience seeking information about her relationship with her granddaughters, impressions or feelings about a subject presented in astronomy class would be inappropriate for an audience wanting factual information on a planet.

Once you think you have a subject you'd like to explore, make sure that you consider *who* might be interested in learning more about the subject and *why* you want to describe a particular subject. Who will form your reading audience and what overall effect do you want to have on that audience?

Practice 10.1   Work with a partner and examine the following subjects for description, filling in a possible audience and purpose for each. The first example has been completed for you.

Subject	Audience	Purpose
1. The internal organs	*A group of pre-med students*	*Offer factual information*
2. The view from the tallest building in the city		
3. An old photograph of a relative		
4. Your favorite restaurant		
5. Jealousy in a relationship		
6. A black widow spider with its prey		
7. Your most meaningful physical possession		
8. An unforgettable person		
9. A necessary piece of equipment for your career		
10. A personalized family ritual ❏		

Focus Range of Subject

As you can see from the list in the preceding practice, your subject may be anything that you first observe and then describe. While some subjects from the list are concrete, others are abstract. Both kinds of subjects are capable of being observed and described using the strategies in this chapter.

- **Concrete subjects** possess physical properties—for example, your cousin Jake or the way the street looks from your bedroom window. You observe concrete subjects with your eyes, ears, and the rest of your senses.

- **Abstract subjects** possess no physical properties but still exist as an idea, concept, or principle. For example, democracy and kindness are concepts that certainly exist even though we cannot see, taste, or hear them; we can only observe examples of democracy or the characteristics of kindness.

Practice 10.2 Return to the list in Practice 10.1 and indicate next to each subject "C" for concrete or "A" for abstract. ❏

In choosing a subject for description, make sure your subject is limited enough to be described vividly. If you're going to write a two- to three-page essay about your grandmother's house, you might be most successful if you restrict your focus to, say, the kitchen and adjacent backyard—describing all the sights, smells, and sounds associated only with these two areas rather than the entire house.

To illustrate, examine a thesis by one student that forecasts his subject for description and includes the writer's dominant impression:

> I'll always remember my grandmother's kitchen and backyard as a place that made me feel secure, warm, and protected from the outside world.
>
> —Bryant Burns, *student*

The kitchen and backyard areas form the writer's subject; the dominant impression is Burns's feeling of security, warmth, and protection.

If your purpose is objective, you will want to keep your own feelings minimal and give your audience only factual information. You might limit your subject as in the following thesis:

> While we know much about our Sun, several of the Sun's characteristics are yet to be fully understood by scientists.
>
> —Charles Kim, *student*

Practice 10.3 Return to the ten subjects you listed under "Audience" and "Purpose" in Practice 10.1. On a separate sheet of paper, write a thesis for each subject, considering carefully the audience and purpose you have indicated. ❏

Select Important Details

You may find that you adjust the focus on your subject after you begin to prewrite to discover important details. Once you have a list or cluster of details, you'll notice that several of these traits tend to develop one dominant impression or controlling idea. At this point, choose those details that focus on your narrowed subject and put aside those that don't seem to relate.

For example, when Burns first began to gather details for his final thesis, he included his grandmother's entire house in his tentative thesis. The following is Burns's preliminary listing for his subject:

Grass in front yard so green it looked unreal, neatly trimmed, had a hill we rolled down

Rose bushes near the porch
From kitchen came smell of fresh bread or biscuits, homemade, pot roast,
    sweet potato pie
Big picture window in living room, fireplace, trophies and awards
    on mantel
Gigantic chairs in kitchen - we used to sit here with big cups of milk
Old fashioned stove, spice rack with little white jars over stove
Another picture window by kitchen table - looked out on back yard
Dog house in back yard, big lemon tree, gate for neighbor, who was a
    creepy old lady
Apricot tree, plum tree
Grass here was like blanket tucked perfectly in a bed
Smells of grass, old leaves, over-ripe fallen fruit, buzzing flies

When Burns reviewed this list, he found that he had many more telling details connected with his grandmother's kitchen and backyard than he did for the rest of the house. At this point, he sorted and selected the details he would use in his description. He set aside details that did not relate to the kitchen or the backyard.

If you are describing an abstract subject, you won't be able to "observe" your subject by using your senses. But you will be able to think about the subject and how you might focus on a particular aspect of it to describe. Let's say you've been asked to write an essay describing your previous work experience. You could use your powers of observation to note all of the jobs you have ever held. Then you could recall in detail your job duties associated with each position.

Whether your subject is concrete or abstract, be sure to keep gathering information in your prewriting until you have more than enough specific detail. That way, you can be selective with what you later choose.

Practice 10.4 Take a few minutes to observe with all your senses the room you are in now. On a separate sheet of paper, cluster or list details about the room that relate to each other. When you've finished, exchange your cluster or list with a partner, and ask your partner to evaluate the effectiveness of your detail. If the person had never seen the room before, would he or she be able to visualize it based on your information, or is the impression of the room vague? If the latter is true, return to your own list or cluster and gather more information.   ❏

Follow a Clear Order

If you reexamine Grant's essay (p. 210–211), you'll notice a spatial order. Grant begins her detailed description in paragraph 2 with her granddaughters' hair, and then she describes the girls' shirts, pants, and shoes. At this point, Grant introduces descriptive detail about the background of the photograph. Spatial order works well for this visual description.

In paragraph 3 of Grant's essay, the concrete subject—the photograph of the two granddaughters—is still being described. At this point, Grant wanted to convey to her audience the connection between this concrete subject, the photo, and what it represents to her: the more abstract subject of her granddaughters' personalities. In this paragraph, Grant's order is logical rather than spatial. Grant describes Alexia's large smile and what it reveals about her personality, and then she discusses Ashley's expression with its revelation of her personality. Grant shifts her focus to the hands of each girl, explaining how their positioning in the photo reveals clues about each granddaughter's personality.

The bottom line for organizing a description is this: Consider your subject, audience, and purpose, and then come up with the best organizational plan to communicate your subject to your readers. Whatever order you decide to use, signal your audience with appropriate cue words, referring if necessary to the list on pages 141–142.

Practice 10.5   Review Burns's thesis and his original prewriting list (p. 213) and then complete the following.

1. Cross out any details in his list that do not clearly relate to his thesis.

2. Number the remaining items in the list in the most effective order for a clear description.   ❏

Use Vivid Words

If your subject for description is concrete, use words or phrases that appeal to your audience's sense of sight, hearing, touch, taste, and smell. For example, when Watson describes Castle's Bowling Alley (p. 209), he uses the phrases "the heavy *clunk* of the ball dropped on wood" and "the *clatter* of pins." Notice that these words appeal much more specifically to his readers' physical world than phrases like "the *sound* of the ball" or "the *noise* of the pins" would have.

If, on the other hand, your subject for description is abstract, you will find it helpful to use comparisons, especially similes and metaphors. Often the thoughtful use of a **metaphor** (an indirect comparison of one thing with another) or a **simile** (a direct comparison of one thing with another using *like* or *as*) will enable your audience to get a clear and instantaneous picture of the subject you are describing. Be advised, however, that an overused or "stale" simile or metaphor will not help you communicate your subject. How do you know whether your comparison is stale or fresh? A good test is the following: If you believe that another person reading your simile or metaphor might be able to finish the comparison without actually reading the entire phrase, you know that this comparison has been overused. For example, if you see "gentle as a _____," you think of *lamb* as the missing word. If you were to see or hear "stubborn as a _____," you'd no doubt think of *mule.* In contrast, fresh similes or metaphors allow the reader to think about the comparison and make connections, rather than tune out the much-used expression.

Practice 10.6   Return to Grant's essay "Double A's, Double Joys" (p. 210) and circle any similes or metaphors you find. Decide whether you think the comparisons Grant uses are fresh or could be improved. For additional practice with comparisons, see the "Responding to Writing" section at the end of this chapter. ❏

Strategies for Writing Description

1. **Purpose**   Determine your audience, then decide whether you want to share factual information, convey your dominant impression about the subject, or both.

2. **Focus**   Choose a concrete or abstract subject, observe it carefully, record your observations, and narrow the subject so that you can describe it fully.

3. **Material**   Gather more than enough details; then choose those that most effectively paint a word picture of your subject. Include sensory as well as factual details when appropriate.

4. **Structure**   Let the nature of your subject guide you in organizing your description. Use cue words to signal your readers.

5. **Style**   Use vivid words whenever possible, and employ effective comparisons, especially when describing abstract subjects.

OPTIONS FOR WRITING DESCRIPTION

Each writing option asks you to use the descriptive strategies you have been practicing. Find a subject for which you have a strong feeling and a fair amount of factual information. In gathering material for your drafts, use your powers of observation to their fullest. If your subject is concrete, you might begin by using your senses to experience and then to record physical features. If your subject is abstract, think about the kinds of comparisons and details that would help make your subject vivid for an audience.

1. Describe a place you have called "home," or a particular part of that home. Use descriptive detail to communicate the impression this special place made on you.

2. Describe a person, place, or animal you have observed over a period of several days. Engage in close observation of your subject, recording your findings in the form of daily notes. Write a descriptive essay detailing your subject.

3. In her essay "Double A's, Double Joys," Grant describes a photograph that affected her. Search for a photo that moves you in some way—this may be a picture of a relative, friend, or total stranger. Write a descriptive essay in which you include information on the person, the clothing, actions, facial expressions, background, and the person's relationship to other objects in the picture. Tie all this descriptive detail together in your thesis indicating the dominant impression the photo has on you.

4. Visit an art gallery on or off campus or find a good-quality reproduction of a painting or drawing. Describe this work of art. You might combine factual information with your dominant impression of the work.

5. Write an essay describing the word *courage.* You might want to describe this word in modern terms and contrast it with a description of the concept in an earlier time, say, the nineteenth century.

6. Write an essay describing an object or an article of clothing, jewelry, or furniture that is symbolic of your ethnic culture or your religious background. For example, you might describe a menorah, a statue of the Virgin of Guadalupe, or a shawl or jacket given to you by a relative. You can begin by observing the object closely, and then you might want to gather more material by recalling the significance and history of the object. You might even interview a family or community member for additional information on your subject.

7. Write a report describing a particular place on your college campus that is in dire need of repair, remodeling, or redesign. If your purpose is to persuade administrators, student body members, or your board of trustees to consider renovation, you will want to remain objective in your report and provide as much detail as possible.

8. Take a notebook and pen or pencil with you to a coffee shop, library, park, or other gathering place. Choose one person to observe and write as many details as you can about that person. For example, you might want to record approximate age, height, weight, clothing colors and style, body build, posture, demeanor, vocal tone, and personality displayed. Compile your information into a fascinating descriptive essay.

9. *(Film and Literature)* After finding information on Malcolm X using the Internet or your college or local library, view Spike Lee's film *Malcolm X.* Describe Malcolm as depicted in the film—what was his personality? His relationship with women? Some strengths and weaknesses?

10. *(Service Learning)* Visit the Big Brothers or Big Sisters organization of your city; ask the authorities there if you could arrange to interview a former participant. In your interview, ask your subject to fully describe his or her experience in the organization. Write an essay describing your subject's experiences.

If both description and definition are based on careful observation, how do these two patterns of essay development differ? Recall the rose mentioned earlier in this chapter. Think again about how you might write a description of a rose: You would want to give your readers so much detail that they could *sense*—see, smell, and feel—that particular rose. Examine the following verse describing two roses:

The red rose whispers of passion
And the white rose breathes of love.

—John Boyle O'Reilly, from "A White Rose"

Now suppose that you were asked to define a rose. You might use description as well as other strategies for defining, but your aim would be to set boundaries for your reader—you would want to communicate all of the essential characteristics differentiating a rose from all other flowers. The following definition establishes these boundaries in only a few words:

> Any of a genus of shrubs . . . with prickly stems, alternate compound leaves, and five-parted, usually fragrant flowers.
>
> —*Webster's New World Dictionary*

CHARACTERISTICS OF DEFINITION

Definition is a statement of the exact nature of a subject, including what the subject is and is not. Defining involves detailing all distinguishing characteristics clearly—so that your audience readily grasps the difference between an *espresso* and other coffee drinks, for example. In your everyday conversation, you probably use definition without being aware of it. Every time someone asks you, "What is that?" you attempt to explain distinguishing features of concrete as well as abstract terms by defining them. "An espresso is a coffee prepared in a special machine that forces steam," you may answer. And in order to define this subject or any other, you need to observe it from a variety of angles to determine its unique traits.

To see how definition works within an essay, read the following:

> In its narrowest sense, violence is defined as an act carried out with the intention of causing physical pain or injury to another. But in real life, severe physical violence is only one extreme of a whole spectrum of aggressive behavior that ranges from "verbal violence"—screaming, shouting, saying vicious, spiteful things—to banging one's fist on the table and slamming doors to actually pushing, hitting, kicking, and throwing things at or beating another person.
>
> —Shari Miller Sims, from "Violent Reactions"

Notice that Sims's definition has the following characteristics:

- **It focuses on an observable subject.**
  As with the subject for description, the subject for definition may be concrete or abstract, but it must be capable of being carefully noticed or studied. Sims's subject is violence, the term she highlights early in the paragraph.

- **It uses a variety of detail to establish boundaries on the subject.**
  For example, Sims defines violence by giving a "narrow" dictionary definition, and then she offers a "real-life" definition—her detail here is a series of examples of violent behavior.

- **It helps readers recognize the subject, even in new or different contexts.**
  After reading Sims's paragraph, readers have a better grasp of the term *violence* and they understand what it is and is not.

To see how definition works within a college essay, read the following model and see how many of these characteristics of definition you can identify.

MODEL WITH KEY QUESTIONS

After reading both "A Black Athlete Looks at Education" by Arthur Ashe (p. 24) and "Ambition" by Perri Klass (p. 348), Ravinder Degun became intrigued by the term *delayed gratification*. She wanted to address an audience of college students who she felt might not understand fully the meaning of this term.

Model 2   ### BETTER LATE THAN NEVER

Ravinder Degun

Ravinder Degun confides that taking writing classes has greatly improved her writing abilities. Having moved from northern India to the United States with her family several years ago, Ravinder works in West Los Angeles as a registered nurse. She hopes to transfer from El Camino to the University of California system, where she plans to receive a B.S. degree in the biological sciences.

1   *Delayed gratification* can be defined as the present hardships and struggles one endures in the hope of achieving a rewarding, satisfying, and brighter future later in life. Through examples presented by two authors of professional readings in our textbook and from firsthand observations, we can see that while situations involving delayed gratification are challenging and far from stress-free, these situations reward the ambitious with life-long gifts.

2   Arthur Ashe in his essay "A Black Athlete Looks at Education" focuses on the concept of delayed gratification. Ashe emphasizes the importance of education within the African-American community, challenging the belief that African-Americans can do better only in entertainment and sports. Ashe prioritizes higher education, believing that although achieving higher education may offer delayed rather than immediate gratification, the outcome is going to last throughout one's life, contrasted with sports and entertainment, which may offer immediate fame and riches, but endure only for a short time. Ashe accepts the fact that African-Americans' greatest heroes of the twentieth century have been athletes like Jack Johnson, Joe Louis, and Muhammad Ali. But he asserts that this is because racial and economical discrimination over the years encouraged African-Americans to channel their energies into athletics and entertainment since these were the only known ways to break out of ghetto existence. Ashe conveys the message to his high school audience that for every hour they spend on the athletic field, they should spend two hours in the library.

3   In her essay "Ambition," Perri Klass also tackles the value of delayed gratification by providing examples of some very ambitious individuals who are so consumed by drive and overdrive that nothing they sacrifice on the way to success has any value at all; everything they do is being done only because it will

one day get them where they want to be. Klass uses medical training as an excellent example of a field requiring delayed gratification. A medical student spends many years in a medical school, then in residency working with a miserable schedule and staying up late most nights, reminding himself or herself that one day all this relentless work will be replaced by a productive and more normal life.

4   The majority of individuals who have experienced the necessity for delayed gratification are somewhat able to succeed and consider it a positive and worthwhile learning experience. In very rare cases, however, especially with some overly ambitious and emotionally or psychologically affected individuals, the outcome of living lives of delayed gratification can be traumatic. A friend, Reena, was brought up by grandparents since her parents had passed away. When she was about ten years old, Reena's grandfather also died. Reena was too young at this time to realize the hardships that her grandmother would have to face raising her. Reena was able to stay in school until graduation because of the grandmother's hard work at home as a sewing machinist. Finally Reena's grandmother revealed that she had been suffering from metastatic breast cancer for almost a year. Reena was traumatized, but nevertheless she took a crash course, became a nursing assistant, and began working night shifts. At the same time this young woman began working on an associate's degree program, advancing from RN to BSN. When Reena's grandmother died, Reena realized how much of an inspiration and a motivator her grandmother had been for her.

5   While having to delay her gratification worked for Reena, in another relative's situation it has been a far from satisfactory experience. For this relative, an only daughter whose overly protective parents voiced high expectations, the pressure to achieve resulted in her falling in with bad company and becoming as rebellious as a wild stallion. However, after the death of her father, this person transformed herself into a serious and completely isolated student. Unfortunately, over the next two years she experienced a nervous breakdown, spent hours in therapy, and remained withdrawn and depressed much of the time. This obviously is a rare case in which the outcome of delaying her gratification did not turn out as positively as might have been hoped.

6   On the whole, the assertions of Arthur Ashe and Perri Klass, as well as personal observations by this writer reveal that while delayed gratification can be precarious for our emotional well-being, it can also build confidence and self-esteem while rewarding us with major long-term benefits.   ○

Key Questions

1. **Purpose**   What clues tell you that Degun is addressing a college audience? By the end of the essay, what have you learned about the term that you didn't know before?

2. **Focus**   Find Degun's thesis and underline it in the essay. After reading the essay, do you agree with her main point? (Support your position with specific evidence.)

3. **Material**   Identify three sources the writer uses for material.

4. **Structure**   How is the essay organized—chronologically, spatially, or logically?

5. **Style**   Find the most memorable phrase in the essay and underline it.

GUIDELINES FOR WRITING DEFINITION

Consider Audience and Purpose

Once you have a tentative subject for your definition, consider the background of your target audience. In your drafting, you will want to think about the level of familiarity your audience has with your subject. If you are defining a term with which your audience is already familiar, such as Smith does with the term *violence*, your purpose might be to introduce a new perspective. If your audience is completely unfamiliar with your subject, as with the term *delayed gratification* in Degun's essay, your purpose might be to educate and inform. For example, you might want to inform by defining sexual harassment to an audience of office workers, defining supply-side economics as part of a research paper for an economics class, defining multiculturalism in an essay for a sociology class, or defining "hip-hop" for a report in a music class.

Practice 10.7 Work with a partner and examine the following subjects for definition, filling in a possible audience and purpose for each. The first example has been completed for you.

Subject	Audience	Purpose
1. The modern family	*A group of family counselors and psychologists*	*Persuade to accept new definition*
2. The term *biodegradable*		
3. A yellow-bellied sapsucker		
4. A star (a celestial body)		
5. A star (a celebrity)		
6. A college freshman		
7. Gay rights		
8. A microchip		
9. The French Revolution		
10. Date rape ❑		

Determine Range of Subject

If your subject is concrete and your purpose is to inform, you might need only a sentence or two for your definition. Many college essays, however, will ask you to write about abstract ideas and issues. For such essays, you will need more than a few sentences to allow your audience to understand your subject.

Depending on your audience and your purpose, you have two kinds of definition strategies to choose from:

- **Simple definition**
  A brief statement describing the exact nature of a subject in one or two sentences. For example, in an essay describing new office technologies for a business class, you might find the following simple definition: "Notebook computers are portable computers, often weighing less than 5 pounds, that can run on either battery or electrical power and can perform all of the functions of a standard desktop computer."

  This one-sentence definition allows the reader to continue the essay without having to stop to look up a technical or specialized term. Simple definitions are often a courtesy to the reader; if your audience is interested in your topic but probably isn't made up of experts, you will want to be alert to places where a simple definition might be helpful.

- **Extended definition**
  Statements describing the exact nature of a subject and involving several sentences, paragraphs, or even an entire essay. This strategy works if your subject is abstract or complex, or if your purpose in providing the definition is to persuade your audience to understand your subject in a unique way. You might also use several strategies rather than just one to define your term. To see how an extended definition works, reexamine the essays by Degun (p. 219) and Naylor (p. 387).

Explore Various Kinds of Definition

In writing definitions, you have several useful strategies available for exploring sources and gathering and organizing material. You can use one strategy or many, depending on the nature and complexity of your subject, your purpose in defining, and your audience.

Dictionary Definition

This strategy is often helpful when you are trying to clarify the distinguishing characteristics of your subject. Avoid beginning your essay with "According to *Webster's*"—a dictionary definition would not be an exciting way to introduce your subject. Instead, use a dictionary definition to develop information within the body of the essay.

You may wish to consult any one of the following references found in college or local libraries or online:

- **Unabridged dictionary**
  A book that contains thousands of alphabetically listed words along with their part of speech, definition, origin, and history of usage.

- **Thesaurus**
  A book that contains an alphabetical list of words along with their **synonyms** (words with similar meaning) and their **antonyms** (words with opposing meaning).

- *Funk and Wagnall's Standard Handbook of Synonyms, Antonyms, and Prepositions*

- *Dictionary of Quotations*, *Bartlett's Familiar Quotations*, and *Gale's Quotations: Who Said What*

Practice 10.8   To see what kind of information you can gather in an essay, refer to the list on page 221 and choose one subject to look up in a dictionary, thesaurus, book of synonyms, or book of quotations. Write down your subject, the information you found, and the source you used. (Be sure to rephrase the information in your own words or use quotation marks to indicate that you found the material in another source.)   ❑

Historical Definition

If your purpose in defining your subject is to help your audience understand it in an expanded time frame, you could use a historical definition. Let's say that you want to show how a word's usage has changed through several centuries. An unabridged dictionary will give you the original meaning as well as the source of a word. Encyclopedias may offer you additional background information on your subject. For example, if you look up the term *anatomy* in an encyclopedia, you may find a long entry that begins with something like the following:

> *Anatomy:* The structural detail and critical analysis of all living organisms. Before 1543, few scientists had dissected the body.

Practice 10.9   Choose a subject that has been around long enough to have some history. Look up the meaning of the word or words in either an unabridged dictionary or an encyclopedia and summarize your findings.   ❑

Comparative Definition

An excellent way of communicating the distinguishing characteristics of your subject is to compare or contrast it with other closely related subjects. The following sentences illustrate this technique:

> *Cripple* seems to me a clean word, straightforward and precise. . . . *Disabled,* by contrast, suggests any incapacity, physical or mental. And I certainly don't like *handicapped.*
>
> —Nancy Mairs, from "On Being a Cripple"

In another kind of comparative definition, you can explain how the term may be misunderstood by stressing what it is *not.* The following is an example of definition by negation:

> Sexual harassment is no joke.
>
> —A. J. Anderson, from "Sexual Harassment Is No Joke"

Practice 10.10 Write a comparative definition to accompany both of the following subjects:

Success:

Prejudice: ❏

Definition by Example

This popular strategy allows your audience to visualize your subject instantly through illustration. Sims uses this strategy in her definition of violence (p. 218): "screaming, shouting, . . . banging one's fist on the table . . ." These phrases define by giving examples of behaviors associated with violence.

Practice 10.11 Return to the two subjects in Practice 10.10. Write down a couple of examples useful in defining each of these subjects. ❏

Practice 10.12 Reread the essays by Degun (p. 219) and Naylor (p. 387). Annotate both essays in the margin indicating the strategies for definition the authors used. ❏

Follow a Clear Order

When you've gathered enough information to define your subject clearly through the use of one or more strategies for definition, you'll want to establish a clear order for your material. If, for example, you are defining a subject using historical background, you might want to use chronological order, beginning with the oldest use of your word and then showing differences or nuances over time. You may find in another essay that spatial order makes a subject easier for readers to understand. For example, if you are defining an object with physical properties—a tornado or a rose—proceeding from bottom to top or from left to right will allow your audience to visualize the subject. Logical order is perhaps the most common method for organizing a definition. You can begin with a simple, easy-to-understand definition and then proceed to more complex strategies, building on your readers' increasing knowledge and ability to handle more intricate material. Refer to the paragraph on page 218 to see how Sims begins with a simple definition and then introduces examples to expand her definition of the term *violence*.

Use Precise Words

Denotative Meaning

The **denotative meaning** of a word is its standard dictionary definition. For example, when you say that you live in a *house*, you're using a denotative term for a place of shelter, a residence. When your audience sees the word *house*, information is conveyed; emotions and images are not.

Connotative Meaning

If, on the other hand, you say that you live in your *home,* your audience mentally notes that you refer to a residence or place of shelter. The dictionary definition is similar to the one for *house*, but your audience also pictures a *home*—quite possibly one with a roaring fire, cozy armchairs, and smells of freshly baked bread coming from the kitchen. **Connotative** words evoke particular emotional associations. *Home* is a connotative word—a word that involves readers more directly than a denotative word would. If you're trying to persuade your audience of the impact a place of residence has on a person, you will want to use connotative language. If, however, your definition is intended for an audience of real estate agents or city surveyors, you would want to use denotative language based on facts and impersonal information.

In drafting and then revising your definitions, be sure that you are using the most effective word or phrase for your purpose.

Practice 10.13   Examine the following list of words. For each word, jot down your reaction—positive, negative, or neutral. Also try to note what you associate or picture with the word. The first item has been done for you.

walk *(neutral) move forward, put one foot in front of the other.*

amble

saunter

grin

leer

smile   ❏

Avoid Circular Definitions

One type of definition strategy to avoid is the **circular definition,** a statement that renames the subject to be defined rather than offering a meaningful explanation. For example, defining *family values* as "the values that families hold dear" is about as helpful as offering no definition at all.

Practice 10.14   Rewrite the following definitions so that they genuinely explain the concept.

1. political correctness—the act of being or seeming correct politically

2. assisted suicide—suicide that is assisted in some way   ❏

Strategies for Writing Definitions

1. **Purpose**   Think about what your readers may already know about a subject, and why you want to provide them with a definition. Do you want to inform them, or do you want to present them with a new concept of the subject? Decide whether a simple or an extended definition will allow your audience to grasp your subject more effectively.

2. **Focus**   Be sure that you have focused on a sufficiently narrow subject to allow you to define it fully; at the same time, make sure that the subject is not too narrow.

3. **Material**   Gather information from a variety of sources: dictionaries, encyclopedias, books of quotations, personal observations, recollection of examples, and your imagination.

4. **Structure**   In an essay using more than one strategy for definition or defining more than one term, organize the material in such a way that you begin with simple definitions and then proceed to the more complex ones.

5. **Style**   Once you have a draft, review it to make sure that all your words—whether denotative or connotative—are precise, and that they are the best words for defining your subject clearly and distinguishing the subject by specific, limiting characteristics. Make sure to revise and eliminate any circular definitions.

OPTIONS FOR WRITING DEFINITION

The following options will allow you to explore in an essay the guidelines for definition you have been reading about and practicing. After choosing a writing option, you'll be focusing on a subject that is either concrete or abstract, just as you did with your descriptive subjects earlier in this chapter. For this assignment, your goal is to communicate the distinguishing characteristics of your subject.

1. Write an essay defining the same article of clothing, jewelry, or furniture that you described in Writing Option 6 (p. 217). This time, you will be using different strategies; rather than telling about an object, you are reporting its distinguishing characteristics. If you are defining a menorah, for example, what differentiates it from a candelabrum? Feel free to consult specialized dictionaries such as a dictionary of religious practices or a dictionary of customs.

2. Reread the paragraph by Monifa Winston in Chapter 6 (p. 116) in which she defines her subject, a college student, by using a series of action words, including the following: "*failed* a test, *read* the wrong pages for homework, *paid* over three hundred dollars for books, *bought* the wrong books." Write an essay in which you define a subject you know something about from your work experience, college major, or special interest. Try to incorporate as many examples as possible into your essay.

3. Define one of the following terms (or another of interest to you). In thinking about your purpose and audience, ask yourself if you want to inform your audience or express your personal definition.

winner	quitter	procrastinator	immigrant
freedom	obsession	tightwad	prejudice
sexual harassment	gay rights	family values	

4. Write an essay defining a term you feel is misused or in some way misunderstood. Use a variety of definition strategies, including at least one outside printed or electronic source.

5. Write an essay in which you define a subject that is a part of modern American culture, but that might not be understood by people from another culture. For example, you could define *situation comedy, yuppies, body piercing, Super Bowl Sunday,* or *fast food.*

6. Choose a term used in one of your past or present classes. This term should be one with which the average person might not be familiar. Write an essay defining this term, trying to use specific language and offering readers any illustrations, explanations, or further detail that will make your definition clear.

7. Imagine that your reading audience has recently landed on earth from Mars. Although fluent in English, these Martians are not familiar with cell phones, computers, televisions, microwaves, pagers, iPods, or other pieces of technology. Choose one of these terms and define it thoroughly in an essay.

8. After rereading the section on plagiarism (p. 170) and brainstorming with one or more class members, define this term using illustrations. Do not feel compelled to limit your illustrations of plagiarism to those taking place in classrooms.

9. *(Film and Literature)* Read Harper Lee's famous novel *To Kill a Mockingbird* and then view the film starring Academy Award–winner Gregory Peck. In an essay discuss the treatment of racism in the film and the book—how is the term defined for the audience?

10. *(Service Learning)* Make an appointment to interview your city council members or your mayor. Ask your interview subject to share with you a definition of *sexual harassment.* There may be printed guidelines or a definition of this term available, or you may want to take careful notes and ask permission to record your subject. Write an essay defining sexual harassment from the city's official point of view.

Challenge Option: Combining Patterns

Thus far in Part 2 of this book, you have read about and practiced narration, illustration, description, and definition as separate patterns that you can use to develop material in your essays. However, many writers use more than one pattern of essay development within a single essay. You will be able to combine patterns of development in your own writing if you choose to write on the challenge option that follows or appears in Chapters 11 and 12.

Writing an essay about a *Shangri-la* will allow you to use three patterns together in an essay—definition, description, and narration.

Shangri-la is defined as "any imaginary, idyllic utopia or hidden paradise." The term came into existence in 1933 as a result of a popular book called *Lost Horizon,* written by James Hilton, in which a place, Shangri-la, became a paradise. Think about the places where you've lived or visited. Pinpoint a special place that seemed like a paradise to you. In prewriting, get down as many details as you can remember. Try to use the following structure for beginning and ending the essay, but arrange the body paragraphs any way you like and don't feel limited to a fixed number of paragraphs if you find you want to expand your material:

- *Introduction:* Hook the audience, mention the subject Shangri-la, and name the particular place that is your personal paradise.

- *Body paragraph:* Define Shangri-la, using strategies for definition covered in this chapter. Consult an unabridged dictionary, encyclopedia, book of quotations, the Internet, or the 1937 film *Lost Horizon,* directed by Frank Capra.

- *Body paragraph:* Narrate your experience in this special place. Here you will be using chronological order.

- *Body paragraph:* Describe your special place. Try to incorporate sensory detail to help your audience visualize your Shangri-la. You may want to use spatial order in this paragraph.

- *Concluding paragraph:* Tie all three patterns—definition, narration, and description—together by closing with your relationship to the place.

JOURNAL WRITING: SENSORY ISOLATION AND WORD ASSOCIATION

The following activities will help you discover details for description and definition. You will be asked to try to concentrate on each of your five senses, recording your observations.

Description

1. Become a camera and record your observations of your visual world. Christopher Isherwood, a writer well known for his astute observations, confided, "I am a camera with its shutter open, quite passive, recording, not thinking." First warm up your "telephoto eye" by looking through a real camera lens, zooming in on various objects and people around you. If you don't have a camera handy, look through a pinhole in a piece of paper to focus your field of vision. Once you feel confident that your camera-like vision is functioning efficiently, you can dispense with the camera or pinhole, but continue to use your "camera eye" as you take your journal with you and record the following observations:

   - An object in your outside world—a bug, flower, leaf on a tree, piece of bark, pet

   - Objects on your desk—pens, pencils, books, stapler

   - A person you know—a relative, friend, spouse, worker

   - A person you don't know—someone waiting for a bus, sipping coffee in a coffee shop, standing in line at the grocery checkout counter

   - A favorite view

For each of these observations, try visually to "zoom in" and "zoom out," noting as you do so what new details present themselves.

2. It is a fact that our senses become more acute when not all are functioning at the same time. For this activity, close your eyes, relax, and don't cheat by peeking. For each "observation station," keep your eyes closed for at least five minutes. Then open your eyes and record everything you heard, smelled, and felt (as in the tactile sense of feeling the chair upholstery or the carpet on your bare feet) before moving to the next location for observation. Record sensory detail by completing this activity in the following locations:

   - An outdoor area such as your yard, a campus lawn, or a park

   - Your room or work area at home

   - A place where friends or relatives gather—a kitchen or family room, for example

   - A crowded place where you know no one—perhaps a coffee shop or a bowling alley, or the campus cafeteria or student union

Definition

1. Take a look at your journal entries for description. Choose a person, place, or object from these entries that seems most interesting to you. In another entry, observe the same subject from the point of view of one who tries to define the subject. This time, think of subjects that are closely related to yours, but different. What can you say about your subject that will allow the reader to understand its distinguishing characteristics? If you described a leaf on a tree before, take that same leaf and look for traits that make it unique from other types of leaves in your yard.

2. In another journal entry, freewrite on any words that set off your personal "hot button." According to a Yale University study, 12 especially potent words in the English language are the following: *save, money, you, new, health, results, easy, safety, love, discovery, proven*, and *guarantee*. What particular words somehow infuriate or inspire you, or perhaps take on special significance? Write down the words and whatever comes to mind in connection with the words without censoring your thoughts.

3. In a third journal entry, take the word you have chosen and think of precise words and effective similes or metaphors that you could use to distinguish your term from others. For example, if your "hot button" word is *health*, you might come up with the images "glowing skin," "sparkling teeth," "shiny hair," and "a gait like that of a conditioned athlete."

When you've completed these journal entries, review your findings. You may discover surprising and significant observations that may be of interest to an audience if they were developed in an essay.

Using the Computer: Developing Descriptions and Discovering New Worlds on the Web

1. You might want to try the following activity as you work through your drafts for essays using description or definition:

   Ask a friend or peer reviewer to read your draft on-screen. The reader should high-light (using bold, italics, or another format that changes the appearance of certain words) what she or he thinks is effective sensory detail. Your reader should save the text. Now reread the highlighted version. When you notice any sections or para-graphs that have few or no highlighted phrases, add additional sensory detail (either from your freewriting, your journal, or new observations). Remember to return all highlighted portions to normal type before printing out your final version.

2. If you could travel anywhere in the world, someplace you've always dreamed about but never actually visited, where would you go? Imagine that you are a travel writer for a popular magazine, and you have been sent on assignment there. To help your readers imagine this place, you will need to use sensory descriptions, and you may need to define local customs and foods. For this assignment, you can "travel" to your dream destination using the World Wide Web. To find information on your destination, see if your Web provider already has a "travel" information option. Or you could try a search engine index. Both *Yahoo!* (**http://www.yahoo.com**) and *The Argus Clearinghouse* (**http://www.clearinghouse.net**) have many options to get you started. Other interesting travel-related sites include the following:

   * *National Geographic Society* (**http://www.nationalgeographic.com**)
   * *Lonely Planet* (**http://www.lonelyplanet.com**)

   Write an article describing an imaginary trip that you take to your chosen destination, using plenty of details and descriptions based on what you learned from the Web. To help organize your article, refer to the "Challenge Option" on page 227.

3. To examine some examples of descriptive paragraphs, visit the following Web site:

   http://leo.stcloudstate.edu/acadwrite/descriptive.html

4. To see a sample definition essay, visit this Web site:

   http://leo.stcloudstate.edu/acadwrite/definition.html

RESPONDING TO WRITING: COMPARISONS

This activity will improve your writing of description and definition. It will also refresh your memory about two kinds of comparisons: simile and metaphor.

Both model essays in this chapter, "Double A's, Double Joys" (p. 210) and "Better Late Than Never" (p. 219), use simile or metaphor. When Grant states in paragraph 3 that Alexia is "like a playful pup" and that Ashley can be "as timid as a mouse," these similes give the reader a clear idea of the subject. Degun uses a simile in paragraph 5. She tells us that her relative became "as rebellious as a wild stallion."

For practice in identifying and evaluating the effectiveness of similes and metaphors, read the following descriptions and definitions, and then complete the exercises that follow for each.

My brother's wet clothes made it easy to see his strength. Most great casters I have known were big men over six feet, the added height certainly making it easier to get more line in the air in a bigger arc. My brother was only five feet ten, but he had fished so many years his body had become partly shaped by his casting. He was thirty-two now, at the height of his power, and he could put all of his body and soul into a four-and-a-half ounce magic totem pole. Long ago, he had gone far beyond my father's wrist casting, although his right wrist was always so important that it had become larger than his left. His right arm, which our father had kept tied to the side to emphasize the wrist, shot out of his shirt as if it were engineered, and it, too, was larger than his left arm.

—Norman Maclean, from *A River Runs Through It*

The chief feature of the landscape, and of your life in it, was the air. Looking back on a sojourn in the African highlands, you are struck by your feeling of having lived for a time up in the air. The sky was rarely more than pale blue or violet, with a profusion of light, weightless, ever-changing clouds towering up and sailing on it, but it had a blue vigour in it, and at a short distance it painted the ranges of hills and the woods a fresh deep blue. In the middle of the day the air was alive over the land, like a flame burning; it scintillated, waved and shone like running water, mirrored and doubled all objects, and created great Fata Morgana. Up in this high air you breathed easily, drawing in a vital assurance and lightness of heart. In the highlands you woke up in the morning and thought: Here I am, where I ought to be.

—Isak Dinesen, from *Out of Africa*

I don't mean to put a damper on things. I just mean we ought to treat fun reverently. It is a mystery. It cannot be caught like a virus. It cannot be trapped like an animal. . . . When fun comes in on little dancing feet, you probably won't be expecting it. In fact, I bet it comes when you're doing your duty, your job, or your work. It may even come on a Tuesday.

—Suzanne Britt Jordan, from "Fun. Oh Boy. Fun. You Could Die from It."

1. In the margin of each paragraph, identify the pattern of development as primarily description or definition.

2. Locate and then underline a simile or metaphor the writer used.

3. Circle the subject being described or defined in the passage.

4. Evaluate the effectiveness of each simile or metaphor in giving the reader a clear picture of the subject. Number the passages in order of effectiveness, assigning 1 to the strongest and 3 to the weakest. Be prepared to defend your choices.

Now return to your own essay drafts for description or definition. Find and underline any similes or metaphors. Evaluate their effect—are these comparisons fresh or stale? If you have none, add at least one or two comparisons.

If you have used a simile or metaphor, but your comparison is less than vivid, revise and strengthen your essay by making the necessary changes.

For more essays using definition, please refer to the following essays in Part 4: "Ambition," "The Meanings of a Word," and "The Geography of the Imagination."

For more essays using description, please refer to the essays "Our Biotech Bodies, Ourselves," and "Crazy for Dysfunction" in Part 4.

CRITICAL THINKING
In Connecting Texts

Return to the opening quotation for this chapter on page 208. In these lines, poet William Blake describes the effects of close observation on a patient and careful observer. Each of the four lines contains a separate metaphor to describe the observer's world. Throughout this chapter, you've read essays and excerpts by writers who have used not only their eyes but also their other senses to observe the world and to convey impressions and information about their subjects. While Grant focuses on concrete subjects in her essay, Degun focuses on abstract ones.

Working with a partner or small group, brainstorm to come up with two lists: one for concrete subjects for describing or defining and one for abstract subjects. Now see if you can agree within your group on a specific purpose, audience, and strategy for describing or defining each subject on your two lists. Continue your brainstorming to come up with at least one metaphor or simile that might be helpful in describing or defining each of the subjects you have listed. Keep a record of this brainstorming session to use as material for future essays.

Chapter 11

Making Connections: Process and Cause/Effect

Like narration, process suggests ongoing movement and continuous action. The emphasis in a process theme, however, is on the how, *rather than the* what.

—Frank D'Angelo, *writing teacher*

In the question of cause and effect, there can be many people who imagine that lightning is the cause of thunder because the thunder comes after the lightning. . . . but is *lightning the cause of thunder?*

—Jostein Gaarder, from *Sophie's World*

Preview

In this chapter you will learn

- How to identify the characteristics of process and cause/effect patterns of essay development
- How to write effective essays using process and cause/effect to tell readers *how* and to show them *why*
- How to use a cause/effect map to gather information and organize points
- How to recognize and use combined patterns of development within an essay
- How to improve your essays by maintaining an essay progress log
- How to create a personal time line
- How to use a computer to access information on the World Wide Web

After reading this chapter and completing its practice exercises, you will be able to use process and cause/effect as patterns of development in your essays.

Let's say your health and safety instructor has asked you to write about the recommended procedures for protecting yourself from lightning danger. To explain the steps, you'd want to use a process pattern of essay development to give your audience necessary "how-to" information. Now let's say your science instructor has asked you to write an essay explaining why lightning occurs, or what happens as a result of a lightning strike. For this essay, you'd choose a cause/effect method of essay development to show why one thing influences another.

As you can see from these examples, process and cause/effect are closely related patterns of thought and essay development. The former explains *how* and the latter investigates *why*. Process and cause/effect allow us to understand, analyze, investigate, and make connections in all aspects of our existence. You might well use both strategies—process and cause/effect—in an essay for a general college audience wanting more information on several aspects of lightning. But you would also use both strategies if you wanted to communicate, either in a conversation or through e-mail, with a group of friends planning a camping trip during a stormy time of year. This chapter will familiarize you with these two patterns of thought by showing you how to apply both process and cause/effect development to your college essays.

CHARACTERISTICS OF PROCESS

Planning a wedding, learning how to create computer files, and changing a car tire are all examples of processes. Like narration, **process** is a writing strategy that presents a series of actions, but rather than focusing on the *what* of events, it explains *how* to do something or how something works. For instance, a narrative might focus on a particular person's experience removing a tree from the front yard in order to communicate the significance of the event for the person involved. A process essay, in contrast, would focus on the steps involved in the tree removal with the intent of informing the reader of the details of the procedure. Process can also explain how something works, for example, how a telephone operates or how a character in a short story is developed. Process writing may include the actions of a person, operations of a machine, or occurrences in nature.

In the following excerpt, the writer has firsthand knowledge of his subject from personal experience, but his essay is not a narrative because he does not focus on the significance of the experience. Instead, his writing focuses on the process of finding a compatible college roommate:

1   The first step to mastering roommate relations is understanding the process by which housing officials match incoming freshmen. Before school begins, colleges send out roommate questionnaires to find out whether you are a morning or night person, whether you smoke, whether you have ever engaged in acts of bestiality, etc. After careful analysis, the officials then take delight in matching you with people whose answers are the opposite of yours. Once it has been determined that the students in each pair will be entirely incompatible, they are made roommates.

2   At this point, it may seem like the best idea is to answer each question the opposite of how you would normally respond. This is risky, because there's always that rare chance you'll be matched with someone who really *is* a peppy morning person whose hobbies include vacuuming.

3   A better idea is to get matched with that one person to whom you are truly best suited: yourself.

4   To ensure a roommate-free abode, leave your survey entirely blank except for the section below:

> Q: Do you have a medical condition?
> A: Yes, I suffer from severe multiple-environmental-allergy syndrome. I am allergic to dust, air, sounds, and all synthetic or natural materials. That John Travolta Movie of the Week, *The Boy in the Plastic Bubble,* was based on my life.

5   If by some fluke the above strategy fails, resign yourself to spending the next year living in an enclosed space with a complete stranger, most likely one who does sleep in a plastic bubble. To pave the way for a smooth transition, most colleges advise contacting your designated roommate before you actually meet. This is a good idea; it allows you to ask personal, probing questions to make sure he or she is the right match for you: (1) Do you own a CD player and/or a TV? (2) A car? (3) Do you have wealthy parents who send generous care packages to share with your roommates? (4) Do you have a girlfriend or boyfriend at a nearby school, where you will spend evenings and weekends? (5) Do you require any special breathing apparatus?

6   Of course, you've arrived early enough on moving day to take the bigger closet, the larger desk, and the unstained mattress before your roommate gets there. When he finally arrives, make him feel like a guest in your home. Show him where he'll be sleeping. Then treat him to dinner at the cafeteria to make others think you have a friend.

7   It is especially important to arrive early if you are placed in a triple. When you live as a threesome, it is standard practice for two to team up against the other. If you show up last, your roommates will have already bonded, and you will be outnumbered.

8   What if you do arrive late on moving day? Seize the opportunity to snoop through your roommates' personal belongings while they are plotting against you in the cafeteria. Flee the premises at once if you come across any of the following warning signs: framed prom picture; Garfield memo board; feathered roach clip; stuffed unicorn; alarm clock; broken glass vial and hypodermic needle.

—Dan Zevin, from "Roommatism"

Notice that Zevin's process demonstrates the following characteristics:

- **The importance, range, or difficulty of the process is clearly indicated.**
  Zevin begins with a thesis that includes the importance of the process: "The first step to mastering roommate relations is understanding the process by which housing officials match incoming freshmen."

- **The process is structured or broken down into a series of separate steps.**
  Zevin outlines the first step in the process in paragraph 1: understanding the process that officials use. In paragraph 2, he proceeds to the second step, filling out the questionnaire. In paragraph 5, Zevin moves from the questionnaire to contacting the roommate; in paragraphs 6, 7, and 8, he continues with the subject of moving day. Zevin uses cue words to delineate each step in the process for his readers. Beginning with the word "first" in paragraph 1, Zevin thoughtfully signals his audience with cue words such as "Before school begins," "After careful analysis," "Once it

has been determined," "At this point," "To pave the way," and "When he finally arrives."

- **The writer includes information on any resources needed for success-ful completion of the process.**
  For Zevin, these materials include a set of specific questions to ask the prospective roommate. For example, in paragraph 5, he asks, "Do you have wealthy parents who send generous care packages to share with your roommates?"

- **Throughout the explanation of the process, the writer maintains a con-sistent tense.**
  Zevin uses the present tense to explain his process: "*leave* your survey entirely blank" and "*resign* yourself to spending the next year."

To see another example of process in a college essay, read the model in the next section.

MODEL WITH KEY QUESTIONS

As you read the following "how-to" essay, try to identify the process character-istics just discussed.

Model 1   TWILIGHT SPECIAL

Rachel Gibson

Rachel's confidence in her writing increased substantially over the course of the semester. At first she found it challenging to generate adequate material in her essays, but when she became convinced that good writing happens in stages rather than all at once, Rachel grew more patient with herself and improved her ability to revise and polish what had begun as a very rough draft.

1   If you're a guy, I know you have the hardest time trying to shop for your mothers, sisters, or especially girlfriends. The perfect solution to your problem is here! Most women love having quiet, romantic evenings in a music-filled room full of soft candlelight. In fact, candles always add a special touch to just about any special event. Making a candle is not as hard as it sounds; it's actually a lot of fun once you get materials and then get the simple steps down.

2   For starters, you will need to get all of your materials together. You can find these at such places as Michael's Craft Shop, or at just about any arts and crafts shop. For the particular candle you'll be working on first, you'll need a few mate-rials and some assorted seashells. The first ingredient you will need is wax: two and one-half cups of Mystic Blue Wax Crystals, which come in a 12-ounce bag. Also you will need one cup of Frosty Wax Crystals. For the mold you will need to get a two-part hexagon mold—the best number to get is 51304. Wicks are sold in a three-or-more pack, but you will need only one for this first candle project. You

will also need one coffee can, one wooden skewer, a disposable tin pin, plastic zip-lock bags suitable for boiling, a disposable tin pan, and a small amount of Planters peanut oil. Finally, you'll need some assorted shells—any shape, size, and color you prefer will do, so don't be afraid to live dangerously and pick shells that reflect you and your mood. Get as many shells as you would like in your candle.

3   Now for your creation: to make a Mystic Blue hexagon candle, take the two-part mold and lightly rub the inside (the part that will be touching the wax) with Planters peanut oil. Then take the half of the mold with the inverted "L" shape grooved in one half of the hexagon mold (standing for "left"). Gently place a wick into the small groove by the "L." Holding one end of the wick in the groove with your finger, bring the other end of the wick straight through the pour spout on the top of the mold. Making sure that the wick stays in place, gently snap the two parts of the mold together, making sure of a tight fit. To fill with wax, measure the appropriate amount of wax and pour into a secured boiling bag. Then fill a two-quart saucepan about one-third full of water. Then place the bag with wax in the water and heat over a medium flame.

4   Don't relax too much and get yourself too distanced from the wax, because once the wax has liquefied, it is ready to pour into the mold. Remove the bag with wax from the stove and wait one full minute before pouring your wax into the mold. Be sure you fill to the bottom of the pour spout. Let this stand in room temperature for at least an hour—now you can relax and perhaps get out those shells and work on creating a design you'll want to incorporate into your candle when the time is right.

5   Also, as the wax begins to harden, poke a few holes around the wick at least two inches down to prevent a vacuum hold from forming in the center of the candle. Reheat the remaining wax in the bag and top off the mold by refilling wax to the bottom of the pour spout. After completing this process, let the mold sit for at least 45 minutes to make sure that no indentations have formed in the middle of the candle.

6   Now you do have to wait, allowing the candle to sit for seven hours before removing it from the mold. To remove, gently pry open the sides of the mold about a quarter of an inch. Then tap the sides all the way around until the candle has been separated from the mold. After removing the candle, snip off any remaining wick from the bottom only.

7   Your last step in the candle-making procedure involves leveling the candle. To do this, heat a disposable tin pan in a 350-degree oven for a few minutes. Remove it from the oven and place the candle bottom in the tin. Move the candle around gently for a few seconds, and then place it on wax paper to cool. Once the candle is cooled, place a skewer in the bottom center of the candle no more than two inches deep. You need to do this to swirl in the wax you are about to melt to add the shells. Next, heat the remaining wax (Frosty Clear Crystals) and pour into a large coffee can. Put smaller shells on a flat surface of wax paper, and then gently dip and swirl the candle. Using a skewer, attach small shells and roll the candle until it is completely covered with shells. If you want to get adventuresome and add larger shells, you can dip a side of the candle in melted wax and gently but firmly press the shell on the candle. Let your candle cool and remove any beads of wax that form by simply scraping them off.

8   This candle-making project, as you can now see, doesn't take infinite amounts of brain power, and when you've finished with your creation, you will be able to show your mother, sister, or girlfriend that you cared about them enough to make a lovely present. So why spend endless hours in shopping malls looking for that perfect gift when for a very moderate cost you can make your own gift to share? ○

Key Questions

1. **Purpose**   What clues do you find in paragraph 1 to reveal Gibson's target audience and her purpose?

2. **Focus**   Underline Gibson's thesis. In what way does the thesis limit the subject of gift-giving?

3. **Material**   Which step in the process is explained in the most explicit detail and why?

4. **Structure**   What steps are involved in the process? Return to the essay and circle all cue words that take readers from one step to another.

5. **Style**   Find one piece of useful information the author shares about the process.

GUIDELINES FOR WRITING PROCESS

Identify Your Purpose and Audience

You will want to choose a process pattern of development for your essay if your subject is how a procedure is performed or how a phenomenon works. If you have an accurate sense of the interests and concerns of your audience, you'll be more likely to write a useful "how-to" essay. Ask yourself what your audience might already know about the process and what strategies you might use to make the procedure easier for them to understand. For instance, if you reread Zevin's essay (p. 234), you'll see that his real purpose is not to explain the process of selecting a suitable roommate; instead, Zevin wants to express his opinion and share his humor with readers. For Zevin, process is a writing strategy that he can use to poke fun at some of the practices that college officials and students engage in when they're involved in roommate selection. If you were asked in a psychology class to write an essay focusing on how to find a compatible roommate, your purpose and your audience would be quite different.

Ask yourself questions about your audience: Do you want to stress to these readers the importance, the complexity, or the humorous nature of the process? Are there positive or negative results that they need to know about? Do you want to convince your audience to begin an activity or learn a new skill?

Practice 11.1   Look at the following process writing situations. In a few words, identify the purpose and the audience's knowledge of the subject. The first example has been done for you.

Subject	Audience	Purpose	Knowledge of Subject
Weight training	Current trainers	*Inform of new procedures*	*In depth*
Weight training	General (no experience)		

Subject	Audience	Purpose	Knowledge of Subject
Computer use	Current users		
Computer use	Nonusers		
Forming campus club ❏	College students		

Focus Your Subject

Once you've identified your purpose and audience, check to make sure that your subject—the process to be explained—is neither too broad nor too limited. For example, let's say that you are experienced in antique refinishing and would like to explain the process to those who might be interested in this hobby. However, as an expert, you become too involved in the prospect of explaining every type of antique refinishing and you wind up trying to write about several different finishes and the steps involved in each. The consequence of your enthusiasm could very well be total reader confusion! Look again at "Twilight Special" (p. 236). Gibson does not attempt to explain the entire process for making many different shapes or kinds of candles, but instead focuses on the process involved in creating one specific kind of candle. Similarly, Zevin knows better than to write about all roommates and thus limits his subject to college roommates.

Practice 11.2 Complete the following sentences and answer the questions, thinking about focusing on a subject for process development.

1. One process I may have more information about than the average person is . . .

2. What type of audience might be interested in learning about the process?

3. If the entire process is too complex to write about in an essay, I might focus on . . .

4. What information could I share on this process that might be particularly useful or enlightening? ❏

Once you've focused on your subject, you will want to create a thesis that names the process and includes a controlling idea. This should include a statement about **range**—the extent of the subject or the boundaries placed on the subject. This controlling idea is the main point you want to make about the process. Looking again at Gibson's essay, you'll see that the thesis in paragraph 1 names the process (making a candle), and the controlling idea (that it's easier than one might think).

Practice 11.3 Examine the following subjects and then create a complete thesis—a sentence that names the process (your subject) and includes a controlling idea (indication of the range, difficulty, or importance of the process). The first subject has been completed for you.

Subject: How to reenter college as an adult student

Controlling idea: *Presents some unique challenges*

Thesis: *Although college reentry presents several unique challenges for an adult, the process can become relatively painless if one follows five simple steps.*

Subject: How to plan a dinner party

Controlling idea:

Thesis:

Subject: How to find employment

Controlling idea:

Thesis:

❏

Structure the Process Using Steps and Cue Words

Have you ever tried to make a cake only to discover that you put the wet ingredients into the dry ones too soon? If you're registering for new classes, what happens if you don't proceed in the required sequence of events? In both cases, this often means starting over again. For successful process writing, a clear step-by-step structure is of the utmost importance to your audience. To make sure that your essay is clearly structured, organize your material by identifying the steps in your process and then ordering those steps in an outline or list. Notice that for Zevin and Gibson, this order is chronological.

Practice 11.4   To test your ability to recognize a sequence of steps in a process, read Craig Swanson's essay "The Turning Point" (p. 356), and complete the series of actions begun in the following list:

- Wedge ball of clay about size of cantaloupe

- Slice in half on a wire

- Slam one-half on wedging board   ❏

When you are organizing your material, try grouping related individual steps into paragraphs. For instance, although Gibson's discussion of candle making includes many individual instructions, she groups those related to the materials to be bought in paragraph 2. When Gibson moves on to the steps involved in making the candle, she groups them according to slight breaks in time in paragraphs 3 through 7. This grouping of material in process development helps your audience to see the main stages or divisions of a whole process, and it can offer you a way to order your paragraphs. Working from an outline that clearly indicates main stages or divisions of a process can also prevent a possibly confusing list of small steps. The larger pattern will help your readers by giving them a sense of the process as a whole.

Practice 11.5 Reread Zevin's excerpt (p. 234). List the three larger groups that Zevin connects with his process.

In addition to using a step-by-step structure, you will want to signal a clear sequence from one step to the next by using cue words and phrases such as *first, second, next, before you add, as you complete this step,* and others found in the table of cue words (p. 141–142). ❏

Explain Every Step with Precise Detail

You will want to gather enough material about your process to make each step totally clear for your audience. You may find it helpful to go through the process based on your outline or rough draft to see if your instructions are adequate. If you write about natural or technical processes, you may need information from outside sources. For example, if you're explaining the procedure for dissecting a frog, you may want to consult your biology notes or text. If you're explaining a social process, such as the procedure for taking a petition to the state legislature, you may need to track down additional information by calling or e-mailing your representative or consulting information in a government booklet or document.

Once you feel that you've gathered enough material to explain your process, use precise language and specific detail to help the reader visualize the process. Notice that Gibson's process is aided by the use of action words; she advises her readers to "place," "snap," "fill," "poke," and "rub," for example.

Check to see that, especially for the more challenging steps of your process, you have given your audience tips, warnings, or concrete suggestions—in other words, any additional information that might be helpful. It's also a good idea to explain *why* certain steps are necessary. For example, rather than just writing, "lay the hubcap on the ground with the screws inside," you might also add, "this will prevent the screws from rolling out into the street or getting lost from your sight."

Practice 11.6 Reread Zevin's essay "Roommatism" (p. 234) and find the following:

- Two effective action words

- One comparison

- A phrase that provides a helpful tip, suggestion, or warning ❏

Maintain a Consistent Tense and Point of View

In drafting your essay, decide on an appropriate tense and point of view, and keep these consistent throughout your writing. If you are offering instructions in your essay, it is best to use the **second person** point of view—*you, your, yours*—and the present tense, as Zevin and Gibson do. If you are explaining a process that you have become familiar with from watching someone else perform it, or if you are explaining how something is done, use the **third person**—*he, his, him* or *she, her, hers*—and the past tense. If you want to emphasize the impersonal nature of the process, use the **passive voice,** a voice in writing in which the subject does not perform any action but instead is acted upon by an outside agent.

To observe the effect of the passive voice, read the following excerpt. Note that the passive voice works for this writer because he wants to convey a sense of helplessness and to convince his audience of the cruelty of the process. The phrases in the passive voice are italicized:

> Off the coast of Costa Rica, the *Maria Luisa,* a tuna fishing boat, sets its net around a school of disporting dolphins. In the eastern tropical Pacific, the presence of dolphins often indicates yellowfish tuna under the surface. A mechanical winch pulls up the net, and a dolphin *is snagged* by its dorsal fin and *raised* high above the ship. The dolphin writhes and twists. The dorsal fin tears off. The net *is pulled* aboard, as more dolphins *are being maimed* and *drowned.* The crew, intent on the tuna catch, rip the mammals from the net. Some are already dead; others still struggle as they *are thrown* into a chute and *dumped* overboard as "food for the sharks." This day, almost 200 dolphins *have been rendered* into shark food in the process of catching only twelve yellowfin tuna, a worse than normal ratio.
>
> —David R. Brower, from *Let the Mountains Talk, Let the Rivers Run*

Define All Necessary Equipment and Terms

Imagine your reader's frustration if you fail to mention any supply or tool essential to the process, no matter how small. Such an omission could very possibly hinder the successful completion of the process you're explaining. In addition, you will need to define or describe any specialized equipment, terms, or words related to steps in the process that your audience might not know, and clearly explain their role in the process.

Practice 11.7 Read the following paragraph explaining the embalming process for a corpse, and then annotate the passage according to the directions that follow.

> The next step is to have at Mr. Jones with a thing called a trocar. This is a long, hollow needle attached to a tube. It is jabbed into the abdomen, poked around the entrails and chest cavity, the contents of which are pumped out and replaced with "cavity fluid." This done, and the hole in the abdomen sewn up, Mr. Jones's face is heavily creamed (to protect the skin from burns that may be caused by leakage of the chemicals), and he is covered with a sheet and left unmolested for a while. But not for long—there is more, much more, in store for him. He has been embalmed, but not yet restored, and the best time to start the restorative work is eight to ten hours after embalming, when the tissues have become firm and dry.
>
> —Jessica Mitford, from *The American Way of Death*

1. Circle the words that indicate the tense. Indicate in the margin whether Mitford has used active or passive voice.

2. Find and put a check by any equipment the writer mentions.

3. Find and underline any terms and their definitions.   ❏

Conclude Thoughtfully

Process can be an enjoyable pattern of essay development to write because sometimes the steps seem to "write themselves" once you start drafting. However, one potential pitfall in creating a successful essay using process occurs when writers stop writing with the last step, mistakenly thinking that they are finished.

Try to go beyond the final step in the process to give your audience a sense that they understand not only the procedure but also the significance of the process. It's not enough that your readers have learned from you how to complete the process. Your essay should also affect readers in some meaningful way—it may make them laugh, as in the case of Zevin's essay, or it may show them the value of learning a new skill, as in the case of Gibson's essay. It may also make them think about an issue in a way that they have never thought about it before, as may be the case with the process paragraph on tuna fishing, which encourages readers to think about wildlife conservation, or the paragraph about embalming corpses, which forces the audience to consider the expense of death in America.

Strategies for Writing Process

1. **Purpose**   Identify your intended audience and what you want them to learn from the process you are writing about.

2. **Focus**   Limit your subject. In your thesis, name the process and include a controlling idea—a comment on the significance, importance, or scope of the process.

3. **Material**   In prewriting, gather sufficient material to explain the process thoroughly and clearly. In drafting and revising, elaborate on every step in the process, explain all equipment needed, and define any unfamiliar terms. Be sure to include suggestions for particularly difficult steps as well as warnings of actions to avoid in the procedure.

4. **Structure**   Organize your essay so that you present a sequence of steps in a chronological order or in the most helpful order to complete the process. If your process is complicated, break the steps into paragraphs, grouping smaller steps within these larger main stages. Use cue words to take your reader from one step to the next.

5. **Style**   Use precise, accurate words and phrases that will help your audience visualize all objects and actions connected with the process.

OPTIONS FOR WRITING ESSAYS USING PROCESS

As you work through any of the following writing options, remember to keep your audience interested by conveying the significance of the process as you explain it.

1. Getting a job requires hard work and planning. If you have experience to draw from, write an essay explaining the process. You might include

sources such as newspaper ads, employment agencies, or college placement centers. You might also discuss the application and interview process, resumes, and follow-up procedures after the interview.

2. Many of us have tried or want to try some personal improvement program. Perhaps you have some knowledge of body building, aerobics, speed reading, or another program. Explain the process involved in a particular area.

3. If you have a particular recipe or special holiday dish that is reflective of your culture or that has been handed down to you from relatives, write an essay detailing the process of creating and serving this dish. If you don't have enough information, interview your relative and get sufficient material to explain the process effectively.

4. Write an essay explaining a process related to your major or hobby. For example, if your major is in a health-related field, you might want to explain the steps in administering CPR. If your hobby is sculpting, you could explain the steps involved in creating a sculpture of the human head.

5. If you or one of your family members is an immigrant to this country, you probably know the many procedures involved in becoming an American citizen. Write an essay explaining this process to an audience of prospective immigrants.

6. Write an essay explaining to a group of potential students how to handle the registration procedures at your college or university.

7. Shopping for and purchasing a car can be a time-consuming and often frustrating experience. Write an essay explaining the steps involved in finding and buying one's dream car.

8. If you have had experience with young children, write an essay explaining to a novice parent how to manage a child. Or, from the point of view of the child, write an essay explaining to another child or teenager how to manage a parent.

9. *(Film and Literature)* Research author Jane Austen, who wrote the novel *Emma* well over a century ago. After viewing the 1995 film *Clueless* (a modern adaptation of *Emma*), write an essay explaining what you think Jane Austen would have thought of her English novel transported to Los Angeles and featuring TVs, cell phones, movies, and CDs.

10. *(Service Learning)* Think about some skill, hobby, or special talent you have. Write an essay carefully explaining the process involved in your skill. Contact your local community's seniors' center and see if you can make an appointment to present your material to interested seniors.

Challenge Option: Combining Patterns

Gibson's essay (p. 236) explains the process of making a candle; Zevin's (p. 234) deals with a relationship—the one you have with a college roommate. Choose another subject related to interpersonal relationships—for example, surviving a job with a boss you hate, succeeding in a required college class when you dislike the instructor, disciplining a toddler, or coping with a drug-addicted family member. Write an essay in which you use two patterns of development: first, *narration* to tell about your own experience, and second, *process* to explain to your readers how something is done.

CHARACTERISTICS OF CAUSE/EFFECT

While a process pattern of development explains *how*, cause/effect development explores *why*. **Cause** is a writing strategy concerned with why something happens; **effect** focuses on results or consequences. Think about watching a game of pool: One ball (let's say the "cause" ball) strikes another, and then this second ball (the "effect" ball) moves as a result. But what if this "effect" ball rolls on and strikes another ball? Doesn't it become a "cause" ball at this point? Even in a basic example such as this one, we can see a model for cause/effect thinking and how a chain reaction can change an effect into a cause. Consider the following:

Causes		Effects
too much rain	*leads to*	flooding
flooding	*leads to*	destruction of crops
loss of crops	*leads to*	shortage of product
shortage of product	*leads to*	rise in market price

Although these examples may seem easy to grasp, sometimes occurrences appear to be related when they are not. Think about the next to last example: "loss of crops leads to shortage of product." The flooding was hindering the orange crop in California, but perhaps the Florida weather was producing an abundant and high-grade orange crop. In this case, shortage of product in California would not lead to a rise in market price nationwide.

A cause-and-effect pattern of development is illustrated in the following excerpt from an essay focusing on college drinking:

1   Since college students have limited responsibilities, they can usually drink heavily without serious repercussions. Drunken college students do sometimes get into trouble, of course. But this is not a drinking problem; it is a drinking *behavior* problem.

2   Students may drink to let off steam, or drink to get drunk, or boast about how much they can drink without puking. But college drinking, by and large, remains social drinking. UO [University of Oregon] students could buy a half-rack of Henry Weinhard's Ale and drink at home. But instead they pay a lot more to drink at [bars like] Rennie's or Max's because they want to be around other people.

3   Drinking isn't only something to do—it's something everyone can do together. It's how many freshmen begin meeting people. "You don't know anybody, and then somebody hands you a beer and pretty soon you're hanging out with a bunch of guys," says Eric, a nineteen-year-old sophomore, remembering his first days in college. Freshmen drink hard early on: A 1995 Harvard study of college freshmen found that 70 percent binge drink in their first semester. But after

students find their social circle (and worship once or twice at the Temple of the Porcelain God), many decide to drink infrequently or not at all.

4   Research finds that college students who drink heavily have lower grades than those who drink moderately or not at all. But these students aren't chemistry majors whose grades and classes will be critical for graduate school and future careers. They tend to be business or social science majors who will probably end up in jobs that have little to do with their academic studies. "The truth is that most students can go out drinking several nights a week and get by," says [Carl] Wartenburg, the Swarthmore dean [of admissions].

5   College students get into trouble not because they drink to get drunk but because they get drunk to be irresponsible. "I was drunk" is a get-out-of-jail-free card for college students who act like idiots, get into fights, climb into construction equipment, or behave in other unacceptable or embarrassing ways. It works because friends know that drinking makes people lose control and they may want to use alcohol as an excuse for their own behavior, especially sexual behavior. According to the Harvard study, 41 percent of frequent binge drinkers engage in unplanned sexual activity, as opposed to only 4 percent for non-binge drinkers.

—Ed Carson, from "Purging Binging"

Notice that Carson's development of cause and effect demonstrates the following characteristics:

- **The writer presents a reasonable thesis connected to logical cause/ effect development. The subject is an event, occurrence, or phenomenon, and the writer focuses on cause, effect, or both.**
  Carson's thesis, the last sentence of paragraph 1, includes the subject, college drinking, and then focuses the subject by stating that the real problem with college drinking is the behavior that results. This controlling idea seems reasonable. Notice also that the thesis presents a situation— college drinking—and then focuses on the effects of this situation.

- **The writer uses detail to develop one or more causes or effects connected with an event or occurrence; the writer may focus on causes, effects, or a combination of both.**
  In paragraphs 2 and 3, Carson discusses some possible causes of college drinking: letting off steam, getting drunk, being able to boast about drinking capacity, meeting new people, or being quickly accepted at parties. In paragraphs 4 and 5, the focus shifts to the effects of this drinking: lower grades, acting idiotically, getting into fights, performing dangerous feats like "climb[ing] into construction equipment," or engaging in unplanned sexual activities.

- **The cause/effect development has a particular structure.**
  You can see that Carson supports his thesis on the problematic effects of college drinking with an overview of the causes and their connection to *social* drinking in college. This structure helps Carson link the troubling effects of campus drinking to supposedly safer "social" college drinking.

To see how cause/effect works within a college essay, read the model in the next section to determine how many of the characteristics previously discussed you can identify.

MODEL WITH KEY QUESTIONS

Student writer Swarupa Reddy has lived in the United States for several years, having come from India as a young woman. Astounded and alarmed by television's impact on American youth, she wanted to share her concern with readers.

Model 2   ## TV AS A CULPRIT

Swarupa Reddy

Swarupa Reddy reports that the strategies she learned in her first college writing class helped her "build the foundation to complete freshman composition and other transfer-level English courses." In addition to raising a family, Swarupa is currently taking courses to prepare for her transfer to a four-year university. She intends to pursue a career in one of the health professions.

1   Our minds are rotting away and we might not know it. This is due to a destructive invention, a culprit known as television. Though television has kept families in their homes with countless hours of entertainment, it has also ended up destroying family ritual, affecting academic performance, and promoting sex and violence.

2   One effect of television in our current time is the destruction of family ritual. Once upon a time, so we have been told, families talked with each other. They actually gathered together and shared ideas, interests, and experiences. Since television, this apparently does not occur in most families. Family meals have taken a definite downward toll since the rise of television. At one time families would actually gather around the table for a meal and some family discussion. This was the place and time that families would work out a lot of problems related to school, sports, work, and relations with the opposite sex. Television has changed this, however, with the family members all staring at the tube rather than looking at each other, and listening to television programs rather than talking. No longer is there the shared mealtime ritual of the family.

3   In addition or possibly as a result of the breakdown of family ritual, television has also affected the schoolwork and performance of children and teenagers. Statistics released recently reveal that many more elementary, junior high, and high school students watch television than twenty years ago, and that these children and teens are watching for more extended periods of time than ever before. The results are discouraging to teachers, parents, and school officials. Studies show that those students who watch ten or more hours of television per week—an increasing number—receive lower grades than their counterparts who do not watch television.

4   Finally, television actually promotes sex and violence. Programs that contain sex and violence may impress upon a child the wrong messages, whereas an adult may know how to distinguish between what is proper and what isn't. In a long-term study on the effect of television on young viewers conducted by Stanford University, participants watched certain programs and were then themselves watched through one-way mirrors. The youngsters "acted out" more violently, hitting, throwing and abusing their toys more frequently after watching such programs. In addition, the carefree and casual use of sex on television has influenced

many viewers to want to engage in sex, without acknowledging any of the dangers of unsafe sex. Young viewers in both instances "do as T.V. does," and then they find that actions that work in the television world have different results in the real world.

5   At the risk of becoming social outcasts for criticizing this accepted American phenomenon, we must start to limit the use of television before this culprit brings about even more destruction to our families, our children, and our way of life. ○

Key Questions

1. **Purpose**   What is the connection the writer wants the reader to make between television and family values?

2. **Focus**   In her thesis, does Reddy focus on causes or effects? Reddy further focuses the subject by including a plan of development in her thesis. What three areas will she explore in her essay?

3. **Material**   What outside sources of information does the writer use for evidence?

4. **Structure**   Do you think Reddy's ordering of her three points is effective? Reread the essay and annotate it by underlining all cue words that signal the reader of a cause or effect relationship. Why do you think Reddy ends with sex and violence as her last point?

5. **Style**   In what way does Reddy's conclusion connect to her introduction and offer the reader a sense of closure? Note specific phrases that reinforce her introduction.

GUIDELINES FOR WRITING CAUSE/EFFECT

Determine Purpose and Audience

You will want to choose a cause/effect pattern of development if your purpose in your essay is to show connections—*why* something happens or what *results* from a situation, occurrence, or even an attitude. For instance, why might you want to explore the causes of homelessness in your city? Would your purpose be to inform your audience, or to convince them to vote differently in the next local election? In searching for a subject, think about topics that interest you. Then ask yourself if these topics could also be of interest to a particular audience.

You can use personal experience to discuss causes or effects, in which case you might want to think about changes that have taken place in your own lifetime. Or, you can write from what you know, or can find out about causes or effects related to a particular situation. When you have a few possibilities written down, ask yourself if you care about this subject enough to explore it in an essay, and what your purpose might be in sharing the causes, effects, or both with your audience.

To illustrate, the excerpt from "Purging Binging" (p. 245) explores the causes and effects of college drinking. Writer Ed Carson had recently graduated from the University of Oregon at the time he wrote his essay. It's probable that Carson felt college drinking was misunderstood by many readers, and that as a recent college graduate, he had a more realistic perspective. He chose to interview college students, engage in more research, and build a body of evidence to persuade his audience that the behavior connected with college drinking is more of a problem than the drinking itself. Once he had determined his purpose and audience, it was relatively easy for Carson to focus his subject on a working thesis and begin to gather information in prewriting.

Practice 11.8   As an idea-generating activity, think about possible subjects of interest to you—situations, occurrences, happenings, attitudes, or phenomena in the physical world. Make a list of the following:

- three subjects that you might consider

- the particular audience you'd like to address for each subject

- your purpose in writing about each subject ❑

Focus Your Subject

Once you have an idea of a subject for cause/effect development, ask yourself whether you are more interested in exploring the subject from the point of view of causes, effects, or both. In prewriting it may be helpful to note both causes and effects connected with a situation so that you can better judge which direction to pursue.

Writers can explore two types of cause/effect connections: *immediate connections*—those that have occurred recently and are fairly obvious—and *remote connections*—those that are not so obvious or that might have come about quite some time ago. For example, Reddy asserts in her thesis that television viewing may not only destroy family ritual and affect academic performance, but also lead to an increase in teen sexual activity and violent behavior. When Reddy brainstormed ways she could focus on her subject, she noticed that many families no longer sit around a table and talk about their day at dinner time. Instead they stare at the television. This negative effect of television on families was immediately visible to the writer. As she continued to explore more remote connections, she remembered reading a study linking violent activities with the viewing of certain television programs, and she decided to pursue this effect also.

Notice that both Reddy and Carson focus on a few specific causes or effects. It would not be practical to discuss all of the causes or the effects of college drinking or television viewing. Ask yourself, "Is this cause or this effect important enough to develop in an essay?" Although Carson knew that two effects of excessive drinking might be throwing up or passing out, he focused on neither of these all-too-obvious effects. To do so would have distracted readers from his thesis.

Practice 11.9   Return to the subjects you indicated in Practice 11.8. Choose a subject for further exploration and complete the first half of the following "Cause/Effect Map." A **cause/effect map** is a prewriting sheet designed for cause/effect essay planning. Such a map can help you discover and begin to organize your main points. Once you have enough information on your subject, read what you have, decide how you will focus your subject, and write a working thesis in the appropriate space at the bottom of the map.   ❑

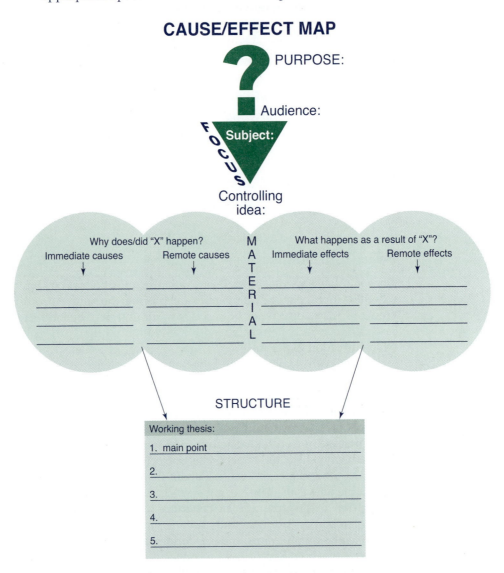

CAUSE/EFFECT MAP

PURPOSE:

Audience:

Subject:

FOCUS

Controlling idea:

Why does/did "X" happen?

Immediate causes   Remote causes

M A T E R I A L

What happens as a result of "X"?

Immediate effects   Remote effects

STRUCTURE

Working thesis:

1. main point

2.

3.

4.

5.

Sketch Out a Structure: Three Alternate Plans

Once you have a working thesis, you will want to decide on a structure for your essay. Three possible plans—(1) Single Cause/Multiple Effects, (2) Single Effect/Multiple Causes, and (3) Chain Reaction—are shown here.

Use the structure called Plan One—which is the one Reddy used in her essay on the effects of television viewing—if you want to emphasize the effects. How do you decide which effect to put first? You might structure your essay from negative to positive effects, or from obvious effects to more subtle ones, or from local to far-reaching effects. You will want to experiment with order—which cause or effect to put first, second, and so forth.

Notice that the structure called Plan Two is the same as Plan One, only reversed. Use this structure if you want to emphasize the causes of an occurrence or situation. For example, for an economics class essay, this would be an effective way to structure an explanation of the multiple causes of the Great Depression.

Plan One: Single Cause/Multiple Effects

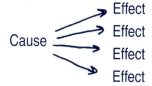

Plan Two: Single Effect/Multiple Causes

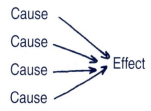

Plan Three: Chain Reaction

Use the structure called Plan Three if your subject has causes or effects that build on each other. For example, if your subject is the celebration of Christmas, your sketch might look something like this:

Original cause for Christmas—Change in holiday to emphasize Santa and gifts—Results in increasing pressure on consumers to spend lots of money—Causes merchants to increase their "hype" and advertising, encouraging consumers to spend—Results in new highs in spending, increased stress on celebrants, less emphasis on original cause for celebration.

Practice 11.10   Return to your subject possibilities in Practice 11.9. Examine your notes on causes and effects and choose a structure that you feel would work for your essay. In preparation for drafting, fill in your main points in the order in which you'll first experiment with presenting them.   ❑

Connect with Cue Words

Because you are seeking to establish a connection between a situation and its causes or its effects, any additional assistance that you can give your audience to help them grasp this relationship is helpful. During your writing, refer to the table of cue words (p. 141–142). Remember that words such as *thus, therefore, because, so, then, consequently, as a result,* and others will help create order in your essay.

Practice 11.11 Reread "TV as a Culprit" (p. 247). Annotate the essay by underlining all cue words that you find. ❏

Use Specific Details

For every cause or effect you connect with your subject, you will want to use specific details from your own experiences or from outside sources. Notice that when Reddy asserts that there are multiple effects of television viewing, she supports each effect by giving specific details. For instance, in paragraph 3 Reddy mentions statistics revealing that more students than ever before watch increased hours of television. She also mentions studies showing that during this same time period, the students who watch more television experience declines in grades and general school performance. She continues in paragraph 4 by telling readers that a long-term study of television viewers by Stanford University reveals that students who watch certain violent programs behave more aggressively and violently to their peers than those who do not watch these television shows.

Avoid Possible Pitfalls

Using cause/effect development successfully in an essay depends not only on your knowledge of a situation but also on your ability to make valid connections between the situation and its causes or its effects. Familiarizing yourself with some common pitfalls of cause/effect writing will make you less likely to make one of these errors in thinking. In reading over your draft or the draft of a fellow student, be sure to point out these errors and revise your draft accordingly.

Oversimplification

One of the most common pitfalls in cause/effect writing is **oversimplification**—attributing only one cause or one effect to a situation. For example, if you tell a friend, "I made a horrible grade on the test because I'm bad at multiple-choice tests," you're probably ignoring some other factors or causes for your poor performance: You did not study enough, you studied the wrong material, or you were not able to think clearly precisely because you fear multiple-choice tests. Quite often we're tempted to oversimplify because we have some bias regarding the subject. To guard against this tendency, avoid subjects that you know you won't be able to approach fairly.

Post Hoc Fallacy

Have you ever washed your car only to have it rain an hour later? You might be tempted to think that it rained *because* you washed your car. You are guilty of what is known as the **post hoc fallacy**—from the Latin phrase *post hoc, ergo propter hoc,* which means "after this, therefore because of this." Don't assume that just because one thing comes before another in time, the first event causes the second to happen. Obviously there will be many times when two events are connected, but when you're writing a college essay, you must be absolutely certain that there is a causal as well as a chronological link in any evidence you present to a reader. For example, when Reddy asserts that television leads to increased sexual activity and violence, she uses the Stanford study of children as a basis of her evidence because these children were observed during the television shows and immediately after. Although Reddy wanted to use an example of a convicted rapist who stated that he had been influenced by television, the writer decided that there was no way of establishing a causal connection in addition to a chronological one.

Practice 11.12   Read the following statements and label them as oversimplification or post hoc fallacy.

1. Increasing numbers of working and single mothers have resulted in uncontrollable and disturbed children.

2. Unemployment has decreased during the present administration; our current president gets credit for employing more Americans than the ex-president.

3. Frank loves to eat; someday he will be obese.

4. Since Julia was unfaithful to her husband during the same summer she viewed a movie featuring promiscuous behavior, the movie caused her infidelity. ❑

Strategies for Writing Cause/Effect

1. **Purpose**   Identify your audience and what you want them to learn from your exploration of the connections between a situation and its causes or effects.

2. **Focus**   Once you have a subject, limit your thesis to the causes, effects, or both that you can most effectively develop to support your purpose.

3. **Material**   In prewriting, gather enough material to develop a clear cause/effect relationship. Look for immediate as well as remote connections.

4. **Structure**   Try organizing your essay according to one of the three plans on page 251. Work from a sketch or outline, remembering to insert cue words to clarify relationships.

5. **Style**   Check your draft for oversimplification and post hoc fallacy, making sure that every word and phrase develops a logical cause/effect connection for your subject. In revising and polishing your introduction and conclusion, be sure that you've captured your readers' interest and made your point about the significance of any causes or effects connected with your subject.

OPTIONS FOR WRITING CAUSE/EFFECT

The following writing options will ask you to use a cause/effect pattern of development in an essay. After you've chosen an option, ask yourself which causes or effects are important and then structure your draft according to one of the alternate plans for this type of development. Examine the draft thoughtfully to identify any pitfalls in reasoning and to determine ways to make the connection between your subject and its causes or effects as clear as possible.

1. Think about a prejudice, attitude, belief, law, or custom that you have questioned. For instance, perhaps you feel the legal driving age should be changed, that women should be allowed in combat situations, or that we should change the way we celebrate the Fourth of July. In an essay, explore possible effects such a change would bring about.

2. Focus on a change or a decision that you've made in your life. What caused you to make the change? Were other people influential in your choice? What happened as a result? In retrospect, are you glad you made the change? Why or why not? In a paragraph, develop the causes or effects connected with your choice.

3. Have you ever fantasized about winning the grand prize in the state lottery, about having millions of dollars to spend? Think about what you would do if this really did happen. Would you travel? Purchase a new car? Spend the money on your family? Make donations to charities? Change the place you live? Quit your job? In an essay, organize the effects of this event into several major changes that would take place and then detail these major changes with specific information.

4. If you have a hobby, pastime, or favorite sport, you know that engaging in this activity gives you pleasure. Write an essay in which you share your reasons for participating in this activity. You can focus on why you became involved, what you get out of the activity, or both.

5. In Reddy's essay "TV as a Culprit" (p. 247), the writer elaborates on three harmful effects of television viewing. In an essay, agree or disagree with Reddy, using specific examples of programs and current or historical events that might support your thesis.

6. In Carson's essay "Purging Binging" (p. 245), the writer enumerates several causes as well as effects of drinking by college students. Think about other behaviors of college students that could be self-destructive or damaging to others. Develop an essay explaining possible causes as well as effects of a particular behavior.

7. Read Amitai Etzioni's essay "McDonald's Is Not Our Kind of Place" (p. 358). Write an essay on the topic of high school or college students working on a part-time or full-time basis while going to school. Whether you agree or disagree with Etzioni on the effects of working while attending school, you will need to develop causes or effects from your own experience or that of others you know. To strengthen your evidence, you may want to interview other students in your class, asking them to recall the causes and effects of working while going to school.

8. After researching in a few print or Internet sources the subject of the golfer Tiger Woods, write an essay discussing some effects of Woods's golf victories.

9. *(Film and Literature)* Find a reliable source on the Vietnam War—you could begin by consulting an online or printed encyclopedia. After

reading about this war, view Francis Ford Coppola's *Apocalypse Now.* Write an essay that elaborates on two or more causes and effects of the Vietnam War.

10. *(Service Learning)* Gather information pertaining to the Meals-on-Wheels program in your community and create an informative essay for students in your college who might want to volunteer. In your essay explain why the organization was founded and what the effects have been both for meal recipients and for volunteers. You may want to interview a member of the Meals-on-Wheels organization.

Challenge Option: Combining Patterns

Most jobs require employees to perform certain procedures. For example, a salesperson goes through a particular process in assisting a customer, answering questions, executing the sale and completing appropriate paperwork, wrapping or packaging the item that is purchased, and explaining the refund policy of the store. If you have held a job in which you executed a procedure, think and write about the immediate as well as the remote effects of performing this procedure many times in the typical workday. Perhaps one effect was that you developed a particular line of greeting for customers; another may be that you found shortcuts for wrapping the sales item or you discovered that you could keep customers from accidentally taking your pen by attaching it to the sales desk. To use both process and then cause/effect patterns of development, here's how you might want to structure your essay:

- *Introduction and thesis:* Capture audience attention and clearly focus on the process and the effects you'll be discussing.

- *Body paragraphs* (one or more): Explain in detail the procedure you executed on the job.

- *Body paragraphs* (one or more): Explore the effects of repeatedly performing this procedure.

- *Conclusion:* Connect the essay's ending to your thesis by thoughtfully commenting on the significance or meaning of these effects on you, on your employers, or on the people you served on the job.

JOURNAL WRITING: CONNECTIONS

Process

Sometimes a mental activity can be clarified by comparing it to a more familiar physical process. Think about some mental activities that you are familiar with, and then see if you can find a physical process with some similarities. For example, maybe studying for an exam is like training for a race; perhaps building your confidence is like weight training. In a journal entry, try to come up with three comparisons. Choose one and write freely about both the overall aspects and the small details, discovering all the connections you can. Try for at least a one-page entry. In another entry, you might respond to this journal writing by noting any new insights or connections you discovered about either the mental activity or the physical process.

Cause/Effect: The Time Line

Remember the billiard balls discussed earlier in this chapter? Now think about an event that happened years ago or quite recently in your own life—one that has caused a sequence of other events to occur. In a journal entry, create a time line, putting approximate dates on each of the effects that resulted from the first event. For example, suppose when you were 16 you left high school and obtained a full-time, low-wage job. This caused several events:

- Your parents asked you to move out.

- You rented your own apartment.

- You realized after two years on the job that you wanted to go back to school.

- You enrolled in college as a part-time student and received limited financial aid.

Your time line might look something like this:

Left school for job	Got apartment Lived with friend	Quit job	Enrolled in college Decided on major	Got help
January 2003	March 2004	May 2004	September 2005	January 2006

If you find that this entry helps you come up with material for your cause/effect essay, try thinking of another important event in your life and create another time line.

Using the Computer: Finding Information on the Internet

1. Have you ever worked in a fast-food establishment? Have you known someone who has? Amitai Etzioni's essay (p. 358) is critical of McDonald's restaurants, especially as places to work. You might have direct experience of your own with working at McDonald's or another fast-food restaurant, and you almost certainly have had experience eating their food! Whether such experiences have been positive or negative, you might be interested in how people have used the Web to promote either a positive or negative image of McDonald's. First, visit McDonald's Web site, **http://www.mcdonalds.com/**.

   What do you notice about this site? What kinds of information does it offer? Look up information on employment opportunities. Does what you read sound like your own, or a friend's, experiences with working in a fast-food restaurant? Next, visit *McSpotlight* at **http://envirolink.org/mcspotlight**. This site includes news, information, discussion groups, and other resources that give an alternative, and mostly negative, view of McDonald's. How is this site different from the "official" McDonald's site? Compare the information both sites offer about a specific issue—the nutritional value of McDonald's food, or working conditions in the restaurants, for example. What do you think?

2. For a brief guide to writing cause and effect essays, visit these Web sites:

   http://www.siskiyous.edu/class/engl1a/reynoldss/ideas4csef.htm

   http://www.delmar.edu/engl/wrtctr/handouts/cause_effect.html

3. For some additional examples of essays using cause and effect, visit this Web site:

   http://grammar.ccc.commnet.edu/grammar/composition/cause_effect.htm

4. For a guide to writing process essays, visit this Web site:

   http://grammar.ccc.commnet.edu/grammar/composition.process.htm

RESPONDING TO WRITING:
KEEPING A PROGRESS LOG

At this point in your English course, you probably have a stash of rough, interim, and final drafts that you have shared with your instructor and perhaps one or more peer editors in your class. In addition, you've probably received written comments on your drafts, verbal comments, perhaps a letter grade, and maybe a list of suggestions. This might be a good time for you to review all your drafts to date and to complete the progress log on the next page. You can then use this information to improve your future essays. The progress log might also form the basis of a writing conference with your instructor.

Before you begin this progress log, find and reread all of your submitted essay drafts. Note all instructor and peer-editor comments. You can now complete each section of the progress log. Enter a plus (+) for any area you feel you've mastered, a minus (–) for any area still needing substantial work, and a checkmark (✓) for any area that is coming along fine.

After you've completed the progress log, examine it carefully to determine your strengths as well as weaknesses in essay writing. According to your progress log, what appears to be your greatest strength to date? What area or areas could use improvement?

Refer to this book's table of contents and index to locate information and activities related to essay-writing skills you would like to improve. Review the appropriate sections and ask your instructor for additional information and advice about improving the quality of your essays.

For other essays using process, refer to "The Turning Point" and "A List of Topics for Writing Practice" in Part 4.

For more essays using cause/effect, refer to the following essays in Part 4: "We're Lying: Safe Sex and White Lies in the Time of AIDS," "Zipped Lips," and "McDonald's Is Not Our Kind of Place."

CRITICAL THINKING
In Connecting Texts

In Swarupa Reddy's essay "TV as a Culprit" (p. 247), the writer claims that television viewing undermines family values in addition to hindering the academic performance of children and teenagers. Furthermore, Reddy maintains that TV "actually promotes sex and violence." In his essay, "TV: A Beautiful Curse?" (p. 180), Brent Monacelli disagrees in part with Reddy's main points. Working with a partner or small group, think about your own experiences with television viewing. If you like, broaden your exploration of the effects of the media to include the Internet and films. Assign a note taker as you brainstorm some immediate as well as long-term effects of these media upon children, teenagers, and families. If time permits, share your findings with the rest of the class.

PROGRESS LOG

	Essay	1	2	3	4	5
PURPOSE						
Introduction engages audience interest						
Purpose is clear						
Point of view is consistent						
FOCUS						
Thesis has subject, controlling idea, appropriate tone						
All main points and details support thesis						
Conclusion connects with thesis						
MATERIAL						
Thesis is adequately and clearly supported						
Information is reliable, accurate, detailed						
STRUCTURE						
Organization of main points is clear						
Cue words signal any shift in thought						
STYLE						
Sentence structure is sound and varied						
Word choice is specific and descriptive						
Surface errors are not distracting						
Manuscript format is correct						
Writer's unique voice comes through						

Chapter 12

Showing Relationships: Comparison/Contrast and Division/Classification

Become aware of the two-sided nature of your mental make-up: one thinks in terms of the connectedness of things; the other thinks in terms of parts and sequences.

—Gabriele Rico, *Writing the Natural Way*

Preview

In this chapter you will learn

- How to identify the characteristics of comparison/contrast and division/classification in essay development
- How to use comparison/contrast to reveal similarities or differences
- How to identify "one-side-at-a-time" versus "point-by-point" organization in comparison/contrast essay development
- How to use division/classification to analyze the relationship of parts to the whole, or to sort and group according to common characteristics
- How to find a unifying principle when using division/classification in an essay
- How to differentiate between types and stereotypes

After reading this chapter and completing its practice exercises, you will be able to use comparison/contrast and division/classification as patterns of development in your essays.

You need a new car, and to help you make a decision, you have drawn up a comparative list of features of your two favorite models. By doing so, you're employing a method of thinking—comparison/contrast—helpful in making decisions as well as understanding how experiences connect.

You're putting the clean laundry away. In sorting and placing your items of clothing in various drawers, you're using another crucial method of thinking in our complex world: division/classification.

Comparison/contrast and division/classification are closely related patterns of essay development as well as ways of thinking. They allow writers to explore a subject by breaking it down into smaller parts and examining those parts. In an essay, this sorting and analyzing helps readers understand how objects and ideas relate. Understanding a subject in depth permits readers to evaluate, and if necessary, to choose among alternatives. This chapter explains how to use comparison/contrast and division/classification patterns of development in your essays.

CHARACTERISTICS OF COMPARISON/CONTRAST

Decisions, decisions! Will you order the juicy cheeseburger and fries or the healthy avocado and sprouts on whole wheat? Do you want to major in biology or business? Should you vote for or against placing height restrictions on new housing developments in your neighborhood? No matter what you do or where you go, you need to make decisions. You may make a choice based on instinctive response, or you may decide by using comparison, which explores the similarities or likenesses of one choice with another, or contrast, which points out the differences.

What subjects might you want to compare or contrast in an essay? Just as choices in real life are limitless, so are the subjects you can choose to write about. You might want to compare or contrast two characters in a short story, two lifestyles, two sports, two movies, two opinions. For an economics class, you might want to compare the past with the present—was our quality of life better or worse in the 1950s than it is now? For a midterm exam in biology, you might contrast two organs in the human body. For a business class, you might compare two management styles. When your essay's purpose is to organize information for clear understanding, to make choices, and to highlight qualities of a subject in more detail, comparison/contrast is an effective strategy.

To examine comparison/contrast development, read the following excerpt:

> As soon as Uncle Frank arrived, his tie loosened and his sleeves rolled up, I felt sorry for my father. It was the way I always felt when the two of them were together. Brothers naturally invite comparison, and when comparisons were made between those two, my father was bound to suffer. And my father was, in many respects, an impressive man. He was tall, broad-shouldered, and pleasant-looking. But Frank was all this and more. He was handsome—dark wavy hair, a jaw chiseled on such precise angles it seemed to conform to some geometric law, and he was as tall and well-built as my father, but with an athletic grace my father lacked.
>
> Frank was witty, charming, at smiling ease with his life and everything in it. Alongside his brother my father soon seemed somewhat prosaic. Oh, stolid, surely, and steady and dependable. But inevitably, inescapably dull. Nothing glittered in my father's wake the way it did in Uncle Frank's.

—Larry Watson, from *Montana 1948*

Notice that Watson's excerpt contains the following characteristics:

- **Two subjects from the same general group are compared or contrasted.**
  Watson's two subjects are brothers: the writer's father and Frank, his uncle. The writer introduces his subjects with his early reference to "Uncle Frank" and "my father"; he further signals the focus of his subject when he states, "Brothers naturally invite comparison. . . ."

- **The structure clearly separates one subject from the other.**
  Watson organizes his writing by contrasting the two brothers point by point. He states that his father was "tall, broad-shouldered, and pleasant-looking" and then switches the focus to his uncle: "Frank was all this and more. He was handsome—dark wavy hair, a jaw chiseled on such precise angles it seemed to conform to some geometric law."

- **The same features are discussed for both subjects—there is a balance to the comparison or contrast.**
  Watson compares the two brothers in height, body build, facial features, and personality.

- **A conclusion results from the comparison or contrast of the two subjects.**
  Watson hints at this conclusion early in the first paragraph: ". . . when comparisons were made between those two, my father was bound to suffer." At the end of the second paragraph, Watson concludes his presentation of the two subjects with a striking image: "Nothing glittered in my father's wake the way it did in Uncle Frank's."

The technique of comparison/contrast works in another way in the following model. As you read, try to identify the characteristics of this pattern of development.

MODEL WITH KEY QUESTIONS

This student writer had recently read a popular book asserting that men and women have different values. She decided to test the author's theory by contrasting her husband's behavior with her own.

Model 1   ## Men Are Makita, Women Are Marigolds

Yen Glassman

Yen Glassman is a mother of two young children, so she attends college on Saturdays. Yen reports that she has found the learning center on her campus very helpful. She enjoys writing essays both for her writing classes and for publication in the college literary magazine. Yen has an interest in gardening, but as far as career plans are concerned, she is undecided, keeping her options open.

1   Men and women have opposite views of shopping. However, do-it-yourself home improvement stores are able to attract both customers (men and women), with different intentions and focus. When Keith and I recently visited Home Depot, I found out that even though men and women respond differently to the same products and displays in the store, these differences really serve to complement each other.

2   When Keith and I decided to remodel our bathroom, we spent a lot of time discussing items needing work. We would go to Home Depot together. This was a rare occasion because Keith was willing to accompany me on a shopping trip. Usually, he would rather stay home with the children. However, Home Depot drew a different reaction from Keith. He was looking forward to it and actually got ready ahead of me and waited in the car.

3   On the other hand, I always love to go shopping, no matter what the circumstances—I'd rather be in a department store shopping for dresses, but a home improvement store has its own charms. For our remodeling project, Keith and I agreed that we would repaint the walls and change the cabinets of our bathroom. I could hardly wait to compare paint chips.

4   When we arrived at the store, each of us headed in different directions. Like many other men, Keith was immediately attracted to the power tool section where there were live demonstrations of the latest technology. After testing several tools, Keith decided to refinish the bathroom cabinets, and he was excited about purchasing a Makita power saw and sanding machine in order to begin work on the cabinets.

5   In contrast, I went to the wallpaper and faucet sections. After seeing several wallpaper sample books, I decided to wallpaper the bathroom with a flower pattern instead of repainting. In addition, I also wanted to replace our old faucet with new porcelain faucets with two gold-plated handles for hot and cold, despite the fact that these did not fit the existing plumbing of our bathroom.

6   When we regrouped, Keith and I realized that each of us was attracted to different products and we had gotten completely off track from our original project. Walking around the store, I observed many different responses of men and women in the shopping mode.

7   For example, on the molding aisle, a lady was driving a male employee crazy by putting back every piece of lumber he had chosen if it contained any knots or had the slightest imperfection. On the other hand, a male construction worker had a list of items and quickly and methodically selected various wood materials with no thought to their small imperfections or roughnesses.

8   As John Gray states in the book *Men Are From Mars, Women Are From Venus,* "Men value power, efficiency and achievement. Women value beauty and romance." The Home Depot appeals to men through gadgets and new power tools, the objects that help them to achieve their projects and goals. In contrast, the store attracts women with its many items for beautifying the home and decorating to express their feelings.

9   However, even though men and women are different in some of their values, they complement each other like lock and key: one cannot work without the other. In addition, the more we understand our differences, the more we can learn to support and respect each other.   ○

Key Questions

1. **Purpose**   What significant point does Glassman make in paragraph 1 about men's and women's responses to shopping?

2. **Focus**   In her thesis, does Glassman indicate that she will be comparing or contrasting?

3. **Material**   Notice that the writer draws from personal experience for her material, but she also relies on two other sources. What are they?

4. **Structure**   Does Glassman develop her essay by exploring all the features of one subject and switching to the other subject, or does she go back and forth from the first to the second subject? Refer to particular paragraphs in support of your answer.

5. **Style**   In what way does Glassman use John Gray's words to connect her conclusion to her thesis?

GUIDELINES FOR WRITING COMPARISON/CONTRAST

Determine Your Purpose and Audience

You will want to choose a comparison/contrast pattern of development in your essay if your purpose involves communicating a significant point about two subjects. Perhaps you want to convince your audience that one career field is better than the other; maybe you want to inform them of the actual differences between two frequently confused mathematical theories or medicines. Use comparison/contrast to organize information about two closely related subjects if you want your audience to be able to make a choice by noticing the features of each subject in more detail.

Practice 12.1   Take a look at the following ideas for subjects and then come up with a possible audience and purpose for each one. The first example has been done for you.

Subject	Audience	Significant point
1. Two brands of sedans	*Potential car buyers*	*One car is better than the other*
2. Two characters in two different short stories		
3. Two Italian restaurants		
4. Two football players		
5. Going to college to obtain marketable skills and going to college to obtain a well-rounded education		
6. Emeralds and diamonds ❏		

Identify Similar Subjects to Compare or Contrast

If you look at the list of subject ideas from the previous practice exercise, you'll notice that the two subjects for each pair are from the same general group. It would be impossible to compare or contrast thoughtfully emeralds and football players, or an Italian restaurant and a short story.

In "Men Are Makita, Women Are Marigolds," Glassman is careful not to contrast men's behavior in a home improvement center with women's behavior in a different environment, such as a boutique or a grocery store. This would invalidate any meaningful conclusion about her two subjects. There are exceptions to this "similar subject" guideline, but in general, unless your instructor specifies, it's a good idea to choose two subjects to compare or contrast that have enough in common to warrant pointing out similarities or differences.

Practice 12.2   Examine the following list and choose appropriate subjects for a comparison/contrast essay, followed by a brief explanation of why you think the subjects are appropriate. If you think a subject is inappropriate, change one of the subject choices to make the combination work. The first example has been done for you.

1. A book about coal miners and a movie about coal miners
    yes—similar subjects

2. A book about coal miners and a movie about Russian aristocracy

3. A book about coal miners and a book about construction workers

4. High school study skills and high school hangouts

5. Constructive addictions and destructive addictions   ❑

Focus Your Subject

In narrowing your thesis for comparison/contrast, try to do the following:

- Name the two subjects to be compared or contrasted.

- Indicate whether the subjects will be compared, contrasted, or both.

- Include a controlling idea in which you mention why you are examining these two subjects. This could be a statement of the significance of the comparison or contrast of the two subjects.

Notice that Glassman's thesis includes her subjects, the limitations of the subjects—different reactions based on gender to a home improvement store visit—and the significant point she wants to make. She states, "I found out that even though *men and women* [subjects] respond *differently* [indication of contrast] to the same products and displays in the store, *these differences complement each other* [controlling idea]."

Practice 12.3 Take a look at the following subjects and audiences. Fill in what you feel could be a controlling idea for each comparison/contrast pair of subjects. The first example has been done for you.

Subject	Audience	Controlling idea
1. Two brands of sedans	Potential car buyers	*One car is better than the other*
2. Two characters in two different short stories	Those familiar with both stories	
3. Two Italian restaurants	People who like Italian food	
4. Two football players	Football fans ❏	

Practice 12.4 To differentiate between an effective and ineffective thesis, read the following thesis statements. Comment on their effectiveness according to the guidelines just discussed:

1. French television sitcoms are quite different from American sitcoms.

2. Although echinacea and goldenseal are both North American herbs useful for various physical ailments, we know quite a bit about the first but almost nothing about the other.

3. When I compare the way I lived before I became a college student with the way I live now, I see a big difference.   ❏

Choose Points and Maintain a Balance

Once you have an effective thesis with a controlling idea, you will want to choose the points to make about your subjects. **Points** are the ideas that are discussed equally for each of two subjects in a comparison/contrast essay. If you want to influence your friend to buy one brand of car instead of another, you wouldn't just say, "Trust me; I know that the Ford is better than the Honda—it's just an all-around better vehicle in every respect." Instead, you would want to draw up a list of points to prove that the Ford is superior. You might want to talk about dependability, price, performance, mileage, comfort, body style, service accessibility, and safety features. You would then discuss each of these eight points for both the Ford and the Honda. But to be fair, logical, and clear in your comparison, you would present the same points for the Ford that you present for the Honda, and in the same order. You wouldn't change the order of points as you go from one subject to the other, because this would only confuse your audience.

You also want to be sure to present a *balanced* comparison or contrast. Notice that when Watson describes the two brothers, he attempts to give his audience equal details about the points—height, body build, facial features, and personality—for each man.

Practice 12.5   Reread "Men Are Makita, Women Are Marigolds" (p. 261) looking for points of comparison or contrast. Complete the following list. The first one has been completed for you.

	Author's husband	**Author**
1. Feelings about shopping trips	*Would rather stay home*	*Enjoys them*
2.		
3.		
4.		

❏

Sketch Out a Structure: Two Possible Plans

You have two options for organizing an essay using comparison/contrast development: the one-side-at-a-time method and the point-by-point method. You can compare the two methods and then decide which one will best serve your purpose. As you are drafting, you may want to experiment by writing two alternative versions and then get feedback from a peer editor or instructor to determine which plan works better.

In the one-side-at-a-time plan, you present all of your information on one subject first and then switch to the "other side"—that is, the second subject being compared or contrasted.

In contrast, both Watson's excerpt and Glassman's essay present the reader with a point-by-point plan—a point is made about one subject and then the same point is used to contrast or compare the other subject. Here is an outline of Watson's structure for the excerpt from *Montana 1948*:

I. Height
   A. Frank
   B. Father
II. Shoulders
   A. Frank
   B. Father
III. Face and hair
   A. Frank
   B. Father

IV. Personality
    A. Frank
    B. Father

Notice that as Watson moves from one subject to the next, point by point, he gives approximately the same amount of detail for both subjects on every point he makes.

Practice 12.6   Reread Glassman's essay and outline the main points.   ❏

Use Cue Words

Signaling your reader that you're moving from one subject to the other is extremely important in comparison/contrast development. If you choose the one-side-at-a-time method, your essay will require fewer transitions than if you use the point-by-point organizational plan. However, regardless of your organizational plan, make clear exactly which point you're making and which of your two subjects you're talking about by using appropriate cue words, such as *in contrast, on the other hand, in a similar manner, in comparison,* and *in the same way.*

Practice 12.7   Review the table of cue words (p. 141–142). Look again at Glassman's essay and annotate it by underlining all cue words or phrases you find.   ❏

Strategies for Writing Comparison/Contrast

1. **Purpose**   Think about why you want to compare or contrast two subjects. Consider the audience that would be interested in these two subjects and their level of knowledge about the subjects.

2. **Focus**   Limit your subject to two situations, people, ideas, or objects. Indicate whether you will develop similarities, differences, or both. Include the significance of the comparison or contrast of your two subjects.

3. **Material**   Choose the same points to compare or contrast for the two subjects, making sure that you gather enough information in prewriting to present meaningful detail on both subjects. Delete any unconvincing or unrelated material.

4. **Structure**   Decide whether your subjects are better suited to a one-side-at-a-time or a point-by-point plan. In revising, make sure you have followed your chosen plan consistently. In polishing, ask yourself where you could insert cue words to help your audience move from one point or subject to another.

5. **Style**   Polish your introduction and conclusion to ensure that they serve your purpose in comparing or contrasting the two subjects.

OPTIONS FOR WRITING COMPARISON/CONTRAST

You will be using your skills of comparing and contrasting when you think about and choose one of the following writing options. When you decide which option you'd like to explore, think about whether you want to emphasize similarities, differences, or both.

1. In her essay (p. 261), Glassman points out several differences in gender response. Perhaps you disagree; maybe you can think of many similarities men and women share in their responses to specific situations. In an essay, compare the two sexes, supporting or refuting Glassman's and John Gray's claim that men and women have different values.

2. Reread the excerpt from *Montana 1948* (p. 260). The author focuses on two brothers and their contrasting qualities. Do you know two relatives or close friends who, in spite of their apparent similarities, possess profound differences? What about you and a sibling or close friend? Write an essay developing the differences or similarities of two people you know well.

3. Have you read a good book only to see it turned into a mediocre movie? Or have you read a good book and then been led to seek out others that were similar? Compare or contrast a book with its movie version, or two books on the same subject written from different points of view.

4. Buy a copy of a local newspaper. (Some of the larger metropolitan papers are also available online.) Choose a favorite section based on your personal interests. Read this section, zeroing in on any article you find of special interest. Read the article twice, annotating it thoughtfully. Now write a carefully composed letter to the editors of the paper, evaluating the article and explaining what you liked and did not like about the piece. Proofread your letter carefully and then mail or send it as an e-mail attachment to the paper's editors.

5. Can you think of a time you underwent a change from one environment to another? Perhaps you want to contrast your life as a college student with your life before. Or it could be that your current situation living with a roommate or living alone has made for a dramatic contrast with your former situation living with your parents or with another relative. Contrast the two environments.

6. Write an essay contrasting two particular brands of car in the same category: for example, you might contrast a Ford with Chevrolet. Be sure that your points of contrast are the same for both cars.

7. Many of us have lived in more than one city or community. If you have, write an essay comparing or contrasting two different places where you have lived.

8. *(Film and Literature)* Write an essay comparing two films of a certain type by evaluating each. For example, you might compare the two World War II films *Saving Private Ryan* and *The Thin Red Line.*

9. *(Film and Literature)* Option 1: Read John Steinbeck's classic short novel *Of Mice and Men* and then view the highly acclaimed John Malkovich film version of the novel. In an essay, contrast the way the characters Lenny and George are portrayed in the book with the way they are presented in the film. Option 2: Read any of the short stories in Raymond Carver's collection entitled *Short Takes.* After viewing the film by the same name, compare and contrast the film and printed versions of the story.

10. *(Service Learning)* Call or visit your local chamber of commerce and ask about particular community service opportunities. After noting these, call or visit the student activities office on your campus and inquire about specific community service or volunteer opportunities for students. Write an essay comparing and contrasting the opportunities offered in your community with those offered on campus. Mention which opportunities are of greater interest to you and why.

Challenge Option: Combining Patterns

This essay asks you to use first cause/effect and then comparison/contrast patterns of development. Think of two significant events in America's history that are recent enough for you to remember. For example, if you're old enough to remember the first human to walk on the moon in 1969, you could pair this event with the discovery of the possibility of life on Mars in 1997. Or you could pair the Jim Jones mass suicide in Guyana in 1978 with the Heaven's Gate mass suicide in 1997.

Once you have chosen two events or occurrences, gather information in prewriting. As you draft your essay, you might want to follow this structure:

- *Introduction and thesis:* Name the two occurrences, indicate whether you will compare or contrast the two, and include the significance of the comparison or contrast to capture the interest of the audience.

- *Body paragraphs* (one or more): Detail the causes or effects connected with the first occurrence.

- *Body paragraphs* (one or more): Show a contrast or a similarity in the two occurrences by detailing the causes or effects connected with the second occurrence.

- *Conclusion:* Make clear the significance of the similar or different causes or effects connected with the two incidents.

CHARACTERISTICS OF DIVISION/CLASSIFICATION

Perhaps one of the first tasks you perform at the beginning of each semester is to buy subject dividers for your notebooks. Dividing a notebook into sections enables you to find notes, essays, handouts, and other class materials easily.

When the schedule of classes is published for your college, you can find the course you're interested in quickly because all course offerings are categorized by subject. All of us make use of the organizational strategies of division and classification every day, often without realizing it. Just as sorting and analyzing are automatic human responses to our complex world, so also are they important methods of essay development. Division and classification permit us to grasp relationships between simple and complex subjects.

Although division and classification are distinct methods of developing an essay, they are quite a bit alike and are sometimes used together within the same essay. Division is a writing strategy that breaks the subject down into smaller parts and analyzes these parts in relation to the whole. Classification is a writing strategy that brings several separate items together under the same "umbrella" or category so that distinguishing characteristics can be closely examined.

To observe how division/classification works, read the following excerpt:

> Men all have different styles of chopping wood, all of which are deemed by their practitioners as the only proper method. Often when I'm chopping wood in my own inept style, a neighbor will come over and "offer help." He'll bust up a few logs in his own manner, advising me as to the proper swing and means of analyzing the grain of the wood. There are "over the head" types and "swing from the shoulder" types, and guys who lay the logs down horizontally on the ground and still others who balance them on end, atop of stumps. I have one neighbor who uses what he calls "vector analysis." Using the right vectors, he says, the wood will practically *split itself.*
>
> —James Finney Boylan, from "The Bean Curd Method"

Notice that Boylan's excerpt demonstrates the following characteristics:

- **A principle or standard is used for breaking the subject into separate parts or types.**
  Boylan tells the reader that his categories are based on "different styles of chopping wood."

- **The subject is broken down into categories or divisions for separate consideration.**
  Boylan states that his subject, wood chopping experts, can be sorted into the following groups: "over the head" types, "swing from the shoulder" types, horizontal log layers, log/stump balancers, and vector analysis proponents.

- **The classifications or divisions of the subject are logical, clearly developed, and detailed sufficiently to explain and differentiate each one.**
  Boylan's categories are all based on his indicated principle of wood chopping styles; he doesn't slip in a category based on these men's appearance, for instance, or pet ownership, or car preference. The categories also proceed in a specific order. For instance, Boylan begins his discussion of the various types with "over the head" types and "swing from the shoulder" types, two styles that Boylan's audience can easily visualize. Because the last three types of wood choppers are slightly more difficult to envision, the writer saves these for the latter part of his paragraph.

See how many of the characteristics of the division/classification pattern of essay development you can identify in the following student model.

MODEL WITH KEY QUESTIONS

Student writer Chuks Ofoegbu wanted to share his experiences in the world of work by focusing on the subject of coworkers. As you read his essay, notice that some of his work experiences point out cultural differences between America and Nigeria.

Model 2   COWORKERS

Chuks Ofoegbu

Chuks Ofoegbu confides, "My writing process started when I was in high school." Born and raised in Nigeria, Chuks is interested in politics and likes to write about contemporary issues. In drafting his essays, Chuks learned the importance of defining all terms that an American audience might not understand. Chuks is currently working as a paralegal with a law firm and reports that he'll be able to think about long-term career plans when his financial situation is solid.

1   "Your boss is not your mother." That's the good news from one of the books I read recently, *Oedipus Wrecks*, by Brian Desroches. The book was named after Oedipus in the Greek legend who, in ignorance and partly from ambition, killed his own father and married his mother. The bad news, on the other hand, is that a lot of us feel and act like our managers or bosses are members of our families. The result is that we coworkers may squabble with one another in the workplace for selfish reasons. Based on the way my coworkers interact with other workers and their bosses, I can place them in three groups: the Butter-ups, the Get-alongs, and the Judases.

2   For the Butter-ups, flattery is the only method to get ahead. For the first year of the five years I worked as a cashier in the Ministry of Finance in Nigeria, I encountered the Butter-ups constantly. Their strategy was to compliment the boss excessively in order to win favorable personal evaluation reports, which were sent to office headquarters. These compliments came in the form of presents given to the boss on his birthday and wedding anniversary, or presents given to him for his wife's or children's birthdays. This group of Butter-ups was comprised of young men and women who needed a promotion and a raise in their salary to enjoy the good things of life. The Butter-ups would give such presents and a shower of praises to the boss even for no apparent reason.

3   Another group of coworkers I came in contact with were the Get-alongs. They just "got along with the boss." They believed in the old fable, "Slow and steady wins the race." I was among this Get-along group. We had a good relationship with the boss because we would often come to work fifteen minutes or more before the official opening hour and we would perform our job assignments efficiently. In spite of the fact that we offered the boss no special gifts or flattery, he had a soft spot for us because our level of neatness in our work, our attire, and our desks was impressive. In addition, our interactions with our coworkers were unruffled.

4   The third group of workers were the Judases, from the Biblical character Judas Iscariot who betrayed Jesus. This group believed in the "divide and rule" method

to gain power. These workers created disharmony between the boss and the other coworkers through back-biting and false allegations. They accused other workers of taking gratifications from members of the public, cheating in promotion examinations, and keeping false records in personnel files at headquarters. Why would they do this? The Judases actually wanted to create this disharmony so that the boss would be toppled. They wanted him out because they had a clash of interest with him over staff control and the way office furniture sent from headquarters had been shared among workers.

5   In the end, the Judases were either posted to handle managerial posts elsewhere or reprimanded through letters to desist from their false accusations. I survived this time of turmoil with the three groups of coworkers. However, colleagues, I would advocate for peace and harmony in the workplace rather than sowing the seeds of disunity and acrimony between coworkers. Just as Oedipus discovered, ignorance and ambition are a dangerous combination. ○

Key Questions

1. **Purpose**   Would you say Ofoegbu's primary purpose is expressive, informative, or persuasive? Support your point of view by citing a word or phrase in his essay.

2. **Focus**   What basis for breaking his subject into groups does Ofoegbu mention in his first paragraph?

3. **Material**   What types of details does Ofoegbu use the most to develop his three categories?

4. **Structure**   Why does the writer order the categories with the Butter-ups first and the Judases last? Circle the cue words that take the reader from one main category to the next in the three body paragraphs.

5. **Style**   Reread the essay, underlining any quoted passages. Now examine these quotations. In what way do they help delineate each category of workers?

GUIDELINES FOR WRITING DIVISION/ CLASSIFICATION

Connect Subject, Audience, and Purpose

You will want to use a division/classification pattern of development in your essay if you have a complex subject that you want to divide into more manageable parts. Dividing and/or sorting will help you impose order and increase your audience's understanding of your subject. Your purpose may be to express humor, as Boylan does (p. 270), or you may want to inform your audience, as Ofoegbu does.

In thinking about your purpose, remember not to bore your audience by presenting them with useless information. Classifying college students' hairstyles into shaved, short, medium, and long would probably result in a real "snoozer" of an essay; separating American freedoms into freedom of speech, freedom of thought, freedom of assembly, and freedom of worship is a nice idea, but unless you offer new information, most readers will tune you out. Once you're assigned a subject or think of an idea for a subject, consider the audience that would benefit from or appreciate having more information on the subject. Then think about how you might break that subject down for this audience.

Practice 12.8   To gain more experience in thinking about division/classification, determine an audience and a purpose for each of the following subjects.

Subject	Audience	Purpose
1. Potential careers for your major		
2. Types of people in the student center		
3. Categories of customers in a retail store		
4. Necessary components of a rock concert		
5. Types of computers ❏		

Identify a Unifying Principle

One potential pitfall for essays using a division/classification pattern involves mixed categories or divisions. Therefore, you will want to make sure you have a **unifying principle**—a basis for breaking down and sorting your subject. For example, in Boylan's essay, men are sorted into categories on the basis of one unifying principle—their particular style of chopping wood.

Practice 12.9   Find the unifying principle for each of the groups below. Cross out the one item that is not categorized as the others are according to the same principle. The first group has been done for you.

1. Swimsuit
a. String bikini
b. Two-piece
c. ~~Nylon~~
d. One-piece
Unifying principle: *suit style*

2. Vacations
a. European
b. South American
c. Asian
d. Summer

3. Workers
a. White-collar
b. Blue-collar
c. Part-time
d. Semiskilled

4. Roommates
a. Shy
b. Outgoing
c. Comical
d. Messy
Unifying principle:

5. Fitness activities
a. Stress
b. Jogging
c. Swimming
d. Tennis

6. Movies
a. Horror
b. Romance
c. French
d. Adventure

❏

Limit Divisions or Categories

Into how many parts should you divide your subject? Boylan comments on five types of wood chopping; Ofoegbu examines three categories of coworkers. Although there is no "correct" number, you will generally want three or more divisions or classifications. You might want to try using as many parts or types as you can develop in sufficient and clear detail for the length of your assigned essay. Also, remember that a few strong components are always preferable to many underdeveloped ones; you don't want your essay to look like a list without any supporting material. The number and quality of these types or categories will determine your plan of development. Be careful not to "invent" a category or a division that doesn't really exist. For example, avoid something like this: "the good friend, the so-so friend, and the best friend."

Your thesis may include the following parts:

- Subject

- Controlling idea—the unifying principle for your division or classification

- Plan of development—an indication of how many parts or categories you've broken your subject into, what these parts or categories are, and the order in which you will discuss them

Notice that Ofoegbu's thesis for his essay contains these parts:

(Controlling idea — Unifying principle)

"Based on the way my coworkers (subject) interact with other workers and their bosses, I can place them in three groups: the Butter-ups, the Get-alongs, and the Judases."

(Plan of development)

Practice 12.10 Choose one of the subjects on page 273 and see if you can come up with a thesis statement that includes these three parts: subject, controlling idea, and plan of development. ❑

Determine a Plan

Once you have a working thesis, you will need to gather material in prewriting to make each division or classification clear and distinct. When you have enough material, consider how you might arrange your information. Oftentimes it is helpful to draft a couple of variations. If you review your purpose and audience, one arrangement will strike you as more effective than the others. It's also helpful to remember that your preliminary organizational plan does not need to be set in stone. For instance, Ofoegbu reversed his original arrangement of categories because his peer editors suggested that the "Judases" would be a dramatic group to end with.

Practice 12.11 Using the same thesis statement you selected in Practice 12.10, decide on an effective ordering for your subject's parts or types. Write out a brief outline, or make a list or a clustering or branching diagram. ❑

Polish for Pizzazz

Once you've written a draft, received feedback, and given yourself time to respond to suggestions of others, go back to your essay and polish it to bring out the pizzazz—the style, energy, spirit, or vigor in writing. Even the most meticulously written draft can get bogged down by mechanical "pigeonholing" of a subject into parts or categories if the writer doesn't give the audience a strong sense of energy and spirit.

Be creative in your introduction. Maybe you'd like to open with a little historical background on your subject, or perhaps you could get the attention of your audience by posing a problem. Check also to make sure that your conclusion is not tedious. Notice that none of the writing samples using division/classification close with a renaming of the parts or categories. Instead, Ofoegbu closes with a bit of personal advice to his colleagues, while Boylan simply comes to the end of his list.

Practice 12.12 To gain experience in polishing an essay for pizzazz, return to the thesis and plan of development which you were working on in Practice 12.11. Think of a creative way you might introduce your subject. Now think of a creative way you might conclude that same essay. (For more information on introductions and conclusions, see Chapter 6.) ❑

Strategies for Writing Division/Classification

1. **Purpose**   Ask yourself what you want to communicate to your audience by sorting a subject into categories or breaking it down into separate parts.

2. **Focus**   State your subject, the categories or divisions you're using, and your unifying principle. Check for overlapping categories or divisions—each should be unique.

3. **Material**   You can use personal experience, but you may want to do a little research to find out more about your subject. Check to see if you have enough material to develop each of the main parts or types fully.

4. **Structure**   Experiment with the most logical and effective order for your particular subject and purpose in dividing or classifying. Use appropriate cue words to signal movement from one division or classification to the next.

5. **Style**   Choose descriptive detail and action words that will make your categories or divisions come alive for the reader. Reread your introduction and conclusion, and then polish them for pizzazz.

OPTIONS FOR WRITING DIVISION/CLASSIFICATION

The following writing options will give you an opportunity to use the strategies for division/classification. Choose an option, decide on a unifying principle for breaking your subject down into parts or types, and then make sure you have sufficient information to develop each part or category.

1. Have you ever felt you were compartmentalized as a person—employee, college student, mother, father, son, daughter, boyfriend, girlfriend, soccer player, amateur bodybuilder, and so forth? Select four major roles that you play and write an essay detailing each of these as a compartment. Make each compartment or role clear by indicating the divisions in your body paragraphs.

2. Are you majoring in a field that has several possible career or job opportunities? For example, the field of nursing offers registered nurse, nurse practitioner, licensed vocational nurse, and certified nurse associate. Divide a major into potential careers and discuss each, perhaps mentioning the salary, job duties, level of education required, and any special skills needed. You might visit the career center on your campus for more information.

3. Do you have a hobby or a special skill? Let's say you know a lot about self-defense. You could write an essay discussing three different types of self-defense: kung fu, jujitsu, and karate. Break your hobby into three or more subdivisions and explore the attributes of each type.

4. Do you like to people-watch? Go to a public place—a library, bar, restaurant, park, or the student center at your college—and try to place people into different categories based on their actions and interactions. For example, in the park your categories might include the loners, reading their books or newspapers on the park bench; the lovers, holding hands and oblivious to all around them; or the young mothers and fathers with their children. Write a paragraph detailing each category.

5. Reading Ofoegbu's essay "Coworkers" may serve to remind you of past or present jobs in your life. If you've ever been a waitress, waiter, salesperson, clerk, or other, could you classify your customers, coworkers, or bosses based on the way they behave? In an essay, detail these categories of people.

6. Each of us traveling on the road has encountered various types of drivers. Write an essay in which you categorize drivers based on their habits and skills (or lack of skill!).

7. From your experience in college, write an essay in which you categorize professors by teaching style in order to inform your audience of effective teaching methods.

8. Write an essay in which you categorize fast-food restaurants in order to inform your audience which particular types of fast-food establishments are better than others.

9. *(Film and Literature)* Write an essay in which you choose one movie genre, such as horror, action, comedy, musical, drama, western, or anime, for example. Subdivide the genre you choose into distinct categories and then discuss some film examples from each category. For instance, if you focus on comedy, you might want to divide this genre into slapstick, romantic, and musical comedy. Now think of three films that each fall into one of the three categories.

10. *(Service Learning)* Visit a nearby animal shelter in order to observe the people who go there. Take notes or tape record what you see and hear. Write an essay in which you categorize the various individuals you saw at the shelter. Put these visitors into distinct groups based on their appearance, their personality, and their interaction with other family members. You might also want to investigate a relationship between particular breeds and size of dogs and the type of visitor they seem to attract. If you like, send a copy of your essay to the administrative head of the shelter and ask him or her to evaluate your findings and get back to you by phone or e-mail.

Challenge Option: Combining Patterns

Write an essay using definition and classification. (For a review of definition, see Chapter 10.) Many of us have encountered times on the job, in school, at home with young children, or in a sport or volunteer commitment when we've been tempted to take the day off and just not show up. In other words, at these times we feel we need a "mental health day." Think about the temptation of taking your own mental health day and write an essay on the subject, using the following structure or another arrangement that you prefer:

- *Introduction:* Grab the interest of the audience; focus your subject and use a clear thesis.

- *Body paragraphs* (one or more): Define "mental health" as this term relates to commitments and/or occasional burnout, frustration, or stress connected to commitments.

- *Body paragraphs* (one or more): Break "mental health days" down into three categories; explore three types of occasions or situations that could make you want to take a holiday from your commitments.

- *Conclusion:* Try to connect your concluding remarks to your introduction and thesis in a meaningful, thoughtful way.

JOURNAL WRITING: TYPES AND STEREOTYPES

Comparison/Contrast

Think about two people whom you know really well—these could be relatives, friends, or coworkers. For a journal entry, draw a line down the middle of your paper, putting one name on the top left side and the other name on the right side. Now think of as many specifics about the person on the left side as you can—looks, personality, way of talking, walking, likes, and dislikes. At the same time, record the corresponding details for the person on the right side. After you have a page or more of material, review what you've written. Would you say these two people are more alike than different? In what respects are they similar? In what other respects do they differ? You may find that you want to develop your journal entry into a comparison/contrast essay.

Division/Classification

When, as a writer, you decide to use classification to develop your essays, you break your subject into **types**—into kinds or groups. The word **stereotypes,** however, means something quite different: preconceived notions that place someone or something into a category. Stereotypes sometimes result from human prejudices, and many times victims of stereotyping suffer discrimination. For example, if you see a person in the market who looks unshaven and is wearing dirty, torn clothing, going up and down the food aisles, you might jump to the conclusion that the person is homeless. This might lead to your next conclusion that he or she is looking for food to steal. This person—who may or may *not* be homeless—then becomes the victim of your stereotyping. In a journal entry, write about a time that:

- You've stereotyped another by labeling or placing the person into a category without enough evidence.
- You've suffered as the victim of someone else's stereotyping.

In the future, check to make sure you are not stereotyping in your writing, and be on the alert to spot this faulty reasoning in the writing of others.

Using the Computer: Comparing and Contrasting Information and Web sites

1. To explore a detailed definition of comparison and contrast essays, visit these Web sites:

   http://leo.stcloudstate.edu/acadwrite/comparcontrast.html

2. To examine a detailed definition of division and classification essays, visit this Web site:

   http://www3.uark.edu/qwct/resources/handouts/classdiv.html

3. To find more information about Daniel Goleman, whose writing appears on page 280 of this chapter, visit this Web site:

   http://www.americanscientist.org/template/InterviewTypeDetail/assetid/30504

4. To find more information on Toni Morrison, a Nobel Prize winner whose writing appears below, visit this Web site:

   http://almaz.com/nobel/literature/1993a.html

5. By now, you have seen many different kinds of Web sites. Some might be very elaborate, with animated characters or even sound and video. Others might be like the newsletters some people send out with holiday cards, describing someone's life and interests for anyone who happens to take the time to read. Setting up a personal Web site is like publishing a book that you have written. You might not ever know who reads it, and you can choose how much or how little information to reveal about yourself. But if you have interests or experiences that you would like to share, you can use your writing skills to "publish" a Web page of your own. You might also want to set up a *blog*—a frequent chronological publication of personal thoughts. Find out if your school allows students to set up their own Web pages. Often, this service is free to students and staff while they are enrolled. (You can also set up your own Web page through a private hosting service.) Next, sign up for any tutorials or classes your school computer lab offers on setting up a Web page. As with all writing you do, there are issues to consider when you set up such a site:

   - Will your page have a main theme or subject? (Besides yourself!)

   - Who will your audience be? What information or entertainment can you provide on your Web page that will attract their interest?

   - What details and experiences can you provide that will enhance your main points? You might want to link your page to other sites, where readers can find additional information. Or you might want to add photographs or sound to your page.

RESPONDING TO WRITING: A SCAVENGER HUNT

If you've ever been on a scavenger hunt, you know that it is a game in which people compete to be the first to find various items on a list. This activity will challenge you to "scavenge" for items found in the following comparison/contrast and division/classification paragraphs. All of the items listed below each paragraph can be found somewhere in the paragraph, and all have been defined and discussed either earlier in this chapter or elsewhere in this book. Annotate the paragraph by labeling each item as you find it. The first example has been done for you.

Subjects

1. **My parents** took issue over the question of whether it was possible for White people to improve. They assumed that Black people were the humans of the globe, but had serious doubts about the quality and existence of White humanity. Thus my father, distrusting every word and every gesture of every White man on earth, assumed that the White man who crept up the stairs one afternoon had come to molest his

daughters and threw him down the stairs and then our tricycle after him. (I think my father was wrong, but considering what I have seen since, it may have been very healthy for me to have witnessed that as my first Black-White encounter.) My mother, however, *believed* in them—their possibilities. So when the meal we got on relief was bug-ridden, she wrote a long letter to Franklin Delano Roosevelt. And when White bill collectors came to our door, it was she who received them civilly and explained in a sweet voice that we were people of honor and that the debt would be taken care of. Her message to Roosevelt got through—our meal improved. Her message to the bill collectors did not always get through and there was occasional violence when my father (self-exiled to the bedroom for fear he could not hold his temper) would hear that her reasonableness had failed.

—Toni Morrison, from "A Slow Walk of Trees"

subject   one-side-at-a-time *plan*
cue word signaling contrast   *specific detail*
thesis

2. Dr. [Harvey] Milkman, in a theory often cited by those who are stretching the boundaries of addiction, proposed in the mid-1980s that there are three kinds of addiction, each marked by the change they produce in emotional states. The first involves substances or activities that are calming, including alcohol, tranquilizers, overeating, and even watching television. The second involves becoming energized, whether by cocaine and amphetamines, gambling, sexual activity, or high-risk sports like parachute jumping. The third kind of addiction is to fantasy, whether induced by psychedelic drugs or, for example, by sexual thoughts.

—Daniel Goleman, from "As Addiction Medicine Gains,
Experts Debate What It Should Cover: Critics Argue That
Too Many Patients Are Called Addicts"

subject   *divisions of subject*
thesis   *cue words that signal order*
unifying principle   *specific detail*

For more essays using comparison/contrast, turn to the following essays in Part 4: "Offering Euthanasia Can Be An Act of Love" (p. 369) and "Who Gets to Choose?" (p. 371).
For more essays using division/classification, turn to the following essays in Part 4: "American Health, Then and Now" (p. 372) and "The Geography of the Imagination" (p. 363).

CRITICAL THINKING
In Connecting Texts

Three of the essays in this chapter focus on behavior: In "Men Are Makita, Women Are Marigolds" (p. 261), Glassman contrasts male and female behavior; in "Coworkers" (p. 271), Ofoegbu classifies workers on the basis of their behavior; in the excerpt by Boylan (p. 270), the writer talks about each man's insistence that his own wood-chopping style is the best. The writers each mention that they have learned something by observing their subjects.

Because America is a land rich in diversity, certain behaviors considered normal by one group of people may be regarded as abnormal by another. For instance, while Westerners tend to stand about 18 to 20 inches apart when they talk, people from Saudi Arabia like to stand closer to their subjects—around 12 to 14 inches apart. Someone born in the United States may feel somehow threatened by this "too intimate" behavior and move away from the speaker; at the same time, the immigrant from Saudi Arabia may perceive the American as unfriendly, distant, and possibly unapproachable. A person from the Southwest may prefer to wear cowboy boots, even in the city. This might seem like strange behavior to someone raised in the city, while the city-bred individual's habit of avoiding eye contact with strangers on the street may appear bizarre to the "cowboy" in the boots.

Work with a small group of people or your entire class to discover other examples of behaviors based on cultural or subcultural differences. Think about the people you see in public places, on campus, in your local neighborhoods, and on the job: baby boomers, Generation-Xers, dog owners, cat lovers, businesspersons, artists, senior citizens, bikers, or joggers. Discuss behavioral differences, including misunderstandings, communication breakdowns, or stereotyping, and then explore possible solutions. Take notes and keep them—you might want to use your notes to write an essay exploring behavioral differences and stereotyping.

Chapter 13

Taking a Stand: Argument

Give me the liberty to know, to utter, and to argue freely according to conscience, above all liberties.

—John Milton, *poet*

Preview

In this chapter you will learn

- To identify the characteristics of argument
- To evaluate arguments on the basis of soundness and validity
- To distinguish among logical, emotional, and ethical appeals
- To recognize and avoid logical fallacies
- To develop skill in writing essays using strategies of argument: stating a claim, supporting the claim with reliable evidence, refuting the opposition, and using appeals fairly

After reading this chapter and completing its practice exercises, you will be able to use argument as a pattern of development in your essays.

When you hear the word *argument*, do you envision a disagreement, perhaps one involving shouts, accusations, or maybe even slammed doors? Think back to the last heated exchange you had with a loved one or friend, a boss or coworker. Were you both behaving logically? Possibly, like many people, you were so emotionally involved that you weren't reasoning carefully or stating your arguments clearly; you might have been too caught up in the heat of the moment.

CHARACTERISTICS OF ARGUMENT

In contrast to this scenario of the fervent quarrel, the writing strategy classified as **argument** involves persuading an audience to agree with you on a controversial issue. To persuade your readers, you use evidence to support your opinion. And although argumentative essays do often include a writer's personal opinion and revolve around a heated or controversial dispute, they need to be controlled and reasonable in order to be effective. In learning about argument and practicing argumentative writing, you'll draw on what you've learned about various methods of essay development in other chapters of this text. In addition, you'll be practicing some new skills.

To see how argument can be used to develop an essay, read the following article, published by the writers of *Opportunity*, asking yourself what these writers want from their audience.

WHERE THE GUYS ARE NOT: THE GROWING GENDER IMBALANCE IN COLLEGE DEGREES AWARDED

1   Although males are 51 percent of the college-age population, in 1997–98 they received just 43.9 percent of the bachelor's degrees awarded in the United States. This was the smallest proportion since 1946 when just 43.1 percent of the bachelor's degrees were awarded to males.

2   Compared to their sisters, young men are struggling to graduate from high school, struggling to continue their educations into college, and finally graduate from college. In a word, males are failing in the educational system. They are failing compared to women, compared to the needs of a college educated workforce, and they are most certainly failing to achieve the potential of their own lives.

3   Over the last three decades, males have moved from superior numbers compared to females at most points in the educational system, to sharply inferior numbers. The story that results from this change could be told in either of two ways: either the success of women, or the failure of men. In reality it is both. Women have made simply stunning progress throughout the educational system over the last 30 years. Men have not.

4   Because *Opportunity* [a monthly postsecondary education publication] tends to focus on the under-represented groups in higher education, we focus here on the plight of males. By any reasonable measure, males are in very serious trouble in the nation's educational system. In a world of escalating demand for college-educated workers, that need has been met almost entirely by women. Men are stuck about where they were in the mid-1970s, in a time-warp, that leaves them oblivious to the growing educational needs of the labor market and the rich rewards for those who prepare through education to meet those needs.

5   While women (and most men) rejoice in the deserved educational success of women, their welfare is also impacted by the poor educational performance of males.

- Many college-educated women will not find college-educated men to marry. When the college-educated women are ready to form their families, too many will then discover the dearth of marriageable men when it is too late to do anything about it. Black women have known this for decades. Women in all other racial and ethnic groups are headed towards the same place.

- Women with fathers, brothers, husbands and sons who are struggling in their lives will share in those struggles. The satisfaction many women derive from the success of their own careers may be compromised by the troubled lives of the males whose lives they share.

- Ultimately, with males disengaging from their traditional family, economic, and civic roles, society faces a challenge about what to do with these

6   disengaged males. The only answer our society has offered so far is to put a rapidly growing share of adult men behind bars.

    Here we update and extend our analysis of data collected by the National Center for Education Statistics on the gender distribution of the academic degrees awarded by American colleges and universities. These data were first collected in 1870. The most recent data have been collected and partially published for 1998.

7   The data on college graduates tell stories of accumulated educational success or failure that spans decades. College degrees are awarded at the end of the education pipeline. They reflect experiences in school, at home, and in neighborhoods accumulated between pre-school and college graduation. The very different numbers of college graduates for men and women at the time of college graduation reflect the very different experiences in the lives and educations of boys and girls when they were growing up. And the end products are very different for males and females. We ought to be asking why.   ○

Notice that this argument demonstrates the following characteristics:

- **The subject is debatable.**
  The writers of *Opportunity* chose American males as their subject. The writers then aired an opinion: Many of these men struggle with their postsecondary education, and this struggle affects their lives and the lives of others.

- **The thesis makes a reasonable claim, a statement that can be supported by evidence.**
  This article's thesis comes near the end of paragraph 2: "In a word, males are failing in the educational system."

- **The opposition is acknowledged and refuted.**
  In paragraph 1, the authors acknowledge that certain events have made college degrees for males less likely than for females. In 1946, the writers continue, "just 43.1 percent of bachelor's degrees were awarded to males" because of World War II. A second acknowledgment of the opposition occurs in paragraph 3: There are those who would say that the number of college degrees for males has decreased because of the "stunning progress" of women in education.

- **The argument is developed with reliable and up-to-date evidence.**
  In paragraph 6, the writers cite data from 1998.

- **Appeals are used to advance the writers' argument.**
  In paragraph 5 the writers assert that in spite of women's success in college, these women are impacted by men's struggles with higher education. The three bulleted examples in this paragraph are logical appeals: They are based on sound reasoning and common sense. The writers later add in paragraph 5, "The only answer our society has offered so far is to put a rapidly growing share of adult men behind bars."

To observe these characteristics of argument at work in a student essay, read the following model and see how many of the characteristics just discussed you can identify.

MODEL WITH KEY QUESTIONS

In his search for an issue of public concern, student Brian Villapudua discovered that he felt strongly about immigration. He decided to gather additional information by consulting online sources and recent articles in periodicals.

LET'S MIX IT UP

Brian Villapudua

Brian Villapudua's essay on the immigration issue reflects the writer's interest in economic affairs. Please note that in March of 2003, the Immigration and Naturalization Services became part of Homeland Security. It is now called U.S. Citizenship and Immigration Services. Brian plans to pursue a bachelor's degree in economics with a French minor. He would then like to become a consultant for an international business firm.

1   Immigration is a touchy subject today and very few people in this country are willing to stick their necks out and take a stand on one side or the other. Either way they look at this muffled debate is bound to raise many questions. Let's take, for example, those who side with the anti-immigrationists. They argue that immigration puts a greater stress on the taxpayers to support immigrants. Anti-immigrationists say immigrants are taking jobs away from U.S. nationals and raising rents, and that too many immigrants are entering too fast to assimilate into "American" culture. However, these people appear to have made rash judgments about the issues when making such arguments, which seem to stem from xenophobic prejudices. Some of us don't like to deal with things that are unfamiliar to us, but immigrants are an invaluable resource to this great nation, which was created by immigrants. Thus, we should strive to increase the number of legal immigrants allowed into our country.

2   One argument anti-immigrationists make is that the taxpayers are burdened by the extra expenses for health, welfare, and other noneducational services that are placed on the system by immigrants. But are immigrants really burdening this country? George Borjas, an economics professor at the University of California at San Diego, discovered that even though immigrants receive more in government benefits than they pay in taxes, they actually produce a net gain for the U.S. economy of about four billion dollars a year.

3   What about immigrants taking away our jobs? This is another question asked by anti-immigrationists. In actuality, the jobs that immigrants accept are usually low-paying ones in restaurants, households, agriculture, and in the manufacturing industry. Dr. Larry Bedard, a hospital board member in a wealthy community, explains, "We want them [the immigrants] to clean our houses, rake our leaves, take care of our children, do the scut work of life."

4   Although some argue that immigrants, both illegal and legal, are destroying the prosperity of this country, they cannot totally blame immigrants for the problems that the U.S. is now facing. Part of the problem is the poor service provided in the past by the U.S. Immigration and Naturalization Services, formally known as the INS. The individual offices of the INS did not have a standardized operation; instead each office operated as it deemed best. In addition, some INS

employees exerted their prejudices on certain ethnic groups, obviously making it more difficult for some to get through the system than for others. Overhauling the INS as the newly created U.S. Citizenship and Immigration Services to provide better, more efficient service for all immigrants will help stop the influx of illegals by increasing the number of legal immigrants into the country. Also, since immigrants get tired of complicated red tape, getting rid of unnecessary forms could lessen the bureaucratic resistance that affects many immigrants.

5   We as U.S. citizens should remember that immigrants provide this country with an invaluable source of labor as well as help the economy through the consumption of goods. If the U.S. is to stop legal immigrants from entering, we are going to lose a part of our country's heritage—the open arms we once stretched out to welcome foreigners during the formative years of our nation. ○

Key Questions

1. **Purpose**   What is the writer's purpose in discussing the immigration issue?

2. **Focus**   State the writer's claim using your own words.

3. **Material**   Find two examples of evidence Villapudua uses and underline them. Search the following Website to discover how the INS has been restructured since March of 2003: **http://uscis.gov/graphics/aboutus/index.htm**

4. **Structure**   Describe the organizational plan Villapudua uses.

5. **Style**   Does the introductory paragraph establish the writer as fair and ethically motivated? Explain and offer support for your point of view.

GUIDELINES FOR WRITING ARGUMENT

Choose a Controversial Subject

When you're picking your brain for a subject for your argument, be aware that certain subjects just won't work for an argumentative essay. You cannot argue about beliefs, preferences, facts, or that which is impossible. Don't "shoot yourself in the foot" by choosing one of these topics. Here is a closer look at four types of subjects that are not appropriate for an essay using argument.

Facts
Because your main purpose in an argument is to persuade your audience to agree with you, **facts**—data that are regarded as true, rather than controversial—do not make appropriate subjects. However, although facts are not appropriate as subjects, they provide excellent supporting evidence to convince your readers to agree with you on a controversial topic.

Preferences
Preferences—personal likes and dislikes that are shaped not by reason but by background and emotions—do not make appropriate subjects for argumentative essays. Personal preferences usually can't be changed. In "Where the Guys

Are Not" (p. 283), the writers don't argue that colleges would be better institutions with a majority of females—instead, these writers argue that males have become an "under-represented group" in colleges.

Beliefs

If you've ever tried to discuss religion with another person, you probably know that **beliefs**—ideas that are held to be true for each individual but can't be proved to others—usually don't make good subjects for argument. For example, the subject in "Let's Mix It Up" (p. 285)—U.S. immigration—has nothing to do with the writer's personal beliefs but instead focuses on his opinion regarding this issue.

Impossibilities

Other subjects to avoid in an argumentative essay are **impossibilities**—proposals that are not possible in the real world. For instance, even though Villapudua speaks out in favor of immigration and asserts that immigrants have made tremendous contributions to our country's resources, he does not argue for unlimited immigration into the United States. He knows that trying to convince an audience of this unrealistic position would be futile.

What *is* an arguable subject? Opinions that can be debated because they have two or more sides or stands are excellent subjects for argumentative essays, especially if the opinions focus on issues of public concern.

In contrast to facts, preferences, beliefs, and impossibilities, **opinions**—issues, especially issues of public concern, about which a person feels strongly—make excellent subjects for an argumentative essay. It's important to differentiate between a personal preference and a reasonable opinion, however. To illustrate, "chocolate ice cream tastes better than vanilla" is a preference. In contrast, the opinion that "yogurt is better for people than ice cream" may be supported by specific evidence about vitamins, minerals, caloric content, and testimony from dietary experts.

Practice 13.1   Read the following sentences to see if they contain debatable subjects for an essay. Identify each as F (fact), P (preference), B (belief), I (impossibility), or O (opinion on an issue of concern to others).

1. In the Civil War, both the North and the South lost many lives.

2. If we as a nation would engage in more recycling, we would make the world a better place for future generations.

3. Short hair is more attractive on men than long hair.

4. God watches all of our actions.

5. Elvis Presley, although rich and famous, was a lonely man.

6. Watching musical groups in concert is more enjoyable than watching solo performers in concert.

7. College instructors should never assign homework to their students.

8. In the United States, the voting age is 18.

9. Most guinea pigs are smaller than most dogs.

10. The best colleges cost the most money to attend.   ❏

Assess Your Audience

Once you've found a debatable subject, think about what kind of audience you will be addressing. Ask yourself how much knowledge of the subject your readers possess, because this will influence the type of evidence and the manner in which you present your material in your argument. How would you categorize your audience in relation to your opinion on the subject? Do you think the average reader would be inclined to agree with you? Would your audience be cautious and possibly undecided, capable of siding with you or against you? Or is your opinion one that is so unpopular or controversial that you predict outright reader hostility?

Practice 13.2 To try your hand at assessing an audience, read the following subjects for arguments and the accompanying situations, and then decide whether you would categorize the audience as friendly, neutral, or hostile. The first item has been done for you.

Subject	Audience	Assessment
1. Violence against women resulting from popular song lyrics	Record companies	*hostile*
2. Violence against women resulting from popular song lyrics	Feminists	
3. More lenient attendance policy for college classes	Students	
4. More lenient attendance policy for college classes	Faculty/ administration	
5. Importance of self-examination for cancer detection	Insurance agencies	
6. Importance of self-examination for cancer detection	High school students	

❏

Practice 13.3 Now that you have a solid understanding of your audience, try making a "My Side/Opposition Side" sheet in order to figure out the best points to discuss in your argumentative essay. To prepare, choose any one of the subjects listed in Practice 13.2 and mentally review both sides of the issue. Pick the side you would like to represent on this issue and then make a list of all the points defending your stand as well as those opposing your stand. When your list is complete, take a look at each point and conclude which of your points is the strongest and which of the opposition's points you feel you should refute. Ask yourself whether your audience would be persuaded enough to change its opinion or to take a course of action.   ❏

Focus Subject with a Reasonable Claim

Once you've determined both a subject and audience for your argument, you'll want to focus your subject with a **claim**—the assertion the writer makes that his or her opinion is valid. The claim forms the thesis statement for an essay using argument, and it sometimes includes a demand or request, using such words as *ought to*, *should*, *must*, or *needs*. An example of a claim can be found in the thesis for "Let's Mix It Up" at the end of paragraph 1: "Thus, we should strive to increase the number of legal immigrants allowed into our country." Notice that this thesis contains a subject (legal immigrants) and a controlling idea (we should strive to increase the numbers).

Practice 13.4   Turn the following subjects into claims, making sure that each claim includes a subject and a controlling idea.

1. Capital punishment

2. Computers and colleges

3. Vitamin E

4. Birth parents and adopted children

5. Violent crime and city living   ❏

Choose a Pattern of Development

Once you have a claim, you might want to use one or more of the following patterns of development (discussed in Chapters 9–12) to support your claim:

- **Definition**
  Many people believe that Internet Websites are tools to educate children, but actually many of these sites are tools for pornography and gambling.

- **Comparison/Contrast**
  Unlike the United States and a handful of other countries, the vast majority of countries in the world do not allow capital punishment.

- **Cause/Effect**
  If the United States continues to allow businesses to pay workers sub-minimum wages, undocumented workers may continue to take jobs from American citizens who would like to be employed.

Practice 13.5   Examine each of the following statements that could be used in an argument. Then identify each by its pattern of development:

1. If more people would purchase gas/electric hybrids, the automobile makers that have not built a hybrid yet might be influenced to produce such a car.

2. Although many people believe that hybrids are cars that need to be plugged into power sources, these cars are actually vehicles that function just like regular gas-powered cars.

3. The Honda Hybrid looks like a Honda Civic but requires a lot less gasoline, and its engine is much more quiet; the Civic is a little cheaper, but the Hybrid comes with a rebate.   ❏

Use a Variety of Reliable, Current, Audience-Appropriate Evidence

You will want to compile **evidence**—support material for claims made within an essay. Evidence can consist of any or all of the following:

- **Facts**
  Information held to be true

- **Statistics**
  A group or list of numerical facts

- **Expert testimony**
  Statement by experts in a relevant field

- **Charts, graphs, tables, surveys**
  Numerical information about a subject

- **Detailed, documented examples**
  Illustrations or models from life

- **Personal interviews**
  Meetings with people who know about the subject

- **Firsthand experience**
  What the writer knows about the subject

- **Observation**
  What the writer has observed about the subject

To develop a sound argument, one that can withstand scrutiny and convince your reader, you will want to use a variety of evidence that is both reliable and current. **Reliable evidence** is support material that comes from qualified sources. Notice that Villapudua uses the findings of a university professor of economics in paragraph 2 of his essay. **Current evidence** is support material that comes from sources that have shared information within the last few years. Sources for "Where the Guys Are Not" are fairly current. When consulting sources and doing research, you should check publication dates. **Audience-appropriate evidence** is support material that serves to convince an audience of the validity of a writer's claim. Although Villapudua offers several sources in support of his claim, he uses the findings of experts to dispel myths about immigrants that many Americans might hold. Villapudua takes into consideration that his audience, concerned American citizens, already possesses a certain amount of knowledge on the issue, but he assumes that their knowledge is incomplete. Therefore, his evidence includes many details, since he must first educate the audience before asking for agreement with his claim.

Practice 13.6   Specific types of evidence are presented in each of the following three paragraphs. Identify the claim that each writer makes and the type of evidence used to support that claim. Refer back to the list of kinds of evidence if you find it helpful.

> Advocates argue that good child care can also benefit employers. Richard Stolley, president of CCAC [Child Care Action Campaign], was instrumental in the development of a day-care center at Time Inc., the large media company where he is editorial director. "It's a productivity issue," he explained. "The number of employees who don't show up or who show up harried because child-care arrangements have fallen through is enormous. Child care is not a women's issue. It has an effect on productivity of men and women, on the whole working family."
>
> —Michael Ryan, from "Who's Taking Care of the Children"

Claim:

Type of evidence:

> Does hate speech harm the individual to whom it is addressed? I can speak to this myself. My parents came to this country nearly four decades ago from the Middle East. I was born in Texas and later grew up in California's Central Valley. My early years were spent constantly trying to conform and avoid the appearance of being different. As a young person in public schools, I often heard comments, jokes, and insults about my ethnicity and the place my parents had once called home. I can assure you that these comments hurt—and in a different way than they might if reversed against those in more populous numbers. If they caused me some pain as a white male, I could only imagine what they must feel like when directed to those already burdened with discrimination in our society.
>
> —Joseph S. Tuman, from "Hate Speech on Campus"

Claim:

Type of evidence:

> More positively, . . . education serves a useful function by upgrading prospective workers' skills—human capital—which in turn boosts earning for individuals and promotes economic growth for society. There is growing evidence to support this view. As the accompanying illustration "How Education Raises Our Income" (p. 292) shows, education and income are strongly related. . . . Economist Dan Burkhead estimates that a 25-year-old man with a college degree can expect to earn within 40 years $365,000 more than a man with a high school diploma can. A 25-year-old female college graduate also can expect to earn within 40 years $144,000 more than a female high school graduate.
>
> —Alex Thio, from "How Education Raises Our Income"

Claim:

Type of evidence: ❏

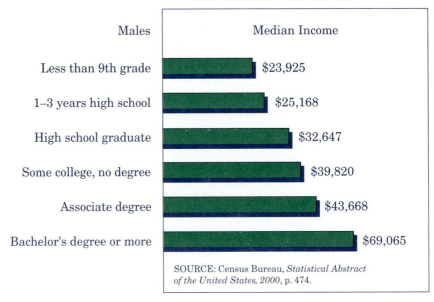

How Education Raises Our Income

Males	Median Income
Less than 9th grade	$23,925
1–3 years high school	$25,168
High school graduate	$32,647
Some college, no degree	$39,820
Associate degree	$43,668
Bachelor's degree or more	$69,065

SOURCE: Census Bureau, *Statistical Abstract of the United States, 2000*, p. 474.

Acknowledge the Opposition

It is important to give credit to the opposing side of your argument. Far from weakening your essay, a clear admission, called a **concession** of the opposition, convinces the audience of your understanding of the issue and your honesty and trustworthiness. Don't be afraid to admit any good points the opposition may have; however, if you can refute the opposing points after giving them, do so. You might also want to mention any "common ground"—for instance, "Johnson and I agree on the necessity of a sales tax increase."

Practice 13.7 After reading the excerpt by Beth Johnson in this chapter (p. 301), find at least one concession and underline it. ❑

Order the Argument: Two Possible Plans

Once you've gathered sufficient evidence to support your claim, you'll want to sketch out a plan for advancing your argument. Stay flexible and give yourself time to experiment with more than one plan; this will allow you to come up with the most effective development for your particular argument.

Claim, Opposition, Evidence
After beginning your essay with a claim, you can then acknowledge the opposition and elaborate with evidence to support your claim. For a model of this plan, look again at "Let's Mix It Up" (p. 285). Here's an outline of Villapudua's structure:

I. Introductory background information and claim (paragraph 1): "Thus, we should strive to increase the number of legal immigrants allowed into our country."

II. Acknowledgment of opposing view (paragraphs 2 and 3): "One argument anti-immigrationists make . . ." and "This is another question asked by anti-immigrationists."

III. Refutation of opposing view (paragraphs 2 and 3): Expert testimony from Borjas and Bedard.

IV. Evidence to support claim (paragraph 4): Information on INS operations and reform efforts of the recently formed U.S. Citizenship and Immigration Services.

Premise, Opposition, Claim

You may also advance your argument by beginning with a **premise**—a specific piece of evidence—proceeding with the acknowledgment of the opposition, offering more evidence that refutes the opposition, and concluding with your claim. For an example of this plan of development, read Derek Humphry's essay "Offering Euthanasia Can Be an Act of Love" (p. 369). Here's an outline of Humphry's structure:

I. Premise (paragraph 1): The American Medical Association decided that "artificial feeding is a life-support mechanism and can be disconnected from hopelessly comatose patients."

II. Premise (paragraph 2): Courts in two other states have also ruled this way.

III. Premise (paragraph 4): People fear life-support equipment use by their loved ones; testimony from Annas about people's rights.

IV. Acknowledgment of opposing view (paragraphs 5 and 6): "Food is a gift from God" and Nazi excesses of the 1930s.

V. Refutation of opposing view (paragraphs 5–8): "A pipe is a manufactured item," not normal feeding; "No terminally ill or comatose person was ever helped to die by the Nazis."

VI. Claim (paragraph 9): Assisting a loved one to die is "good medicine" and demonstrates a "caring society" willing to demonstrate "an act of love."

Practice 13.8 Think about sketching out an appropriate argumentative plan. Work with a partner and compose an outline for the following claim: "Colleges should make freshman composition a pass/fail rather than a graded course." ❏

Use Cue Words to Advance Argument

When you are revising and polishing, check the table of cue words (p. 141–142) to make sure that you move your audience logically and smoothly from one part of your argument to the next. In addition to the cue words listed in the table, the following transition words or phrases may be helpful in advancing your argument clearly:

- Phrases that signal that the writer is acknowledging the other side: *my opponents, the opposition believes, although many people think, there are some who say, it is often thought that, in all fairness*

- Phrases that signal that the writer is being fair or attempting to put some limits on the claims made: *apparently, frequently, appears, most of the time, sometimes, may, might, on several occasions*

Include Appropriate, Fair-Minded Appeals

In your argument, you will be appealing to your audience to side with you on the issue being discussed. These appeals can be of three types: logical, emotional, and ethical.

Logical Appeals

Logical appeals are a writer's calls for help based on sound reasoning and good common sense. These are the appeals that a writer will use to take the reader from point A to point B, no matter what plan of development will be followed. For example, when Villapudua poses the question, "What about immigrants taking away our jobs?" he answers the question with details from a reputable source. The source states that the only jobs immigrants appear to "take away" are low-paying ones that few others are willing to take. Villapudua appeals to the reader's ability to think reasonably on this point.

Emotional Appeals

Much of what we read in advertising copy or see in television commercials uses **emotional appeals,** which are often advanced by a writer's choice of words, to persuade an audience. (For more information about the power of word choice, see the sections on connotative and denotative meanings in Chapter 10). For example, when the writers of the article " Where the Guys Are Not" (p. 283) use phrases such as "stuck . . . in a time-warp" and "troubled lives of males," their word choice evokes an emotional response from their audience.

Ethical Appeals

Ethical appeals enlist audience support on the basis of the writer's fairness or sense of moral values. For example, when an advertisement for America's Chemical Industry states, "Landfills, if *properly* designed, operated, and monitored, are one of the best ways to dispose of certain kinds of solid wastes," the writers of the ad appeal to readers by convincing them that they should have faith in the chemical industry because it is ethical enough to act responsibly and design proper landfills.

Which kind of appeal and how many appeals should you include in your argument? This is a sticky question. Throughout your argument, if you use a fair and unbiased tone, you'll be appealing ethically. And certainly you'll want to develop as many logical appeals as you can. Then you can enhance your argument by using emotional appeals, as long as you have the logic to back them up. Just make sure the facts justify the emotion you're arousing in your audience.

Practice 13.9 For practice in identifying appeals, read the excerpts from the two essays by Louis Nizer and Beth Johnson on America's drug problem (pp. 301–302). Find one example of each type of the following appeals: logical, emotional, and ethical. ❏

Avoid Logical Fallacies

In your zeal and enthusiasm to influence others, you risk using **logical fallacies**—errors or flaws in reasoning or logical thinking. Although some writers may be guilty of knowingly using a logical fallacy to persuade a reader, more often, writers unknowingly fall into the fallacy trap even though they would like to present a balanced, well-supported argument. Learn to recognize the following fallacies in the writings of others and try to avoid them in your own writing.

Some Frequently Occurring Logical Fallacies

Fallacy: ad hominem   **Definition:** attack on the person rather than the person's arguments

Example: Senator Wilson's bill on air pollution should not be taken seriously because he has been accused of misusing travel funds.

Fallacy: appeal to authority   **Definition:** reliance on an authority to lend credibility in an area the authority may know nothing about

Example: Sandra Day O'Connor was a brilliant Supreme Court judge and she loves this brand of chocolate chip cookies—they must be good!

Fallacy: bandwagon   **Definition:** suggestion that readers should accept something because it is popular

Example: The majority of U.S. citizens own at least one television—it can't be that harmful.

Fallacy: begging the question   **Definition:** acceptance as a conclusion of something that needs to be proved

Example: Football is a dangerous sport because lots of players get injured.

Fallacy: equivocation   **Definition:** use of vague or unclear words to mislead the reader

Example: Your honor, I should not be held responsible for plate damage because the restaurant is called "Smashing Food."

Fallacy: false cause   **Definition:** assumption that because two events are related in time, the first event caused the second

Example: I listened to my favorite CD last night while I studied for my French test; I got an "A" on the test, so listening to my music helped me study more efficiently.

Fallacy: false dilemma   **Definition:** presentation of only two sides of an issue

Example: America—love it or leave it.

(continued)

Fallacy: hasty generalization

Definition: conclusion based on inaccurate or insufficient evidence.

Example: The student body is very community service–oriented. Just look at our Big Sisters club!

Fallacy: red herring

Definition: introduction of an irrelevant point to divert the reader's attention from the main argument

Example: Why worry about global warming when we haven't solved the plight of our homeless?

Fallacy: slippery slope

Definition: assertion that one change will lead to a drastic second change, even when the two are unrelated

Example: If we don't allow some wiretapping of phone conversations, terrorists will take over our country.

In the revising and polishing stages of your essay writing, check carefully to be certain you have not committed any of the these errors in reasoning that could weaken your essay. If you find one or more logical fallacy, revise accordingly.

Practice 13.10 For practice in identifying logical fallacies, read the excerpts from the two essays by Nizer and Johnson (p. 301) and then answer these two questions:

1. Search for and record logical fallacies in Nizer's argument. When you've found one, write the phrase and identify the type of fallacy. Refer back to the list of logical fallacies for review.

2. Now search for logical fallacies in Johnson's argument. Write down any that you find, also identifying the type of fallacy. ❏

Strategies for Argumentation

1. **Purpose**   Choose a subject of public concern that you feel strongly about—avoid facts, preferences, beliefs, and impossibilities. Define your audience; figure out exactly whom you want to address and why you'd like to advance your argument on the issue.

2. **Focus**   State your claim, making sure that it is reasonable and that your tone presents you as a fair person.

3. **Material**   Gather enough evidence to advance your argument effectively. Check to see that you use current and reliable sources, including several of the following: facts, statistics, expert testimony, charts, graphs, tables, surveys, examples, personal

interviews, firsthand experience, observation. Make sure that you do not manipulate the facts to suit your argument's purpose.

4. **Structure**   Use the most effective organization of your material to advance your argument. Experiment with alternative plans—from claim to specific evidence and from evidence to claim. Place your acknowledgment of the opposing side wherever this will be most appropriate. Use cue words to move from one piece of evidence to the next.

5. **Style**   Use logical as well as ethical and emotional appeals. Make sure you have the facts to support these appeals. In revising and polishing, search your draft for logical fallacies, revising when appropriate. In your introduction, make sure you're conveying your stand on the issue clearly to your audience; in your conclusion, ask yourself if you've communicated what action you want your readers to take in response to your essay.

JOURNAL WRITING: AN OPINION INVENTORY

Your journal can be helpful in generating ideas for an essay using argument. In an entry, create an inventory of issues that interest you. First, try to list ten or more issues that you might like to write about. Think about what has been in the papers recently or discussed by television newscasters. Explore your feelings about political situations in the United States and abroad. Don't forget to think about campus issues also. Is your tuition increasing? Is student parking scarce? Are computers hard to find on campus? If you are taking a night class, do you feel safe walking to your car? You might also think about issues of local concern in your community. Do people with loud music or power tools interfere with your peace and quiet? Are your parks or streets in need of repair?

Once you've created a substantial inventory, choose two or three of these issues to explore further. Then in another journal entry, answer the following questions for each issue:

- What is my stand on this issue?

- Why do I feel this way about the issue?

- Who would disagree with me and why?

- What evidence do I already have that I could use to advance an argument?

- What kinds of additional evidence would be particularly helpful in developing an argument on this issue?

Your opinion inventory and the resulting answers to questions associated with issues should help you focus on some exciting subject possibilities for essays using argument.

Using the Computer: Writing, Developing, and Observing Arguments

1. You can use the Internet in developing your argumentative strategies. First, find an ongoing discussion about a controversial issue that interests you and about which you might write an essay. Then, "listen" in on how people are discussing the topic. You might try one of the following chat groups:

   http://www.talkcity.com

   http://chat.yahoo.com

   http://www.hotbot.lycos.com

2. In addition, many newspapers and magazines have Websites that invite reader response. (If a chat room is like a debate on a bus or in a bar, these response forums are more like a letters-to-the-editor page where every response is printed, and the letter writers can also respond to each other.) Unfortunately, some people use the anonymity of the Web to say things that they wouldn't usually admit, and some people can be very crude in their opinions and in their responses to other chat room participants. Does this seem to be an effective way of arguing in an online environment? How do other participants in the chat room respond to rude or arrogant postings?

3. It is possible to find many new perspectives on an issue being expressed in a chat room. Do you recognize good argument strategies in any of the postings? Print out examples of rude or unproductive arguing, and examples of smart and considerate arguing, and share them with the class. Be prepared to discuss what makes a particular posting an effective or ineffective style of argument.

OPTIONS FOR WRITING ARGUMENT

The following writing options encourage you to take a stand on an issue of public concern. As you work through your essay, think about where you can gather solid, convincing evidence to advance your argument.

1. Euthanasia, life-support systems, living wills, artificial feeding—these terms have today become increasingly controversial. Read the two essays, "Offering Euthanasia Can Be an Act of Love" (p. 369) and "Who Gets to Choose?" (p. 371), and then explore the issue both authors consider by making a claim of your own about the subject. Support your claim in an essay. To find more information, you can browse the Web, use an online subject index (see p. 161), use the *Readers' Guide to Periodical Literature* at your college library, or interview a local hospital administrator, nurse, or doctor. Try the keywords *euthanasia, life-support systems, living wills, artificial feeding,* or *Kevorkian* (a doctor who supported and performed euthanasia for his terminally ill patients). In compiling your information, be sure

you have found material on both sides of the issue so that you can present a sound, balanced argument.

2. Think about an issue of campus concern that impacts you in some way—for example, student parking, tuition increases, attendance policy, food service, sexual harassment policy, or the need for a child-care center. If several of the students in your class are exploring the same campus issue, you can break into "pro" and "con" teams at random. Engaging in such a mini-debate should allow you to discover specific points for both sides of the issue. Beware of logical fallacies presented by either side. Take notes and then develop an essay arguing for one side of this campus issue. Explore the possibility of interviewing a faculty or staff member, an administrator, or other students about the issue.

3. Although some major corporations and companies promote their products through responsible advertising, many others use misleading or deceptive advertisements and commercials. Just flip through any popular magazine or watch an hour of prime-time television, and you can find several examples of blatant deception. Argue for more responsible advertising, more educated and wary consumers, or tighter government controls on advertising. Part of your evidence might come from specific ads and commercials. Find those that make use of emotional appeals with little or no appeal to logic. You might also look for ads that thrive on logical fallacies.

4. Although Nizer in "Low-cost Drugs for Addicts?" (p. 301) and Johnson in "Our Drug Problem" (pp. 301–302) have divergent viewpoints on the issue of drug legalization, both clearly recognize drug use as a major problem in the United States. Write an essay in which you take a stand on the legalization of "street drugs." Feel free to discuss points not raised by either of these writers or to use their material to support your own position.

5. Many students hold full- or part-time jobs, and some of these jobs may be for companies that require drug testing before hiring. Brainstorm with one or more classmates to discover which companies in your area require drug testing and how often, when, and how the testing is accomplished. You can also research the subject on the Web on one or more of these sites:

   http://bbs.cartserver.com/bbs/b/4284
   http://www.cmrtesting.com

   After you have explored and discussed the issue, write an argumentative essay supporting or condemning mandatory on-the-job drug testing.

6. Explore the issue of organ and tissue donation. You can find information on the following Websites:

   http://www.organdonor.gov/
   http://www.shareyourlife.org/
   http://www.donor-awareness.org/

   Write an essay arguing for or against increasing organ and tissue donation awareness.

7. Kay Hymowitz in her book *Ready or Not* asserts that current print ads and television commercials in America have succeeded in deconstructing childhood by portraying 8- to 12-year-olds with hipness and attitude that encourages these young consumers to be the rulers of their classrooms and their households. Write an essay agreeing or disagreeing with Hymowitz. Attempt to sway your audience to become involved in children's media exposure if you agree with Hymowitz.

8. Write an essay arguing for or against driving limitations for those over a certain age. Be sure to investigate some reliable sources rather than using as evidence encounters you have had with senior drivers.

9. *(Film and Literature)* Find a reliable plot summary of the French play *Cyrano de Bergerac*—you might try the Masterplots series available in most college libraries and large public libraries. Read the plot summary carefully and then view Steve Martin's film *Roxanne*. Write an essay in which you either support Martin's film adaptation of the classic play or criticize his film by pointing out specific weaknesses.

10. *(Service Learning)* Visit the hazardous waste facility closest to you. Interview someone working there, collect any printed informational material

you can, and write an essay urging fellow students and community members to become more educated in the effects of these wastes and more active in the prevention of improper hazardous waste disposal.

RESPONDING TO WRITING: ASSESSING STRATEGIES FOR WRITING ARGUMENT

Recognizing the strengths and weaknesses in the strategies of other writers will help you identify strong points as well as troublesome areas when writing argument. Read the following two excerpts at least twice before answering the prompts that follow. As you read these two opposing arguments, keep an open mind and avoid being swayed by any personal beliefs you may have.

1   We are losing the war against drug addiction. Our strategy is wrong. I propose a different approach.

2   The government should create clinics, manned by psychiatrists, that would provide drugs for nominal charges or even free to addicts under controlled regulations. It would cost the government only 20 cents for a heroin shot, for which the addicts must now pay the mob more than $100, and there are similar price discrepancies in cocaine, crack, and other such substances.

3   Such a service, which would also include the staff support of psychiatrists and doctors, would cost a fraction of what the nation now spends to maintain the land, sea, and air apparatus necessary to interdict illegal imports of drugs. There would also be a savings of hundreds of millions of dollars from the elimination of the prosecutorial procedures that stifle our courts and overcrowd our prisons. . . .

4   Many addicts who are caught committing a crime admit that they have mugged or stolen as many as six or seven times a day to accumulate the $100 needed for a fix. Since many of them need two or three fixes a day, particularly for crack, one can understand the terror in our streets and homes. It is estimated that there are in New York City alone 200,000 addicts, and this is typical of cities across the nation. Even if we were to assume that only a modest percentage of a city's addicts engage in criminal conduct to obtain the money for the habit, requiring multiple muggings and thefts each day, we could nevertheless account for many of the tens of thousands of crimes each day in New York City alone.

5   Not long ago, a Justice Department division issued a report stating that more than half the perpetrators of murder and other serious crimes were under the influence of drugs. This symbolizes the new domestic terror in our nation. This is why our citizens are unsafe in broad daylight on the most traveled thoroughfares. This is why computers and television sets are stolen from offices and homes and sold for a pittance. This is why parks are closed to the public and why murders are committed. This is why homes need multiple locks, and burglary systems, and why store windows, even in the most fashionable areas, require iron gates.

—Louis Nizer, from "Low-cost Drugs for Addicts"

1   In the eyes of some, legalizing narcotics is a tantalizing cure-all for America's drug problem. It's time, they say, to stop pouring enormous resources into the

war on drugs. The war has been lost. Drug use, they argue, is here to stay. Ignoring evidence that drug legalization can produce a permanent underclass of hopelessly addicted people, as has happened in Holland, they advocate removal of all legal restrictions on drug use. . . .

2   The only thing more costly than continuing the current war on drugs would be the legalization of narcotics; such a measure would claim innumerable human lives. Government figures estimate that crimes involving drug use cost society more than $58 billion a year. Substance abuse is linked with 52 percent of rapes committed; 49 percent of murders; 62 percent of assaults; and 50 percent of traffic fatalities and incidents of spousal abuse. The legalization of narcotics could only push those figures higher.

3   Currently, drug abuse costs American industry as much as $75 billion per year in lost productivity, liability for errors committed by substance-abusing employees, and drug-related injuries. Imagine how that figure would soar if legal restraints were removed. If people didn't have to drive into a seedy neighborhood, didn't risk arrest and disgrace, how many more would try addictive drugs? Moreover, what would be the fate of addicts if narcotics were available legally? In the words of one cocaine addict, "I'd be dead. . . . I'd just sit down with a big pile of the stuff and snort it until I dropped."

4   Why, then, would anyone recommend legalizing narcotics? The answer has to do with racism, elitism, and sheer indifference to the suffering of others. "These people are going to kill themselves anyway," many middle-class Americans reason. "I'm not going to have my tax dollars used to try to save them. Besides, what does it matter if drugs wipe out a generation—as long as it's a generation of Black and Hispanic kids?"

5   Legalizing narcotics, then, . . . is not the solution; it's simply another way of ignoring the problem. Making drugs legal won't make them go away. What is needed is an all-out attack on the conditions that lead to drug abuse. Improved education, more affordable housing, new employment opportunities—these are the only effective weapons against drugs.

—Beth Johnson, from "Our Drug Problem"

1. Find and label the claim in each argument. Remember that the claim does not always come before the evidence.

2. Find and label three kinds of evidence Nizer uses to support his argument.

3. Find and label three kinds of evidence Johnson uses to support her argument.

Now that you've examined both arguments on this same issue in greater detail, ask yourself which writer advances his or her point of view more effectively. In responding to your own essays, make sure you recognize any weaknesses that could undermine your stand, and then make necessary changes to strengthen your argument.

For more essays using argument, read the following essays in Part 4: "Zipped Lips," "Offering Euthanasia Can Be an Act of Love," "Who Gets to Choose?" "Whose Eyes Are Those, Whose Nose?" and "The Salsa Zone."

CRITICAL THINKING
In Connecting Texts

Several of the readings in this chapter focus on issues involving survival. The writers of "Where the Guys Are Not" argue that American males are failing to survive the educational system; Villapudua mentions that many Americans feel immigrants threaten the future economy of our country; Nizer and Johnson explore solutions to drug addiction. In a small group, brainstorm a list of solutions to any one of these problems. Save your notes—they could be of help if you decide to write an essay on this subject.

PART THREE

Exploring Other Options: A Writer's Toolkit

UNIT 1 Timed Writing

UNIT 2 Writing about Film and Literature

UNIT 3 Connecting with Your Audience: Public Speaking and Public Writing

Unit 1

Timed Writing

Preview

In this unit you will learn

- The characteristics of timed writing
- How to prepare yourself before a timed writing
- How to use strategies while completing a timed writing

Examining strategies for timed writing will enable you to feel more comfortable and more prepared to write under pressure. Throughout your college career, you'll be asked in various classes to write in-class essays and short-answer exams. In addition, skills and confidence in timed writing will serve you well in your career path: People in the workforce are often asked to present a report, summarize a situation, or compose a business memo more or less "on the spot."

Although the format may vary tremendously by subject and instructor, each timed writing possesses the following characteristics:

- **It focuses on a subject.**
  You may or may not be given a choice of subject, but you will be asked and expected to respond specifically to a subject.

- **It is administered within a fixed, predetermined period of time.**
  For some in-class essays, you may be given three hours; others may be timed writings of 10 to 15 minutes. Whatever the time limit, it will help you to know that all students will be feeling the same time constraints. If you do not turn your essay in at the end of the allotted time, it cannot be evaluated.

- **It may be written by hand, using pen and paper in a classroom.**
  There are increasing exceptions to this rule today with computer labs and personal laptop computers becoming more common in class.

- **It resembles the regular college essay in much of its structure: thesis, development, conclusion.**
  Whether you're asked to write a brief essay response in ten minutes, or a longer one because you are given two hours of writing time, the in-class essay focuses on a thesis, develops that thesis, and then concludes.

SAMPLE TIMED WRITING

The writing instructor who administered the following timed writing asked students to prepare for the assignment by reading and discussing two editorials in the campus newspaper. The editorials focused on whether or not American tobacco makers should be held financially responsible for smoking-related illnesses. A week before the timed writing, the instructor informed students that they would have two hours (the regular class time for this course) to complete the writing assignment, and that they could use no notes or outside sources.

When Russell Fullerton and the other students in his class arrived on the day of the timed writing, they were given the following essay question:

> Should American tobacco makers take financial responsibility for smoking-related illnesses? In developing your essay, discuss the issue by using examples to support your thesis.

Fullerton wrote the following in-class essay in response to the essay question.

COFFIN NAILS

Russell Fullerton

Russell Fullerton confides that he has never found writing difficult but that he really didn't try hard to write clearly until coming to college. Russell states that he has little trouble organizing or developing his ideas. When he's writing on a computer, he knows how to solve most of his spelling problems, but when writing a timed, handwritten assignment, Russell still grapples with spelling errors. Russell describes his interests and prospective major as follows: "Computers, computers, . . . uhm . . . computers."

1   Despite the knowledge that smoking cigarettes has been proven to cause many health problems, millions of people still go through a pack or more a day and many new smokers pick up their first cigarette each day. This is an exercise of their freedom of choice—perhaps not the smartest choice, but their choice nonetheless. There are many products on the market that may not be as addictive or harmful as cigarettes but are, however, destructive to the user: chocolate when eaten in excess, ergonomically challenged school and office furniture, Häagen-Dazs ice cream, or even roller blades (unsafe at any speed). Even though these products pose health hazards, their manufacturers are not asked to pay for the effects their products have on the people who use them. Yet the tobacco industry is being asked to pay for the effects caused by its product, even though the people who smoke have freely chosen to do so. The American tobacco industry should not be forced to take financial responsibility for smoking-related illnesses.

2   Once the American public did not know exactly how dangerous it was to smoke, but for years now, every thinking person has been aware of the health hazards. My parents had both smoked for twenty-five years before they quit eight years ago—cold turkey. And now, eight years later, they have started smoking again. Both of my parents are fully aware of the risks, but they have chosen to smoke again, most likely for the rest of their lives. When asked why he started again now, my father says he

would rather enjoy himself for the time he has left than live forever and not have any fun. My father, mother, and many other smokers have made an informed choice, and the tobacco industry should not have to pay for this choice.

3   Many parents are angry because tobacco advertisements target children with their cartoon camels and smoking cowboys. These parents claim that their children will be influenced to smoke by these images. They assume that children are not old enough to take responsibility for their choices; in this they are correct. That is why it is illegal for children to smoke. It is the parents' responsibility to guide their children to make the right choices in this confusing world. The tobacco industry is not alone in using advertising to promote potentially harmful products among both children and adults. Images of beautiful and healthy people surround us constantly, guzzling down alcoholic beverages, caffeine, and "perfectly safe" diet pills, for example. In a recent McDonald's commercial, a group of children ask Ronald McDonald where hamburgers come from. Instead of taking the children to the slaughterhouse, Ronald takes them to the "hamburger patch" where the talking hamburgers grow on trees. Is what the tobacco industry has done worse than this?

4   Selling cigarettes does not kill people. Smoking cigarettes can kill people—and that's a smoker's responsibility. If we are going to prosecute the tobacco industry for creating the cigarettes, perhaps we should then prosecute the individuals who smoke the cigarettes. They are the manufacturers of the clouds of secondhand smoke, which have proven to be more deadly than the cigarettes themselves. However, when we start prosecuting manufacturers or consumers for making or using products, then we chip away at the freedoms we have fought to preserve for so long. Freedoms come with responsibility—the freedom to make good and bad choices, and the freedom to live with the effects of those choices. When these freedoms are taken, they are not just taken from the manufacturers, but from the consumers as well. ○

GUIDELINES FOR TIMED WRITING

Make Preparations

What you do *before* the actual in-class essay day can help you to stay calm and complete an effective timed writing. Go over any notes, review chapters from which you believe information will be asked, and think about the subject and the essay question, if you know them. Ask your instructors what kinds of in-class writing assignments they give, what materials you will be permitted to bring with you, and if they have any suggestions for preparation before the actual day of the timed writing.

Make sure that you have all your supplies ready and in good order: a couple of functioning erasable pens (in case one of them runs out of ink); paper or bluebook if required; paperback dictionary if you are allowed to use one; a wristwatch, especially if there is no clock in your classroom; and any other materials you may need and are permitted to bring. If you will be writing on a computer, you will need a formatted disk with your name printed on it. Fellow students may not appreciate last-minute borrowing on the in-class essay day.

On the day of the timed writing, make every effort to get to class on time or even five minutes early. Your early arrival could result in that extra few minutes for proofreading at the end of class time. Finally, after you have prepared mentally and your supplies are ready, relax. Once you start reading the assignment and thinking about it, you may even find that you enjoy the challenge of writing under pressure.

Understand the Question

Once you receive the question or writing prompt, read it carefully. If it is written on the board, jot it down quickly on a piece of scratch paper so that you can think about it and refer to it more easily. Underline **directives**—the instructive words, usually verbs, that tell what is expected of you in the timed writing. For example, Fullerton focused on the directives "discuss" and "use examples" before beginning to write his in-class essay. After he underlined these two directives, he knew which strategy he would use to organize and develop his material. The following are some of the most commonly used directives in timed writing:

Directives Used in Timed Writing

- **Explain** Show or make clear, establish connections, tell why, how, or what, depending on the subject.

- **Compare** Develop the similarities between one subject and another.

- **Contrast** Explore the differences between two subjects, pursuing ways in which the two subjects are not alike.

- **Define** Establish boundaries for, or set limits on, a subject. Tell what the subject is by differentiating it from other closely related subjects; possibly tell what it is not.

- **Illustrate** Explain by example and detail.

- **Identify** Distinguish, know, and list the various parts of the subject.

- **Describe** Paint a word picture with sensory details. Sometimes instructors use this directive more broadly to mean "discuss" or "explain."

- **Interpret** Share your understanding of the subject. Go into the significance of the idea, event, or process in order to explain its meaning to your audience.

- **Trace** Detail in chronological order events or situations or occurrences connected with the subject.

- **Evaluate** Explore the value of the subject. To evaluate, you need criteria to judge the worth of a subject.

- **Discuss** Literally, this means "talk about." When you get this directive, be careful—even though it may appear that you've been given the "green light" to talk about any aspect of the subject, create a thesis that will steer you away from vagueness and into specific territory that you can support with details.

- **Analyze** Divide the subject into its components so that you can take a more in-depth look at each part in relation to the whole.

- **Summarize** Explain the subject briefly in your own words. If you're asked to summarize, the instructor wants to see whether you can recall the important aspects of a subject and put them in your own words.

Allocate Time

Once you know what you will be expected to cover in your timed writing and the strategy your instructor wants you to use, schedule your time to allow you to plan your main points, write the draft, revise it, and then proofread it. If you have only one essay question, as Fullerton did for his essay "Coffin Nails," you might come up with a time allocation like this:

> 5 minutes to reread the question and decide on a strategy
> 10 minutes to organize main points and find a thesis
> 1 hour and 20 minutes to write
> 15 minutes to revise and polish
> Total: 1 hour and 50 minutes

Resist the temptation to begin writing before you have completed your preparations. The biggest problem students have with in-class essays is not that they write too little, but that too often they write without thinking about the essay question and mapping out a plan first. Often this results in rambling, vague, or off-topic answers.

Find a Thesis and Sketch a Plan

Sometimes you may get an idea for a working thesis after you've read the essay question; at other times, you may have no idea for a thesis but you do know that you can make several main points related to the subject and the specific directives. In many cases, you can take your essay question, and with a little careful rewording, turn it into a statement that becomes your thesis. If you reread "Coffin Nails," you will see that Fullerton turned the essay question into a thesis in paragraph 1.

Whether or not an idea for a working thesis comes to you, get started by jotting down your main points in a **scratch outline**—a brief, quickly written outline of main points. If you do not have a working thesis to begin with, you will probably feel more capable of creating one after looking over your scratch outline. To see what a scratch outline looks like, examine Fullerton's scratch outline, which follows, written in preparation for "Coffin Nails."

Sample Scratch Outline

(Should) American tobacco makers take financial responsibility for smoking related illnesses? In developing your essay, discuss the issue by using examples to support your thesis.

No!

adults know dangers of smoking
* – my parents*
* – dad's comment*

issue of misleading ads

— children-Joe Camel
            Ronald McDonald
            cowboy w/cigarette
adults + ads
— coffee
— beer
— diet pills
— junk food

Draft and Reread

Working from your scratch outline and thesis, begin to draft your written response. Begin with your thesis, and then launch into your main points and supporting details. While you're drafting, glance at your watch every now and then to make sure that you're following your allocated schedule. As you write, try to keep the assigned question uppermost in your mind so that you stay on the subject.

Revise and Polish

One major difference between an essay assigned as homework and a timed writing is that the latter does not get worked through multiple drafts. Often you'll have time only for a scratch outline and then one draft. Once you have a scratch outline, write the draft that you are going to turn in, leaving sufficient time for revising and polishing of this draft.

When you have finished the draft, ask yourself if you have answered the essay question thoroughly and clearly. If you find that you've left out something crucial to your development, you can always write this sentence or even paragraph in the margin or on a separate sheet of paper, marking it with an asterisk (*) or drawing an arrow to indicate where the additional information belongs. If you are drafting on a computer, familiarity with the editing tools *Copy, Paste, Cut,* and *Find* can be helpful.

After you've read the draft for content, read it again to make sure that your spelling is correct (you may be permitted to use your dictionary), that all sentences are correctly punctuated, and that every word is the most specific word possible for clear communication of your thesis. If you are writing your essays by hand and you find any errors or off-topic phrases or sentences, correct or delete them even if this means crossing out words, phrases, or whole sentences. You can also insert words with a caret (^). Title your essay, check to see that your name is on the essay, and make sure that your pages are in the right order.

Strategies for Timed Writing

1. **Purpose**   Read and reread the question or writing assignment, underlining the directives. Think carefully about what is expected of you in the timed writing.

2. **Focus**   If possible, restate the question in the form of a thesis statement. If this won't work, begin to jot down all the main points you can make about the subject. After reviewing your list, draft a thesis that addresses the subject and fits the main points you've listed.

3. **Material**   Use a strategy for developing your material suggested by the directives in the essay question. Check the question to make sure that you are using material appropriate to the subject.

4. **Structure**   Before drafting your timed writing, write a scratch outline. Refer to this outline during drafting.

5. **Style**   In revising, make appropriate and legible additions and deletions. Check word choice and replace any vague words with specific ones. Check punctuation, spelling, title, page order, and name placement.

Writing about Film and Literature

Preview

In this unit you will learn

- How to define important terms in literature and film
- How to answer key questions relating to literature and film
- How to write an essay analyzing one or more elements in literature and film
- How to define important terms in poetry
- How to examine a poem

We read various types of literature and we view different genres of films for pleasure, escape, and knowledge. Oftentimes after reading a novel or short story or watching a movie, we discover that the writer or director has raised moral or ethical questions without giving us any direct answers—we are left to ponder the situation presented, make certain inferences based on evidence given, and arrive at a personal opinion, evaluation, or solution.

In your college classes, you may be asked to write about a piece of literature you have read or a film you have viewed. In order to communicate your views clearly to your audience, you will need to familiarize yourself with several key terms.

Key Terms in Film and Literature

Exposition: the basic information the reader or viewer needs at the beginning of a story or film

Plot: an arrangement in a certain order of events or episodes that occur in a story or film

(continued)

Subplot: a minor complication that relates to the main plot but is not the main focus of the film or work of literature

Dialogue: words, phrases, or sentences spoken by one or more characters

Character: the person or people in the story. Some are *static* (they remain the same throughout the story) and some are *dynamic* (they change in the course of the story).

Theme: the central or main idea conveyed by the story

Setting: the time and place in which the story occurs

Symbol: something that suggests or stands for an idea, quality, or concept

Motif: a pattern of identical or similar images recurring throughout a work of literature or a film

Tone: the attitude a writer or director conveys toward his or her subject and audience

Mood: the emotional content of a scene, usually described in terms of feeling (for example, *gloomy, jubilant, anxious*)

Point of view: the position from which an action or subject is seen, often determining its significance. Objective POV: not confined to any one person's perspective. Subjective POV: seen through a particular character's eyes.

Shot (film term): a continuously exposed and unedited image made up of a number of frames

Frame: the borders of the image within which the subject is composed

Editing (film term): transitions between scenes

Crosscutting (film term): a film editing technique. Pieces from two separately shot scenes are intermixed, creating a sequence that moves back and forth between them.

QUESTIONS FOR ANALYZING FILM

These questions can help you understand films. If you are planning to write an essay about a film, you can generate much of the material for your essay by writing out the answers to these questions.

1. Does the film follow the normal dramatic structure? (exposition, conflict, climax, resolution)

2. What is the setting?

3. How do the camera work and editing mark the structural transitions within the film?

4. Is there crosscutting in the film? What comments do the crosscut scenes make upon each other?

5. What images are repeated or emphasized in the film?

6. Do you notice the use of camera angles other than eye-level shots? What is their effect?

7. What is the filmmaker's point of view? Does it limit the viewer's vision in any way?

8. What appears to be the style of the film?

9. What characters seem static?

10. What characters appear to be dynamic?

11. What appears to be the overall theme of the film? State the theme in one sentence.

12. What is the significance of the film's title?

QUESTIONS FOR ANALYZING LITERATURE

These questions can help you understand short stories, novels, poems, or plays. If you are planning to write an essay about a literary work, you can generate much of the material for your essay by writing out the answers to these questions.

1. Who is the main character? During the course of the work, does this character change?

2. Who are the minor (less important) characters? Why are they necessary for the story?

3. Are there any images, motifs, or use of symbolism? What are they?

4. What is the setting of the story?

5. What is the mood of the story? How does the writer create this mood?

6. Who is the narrator? (From whose point of view is the story told?) Is this narrator trustworthy or not? Why?

7. What is the theme of this literary work? State the theme in one sentence, being as specific as you can.

MODEL ESSAYS

Let's assume you were given the following writing assignment:

Read F. X. Toole's short story "Million Dollar Baby." Then view the 2004 film by the same name. Write an essay tracing significant differences between the short story and the film.

FRANKIE, MAGGIE, AND THE RING

1   F. X. Toole's not-so-short story, "Million Dollar Baby," was recently turned into an Academy-Award-winning film by the same name. In many respects filmmaker Clint Eastwood and screenwriter Paul Haggis have been true to the original story, but in three major respects, the film has been significantly altered.

2   For one thing, the film gives the character Frankie (played by Eastwood) a background that does not exist in the story. While the minimalist writing of Toole allows us no clues as possible reasons for Frankie's troubled past, in contrast, the film offers hints that excite us into thinking we might get to the bottom of his past life's problems, only to discover that we will never be told specifics. For example, in the film Frankie attends Mass and harrasses an irate priest with challenging religious questions. However, we never get to know the nature of the guilt driving Frankie to Mass, the nature of his personal faith, and the reason his daughter persists in returning his letters to her unopened.

3   Another digression from Toole's story in the film involves the creation of the character of Scrap-Iron (played by Morgan Freeman). The insertion of Scrap-Iron affords Eastwood the chance to have a narrator that is trustworthy and involved in the action. Scrap-Iron is an ex-boxer who now works as a live-in custodian of Frankie's Hit Gym. Making the narrator a visible character layers the film version of the story with additional history. This addition also gives viewers the chance to see not only Frankie's, but also the narrator's, reaction to Maggie's growth as a boxer.

4   A third alteration from short story to film involves the large amount of time devoted to Maggie's training at the gym "after hours." Director Eastwood wisely understands that film enables viewers to witness Maggie's dogged devotion to her workouts, including those dimly lit, long, lonely hours at the punching bag. In the film version, we get a much more detailed picture of Maggie's slow but solid transformation from novice to expert boxer than Toole furnishes readers in his short story.

5   After reading the story and viewing the film, we can see that Eastwood deserves his Academy Award—he had the filmmaker's vision to foresee what he could do on film with this powerful piece of literature.   ○

In preparation for writing about a piece of literature you have read, you will need to use active reading skills. Read the following chapter excerpt from the novel *Car Camping* by Mark Sundeen, a travel writer for the *New York Times*. Then answer the questions that follow.

Car Camping: "Down Here in the Hobbit Hole"

1   My first adventure was to Joshua Tree when I was fifteen. Donny Brown taught me to rock climb. He showed me which knots to tie, how to wedge a chock in a crack then pop it out with a screwdriver, and how to smear the soles of my boots on the rock so that I could balance without my hands. We were the same age, but he was the one who knew what to do.

2   One night it snowed. Young Tom and Alfy the cobbler, who lived out there, walked into our camp and stood by the fire with a pot of hot soup to share. The snow didn't stop so we all crowded into a small foreign station wagon that smelled bad and passed around the soup.

3   When we got out of the car, the sky was clear. Most of the snow had melted and the ground was glowing beneath the round moon. The rocks were like lumps of ice cream starting to melt.

4   We sprinted across the desert and leapt over chollas and yuccas and quartzite boulders. We could run forever. I looked over at my cousin Donny Brown. He was smiling. He was not looking at me.

5   We ran faster.

6   Donny Brown was a screen. He crossed the landscape like a fishnet through a clear pond. He gulped up clusters of stars and they danced out the back of his head.

7   I wanted to be him, for life to rush through me as fast as it arrived, not caught up in thoughts or thinking. That's the only thing I've really wanted. ◯

Questions for "Down Here in the Hobbit Hole"

1. Who appears to be the narrator?

2. What do we learn about Donny Brown?

3. What is the setting?

4. What is the only thing the narrator has "really wanted"?

5. How old do you think the narrator is?

6. The narrator tells us that Donny Brown "crossed the landscape like a fishnet through a clear pond. He gulped up clusters of stars and they danced out the back of his head." Are these images symbolic? What idea does the writer communicate here?

7. In a sentence, state the theme of this excerpt.

Responding to Poetry

Literature includes short stories, plays, novels, and also poems. Poetry is the oldest form of literature, mimicking not ordinary speech as fiction does, but extraordinary speech in its language, rhythm, and rhyme. Poetry is often filled with rich sensory images and various figures of speech. Although reading a short story or a novel once will usually allow one to understand what's going on, often a poem requires several readings for understanding. However, having a basic knowledge of several terms used in poetry can help readers understand a poem.

Key Terms in Understanding Poetry

alliteration: repetition of consonant or vowel sounds at the beginning of words

assonance: the use of similar vowel sounds in adjacent or nearby words

blank verse: unrhymed lines of a iambic pentameter (unstressed followed by stressed syllables)

free verse: poetry that relies more on rhythm than on regular meter for its effectiveness

metaphor: a comparison of one object or emotion with another unlike it

meter: a rhythmic pattern in a poem (created by alternating stressed and unstressed syllables)

personification: giving nonhuman things human characteristics or attitudes

rhyme: words on adjacent lines of poetry that sound the same or almost the same

(continued)

rhythm: the regular repetition of stressed syllables
simile: a comparison of two things with the word *like* or *as*
speaker: person or object that appears to be speaking in a poem
stanza: a part of a poem separated from the next part by extra spacing

Read the poem "Monet Refuses the Operation" by Lisel Mueller. After a second reading, answer the questions that follow the poem, referring to "Key Terms in Understanding Poetry" if helpful.

Monet Refuses the Operation

Doctor, you say that there are no haloes   1
round the streetlights in Paris
and what I see is an aberration
caused by old age, an affliction.
I tell you it has taken me all my life   5
to arrive at the vision of gas lamps as angels,
to soften and blur and finally banish
the edges you regret I don't see,
To learn that the line I called the horizon does not exist and
sky and water,
so long apart, are the same state of being.   10
Fifty-four years before I could see
Rouen cathedral is built

of parallel shafts of sun,
and now you want to restore
my youthful errors: fixed   15
notions of top and bottom,
the illusion of three-dimensional space,
wisteria separate
from the bridge it covers.
what can I say to convince you   20
the Houses of Parliament dissolve
night after night to become
the fluid dream of the Thames?
I will not return to a universe
 of objects that don't know each other,   25
as if islands were not the lost children of one great continent. The world
is flux, and light becomes what it touches,
becomes water, lilies on water,
above and below water,
becomes lilac and mauve and yellow   30
and white and cerulean lamps,
small fists passing sunlight
so quickly to one another
that it would take long, streaming hair
inside my brush to catch it.   35
To paint the speed of light!
Our weighted shapes, these verticals,
burn to mix with air
and changes our bones, skin, clothes
to gases. Doctor,   40
if only you could see
how heaven pulls earth into its arms
and how infinitely the heart expands
to claim this world, blue vapor without end.

Questions for "Monet Refuses the Operation"

1. Who is the speaker in the poem and what do we know about him/her?

2. What appears to be the situation the speaker describes?

3. What is the setting?

4. Find a line in the poem that contains vivid imagery and annotate accordingly.

5. Is the poem written in blank verse or free verse?

6. Find a simile and a metaphor. Annotate your poem in the margins.

7. In one sentence state why Monet refuses the operation.

8. Examine the painting by Monet on page 318. Search the Internet or your library for pictures of other paintings by Claude Monet. After

examining copies of some of Monet's paintings, do you believe that by having the operation, Monet might have been losing a special, unique sight? Why?

For additional practice in responding to poetry, read Jane Yolen's poem "Grant Wood: American Gothic." (p. 368–369.)

Strategies for Using the Five Keys when Writing about Film and Literature

1. **Purpose**   Your main idea should never include supporting an opinion about a work of film or literature that cannot be grounded in ample evidence from the work itself.

2. **Focus**   Be sure that your thesis can be supported by details and is clearly phrased and related to a particular element in the film or literary work.

3. **Material**   Use quoted material to support your thesis, but be sure to use "the sandwich" (see page 168) to introduce quotes as well as to clarify them. Also, avoid any unnecessary plot summary. Your purpose is to analyze, not summarize. Therefore, you should include plot details only if they are clearly needed to support a point that you are making to support your thesis.

4. **Structure**   Try to take supportive examples from most or all stanzas if you are writing about a poem, or from several different parts of a short story, novel, or film. Going from the beginning to the end of the work rather than starting in the middle of a poem or short story makes it easier for readers to follow your thoughts.

5. **Style**   Make sure that you follow literary conventions: Include the full name of the author/poet/playwright/filmmaker and the complete name of the work in your introductory paragraph. Remember that most essays about literature or film are written in the "literary present tense." Finally, for quotations from short stories or novels, include page numbers in parentheses, and for quotations from poems, include line numbers in parentheses.

Connecting with Your Audience: Public Speaking and Public Writing

Preview

In this unit you will learn

- How to prepare for an oral presentation
- How to use strategies to build self-confidence in public speaking
- How to identify different types of public writing
- How to engage in public writing associated with service learning

PUBLIC SPEAKING

In college, career, and personal and civic life, you will be asked to speak in front of an audience—perhaps because your company asks you to present a proposal, possibly because as a PTA officer you need to share some findings, or maybe because your history professor has assigned an oral report to your class. Although many people view oral presentations of any sort as horrifying—using the five "keys"—PURPOSE, FOCUS, MATERIAL, STRUCTURE, and STYLE—will help you cope with the stress of speaking before the public and will allow you to present an effective, clear speech with confidence.

Purpose

To your advantage, you will usually know your specific audience in advance; you may not know exactly how many people will be present, but you will know the interest or bias of your prospective audience. If you take the time to analyze the demographics and attitude of this audience, you can decide on a strategy for your speech based on this audience's likely knowledge of your subject as well as the age, gender, and ethnicity represented, and the occasion and circumstances of your presentation. To assure your speech's effectiveness, you might want to interview a few selected audience members or ask a group of people with related characteristics to complete a survey questionnaire you have composed. Your questions might include the following: What do you know about the subject? What about the subject do you not understand? Where did you get your information on the subject?

Practice   **Practice on Purpose**

Once you have a specific audience in mind for your speech, answer the following questions:

1. What is the main goal of your speech?

2. What is the median age of your audience?

3. Are there more people of one gender than the other, or are the genders evenly balanced?

4. What is the average educational level of the audience?

5. Into what socioeconomic group does your audience fall?

6. Can you identify any predominant beliefs or values your audience shares? What are they?

7. What terms might you need to define in order for your audience to understand your content fully?

8. Will your audience be interested in your topic?

9. How could you get your audience to be more interested?   ❏

Focus

If you are given a specific subject to explore in your speech, your thesis will really have been chosen for you. However, if you have the freedom to choose your topic, consider your own background, interests, knowledge, and goals in your speech as well as your time constraints. Decide what type of speech you will be presenting:

- Summary or overview of a long report

- Persuasive speech that tries to change the audience's beliefs and attitudes in **order** to show that a certain course of action is best

- Informative speech that explains a concept or analyzes a subject

- Explanatory speech that gives the audience necessary information for completing a particular task

- Group presentation that features two or more people presenting individual elements

You can develop a list of possible subjects and then brainstorm by making a **concept map,** which is similar to clustering (Chapter 3, p. 53–54). The following concept map depicts the flow of an idea from general (vacations) to specific (Yosemite).

Europe	*American Southwest*	*hiking*	*fishing*
VACATIONS	*mountains*	*YOSEMITE*	*camping*
Pacific Islands	*Sightseeing*	*Relaxing*	*Rockclimbing*

Once you have an idea of what subject you want to explore, choose two to five main areas of that subject. Based on the previous concept map, for example, you might decide to discuss Yosemite as a vacation spot offering hiking, fishing, camping, and rockclimbing.

Practice | Practice on Focus

1. What do you know about the topic?

2. What do you need to find out about the topic?

3. Where could you go to get this information?

4. Write a thesis—a statement of your main idea in the speech.

5. Examine the thesis—does it have a subject, controlling idea, appropriate tone, and specific language? (See Chapter 4.)

6. Evaluate your thesis, making sure it is neither too broad nor too narrow for the amount of time you have been allotted for your speech. ❏

Material

You might want to limit the number of points you plan to make in your speech since listening is hard work, and most listening audiences have trouble grasping more than five main points in an oral presentation. Listeners have a limited attention span and are often less tolerant than readers for a large amount of abstract information, so remember to support each of your main points with specific examples as evidence. Public speaking also permits you to use visual aids such as overhead transparencies, slides, flip charts, handouts, physical objects, audio and video clips, and computer-generated images. If you choose to use any of these aids, it is extremely important that you practice using the aid before the actual speech—make sure you know how to operate the equipment. Also, although visual aids can be extremely effective, try to keep their use to a minimum—they work best when highlighting your main points, serving as "cue cards" to remind you of important points. According to recent studies, an audience remembers visual parts of speeches better than they remember verbal parts.

Practice | Practice on Material

1. Write down three to five main points you want to make in your speech.

2. Assess the evidence you have to support each point—is there enough? Is the evidence reliable? Up-to-date? Unbiased?

3. What visual aid(s) will you use? ❏

Structure

The structure of your speech can be quite similar to that of the college essay: you will want an introduction, a body section making specific points, and a conclusion. Because your audience will be listening rather than reading, you will want the structure of your speech to be more obvious than the structure of a written paper. Using lots of verbal cues will let people know when you're making a main point and when you're moving on to your next point. (For a list of transition words, see pages 293–294.) Three types of organization are popular for speeches:

- *Chronological:* Mentions the main points in time sequence.

- *Topical:* Breaks a speech into several connected topics and elaborates of those topics.

- *Problem/solution:* Can be used in situations where a problem is stated and a solution is proposed.

Practice   **Practice on Structure**

1. Put your main points and supporting evidence in the best possible order for favorable audience reaction.

2. Check to make sure you use transitions to let your audience follow your speech content clearly. (See Chapter 7, "Cue Words" pp. 141–142.)

3. Examine your speech's introduction—does it capture the attention of your audience? Does it state your main purpose?

4. Examine your conclusion—does it tie up all loose ends and offer your audience a sense of closure?   ❏

Style

Even though your speech is oral, you may want to write down everything you're going to say. However, some speakers prefer to familiarize themselves with the main points of their speech but be somewhat open to responding moment-to-moment to their audience's reaction. A "speaking draft" allows you to collect and organize all your ideas in advance. It also permits you to practice making your speech in front of a mirror, a friend, relative, classmate, or coworker. Finally, using this draft or a much more simplified one (as in the scratch outline on page 309), recorded on index cards, will allow you to keep track of your place as you present your speech before your real audience. Once you have practiced several times, it's better to use your scratch outline rather than the complete draft because you'll be less tempted to read the speech from the paper, word for word. Be sure to number your pages or index cards so that you won't experience the "Where is my next page?" panic reaction that can occur if you lose your place.

If you worry about "stage fright," here are a few strategies that will make you feel more confident and less nervous:

- Practice in front of a person or people using visual aids and standing as you intend to stand for your presentation. Ask for honest feedback from this audience.

- Try to practice at least once in the location in which you'll be speaking, making use of any visual aids as you speak.

- If possible, audiotape or videotape your practice presentation—then listen to the tape and adjust accordingly.

- On the day of your speech, do some deep breathing and stretching exercises to relax your body and mind.

- Remind yourself that the more you deliver speeches, the easier public speaking will become for you.

At the time of your speech, when you approach the podium or the area in front of the room, take a few moments to arrange your notes and papers rather than jumping right into your speech. Make sure that you have your audience's complete attention before beginning. During the course of your speech, don't hesitate to use hand movements to stress your points. Remember to make eye contact with people in different areas of the room, and try to speak distinctly and loudly enough for those in the rear of the room to hear you. One good strategy for keeping your audience engaged is to ask them to do something: perhaps work on a brief activity with a partner, read a handout, or think of an example. As a part of your conclusion, it is often helpful to call for questions. You can prepare yourself for the ability to answer questions satisfactorily by having some friends listen to your presentation and then ask you challenging questions.

| **Practice** | **Practice on Style** |

1. Do you have legible, clearly numbered index cards for your speech?

2. Have you practiced in front of a mirror and then for a friend, relative, or classmate?

3. Have you practiced with whatever visual aid(s) you will use? Have you written on your index cards exactly when you will use the visual aid?

4. Have you timed your speech, making sure you are enunciating clearly and allowing pauses in your speaking when appropriate?

5. Have you practiced using gestures to stress at least a couple of your important points?

6. Have you anticipated questions that might be asked as well as your answers to these questions?   ❏

Here is a speech written and delivered by student Emily Anderson for her history class:

Two Ways to Achieve Social Change

Emily Anderson

Emily Anderson confides that she likes writing but gets a little nervous when faced with a speaking assignment. She is currently a junior at UCLA.

1   Both Martin Luther King and Malcolm X used very different means to achieve social change. Nonviolence, which was activated by Reverend King, worked in situations where aggressors were more easily touched through moral persuasion and self-realization than because they were forced to change.

2   King sought to persuade fellow Christians by using moral arguments and protest methods supported by the Bible (for example, "turn the other cheek"). King used restaurant sit-ins and freedom rides—completely active but nonviolent means of getting the attention of some racist Southerners. The idea behind these actions was to get media coverage that would publish or broadcast these stories and therefore allow the public to see pictures of blacks occupying space while being nonviolent.

3   After the Voter Registration Laws passed, they were not always enforced in the South. When black student James Meredith was denied entrance to Ole' Miss School, he was met with racism and resistance. Finally, the government had to send federal troops to ease the situation. After seeing the response that this situation received from the government, King asserted from the Birmingham Jail that the government responds only to crisis. He concluded that nonviolence brings about change only when the situation is tense and in crisis mode. King and other followers marched from Selma to Montgomery to protest the denial of black voters. Even though this march did not directly pass the voting rights act, it definitely heightened the public's attention to the situation and showed the government the urgency of King's and the marchers' cause. Within four years of the march, 55 percent of Mississippi's blacks voted in state elections.

4   Someone who advocated a more direct and aggressive approach, as Malcolm X did, would have stated that having only 55% of blacks voting in the South was absurd. He advocated black pride and nationalism, being aggressive towards aggressors, and a different approach to the civil rights movement. He believed that the current struggle on civil rights clearly should be based on human rights. Governments operating under United Nations supervision could not deny blacks human rights because the United Nations had a committee to help end violations of human rights. Malcolm X did not believe that America could be convinced through moral persuasion because Americans have no morals.

5   Probably the idea of nonviolence worked more effectively than Malcolm X's approach in speeding up achievement of the civil rights movement's goals. Although Malcolm X encouraged his followers to have a strong sense of pride and power, he did not help create as many laws and change as many injustices as King did. Although King is remembered for his flowery speech in Washington, he had a stronger political agenda than Malcom X—King's agenda helped the civil rights act, bus desegregation, and black voting. The passing of these laws showed Americans that our government might not have acted with strong morals on a day-to-day basis, but when there was crisis, it would respond and attempt to undo injustices or at least try to escape from potential embarrassment resulting from the weaknesses of its pro-equality laws.

6   Before King's march, Gallup polls indicated that only 49% of the public wanted to segregate schools, and 60% of people surveyed thought the protests were doing

more harm than good. With these statistics, one can speculate that if Malcolm X's more aggressive means had been taken during this time to promote black equality, the government would not have supported these methods of social change.   ●

Once she had written and reviewed her speech on King and Malcolm X, Anderson decided to use several slides to help her audience visualize certain key points. When she presented the speech, she had become so familiar with its contents that she was able to use only the following two index cards—note that these two cards cover her main points and also indicate where she would use visual aids:

TWO DIFFERENT WAYS TO ACHIEVE ① slide 1
SOCIAL CHANGE
MLK & Malcolm X used very diff. means to achieve
social change. Non-violence (K) sit. where aggressors
morally more touched. K convinced Christians by
support from Bible.
(ex.) sit-ins
Freedom Rides } media coverage

Voter reg. Laws
James Meredith – Ole'Miss = Fed. Troops
K + Birmingham jail = non-violence.
Brings change only when tense crisis mode.
March from Selma to Montgomery.
slide 2

---

1 yr after– March, 55% Miss. blacks voted in state ②
elections.
→ Malcolm X-more direct & aggressive.
slide 3
Diff. View of 55%. View based on human rights.
U.N.   no morals in Am.

→ Malcolm X = sense of pride & power but
slide 4 not many laws & changes

King – flowery speech, strong political agenda =
civil rights, bus deseg., black voting.
Gallup polls before K's march = more aggressive
means of Malcolm would not have been supported.

PUBLIC WRITING

Much of our writing is private—when we write a letter addressed to a particular person, when we keep journals or diaries, or when we make grocery lists or scribble on paper while talking on the phone, these are **private writings.** They are addressed to ourselves or to a select, small audience interested in us personally. In contrast, **public writing** is that writing meant to be read by a larger audience. Examples of public writing include the following: college essays, memos, reports, business letters, resumes, graffiti, bulletin boards, letters to the editor of a newspaper or magazine, and signs for a garage sale or a car wash. In addition to these types of public writing, there are kinds of public writing that are the products of community members working individually or together and motivated by a cause or a civic-minded interest. Such writings include flyers, pamphlets, newsletters, fact sheets, position papers, letters to prospective supporters, mission statements or statements of principles, grant proposals, calls to action, minutes of meetings, letters to officials, and petitions.

Have you ever wished that you could be a member of an outreach program? Would you feel challenged as well as enriched by helping the local elderly, or do you think you might like to organize and then help oversee a 10K run in your community? Working with your class or alone, you may want to become involved in a type of writing connected with service learning. This type of public writing connects you quite closely in a variety of ways with your community, whether it be college, work, neighborhood, state, or even your national or global community.

Public writing allows students who can think critically about particular social problems the chance to support arguments for a policy or cause of action; to explain, inform, or counsel for the public good; and to take actions to solve or lessen these problems while sharing their knowledge and skills. Although demanding, this process can be rewarding for college participants as well as for community members. Students and community members may be brought together by their shared interest and use of college or university facilities such as libraries, computer technology centers, and expert opinions of professors, administrators, and public citizens of different ages and backgrounds.

"Okay, but what's in it for me?" If you find yourself asking this question, you might want to know that in any public writing situation, people will really be counting on your writing to help them in tasks that are extremely important to them and that may have a very real impact on their lives. For example, perhaps your local humane society has an overflow of dogs and cats due to a recent flash flood. This organization might be grateful for your ability to produce literature, flyers, and public bulletins to promote pet adoption. Perhaps your church, temple, or mosque could use your help in writing flyers to advertise a boutique, holiday fundraiser, or need for food kitchen volunteers. Possibly you could become involved with local government by writing informational material for mayoral or city council candidates, a position paper on zoning changes, or a pamphlet on alternatives to animal testing of cosmetics. Whatever your area of interest, helping a local group will hone your writing skills and prepare you for the many formidable tasks of the civic and employment world. Public writing is also personally enriching because you will probably learn some "real-world" skills involved in meeting deadlines, writing for a variety of nonacademic audiences, and possibly speaking publicly.

If your class engages in the kind of public writing that includes student participation in community service tasks, you will be involved in **service learning.** Service learning is a concept that combines service objectives with learning objectives. These activities change the recipient (the community) and the provider of the service (students). In other words, your service alters or transforms the community—for example, if your English class engages in weekly tutoring at a local elementary school, the students and the teacher of the class gain from your shared time, interest, and abilities. In addition, you and your class are affected by your experience with these elementary students and by your written reflections on this tutoring.

Although avenues for public writing and service learning may vary tremendously, they do seem to share the following characteristics:

- As college class members, you collaborate with members of your local community.

- In collaborating with the local community on a particular issue, you as students essentially become members of the local community regardless of your original home community before coming to college.

- You share college or university resources such as computer facilities and libraries with the local community.

- As class members, you work either independently or together to create a public document with or for a particular group within the community.

- You learn to interact with groups and individuals from different backgrounds, ages, and interests.

- You learn the value of flexible scheduling and receptivity to various points of view.

How can you get started? Just as in other kinds of writing, using the five "keys"—PURPOSE, FOCUS, MATERIAL, STRUCTURE, and STYLE—will help you engage in public writing. In the "Options for Writing" section of each chapter in Parts 1 and 2 of this text, you will find that the tenth writing option is labeled "Service Learning." Using the detailed table of contents in the front portion of the book, locate the service learning options and decide on one you'd like to pursue individually or with one or more classmates. Also, if you think of a project that interests you, approach your instructor for tentative approval. There may be some area that you'd love to become involved with, but you'll need to remember that if your project puts you in the role of a "do-gooder," you may experience resentment from some members of the group. Also, be aware of logistics: will you be able to attend your required classes, fulfill your other off-campus obligations, and still have the time to take on this service project? It might be a good idea to map out a rough schedule for yourself to make sure the project is feasible.

One starting point is to brainstorm with several other class members to create a list of groups of local residents who might need your help. Once you have a list, discuss what you think your primary goal should be. In other words, what would you and your group members really like to do for this group? Once you have some goals in place, engage in a group discussion with a note taker. When you can all agree on one group on your list considered particularly worthy of your help, meet with your instructor. (Note: Try to avoid choosing a group and project that is too far away from the college to be feasible.)

If your instructor gives you the green light, set up an appointment with the group you want to help. When you meet with the group, try to explain your purpose clearly. After your meeting, think about the people you met to make sure that you are able to work intelligently and responsibly with the involved parties. If you are considering a project that appears to be quite large in scope, you may want to recruit several more class members.

In addition to the writing assignments labeled "Service Learning" under "Options for Writing" in Chapters 1 through 13, the following are some additional service learning/public writing possibilities:

- Convalescent home visitation—is there a home near your college or home? If so, might you be able to offer your services to one of the residents so that he or she could tell you his or her life story? According to recent studies, many older adults feel tremendous gratification sharing their past with someone who can write it down for them and organize a personal narrative.

- Contact the Center for Campus Organizing online at http://www. organizenow.net/cco/canet/index.html or write or call Box 748, Cambridge, Mass. 02412, (617) 354-9363. This resource promotes the creation of alternative newspapers and student-initiated social justice efforts through its Website and a national magazine, *Infusion*.

- Call your local chamber of commerce and ask about particular community service opportunities.

- Find out if there is an office that coordinates service learning efforts at your college. If so, contact instructors who offer service learning courses and ask them about the kinds of projects they have worked on.

- Contact a child abuse and family violence hotline or center in your area, arrange an interview with an employee, and write an informative essay for public awareness.

- Obtain literature pertaining to unsafe household products. Create a flyer for public awareness.

- Find out how you can become a volunteer for your state department of conservation. Interview an authority on the subject of recycling.

- Gather information pertaining to the Meals-on-Wheels program and create an informative essay for interested volunteers in your college.

- Visit the Big Brothers or Big Sisters of your city; ask the authorities there if you could arrange to interview one or two former participants.

- Contact the national site for service-learning information: **http://www. servicelearning.org/welcome/SL_is/index.html**

Living History Project

An English instructor at a community college wanted to establish a service learning project in which students in her class would visit a senior citizen center every week. Each student was paired with a senior, and the goal was the creation of a "life story" as public document. The material for this project was the information given by the senior about some important event in his or her life in interviews with each student. The students' responsibility included

- Attentive listening

- Good follow-up questions

- Clear note taking

At the end of four meetings at the senior center, each student brought a typed working draft of the senior's story. At this point, senior and student agreed on revisions, editing, and any format changes. Next, the student/senior team met to agree on the final draft, with the student making any necessary changes. Then the students, instructor, seniors, and family and friends met at a preassigned time at the senior center to have punch, a celebratory cake, and listen to public readings of the seniors' "life stories." Each student gave his or her senior partner a computer-generated copy of the story, some accompanied by pictures and illustrations. What each student was given, in addition to the opportunity to forge a meaningful friendship with a much older adult, were the memories of each meeting with the senior that the student had tracked and reflected on in his or her personal journal.

If you are interested in additional information in the service learning field, you can log on to the following Websites:

Action Without Borders, Inc. **(http://www.idealist.org)**
America Reads Challenge **(http://ed.gov/inits/americareads)**
American Association of Community Colleges **(http://www.aacc.nche.edu/
    Template.cfm?Section=CommunityBuildings&template=/
    ContentManagement**
Oxfam America **(http://www.oxfamamerica.org)**
Kaboom! Headquarters **(http://www.kaboom.org)**

PART FOUR

Exploring Other Writers:
A Collection of Readings

Thematic Contents

College Community

Work Community

Civic Community

COLLEGE COMMUNITY

GENERATION 9/11

Kay Randall

Kay Randall is affiliated with the University of Texas and its Office of Public Affairs/College of Education. She wrote this piece as a feature story for an online University of Texas magazine.

1   It may be due to the year you were born or the fact that you drove a white BMW and loved Gap khakis a little too much back in the '80s, but, whatever the reason, you've been packaged and labeled.

2   If you entered the world in 1966, you're a Gen X-er. If you came of age during the Great Depression and World War II, Tom Brokaw was kind enough to deem you a member of "The Greatest Generation." If you lived in an urban loft, pulled down a six-figure salary, had 25 pastel Izods, and boasted a swanky college pedigree during the Reagan years, you were a yuppie.

3   But, if you were in high school or college when radical Islamic terrorists attacked America on Sept. 11, 2001, are you Generation 9/11?

4   Dr. Patricia Somers, an associate professor in The University of Texas at Austin's College of Education, is intrigued by that question and has decided to go to the source for some answers. Currently in the first stage of a planned five-year series of studies, Somers and her research colleagues have surveyed about 50 students at colleges and universities in the Midwest to gather preliminary data on student responses to the most deadly attack on U.S. soil in more than 300 years.

The destruction of the World Trade Center Towers, September 11, 2001.

5   "I study higher education, specifically college students," says Somers, who is in the Department of Education Administration, "and have become very interested in how university students may have reacted differently from other populations to the events of 9/11.

6   "This preliminary, exploratory study examines both the direct and indirect effects of 9/11 on students at two-year and four-year, residential and non-residential colleges. Significant shifts in college students' attitudes will have an effect on the future—politics, economics, and social policy–so what we're looking for are trends and to see if there's any evidence of an emerging.

7   As a theoretical framework for the study, the researchers chose terror management theory (TMT), a relatively new system of principles that was first used to analyze Americans' psychological response to the Sept. 11 attacks.

8   "Terror management theory states that when humans are faced with their own mortality by random acts of terror, they respond in ways that show their lives have meaning and purpose," says Somers.

9   According to TMT, immediately following 9/11 most Americans shared similar reactions to the catastrophe. The first reaction was shock and disbelief, or an inability to absorb the reality of an attack on an American city. The second was the search for some sort of distraction that would take their minds off the event, and the third tendency was to withdraw from society and take actions to protect themselves should more attacks occur.

10   Somers' interviews at five universities revealed that students did share some of the same reactions as the general population. About 65 percent of all students interviewed reported feeling shock as a primary response to the terrorist attacks, with one student stating, "I just couldn't think . . . it was all kind of blank at that point, and I went into the bathroom and threw some water on my face and didn't even talk to anybody."

11   Mirroring the disbelief of the rest of the nation, one interviewee said, "I thought it was a joke—the stupid radio program and people thinking they were really funny. I seriously felt like it was Orson Welles' 'War of the Worlds' or something."

12   Although most students who were interviewed did not report engaging in efforts to escape coverage and reminders of the event, about 40 percent did recall feeling an overwhelming desire to be with their families and 45 percent said that they felt a strong urge to be "part of a community." Some sought out the religious community or gained comfort from attending candlelight vigils, while others banded with fraternity brothers or residents of their dorms or stayed at a friend's apartment for prolonged stretches of time.

13   "I remember that night everyone—all the Maryland students and all of the D.C. students—just wanting to talk to each other, "said one student who was interviewed. Another vividly recalls her very frightened friend calling to tell her about the first plane hitting the World Trade Center, and she remembers responding, "Maybe we need to get together to say goodbye. Maybe this is the end. . . ."

14   According to Somers and her colleagues, the "huddling" impulses that students felt and acted upon did not fit the predictions of terror management theory. Neither did the direct reaction of anger toward the U.S. government and the media that 45 percent of students reported feeling.

15   Related to this anger was a direct response of fear for others' safety. About 33 percent of the students who were interviewed stated that they were afraid retaliation would needlessly claim more innocent American lives and members of the American Muslim community would suffer a backlash.

16   "I was so scared because I knew that from then on, no Muslim or anyone who looked like they could possibly be Muslim would ever be the same again," stated one student who was interviewed.

17   In addition to the direct and immediate responses of shock and confusion, terror management theory also asserts that people experience a distal, or delayed and indirect, reaction to terrorism. When Somers and her colleagues asked students about indirect responses, they instructed the interviewees to focus on the six months following the catastrophe

18   With the 9/11 tragedy, TMT analysts found that in the weeks and months following the attacks, most Americans actively searched for information that would help them understand the catastrophe and make sense of a chaotic and dangerous world. Statistics show that Bible sales increased after the attacks, for example, and religious service attendance increased as people sought answers.

19   Americans also experienced a surge in patriotism, and the evidence of this allegiance was very visible. Sales of flags skyrocketed and flag images were displayed on everything from shirts and hats to homes and vehicles. Patriotism pushed President Bush's ratings to an all-time high, and strong support for members of the military was voiced.

20   TMT analysts found that many Americans felt much less tolerance for free speech in the months after 9/11 and that an increased level of censorship prevailed along with an increase in bigotry. Newspapers were filled with accounts of hate crimes against Americans of Arab descent and mosques from coast to coast were vandalized.

21   "So how closely did our college students reflect the distal responses of the general population? It was very interesting," states Somers. "Around 50 percent of the students at three of the five institutions said they felt an increased sense of patriotism, and about 65 percent definitely expressed a desire to gather more information in the weeks and months after 9/11.

22   "Some students reported watching CNN all day and doing their homework a lot less, and at the one public research university that was surveyed there was increased enrollment in world politics and religion courses and signs of a greater level of interest in international and national news. But with the distal responses, we also started seeing some trends that were *not* predicted by terror management theory."

23   Although a majority of students experienced feelings of nationalism, Somers and her colleagues found that the mindset of many could more accurately be described as *"skeptical patriotism."* An overwhelming 80 percent of the students surveyed at the intellectually elite public research university hastened to define patriotism in a way that distinguished loyalty from pride in America.

24   One student commented, "I think patriotism blinds people to what's really going on," while many were repulsed by the songs calling for

retaliation and the "cheering for America as if it were a football team." Some noted that the superficial, widespread visible signs of patriotism were "hypocritical and false," while others were concerned that Americans had stopped viewing the U.S. government's actions objectively and were following the emotional tide, "waving a flag."

25   In addition to revealing skeptical patriotism, students who were interviewed also differed from the population discussed in TMT literature in their increased global awareness, heightened political awareness, and desire for more civic engagement.

26   About 47 percent of all students interviewed stated that they felt a greater interest in the global community post-9/11 and, although only two respondents reported changing their political views as a result of the terrorist attacks, most stated that the attacks intensified their existing political views.

27   One student commented, "I'm a liberal, I've always been a liberal and Sept. 11 did not make me any less of a liberal. It may even have made me more of an activist about it." Another student at the other end of the political spectrum but with the same inclination said, "It [9/11] put foreign policy and foreign affairs at the forefront of what I cared about, politically speaking–it might have made me stronger as a conservative Republican."

28   Perhaps most striking was the number of students who could point to specific actions they had taken to become more civically involved and contribute to the community at large. About one third of the interviewees reported increased levels of civic engagement after 9/11.

29   One student organized a campus forum called "Patriotism, Can it Lead to Hate?" and stated, "I remember that from then on, I always tried to think about the other side of the story." Others participated in community events that related to diversity and encouraged open dialogue or joined social justice-oriented organizations. About 20 percent of the students said that they were altering their academic or career path because of the terrorist attacks.

30   "Although we're just beginning our studies, there does seem to be some evidence of the emergence of a more civically inclined, altruistic generation that takes a world view and will be better equipped to deal with global politics and a world economy," says Somers. "We're continuing our research and will begin interviews for the second part of our study in the spring, along with further analysis by gender and ethnicity of our current data."

31   Whether today's young adults will march through history with the badge "Generation 9/11" has yet to be seen. Civic-mindedness may be short-lived and interest in global affairs may subside.

32   "Only time will tell if Sept. 11, 2001 was a defining moment for an entire generation and the beginning of a new era in American history," says Somers, "or just a terrible national tragedy that occupied our mind and wrenched emotions for a short while before it faded into memory."

Questions on Content

1. Explain the purpose of the five-year study Dr. Patricia Somers is working on.

2. What does TMT stand for?

3. What were 33 percent of the students afraid would happen after 9/11?

4. What two things increased soon after the 9/11 attacks?

5. How many students did Dr. Somers survey, and where did she find these students?

Questions on Strategy

1. This essay opens with brief descriptions of different generations and how they are stereotyped: "Gen X-er," "the Greatest Generation," "yuppie." Is Randall's introductory strategy successful in grabbing our attention?

2. Notice that Randall uses direct quotes from Somers to explain the nature of the study. Do you think direct quote is better than paraphrase for this purpose? Why or why not?

3. When Randall introduces a term that might not be familiar to readers, TMT, she explains what the letters stand for and gives a brief definition of the term. Does her explanation help you to understand her point?

4. Although several students surveyed are quoted in this article, the writer does not reveal their names. Why not? What expression does the writer use to identify the students being quoted?

* * *

Reading 2 　　**THE PATH OF BOOKS AND BOOTSTRAPS**

Jill Leovy

Jill Leovy is a staff writer for the L.A. Times. She is a journalist known for her special reports on education and community service.

1　　When Alex Garcia talks about his life, he absently repeats the words, "I can't believe it." He says it when he talks about his life before—running with a gang, dropping out of school, getting arrested. He says it again when he reflects on his life now, as a Glendale College student earning straight A's. "Every day," he said, "everything gets better." Garcia is the first in his family to go to college. As such, he represents a vast group that educators must pull in if the state is to fulfill its historic promise of universal access to college.

2　　First-generation college students are made up disproportionately of minorities and immigrants, and tend to be older and poorer than peers from college-educated families. They are more likely to attend two-year colleges, less likely to get advanced degrees, more likely to get vocational certificates, and more likely to drop out. They are impoverished immigrants, single parents, students who fall into college as if by accident. In short, they are archetypal community college students—especially in urban Los Angeles where some colleges' enrollments are 70 percent or more first-generation.

Colleges Focusing on Such Students

3   As California colleges and universities strain to increase diversity on their campuses without race-based affirmative action, they are paying more heed to such students, particularly at community colleges, where most minority students enter higher education.

4   Garcia is in a counseling program for first-generation students that has been expanded to several local community colleges in recent years. In addition, California community colleges may soon begin tracking first-generation status of applicants with an eye toward ushering them more effectively through school.

5   The University of California, meanwhile, has agreed to try to boost community college transfers—a means of reaching out to such statistically disadvantaged students without specifically targeting race.

6   Poor, Latino, a school dropout, and the son of a single mother from Guatemala who didn't finish grade school, Garcia typifies the first-generation student who is making it through college against the odds.

7   He also makes clear why ushering new groups into higher education involves more than recruiting. It's a matter of finding the A students hidden among C students. UC recruits among high school dropouts, lost kids like Garcia who turn out to be whizzes at math. It's a matter, said Scott Spicer, a Glendale College administrator, "of staying with students and not giving up on them."

8   Wiry and often wearing a wide bad-boy grin, Garcia grew up in Atwater Village. He dropped out of high school in the 11th grade. His mother, a seamstress, lost her job and needed him to work.

9   He was a troublemaker and never a good student. A science teacher once pulled him aside to tell him he was smart and urged him to work harder. Garcia shrugged it off.

10   He drank and brawled with his gang. He shoplifted, violated his probation and spent time in juvenile camp. Asked to describe himself then, Garcia laughs, his hands tracing the course of an imaginary bowling ball. "Gutter ball," he says.

11   When it came to discipline, Garcia remembers his mother trying to lay down the law: Don't do drugs, she told him. Don't bring home a pregnant girl. As for school, "She didn't encourage me," he said. "But she never told me not to go to school either. We just didn't talk about school."

12   He did get his GED, and briefly held a job as a shoe salesman in the Glendale Galleria earning $200 a week. "Now I see it wasn't much money," he said. "But then, wow, it was so much money."

13   When that job ended, manual labor seemed his only option. But, "I didn't want to break my back lifting boxes—I'm just 5-7, a little guy," he said.

14   So, being short, he went to college.

15   It was a major turnaround, but not decisive. Rather, Garcia followed a pattern counselors say is typical of many first-generation students: He muddled along, barely passing his classes. To him a C was good enough, more than good enough. What happened next is a bit of a mystery.

16   Glendale College had recently started a program for first-generation freshmen called First-Year Experience. It is an outgrowth of TRIO, a federal program rooted in 1960s Great Society reforms.

17   At Glendale, the program was designed to target troubling patterns educators noticed in first-generation freshmen: low expectations, poor study habits, and abysmal grades in the first semester.

18   Garcia embodied the problem. His counselors could tell he was bright. But his grades were low. They nagged him, but he seemed unmoved.

19   Then he pulled a B in a difficult sociology course. Something caught fire.

20   Spicer, who taught the class, said tutoring may have helped. But he thinks there was more to it, something to do with confidence.

21   Garcia "was someone that had been influenced by gangs . . . He was pretty removed from the mainstream," he said. "But I remember one thing: He said he could go home and talk about the class. He got excited about that, about talking about the world and seeing the world from an analytical perspective. I think that gave him a sense of power. . . . He saw that the world was interesting and he could talk about it."

22   The next semester Garcia showed up in Ted Lavatter's speech class and lingered afterward, eager for attention.

23   Lavatter sensed that "underneath all that baggage there was a real intelligence," and took an interest. Garcia ended up getting his first A.

Bachelor's Degree Is Key to Middle Class

24   And that was that. Garcia has been getting A's ever since, even in challenging science and math courses. "It was in me all along," said Garcia. "I just had to bring it out."

25   First-generation status is not the only marker of disadvantage among college students. But it does offer a way to judge whether the system is providing opportunities for all groups.

26   Society is fast closing the door to middle-class status for people whose scholastic achievement is limited to high school diplomas or less, said Patrick Callan, president of the National Center for Public Policy and Higher Education in San Jose.

27   The earnings gap between holders of four-year college degrees and people with only high school diplomas has nearly doubled since 1979 to 71 percent according to the U.S. Department of Labor.

28   The bachelor's degree is the great equalizer. Although first-generation students start out much poorer than their peers from college-educated families, they earn comparable salaries if they get a bachelor's, according to the study by MPR Associates of San Francisco.

29   "As a society," said Ed Gould, a vice chancellor for California Community Colleges, "we can't afford to lose these students."

Questions on Content

1. Name three or more qualities of first-generation college students that Leovy mentions.

2. What has the University of California agreed to do?

3. An MPR study of first-generation college students found that these students encounter what particular problems?

4. The author states that the "earnings gap between holders of four-year college degrees and people with only high school diplomas has nearly doubled since 1979 to 71 percent." Do you know of any exceptions to this earnings gap? Are there friends, relatives, or acquaintances of yours who did not pursue their studies beyond high school but who now earn a good, solid living according to today's standard of living?

Questions on Strategy

1. What is Leovy's strategy in beginning her article with descriptive details and dialogue?

2. How and where does the writer shift from description of one student, Alex Garcia, to hard evidence in the form of statistics and sources such as the MPR Associates study?

* * *

WE'RE LYING: SAFE SEX AND WHITE LIES IN THE TIME OF AIDS

Reading 3

Meghan Daum

When this article appeared in the New York Times *Magazine, the subject and controversial opinion of writer Meghan Daum prompted much discussion and a number of letters to the editors of the magazine.*

1   We grew up with simple, cozy absolutes. Our high school educators knew what they were doing. They taught what they were taught to teach. . . . They told us how to act like the "adults we were becoming," never to drink and drive, never to "experiment" with "cannabis," and never to have sex or even go to third base as the result would be emotional trauma of unimaginable proportions, not to mention pregnancy, which could mean nothing other than ruined lives, missed proms, the prophecy of the sack of flour we carried around for health class finally realized.

2   It wasn't until college that I heard the AIDS speeches. Suddenly we were on our own and didn't have to bring the car back by midnight, so it seemed incumbent upon all those dorm mothers and counselors to give us the straight talk, to tell us never, ever to have sex without condoms unless we wanted to die, that's right *die*, shrivel overnight, vomit up our futures, pose a threat to others (and they'd seen it happen, oh yes they had).

3   Suddenly, pregnancy's out the window concern-wise. It's a lesser evil, a math class rather than a physics class, Chaucer and not Middle English survey. Even those other diseases, the ones they had mentioned in health class, like gonorrhea and even the incurable herpes, seem inconsequential. AIDS

is foremost in our malleable minds, a phantom in our not-yet-haunted houses. They tell us we can get it, and we believe them and vow to protect ourselves, and intend (really, truly) to stick by that, until we don't because we just can't, because it's just not fair, because our sense of entitlement exceeds our sense of vulnerability. So, we blow off precaution again and again and then we get scared and get an HIV test and everything turns out okay and we run out of the clinic, pamphlets in hand, eyes cast upwards, saying we'll never be stupid again. But of course we are stupid, again and again. And the subsequent testing is always for the same reasons and with the same results and soon it becomes more like fibbing about SAT scores ten years after the fact than lying about practicing unsafe sex, a lie which sounds like such a breach in contract with oneself that we might as well be talking about putting a loaded gun to our heads every night and attempting to use our trigger finger to clean the wax from our ear.

4   I have been tested for HIV three times; the opportunities for testing were there, so I took them, forgetting, each time, the fear and nausea that always ensues before the results come back, those minutes spent in a publicly funded waiting room staring at a video loop about "living with" this thing that kills you. I've been negative each time, which is not surprising in retrospect, since I am not a member of a "high-risk group." Yet I continue to go into relationships with the safest of intentions and often discard precaution at some random and tacitly agreed-upon juncture. Perhaps this is a shocking admission, but my hunch is that I'm not the only one doing this. My suspicion is, in fact, that very few of us—"us" being the demographic frequently charged with thinking we're immortal, the population accused of being cynical and lazy and weak for lack of a war draft and altogether unworthy of the label "adult"—have really responded to the AIDS crisis in the way the federal government and the educational system would like to think. My guess is that we're all but ignoring it and that almost anyone who claims otherwise is lying.

5   It's not that we're reckless. It's more that we're grasping at straws, trying like hell to feel good in a time when half of us seem to be on Prozac and the rest of us have probably been told that we need it. When it comes down to it, it's hard to use condoms. Even as a woman, I know this. Maybe the risk is a substitute for thrills we're missing in other areas of life. Maybe there's something secretly energizing about flirting with death for a night and then checking six months later to see if we've survived. This, at least, constitutes intensity of experience, a real, tangible interaction with raw fear. It's so much more than what we get most of the time, subject as we are to the largely protected, government approved, safety first-ness of American society. For my peers and myself, it's generally safe to assume that our homes will not be bombed while we sleep, that our flight will not crash, that we will make the daily round trip from our beds to the office and back again without deadly intervention somewhere in between. We live in the land of side-impact air bags, childproof caps on vitamins, "do not ingest" warnings on deodorant bottles. We don't intend to die in childbirth. Even for those of us, like myself, who live in cities, who read in *USA Today* polls that we'll probably get mugged eventually, who vaguely mull over the fact that the person shot on the corner last week could have been us, fear

continues to exist in the abstract. We've had it pretty cushy. We've been shielded from most forms of undoing by parents and educational institutions and health insurance. But AIDS is housed in its own strange caveat of intimate conversations among friends and those occasional sleepless nights when it occurs to us to wonder about it, upon which that dark paranoia sets in and those catalogs of who we've done it with and who they might have done it with and oh-my-god-I'll-surely-die seem to project themselves onto the ceiling the way fanged monsters did when we were kids. But we fall asleep and then we wake up. And nothing's changed except our willingness to forget about it, which is, in fact, almost everything.

6   Much of the discourse surrounding AIDS in the early 1990s was informed by a male homosexual community, which, in the interests of prevention, assumed an alarmist position. In a *Village Voice* review of two books about the AIDS crisis and gay men, writer Michael Warner described HIV negative status as "living around, under, and next to crisis for that indefinite, rest-of-your-life blank stretch of time." And even though he is speaking largely of the crisis as it relates to gay men, he points out that for homosexuals and heterosexuals alike, "negative status is always in jeopardy and has to be preserved through effort." These sorts of statements are, in many ways, a legitimate tactic for HIV prevention in the gay community, which has been devastated by the disease in staggering proportions. But when words like "crisis" and "effort" are aimed at the heterosexual population as well, a lot of us tend to stop listening. What constitutes strenuous effort for one person may be routine behavior for another. For better or worse, guidelines for HIV prevention among straight people are often a matter of interpretation.

7   The message is that trusting anyone is itself an irresponsible act, that having faith in an intimate partner, particularly women in relation to men, is a symptom of such profound naiveté that we're obviously not mature enough to be having sex anyway. That this reasoning runs counter to almost any feminist ideology—the ideology that told us, at least back in the 70s, that women should feel free to ask men on dates and wear jeans and have orgasms—is an admission that few AIDS-concerned citizens are willing to make. Two decades after *The Joy of Sex* made sexual pleasure accessible to both genders and the pill put a government approved stamp on premarital sex, we're still being told not to trust each other. Women are being told that if they believe a man who claims he's healthy, they're just plain stupid. Men are wary of any woman who seems one or more steps away from virginhood. Twenty years after the sexual revolution, we seem to be in a sleepier, sadder time than the 1950s. We've entered a period where mistrust equals responsibility, where paranoia signifies health.

8   Since I spent all of the 1970s under the age of ten, I've never known a significantly different sexual and social climate. Supposedly this makes it easier. Health educators and AIDS activists like to think that people of my generation can be made to unlearn what we never knew, to break the reckless habits we didn't actually form. But what we have learned thoroughly is how not to enjoy ourselves. Just like our mothers, whose adolescences were haunted by the abstract taboo of "nice" girls versus some other kind of girl, my contemporaries and I are again discouraged

from doing what feels good. As it was with our mothers, the onus falls largely on the women. We know that it's much easier for women to contract HIV from a man than the other way around. We know that an "unsafe" man generally means someone who's shot drugs or slept with other men, or possibly slept with prostitutes. We find ourselves wondering about these things over dinner dates. We look for any hints of homosexual tendencies, any references to a hypodermic moment. We try to catch him in the lie we've been told he'll tell.

9   What could be sadder? When I was a young teenager, . . . I looked forward to growing up and being able to do what I wanted, to live without a curfew, to talk on the phone as long as I wanted, and even to find people whom I could love and trust. But trust is out of vogue. We're not allowed to believe anyone anymore. And the reason we're not isn't because of AIDS but because of the lack of specificity in the anxiety that ripples around the disease. The information about AIDS that was formerly known as "awareness" has been subsumed into the unfortunate—and far less effective— incarnation of "style." As in *Kids*, where violence and ignorance are shown so relentlessly that we don't notice it by the end, AIDS awareness has become so much a part of the pop culture that not only is it barely noticeable, it is ineffectual. MTV runs programs about safe sex that are virtually identical to episodes of "The Real World." Madonna pays self-righteous lip service to safe sex despite basketball star Dennis Rodman's claim that she refused to let him wear a condom during their tryst. A print advertisement for the Benetton clothing company features a collage of hundreds of tiny photographs of young people, some of whom are shaded and have the word AIDS written across their faces. Many are white and blond and have the tousled, moneyed look common to more traditional fashion spreads or even yearbooks from colleges like the one I attended. There is no text other than the company's slogan. There is no explanation of how these faces were chosen, no public statement of whether these people actually have the disease or not. I called Benetton for clarification and was told that the photographs were supposed to represent people from all over the world and that no one shown was known to be HIV positive. Just as I suspected, the advertisement was essentially a work of art, which meant I could interpret the image any way I liked. This is how the deliverers of the safer sex message shoot themselves in the foot. By choosing a hard sell over actual information, people like me are going to believe what we want to believe, which, of course, is the thing that isn't so scary. So, I turn the page.

10   Heterosexuals are being sent vague signals. We're being told that if we are sufficiently vigilant, we'll probably be all right. We're told to assume the worst and not to invite disaster by hoping for the best. We're encouraged to keep our fantasies on tight reins, otherwise we'll lose control of the whole buggy, and no one will be able to say we weren't warned.

11   But I've been warned over and over again and there's still no visible cautionary tale. Since I'm as provincial and self-absorbed as the next person, I probably won't truly begin to take the AIDS crisis personally until I see either someone like me succumb to it or concrete statistics that show that we are. Until then, my peers and I are left with generalized anxiety, a low-grade fear and anger that resides at the core of everything we do. Our attitudes

have been affected by the disease in that we're scared, but our behavior has stayed largely the same. The result of this is a corrosion of the soul, a chronic dishonesty and fear of ourselves that will, for us, likely do more damage than the disease itself. In this world, peace of mind is a utopian concept.

Questions on Content

1. What does Daum mean by "demographic" in paragraph 4?

2. Name at least one lie "going around" according to the author.

3. What specific support does Daum give for her assertion that AIDS awareness has become a part of pop culture?

4. What is it that advertisers have done with the AIDS problem, according to Daum? Do you agree or disagree with her?

5. Why do the people in Daum's group continue to disregard the message that "sex kills"?

6. Daum asks in paragraph 9, "What could be sadder?" Do you agree or disagree that not being able to trust one's intimate partner is one of the terrible effects of the AIDS crisis? (State your reasons for your position.)

Questions on Strategy

1. Describe in a few words Daum's voice and tone in the introductory paragraph.

2. What introductory strategy does the author use to grab the audience's attention?

3. What are two images used in the introduction to help the reader visualize the scene?

4. Throughout the essay, Daum targets a particular audience. When she repeatedly uses "we," to what group is she referring?

5. The following expressions are found in Daum's conclusion: "low-grade fear," "chronic dishonesty," and "corrosion of the soul." What is her strategy in concluding with these images?

* * *

WORK COMMUNITY

Reading 4   ## AMBITION

Perri Klass

In the following essay Perri Klass discusses ambition—what it has meant through the ages, what it meant to her as a college student, and what it means to her today as a mother, professional writer, and pediatrician. Klass was born in Trinidad but came to the United States at an early age. Her mother and father as well as her sisters and brothers are all published authors. Klass acknowledges that ambition and expectations played a large role in her upbringing.

1   In college, my friend Beth was very ambitious, not only for herself but for her friends. She was interested in foreign relations, in travel, in going to law school. . . . I was a biology major, which was a problem: Beth's best friend from childhood was also studying biology, and Beth had already decided *she* would win the Nobel Prize. This was resolved by my interest in writing fiction. I would win *that* Nobel, while her other friend would win for science.

2   It was a joke; we were all smart-ass college freshmen, pretending the world was ours for the asking. But it was not entirely a joke. We were *smart* college freshmen, and why should we limit our ambitions?

3   I've always liked ambitious people, and many of my closest friends have had grandiose dreams. I like such people, not because I am desperate to be buddies with a future secretary of state but because I find ambitious people entertaining, interesting to talk to, fun to watch. And, of course, I like such people because I am ambitious myself, and I would rather not feel apologetic about it.

4   Ambition has gotten bad press. Back in the seventeenth century, Spinoza thought ambition and lust were "nothing but species of madness, although they are not enumerated among diseases." Especially in women, ambition has often been seen as a profoundly dislikable quality; the word "ambitious" linked to a "career woman" suggested that she was ruthless, hard as nails, clawing her way to success on top of bleeding bodies of her friends.

5   Then, in the late Seventies and the Eighties, ambition became desirable, as books with titles like *How to Stomp Your Way to Success* became bestsellers. It was still a nasty sort of attribute, but nasty attributes were good because they helped you look out for number one.

6   But what I mean by ambition is dreaming big dreams, putting no limits on your expectations and your hopes. I don't really like very specific, attainable ambitions, the kind you learn to set in the career-strategy course taught by the author of *How to Stomp Your Way to Success*. I like big ambitions that suggest that the world could open up at any time, with work and luck and determination. The next book could hit it big. The next research project could lead to something fantastic. The next bright idea could change history.

7   Of course, eventually you have to stop being a freshman in college. You limit your ambitions and become more realistic, wiser about your potential, your abilities, the number of things your life can hold. Sometimes you get close to something you wanted to do, only to find it looks better from far away. Back when I was a freshman, to tell the truth, I wanted to be Jane Goodall, go into the jungle to study monkeys and learn things no one had ever dreamed of. This ambition was based on an interest in biology and several *National Geographic* television specials; it turned out that wasn't enough of a basis for a life. There were a number of other early ambitions that didn't pan out either. I was not fated to live a wild,

adventurous life, to travel alone to all the most exotic parts of the world, to leave behind a string of broken hearts. Oh well, you have to grow up, at least a little.

8   One of the worst things ambition can do is tell you you're a failure. The world is full of measuring tapes, books and articles to tell you where you should be at your age, after so-and-so many years of doing what you do. . . .

9   The world is full of disappointed people. Some of them probably never had much ambition to start with; they sat back and waited for something good and feel cheated because it never happened. Some of them had very set, specific ambitions and, for one reason or another, never got what they wanted. Others got what they wanted but found it wasn't exactly what they'd expected it to be. Disappointed ambition provides fodder for both drama and melodrama: aspiring athletes (who coulda been contenders), aspiring dancers (all they ever needed was the music and the mirror).

10   The world is also full of people so ambitious, so consumed by drive and overdrive that nothing they pass on the way to success has any value at all. Life becomes one long exercise in delayed gratification; everything you do, you're doing only because it will one day get you where you want to be. Medical training is an excellent example of delayed gratification. You spend years in medical school doing things with no obvious relationship to your future as a doctor, and then you spend years in residency, living life on a miserable schedule, staying up all night and slogging through the day, telling yourself that one day all this will be over. . . .

11   As you grow up, your ambitions may come into conflict. Most prominently nowadays, we have to hear about Women Torn Between Family and Career, about women who make it to the top only to realize they left their ovaries behind. Part of growing up, of course, is realizing that there is only so much room in one life, whether you are male or female. You can do one thing wholeheartedly and single-mindedly and give up some other things. Or you can be greedy and grab for something new without wanting to give up what you already have. This leads to a chaotic and crowded life in which you are always late, always overdue, always behind, but rarely bored. Even so, you have to come to terms with limitations; you cannot crowd your life with occupations and then expect to do each one as well as you might if it were all you had to do. I realize this when I race out of the hospital, offending a senior doctor who had offered to explain something to me, only to arrive late at the daycare center, annoying the people who have been taking care of my daughter.

12   People consumed by ambition, living with ambition, get to be a little humorless, a little one-sided. On the other hand, people who completely abrogate their ambition aren't all fun and games either. I've met a certain number of women whose ambitions are no longer for themselves at all; their lives are now dedicated to their offspring. I hope my children grow up to be nice people, smart people, people who use good grammar; and I hope they grow up to find things they love to do, and do well. But my ambitions are for *me*.

13   Of course, I try to be mature about it all. I don't assign my friends Nobel Prizes or top government posts. I don't pretend that there is room in my life for any and every kind of ambition I can imagine. Instead, I say piously that all I want are three things: I want to write as well as I can, I want to have a family and I want to be a good pediatrician. And then, of course, a voice inside whispers . . . to write a bestseller, to have ten children, to do stunning medical research. Fame and fortune, it whispers, fame and fortune. Even though I'm not a college freshman anymore, I'm glad to find that little voice still there, whispering sweet nothings in my ear.

Questions on Content

1. Although Klass explores the merits of ambition, she also sets limits, hinting that too much ambition is not good. Find the paragraph in which she discusses the negative effects of ambition. What is one negative consequence you found?

2. Search the body paragraphs of the essay and name two sources for the author's material.

3. Explain what Klass means in her concluding paragraph when she mentions a little voice "whispering sweet nothings in my ear."

Questions on Strategy

1. Note any details in the first paragraph that might draw you as a reader into the essay and make you want to read further.

2. In your estimation, does the material presented in body paragraphs offer effective support for Klass's views? Explain.

3. Throughout the essay, the author moves from an examination of the negative aspects of ambition to an indication of its benefits. Find an example of this pattern. Why is this an effective strategy?

4. Find several specific examples of ambition that help to illustrate the author's general ideas for you by "showing" as well as "telling."

5. How does the author emphasize her main point in the conclusion?

* * *

Reading 5   ## ZIPPED LIPS

Barbara Ehrenreich

Even though America has long held sacred an individual's freedom of speech, that same individual cannot yell "Fire!" in a crowded public building, jeopardizing the lives of others when there is no real danger. The following essay explores the prickly question of freedom of speech and its limitations in the workplace. Author Barbara Ehrenreich, highly respected for her political and social commentary, released her bestseller Nickle and Dimed: On (Not) Getting By in America *in 2002. As you read this essay, pay particular attention to the various kinds of support she uses for her topic sentences in each body paragraph.*

---

1   Earlier this month a fellow named Sam Young was fired from his grocery-store job for wearing a Green Bay Packers T-shirt. All right, this was Dallas, and it was a little insensitive to flaunt the enemy team's logo on the weekend of the N.F.C. championship game, but Young was making the common assumption that if you stay away from obscenity, libel, or, perhaps in this case, the subject of groceries, it is a free country, isn't it? Only problem was he had not read the First Amendment carefully enough: It says *government* cannot abridge freedom of expression. Private employers can, on a whim, and they do so every day.

2   On January 10, for instance, a Peoria, Illinois, man was suspended from his job at Caterpillar Inc. for wearing a T-shirt bearing the words "Defending the American dream," which happens to have been one of the slogans of the United Auto Workers in their seventeen-month strike against Caterpillar. Since the strike ended in early December, the firm has forbidden incendiary slogans like "Families in Solidarity" and suspended dozens of union employees for infractions as tiny as failing to shake a foreman's hand with sufficient alacrity. A 52-year-old worker who failed to peel union stickers off his toolbox fast enough was threatened with loss of retirement benefits.

3   It is not just blue-collar employees who are expected to check their freedom of speech at the company door. In mid-December, Boston physician David Himmelstein was fired for going public about the gag clause in his employer's contract with doctors, forbidding them to "make any communication which undermines or could undermine the confidence . . . of the public in U.S. Healthcare . . . " or even revealing that this clause is in their contract.

4   So where are the guardians of free speech when we need them? For the most part, they are off in the sunny glades of academe, defending professors against the slightest infringement of their presumed right to say anything, at any volume, to anyone. Last fall, for example, history professor Jay Bergman was reprimanded by his employer, Central Connecticut State University, for screaming at a student he found tearing down a flyer he had posted. Now the Anti-Defamation League and the National Association of Scholars are rallying to have the reprimand rescinded. Reprimand, mind you, not firing or suspension.

5   Or, in 1991, you would have found the New York Civil Liberties Union defending crackpot Afrocentrist professor Leonard Jeffries of New York's City University. Thanks to such support and the fact that CUNY is a public-sector employer, Jeffries still commands a lectern, from which he is free to go on raving about the oppression of blacks by "rich Jews" and how melanin deficiency has warped the white brain.

6   Most workers, especially in the private sector, have no such protections. Unless their contract says otherwise, they can be fired "for any reason or no reason"—except when the firing can be shown to be

discriminatory on the basis of race, sex, or religion. In addition, a few forms of "speech," such as displaying a union logo, are protected by the National Labor Relations Act, and the courts may decide this makes Caterpillar's crackdown illegal. But the general assumption is, any expansion of workers' rights would infringe on the apparently far more precious right of the employer to fire "at will." So the lesson for America's working people is: If you want to talk, be prepared to walk.

7   Obviously there are reasonable restrictions on an employee's freedom of speech. A switchboard operator should not break into Tourette's-like torrents of profanity; likewise, professors probably *should* be discouraged from screaming at students or presenting their loopier notions as historical fact. But it's hard to see how a Green Bay Packers T-shirt could interfere with the stocking of Pop-Tarts or how a union sticker would slow the tightening of a tractor's axle. When employers are free to make arbitrary and humiliating restrictions, we're saying democracy ends, and dictatorship begins, at the factory gate.

8   So we seem to have a cynical paradox at the heart of our political culture: "Freedom" is our official national rallying cry, but *un*freedom is, for many people, the price of economic survival. At best this is deeply confusing. In school we're taught that liberty is more precious than life itself—then we're expected to go out and sell that liberty, in eight-hour chunks, in exchange for a livelihood. But if you'd sell your freedom of speech for a few dollars an hour, what else would you sell? Think where we'd be now, as a nation, if Patrick Henry had said, "Give me liberty or give me, uh, how about a few hundred pounds sterling?"

9   Surely no one really believes productivity would nose-dive if employees were free to wear team logos of their choice or, for that matter, to raise the occasional question about management priorities. In fact, the economy could only benefit from an increase in democracy—and enthusiasm and creativity—on the shop floor. Or does the "free" in "free market" apply just to people on top?

10   When employers have rights and employees don't, democracy itself is at risk. It isn't easy to spend the day in a state of servile subjugation and then emerge, at five p.m., as Mr. or Ms. Citizen-Activist. Unfreedom undermines the critical spirit, and suck-ups make lousy citizens.

Questions on Content

1. What is the First Amendment, in your own words?

2. According to Ehrenreich, why would Caterpillar object to particular T-shirt slogans?

3. What is meant by a "gag clause" in paragraph 3?

4. According to the author, what differences are seen in free speech rights on campuses and in the private business sector?

5. What is the paradox mentioned in paragraph 8 that is "at the heart of our political culture"?

Questions on Strategy

1. What kind of support does Ehrenreich use in her first body paragraph?

2. What is the purpose of paragraph 8? Does the author achieve her purpose in this body paragraph? (Support your answer with specific comments.)

3. Does paragraph 5 lose focus and veer off-topic, or does it support Ehrenreich's thesis in the essay? Explain your answer.

4. What important words does Ehrenreich repeat for emphasis in several of her body paragraphs?

5. Why do you think Ehrenreich's style becomes more informal in her concluding sentence?

* * *

Reading 6 — DELIVERING THE GOODS

Bonnie Jo Campbell

Bonnie Jo Campbell decided to write a book about people's workday experiences. The following narrative essay is taken from her book Getting By: Stories of Working Lives. *As you read, notice Campbell's use of dialogue in several paragraphs.*

1   Last year, after school was out, I found myself staring six weeks of unemployment in the face. My mother quickly got wind of this and lined up myriad farm chores to occupy me—including mucking out her horse barn. The manure was so deep in some parts that the horses were scraping their heads on the ceilings.

2   "How are we going to get rid of this stuff?" I asked.

3   "We're going to sell it," she said.

4   She put ads in the *Kalamazoo Gazette* and the *Kalamazoo Shopper* offering manure for $35 a truckload. My portion for doing the physical work was $20; Mom got $15 for providing the truck and the product. Right away we got calls. A surprising number of people wanted the stuff we were anxious to get rid of.

5   I spent a lot of time inside that barn with my pitchfork, moving layer after layer of manure and urine-soaked straw. The sweat poured out of me like I was a marathon runner. My mother brought me glasses of iced tea to keep my spirits and electrolytes up. Oddly enough, I wasn't feeling wretched. As my thoughts wandered, I found myself filled with good cheer. After months of sitting in class listening to professors, I felt like I finally had rejoined the world of the living. Moving my muscles was reviving me.

6   Making the delivery was a little embarrassing at first. The body of my mother's pickup truck was rusting away; the two sides of the bed were held together with shock cords. Some days, with the temperature in the

90s, a half ton of manure in the back, and the truck stuck in a traffic jam on West Main, we made quite a sensation. I put my hand over my face and hoped I wouldn't see anyone I knew.

7　　Within a week, however, I began to see the absurdity of our situation as liberating. As we rattled through well-kept neighborhoods in a half-ton pickup full of stinking manure, I hung my leg out the window, and, strangely, felt like the master of all I surveyed. Perhaps this is how a prostitute feels toward a wealthy, respectable client: I might be dirty, but I have something you need.

8　　Mom and I provided an excellent-quality product at a fair price to decent folks. They were nice—after all, only very earthy people order manure from the farm rather than buying it in bags at the store. Customers often tried to help me shovel, but after I rebuffed their advances, they stood back and smiled at the cascading dung. Hands on hips, eyes sparkling, they perhaps were fantasizing about midsummer gardens brimming with vegetables.

9　　One man was planting a full acre of garden. After I unloaded the truck he took Mom and me to admire a mound on the other side. "Do you know what this is?" he asked. "That's llama manure. And this pile over here, that's pig manure. And that's chicken." His enthusiasm was touching. I felt proud that our manure was out in the world, mingling with other manures, making things grow.

10　　There is no vocation more honest than selling manure. Consider what most people do for a living. They build crap, or sell crap, or move crap, or spin a line of bull over the telephone, all the while pretending that their product is something other than crap. When I delivered a load of manure to someone's garden, the customer and I were both upfront about what we were dealing with. All I had to do was ask, "Where do you want this shit?"

11　　This experience made me reflect on the idea of work in general. Any job is an important job, whether it's selling manure or selling insurance. People should take pride in what they do, and not assume that a dirty job makes them second-class citizens. Even the smelliest job, done well, has its rewards.

12　　My husband works second shift at a paper-converting plant in town. "What are you doing this afternoon?" he asked me one day as I walked him out to his truck. I told him I was going to pitch manure.

13　　"Aren't we all," he said, nodding. "Aren't we all."

Questions on Content

1. Explain how the title of the essay relates to its content.

2. Why was Campbell at first embarrassed by her summer job?

3. What insight has Campbell gained from her job experience?

Questions on Strategy

1. How is the dialogue in paragraph 9 effective in giving readers more information about the man with the garden? What difference would there

have been if Campbell had chosen to tell the reader about this man rather than use his own words in the form of dialogue?

2. In which paragraphs does Campbell make use of humor?

3. Why do you think Campbell compares herself to a prostitute in paragraph 7?

4. What appears to be Campbell's purpose in the second half of the essay?

5. If reading the essay caused you to recall particular jobs you've held in the past, does Campbell seem to want you to take the next step in your thinking? What would this be?

* * *

Reading 7

THE TURNING POINT

Craig Swanson

Craig Swanson majored in math and computer science, completed his graduate work in artificial intelligence, and loves to write. He asserts, "If I could write all day long, I'd be a very happy man." As you read the following essay, notice how Swanson combines personal narrative with process: at the same time Swanson tells about his father and what his hobby means to him, he explains how to "throw" a pot, and he also hints at the significance of finding something in life that is really enjoyable.

1   Dad lost his job last summer. They say that it was due to political reasons. After twenty years in the government it was a shock to us all. Dad never talked much about what he did at work, although it took up enough of his time. All I really know was his position: Deputy Assistant Commissioner of the State Department of Education. I was impressed by his title, though he rarely seemed to enjoy himself. Just the same, it was a job. These days it's hard enough to support a family without being out of work.

2   Apparently his coworkers felt so bad about the situation that they held a large testimonial dinner in his honor. People came from all over the East Coast. I wish I could have gone. Everyone who went said it was really nice. It's a good feeling to know that your Dad means a lot to so many people. As a farewell present they gave Dad a potter's wheel. Dad says it's the best wheel he's ever seen, and to come from someone who's done pottery for as long as he has, that's saying a lot. Over the years Dad used to borrow potter's wheels from friends. That's when I learned how to "throw" a pot.

3   When I came home for Thanksgiving vacation the first thing I did was rush down to the basement to check it out. I was quite surprised. Dad had fixed the whole corner of the basement with a big tabletop for playing with the clay; an area set up for preparing the clay, including a plaster bat and a wedging board; the kiln Walt built for Dad one Christmas;

one hundred and fifty pounds of clay; nine different glazes; hand tools for sculpting; and the brand new potter's wheel. It had a tractor seat from which you work the clay. It could be turned manually or by motor, and it offered lots of surface area, which always comes in handy. Dad was right, it was beautiful. He had already made a couple dozen pots. I couldn't wait to try it.

4   The next day I came down into the basement to find Dad in his old gray smock preparing the clay. I love to watch Dad do art, whether it's drawing, painting, lettering, or pottery. I stood next to him as he wedged a ball of clay the size of a small cantaloupe. He'd slice it in half on the wire and slam one half onto the wedging board, a canvas-covered slab of plaster; then he'd slam the other half on top of the first. He did this to get all the air bubbles out of the clay. You put a pot with air bubbles in the kiln, the pot'll explode in the heat and you've got yourself one heck of a mess to clean up. Dad wedged the clay, over and over.

5   When he was finished he sat down, wet the wheelhead, and pressed the clay right in the center of the wheel. Dad hit the accelerator and the clay started turning. He wet his hands and leaned over the clay. Bracing his elbows on his knees he began centering the clay. Steady right hand on the sides of the clay. Steady left hand pushing down on the clay. Centering the clay is the toughest part for me. The clay spins around and around and you have to shape it into a perfectly symmetric form in the center by letting the wheel do all the moving. Your hands stay motionless until the clay is centered. It takes me ten or fifteen minutes to do this. It takes Dad two. I shake my head and smile in amazement.

6   Dad's hands cup the clay, thumbs together on top. He wets his hands again and pushes down with his thumbs. Slowly, steadily. Once he's as far down as he wants to go he makes the bottom of the pot by spreading his thumbs. His hands relax and he pulls them out of the pot. Every motion is deliberate. If you move your hands quickly or carelessly you can be sure you will have to start again. Dad wipes the slip, very watery clay, off his hands with a sponge. It is extremely messy.

7   To make the walls Dad hooks his thumbs and curls all of his fingers except for his index fingers. Holding them like forceps, he reaches into the pot to mold the walls to just the right thickness. He starts at the bottom and brings them up slowly, making the walls of the pot thin and even all the way up, about 12 inches.

8   Dad sponges off his hands, wets them, and then cups his hands around the belly of the pot. Slowly, as the pot spins around, he squeezes his hands together, causing it to bevel slightly. Dad spends five minutes on the finishing touches. He's got himself a real nice skill.

9   It is a rare treat to watch Dad do something that he enjoys so much.

Questions on Content

1. How did Swanson's father feel about his job?

2. How does Swanson's father feel about his hobby?

3. Why is it important to get all the bubbles out of the clay?

Questions on Strategy

1. If the writer's focus is on the process of "throwing" a pot, why does Swanson begin the essay with a fairly lengthy discussion of his father's job situation?

2. What tense does the writer use in the first five paragraphs?

3. What tense is used for the rest of the essay?

4. Why does the author change tense?

5. Reread the essay, underlining all words that help you visualize the process of "throwing" a pot.

* * *

Reading 8 — MCDONALD'S IS NOT OUR KIND OF PLACE

Amitai Etzioni

This essay focuses on high school students working in places such as fast-food franchises. Amitai Etzioni—an associate professor of sociology at Columbia University whose writings on war, peace, and social change have won many awards—states that many teen jobs are worse than uneducational. He contends that they can teach teens to become liars and cheats and to waste their money on trendy fashions. Although Etzioni has lived in the United States for many years, he was born in Germany, and his stand on the issue of teen employment may be a reflection of his European background. While you may disagree with many of Etzioni's assertions, he offers his audience some strong support of his thesis. As you read, see if you can determine any important effects of teen employment that Etzioni fails to mention.

1   In today's reality you need to look beyond the school itself to examine those factors that hinder or provide opportunities for generating educational experiences that enhance character formation and moral education. Today's high school students spend much time outside the school and within the work environment. It would be shortsighted to ignore the educational effects of this context. As I have stressed, much of the education of children takes the form of experiences; since work has become such an important part of many high school students' lives, it too must be examined in this light: Is it educational?

2   I regret to report that from this viewpoint, McDonald's (and other companies like it, from Roy Rogers to Dunkin' Donuts) are far from benign creations. McDonald's is bad for your kids. I don't mean the flat patties and the white-flour buns. I mean the jobs it takes to mass-produce these delicacies. About two-thirds of high school juniors and seniors these days have part-time paying jobs, many in fast-food chains, of which McDonald's is the pioneer, trendsetter, and symbol. Such employment would seem to be straight from the pages of the Founding Fathers' moral education manual on how to bring up self-reliant, work-ethic-driven

youngsters. From lemonade stands to newspaper routes, it is a longstand-ing tradition that American youngsters hold paying jobs. Here, kids learn the fruits of labor and trade and develop the virtue of self-discipline.

3   Hardee's, Baskin-Robbins, Kentucky Fried Chicken, and the like ap-pear to be nothing more than a vast extension of the lemonade stand. They provide large numbers of steady teen jobs, test the teenagers' stamina, and reward them quite well compared with many other teen jobs. Upon closer examination, however, the McDonald's kind of job is rather uneducational in several ways. Far from providing an opportunity for self-discipline, self-supervision, and self-scheduling, like the old-fashioned paper route, it is highly structured and routinized. True, students still must mobilize themselves to go to work, but once they don their uniforms, their tasks are spelled out in minute detail. The McDonald's Corporation dictates for thousands of local outlets the shape of the coffee cups; the weight, size, shape and color of the patties; the texture of the napkins (if any); how of-ten fresh coffee is to be made (every eight minutes); and so on. There is little room for initiative, creativity, or even elementary rearrangements. Thus, fast-food franchises are breeding grounds for robots working for yesterday's assembly lines and not practice fields for committed workers in tomorrow's high-tech posts.

4   Although it is true that these workplaces provide income and even some training to such low-skilled youngsters, they also tend to perpetu-ate their disadvantaged status. Such jobs provide no career incentives and few marketable skills, and they can undermine school attendance and involvement.

5   The hours are long. Often the stores close late, and after closing work-ers must tally and clean up. There is no way that such amounts of work will not interfere with schoolwork, especially homework. Fifty-eight per-cent of the seniors at Walt Whitman High School in Montgomery County, an affluent area in Maryland, acknowledge that their jobs interfere with their schoolwork.

6   One study did find merit in jobs at McDonald's and similar places. The study reported that this work experience teaches teamwork and working under supervision. That may be true, but it must be noted, how-ever, that such learning is not automatically educational or wholesome. For example, much of the supervision in fast-food places leans toward teaching the wrong kinds of compliance (blind obedience or being pissed off with the world, as the supervisors often are). Also, such compliance helps very little to develop the ability to form quality-of-work circles, in which employees and supervisors together seek to improve operations.

7   Supervision is often both tight and woefully inappropriate. In the days before industrialization and capitalism, the young were initiated into the world of work in close personal relations such as between a mas-ter (adult) craftsman and an apprentice. Even when a young person worked for someone other than his parents, he lived in the master's or farmer's home and was integrated into his family; he was not part of a teen horde.

8   Today, fast-food chains and other such places of work (record shops, bowling alleys) keep costs down by having teens supervise teens, often

with no adult on the premises. There is no mature adult figure to identify with, to emulate, or to provide a role model or mature moral guidance. The work culture varies from one store to another: some places are tightly run shops (must keep the cash registers ringing); in other places the employees may "party," only to be interrupted by the intrusion of customers. Rarely is there a "master" to learn from; rarely is there much worth learning. Indeed, far from being places where solid work values are being transmitted, these are places where all too often teen values dominate. Typically, when one of my sons was dishing out ice cream for Baskin-Robbins in upper Manhattan, his fellow teen workers considered him a sucker for not helping himself to the till. Most of them believed they were entitled to a self-awarded "severance pay" of fifty dollars on their last day on the job.

9   The money raises additional issues. The lemonade stand and paper route money was your allowance. Apprentices, to the extent that they generated a significant flow of income, contributed most, if not all, of it to their parents' household.

10   Today's teen pay may be low by adult standards, but it is often substantial. Especially among the middle class, it is largely or wholly spent by the teens. That is, the youngsters live free at home and are allowed to keep considerable amounts of money. Where this money goes is not quite clear. Some use it to support themselves, especially among the poor. Some middle-class youngsters set money aside to help pay for college or save it for a major purchase, like a car. But large amounts seem to pay for an early introduction into trite elements of American consumerism: trendy clothes, trinkets, and whatever else is the fast-moving teen craze.

11   One may say that this is only fair and square: the youngsters are just being good American consumers, working and spending their money on what turns them on. At least, a cynic might add, the money isn't going to buy illicit drugs and booze. On the other hand, an educator might bemoan that these young, as-yet-unformed individuals are driven to buy objects of no intrinsic educational, cultural, or social merit. They learn early and quickly the dubious merit of keeping up with ever-changing mass-merchandising fads.

12   Moreover, many teens find the instant reward of money, and the youth status symbols it buys, much more alluring than credits earned in algebra, American history, or French. No wonder quite a few would rather skip school, and certainly homework, to work longer hours at a Burger King.

Questions on Content

1. According to Etzioni, what percentage of high school juniors and seniors have part-time jobs?

2. What advantages does the author cite for these jobs?

3. What disadvantages does he stress?

4. Name three fast-food franchises other than McDonald's that Etzioni targets.

Questions on Strategy

1. Reread the essay, and find the places where the writer does give credit to some positive effects of these jobs.

2. Is Etzioni's use of outside sources as well as the experience of his son sufficient to convince you of his thesis? Why or why not?

3. Do you think the writer has a European bias? If so, where do you find evidence of this bias?

4. Is Etzioni guilty of oversimplification in any part of his essay? If so, in which paragraph?

* * *

Reading 9   ## FACING DOWN ABUSERS

Im Jung Kwuon

Working in Los Angeles as a counselor in a domestic-violence-prevention program is Im Jung Kwuon's life's work. She is also an Advisory Council Member of the Center for Cultural Fluency in Los Angeles.

1   I always wanted a safe life after recovering from alcoholism, two suicide attempts and abusive relationships. But could I truly be safe if others were in danger? Helping families became part of my recovery. Now I work with men who beat and sometimes kill the women they love. I counsel those who are court-ordered attendees to a yearlong domestic-violence prevention program. Some people hearing this step back startled, cringing at a familiar memory of abuse. Others glare, accusing me of coddling bad guys by teaching them anger-management skills.

2   Even cops twice my size say they would be scared to go into my classes. They say that domestic calls are the worst, too dangerous. I tell them "Hey, my groups are as safe as you'll get. Come see what it's like. I'll protect you." They look skeptical since I'm a petite, 40-year-old, Korean-American woman. My bravado hides the fact that I've shopped for a bullet-proof Kevlar vest. I've fingered the high-tech, impenetrable material, wondering if it would be a good investment. I choose not to buy one, because fear is my worst enemy.

3   I wish I had been wearing a vest when enrolling some batterers into the classes. They scream curses and pace threateningly. They rarely admit to having beaten their partners or children. When they do, most cling to a justification. "She made me punch her." I always suggest they take a timeout to cool off until the next class. When they choose to de-escalate, both classmates and family are less likely to get hurt.

4   Recovery begins when men can express anger without intimidating others. It continues when they can recount how often they saw their mothers slapped, choked or hit with a two-by-four. I encourage them to share painful childhood experiences, but remind them there is no excuse for abuse.

5   I remain on guard even after healing days. When a group member shakes my hand or brings flowers in gratitude, I remember that emotional intimacy is dangerous for both victims and victimizers. Batterers usually injure only those they care about. Getting close to one is like building a home on the slopes of a dormant volcano. Occasionally, I hear encouraging reports from partners of former clients. One joyful wife called a year after her husband finished the class. She gushed, "We had a big fight and he didn't hit me. I should've called the police 10 years ago."

6   After working with batterers for four years, I no longer have unrealistic expectations of success. I remember a young man I'll call Joey. He attended 14 classes, entertaining us with clever jokes and reassuring us that he was getting along with his girlfriend. Then he dropped out. Two months later, I saw on TV that Joey had shot her in the chest and killed her. Six months earlier, she had given birth to their second son.

7   For weeks I cried and lost sleep, wondering if I could have saved her life. I pored over the newspaper, looking for names of former clients charged with homicide. Can the chain of domestic violence ever be broken? Recovery frequently includes relapse. So it wasn't surprising when a man called me after getting my number from his cellmate, a former client doing hard time for a second spousal-abuse charge. I reflected back to a decade ago when domestic-violence calls were less frequent and counseling haphazard. Today, an arrest often follows a 911 call. A criminal charge plus 52 classes encourage an abuser to give up violence and intimidation as control strategies. Families benefit because batterers can learn to become safer partners and fathers.

8   Without help abusers can also lose their lives. Last year after Father's Day weekend, one group talked about who among them got drunk, who picked a fight, who walked away for a timeout. Near the end of that session, a man I'll call John revealed how he had lost his father that past Sunday. "Just before midnight, my mom called me for help. Dad was drinking and beating her. Like times before, he pointed a shotgun at her, but this time they wrestled with it and she shot him." John choked up. "I got there too late," he explained.

9   John stayed behind to confess, "I know it was an accident. This has been going on since I was a kid, but even at Dad's funeral, I couldn't forgive her. I couldn't look at my mom's face." He added, "I can't come back for a while." I hugged him goodbye, encouraging him to return soon.

10   I knew he needed our support as much as the group needed him. John's courage in telling other batterers about his loss could help prevent tragedy in their lives now. Confronting abusers with the consequences of their behavior increases the chance their families will survive and recover. Unfortunately, counseling cannot save or heal people who never try it. As a young adult, I took up with increasingly abusive boyfriends. I remember standing mute when a boyfriend punched a wall. He said my anger provoked him. I felt I was going to be hit next. Being a paralyzed victim and witness supports abusers. I learned this the hard way.

11   After salvaging my life through counseling, I've realized how powerful batterers are. They scare the world, because no one wants to face them. Often they are our family leaders. We still struggle to love and be loyal to

them. I teach abusers how to be safe physically and emotionally. But no one is safe until every batterer is held accountable for his behavior.

12   For me, safety means that I'm prepared to call the police if anyone becomes violent. This rule applies even to family and friends. But strengthening my basic security doesn't shield me from sadness and pain.

13   When I watched John walk away, I realized I had embraced someone experiencing my ultimate nightmare. No one in his family called 911 to report the domestic violence, just the death. Breaking the chain of family abuse is a good job, even if it hurts.

Questions on Content

1. According to police, what kinds of calls are the most dangerous?

2. Who is the man Kwuon refers to as "Joey," and why does the thought of him sadden Kwuon?

3. When the author states that she has no "unrealistic expectations of success," what point does she seem to be making about abusers?

4. Kwuon states that a decade ago, "domestic-violence calls were less frequent." Why do you think the calls have increased?

Questions on Strategy

1. What kind of introductory strategy does the author use in this essay? Is it effective? Why or why not?

2. Notice Kwuon's use of dialogue in several of her body paragraphs. She quotes police officers, battered wives, abusers themselves, and children of abusers. After a close reexamination of the essay, explain whether you think the use of this dialogue strengthens or weakens her essay.

3. Annotate this essay by underlining Kwuon's insertion of her personal history. Do you feel that Kwuon's commentary of her own story reinforces her essay? Support your opinion with specific reference to the text.

* * *

CIVIC COMMUNITY

Reading 10 — THE GEOGRAPHY OF THE IMAGINATION

Guy Davenport

Guy Davenport was a poet, short story and essay writer, painter, professor of English, and recipient of numerous awards. "The Geography of the Imagination" is one of forty essays published in 1981. As you read the essay, refer to the copy of the painting American Gothic.

Grant Wood, *American Gothic*, 1930

1   A geography of the imagination would extend the shores of the Mediterranean all the way to Iowa.

2   Eldon, Iowa—where in 1929 Grant Wood sketched a farmhouse as the background for a double portrait of his sister Nan and his dentist, Dr. B. H. McKeeby, who donned overalls for the occasion and held a rake. Forces that arose three millennia ago in the Mediterranean changed the rake to a pitchfork, as we shall see.

3   Let us look at this painting to which we are blinded by familiarity and parody. In the remotest distance against this perfect blue of a fine harvest sky, there is the Gothic spire of a country church, as if to seal the protestant sobriety and industry of the subjects. Next there are trees, seven of them, as along the porch of Solomon's temple, symbols of prudence and wisdom.

4   Next, still reading from background to foreground, is the house that gives the primary meaning of the title, *American Gothic*, a style of architecture. It is an example of a revolution in domestic building that made possible the rapid rise of American cities after the Civil War and dotted the prairies with decent, neat farmhouses. It is what was first called in derision a balloon-frame house, so easy to build that a father and his son could put it up. It is an elegant geometry of light timber posts and rafters requiring no deep foundation, and is nailed together. Technically, it is, like the clothes of the farmer and his wife, a mail-order house, as the

design comes out of a pattern book, this one from those of Alexander Davis and Andrew Downing, the architects who modified details of the Gothic Revival for American farmhouses. The balloon-frame house was invented in Chicago in 1833 by George Washington Snow, who was orchestrating in his invention a century of mechanization that provided the nails, wirescreen, sash-windows, tin roof, lathe-turned posts for the porch, doorknobs, locks, and hinges—all standard pieces from factories.

5   We can see a bamboo sunscreen—out of China by way of Sears Roebuck—that rolls up like a sail: nautical technology applied to the prairie. We can see that distinctly American feature, the screen door. The sash-windows are European in origin, their glass panes from Venetian technology as perfected by the English, a luxury that was a marvel of the eighteenth century, and now as common as the farmer's spectacles, another revolution in technology that would have seemed a miracle to previous ages. Spectacles begin in the thirteenth century, the invention of either Salvino degl'Armati or Alessandro della Spina; the first portrait of a person wearing specs is of Cardinal Ugone di Provenza, in a fresco of 1352 by Tommaso Barisino di Modena. We might note, as we are trying to see the geographical focus that this painting gathers together, that the center for lens grinding from which eyeglasses diffused to the rest of civilization was the same art of Holland from which the style of the painting itself derives.

6   Another thirteenth-century invention prominent in our painting is the buttonhole. Buttons themselves are prehistoric, but they were shoulder-fasteners that engaged with loops. Modern clothing begins with the buttonhole. The farmer's wife secures her Dutch Calvinist collar with a cameo brooch, an heirloom passed down the generations, an eighteenth-century or Victorian copy of a design that goes back to the sixth century B.C.

7   She is a product of the ages, this modest Iowa farm wife: She has the hair-do of a mediaeval Madonna, a Reformation collar, a Greek cameo, a nineteenth-century pinafore.

8   Martin Luther put her a step behind her husband; John Knox squared her shoulders; the stock-market crash of 1929 put that look in her eyes.

9   The train that brought her clothes—paper pattern, bolt cloth, needle, thread, scissors—also brought her husband's bib overalls, which were originally, in the 1870s, trainmen's workclothes designed in Europe, manufactured here for J. C. Penney, and disseminated across the United States as the railroads connected city with city. The cloth is denim, from Nimes in France, introduced by Levi Strauss of blue-jean fame. The design can be traced to no less a person than Herbert Spencer, who thought he was creating a utilitarian one-piece suit for everybody to wear. His own example was of tweed, with buttons from crotch to neck, and his female relatives somehow survived the mortification of his sporting it one Sunday in St. James Park.

10   His jacket is the modification of that of a Scots shepherd which we all still wear.

11   Grant Wood's Iowans stand, as we might guess, in a pose dictated by the Brownie box camera, close together in front of their house, the farmer looking at the lens with solemn honesty, his wife with modestly averted eyes. But that will not account for the pitchfork held as assertively as a minuteman's rifle. The pose is rather that of the Egyptian prince Rahotep,

holding the flail of Osiris, beside his wife Nufrit—strict with pious recti-
tude, poised in absolute dignity, mediators between heaven and earth,
givers of grain, obedient to the gods.

12   This formal pose lasts out 3,000 years of Egyptian history, passes to
some of the classical cultures—Etruscan couples in terra cotta, for instance—but does not attract Greece and Rome. It recommences in northern Europe, where (to the dismay of the Romans) Gaulish wives rode
beside their husbands in the war chariot. Kings and eventually the merchants of the North repeated the Egyptian double portrait of husband
and wife: van Eyck's Meester and Frouw Arnolfini: Rubens and his wife
Helena. It was this Netherlandish tradition of painting middle-class folk
with honor and precision that turned Grant Wood from Montparnasse,
where he spent two years in the 1920s trying to be an American post-
Impressionist, back to Iowa, to be our Hans Memling.

13   If Van Gogh could ask, "Where is my Japan?" and be told by Toulouse-
Lautrec that it was Provence, Wood asked himself the whereabouts of his
Holland, and found it in Iowa.

14   Just thirty years before Wood's painting, Edwin Markham's poem
"The Man with the Hoe" had pictured the farmer as a peasant with a life
scarcely different from that of an ox, and called on the working men of the
world to unite, as they had nothing to lose but their chains. The painting
that inspired Markham was one of a series of agricultural subjects by Jean
Francois Millet, whose work also inspired Van Gogh. A digging fork appears in five of Van Gogh's pictures, three of them variations on themes
by Millet, and all of them are studies of grinding labor and poverty.

15   And yet the Independent Farmer had edged out the idle aristocrat for
the hand of the girl in Royal Tyler's "The Contrast," the first Native
American comedy for the stage, and in Emerson's "Concord Hymn" it is
a battle-line of farmers who fire the shot heard around the world. George
III, indeed, referred to his American colonies as "the farms," and the two
Georges of the Revolution, Hanover and Washington, were proudly farmers by etymology and in reality.

16   The window curtains and apron in this painting are both calico printed
in a reticular design, the curtains of rhombuses, the apron of circles and
dots, the configuration Sir Thomas Browne traced through nature and art
in his Garden of Cyrus, the quincunxial arrangement of trees in Orchards,
perhaps the first human imitation of a phyllotaxis, acknowledging the
symmetry, justice, and divine organization of nature.

17   Curtains and aprons are as old as civilization itself, but their presence
here in Iowa implies a cotton mill, a dye works, a roller press that prints
calico, and a wholesale-retail distribution system involving a post office,
a train, its tracks, and, in short, the Industrial Revolution.

18   That revolution came to America in the astounding memory of one
man, Samual Slater, who arrived in Philadelphia in 1789 with the plans of
all Arkwright's, Crompton's, and Hargreaves's machinery in his head,
put himself at the service of the rich Quaker Moses Brown, and built the
first American factory at Pawtucket, Rhode Island.

19   The apron is trimmed with rickrack ribbon, a machine-made substitute
for lace. The curtains are bordered in a variant of the egg-and-dart design

that comes from Nabataca, the Biblical Edom, in Syria, a design which the architect Hiram incorporated into the entablatures of Solomon's temple— "and the chapiters upon the two pillars had pomegranates also above, over against the belly which was by the network; and the pomegranates were two hundred in rows round about" (1 Kings 7:20)—and which formed the border of the high priest's dress, a frieze of "pomegranates of blue, and of purple, and of scarlet, around about the hem thereof; and bells of gold between them round about" (Exodus 28:33).

20   The brass button that secures the farmer's collar is an unassertive, puritanical understatement of Mathew Boulton's eighteenth-century cut-steel button made in the factory of James Watt. His shirt button is mother-of-pearl, made by James Boepple from Mississippi fresh-water mussel shell, and his jacket button is of South American vegetable ivory passing for horn.

21   The farmer and his wife are attended by symbols, she by two plants on the porch, a potted geranium and sansevieria, both tropical and alien to Iowa; he by the three-tined American pitchfork whose triune shape is repeated throughout the painting, in the bib of the overalls, the windows, the faces, the siding of the house, to give it a formal organization of impeccable harmony.

22   If this painting is primarily a statement about Protestant diligence on the American frontier, carrying in its style and subject a wealth of information about imported technology, psychology, and aesthetics, it still does not turn away from a pervasive cultural theme of Mediterranean origin—a tension between the growing and the ungrowing, between vegetable and mineral, organic and inorganic, wheat and iron.

23   Transposed back into its native geography, this icon of the lord of metals with his iron sceptre, head wreathed with glass and silver, buckled in tin and brass, and a chaste bride who has already taken on the metallic thralldom of her plight in the gold ovals of her hair and booch, are Dis and Persephone posed in a royal portrait among the attributes of the first Mediterranean trinity, Zeus in the blue sky and lightning rod, Poseidon in the trident of the pitchfork, Hades in the metals. It is a picture of a sheaf of golden grain, female and cyclical, perennial and the mother of civilization; and of metal shaped into scythe and hoe: nature and technology, earth and farmer, man and world, and their achievement together.

Questions on Content

1. According to Davenport, what hinders us from really seeing the painting *American Gothic?*

2. Why does the woman in the painting look away, according to Davenport?

3. Make a list of all the items Davenport mentions (for example, bamboo, sunscreen, buttonhole). What does Davenport's discussion of each item reveal about the history of America?

4. In paragraph 8, Davenport says of the woman in the painting, "Martin Luther put her a step behind her husband; John Knox squared her

shoulders; the stock market crash of 1929 put that look in her eyes." Explain the meaning of each of these phrases.

5. Explain your understanding of the pose in this painting.

6. A theme Davenport mentions in paragraph 22 is "a tension between the growing and ungrowing, between vegetable and mineral, organic and inorganic, wheat and iron." What does the writer mean? Support your answer with specific details from the picture.

Questions on Strategy

1. After reading Davenport's essay carefully, explain the meaning of the first sentence.

2. Examine the structure of the essay. What part of the painting does Davenport concentrate on first? Second? Third? Is there any reason for this organization plan? Is the organization effective? Why or why not?

3. In paragraph 22, Davenport asserts that "this painting is primarily a statement about Protestant diligence on the American frontier." Why does the writer wait until almost the end of the essay to make this assertion?

* * *

Reading 11 GRANT WOOD: AMERICAN GOTHIC

Jane Yolen

Jane Yolen, author of over 200 books, composes songs, writes fiction as well as poetry, and is a professional storyteller. All of Yolen's works are rooted in her sense of family and self. In Yolen's poem "Grant Wood: American Gothic," the poet responds to the painting in a way quite different from Davenport.

Grant Wood: American Gothic

Do not dwell on the fork,   1
the brooch at the throat,
the gothic angel wing
of window pointing toward
a well-tended heaven.   5
Do not become
a farmer counting cows
as if the number of the herd
defines you.

Look behind the eyes,   10
to see who looks out at you.
We are not what we own
We own what we would be.

Questions on Content

1. Who is the speaker in the poem?

2. What are readers told *not* to do?

3. What are readers told to do?

4. How does Yolen's point of view differ from Davenport's?

Questions on Strategy

1. Where can you find three distinct breaks in the poem?

2. Why does the speaker place negative instructions first and positive instructions last? Is this strategy successful?

3. In what way is Yolen's last line in the poem dependent on the next-to-last line?

4. Although the picture upon which the poem is based was painted in 1930, is the poem's theme timeless? In other words, is the theme of the poem pertinent today?

* * *

Reading 12 ── OFFERING EUTHANASIA CAN BE AN ACT OF LOVE

Derek Humphry

Derek Humphry takes a strong stand on the issue of euthanasia in his essay. (If you don't know the meaning of euthanasia, *be sure to look it up in a dictionary.) As you examine the essay, notice Humphry's technique for acknowledging and then refuting the opposition.*

1   The American Medical Association's decision to recognize that artificial feeding is a life-support mechanism and can be disconnected from hopelessly comatose patients is a welcome, if tardy, acceptance of the inevitable.

2   Courts in California and New Jersey have already ruled this way, and although a Massachusetts court recently ruled in an opposite manner, this is being appealed to a higher court.

3   The AMA's pronouncement is all the more welcome because it comes at a time when the benefits of some of our modern medical technologies are in danger of being ignored because of the public's fear that to be on life-support machinery can create problems.

4   People dread having their loved ones put on such equipment if it means they are never likely to be removed if that proves later to be the more sensible course. As medical ethicist and lawyer George Annas has said, "People have rights, not technologies."

5   The argument by the pro-life lobby that food is a gift from God, no matter how it is introduced, and thus to deprive a comatose person of pipeline food is murder, is fallacious. A pipe is a manufactured item; the skill to introduce it into the body and maintain it there is a medical technology. Without the pipeline, the person would die. Food is common to all humans, but taking it through a pipeline is a technique carried out because the person has sustained an injury or suffers an illness which prevents normal feeding.

6   The pro-life lobby also harks back to Nazi excesses of the 1930s and '40s as part of its argument for continued pipeline feeding. True, Nazi Germany murdered about one hundred thousand Aryan Germans who were mentally or physically defective because it considered them "useless eaters," detracting from the purity of the German race.

7   But neither the views of the victims nor their relatives were ever sought: they were murdered en masse in secret fashion and untruths concocted to cover the crimes.

8   No terminally ill or comatose person was ever helped to die by the Nazis. Moreover, their barbarous killing spree took in 6 million Jews and 10 million noncombatant Russians, Slavs, and gypsies. Life was cheapened by the Nazis to an appalling degree. What connection is there between the Nazis then and the carefully considered euthanasia today of a permanently comatose person who might, as Karen Quinlan did, lie curled up for ten years without any signs of what most of us consider life?

9   Helping another to die in carefully considered circumstances is part of good medicine and also demonstrates a caring society that offers euthanasia to hopelessly sick persons as an act of love.

Questions on Content

1. On what issue have the courts recently ruled?

2. In what paragraph do you find Humphry's claim?

3. Why does Humphry point out that a pipe is a "manufactured item"?

Questions on Strategy

1. Evaluate the effectiveness of Humphry's distinction of Nazi murder of "useless eaters" and his own stand on artificial feeding. Does he make a clear and valid distinction between the two? Explain and support your view.

2. Find one or more emotional appeals in the essay and note them.

* * *

Reading 13   ## WHO GETS TO CHOOSE?

Jean Nandi

Jean Nandi, a member of the California Disability Alliance, is one of many who oppose euthanasia. The alliance receives grants from the Disability Rights Advocates Fund of the San Francisco Foundation and the Milbank Foundation for Rehabilitation. The following article by Nandi was published as an editorial in the Oakland Tribune.

1   On the face of it, Dion Aroner's "Death with Dignity Act," A.B. 1592, seemed like a good idea. Why not give dying folks the right to choose a dignified, early end to hopeless suffering? But close examination reveals the dangers lurking in this apparent liberty.

2   **1. Not everyone will get to choose.**

You may choose suicide only if two physicians have attested to your mental "competence." If you are depressed (surely a likelihood if contemplating suicide), you might be counseled by a psychiatrist, but only if your physician thinks you are mentally unbalanced. And if you are too sick or disabled to take a whopping dose of poison on your own, you will not be eligible for the opportunity to kill yourself with your doctor's help.

3   **2. Your choice may be cost driven.**

Inadequate home health services may force you into a nursing home, and the quality of your life is likely to deteriorate immediately. Your health plan may deny services which could prolong your life and ease your suffering, and your physician may not be adept at managing your pain. If you are compelled to choose suicide because adequate medical treatment and care is likely to result in your family's financial ruin, is this free choice?

4   **3. Doctors are not omniscient.**

Two physicians must agree that you are "likely" to die within six months. But how often have you heard of "miraculous" recoveries? Physicians are not always right, and many of us with disabilities are alive in spite of dire predictions—and some of us in spite of our physicians! I have lived 45 years beyond the first time doctors pronounced my cancer "terminal"—45 rich, full years that I might have needlessly discarded. A.B. 1592 mistakenly presumes that doctors can predict your death with scientific certainty.

5   **4. Few doctors are truly knowledgeable about alternatives.**

Your physician must inform you about other options prior to prescribing a fatal dose. But those of us living with disabilities know only too well that doctors often undervalue our lives, are too frequently unaware of resources within ourselves and our communities which make our lives meaningful and even happy. In hospitals, persons with disabilities are frequently tricked or subtly pressured into signing "Do Not Resuscitate" orders. Managed care reviews deny potentially costly care that appears "futile" or wasteful of money or resources. It is in this setting that you will need to make your choice.

6   **5. We have choices today.**

New legislation is not necessary to provide painkilling drugs to ease one's suffering, even opiates adequate to end one's life "early" if they are prescribed for the purpose of ending pain. New legislation is not needed to allow one to request that treatment or even nutrition be withdrawn, nor is it needed to give one the choice of refusal of treatments that one feels too onerous to bear. The proposed new legislation is bound to harm many, and to help almost none, and we find it unsupportable despite the public's uninformed enthusiasm.

7   We believe that A.B. 1592—or any similar bill legalizing physician-assisted suicide in any form—cannot bring wisdom to our medical profession or protections to our uninsured or underinsured frail and vulnerable seniors, disabled and poor. Rather let us reeducate our caregivers and provide quality health care for all. Let us have Life, not Death, with Dignity!

Questions on Content

1. State in your own words the first reason Nandi opposes the "Death with Dignity Act."

2. What does Nandi find possibly erroneous regarding the decision of two physicians?

3. What solution does Nandi offer?

Questions on Strategy

1. In her opening paragraph, the author uses a couple of emotionally charged words. Find these and underline them.

2. Do Nandi's five points against euthanasia reveal that there are dangers inherent in the proposal?

3. Is Nandi's strategy in organizing her main points effective, or would you recommend a rearrangement of any of these? Explain why or why not.

4. Who appears to be the target audience for this writer's essay?

* * *

Reading 14   ## AMERICAN HEALTH, THEN AND NOW

Bryan Williams and Sharon Knight

The following reading is taken from a current health textbook, Healthy for Life, *written by Bryan Williams and Sharon Knight.*

1   During the past century, life expectancy has risen because of improvements in public health, drugs and medical technology, and better lifestyle. Still, a great many Americans are in ill health, and many suffer premature deaths—young people principally from injuries and violence, adults from cancer and heart disease—most of which are preventable by lifestyle changes. The lesson is: your habits matter.

2   More than a century ago, people were pretty much obliged to look after their own health, because the "health authorities" themselves were not much more knowledgeable. Then came the revolutions that have led to modern medicine.

From Public Health to Lifestyle

3   Over the past 100 years or so, death rates have declined through three stages, according to Donald M. Vickery (see Figure 1, on page 374).

- *Age of Environment—Improved public health:* From about 1885 until the 1930s, public health policies and improvements in the environment dramatically lowered death rates, especially those for infant mortality. During this period, city health departments were established, city water supplies were cleaned up, milk became pasteurized, and public health campaigns were introduced.

- *Age of Medicine—Improved drugs and technology:* In the 1930s, sulfa drugs, penicillin, and other antibiotics were introduced, further accelerating the drop in death rates. However, in the early 1950s, life-expectancy rates stopped increasing, even though many high-tech innovations—open-heart surgery, polio vaccine, and so on—continued to be introduced.

- *Age of Lifestyle—Better living habits:* It was not until the 1970s that life-expectancy rates began to increase again. This coincided with attempts to deal with what are called **lifestyle disorders**—ill health brought about by individuals' behavior patterns, such as those involving eating, safety, and drug use.

4   Today we are still living in the Age of Lifestyle. Unfortunately, people find lifestyle a lot less fascinating than medical wizardry. "We're so in love with the chrome and glitter of high-tech medicine," says medical-ethics consultant Bruce Hilton, "we forget to ask how the patient got this way. . . . How many people remember that Barney Clark, the first artificial-heart patient, whose bravery we all admired, had been a lifelong chain smoker?"

Is *Everyone* Sick?

5   Where have these ages of health advancement brought us today? A researcher on the staff of former U.S. surgeon general C. Everett Koop added up the numbers of Americans suffering from various diseases. He found, according to Koop, "that the total exceeded by a good measure *the entire population of the United States*" (our emphasis added). More remarkable,

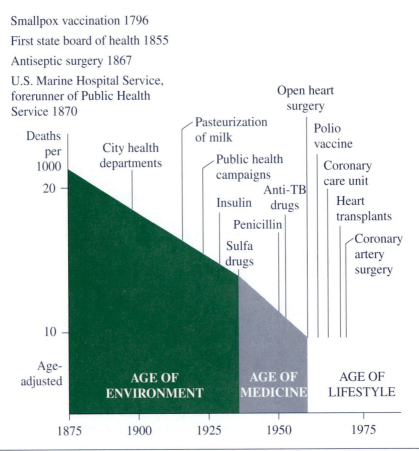

Smallpox vaccination 1796

First state board of health 1855

Antiseptic surgery 1867

U.S. Marine Hospital Service, forerunner of Public Health Service 1870

FIGURE 1   One hundred years of health advancement

Physician Donald Vickery describes three stages of health advancement in the United States that took place in the 100 years between 1885 and 1985:

- In stage 1, the *Age of Environment* (approximately 1875–1935), 70% of the decline in the death rate occurred *before* the introduction of wonder drugs and organ transplants—the result of improvements in the environment and public health policy.
- In stage 2, the *Age of Medicine* (aproximately 1935–1955), there was further progress resulting from antibiotics and other drugs.
- In stage 3, the *Age of Lifestyle* (aproximately 1955–present), for several years life-expectancy rates no longer improved, despite the introduction of many high-tech innovations such as open-heart surgery. Then, in the early 1970s, death rates began to decline again as the effects of lifestyle programs took hold, with their emphasis on less fat in the diet, more exercise, and reduction in tobacco use.

this total was for physical ailments only. It did not include the estimated 30 million with mental illnesses and psychiatric disorders, Koop says.

6   It should not be surprising, therefore, that the research assistant concluded that pretty "near everyone in this country is sick!" Some researchers might object that many of the people measured had multiple disorders that were counted singly. Even so, the great majority of Americans, says Koop, "are victims of chronic, crippling, or incapacitating diseases ranging from

alcoholism to Alzheimer's. Sexually transmitted diseases alone have infected 40 million." (**Chronic** means of long duration or recurring, as opposed to an **acute** disorder, which is of short duration.)

7   However one may argue about numbers, the news from the health front is not good. For instance, Koop was also part of a commission of physicians and educators looking into what schools and communities might do to improve adolescent health. The panel concluded that the United States is raising a generation of adolescents plagued by pregnancies, illegal drug use, suicide, and violence. Although you might not consider pregnancies, drunkenness, arrests, and homicides parts of the usual definition of ill health, they are indicative of frightening trends—signs of massive declines in the quality of American life.

The Importance of Prevention

8   It should be clear by now that a lot of ill health is *preventable*. Consider the age group you are in, which most likely is either ages 15–24 (adolescents and young adults) or ages 25–64 (adults).

- *Adolescents and young adults:* There are two categories of preventable health problems found among people between the ages of 15 and 24.

9   The first category consists of *injuries and violence* that kill and disable them while they are still young.

10   The second category consists of *emerging lifestyles,* such as those having to do with diet, physical activity, use of alcohol and other drugs, safety, tobacco use, and sexual behavior. These are important because they affect one's health many years later.

- *Adults*: Many of the principal areas of ill health for people between the ages of 25 and 64 are also preventable, in whole or in part through changes in lifestyle, such as tobacco and alcohol use, diet, exercise, and safety.

11   For adults in this age group, the leading causes of death are cancer and heart disease. Cancer is actually not one but many diseases, the significant ones being lung cancer, cancers of the colon and rectum, breast cancer, cervical cancer, and cancer of the mouth and throat. Other leading causes of death are heart disease and stroke (blood clot in the brain), and injuries, as from car crashes. (See Figure 2, on page 376)

Health and Personal Responsibility

12   No doubt you know of someone who avoided all the standard advice for a healthy life and lived to a ripe old age. Or, conversely, you know someone who ate and did all the right things and still developed a severe illness. We need, then, to point out a fundamental fact: health-promoting habits *are not guarantees.* As health writer Jane Brody points out, "they do not offer 100% protection, like a vaccine against a disease. Good habits merely weight the odds in one's favor."

13   Physician Gary Williams, director of medical sciences at the American Health Foundation, a health research organization, has ranked the value

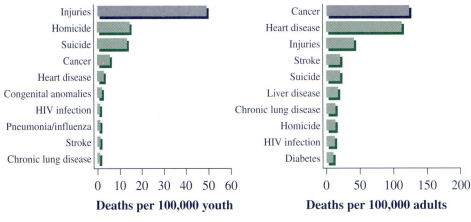

Deaths per 100,000 youth

Deaths per 100,000 adults

Leading causes of death for youth ages 15–24 (in 1987)   Leading causes of death for adults ages 25–64 (in 1987)

FIGURE 2 Leading causes of death for youth and adults

of various recommendations in preventing particular illnesses, based on thousands of studies. Although his analysis is not all-inclusive, it does show that lifestyle makes a difference.

14   The lesson is clear: *Your habits matter.* The lifestyle choices you make today could have a tremendous influence on the quality of your life, both now and later.

Questions on Content

1. Which of the three stages of health advancement in the United States are we living in now?

2. What health problems plague adolescents in the United States, according to a commission of physicians and educators?

3. What are the leading causes of death for people between the ages of 25 and 64?

4. Find and underline the definitions given in the text for *chronic* and *acute.* Think of an example for each kind of disorder.

Questions on Strategy

1. Describe the technique the writers use to get your attention in the first paragraph.

2. Figure 1 is accompanied by a boxed explanation. Does this information help you to understand the figure? How?

3. Why do you think the writers omit any boxed explanation for Figure 2?

4. What strategy have the writers used to break down the information into separate sections?

5. Skim the entire reading, looking for direct quotes from individuals. How many different quotes do you find? Why do you think the writers have included these comments?

* * *

Reading 15 ⎯ OUR BIOTECH BODIES, OURSELVES

James Pethokoukis

James Pethokoukis is a senior editor at U.S. News and World Report. *His articles have also appeared on the Web site* **http://techcentralstation.com.** *This article first appeared in the May 31, 2004, issue of* U.S. News and World Report. *The writer explores the controversial question of whether humans should be bioengineered.*

1   What if, by taking a drug, you could possess an IQ of 250? Or by tinkering with your genes, have the athletic prowess of a decathlete? Or by injecting yourself with stem cells, live to be 160? Would you do it? Would these enhancements make you less human? If everyone did this, would the world become a paradise full of self-actualized superpeople? Or a dystopian Stepford society devoid of essential human values such as compassion for the less blessed?

2   What seems like fodder for a science fiction potboiler has become a matter of deadly serious debate among scientists and ethicists. In a speech last year before a gathering of enhancement advocates, William Sims Bainbridge, a deputy director at the National Science Foundation who studies the societal impact of technology, warned that "scientists may be forced into rebellion in order to carry out research prohibited unnecessarily by powerful institutions."

3   A few months later, Leon Kass, chair of the President's Council on Bioethics, was expressing the advisory panel's profound "disquiet" with a biotech-enabled, post-human future that "cheapens rather than enriches America's most cherished ideals." The council's 325-page report, *Beyond Therapy: Biotechnology and the Pursuit of Happiness*, takes a decidedly dim view of the impact of such issues as radical life extension, mood and intelligence-enhancing drugs, and genetic therapies.

4   At the core of the conflict lies a fundamental question: How far should homo sapiens be allowed to go? Nascent technologies like genetic engineering, stem-cell therapy, and neuropharmacology promise not only to cure our disease but to enhance our bodies, even to turn us all into the Six Million Dollar Man—better, stronger, and faster.

Clash

5   But not everyone thinks humans should be bioengineered. "Our increasing ability to alter our biology and open up the processes of life is now fueling a new cultural war," says Gregory Stock, director of the University of California–Los Angeles's Program on Medicine, Technology, and Society and author of the pro-enhancement book *Redesigning Humans*.

6   Yet isn't arguing about whether mankind should transform itself into a race of superhumans a little like arguing about whether the first Mars colony should have a bicameral or unicameral legislature? Kass doesn't think so. "These topics are not futuristic," he says. "Some of these issues are already here. Choosing the sex of your children is here. The use of stimulants on children to improve performance is here. Steroid use is here. Drugs that affect mood and temperament are here. . . . There is something profound going on here that will affect our identities and the society we live in."

7   Indeed, there are hints that genetic engineering might be able to alter mankind in some astounding ways. Researchers at the University of Pennsylvania have boosted levels of a protein in mice that makes them more muscular throughout life. Southern Illinois University scientists extended one mouse's life span to nearly twice the normal length.

8   But governments around the world are already putting brakes on this type of research, especially as it applies to humans. President Bush famously banned the federal funding of research on new embryonic stem-cell lines in 2001. A year later, the South Korean government raided BioFusion Tech, a company backed by the Raelian religious sect, after the group announced that a Korean woman would give birth to a clone—even though cloning isn't illegal there. And at least 17 countries have banned germ-line modification, which alters reproductive cells so that genetic tweaks will be passed down to future generations.

9   "How we respond to these threats to enhancement today will lay the groundwork for dealing with the ones that emerge in the future," says enhancement activist James Hughes, a lecturer in health policy at Trinity College in Hartford, Connecticut. Political scientist Francis Fukuyama agrees that policies need to be shaped before these technologies fully ripen—although Fukuyama, member of the bioethics council and author of *Our Posthuman Future*, counts himself a bioconservative. "If you don't shake people up now, then you will get these gradual changes that are going to end up leading us to a place that we're not going to be comfortable with," he says.

Side Effects

10   Why worry about human enhancement? After all, what's not to like about, say, doubling the average human life span? But the bioethics council wonders in its report whether we would achieve a "stretched rubber band" version of longevity in which our active, healthy years would be extended, but so would our years of decline and decay. "Having many long, productive years, with the knowledge of many more to come, would surely bring joy to many of us," says panel member William Hurlbut, a bioethicist at Stanford University. "But in the end, these techniques could also leave the individual somewhat unhinged from the life cycle. Do I want to live to be 100? Sure. But to 250 or some other dramatic extension? No."

11   Bioconservatives acknowledge, however, that human enhancement may be inevitable. Even Kass admits that the council's report focused on the problems of enhancement rather than its benefits because the advantages of longer lives and better brains are so obvious "they don't need

articulating." It's easy to argue the "con" position, says UCLA's Stock, about issues like the use of embryonic stem cells as long as the benefits are merely theoretical. Once those benefits become tangible, though, "the debate will be over," says Stock. Indeed, the potential therapeutic value of stem-cell research has already prompted more than 200 House members and Nancy Reagan to urge Bush to alter his ban.

12   With the proliferation of plastic surgery, for example, or the use of Ritalin by achievement-crazed students hoping to score better on the SAT, enhancement seems to be the wave of the future. Even Bush's Department of Commerce appears to be buying into it. In a 2002 joint report with the National Science Foundation (coauthored by Bainbridge among others), the agency recommended a national research-and-development effort to enhance humanity in order to create a world where human brains communicate directly with machines, and scientists "control the genetics of humans" to make bodies "more durable, healthier . . . and more resistant to many kinds of stress, biological threats, and aging processes." If successful, the effort will "create a golden age that would be a turning point for human productivity and quality of life."

13   Or not. Science could render all this high-flying rhetoric just that. Stem-cell and protein therapies, after all, have yet to spawn any successful treatments for disease, much less provide the catalyst for launching a new stage of human evolution. In 2000, researchers used gene therapy to cure two French boys of an inherited immune-system disorder but in the process gave them leukemia. Who knows what other dangerous side effects these new therapies will bring? It is, as they say, too early to tell— but judging by the intensity of the debate, not any too early to fight.

Questions on Content

1. What issue has the President's Council on Bioethics recently explored?

2. According to Gregory Stock, what "issues are already here"?

3. How has genetic engineering affected mice?

4. Why have 17 or more countries banned germ-line modification?

5. Why should we worry about human enhancement?

6. Have stem-cell and protein therapies led to any successful treatments for disease?

Questions on Strategy

1. What introductory device does Pethokoukis use in his essay?

2. Notice the author's strategy of using direct quotes from experts in the field. How many such sources does the writer use?

3. In paragraph 6, Pethokoukis asks, "Yet isn't arguing about whether mankind should transform itself into a race of superhumans a little like arguing about whether the first Mars colony should have a bicameral

or a unicameral legislature?" Look up the words *bicameral* and *unicameral*. What point is the writer making with this question?

4. What strategies does Pethokoukis use to show the reader his objectivity? Is he successful in his use of these strategies, or is his bias in one direction revealed? Support your answer with evidence from the article.

* * *

WRITER'S COMMUNITY

Reading 16   ## WELCOME TO THE E-MAIL COMBAT ZONE

Patricia T. O'Conner and Stewart Kellerman

Patricia T. O'Conner and Stewart Kellerman have written a book on e-mail entitled You Send Me. *In this article written for the* The New York Times, *the two authors attempt to establish some standards for our new form of cyber-communication.*

1   Even the nicest people sometimes adopt a take-no-prisoners attitude when they sit down at the computer. As a result, too many e-mail exchanges resemble hand-to-hand combat.

2   Herewith, a report from the trenches. A friend of ours in the entertainment business complains that all the abrupt, rude and belligerent e-mail he gets at work has turned his electronic in-basket into a "testosterone-enhanced war zone."

3   "E-mails are forms of assault," he told us. "Sentences are shortened to be only commands, written in the form of quick barks. In fact, I've been in cognitive therapy for the last year trying to come to terms with how much e-mail upsets me, believe it or not."

4   The very structure of e-mail encourages behavior that's nasty, brutish, and short. The blank subject line is a signal to state your business and get on with it, and almost precludes a warm message. The To and From fields seem to make greetings and closings redundant or at least unnecessary. All in all, it's the ideal breeding ground for rudeness.

5   What's more, the things so many people like about e-mail—the speed, the informality, the brevity, the disengagement—give words a sharp edge. Clipped, telegraphed messages seem brusque and curt. Small slights are magnified. A tiny, half-joking pout looks like a major hissy fit. A mild suggestion sounds like a dressing down. And attempts at subtlety, irony or sarcasm land with a thud more often than not. As for the quality of the writing, perhaps some things are better left unsaid.

6   So what's the answer? Is there no room for civility online? Maybe the real question is, What is e-mail, anyway?

7   When we polled friends and acquaintances, most thought an e-mail message fell somewhere between a letter and a phone call. Not surprisingly, those who thought e-mail was closer to letter-writing were pickier

about the niceties—manners as well as spelling, grammar, punctuation and such. Those who thought e-mail was closer to speech were more likely to ignore the pleasantries along with their spell-checkers. Swell people, every one of them, but you can imagine which group came across as the more civil—and readable.

8   Why do good people send bad e-mail? Maybe they forget that what they're doing at their computers is writing. And the purpose of writing—whether with a pen, a typewriter or a laptop—is to connect with others. When people write well, they connect. When they write badly, they don't.

9   With that in mind, we've tried to imagine the kind of virtual message we'd like to get, a Platonic ideal of e-mail perfection. Here's what our dream e-mail looks like.

- It's written in good English: clear, plain, and, above all, understandable.

- It's polite, asking instead of demanding and using such quaint terms as "Please," "Thank you" and "Sorry." (Our ideal e-mailers never send in anger. They sleep on it.)

- It gets to the point in the first screenful. We computer users have short attention spans.

- It has a helpful subject line; the reader knows at a glance what it's about and how urgent it is.

- It's discreet and protects the privacy of everyone involved.

- It mentions what it's replying to (a cryptic "Fine" or "Nope" or "Maybe" isn't enough).

- It capitalizes properly. Writing that's all upper- or lowercase is hard to read.

- It uses shorthand sparingly. Not everybody understands those smileys, abbreviations, and techie terms.

- It has obviously been reread—yes, just like "real" writing. Fortunately the Age of E-mail is still young.

Questions on Content

1. According to O'Conner and Kellerman, why do some people seem offended by e-mail messages?

2. Name two ways in which the structure of e-mail "encourages behavior that's nasty, brutish and short."

3. Define "hissy fit," a term used in paragraph 5.

4. In paragraph 9, the writers refer to "a Platonic ideal of e-mail perfection." Who was Plato? After finding information on this philosopher, explain what you believe the writers meant by "a Platonic ideal of e-mail perfection."

5. Define the words *cryptic* and *smileys* in paragraph 9.

Questions on Strategy

1. What are O'Conner and Kellerman attempting to accomplish with their title? Is the title effective?

2. Find examples of military language used in the essay.

3. This short essay's content is divided into two distinct parts. Find this break in thought and explain why you think the writers organized their essay in this manner.

4. O'Conner and Kellerman's conclusion is "open-ended." What is the implication of the concluding sentence? Do you think the authors would have influenced readers more if the conclusion had been stated rather than implied? Why or why not?

* * *

Reading 17   # A LIST OF TOPICS FOR WRITING PRACTICE

Natalie Goldberg

Natalie Goldberg is a writer and teacher. She reports that she has written a book on writing because even though there is no "logical A-to-B-to-C way to become a good writer," the discovery and consistent practice of different techniques and methods will help writers build confidence and skill. In this excerpt from her book Writing Down the Bones, *Goldberg focuses on some techniques to help writers get started in generating material. Toward the end of the selection, the author offers a large list of writing ideas.*

1   Sometimes we sit down to write and can't think of anything to write about. The blank page can be intimidating, and it does get boring to write over and over again for ten minutes of practice, "I can't think of what to say. I can't think of what to say." It is a good idea to have a page in your notebook where you jot down, as they come to you, ideas of topics to write about. . . .

2   Making a list is good. It makes you start noticing material for writing in your daily life, and your writing comes out of a relationship with your life and its texture. In this way, the composting process is beginning. Your body is starting to digest and turn over your material, so even when you are not actually at the desk physically writing, there are parts of you raking, fertilizing, taking in the sun's heat, and making ready for the deep green plants of writing to grow.

3   If you give your mind too much time to contemplate a beginning when you sit down to write, your monkey mind might meander over many topics and never quite get to putting a word on the page. So the list also helps to activate your writing quickly and cut through resistance. Naturally, once you begin writing you might be surprised where your mind takes the topic. That's good. You are not trying to control your writing. You are stepping out of the way. Keep your hand moving.

4   But until you get your own list, here are some writing ideas:

1. Tell about the quality of light coming in through your window. Jump in and write. Don't worry if it is night and your curtains are closed or you would rather write about the light up north—just write. Go for ten minutes, fifteen, a half hour.

2. Begin with "I remember." Write lots of small memories. If you fall into one large memory, write that. Just keep going. Don't be concerned if the memory happened five seconds ago or five years ago. Everything that isn't this moment is memory coming alive again as you write. If you get stuck, just repeat the phrase "I remember" again and keep going.

3. Take something you feel strongly about, whether it is positive or negative, and write about it as though you love it. Go as far as you can, writing as though you love it, then flip over and write about the same thing as though you hate it. Then write about it perfectly neutral.

4. Choose a color—for instance, pink—and take a fifteen-minute walk. On your walk notice wherever there is pink. Come back to your notebook and write for fifteen minutes.

5. Write in different places—for example, in a laundromat, and pick up on the rhythm of the washing machines. Write at bus stops, in cafés. Write what is going on around you.

6. Give me your morning. Breakfast, waking up, walking to the bus stop. Be as specific as possible. Slow down in your mind and go over the details of the morning.

7. Visualize a place that you really love, be there, see the details. Now write about it. It could be a corner of your bedroom, an old tree you sat under one whole summer, a table at McDonald's in your neighborhood, a place by a river. What colors are there, sounds, smells? When someone else reads it, she should know what it is like to be there. She should feel how you love it, not by your saying you love it, but by your handling of the details.

8. Write about "leaving." Approach it any way you want. Write about your divorce, leaving the house this morning or a friend dying.

9. What is your first memory?

10. Who are the people you have loved?

11. Write about the streets of your city.

12. Describe a grandparent.

13. Write about:
    swimming
    the stars
    the most frightened you've ever been
    green places
    how you learned about sex

your first sexual experience
the closest you ever felt to God or nature
reading and books that have changed your life
physical endurance
a teacher you had

Don't be abstract. Write the real stuff. Be honest and detailed.

Questions on Content

1. What is the "composting process" Goldberg refers to in paragraph 2?

2. Why do you think Goldberg suggests as a writing idea choosing a color and then taking a walk to notice that color? What is to be gained from this activity from a writer's point of view?

3. What does Goldberg mean after number 13, "Don't be *abstract*"? Look up the word and then write your own definition.

Questions on Strategy

1. Why do you think Goldberg begins with specific examples?

2. Find at least two places in her list of writing ideas where Goldberg uses specific images of sight, smell, sound, or touch in order to convey the importance of these specific details in writing to her audience.

3. Who would you say Goldberg's specific audience is, and how carefully does she consider them? Find evidence of audience consideration and the writer's purpose in the excerpt.

* * *

FAMILY COMMUNITY

Reading 18   ### WHOSE EYES ARE THOSE, WHOSE NOSE?

Margaret Brown

As a college freshman in Austin, Texas, Margaret Brown wrote this essay exploring her roots. This exploration proved to be fraught with disappointments and obstacles.

1   I've had this recurring dream of floating through darkness where I am whirling faster and faster through some nameless, timeless, almost unearthly region. I get weary and want to put my feet down to stand so I can gather myself together. But there's nothing to stand on. This is my nightmare—I'm a person created by donor insemination, someone who will never know half of her identity. I feel anger and confusion, and I'm filled with questions. Whose eyes do I have? Why the big secret? Who

gave my family the idea that my biological roots are not important? To deny someone the knowledge of his or her biological origins is dreadfully wrong.

2   Beginning with the selection of a sperm donor, the process is centered around deception. From hair and eye color to religious and musical preferences, a donor is carefully matched to the mother or to her husband if she is married. Usually there is multiple insemination, a kind of potluck technique of fertilization, often involving a different donor each time, so determining the exact biological father can be next to impossible. In many cases records are eliminated after conception (though I believe there are a few sperm banks that release donor identities). Couples are counseled not to tell anyone they're considering donor insemination. Some doctors encourage the couple to lie, to say that the husband's infertility has been treated successfully. Then friends and family will assume the child is the natural offspring of the husband and wife.

3   I only recently found out my father was not really my father. My parents divorced when I was seven, and I have had very little contact with him since then. Two years ago, at sixteen, when I expressed interest in seeing him again, my mother decided to tell me that my "dad" wasn't my father and that my father's half of me came from a test tube. With no records available, half my heritage is erased. I'll never know whose eyes I have inherited. I've searched family photo albums to no avail.

4   The news has affected my sense of identity and belonging. "Who am I?" is a hard question to answer when I don't know where I came from. I'd like to have the comfort of knowing whom I resemble. It's amazing how one can miss a sense of identity and wholeness because no one has ever said, "You act just like your mama when she was young." I guess I act like my donor. And, as my thoughts, opinions and behavior are almost 180 degrees from those of most of my family members, I've never felt like a "piece of the puzzle" at family gatherings, especially around my father's side of the family. This isn't something I sensed strongly—I thought I acted differently because I was from Tennessee and they were from Texas—but the feeling was always there. I'll admit putting it into words is hard. As well as grappling with who I am and where I belong, I have a more difficult obstacle since the secret's been out: trust. I've wondered if there are other secrets being kept from me. I shouldn't have to doubt my mother. But I've found myself questioning whether I was told the truth. How can I know for sure that there was a donor as she says?

5   Advocates of donor babies argue that biology is not an issue in parenting; the love and care a child receives is all that matters. I can understand a couple's desire for a child, and I don't deny that they can provide a great amount of love and caring, no matter how conception occurs. In a world where history is a required academic subject and libraries have special sections for genealogy, I don't see how anyone can consciously rob someone of something as basic and essential as heritage. Parents must realize that all the love and attention in the world can't mask that underlying, almost subconscious feeling that something is askew. I greatly appreciate the sacrifices my mother has made and the love my family has given me. But even while being enveloped in my father's sister's

warmest embrace, I feel a strange little twinge of something deep inside me like I'm borrowing someone else's family.

6   What is even more astounding, given society's present attitude toward protecting children's rights—even the unborn—is that decisions about insemination are made in the interests of the parents' and the physicians' privacy, rather than those of the child. A donor is matched to the recipient's husband so the couple can pass the child off as their own. The procedure is kept secret so the couple can avoid accusations of immorality and adultery. That the child deserves the right to know of a biological father is not a consideration. One couple that Elizabeth Noble, author of *Having Your Baby by Donor Insemination*, interviewed said that telling the child "would serve absolutely no useful purpose whatsoever." That assumes the child would have no thoughts on the matter of paternity because the parents don't. It seems no one thought I might want to know of the other half of my genetic makeup. But children are not commodities or possessions. They are people with an equal stake in the process.

7   Future donor-recipient parents must step out of their own shoes and into those of the person they are creating. Parents can choose to raise a child honestly—fully respecting the child's individuality—without the self-imposed pressure to deceive. If there is honesty and openness in donor insemination, it could become a process similar to adoption—at least giving young adults a possibility to find out about their biological fathers.

8   So, to couples seeking babies this way, I propose that you find out who your donors are, keep records and let your children know where they came from. And to a possibly brown-haired man who attended University of Tennessee Medical School in 1974 and made a donation on my mother's behalf, I thank you for the gift of life. I think I have your eyes, your jaw and your personality. I just wish I could find out for sure.

Questions on Content

1. What specific facts do you learn about donor insemination?

2. How does the news that Brown's supposed father isn't really her father affect her?

3. What is the "more difficult obstacle" to which the writer refers?

4. Reread paragraph 7 of this essay. Because the writer makes a call for action on the part of her readers, have you been moved to agree with her? Why or why not?

Questions on Strategy

1. Brown takes a strong stand at the end of paragraph 1. Is this claim one you readily agree with, or do you prefer to hold off on your response until you've read further in the essay?

2. In paragraph 2, does Brown support her claim adequately that donor insemination is "centered around deception"?

3. In which paragraph does Brown acknowledge the opposition?

4. Evaluate Brown's introduction of expert testimony in paragraph 6.

* * *

Reading 19   THE MEANINGS OF A WORD

Gloria Naylor

A telephone operator while she was in college and later a missionary for the Jehovah's Witnesses, Gloria Naylor became a writer of novels and stories detailing the African-American woman's condition. In the following essay, Naylor examines a word that shocked her when she heard it in her third-grade classroom.

1   Language is the subject. It is the written form with which I've managed to keep the wolf away from the door and, in diaries, to keep my sanity. In spite of this, I consider the written word inferior to the spoken, and much of the frustration experienced by novelists is the awareness that whatever we manage to capture in even the most transcendent passages falls far short of the richness of life. Dialogue achieves its power in the dynamics of a fleeting moment of sight, sound, smell, and touch.

2   I'm not going to enter the debate here about whether it is language that shapes reality or vice versa. That battle is doomed to be waged whenever we seek intermittent reprieve from the chicken and egg dispute. I will simply take the position that the spoken word, like the written word, amounts to a nonsensical arrangement of sounds or letters without a consensus that assigns "meaning." And building from the meanings of what we hear, we order reality. Words themselves are innocuous; it is the consensus that gives them true power.

3   I remember the first time I heard the word *nigger.* In my third-grade class, our math tests were being passed down the rows, and as I handed the papers to a little boy in back of me, I remarked that once again he had received a much lower mark than I did. He snatched his test from me and spit out that word. Had he called me a nymphomaniac or a necrophiliac, I couldn't have been more puzzled. I didn't know what a nigger was, but I knew that whatever it meant, it was something he shouldn't have called me. This was verified when I raised my hand, and in a loud voice repeated what he had said and watched the teacher scold him for using a "bad" word. I was later to go home and ask the inevitable question that every black parent must face—"Mommy, what does *nigger* mean?"

4   And what exactly did it mean? Thinking back, I realize that this could not have been the first time the word was used in my presence. I was part of a large extended family that had migrated from the rural South after World War II and formed a close-knit network that gravitated around my maternal grandparents. Their ground-floor apartment in one of the buildings they owned in Harlem was a weekend mecca for my immediate family, along with countless aunts, uncles, and cousins who brought along

assorted friends. It was a bustling and open house with assorted neighbors and tenants popping in and out to exchange bits of gossip, pick up an old quarrel, or referee the ongoing checkers game in which my grandmother cheated shamelessly. They were all there to let down their hair and put up their feet after a week of labor in the factories, laundries, and shipyards of New York.

5   Amid the clamor, which could reach deafening proportions—two or three conversations going on simultaneously, punctuated by the sound of a baby's crying somewhere in the back rooms or out on the street—there was still a rigid set of rules about what was said and how. Older children were sent out of the living room when it was time to get into the juicy details about "you-know-who" up on the third floor who had gone and gotten herself "p-r-e-g-n-a-n-t!" But my parents, knowing that I could spell well beyond my years, always demanded that I follow the others out to play. Beyond sexual misconduct and death, everything else was considered harmless for our young ears. And so among the anecdotes of the triumphs and disappointments in the various workings of their lives, the word *nigger* was used in my presence, but it was set within contexts and inflections that caused it to register in my mind as something else.

6   In the singular, the word was always applied to a man who had distinguished himself in some situation that brought their approval for his strength, intelligence, or drive:

7   "Did Johnny *really* do that?"

8   "I'm telling you, that nigger pulled in $6,000 of overtime last year. Said he got enough for a down payment on a house."

9   When used with a possessive adjective by a woman—"my nigger"—it became a term of endearment for her husband or boyfriend. But it could be more than just a term applied to a man. In their mouths it became the pure essence of manhood—a disembodied force that channeled their past history of struggle and present survival against the odds into a victorious statement of being: "Yeah, that old foreman found out quick enough—you don't mess with a nigger."

10   In the plural, it became a description of some group within the community that had overstepped the bounds of decency as my family defined it. Parents who neglected their children, a drunken couple who fought in public, people who simply refused to look for work, those with excessively dirty mouths or unkempt households were all "trifling niggers." This particular circle could forgive hard times, unemployment, the occasional bout of depression—they had gone through all of that themselves—but the unforgivable sin was a lack of self-respect.

11   A woman could never be a "nigger" in the singular, with its connotation of confirming worth. The noun *girl* was its closest equivalent in that sense, but only when used in direct address and regardless of the gender doing the addressing. *Girl* was a token of respect for a woman. The one-syllable word was drawn out to sound like three in recognition of the extra ounce of wit, nerve, or daring that the woman had shown in the situation under discussion.

12   "G-i-r-l, stop. You mean you said that to his face?"

13   But if the word was used in a third-person reference or shortened so that it almost snapped out of the mouth, it always involved some element of communal disapproval. And age became an important factor in these exchanges. It was only between individuals of the same generation, or from any older person to a younger (but never the other way around), that *girl* would be considered a compliment.

14   I don't agree with the argument that use of the word *nigger* at this social stratum of the Black community was an internalization of racism. The dynamics were the exact opposite: the people in my grandmother's living room took a word that Whites used to signify worthlessness or degradation and rendered it impotent. Gathering there together, they transformed *nigger* to signify the varied and complex human beings they knew themselves to be. If the word was to disappear totally from the mouths of even the most liberal of white society, no one in that room was naive enough to believe it would disappear from white minds. Meeting the word head-on, they proved it had absolutely nothing to do with the way they were determined to live their lives.

15   So there must have been dozens of times that *nigger* was spoken in front of me before I reached the third grade. But I didn't "hear" it until it was said by a small pair of lips that had already learned it could be a way to humiliate me. That was the word I went home and asked my mother about. And since she knew that I had to grow up in America, she took me in her lap and explained.

Questions on Content

1. What does Naylor mean by the sentence in paragraph 2, "Words themselves are innocuous; it is the consensus that gives them true power"? Rephrase this thought in your own words.

2. What do paragraphs 4 and 5 have to do with Naylor's subject? Explain.

3. Annotate Naylor's essay by underlining each definition she offers. How does Naylor's hearing of the word *nigger* within her Black community contrast with her hearing of the same word by "a small pair of lips that had already learned it could be a way to humiliate me"?

Questions on Strategy

1. Why does Naylor delay the focus on her subject until the beginning of paragraph 3? Does this strategy work? Why or why not?

2. What strategy or strategies does Naylor use to define her subject in paragraphs 8, 9, 10, and 11?

3. Why does the writer conclude the way she does? What is the impact of this ending on her audience?

4. What is Naylor's purpose in this essay?

* * *

Reading 20   C̲RAZY FOR D̲YSFUNCTION

Douglas Cruickshank

A senior writer for Salon.com, *Douglas Cruickshank has also written for the* San Francisco Chronicle *and the* Readerville Journal. *This essay appeared in* Salon.com *on May 3, 2002. The writer reports that dysfunctional families appear regularly on television, in film, and in memoirs.*

1   Once upon a time, the dysfunctional family was an aberration, an entity feared and shunned by normal families—good families—who modeled themselves on the Cleavers, the Nelsons, the Andersons, and the Stones (as in Donna Reed, not Mick and Keith). The designation was uttered almost exclusively by experts in the dreaded "professional help" category. And such was the shame of dysfunction that the dysfunctional would go to extreme lengths to hide their flaws in function, believing an appearance of normalcy might actually move them closer to it, or at the very least make life easier for everyone, most of all the neighbors.

2   Which brings us, several decades later, to *The Osbournes,* a TV family of daunting popularity that features drug-addled dinosaur rocker Ozzy Osbourne and his real-life wife, son and daughter. They go about their daily business before cameras, flipping each other off and peppering their conversations with the F-word. Much to the satisfaction of MTV, every obscenity, drug reference and unadorned outburst of intrafamilial angst brings more viewers, making the weekly Ozzyfest the second most popular show on cable (wrestling is first) and a favorite of President Bush.

3   Clearly, the dysfunctional family has been rehabilitated. What was once considered dark and unmentionable now constitutes high-quality entertainment. Profane kooks and apprentice psychopaths have become endearing TV stars, while televised confessions of supposed stigmas—incest, drugs, alcohol, emotional abuse, and relationships without civility—have become a viable path to fame, wealth and warm societal acceptance.

4   "Lovable but dysfunctional families have been a trademark for Fox going back to the days of *Married . . . with Children,*" wrote Nellie Andreeva recently in the *Hollywood Reporter.* "The network hopes to keep that string alive." Indeed, Fox has at least five new shows in the works based on the dysfunctional-family premise, Andreeva reports. But the upstart network, which kicked things off with *Married . . .* in 1987, now faces stiff competition.

5   And that's just what can be found in *TV Guide.* The dysfunctional family is a star of stage and screen, as well as a cavalcade of memoirs that take the very idea of a damaged family dynamic out of the shadow land it inhabited when it was mined only by a handful of high-culture writers such as Eugene O'Neill and Tennessee Williams, whose dysfunctional backgrounds served as source material, and into the down-market glare of the popular mass media. Most recently on the big screen, *The Royal Tenenbaums,* a film about a tortured clan of social misfits, though not a blockbuster, has—as of early April—grossed nearly $52 million—more than twice its production budget.

6   Meanwhile, intimate memoirs overflowing with kink and confession, such as Marry Karr's *Liar's Club* and its follow-up, *Cherry,* as well as Kathryn Harrison's *The Kiss,* have given amazing firepower to the literary market niche in recent years. Last and loudest, daytime TV shows such as those hosted by Jerry Springer, Jenny Jones and Sally Jesse Raphael have turned the most revealing personal confessions into a lucrative, if ethically questionable, entertainment product.

7   But then perhaps we never really understood the meaning of the word *dysfunctional* in the first place. Like a whole passel of other therapeutic terms, this is an adjective that seems to have slipped into the layman's language via the sloppy phenomenon known as psychobabble. Yet just as it is vague when used in everyday conversation, so does the "dysfunctional family" lack a precise definition even in the realm of psychology. The phrase encompasses a vast range of behaviors and can mean most anything the person using it wants it to, but a broad, generally accurate definition is: *a family that functions poorly or not at all and communicates or behaves in ways that are emotionally unhealthy; a family that creates a negative environment that can be detrimental, or even catastrophic, to the development of its members.*

8   Great, but what's family? The nuclear family—mom, dad, kids—now constitutes a minority of the adult/child groups living together in the United States. So, not only has "dysfunctional" undergone an apparent transmogrification, the term "family" has outgrown its original meaning. At the same time that the emotional tangles of family life have begun to see the light of day, the nature of families has radically changed to include a growing cast of characters, making the entanglements more complex.

9   A brief history of semantics doesn't necessarily explain our fondness for families, whatever their composition, that are rife with "issues," as they are now called. But the morphing of the nuclear family surely has a role in the media celebration of messed-up domestic groups. If television means to offer a reflection of real life—or, more recently, real life itself—dysfunction is going to pop up, now perhaps more than ever. Beaver, Bud, Princess and Kitten—every episode of their fictional lives involved a crisis, but it was a crisis fit for the times. Telling a fib was big news in the world of Ricky Nelson; it could be that Ozzy badgering his daughter Kelly about a gynecologist's appointment is the moral equivalent. What was dysfunctional in the old sense is still called dysfunctional, but these days it is also typical, much to everyone's relief.

10   Robert J. Thomson, founding director of the Center for the Study of Popular Television at Syracuse University, says that even what many consider the most dysfunctional TV families are "very functional at their roots." Of the three shows with the most beloved dysfunctional families—*The Simpsons, Roseanne* and *Married . . . with Children*—only the last had a family "that was really, truly dysfunctional," says Thompson.

11   "You could make the argument that all four of the people in that show would've been better off if they were not in that family," he says. "But in the case of *Roseanne* and *The Simpsons,* for all the trashy qualities on the surface, they are basically families that love each other, support each other, and all the rest of it, though not necessarily in traditional fashion."

12   (Thompson says he doesn't address the pioneering *All in the Family*, which first aired in 1971, because the show featured no young children among the core performers.)

13   "*The Osbournes*," Thompson adds, "proves that even a guy like Ozzy Osbourne, once best known for biting the head off a bat during a concert, has absorbed himself in what amounts to a bizarre, kooky and relatively foul-mouthed family, but it's a family nevertheless. People are together, they're coming home every night, it's completely functional. So, ironically enough, on one level, pop-culture entertainment has really not let go of the notion of the ideal family."

14   In the venue of publishing, as in the realm of issue-obsessed daytime TV, where the raw confessional memoir—on the page or in front of the camera—dominates, the ideal family has been dismissed as myth. Nothing is forbidden, nothing is particularly embarrassing, all of it—literate accounts of incest, shouting matches about paternity—is aired, ostensibly in the pursuit of mental health. And it may well be mentally healthy for the writer and the blurter as well as for their audiences. These are vehicles, Thompson says, "that introduce us to things going on with our fellow citizens that we may not be aware of."

15   Carl Pickhardt, a psychologist and novelist, calls the function of books like Karr's and Harrison's "a memoir catharsis." The writing has "allowed the expression of the dark side of family life to come to the surface," he says. "And I think that's good. It's also allowed some people to talk about and identify behavior that they previously took for granted and never thought had any particular formative effects."

16   In the process, Pickhardt says, "we've re-normed our view of family life. When we look at it now, we say that every family is a mix: The old notion of the idealized TV family isn't exactly true, but by the same token, the extraordinarily painful and traumatic vision given by a lot of these memoirs is not the whole story either."

17   Pickhardt, who has a private practice in Austin, Texas thinks there's also been a shift in how therapists see troubled family relations—and a change in their approach to helping. In the past, he says, "there was a view [on the part of therapist] of what wasn't there but should have been there, of negative things going on that were having destructive effects, and the power of the past. That needed to be investigated in order to help people heal from what had happened."

18   "That's still of therapeutic concern," Pickhardt adds, "but there's been somewhat of a shift so that now there's also an appreciation of taking a look at what is positively present, and focusing on what can be done in the present."

19   Therapists also tend to use the term *dysfunctional* with much more restraint than civilians. "We describe families in terms of what their specific issues or problems are," says Dr. Leigh Leslie, a psychologist, family therapist and associate professor of family studies at the University of Maryland. "We have our diagnostic manuals. But [the language in them] is not what's common to the general public. That's not to say that professionals don't use the term, but when they do, they talk about what *kind* of dysfunctional family. It's not a term professionals use a lot."

20   Meanwhile, plain folks toss around the word with abandon. "Psychological terms are second nature to us because psychologists are part of our everyday dialogue," says Deborah Tannen, the author of *I Only Say This Because I love You* and a professor of linguistics at Georgetown University. The downside of this trend, Tannen says, "is what I see as a tendency to pathologize. Sometimes we over-apply these psychological interpretations: We're calling people pathological when in fact they just have a different style.

21   "So, for example, the New Yorker who talks to the Californian is accused of being hostile when maybe she's just being blunt," Tannen continues. "Or you're accused of being pathologically secretive because you don't think it's right it's right to talk about your personal life. You try to say what you want in an indirect way, you're called passive aggressive, you're called manipulative."

22   At first, some mental health professionals thought that incorporating psychological terms in common conversation was a good thing. "It showed some awareness," Leslie says. "But it does get to the point where now if someone tells me, 'I'm an enabler,' I have to ask, 'What do you mean by that?' Because it's come to mean so many different things, it loses its meaning for professionals. Psychological jargon has infiltrated our culture. I don't know that it always helps us communicate any better, but at least there is openness to it."

23   There is no disputing the dysfunction and pathology of those who occupy the hot seats on *The Jerry Springer Show, Jenny Jones Show* and others like them. They're programs, Thompson says, in which viewers see "the real nuts and bolts of family dysfunction . . . you actually look into the heart of darkness of where a real American family can go, as opposed to a fictional one.

24   "What they've done," he says, "are two things: one very healthy, one perverse. The healthy part is what has brought a lot of this stuff out of the closet. That's a good thing—they've taken the taboo out of speaking about this."

25   But the unhealthy part, Thompson says, "is that in packaging dysfunction as a form of entertainment it's become the only way in which a lot of people could ever achieve celebrity. By simply confessing, letting go, and paying the price of your self-respect and privacy, one is able to instantly get this kind of recognition that, of course, human beings long for."

26   This is, in Thompson's words "a little bit sick." But more important, it takes the confessional catharsis beyond the constructive point, when it demonstrates that we all have similar problems, to a place in which dysfunction becomes a badge of legitimacy. Suddenly, the most messed-up person wins the prize. Dysfunction, says Thompson, "turns out to be something that is valued in its own right as a means to keep the *Springer* show and the *Jenny Jones* show going. And that's the disturbing part."

27   Says Tannen, "People watch *The Jerry Springer Show* and think, 'Those people are really sick. I can't believe they're on TV.' It's very different from what Oprah did, which in my mind was the opposite thing—creating a sense of connection: 'Oh, there's someone talking about her

problem. I had the same problem and I thought I was the only one. This is such a load off my mind. I'm *not* the only one.'" Jerry Springer, she says, "breaks that connection."

28   By the same token, though, shows like Springer's offer more selfish relief. The viewer might say, "I am so glad I don't have that problem. I'm better off than I thought I was." At that point, "dysfunctional family" reverts to its old definition, reserved for the truly hopeless and lost. Judging from the popularity of the Springer-like shows, that meaning maintains its charm as a nifty means of establishing superiority.

29   "People who use the term 'dysfunctional family' have no idea what they've talking about," Leslie says. "They know what their definition is, but is it a shared definition? Well, there is no shared definition other than it's a family that is having, or has had, some kind of severe problems.

30   "What people have become aware of is this notion that all families have problems, that it's normal to have problems, and the problem-free ideal family doesn't exist," she continues. "Terms like 'dysfunctional family' are not at all helpful to anybody, because it describes nothing and everything."

Questions on Content

1. What is the second most popular show on cable TV, according to the author?

2. What examples of dysfunctional families on film and in memoirs does the writer give?

3. Name the three families that Robert Thompson states are the "most beloved dysfunctional families on TV."

4. Explain the change Carl Pickhardt says has taken place in how therapists see troubled family relations.

5. According to Deborah Tannen, what are the dangers of incorporating psychological terms in our common conversation?

Questions on Strategy

1. Why does Cruickshank use the title "Crazy for Dysfunction"? What is ironic about the title?

2. Notice how Cruickshank transitions from families on TV to those in film and in memoirs (paragraph 14). Is this transition successful? Why or why not?

3. Cruickshank makes use of many sources in his essay. Whenever he introduces a new source, what information does he include in addition to the person's name? Why?

4. Find two or more places in the essay where Cruickshank uses comparison and contrast. How does this strategy help readers?

* * *

GLOBAL COMMUNITY

Reading 21 — THE SALSA ZONE

Richard Rodriguez

A writer holding controversial views regarding affirmative action, Richard Rodriguez is well known for his autobiographical works Hunger of Memory *and* Days of Obligation. *Currently Rodriguez is an editor at Pacific News Service.*

1   Last week after Mexicans elected Vicente Fox their new president, a U.S. journalist gushed: "The Cactus Wall has fallen."

2   In more ways than one, I'd say. For what we are witnessing in Mexico is also apparent throughout the United States. The line separating "us" from "ellos" is blurring.

3   Consider Mexico: Not so long ago, Mexicans would refer to citizens of the United States as *norteamericanos*. But then the North American Free Trade Agreement [NAFTA] forced Mexicans to look at the map: Mexico is a North American country.

4   Last week, Fox appeared on U.S. television, wearing a Reaganesque grin. He urged the formation of a "common market" of Mexico and its fellow North American neighbors. He made the suggestion in English.

5   Fox speaks fluent English. He's not the first Mexican president to do so. But he is the first to be so unguarded. (Earlier presidents, for reasons of Mexican pride, were more cautious about speaking English in public.)

6   Last week, while Fox was holding an unprecedented bilingual press conference in Mexico City, Texas Gov. George W. Bush, on a swing through California, was insisting to audiences that the GOP has *corazon,* and Vice President Al Gore was mocking his Republican rival for promising voters only *palabras.*

7   Clearly, some change is going on—on both sides of the border. Mexico is becoming North Americanized. The United States is becoming—what shall we say?—Latinized.

8   Because, in centuries past, a large part of the United States was ruled by Spain, then Mexico, it is perhaps ludicrous to speak of the Latinization of the United States today as something "new." Yet, of course, it is.

9   England and Spain left more of their mark on the New World than any other European countries. But they were Renaissance rivals. Antagonism marked the borders that separated each culture from the other. To this day, one hears of cafeteria battles between "Hispanic" and "Anglo" high school students, proxies in a sea battle between the Spanish Armada and Queen Elizabeth's navy.

10   But now, a change. Mexico's new president carries an English surname and is not shy about his knowledge of English. Texas, a state with a long history of friction between Tex and Mex, has a governor who is not shy about his Spanish fluency and has Mexican in-laws.

11   Pity the nativists on both sides of the border!

12   Because Mexico is the smaller country and poorer, the Mexican nativist perhaps could have anticipated our brave new *mundo*. American nativists have more reason to be surprised, but they would do well to remember that none other than President Richard M. Nixon was the father of today's Hispanic America.

13   In 1973, the Nixon administration described America as a pentagon: no longer just a black-and-white dialectic between Europe and Africa. Nixon colorized America. His administration proposed five possibilities on the affirmative-action form. There is white, there is black, there is Asian/Pacific Islander, there is American Indian/Alaskan Native, and— last but not least—there is Hispanic. (Choose one.)

14   Initially, many Mexican Americans resisted the Nixonian label. After all, Mexicans in America represent 70 percent of the total number of Hispanics. So many felt their story and status were diminished by Nixon's sweeping Hispanic category.

15   Others regarded the English word as too colonial and chose "Latino," the word that remains today the more politically correct. In truth, however, Latino is doubly colonial. For it is after all, a Spanish word, and it connects the descendants of Latin America to the far shores of the Latin empire, which is southern Europe.

16   I prefer Nixon's term. Hispanic is appropriate to our confused state of affairs. Here is an English word that describes the descendants of Latin America, living in the United States.

17   *Soy Hispanic.*

18   The purpose of Nixon's five categories was to flatten differences, rather than to compartmentalize us from each other. What Nixon would have said, I think: To get rid of a minority, to make it disappear into America, throw money at it—and affirmative-action privileges and little flatteries.

19   In 19th-century America, Irish and Italian immigrants were told that they were "white." (America is a country of broad strokes.) Just so, does America today tell Peruvian and Salvadoran immigrants that they are, alike, Hispanics. The immigrant may refuse the label. But with time, the experience of America forces it.

20   If you are Mexican and live in the United States, you end up knowing more Salvadorans than you ever would in Mexico. If you are Cuban in Miami, you hear a standardized Spanish accent on Spanish-language television. If you are a Dominican in Hartford, Conn., you end up hearing politicians call you Hispanic; after a while, you come to believe them.

21   Those of us today who call ourselves Latino or Hispanic are, in fact, merely acknowledging our Americanization. We're like the Vietnamese teenager who told me recently that she only dates "Asian" or the woman who cares for my parents and who calls herself a "Pacific Islander"—we have all become children of Nixon's America.

22   Today politicians try to come up with a Hispanic agenda, to seduce voters. But neither side has come up with anything more than a middle-class American agenda. For by the time Hispanics assume a public face

and a voice, by the time we begin to vote and assume our full place in this country, we want what other middle-class Americans want: jobs, health insurance and good schools. We want mobility for our children.

23   My nieces and nephews, the next generation, already live behind Scottish and Dutch and German surnames. I look at them and think that the rise of the Hispanic today marks also our decline as a distinct political force. Within a decade, many of today's Hispanics will disappear into the American mass as we marry out of the group and into the nation.

24   But here is the curious part: Even while Nixon's label Americanized us, it simultaneously Latinized you. That little noun—from the start—became synonymous with fertility and ascending totals. Government statisticians kept score. Nineteen million Hispanics became 22 million, which became 25 million, then thirtysomething.

25   The persons who first realized the significance of growing Hispanic numbers were not politicians but businessmen. By the 1980s, for example, Coors was paying for billboards that heralded the "decade of the Hispanic." Advertising agencies, by then, were describing America as one of the largest Spanish-speaking countries in the world. Thus were Ford and McDonald's and Colgate-Palmolive convinced to speak Spanish on radio and television.

26   A few years ago, several Hispanic mothers in Southern California began a campaign to undo bilingual education and to free their children to learn American English. They were ultimately successful.

27   But even while bilingual education was outlawed in the California classroom, Spanish became the unofficial second language of the United States. You see and hear it everywhere. Now (non-Hispanic) friends of mine wonder if, perhaps, I know a Hispanic woman who might be willing to come to their houses for minimum wage, to do the housework, while teaching the kids some Spanish.

28   The best thing about Hispanic numbers is that they force Americans, at last, to realize that Latin America is not far away. Latin America lives within our borders. Young Americans (not Hispanic) do not find it surprising, consequently, to find salsa, rather than ketchup, on the kitchen table or to hear Tito Puente's music, happily sounding everywhere in the city, from the grave.

29   The danger of Hispanic numbers is that they will be used as a way of ignoring American blacks. One regularly hears from the Census Bureau, for example, that Hispanics are soon to outnumber blacks and become America's largest minority. The prediction is an absurdity, because you cannot compare a racial group—blacks—to an ethnic group—Hispanics.

30   My best hope is that Hispanicity might release blacks from the old black-and-white dialectic, which white liberals insist on maintaining. To a country where blood has been crucial to identity, Hispanics bring a vocabulary for mixed blood, like "mestizo" and "mulatto." Most important, Hispanicity is culture or the illusion of it, the memory of ancestors or their ghosts. Today, white Cubans describe themselves as Hispanic, not white; and there are black Dominicans who describe themselves as Hispanic, not black.

31   In this way is America becoming a Hispanic nation: Everywhere around us, culture is overcoming race. There is Chinese hip-hop in Dallas. The best golfer in America—and the world—is an African American Indian Thai. The Idaho skinhead's favorite food is burritos. Maya Indians sing Baptist hymns in Georgia. And politicians run for the American presidency in the year 2000, speaking the language of the 16th-century conquistadors.

Questions on Content

1. What does "the Cactus Wall" refer to?

2. What proof does Rodriguez offer that the United States is becoming Latinized?

3. Why did many Mexican-Americans resist the label "Hispanic"?

4. Rodriguez points out the advantages as well as the danger of Hispanic numbers. Explain in your own words both advantages and dangers.

Questions on Strategy

1. In his introductory paragraph, Rodriguez begins his essay with a political occurrence: the election of Mexico's new president, Vicente Fox. Discuss how this occurrence links with Rodriguez's theme.

2. Notice Rodriguez's use of illustrations in several body paragraphs. Do these illustrations serve to add credibility to the author's thesis? If so, how?

3. In his conclusion, Rodriguez states, "Everywhere around us, culture is overcoming race." Do the examples in this final paragraph support this main idea, or could the author have used other examples?

* * *

Reading 22   ## ILLUSIONS ARE FOREVER

Jay Chiat

Jay Chiat revolutionized the advertising industry, founding the Chiat/Day agency in 1967 and going on to engineer many innovative ad campaigns and make the Super Bowl into the advertising showcase it currently is. "Illusions Are Forever" was first published in the October 2000 issue of Forbes *magazine.*

1   I know what you're thinking: That's rich asking an adman to define truth. Advertising people aren't known either for their wisdom or their morals, so it's hard to see why an adman is the right person for this

assignment. Well, it's just common sense—like asking an alcoholic about sobriety, or a sinner about piety. Who is likely to be more obsessively attentive to a subject than the transgressor?

2   Everyone thinks that advertising is full of lies, but it's not what you think. The facts presented in advertising are almost always accurate, not because advertising people are sticklers but because their ads are very closely regulated. If you make a false claim in a commercial on network television, the FTC will catch it. Someone always blows the whistle.

3   The real lie in advertising—some would call it the "art" of advertising—is harder to detect. What's false in advertising lies in the presentation of situation, values, beliefs, and cultural norms that form a backdrop for the selling message.

4   Advertising—including movies, TV, and music videos—presents to us a world that is not our world but rather a collection of images and ideas created for the purpose of selling. These images paint a picture of the ideal family life, the perfect home. What a beautiful woman is, and is not. A prescription for being a good parent and a good citizen.

5   The power of these messages lies in their unrelenting pervasiveness, the twenty-four-hour-a-day drumbeat that leaves no room for an alternative view. We've become acculturated to the way advertisers and other media-makers look at things, so much so that we have trouble seeing things in our own natural way. Advertising robs us of the most intimate moments in our lives because it substitutes an advertiser's idea of what ought to be—What should a romantic moment be like?

6   You know the De Beers diamond advertising campaign? A clever strategy, persuading insecure young men that two months' salary is the appropriate sum to pay for an engagement ring. The arbitrary algorithm is preposterous, of course, but imagine the fiancée who receives a ring costing only half a month's salary? The advertising-induced insult is grounds for calling off the engagement, I imagine. That's marketing telling the fiancée what to feel and what's real.

7   Unmediated is a great word: It means "without media," without the in-between layer that makes direct experience almost impossible. Media interferes with our capacity to experience naturally, spontaneously, and genuinely, and thereby spoils our capacity for some important kinds of personal "truth." Although media opens our horizons infinitely, it costs us. We have very little direct personal knowledge of anything in the world that is not filtered by media.

8   Truth seems to be in a particular state of crisis now. When what we watch is patently fictional, like most movies and commercials, it's worrisome enough. But it's absolutely pernicious when it's packaged as reality. Nothing represents a bigger threat to truth than reality-based television, in both its lowbrow and highbrow versions—from *Survivor* to A&E's *Biography* The lies are sometimes intentional, sometimes errors, often innocent, but in all cases they are the "truth" of a media-maker who claims to be representing reality.

9   The Internet is also a culprit, obscuring the author, the figure behind the curtain, even more completely. Chat rooms, which sponsor intimate conversation, also allow the participants to misrepresent themselves in every way possible. The creation of authoritative-looking Web sites is within the grasp of any reasonably talented twelve-year-old, creating the appearance of professionalism and expertise where no expert is present. And any mischief-maker can write a totally plausible-looking, totally fake stock analyst's report and post it on the Internet. When the traditional signals of authority are so misleading, how can we know what's for real?

10   But I believe technology, for all its weaknesses, will be our savior. The Internet is our only hope for true democratization, a truly populist publishing form, a mass communication tool completely accessible to individuals. The Internet puts CNN on the same plane with the free-lance journalist and the lady down the street with a conspiracy theory, allowing cultural and ideological pluralism that never previously existed.

11   This is good for the cause of truth, because it underscores what is otherwise often forgotten—truth's instability. Truth is not absolute: it is presented, represented, and re-presented by the individuals who have the floor, whether they're powerful or powerless. The more we hear from powerless ones, the less we are in the grasp of powerful ones—and the less we believe that "truth" is inviolable, given, and closed to interpretation. We also come closer to seeking our own truth.

12   That's the choice we're given every day. We can accept the very compelling, very seductive version of "truth" offered to us daily by media makers, or we can tune out its influence for a shot at finding our own individual, confusing, messy version of it. After all, isn't personal truth the ultimate truth?

Questions on Content

1. According to Chiat, what is the real lie in advertising?

2. What does advertising have to do with engagement rings?

3. In addition to advertising, what other culprits are guilty of misrepresenting truth, according to Chiat?

4. The writer asserts that something will be our savior. What will this savior be and how will it save us?

5. Agree or disagree that "personal truth [is] the ultimate truth." Support your claim with specific evidence.

Questions on Strategy

1. What strategy does Chiat use in his introduction to get readers' attention? Is this strategy successful? Why or why not?

"I can't decide. I'm having a brand identity crisis."

2. Why might readers be inclined to believe what Chiat says about advertising even though he offers no evidence from other experts?

3. Chiat presents a force as a culprit but also a savior in paragraphs 9 and 10. Is this strategy a plausible one? Support your answer with specific evidence.

* * *

Editing Essays: A Concise Handbook

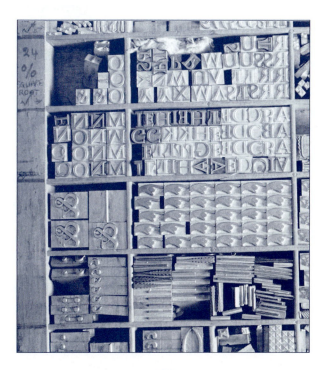

Guide to the Handbook

DIAGNOSTIC TEST

No two students enter a writing class with identical strengths and weaknesses in their writing. The following diagnostic test will allow you and your instructor to obtain a better idea of the areas that will need more attention from you versus those in which you already have expertise. Please follow all directions carefully as you work your way through this exam. Remember that you will not be given a grade for this test so try to do your best, but don't worry if you don't know some or even many of the answers right now.

After you have read, practiced, and become more familiar with the information in this handbook, you will find that your skills and confidence in your writing will increase. You can also feel more at ease knowing that whatever writing assignment or project you will be working on in your academic future or professional career, you can use this book as a quick and thorough guide. In addition, consulting the Diagnostic Test Error Analysis Chart (pp. 417–418) will allow you to see at a glance just what areas of grammar and usage are giving you trouble.

Part One: Grammar

Directions: Identify the one item/sentence in each question that is *incorrect* based on the italicized phrase at the beginning of the section.

Fragments, Comma Splices, Run-ons

(errors in which part of a sentence is punctuated as a complete sentence, or two complete sentences are incorrectly joined)

_____ 1. A. Eight months after receiving the job promotion, Mario had still not received a raise.
   B. Major sales are being offered in clothing items, home furnishings, and cosmetics.
   C. Flies landing on food products leaving bacteria and endangering lives.
   D. Books read by students help increase their knowledge of the subject.

_____ 2. A. The computer malfunctioned when the power supply was lost.
   B. Doctors, patients, and medical staff agreed to meet in the new facility.
   C. Creating music with a synthesizer was the topic of the discussion.
   D. Vitamin C has been added to some sodas, what will manufacturers think of next?

_____ 3. A. Unfortunately, the college's parking is terribly bad, sometimes I circle the campus for half an hour or more.

B. An introduction to Internet use is being given on Tuesday; it lasts from 12 to 5 and costs 75 dollars.

C. The Jolly Green Giant is a familiar trademark.

D. The nearest telephone booth is nearly a mile away.

_____ 4. A. As the day continued, our condition became more perilous, and our fate became more difficult to accept.

B. The pizza place is on the right, one block past the library.

C. Jobs at this restaurant are available, but nobody seems to be applying for them.

D. Richard Wright waited until he had finished the novel *Native Son* to write the introductory chapter he felt he could write about these characters more realistically only after he had taken them to the end of their story.

_____ 5. A. The pickers moved from Merced to Fresno and worked for three months. Then they were laid off.

B. Esperanza never learned to drive, every time she needed to go somewhere, she asked one of her brothers or sisters for a ride.

C. The use of symbolism in medieval literature is discussed in the text.

D. During the game, the referee told the players that they were ignoring one of the primary rules. He told them to sit on the bench.

_____ 6. A. The in-class essay will begin at nine in the morning the students will need to be in the classroom on time and prepared with all materials.

B. One customer asked if there would be sales in the future, and another wanted to know if there would be refunds for faulty merchandise.

C. Surfing was Mike's favorite sport; basketball was his least favorite.

D. The siren caused the passengers great surprise, forcing them to stop all movement at once.

_____ 7. A. Two members of the class were majoring in mathematics even though they hoped to become engineers.

B. One hour after the repair service had been called, a mechanic had still not arrived.

C. Businesses, homes, schools—all were destroyed by the San Francisco earthquake.

D. Nelson's birthday gift from his grandmother was another tie. Not the new CD he had hoped to receive.

Verbs

(errors in verb tense and form)

_____ **8.** A. When the snow began to fall, Mario was sorry that he had forget his gloves.

B. The copy center will not be able to complete the job by your requested deadline time.

C. The sweet old grandfather hoisted his grandchild and set him on the pony so that the young child could take a ride.

D. Having exhausted all of his pick-up lines, the young man at the bar gave up and headed home.

_____ **9.** A. Did Copernicus believe that the sun was the center of the solar system?

B. Transcendentalists believe in the interconnectedness of man, animals, and nature.

C. Aristotle believed that the earth was the center of the universe.

D. Today, do most people believe that the earth was flat?

_____ **10.** A. Since the exam will be next week, Jason is studying this week.

B. When the market prices go up, more customers start using their coupons.

C. The Fourth of July will come on a Friday next year.

D. The textbooks were bought after the bookstore opens.

Subject-Verb Agreement

(errors in subject-verb agreement, such as a singular subject with a plural verb)

_____ **11.** A. Staplers are in the top drawer; tape dispensers are in the side cabinet.

B. Neither cereal nor milk were available in the new grocery store.

C. Here is the pair of scissors that needs repairing.

D. Either *Catcher in the Rye* or *For Whom the Bell Tolls* was the winner of the literary prize.

_____ **12.** A. What is onomatopoeia?

B. The group of players quickly gets into a huddle to discuss the next play.

C. Practice as well as talent are needed for successful piano playing.

D. Measles was the illness that Joanna suffered from.

_____ **13.** A. Constantin Stanislovski, one of Russia's first acting teachers and directors, believed that actors needed to find a "subtext," the unspoken thoughts and emotions that characters experienced.

B. In America, Stanislavski's techniques were adopted by theater coaches and instructors who came to call this kind of acting "method acting."

C. Actors in the 1950s and 1960s such as Marlon Brando is known for their use of "method acting."

D. Karl Malden was praised for his moving performances in American films of the 1950s, 1960s, and 1970s.

Pronouns

(errors in pronoun use, such as ambiguity, lack of agreement between a pronoun and its antecedent, or use of incorrect case form)

_____ 14. A. Juan and Felicia mailed packages to their relatives in Milan and looked forward to their visit.

B. The team decided on its strategy for the game.

C. Everybody took the dessert he or she desired.

D. Each parent needs to learn how to love his or her child.

_____ 15. A. I took her with me to the store, and later we stopped for coffee.

B. The movie that him and me saw last week was really good.

C. Please feel free to invite whomever you like to this party.

D. Bill, Jefferson, Grant, and I were all nominated by the class.

_____ 16. A. In many classes on this campus are students who we know come from diverse backgrounds.

B. Each of them tables is clean and ready for service.

C. I called her because she told me she'd help me.

D. Franceli believed that no one could make enchiladas as well as she.

_____ 17. A. This backpack is either yours or Charlie's.

B. The floor was covered with sand that had been tracked in by the guests.

C. The alarm clock awakened Shelly and me after our plane had departed.

D. Neither of the dancers was prepared for the reaction of their audience.

_____ 18. A. The attorney acknowledged her approval of her client's courtroom attire.

B. The committee began the meeting in the conference room, but then they moved to the auditorium.

C. Jackie du Prie was a brilliant musician who produced her most memorable performances before battling a severe illness.

D. The waiter who brought our food forgot to bring our drinks.

_____ **19.** A. *Citizen Kane*, which made Orson Welles famous, was released in 1941.

B. The skateboard was new enough for him and Ted to take to the competition.

C. The first lady confided that she had developed her social skills.

D. Between her and me sat our two children who we were taking to the play.

_____ **20.** A. The Red Sox team was slowly overcome by the opposing team and hated this.

B. The wedding rehearsal went badly, yet the bride and groom remained calm then finished the ceremony.

C. The veterinarian felt carefully down the leg of the golden retriever, who stood poised on the vet's medical bed.

D. For several minutes after the bank opened, the customer was not really certain that they would be able to cash the check.

Adjectives and Adverbs

(errors in adjective/adverb use)

_____ **21.** A. Walking into the bar, Jose saw that each person truly was in costume.

B. An evening spent joyously proved quite surprising.

C. Each day was brighter and beautifuller than the day before.

D. Sometimes the mixer must be held horizontally in order to reach the deepest batter in the bowl.

_____ **22.** A. The white Ford sitting in that driveway is really sharp.

B. The pitcher threw the ball quite good.

C. Both delicatessens have a solid reputation, but the one on the corner is slightly better because it has hot pastrami.

D. Artichokes taste better when they are served with melted butter or with mayonnaise.

_____ **23.** A. Initiation into adulthood is critics' most favoritest theme in James Joyce's short story "Araby."

B. The old gray blanket felt rough against his cheek.

C. The college senate thought that expelling a student for blatant plagiarism was a harsh but necessary action.

D. Although Francisco was tired, he dazzled the audience with his humorous stories.

Part Two: Effective Sentences

Directions: Identify the one item/sentence in each question that is *incorrect* based on the italicized phrase at the beginning of the section.

Parallelism

(errors in parallelism in equivalent sentence parts)

_____ 24. A. The patient would have received his vaccination today, but no one was in the office to give it.

B. Cleaning off her boots and watching the early news, Sandra relaxed at the end of the day.

C. If you love to travel and speak different languages, you may want to take this trip.

D. Happy and showing exhilaration, the two barbers celebrated the success of their new shop.

_____ 25. A. Jennifer got the job because of her filing, and she was a good typist too.

B. The tornado came down on the town, and the residents took cover in cellars.

C. The clerk states that she got the call that night and thought about how to handle it.

D. Notebooks that had been left behind and textbooks that had been forgotten started to pile up on the classroom's podium.

_____ 26. A. If the sun would come out, then the players could assemble and the game could begin.

B. Explain the plot of the story, and then you are to analyze the two main characters.

C. Snowboarders abound in large numbers—at the local ski re-sorts, the out-of-state centers, and the larger mountains.

D. First the cutting board is covered with flour, and then the dough is rolled with a rolling pin.

_____ 27. A. An instructor explained the difference between a simile and a metaphor.

B. The architect's renderings are elegant, yet they are possessed of impracticality.

C. A play lover who buys a ticket to see a well-reviewed play and who discovers that the play has been cancelled is likely to be irate and unhappy.

D. Alma and John gave two percent of their yearly salaries to the community's nonprofit ballet company.

_____ 28. A. Papers to be turned in may be left under the office door, and late papers may be given to the department's office.

B. The essay is incomprehensible, not because of the vocabulary used but because the grammar is incorrect and the tone is confusing.

C. Either the vacation cottage will be too cold and damp, or it will be too warm and muggy.

D. A *header* in soccer is the contact of the soccer ball with a player's head.

_____ **29.** A. The art company's policy was to reject all unacceptable portfolio drawings but to send each aspiring artist a personal note.

B. The china and crystal were nicely set and neatly arranged.

C. To conserve electricity, overhead lights and oven lights are not permitted.

D. Sheila Finch is an English instructor and one who loves writing science fiction.

Positioning Modifiers

(errors in the placement of a modifier in a sentence)

_____ **30.** A. To sew a button, find thread of an approximate match in color with the button, thread a needle, tie off the thread at the end with a knot, and then place the button on the piece of clothing to be sewn.

B. Bottled water today is one dollar per bottle; by next year, perhaps one water bottle will be two dollars!

C. Only three days old, the giant teddy bear is the wrong gift for Anthony.

D. After the concert, Inez and Frank bought their boxed dinners and ate them before remembering their picnic basket in the back seat of their car.

_____ **31.** A. To arrive on time for class, the alarm clock should be set an hour early.

B. The salesperson announced the opening of a new opportunity: a table of wool sweaters of various colors and sizes.

C. Feeling that if he brought her flowers she would adore him, Zeppo laid a dozen red roses at the feet of Maria.

D. Actually, she discovered that eating mango skins caused her upper lip to break out in a rash.

_____ **32.** A. The gentleman in the dark hat turned out to be the new prime minister.

B. The murderer was finally and irrevocably sentenced.

C. A book on healthy diets that has made a splash in all the papers appeared in the bookstore today.

D. To speak Vietnamese as well as his uncle was Tran's goal.

_____ 33. A. Last week the site of the old fort where tourists used to visit was declared unsafe.

B. Precautions and directions on eye ointment bottles found in supermarkets are sometimes hard to read.

C. After having trouble with math and science twice a week, Elaine was tutored.

D. The parking fee that students of the college pay depends on where their particular lot is located.

Part Three: Punctuation

Directions: Identify the one item/sentence in each question that is *incorrect* based on the italicized phrase at the beginning of the section.

Use of Commas

(errors in the use of commas)

_____ 34. A. The idea of offering free popcorn and beverages as well as a T-shirt to those that participate in the city's 10K run was opposed by the local merchants.

B. The resort offered golf, hiking, swimming, craft making, and tennis to its patrons.

C. The mall's directory which is next to impossible to find, is supposed to assist mall patrons in finding their way around.

D. Some dwellings that will be included in the project include apartments, condominiums, houses, and cabins.

_____ 35. A. Janice's garden had an abundance of cucumbers, cauliflower, and tomatoes, and she has given many of these vegetables to her neighbors.

B. Takisha, the young woman in the suede jacket, will begin the ceremony.

C. After the birth of Tuan and Sara's baby, Marion Nguyen Tuan's aunt, gave the little boy a quilt she had made for him.

D. Pushed to the very back of the cabinet was the box of candy that she had been searching for all morning.

_____ 36. A. After it was washed and waxed the old car looked incredibly good.

B. The luncheon having begun, the speaker approached the podium at the front of the grand hall, where he gave his speech.

C. The writer Anne Lamott, who wrote *Bird by Bird*, was the daughter of a writer.

D. Frank, your breakfast awaits you.

_____ 37. A. Plot, character, and theme are three major elements in works of fiction.

B. Eleanor Roosevelt, who believed in the responsibility of Americans to help those less fortunate across the world, helped to found the United Nations.

C. Some writers like Faulkner and O'Connor, are representative of Southern writers.

D. The keys to successful writing are purpose, focus, material, structure, and style.

Use of Semicolon and Colon

(errors in the use of semicolons and colons)

_____ **38.** A. The map indicated that the house would be the second from the end of the street; however, we discovered that the map was wrong.

B. Fernando loves poached pears with wine sauce; Jennifer prefers chocolate mousse with whipped cream.

C. When Bush agreed to a press conference; he had no idea that his comments would be misinterpreted by press and public.

D. John Steinbeck attended Stanford; he did not remain there for long.

_____ **39.** A. The young man looked forward to his first day on the job: his supervisor seemed cordial and considerate.

B. The piano needs a little tuning; otherwise, it is in great shape.

C. Richard Wright, who spent much of his time in Chicago, Illinois, and Paris, France, was born in the state of Mississippi.

D. The couple lived for brief times in the following cities: Tulsa, Oklahoma, Amarillo, Texas, Scottsdale, Arizona, and Los Angeles, California.

_____ **40.** A. John entered the convenience store and bought: eggs, milk, cereal, and juice.

B. Nyla's grandmother remembered her childhood despondently: "When I played by myself in our front lawn, my mother never stopped checking on my safety from our big front picture window."

C. The proprietor of the establishment told the customer that he would receive a senior's discount on the room.

D. Studies have shown that humans often obey automatically rather than question authority; psychologists believed that the reverse would be true.

Use of Quotation Marks and End Punctuation

(errors in the use of quotation marks and end punctuation)

_____ **41.** A. "Jacob," asked the doctor, "have you been plagued by headaches?"

B. "Get lost!" shouted the infuriated manager.

     C. The decision of whether to save on the hard drive or on disk depends on how the information stored will be used?

     D. One cannot predict the end result of increased media involvement (for example, television, film, Internet) on young children and teenagers.

_____ 42. A. "You decided to use extra nutmeg in this casserole, didn't you?" asked Laura.

     B. Many people have read and discussed certain American short stories: "The Telltale Heart," "Barn Burning," "The Lottery," and "The Lady or the Tiger"?

     C. Did you know that Geoffrey Chaucer, a medieval writer in England, never completed all of his intended *Canterbury Tales?*

     D. A student who cheats on tests and often comes unprepared to class is no "student."

_____ 43. A. The two chapters of this book that we most wanted to read were "Index Cards" and "The Moral Point of View".

     B. "I would like to invite the whole family to my flute performance, entitled 'A Classical Evening,'" Derek announced.

     C. "Actually, argument continues over what prompted Nixon to lie to Americans," stated the author.

     D. "When do you think he will appear?" Jackson asked his father.

_____ 44. A. Many colleges and universities offer the following degrees: B.A., M.A., M.F.A., and Ph.D.

     B. Kyle decided to join the group in spite of its wild behavior.

     C. Please remove your shoes before entering the house.

     D. In her paper, Jessica asked the reader the questions how will we solve this problem and where will the funding come from?

Use of the Hyphen

(errors in the use of the hyphen)

_____ 45. A. There was a half-eaten apple turning brown on the edge of the kitchen counter.

     B. This extremely well known tennis player will be featured on the talk show.

     C. Highly sought after, the replica appears almost as perfect as the original sketch.

     D. It is the time-honored tradition to wrap the body in the country's flag.

_____ 46. A. The end of classes occurs on the twenty first of May.

     B. The almost perfect pirouette landed her a prize in the contest.

     C. Adrienne Rich's poems are well liked by most of the readers in the group.

     D. In December, sales of cinnamon, sugar, and nutmeg reach a yearly high point.

Use of the Apostrophe
(errors in the use of the apostrophe)

_____ **47.** A. Lisandra and Bill's new house is really spectacular.

B. Greg's mother-in-law is an expert trial attorney.

C. The family plans to go to the beach since its such a lovely, sunny day.

D. The old saying, "A day's work for a day's pay," is true in this case.

_____ **48.** A. "Should I wear my bear costume?" asked the team's mascot.

B. At the ceremony, the class of 00 and that of 01 were honored.

C. The women's room is temporarily closed for repairs.

D. The next line in the film was delivered by the lead actor: "You're going to get more than you bargained for, and I'm not going to be too sorry."

Part Four: Mechanics

Directions: Identify the one item/sentence in each question that is *incorrect* based on the italicized phrase at the beginning of the section.

Use of Italics
(errors in the use of italics)

_____ **49.** A. Jane Austen's novel "Sense and Sensibility" has been made into a film starring Emma Thompson and Hugh Grant.

B. The tourists were advised to leave Ecuador before political conflict developed.

C. Janica was disappointed to discover that the *Mona Lisa* is behind glass.

D. Every Sunday, they sit in a sunny café and read the *New York Times*.

_____ **50.** A. The soup was a mixture of herbs and vegetables.

B. The first short story in Boyle's collection is entitled *Greasy Lake*.

C. The novel *For Whom the Bell Tolls* was written by Ernest Hemingway.

D. The author wrote his masterpiece when he was 17.

Capitals
(errors in the use of capital letters)

_____ **51.** A. Alice felt she should drop the course in French since she had missed too many classes.

B. Leland Stanford was governor of California and the founder of Stanford University.

C. Give the note to Vincent Ramirez, president of the company.

D. The Chevron Company hired a person who had worked for ford.

_____ 52. A. Although the president is highly regarded, Americans seem to value him more than the people of other countries.

B. The Democrats and the Republicans have perpetually been at each other's throats.

C. During the Great Depression, people from Oklahoma were shunned as Okies.

D. The Three Musketeers candy bar has been a popular one for half a century.

Part Five: Diction (Word Choice)

Directions: Identify the one item/sentence in each question that is *incorrect* based on the italicized phrase at the beginning of the section.

Word Choice and the Use of Idioms

(errors in the choice of words and in the use of idiomatic expressions)

_____ 53. A. The senior class thought that this year's prom was like totally awesome.

B. Many physicians are now urging Americans to cut down on intake of red meat, and most health-conscious citizens of this country are attempting to follow that advice.

C. Last night the blackout in New York City frightened many people, but no one was hurt.

D. Someone who has graduated from an institution is referred to as an *alumna* or *alumnus*.

_____ 54. A. Everyone except Sharon enjoyed the play; Sharon was in the hospital.

B. Each committee member felt compelled to veto the proposal that was introduced.

C. The student was such a troublemaker that he was sent to the principle's office last Tuesday.

D. Please feel free to give the recipe to whomever you know who might use it.

_____ 55. A. When Asako wanted a job application, he visited the personal office of the company.

B. Because he had not been perfectly honest during the conversation, his conscience began to bother him later.

C. Clare decided to have her brakes checked because she noticed a grinding noise when she was driving.

D. The students were careful to listen to and heed the advice of their counselors.

Diagnostic Test Error Analysis Chart

Question Number	Missed	Topic	Handbook Page
1.	X	Fragments	426
2.		Fragments	426
3.		Comma splices	427
4.		Run-ons	427
5.		Comma splices	427
6.		Run-ons	427
7.		Fragments	426
8.		Irregular verbs; tense	433
9.		Tense shift	437
10.		Tense shift	437
11.		Subject/verb agreement	434
12.		Subject/verb agreement	434
13.		Subject/verb agreement	434
14.		Pronoun reference	443
15.		Pronoun case	442
16.		Pronoun case	442
17.		Pronoun agreement	441
18.		Pronoun agreement	441
19.		Pronoun case	442
20.		Adjective/adverb use	446
21.		Adjective/adverb use	446
22.		Adjective/adverb use	446
23.		Adjective/adverb use	446
24.		Parallelism	431
25.		Parallelism	431
26.		Parallelism	431
27.		Parallelism	431
28.		Parallelism	431
29.		Parallelism	431
30.		Dangling modifier	449
31.		Dangling modifier	449
32.		Misplaced modifier	449
33.		Misplaced modifier	449
34.		Comma	452
35.		Comma	452
36.		Comma	452
37.		Comma	452
38.		Semicolon	455
39.		Semicolon	455
40.		Colon	456
41.		End punctuation	458
42.		Quotation marks	460
43.		End punctuation	458
44.		Quotation marks	460
45.		Hyphen	462

Question Number	Missed	Topic	Handbook Page
46.		Hyphen	462
47.		Apostrophe	459
48.		Apostrophe	459
49.		Italics	461
50.		Italics	461
51.		Capitalization	467
52.		Capitalization	467
53.		Word choice	474
54.		Word choice	474
55.		Word choice	474

Editing Essays: A Concise Handbook

REVIEWING PARTS OF SPEECH

We can label all words according to the way we use them in sentences. The eight labels we use, called the **parts of speech,** are nouns, pronouns, verbs, adjectives, adverbs, prepositions, conjunctions, and interjections. The three words *a, an*, and *the* are not parts of speech; they are called **articles.**

Nouns

Nouns refer to persons, objects, places, or ideas.

Common nouns are general words for persons, objects, places, or ideas: *student, beeper, corner, advantage, suggestion.* Do not capitalize common nouns.

Proper nouns are specific names of persons, objects, institutions, places, or ideas: *Jerry Seinfeld, Pepsi Cola, Venezuela, Protestantism.* Always capitalize proper nouns.

Singular nouns refer to one person, object, place, or idea: *a student, a beeper, the corner, an advantage.* **Plural nouns** refer to two or more persons, objects, places, or ideas: *students, beepers, corners, advantages, suggestions.*

Pronouns

Pronouns take the place of nouns. Pronouns come in six categories.

Personal pronouns include all forms of *I, we, you, she, he, they,* and *it,* as well as the reflexive pronouns *myself, ourselves, yourself, yourselves, himself, herself, itself,* and *themselves.*

Possessive pronouns show ownership. They include *my, mine, your, yours, his, her, hers, its, our, ours, their,* and *theirs.*

Indefinite pronouns are words that refer to a number of persons or things, like *everyone, something, all, many,* and *each.*

Relative pronouns introduce clauses that relate to or modify other parts of a sentence. These pronouns include the forms of *who,* as well as *which* and *that.*

Interrogative pronouns, used to begin questions, include *who, which,* and *what.*

Demonstrative pronouns point out persons, places, or things. Demonstrative pronouns include *this, that, these,* and *those.*

Verbs

Verbs designate action or a state of being. **Action verbs** include words like *swim, drive, dance,* and *write.* **State of being verbs** include *be* (in all its forms—*is, was, were,* etc.), *seem, become, feel, look, remain, smell,* and *taste.* In number, verbs are either singular (referring to one: the boy *runs*) or plural (referring to more than one: the boys *run*). In person, verbs refer to the first person (*I, we*), second person (*you,* either singular or plural), or third person (*he/she/it, they*). In tense, verbs indicate time periods: present, past, and future—and shades of differences within each category.

Adjectives

Adjectives describe or modify nouns. Some adjectives, like *green, heavy, beautiful,* and *happy,* tell what kind of person or thing is being described. Others, like *twenty, few,* and *innumerable,* tell how many persons or things are being described. A few adjectives, like *this, that, these,* and *those* (which are pronouns when they stand alone), identify which person or thing is being described.

Adverbs

Adverbs describe verbs, adjectives, and other adverbs. Adverbs can designate how, when, or where an action occurs. Many adverbs, like *quickly, permanently,* and *happily,* are formed by adding *ly* endings to adjectives.

Prepositions

Prepositions are small words or word combinations that show relationship or direction. Prepositions include words like *in, of, on, above, beneath,* and *through,* as well as word combinations like *by means of, on behalf of,* and *in regard to.* **Prepositional phrases,** such as *of the students, in the film,* or *with an attitude,* contain prepositions and their objects (the nouns or pronouns that come after them).

Conjunctions

Conjunctions are connectors that link words, phrases, or clauses.

Coordinating conjunctions (*for, and, nor, but, or, yet,* and *so*) join equal parts of a group of words, such as two words (bread *and* butter), two phrases (above the ankles *but* below the knees), or two clauses (she wanted to apply for the job, *yet* she had doubts about it). Coordinating conjunctions are used to join parts of **compound sentences.**

Correlative conjunctions, such as *either/or, not only/but also,* and *both/and,* are used in combination to join words, phrases, or whole clauses.

Subordinating conjunctions, such as *because, when, if, although,* and *since,* connect **independent clauses** with **dependent clauses** in **complex sentences.** (*Since it was raining, they decided to go to a movie.*)

Interjections

Interjections are inserted exclamations. These are short words like *oh, well, yes,* and *sure,* and phrases like *good heavens!* or *good grief!* that express strong feeling or surprise. Put commas or exclamation points after interjections.

Practice in identifying words by how they are used in a sentence will help you in checking your own writing for correct sentence formation. Label each word in the following sentences (omitting *a, an,* and *the*) by writing the part of speech just above the word. Use abbreviations for the eight parts of speech: *n.* (noun), *pro.* (pronoun), *v.* (verb), *adj.* (adjective), *adv.* (adverb), *prep.* (preposition), *c.* (conjunction), *i.* (interjection). The first sentence has been done for you.

1. *n.* *n.* *v.* *n. prep. n. c. v.*
   Dolores Whittaker placed the plant in the sun and waited.

2. Immediately after Jay logged on, his computer froze and he screamed, "Great!"

3. Pamela Nguyen announced her new and exciting job offer to the board members.

4. Professor Matson wanted to plant a seed of curiosity in the minds of her students, so she ended the class with three questions.

5. You have only one choice: come before the board with the whole story or resign your position.

6. The college lawn was the scene of much merriment last Thursday during activity hour.

7. Well! I waited in line patiently for over an hour!

8. This college has had a sexual harassment policy in place for ten years. ❏

WRITING SENTENCES

Every sentence contains a subject and a verb.

Subjects

The **subject** of a sentence names the person or thing the sentence is about. Subjects are usually nouns or pronouns.

Sentences with Noun Subjects:

A *degree* in hotel management makes you eligible for the job.

These *videotapes* belong to the college library.

Sentences with Pronoun Subjects:

> *We* discovered a new way to drive to New Orleans.

> After much thought, *she* entered the bike race.

Verbs

A **verb** is a word that shows an action or a state of being.

Sentences with Action Verbs:

> The members of the Spanish Club *eat* lunch together every Tuesday.

Sentences with State of Being Verbs:

> The Edmonton Oilers *are* ahead of the Dallas Stars by one goal.

> Jay Leno *became* host of the *Tonight Show* in May 1992.

To be complete, action and state of being verbs sometimes must be accompanied by one or more **helping verbs,** like a form of *be (be, is, are, was, were, will),* *have (have, has, had),* and *do (do, does, did).* Other helping verbs include *can, could, may, might, must, shall, should,* and *would.* A main verb with its helping verbs is called a **verb phrase.**

Sentences with Verb Phrases:

> In the manual, you *will find* the most frequently asked questions.

> They *could have seen* a silent movie at the film festival.

> *Do* the prices on the menu *include* dessert?

Clauses

A **clause** is a group of words that has a subject and a verb. An **independent clause** can stand alone and function as a complete sentence.

Independent Clauses (Complete Sentences):

> subject verb
> Action *movies give* Ronald a headache.

> subject   verb
> Stretching *exercises are* helpful before distance running.

A **dependent clause** has a subject and a verb but does not express a complete thought and therefore cannot function as a complete sentence.

Dependent Clauses:

> Although the three brothers grew up in different families.
> [The word *although* makes the clause dependent. We are "dependent" on another thought to understand what happened.]

Although the three brothers grew up in different families, they all loved to read.
[It is now a complete sentence.]

People who write films.
[The dependent clause is *who write films*. The subject of the clause is *who*, and the verb is *write*, but *who write films* does not express a complete thought.]

People who write films have special talents.
[This is now a complete sentence.]

Types of Sentences: Simple, Compound, Complex, Compound-Complex

Simple Sentences:

A **simple sentence** has one independent clause, with one subject-verb combination.

subject   verb
Jennifer works in a restaurant on weekends.

Compound Sentences:

A **compound sentence** has two independent clauses joined together. Each clause has its own subject-verb combination.

subject   verb   subject   verb
Stephanie buys lottery tickets every week, but *Franklin spends* his money on compact disc recordings.
[The sentence contains two independent clauses joined by *but*.]

Complex Sentences:

A **complex sentence** has one independent clause and one (or sometimes more than one) dependent clause. Each clause has its own subject-verb combination. The dependent clause can appear before, after, or in the middle of the independent clause.

Dependent Clause before Independent Clause:

Because the divorce rate has increased, many families are headed by one parent.

Dependent Clause after Independent Clause:

We arrived at Danceteria *before the crowds made dancing impossible.*

Dependent Clause between words of Independent Clause:

We *who are about to die* salute you.

Compound–Complex Sentences:

A **compound-complex sentence** has two or more independent clauses and one or more dependent clauses.

dependent clause
Although many people are interested in space exploration,

independent clause   *independent clause*

most underestimate the vastness of space, and some cannot tell the difference between a planet and a star.

SENTENCE COMBINING

Knowledge of the four types of sentences just covered will allow you to build sentences in varied and interesting ways. With this knowledge, you can convey to your audience relationships between two or more ideas. If you want to present two or more ideas or pieces of information as having equal importance, you can use **coordination.** If you want to make an idea or piece of information less prominent than another, you can use **subordination.**

COORD

Coordination

A compound sentence can be formed by **coordination**—joining two independent clauses with a comma followed by a coordinating conjunction. The coordinating conjunctions are the short connecting words *for, and, nor, but, or, yet,* and *so.* The first letters of the coordinating conjunctions spell FANBOYS, which is an easy way to remember the words.

Two Independent Clauses (Sentences):

A comet appears small in the night sky.

It can be millions of miles long.

Compound Sentence:

A comet appears small in the night sky, *but* it can be millions of miles long.
[Two independent clauses are joined by a comma and the coordinating conjunction *but.*]

Two Independent Clauses (Sentences):

Courses in technical writing are useful.

They can lead to high-paying jobs.

Compound Sentence:

Courses in technical writing are useful, *for* they can lead to high-paying jobs.
[Two independent clauses are joined by a comma and the coordinating conjunction *for.*]

SUBORD

Subordination

A complex sentence can be formed by **subordination**—joining two independent clauses with a subordinating conjunction. The subordinating conjunction makes one of the clauses dependent on (subordinate to) the other.

Two Independent Clauses (Sentences):

The concert conflicted with commencement exercises.

The date of the concert was changed.

Complex Sentence:

Because the concert conflicted with commencement exercises, the date of the concert was changed.
[The addition of the subordinating conjunction *because* makes the first clause dependent. When the first clause is dependent, it is almost always followed by a comma.]

Two Independent Clauses (Sentences):

Utility bills go up.

Air conditioning consumes a large amount of electricity.

Complex Sentence:

Utility bills go up *when* air conditioning consumes a large amount of electricity.
[The addition of the subordinating conjunction *when* makes the second clause dependent. When the dependent clause comes second, usually no comma is needed.]

You can also use a relative pronoun, like *which, that, who, whoever,* or *whomever,* to create complex sentences.

Two Independent Clauses (Sentences):

The students felt nervous.

They had an exam that morning.

Complex Sentence:

The students *who* had an exam that morning felt nervous.
[The addition of the relative pronoun *who* makes the second clause dependent. No commas set off the dependent clause because the clause is crucial for the meaning of the sentence.]

Two Independent Clauses (Sentences):

At the party I met someone from my old high school.

That high school was torn down years ago.

Complex Sentence:

At the party I met someone from my old high school, *which* was torn down years ago.
[The addition of the relative pronoun *which* makes the second clause dependent. A comma precedes *which* because the dependent clause is not crucial to the meaning of the sentence.]

PROBLEM-SOLVING
Practice 2   On a separate sheet of paper, use coordination (a coordinating conjunction) or subordination (a subordinating conjunction or a relative pronoun) to combine each of the following pairs of sentences.

1. Experts once predicted that computers would make books obsolete. That has not happened.

2. The computer age began in the 1960s. Book publication has grown.

3. The use of computers itself has increased the number of books. Many of the books have been written about computers.

4. Books on word processing appear every month. They have become too numerous to count.

5. Other areas of activity have expanded as well. Computer technology has had an impact on them.

6. Teachers once feared they would be replaced by computers. They have discovered that their role is even more important than before.

7. Computers have enhanced rather than eliminated teachers' jobs. Teachers can use computers to take over repetitive drills.   ❏

SOLVING SENTENCE PROBLEMS

FRAG

Fragments

A **fragment** is an incomplete sentence. To be a complete sentence, a group of words must contain a subject and a complete verb, and express a thought that can stand by itself. To solve a fragment problem, either rewrite the sentence or connect the fragment to a complete sentence.

Fragment: Picked up a virus last week.
[The sentence is missing a subject. *Who* or *what* picked up a virus?]

Corrected: *Jeanne's computer* picked up a virus last week.

Fragment: The skunk-ape, which is a foul-smelling creature.
[The sentence is missing a main verb. What does the skunk-ape *do*?]

Corrected: The skunk-ape, which is a foul-smelling creature, *has surprised* fishermen in Florida since the 1920s.

Fragment: Because the siren made an earsplitting sound.
[The subject is *siren*, and the verb is *made*. The word *because*, however, makes the thought incomplete. We don't know what happened as a result of the siren's earsplitting sound.]

Corrected: The siren made an earsplitting sound.
[The sentence has been rewritten to omit *because*; the sentence now expresses a complete thought.]

Corrected: Because the siren made an earsplitting sound, *the cyclist veered toward the oncoming traffic.*
[The fragment has been attached to an already complete sentence.]

PROBLEM-SOLVING
Practice 3

Write F next to all fragments and S next to all complete sentences. On a separate sheet of paper, turn the fragments into sentences.

1. _____ People in the suburbs who carpool to work.

2. _____ After allowing for tuition and books.

3. _____ Along the highway were many annoying billboards.

4. _____ Because Spanish 2 has a prerequisite.

5. _____ In February, we usually go skiing in Vermont.

6. _____ Except for those who travel by bus.

7. _____ The governor and his wife appearing on camera together.

8. _____ During the last episode of a soap opera I saw recently.

9. _____ When spring comes, the water level rises.

10. _____ Having passed the bar exam, she felt exhilarated.

Problem-solving for Fragments

Edit the following paragraph for fragments. When you discover a sentence fragment, correct it by using one of the solutions previously suggested.

> Frank seems to be the all-American guy. Described as a handsome, tall man who is a doctor. Frank is also known as a war hero in his home town. For instance, "Under heavy enemy fire he [Frank] carried . . . just like in the movies three wounded soldiers from the battlefield to safety," describes David. Frank seems to be more cherished by his father than his brother. For example, according to David, "Grandfather did not say, 'My son the veteran. . . .' He simply said, 'My son.' Seems to acknowledge he has one son rather than two. Frank is also a prejudiced person. For instance, when he talks about Indian Americans and how they get cured. Frank doesn't like Indians. Ridicules them and sexually assaults Indian young women.
>
> —Darlene Cabrales, *student*   ❏

**R/O
c/s**

Run-ons and Comma Splices

A **run-on** is two (or more) sentences run together without any punctuation between them.

> Brazil became independent in 1828 it was called an empire until 1889.

A **comma splice** is two (or more) sentences linked by commas instead of being separated by periods.

> Emil attends the University of Texas, he finds his courses stimulating.

Advice: Do not attempt to solve a run-on sentence problem by inserting a comma between two complete sentences. To do so will only turn a run-on into a comma splice.

Here are five ways to correct either a comma splice or a run-on.

1. Use a period to separate the sentences. Remember to start the second sentence with a capital letter.

   > **Comma splice:** Kepler's Law explains the motion of the planets around the sun, most astronomy students master the concepts early in their studies.

Run-on: Kepler's Law explains the motion of the planets around the sun most astronomy students master the concepts early in their studies.

Corrected with a period: Kepler's Law explains the motion of the planets around the sun. Most astronomy students master the concepts early in their studies.

2. Use a semicolon to make one long sentence with two parts. Begin with a lowercase letter after the semicolon.

   Comma splice: A float rolled slowly toward the middle of the field, it was circled by cheerleaders and a marching band.

   Run-on: A float rolled slowly toward the middle of the field it was circled by cheerleaders and a marching band.

   Corrected with a semicolon: A float rolled slowly toward the middle of the field; it was circled by cheerleaders and a marching band.

3. Use a comma and a coordinating conjunction: *for, and, nor, but, or, yet, so.* (Don't forget the acronym FANBOYS, which can help you remember the seven coordinating conjunctions.)

   Comma splice: The tenants sent many letters to the landlord about the lack of heat, he did not reply.

   Run-on: The tenants sent many letters to the landlord about the lack of heat he did not reply.

   Corrected with a coordinating conjunction: The tenants sent many letters to the landlord about the lack of heat, *but* he did not reply.

4. Use a subordinating conjunction, such as *after, although, because, before, if, since, when, where, while.* The subordinating conjunction turns one of the sentences into a dependent clause.

   Comma splice: I returned home from work last night, someone had already made dinner.

   Run-on: I returned home from work last night someone had already made dinner.

   Corrected with a subordinating conjunction: *When* I returned home from work last night, someone had already made dinner.

5. Use a relative pronoun, such as *that, which, who, whose.*

   Comma splice: Computer experts refer to Moore's Law, it says that the speed of personal computers doubles every 18 months.

   Run-on: Computer experts refer to Moore's Law it says that the speed of personal computers doubles every 18 months.

   Corrected with a relative pronoun: Computer experts refer to Moore's Law, *which* says that the speed of personal computers doubles every 18 months.

PROBLEM-SOLVING
Practice 4   On a separate sheet of paper, correct all comma splices and run-ons, using one of the five solutions above. If a sentence is correct, write C next to it.

1. _____ Scientists disagree about what caused dinosaurs to become extinct.

2. _____ One theory is that dinosaurs vanished about 65 million years ago an asteroid crashed into the earth.

3. _____ Plants, the dinosaurs' main food supply, may have died out, the collision darkened the sky for months.

4. _____ Geologists believe that such a catastrophe might have eliminated half of all life on earth.

5. _____ They have even found a layer of underground clay containing iridium, it is an element often present in objects from outer space, it matches the period when dinosaurs disappeared.

6. _____ There is evidence to support the asteroid theory some scientists think that dinosaurs died out gradually.

7. _____ Some evidence indicates that dinosaurs became extinct before the collision supposedly occurred the asteroid theory cannot be considered proven.

8. _____ More exact methods of dating fossils may be discovered then we may know more about what happened.

Problem-solving for Run-ons and Comma Splices

Edit the following paragraph for comma splices and run-on sentences. When you discover either, correct the sentence by using one of the solutions previously suggested.

I can't remember if it was my freshman or sophomore year when I read *Frankenstein*. I was by myself in the living room my parents had just left for my grandmother's house. I was alone by myself, for some weird reason none of my friends were home. There was nothing to do, so I decided to open up the hard cover of this book. This was to be the first book I was going to read usually I just read the Cliff notes. So I started reading about noon, and I read right through the day! Soon one hour passed and then two I wasn't getting tired of reading for some reason. I began to realize that I couldn't stop reading, I was addicted. I was imagining every sentence in my head, I saw the monster be created. I could see everything, even Frankenstein's son being murdered in my mind, the monster walking through the snow, it was all so clear for the first time. Time had flown and next thing I knew it was dinner time.

—David Estrada, *student*   ❏

Problem-solving in Essay Editing

Edit the following student essay by discovering and correcting as many "surface errors" as you can. These will include fragments, run-ons, and comma splices.

A Safer Driver

Jorge Arellano

1   I've always been told that I'm not a safe driver however, I never believed it until the day I was sideswiped. After getting into an accident only two blocks away from home. I experienced the struggles of having no car.

2   Family and friends have always warned me to slow down and to drive carefully. In the first week of school, I came home on a Thursday evening, I was tired and hungry. As I came to an intersection to turn left, thinking there was no car coming after a van, how wrong I was! The van blocked my view of a car behind it by then I had already hit the gas to make the left turn. In a split second, I made eye contact with the driver and floored it, my back wheels spun in place and lost traction for a second. The brown Mercury Cougar hit its brakes it was too late and the car slammed into the back right tire of my beautiful Thunderbird. My car then spun around from the impact it finally stopped and blocked traffic.

3   When the car came to a stop. I put it in "Park," turned off the car, and turned on my emergency lights. By the time I got out of the car, a large crowd had already formed, the other driver had left, not knowing whether I was alive or hurt. My face burned with anger when witnesses to the accident told me he had left I changed when I saw that his license plate was stuck to my car! My back tire was bent in close to the back window. I could not bear to see my car.

4   Since my once-beautiful vehicle had been mangled. I called the police on my cell phone, I then called my mom. It took police 15 minutes to get to my location. My mom, 2 minutes. Luckily, a former classmate of mine had been behind me making a left turn also she saw the whole thing as it had happened. We told police that the light had been yellow and about to turn red when out of nowhere, a car had come rushing at me. After I was interviewed for about a half an hour. The tow truck came. It was the second time I had seen my car being towed away that same year.

5   I now have another car, the same model however, now I know I will take care

of it better than its sister Thunderbird. I no longer drive with an urgency. I now

use turn signals more often than before. I guess I'm finally taking the advice of my

family and friends I am a slower and more careful driver.   ○

Faulty Parallelism

Faulty parallelism results when similar thoughts are expressed in dissimilar ways. To make your sentences flow smoothly, use parallel constructions whenever possible.

Faulty parallelism: The marathon went *along the avenue, over the suspension bridge,* and *then it turned into the park.*

Corrected: The marathon went *along the avenue, over the suspension bridge,* and *into the park.*
[Each description of the marathon's course is expressed as a prepositional phrase.]

Faulty parallelism: The party was *wild, noisy,* and *it had a note of hilarity.*

Corrected: The party was *wild, noisy,* and *hilarious.*
[Each description of the party is expressed as an adjective.]

Mixed Construction

Mixed constructions result when someone's writing process and thinking process don't quite match. Solve mixed-construction problems by rethinking and then rephrasing the sentence for clarity.

Mixed construction: I wondered was she the right girl for me.

Corrected: I wondered if she was the right girl for me.

Corrected: Was she the right girl for me?

Mixed construction: By agreeing to their demands was a sure way to invite further demands.

Corrected: Agreeing to their demands was a sure way to invite further demands.

Corrected: By agreeing to their demands, we will surely invite further demands.

PROBLEM-SOLVING
Practice 5   In the space at the left of each sentence, write FP for faulty parallelism, MC for mixed construction, or C for correct sentence. On a separate sheet of paper, revise all the incorrect sentences.

1. _____ In studying the review sheets helped him do well on the test.

2. _____ After growing up in San Francisco was why she liked art and culture.

3. ____ They wanted to advance in their jobs, earn a lot of money, as well as enjoying their work.

4. ____ The visit to Eastern Europe left her better informed, more tolerant, and an optimist.

5. ____ Tony wanted to know did they believe everything they heard on television.

6. ____ I got a headache from too little sleep and because I was anxious about the examination.

7. ____ Murphy's Law states that whatever can go wrong will go wrong.

8. ____ The vehicle started, stopped suddenly, and was going in reverse.

Problem-solving for Faulty Parallelism and Mixed Construction

Edit the following paragraph for faulty parallelism or mixed construction.

It was time to face my fears once I was ready to be interviewed. I was invited into a stock room, which was the store office, in addition to being not the cleanest office I've seen. There were four females there and managers all. They were nice too. I always thought any manager would be mean, stressed, and having to be grumpy, but they asked me very simple questions like "Did you enjoy your senior year at high school?" and "What influenced you to want to work at a bookstore?" Then they asked, "Can you provide good customer service?" I thought these questions were easy. After five minutes the interview was over, after two hours my house was called, and finally they told me I had been hired. I was pretty happy at that moment, but as soon as I hung up, I got scared again. Now I was afraid that something on my employment record might show up on what I had done a long time ago. The pressure was building.

—Dylan Covert, *student*   ❏

SOLVING VERB PROBLEMS

Verb Tenses

There are three basic verb tenses.

Present:	Phyllis *enjoys* racquetball.
Past:	Phyllis *enjoyed* racquetball.
Future:	Phyllis *will enjoy* racquetball.

Present Tense

In the **present tense,** most verbs take *s* endings (third person singular) or no endings (first and second person singular; all plural forms).

	Singular	Plural
First person:	I succeed	We succeed
Second person:	You succeed	You succeed
Third person:	He, she, it succeeds	They succeed

Forms of Be, Have, and Do

The irregular verbs *be, have,* and *do* have more forms than other verbs. Instead of just adding an *s* ending, *be* has these forms in the present tense:

	Singular	**Plural**
First person:	I am	We are
Second person:	You are	You are
Third person:	He, she, it is	They are

   Have has two forms in the present: *has* for third person singular and *have* for all other subjects.

   Do also has two forms: *does* for third person singular and *do* for all the others.

Past Tense

In the **past tense,** verbs fall into two categories: **regular verbs,** which take *d* endings, and **irregular verbs,** which change their spelling and do not take *d* endings.

Regular Verbs

Present	**Past**
discuss	discussed
doubt	doubted
kiss	kissed
stampede	stampeded
succeed	succeeded
walk	walked
wander	wandered

Irregular Verbs

Irregular verbs never take *d* endings. Instead, they change in different ways—*go* changes to *went, think* to *thought,* and so on.

   The irregular verb *be* will take different forms than other verbs in the past tense. These forms include the following:

	Singular	**Plural**
First person:	I was	We were
Second person:	You were	You were
Third person:	He, she, it was	They were

Future Tense

All verbs form the **future tense** by adding the helping verb *will* to the main verb *with no ending.*

will be	will register
will deliver	will spend

will do	will study
will have	will succeed
will jog	will work

S/V AGR

Subject/Verb Agreement

If the subject of a sentence is singular, the verb must be singular. If the subject is plural, the verb must be plural.

singular   singular
subject   verb

Paula usually *arrives* on time.

plural   plural
subject   verb

We, on the other hand, often *arrive* late.

Compound Subjects

Two or more subjects joined by *and* are called a **compound subject.** A compound subject takes a plural verb.

compound   plural
subject   verb

Manuel and I usually *invest* our money in mutual funds.

Either/Or (Neither/Nor)

Two or more subjects joined by *either/or* or joined by *neither/nor* take a singular verb if both subjects are singular.

singular subjects   singular
with neither/nor   verb

Neither Jack nor Melanie plans to videotape the performance.

If one subject is singular and the other is plural, the verb agrees with the subject that is closer to it.

plural subject   plural
closer to verb   verb

Either Kamal or his *brothers are going* to represent the family at the ceremony.

singular subject   singular
closer to verb   verb

Either the brothers or *Kamal is going* to represent the family at the ceremony.

Collective Nouns

Collective nouns name groups that act together: for example, *class, committee, company, family, group, jury, school, team.* A collective noun usually takes a singular verb.

collective   singular
noun   verb

Our *family meets* for a reunion every year.

> *collective*   *singular*
> *noun*   *verb*

The *committee has reached* its decision.

If the group does not act as a unit, however, the collective noun takes a plural verb.

> *collective*   *plural*
> *noun*   *verb*

The *jury disagree* about what happened on the night in question.
[The members of the jury have different opinions.]

> *collective*   *plural*
> *noun*   *verb*

The *team are taking* their places on the field.
[The team members act individually.]

Singular Nouns Ending in s

Nouns ending in *s* that have a singular meaning take a singular verb.

> *singular*   *singular*
> *subject*   *verb*

The *news* of her appointment to the court *is* exciting.

Indefinite Pronouns

The indefinite pronouns *anybody, anyone, everybody, everyone, nobody, no one, somebody,* and *someone* are singular and take a singular verb.

> *singular*   *singular*
> *subject*   *verb*

Everybody wants to help you find your watch.

> *singular*   *singular*
> *subject*   *verb*

Somebody has spotted it.

Other indefinite pronouns *(each, one, neither, none)* are often separated from the verb by a prepositional phrase that includes a plural noun. The verb must be singular to match the singular subject.

> *singular*   *singular*
> *subject*   *verb*

Each of the laid-off workers *has found* a new job.

> *singular*   *singular*
> *subject*   *verb*

One of the stations on the express line *was closed* last week.

The indefinite pronouns *all, half, some, most,* and *more* usually take a plural verb.

> *plural*   *plural*
> *subject*   *verb*

All of the visitors *have* badges.

plural   plural
subject   verb

Some of the customers *find* the restaurant's prices too high.

When the indefinite pronouns *all, half, some, most,* and *more* refer to a singular noun or pronoun, they take a singular verb.

All of the cake *has been eaten.*
[The indefinite pronoun *all* refers to the singular noun *cake;* therefore, all takes the singular form *has.*]

Half of the fee *is* due tomorrow.
[The indefinite pronoun *half* refers to the singular noun *fee;* therefore, *half* takes the singular verb *is.*]

Sentences Beginning with **Here** or **There**

The words *here* and *there* are adverbs, not nouns, and therefore are never the subject of a sentence. Look for the true subject to determine whether the verb should be singular or plural.

There *are* many *reasons* for her decisions.
[The subject of the sentence is *reasons.* To agree with the subject, the verb, *are,* must be plural.]

Here *comes* the *band!*
[The subject of the sentence is the collective noun *band.* To agree with the singular subject, the verb, *comes,* must be singular.]

Inverted Subjects

When the usual sentence order of subject followed by verb is reversed, the verb must still agree with the subject.

From understanding, respect, and kindness *grows love.*
[The sentence begins with a prepositional phrase instead of with the subject. The singular verb *grows* agrees with the singular subject, *love.*]

Under the apple tree *lie you and I.*
[The sentence begins with the prepositional phrase *under the apple tree.* The plural verb *lie* agrees with the plural compound subject, *you and I.*]

Relative Pronouns

When a verb follows a relative pronoun *(that, which, who),* the verb agrees with the antecedent of the pronoun (the noun to which the pronoun refers).

The *paper that is* single-spaced should be reformatted.
[The relative pronoun *that* refers to the singular noun *paper;* therefore, the verb, *is,* must be singular.]

Monica is one of those *people who surf* the World Wide Web daily.
[The relative pronoun *who* refers to the plural noun *people;* therefore, the verb, *surf,* must be plural.]

PROBLEM-SOLVING
Practice 6   Underline the subject or subjects and circle the correct form of the verb in parentheses.

1. Half of the money (has, have) already been spent.

2. Most of the assistants in the program (is, are) graduate students.

3. A stimulating environment with caring family members (contribute, contributes) to an infant's healthy development.

4. Inside the entrance to the business school (hangs, hang) pictures of two former deans.

5. Physics (is, are) a course I want to take before I leave school.

6. Graduates who (donate, donates) large amounts of money are invited to attend the honors convocation.

7. Either cable television channels or the local radio station (announce, announces) school closings during snowstorms.

8. Jerry is one of those students who (miss, misses) the homework assignment because he leaves class early.

9. Here (is, are) the first batch of applications we have received.

10. The company changed (its, their) logo last month to project a more up-to-date image.

Problem-solving for Subject/Verb Agreement

Edit the following paragraph to correct any errors in subject/verb agreement that you find.

Have you ever been awakened from a sound sleep by a vociferous cry, only to realize that it is an unspeakable hour of the morning and you were just awakened by the same sound a few hours earlier? This is usually how my day begin while caring for my newborn infant. I stumble out of bed and finds my way to the kitchen, feeling like a drunken zombie. I open the refrigerator and pull out a pitcher of ready-to-feed infant formula. I pour it into a four-ounce bottle and tightly secure the nipple. I put the bottle into the microwave for about 45 seconds and removes the bottle from the microwave, beginning to shake it vigorously to make sure the heat is evenly distributed. I squirt some of the formula on the inner part of my wrist to test the temperature. I walk briskly to the baby nursery to appease my daughter's alarming cries. Picking the baby up from her crib, remembering to support her neck, I sit down in a chair, holding the baby in a semi-upright position so as not to causes ear infections while feeding. The crying stop instantly and there is a serene moment of peace. The baby and I gaze lovingly into each other's eyes, establishing a wonderful bond between mother and child as my daughter indulges in her bottle of milk.

—Rafiekki Boykin, *student* ❏

Tense Shifts

Tense refers to the time frame (past, present, future) of a verb. Keep your verbs in the same time frame unless you deliberately want to signal a time change.

Unnecessary shift from past (first sentence) to present (second sentence): When I *got* up this morning, I *felt* excited. I *know* I *have* an exam at 11 o'clock, but I *am* ready for it because I *study* hard the night before.

Corrected (all verbs in past): When I *got* up this morning, I *felt* excited. I *knew* I *had* an exam at 11 o'clock, but I *was* ready for it because I *had studied* hard the night before.

Unnecessary shifts within each sentence: This story *is* about two girls who *lived* in the South. Although they *are* sisters, one of them *was* cheerful while the other *complains* all the time. The mother *tries* to be a good parent to both, but she *could* not treat them the same way.

Corrected (all verbs in present): This story *is* about two girls who *live* in the South. Although they *are* sisters, one of them *is* cheerful while the other *complains* all the time. The mother *tries* to be a good parent to both, but she *cannot* treat them the same way.

Voice

VOICE

Passive voice means that the subject of the sentence does not perform the action of the sentence. **Active voice** means that the subject carries out the action.

Passive voice: The question was answered by both contestants simultaneously.
[The subject of the sentence, *question,* does not perform the action.]

Active voice: Both contestants answered the question simultaneously.
[The subject, *contestants,* performs the action: *contestants answered.*]

For strong writing, use the active voice whenever possible.

Weak: Loud rock music *was heard* on the bus.

Stronger: Everyone on the bus *heard* the loud rock music.

Weak: Much dissatisfaction *is being felt* over the new city tax.

Stronger: Citizens *feel* much dissatisfaction over the new city tax.

Sometimes, however, the person(s) or thing(s) performing the action is not as important as the person(s) or thing(s) acted upon. In such a case, use the passive voice for emphasis:

Weaker (active voice): The police *took* three suspects to police headquarters for questioning.

Stronger (passive voice): Three suspects *were taken* to police headquarters for questioning.

Faulty Predication

PRED

Avoid writing sentences with a subject and a verb that don't belong together. Mismatched subjects and verbs can result in illogical or meaningless statements.

Faulty predication: *Increases* in federal funds for education *are expected to rise* next fall.
[*Increases* don't rise. The word *increases* itself means the act of rising.]

Corrected: Federal funds for education *are expected to increase* next fall.

Corrected: *Increases* in federal funds for education *are expected* next fall.

Faulty predication: A *bounced check* is when there are not enough funds in an account to cover payment of the check.
[*A bounced check is when* does not make sense. A check is a *thing.*]

Corrected: A bounced check is the result of overdrawing funds in an account.

Corrected: A bounced check results from overdrawing a checking account.

© 2008 by Pearson Education, Inc.

PROBLEM-SOLVING
Practice 7   Correct unnecessary tense shifts, inappropriate passive voice, and faulty pre-dication in the following sentences. Cross out the errors and insert your corrections.

1. Because people were worried about the authority of police meant that all law-enforcement officers had to leave their guns at headquarters.

2. The poem was read aloud in class by Margaret.

3. His personal computer was given to Sampson by his parents.

4. The moon was landed on by the *Apollo 11* crew in 1969.

5. He hit the ball and runs to first base.

6. The athletes were putting on their uniforms and jokes with each other.

7. A stranger approaches and slipped a flyer under the door.

8. Satisfaction with this product is expected to appease customers in the future.

Problem-solving for Tense Shift, Faulty Predication, and Voice
Edit the following paragraph to correct problems with tense shift, faulty predication, and voice.

Although some believe otherwise, actually employees do have as much freedom of speech as employers enjoy in the workplace. For example, employees at UCLA's hospital exercise their freedom of speech when their cafeteria discount was taken away. The employees felt that this was an unfair act, so they present their case to the union. After not being able to come to an agreement with their employer, the media were invited to report on this injustice so that the public had been informed of the disagreement in the workplace. Employees picketed in front of the hospital and boycott the cafeteria and finally employers overturn the decision and the discount was reinstated. In another example, freedom of speech can also be exercised by employees with wage disputes. At Wells Fargo Contract Security Company, an armed guard worked 12 hours per day for four days. When a paycheck was issued to him for the hours he had worked, he was paid 40 hours regular time and 8 hours of overtime. His regular shift was for 8 hours per day, so he should have received 4 hours overtime for each of the four days he works. When he presents his check to his employers because he thought they had made a mistake, they disagree with him and refuse to discuss the matter, so he took his case to the Labor Board. The Labor Board agreed with his case and had the employers adjust the pay of the employee for that week of hours worked.

—Sherie Amos, *student*   ❏

Edit the following student essay by discovering and correcting as many "surface errors" as you can—these will include any errors in verb use (refer to pages 432–438 in your handbook for examples):

A Blessing in Disguise

Fredrick C. Kessee

1   As Herman Cain once said, "Nobody motivates today's workers. If it doesn't come from within, it doesn't come. Fun helps remove the barriers than allow people to motivate themselves." That is very true for me. I work at Company X for four months, and in those four months I was very unhappy. My motivation was lackluster and the fun I was having was nonexistent. Before obtaining the job, I feel it would be great to work for this company. It is an electronics store, and I am extremely fond of electronics. Yet when a person becomes one of the gears which keep the store running, he or she will feel the friction between the gears. The job will be neither fun nor motivating for me. It required me to "offer things that people did not want and that did not connect with their personality. I quit my job due to an unforeseen circumstance. But now as I look back at the situation, I see that this was meant to happen. Quitting my job showed me that some misfortunes can be blessings in disguise. I'm currently searching for employment, but I feel as if a huge weight has been lifted off my shoulders.

2   Before I receive the job at company X, I apply there on many occasions, but every time I applied, the company will not respond. So in July, I applied there once more. Two days passed and there was no response, so I decided to call. The personnel director tells me to come in for an interview. I was excited with the development of the situation. During the interview process, I was told that I was going to be "offering" extended warranties for certain items. I replied that I was comfortable with that because I've "offered" things in the past. Now in my mental dictionary, "to offer" means to present something to someone in order to see whether he or she wants to take it or not. After the interview, I was told I had the job. As my job progressed, however, I begin to see that their definition of "offering" was different from mine.

3   As a customer steps to my register with an item, I was supposed to "offer" the warranty. I would offer the warranty to the customer and tell him or her all the benefits of owning the warranty. The customer will be saying, "No." I would say, "Okay." To me, this was an "offer." Yet what Company X wanted me to do was to tell customers about the warranty and keep pressuring them to buy until they said "yes," or became very angry and said, "no." I have never believed in pressuring people to do things they did not want to do. My respect for the store dropped from its skyscraper height.

4   In late September, I was forced to resign due to an unforeseen incident. I was told either I would have to quit or be terminated. I could have fought the decision, but I did not. After quitting, I felt as if I had just removed a giant boulder from my back. I will be feeling free. Fun is the key to motivation. Those words by Herman Cain are words that should be taken to heart. Without fun there is no motivation. Without motivation there was no effort. Losing a job may be a disaster at the moment, yet in the end it may be a key to an even better future.   ○

SOLVING PRONOUN PROBLEMS

Pronoun Agreement

PRO AGR

A pronoun is a word that takes the place of a noun. Use pronouns that agree in number and gender with the nouns to which they refer.

John lost *his* book.
[The pronoun *his* agrees in number (singular) and gender (male) with the noun to which it refers, *John.*]

Both *companies* changed *their* names.
[The pronoun *their* agrees in number (plural) and gender (neuter) with the noun to which it refers, *companies.*]

Use singular pronouns with *everyone, everybody, anyone, someone, each,* and *nobody.*

Incorrect: Everyone among the women here knows this is true for *them.*

Correct: Everyone among the women here knows this is true for *her.*

Incorrect: *Each* of the apples must be carefully polished and then put in *their* container.

Correct: *Each* of the apples must be carefully polished and then put in *its* container.

Avoid sexist language by using *one, he or she, him or her,* or *his or her* if the gender of the noun in question is unknown. You can also change your subject to the plural if you feel that repeated use of *he or she, him or her,* or *his or her* will become distracting.

Incorrect: A *firefighter* who stays on the force for 20 years receives *his* retirement benefits.

Correct: A *firefighter* who stays on the force for 20 years receives *her or his* retirement benefits.

Correct: *Firefighters* who stay on the force for 20 years receive *their* retirement benefits.

Incorrect: *Anyone* who does that is putting *his* life at risk.

Correct: *Anyone* who does that is putting *his or her* life at risk.

Correct: *Those* who do that are putting *their* lives at risk.

CASE

Pronoun Case

If a pronoun is the subject of a sentence, use the subjective case: *I, you, she, he, it, we, they,* or *who (whoever)*. To determine how the pronoun is used in a sentence, mentally delete any nouns that are joined to the pronoun. Then try reading the sentence with the intervening words deleted.

Incorrect: *Him* and Sheryl gave voice lessons to the children.
[Mentally delete the words *and Sheryl.*]

Correct: *He* and Sheryl gave voice lessons to the children.

Incorrect: *Us* three applicants will hear about the job tomorrow.
[Mentally delete *three applicants.*]

Correct: *We* three applicants will hear about the job tomorrow.

The verb *to be* in all of its forms always takes the subjective case.

Incorrect: *Whom* will be the captain of the team?

Correct: *Who* will be the captain of the team?

If the pronoun is an object of a verb or a preposition, use the objective case: *me, you, her, him, it, us, them,* or *whom (whomever)*.

Incorrect: The employment officer interviewed we three applicants.
[Mentally delete the words *three applicants.*]

Correct: The employment officer interviewed *us* three applicants.

Incorrect: The professor gave voice lessons to Alan and *she.*
[Mentally delete the words *Alan and.*]

Correct: The professor gave voice lessons to Alan and *her.*

Turning questions into statements can help you decide whether to use the subject *who* or the object *whom*.

Incorrect: *Who* will Mr. Jones hire?
[Turn the question into a statement: Mr. Jones will hire . . . The verb needs an object, not a subject.]

Correct: *Whom* will Mr. Jones hire?

Sometimes you may need to mentally complete a sentence to know whether to choose a subject or an object pronoun.

Incorrect: Franco likes Chinese food more than *her*.
[Complete thought: Franco likes Chinese food more than she does. Otherwise, the sentence means that Franco likes Chinese food more than he likes the woman.]

Correct: Franco likes Chinese food more than *she*.

Incorrect: Lucy is taller than *me*.
[Complete thought: Lucy is taller than I *am*.]

Correct: Lucy is taller than *I*.

Pronoun Reference

REF

Make sure that any pronoun you use clearly refers to another noun or pronoun. Sometimes you can solve unclear pronoun reference problems by replacing a pronoun with a noun.

Incorrect: When Betty put the rich cake on the table, *it* fell.
[It is unclear whether the cake or the table fell.]

Correct: When Betty put the rich cake on the table, the *table* fell.
[For clarity, a noun is used instead of a pronoun.]

Incorrect: Because the writer's tone is ironic and his settings are symbolic, *this* sometimes frustrates readers.
[It is unclear whether *this* refers to the tone, the setting, or both.]

Correct: The writer's ironic tone and symbolic settings sometimes frustrate readers.
[Sentence is rephrased for clarity.]

Pronoun Shift

PRO S

Be careful not to shift the point of view from one person to another when you use pronouns.

Pronoun shift: *I* love going to the beach early in the morning because *you* can see the dolphins jumping in the waves.

Correct: *I* love going to the beach early in the morning because *I* can see the dolphins jumping in the waves.

Pronoun shift: Most *students* realize that college has changed a lot since *your* parents' time.

Correct: Most *students* realize that college has changed a lot since *their* parents' time.

Pronoun shift: *One* often has to take on large debts before *you* graduate nowadays.

Correct: *You* often have to take on large debts before *you* graduate nowadays.

Correct: *One* often has to take on large debts before *one* graduates nowadays.

Correct the following sentences for errors in pronoun agreement, pronoun case, pronoun reference, and pronoun shift. Cross out the incorrect words and insert correct ones. You may need to change a verb form to agree with a new pronoun.

1. A law that is not enforced loses their validity.

2. Because he has taken the recommended steps, John has more confidence than her about passing the course.

3. A person who wants to do well in this sport must consider how much time they are willing to spend practicing.

4. Angie, Bill, and him are eager to see the new play.

5. Although a man may be born in poverty, you can set your own course in America.

6. Please put your briefcase next to the bookcase and be careful not to tip it over.

7. Our impression of an essay's introduction is as important as one's impression of the essay's conclusion.

8. Whom will be the best administrator for the company?

9. Everyone on the *Titanic* was certain they were going to have a peaceful cruise.

10. If a parent is too permissive, some people believe you will raise an irresponsible child.

Problem-solving for Pronoun Use
Edit the following paragraph for errors in pronoun agreement, pronoun case, pronoun reference, and pronoun shift.

Growing up, I never knew the true value of such words as *honesty* and *truth*. In my Italian neighborhood, words like *silence, loyalty,* and *respect* were revered. If you were honest about certain things, you could often put friends or loved ones in danger, so one always took a code of silence. Organized crime ran the neighborhood, and as I grew older you saw how businesses were really conducted. The storefronts on Frankfort Avenue were often fronts to launder other income. For every dollar made legally, the average person pulled in five dollars illegally. Everyone pulled in extra money from the street. If you weren't one to acquire money from the street, eventually the street found a way to make money off of you. This was a tough town with tough rules, and honesty was not always the best policy. Later in life, I did eventually learn the value of honesty as I traveled away from my culture, but we still know there are places in this world where there are different codes of ethics. Rather than the moral code of honesty, there is the survival code of the neighborhood.

—Shawn Marzulli, *student*

Edit the following student essay by discovering and correcting as many "surface errors" as you can—these will include any errors in pronoun usage (refer to pages 441–444 in your handbook for examples):

My Brothers

Jose Garcia

1   Edin and Marvin played an important part in my youth. Edin is 23 years old and Marvin is 21. As brothers, we are different in physique and personalities, but we have something in common: our voice and birthmarks. Now that he is older, they have taken different paths, and each of we is separated from the others. Although we still live together, my brothers and I never do anything together. The last time we were together is immortalized in a photo I like to call "The End of the Three Musketeers."

2   When I'm in his room, I look at the picture and remember that day; I remember that it was ours very first Communion. Their mom had bought us identical suits, so we all looked the same. He dressed Marvin and I, but Edin wanted to be independent so he dressed himself. He did it fine, but he couldn't fix the red bow tie he had to wear, and so he just wore it backwards as shown in the picture. My mom told his to fix his hair as we had done, but he was loyal to his own style and combed his hair down. Before the picture was taken, we imitated the Three Musketeers—we always did that. We used our Communion candles as swords, and we played until my candle and Marvin's broke. Marvin always broke anything that she had in his hands, but Edin was more cautious with his toys. In the picture, Marvin tried to make the candle straight by grabbing it where they was broken. In the picture's background, there is a cross surrounded by white flowers and also two chair—one black and one white, which tell that the picture was taken in front of the altar of a church.

3   My brothers' personalities are quite different. Edin with his smile shows

friendliness and a great enjoyment of life. He also shows his authority as the older

brother. Marvin, serious as he is, is always the odd one, the one that hides its feel-

ings, the unfriendly one, and the untruthful one. He is also the one that often

screws everything up, like holding his Communion book backwards in the picture.

4   This photo brings back old memories, but I realize that my memories of this

former time are fading and that I have separated from my brothers as well. This

was perhaps meant to happen sooner or later, but with we, it happened sooner,

which made it easier for us because none of us misses those times that much even

though they played an important part in my life.   ○

SOLVING ADVERB AND ADJECTIVE PROBLEMS

ADV/ADJ

Adverb and Adjective Usage

To decide whether to use the adjective or the adverb form of a word, ask yourself the following questions:

- Does the word answer the question *which, what kind of,* or *how many* about
  a noun or pronoun? If it does, use an adjective.

- Does the word answer the question *how, when,* or *where* about a verb, an
  adjective, or an adverb? If it does, use an adverb.

Many adverbs end in *-ly.* For example, *badly, beautifully, poorly, really,* and *surely*
are adverbs. The corresponding adjectives are *bad, beautiful, poor, real,* and *sure.*

Incorrect: I feel *real* happy today.

Correct: I feel *really* happy today.
[The adverb form is needed because it modifies the adjective *happy.*]

Incorrect: My computer screen is not lit *bright* enough.

Correct: My computer screen is not lit *brightly* enough.
[The adverb form is needed because it modifies the verb *lit.*]

The words *good* and *bad* are adjectives; they modify nouns and pronouns.
The words *well* and *badly* are adverbs, although *well* can also be used as an
adjective.

Incorrect: My friend Erica *plays* the piano *good.*

Correct: My friend Erica *plays* the piano *well.*
[The adverb form is needed because it modifies the verb *plays.*]

Incorrect: She *feels well* about her courses this term.

Correct: She *feels good* about her courses this term.
[Adjectives are used after state of being verbs.]

But also correct: I *feel well* today, thank you.
[*Well* is used as an adjective meaning "healthy."]

Double Negatives

DN

A *negative* word changes the meaning of a sentence. Don't use two or more negatives in the same sentence. Negative adverbs include *barely, hardly, never, not,* and *scarcely.* The most common negative adjective is *no.* These words should not be used with negative nouns (for example, *none, nothing*) or with words that are contractions for a verb plus *not* (for example, *can't, couldn't, didn't, don't, hadn't, hasn't, haven't, won't, wouldn't*).

Double negative: I *don't* have *no* time for sports this week.

Correct: I *don't* have *any* time for sports this week.
[To keep the negative *don't,* change the negative *no* to the positive *any.*]

Correct: I have *no* time for sports this week.
[To keep the negative *no,* drop the negative *don't.*]

Double negative: We *couldn't* see *nothing* on the stage.

Correct: We *couldn't* see *anything* on the stage.
[To keep the negative *couldn't,* change the negative *nothing* to the positive *anything.*]

Correct: We *could* see *nothing* on the stage.
[To keep the negative *nothing,* change the negative *couldn't* to the positive *could.*]

Faulty Comparison

COMP

Comparative Forms
With adjectives of one syllable, use the ending *-er* to show a comparison of two items. With adjectives of two syllables that end in *-y,* change the *y* to *i* and add *-er.*

Incorrect: This book is *more light* than that one.

Correct: This book is *lighter* than that one.

Incorrect: This was the *more happy* of the two films.

Correct: This was the *happier* of the two films.

Superlative Forms
Use the ending *-est* to show a comparison of three or more items.

Incorrect: She is the *wealthier* of the three cousins.

Correct: She is the *wealthiest* of the three cousins.

Incorrect: This is one of the *greater* efforts of filmmaking we've ever seen.

Correct: This is one of the *greatest* efforts of filmmaking we've ever seen.

With some adjectives of two or more syllables, do not change the ending but instead use *more* or *less* to compare two items and *most* or *least* to compare three or more.

Incorrect: Professor Griswold is *cheerfuler* than Professor Stanton.

Correct: Professor Griswold is *more cheerful* than Professor Stanton.

Incorrect: Of the four possibilities, this one is the *less precise* instrument for measuring.

Correct: Of the four possibilities, this one is the *least precise* instrument for measuring.

Most adverbs also take *more* or *less* for comparing two items and *most* or *least* for comparing three or more items.

Incorrect: This jar will open *most easily* than that one.

Correct: This jar will open *more easily* than that one.

Incorrect: Of the five men, Bart is the *less happily* married.

Correct: Of the five men, Bart is the *least happily* married.

The adjectives *good* and *bad* and the adverbs *well* and *badly* change their forms completely when they are used to compare:

	Comparative	Superlative
good, well	better	best
bad, badly	worse	worst

PROBLEM-SOLVING
Practice 9   Complete the following sentences by writing the comparative or superlative form of the adjective or adverb (in parentheses) in the blank.

1. Many people enjoy films that are _____ (long) than the usual ones.

2. Length, of course, does not make a boring film _____ (enjoyable).

3. Still, audiences often expect a long film to provide a _____ (rich) experience than a short one.

4. One of the _____ (long) films was *The Human Condition*, which lasted 9 hours and 29 minutes.

5. Robert moves _____ (quick) than his opponent.

6. Many people find that grammar is _____ (interesting) than bungee jumping.

7. Antonio did _____ (good, well) in the class because he worked hard.

8. Your comments about your physical health lead me to believe you haven't been feeling _____ (good, well).

9. This is the _____ (extreme) case of chicken pox I've ever encountered.

10. Ionna said that her blind date last week was the _____ (bad) experience of her life.

Problem-solving for Faulty Comparison

Edit the following paragraph for errors in faulty comparison.

> My grandma was a generous and fascinating person. She used to take night classes to learn how to decorate cakes. She would bake beautiful cakes and give them away to students who learned a new prayer. She used to teach catechism every Sunday at church. She also used to belong to a club called Swinging Singles, which used to meet every Wednesday and were the unselfishest people in the congregation. The club members would put food in bags and give it away to needy people. When I was in third grade, my grandma had an operation. She had cancer but never told me that she felt most sick than I ever knew. Every day after school, I would go running to the bench where she would sit, and I'd hug her. When I used to hug her, I could feel her soft and gentle arms and smell her perfume. Being hugged like that, I felt that she was okay and that she was never going to leave me. I only saw her cry once, and she put her head down and put her shawl over her so I wouldn't see. She didn't want to make me cry. She used to kiss me and leave Estee Lauder "Cherries in the Snow" lipstick on my cheek. Finally I knew something was wrong with her. She was my most best friend and she still is because I keep all the most greatest memories in my heart.
>
> —Laura Ballesteros, *student* ❏

SOLVING MODIFIER PROBLEMS

A **modifier** is a word or group of words that describes another word or group of words in a sentence.

Dangling Modifiers

DM

Dangling modifiers most often appear at the beginning of a sentence; they lack a clear, logical relationship with other words in the sentence. Dangling modifiers can be corrected by adding proper subjects to the main clauses or by clarifying the wording of the sentence.

Incorrect: *While drying her hair,* the clock radio suddenly began blasting.

Correct: *While Jenna was drying her hair,* the clock radio suddenly began blasting.
[A subject and helping verb have been added.]

Incorrect: *As a teenager,* school became boring and homework a drag.

Correct: *As a teenager,* Peter found school boring and homework a drag.
[A subject has been added and the sentence reworded.]

Misplaced Modifiers

MM

Misplaced modifiers result from the failure to place a word or phrase near enough to the word it describes. Reposition words or phrases for clarity.

Incorrect: She wanted an apartment with space enough for two children *with plenty of light*.
[The phrase *with plenty of light* does not make sense as a description of the two children; it belongs next to the word *apartment*.]

Correct: She wanted an apartment *with plenty of light* and space enough for two children.

Incorrect: Several customers sent the lamb stew back to the chef, *which was too salty.*

Correct: Several customers sent the lamb stew, *which was too salty*, back to the chef.

PROBLEM-SOLVING
Practice 10   Circle any dangling or misplaced modifiers in the following sentences. Use arrows to reposition the modifiers. If necessary, reword phrases.

1. Susan gave Ted a poster for his room in the dormitory that looked like a spring landscape.

2. After buying three tickets, on the way home it became apparent that they would need four.

3. Julio had to drive his old pickup truck to get to the party on time without a spare tire.

4. Learning how to use a home computer, a surprising number of tasks suddenly became easier.

5. Checked three times by the examiners, his answers nevertheless proved all correct.

6. While using the hair dryer, the doorbell was inaudible.

7. The people usually vote for a candidate they see on television with charm and poise.

8. Sally gave the names of three dentists to Tom's cousin listed in the phone directory.

9. In V formation, we watched the jets flying overhead.

10. Eating an ice cream cone, the truck almost collided with the boy.

Problem-solving for Dangling and Misplaced Modifiers
Edit the following paragraph for dangling and misplaced modifiers. This may involve circling certain phrases, using arrows, and adding or changing words or phrases.

The first step in attaining your dream body involves making out a schedule that is good for you. You have to plan to work out for about two hours. Find a good time that you will not feel rushed or worried about anything in your schedule. When you have made your schedule for the times that you want to work out, make another schedule that you are going to eat for the foods. Stop eating junk foods and foods that have fat, are high in calories, and also have sugar. You have to eat three to five servings of fruit or vegetables a day, and drink glasses of water three to five or even more. Eating foods that have a lot of fat after you exercise, your workout plan will not succeed.

—Sam Roham, *student* ❏

Problem-solving in Essay Editing

Edit the following student essay by discovering and correcting as many "surface errors" as you can—these will include adjective and adverb problems, double negatives, faulty comparisons, and dangling and misplaced modifiers (refer to pages 449–450 in your handbook for examples):

LEARNING TO TEACH AND TEACHING TO LEARN

Jessica Madrid

1   In the summer of my senior year, I was hired at the YMCA to be a dance teacher. Through this job, I learned how to have patience with students, how to teach differently age groups, and how to nod my head and smile whenever a parent would try to tell me what to do.

2   Patience was never one of my stronger qualities, but it was something I needed for this job. From three years old to fourteen years of age, my patience was always being tried by my students. Not wanting to do a particular dance step, I found that students would complain and refuse to do the step. Sometimes they would complain about the music and ask for music that I could not play. But instead of getting mad at a student who did not get the step right away, I would just take a deep breath and say, "That's okay—all you have to do is practice and you will eventually get it." Teaching kids can be very frustrating since I never could know what wouldn't happen next.

3   From three to fourteen years of age, another aspect of teaching I had a hard time with was that I had to teach a variety of age groups. I always needed to have a variety of activities planned for each day, making sure that I didn't have too many hardly steps for the little kids and not too many easily steps for the older kids. Every class I needed to do a least bit of review and also have new steps for them to learn.

4   The third aspect of teaching I had a hard time with occurred when a parent would come up to me and try to tell me how to teach. Sometimes, wanting not to appear appreciative of their contributions, parents would give me suggestions on a new dance or how to teach a new step. This was frustrating to me because I needed to follow strict the curriculum that I received. However, instead of getting mad at these parents, their suggestions were taken and I would go on with what I was doing. The parents didn't never seem to understand my responsibilities as a teacher.

5   Overall, being a dance teacher for the YMCA has been the greater experience because it has helped me become a better person with more patience and under-standing. ○

SOLVING PUNCTUATION PROBLEMS

Commas

Use a comma to separate two complete thoughts connected by a coordinating conjunction (any of the FANBOYS: *for, and, nor, but, or, yet, so*). Place the comma before the conjunction.

> I like to study with the radio on, *but* this music makes me nervous.

> You can turn left at the next light, *or* you can follow the main highway for three blocks.

Use a comma after introductory words, phrases, and clauses.

> Yes, this segment of the soap opera is certainly absorbing.
> [Introductory word is set off.]

> Taking her baby along, Phyllis joined Shane on a business trip to Orlando.
> [Introductory phrase is set off.]

> When the results came back positive, the patient was advised to return to the doctor.
> [Introductory clause is set off.]

Use a comma before and after nonrestrictive words, phrases, and clauses. Non-restrictive words, phrases, and clauses are not essential to the meaning of the sentence.

> Her husband, Bill, will sail to Bermuda this summer.
> [Bill is not essential; it renames the word *husband*. If *Bill* was restrictive—essential to the meaning of the sentence—then no commas would be used, and the sentence would mean "her husband Bill" as opposed to "her husband Fred" or "her husband James." That is, *Bill* would be one of her three husbands.]

Electronic mail, *which sends messages instantaneously,* is beginning to replace "snail mail," as some call the postal service.

Philip Johnson, *who designed some of America's most interesting buildings,* failed the New York State licensing examination.

Samuel Taylor Coleridge, *a Romantic poet of the nineteenth century,* was a heavy user of opium.

Do not use commas to set off restrictive words, phrases, or clauses. Restrictive words, phrases, and clauses are essential to the meaning of the sentence. Do not use a comma with clauses beginning with *that.* The word *that* always introduces an essential clause.

Incorrect: The novel, *Beloved,* earned Toni Morrison the Pulitzer Prize.
[The name of the novel is essential to the meaning of the sentence.]

Correct: The novel *Beloved* earned Toni Morrison the Pulitzer Prize.

Incorrect: Students, *receiving A grades,* may skip the second course.
[Without the phrase *receiving A grades,* the sentence has a different meaning.]

Correct: Students *who receive A grades* may skip the second course.

Incorrect: The essay, *that won the prize,* was about illiteracy.
[Without the clause *that won the prize,* the sentence does not specify which essay was about illiteracy.]

Correct: The essay *that won the prize* was about illiteracy.

Use a comma after each element in a series except the last one.

Books, records, and *magazines* lay on the table.

The company preferred *sales managers who were cordial with employees, knew the business,* and *demonstrated loyalty to the organization.*

Use a comma between adjectives that modify the same noun. If you can put *and* between the adjectives, separate the adjectives with commas.

Incorrect: The Lakers had an *intimidating overpowering* defense.
[You can mentally insert *and* between *intimidating* and *overpowering.*]

Correct: The Lakers had an *intimidating, overpowering* defense.

Incorrect: The class enjoyed the *enchanting imaginative subtle* performance.
[You can mentally insert *and* between *enchanting,* and *imaginative,* and *subtle.*]

Correct: The class enjoyed the *enchanting, imaginative, subtle* performance.

Incorrect: He spread a *navy, blue, beach* towel on the sand.
[You cannot insert *and* between *navy, blue,* and *beach.*]

Correct: He spread a *navy blue beach* towel on the sand.

Use a comma to set off interrupters from the rest of the sentence. Use one comma if the interrupter appears at the beginning or at the end of the sentence; use two commas if the interrupter appears in the middle of the sentence.

However, the check will not be honored at this bank.

Some new cars have too much fiberglass, *for example.*

She knew, *by the way,* that the television didn't work.

Use a comma (or commas) to set off a noun of direct address from the rest of the sentence.

Barbara, will you please give me some advice.

I hope, *Dr. Jones,* to see you soon.

Use a comma with direct quotations. Before quoting a whole statement, put a comma after the introductory words.

He said, "This is the road to Seattle."

Do not use commas with short quoted phrases that fit smoothly into the rest of the sentence.

Incorrect: Trevor called his brother a, "universal genius."

Correct: Trevor called his brother a "universal genius."

Incorrect: Shakespeare called music the, "food of love."

Correct: Shakespeare called music the "food of love."

At the end of quoted material, put the comma *inside* the quotation marks.

"After dinner, let's play Scrabble," Sue suggested.

Put a comma inside the question mark and after words like *he said* and *she asked* if a quoted sentence is interrupted.

"Don't leave any questions blank," the instructor said, "even if you have to guess at the answer."

Use commas with dates and place names.

Jackie Robinson was born on January 31, 1919, in Cairo, Georgia.

The address is 1600 Broadway, New York, New York 10019.
[Do not use a comma to separate the state from the ZIP code.]

PROBLEM-SOLVING
Practice 11   Correct the following sentences by inserting missing commas and crossing out unnecessary ones.

1. We toured China Japan the Philippines and Bali.
2. The counselor was prepared for the quarrelsome rebellious student.
3. The antiques dealer looked longingly at the fine, old chair.
4. Nevertheless he washed his car every Saturday.
5. Alfred Kinsey who was a pioneer in sex research was known in high school as a boy who never had a girlfriend.
6. My only sister Karen will join us.

7. "You know Steve that the rest of us agree with you."

8. "Let's meet in the cafeteria for lunch" Tamoy suggested.

9. "I admire your determination" the manager said "but there are some errors in the reports."

10. Leilani asked "Why should we wait for them to call us?"

11. She was born on Wednesday October 10 1968.

12. She adores the man who works at 10990 Wilshire Boulevard Los Angeles California 90024.

Problem-solving for Commas

Edit the following paragraph for comma errors by inserting missing commas and crossing out unnecessary commas.

> Disneyland has been attracting people for over fifty years and for each person it leaves a different impact no matter what their age ethnicity or background. This place contains a haunted mansion a little bit of New Orleans where the Disney projection of *Fantasmic* takes place where pirates that sing "Yo, ho, ho" and other rides and shows. The Haunted Mansion is the biggest memory-maker I have ever been to. It has the most background and history as far as characters in the Mansion and it has made the most memories for me personally. As a kid I remember trembling when walking up to the eerie doors not knowing what to expect. On my first date to Disneyland my first real kiss occurred in the shadows of the ballroom with dancing ghosts around us. Now every time I visit the Haunted Mansion I consider how my life has changed even though this spooky house has remained the same.
>
> —Greg Reilly, *student*   ❏

Semicolons

Use a semicolon to separate two complete thoughts that are closely related and that are not linked by a coordinate conjunction (*for, and, nor, but, or, yet, so*).

Incorrect: The road was bumpy, it caused many blowouts and accidents.

Correct: The road was bumpy; it caused many blowouts and accidents.

Incorrect: We used to go surfing every Saturday afternoon then we would bake clams on the beach.

Correct: We used to go surfing every Saturday afternoon; then we would bake clams on the beach.

Use a semicolon to separate two complete thoughts linked by a conjunctive adverb (a word like *consequently, however, meanwhile, moreover, nevertheless, therefore*). Put a comma after the conjunctive adverb.

Separate conference rooms are available for the two meetings; *however,* you may convene together afterward if you like.

We have sent you an application form; *meanwhile,* we will check your references.

Use semicolons in a series when the parts already have commas within them.

Incorrect: She had lived in Dallas, Texas, San Mateo, California, and Stamford, Connecticut.

Correct: She had lived in Dallas, Texas; San Mateo, California; and Stamford, Connecticut.

Incorrect: You will have to pass a reading test, given in multiple-choice format, a writing test, administered in the form of a one-hour essay, and a mathematics test, given on a computer.

Correct: You will have to pass a reading test, given in multiple-choice format; a writing test, administered in the form of a one-hour essay; and a mathematics test, given on a computer.

PROBLEM-SOLVING
Practice 12   Correct the following sentences by inserting or deleting semicolons.

1. A medical checkup every few years may not seem necessary however, it could save your life.

2. Three special dates in Nicole's life are January 15, 1985, May 24, 1987, and October 10, 1991.

3. The course is too easy you should take a more advanced one.

4. After you lay the wooden pieces on the diagram; glue them together at the corners.

5. The police had not enforced the law against selling marijuana, therefore, the two men were surprised to be arrested.

Problem-solving for Semicolons
Edit the following paragraph for correct use of semicolons.

The first step is to send an application to the California Highway Patrol office in your local area. Fill out the application and mail it then you will receive a testing date in about a month. The test is pass or fail it consists of 400 questions and a two-page essay. The questions consist of grammar, spelling, math, and motor skills therefore if you can brush up in these subjects, you might do just fine. The essay will probably be on a situation in your life that you had to take control of. If you are fortunate enough to have passed this test, you will move on to the physical agility test. This test is pass or fail it consists of running 500 yards, completing an obstacle course, evaluation of abdominal and shoulder strength, grip pressure, and flexibility. Very few applicants fail on this physical portion of the testing process the biggest problem they encounter is the running. After completing and passing this portion of the test, you can sign up for an oral interview at this point you will be mailed a background packet and a confirmation packet.

—Daniel Hollywood, *student*   ❑

Colons

Use a colon to introduce a list.

She called out the following names: Roberta, Carl, Tracy, Juanita, Janice, and Lamont.

Open the bottle like this: Press down on the lid, align the arrows, and turn the lid to the left.

Do not use a colon with *to be* verbs.

Incorrect: The book's shortcomings *are:* its unrealistic plot, its difficult style, and its improbable ending.

Correct: The book's shortcomings *are* its unrealistic plot, its difficult style, and its improbable ending.

Use a colon to introduce a direct quotation when the introductory words form a complete statement.

In the owner's manual, the section on maintenance clearly warns the consumer with these words: "The chemicals in this packet may be harmful if inhaled."

Use a colon to introduce a word, phrase, or clause that explains or summarizes the first part of the sentence.

Incorrect: Joan approached the interview with only one thought in mind, she intended to prove that she understood the job.

Correct: Joan approached the interview with only one thought in mind: She intended to prove that she understood the job.

PROBLEM-SOLVING
Practice 13   Correct the following sentences by inserting the necessary colons.

1. In the spring of 1997, scientists made an important announcement a sheep had been successfully cloned.

2. Exciting breakthroughs raised speculations in the following areas of study biology, physics, philosophy, psychology, and law.

3. Some religious leaders have expressed disapproval of human cloning in the following ways calling for laws banning the cloning of human beings, preaching against human cloning, and expressing moral outrage in television interviews and debates.

4. Laws in the United States against cloning human beings will not prevent the practice for one chief reason U.S. laws do not control what scientists do in other countries.

5. There is one question people are asking each other everywhere who is the person you would most like to see cloned?

Problem-solving for Colons
Insert colons where appropriate in the following paragraph.

The tobacco scandal has outraged many people because the industries choose to make more money instead of saving lives. For decades the tobacco industry has made it a business to kill huge numbers of people twenty-seven years from now five hundred people worldwide will die of tobacco-related diseases. We can see the extent of human carnage by putting this in terms of minutes and seconds there's a death every 1.7 seconds or about two hundred and fifty people would have been dead during the time it takes you to read this essay. The industry predicted these results and they still decided to package, advertise, and sell this product. The industry knows the consequences of selling tobacco disease and death for many. In front of the nation, the tobacco industry swore under oath that its product was not addictive or dangerous, nor does the industry admit to marketing their tobacco for use by minors. The industry has finally confessed that it marketed its tobacco to children under thirteen an unforgivable sales strategy.

—Azucena Zepeda, *student*   ❏

End Punctuation

Use periods to end statements, requests, and indirect questions.

Incorrect: Would you please send me an application form?

Correct: Would you please send me an application form.
[This is a request, not a question.]

Incorrect: Sam asked whether the store was having a sale?

Correct: Sam asked whether the store was having a sale.
[This is an indirect question, not a direct one.]

Use question marks after direct questions.

Is this book overdue?

Why, if no one objects to the proposal, are we waiting until March to begin?

Use exclamation points after sentences or words that express excitement or strong feeling.

Watch out for that elephant!

Stop, thief!

PROBLEM-SOLVING
Practice 14   Place the correct end punctuation after these sentences.

1. The instructor asked whether the class had read the assignment

2. If you want help, why don't you ask one of us for it

3. Get out of that van It's going to explode

4. Would you please send me travel literature and maps of Florida

5. Will you be spending your vacation in Greece

Problem-solving for End Punctuation
Edit the following paragraph by adding the appropriate end punctuation.

I was ready to go, my seat adjusted, my hearing helmet working, and the vehicle turned on My sergeant told me to drive forward at a slow pace. At first, he had me drive on some nice paved roads. He then decided that it was time for me to go to the hills and rocky roads. I was so scared at this point, I couldn't believe it At first he had me drive on some nice paved roads. Can you believe what he did next He had decided it was time for me to go on the hills and rocky roads The shift was on speed 1-3 as I started to go up a hill. I started to press on the accelerator really hard but the hill was too steep, and my smoke track wouldn't continue to go up the hill. I could then hear my sergeant's voice telling me step by step how to continue to go up the hill. The shift was now on 1-1, and the track was slowly going up the hill. It didn't help that there were some huge rocks around We finally made it to the top. That hill was not as big as I thought it had been. I have since driven those vehicles so much and so carefully that I have received awards for it. Everything we learn will at first seem difficult but in the end it will bring a satisfaction that is unique.

—Janet Vidaurre, *student*   ❑

Apostrophes

Use an apostrophe in contractions—words in which letters have been left out.

The English language doesn't go back in history as far as Latin or Greek.
[*Doesn't* is a contraction of *does not*. An apostrophe replaces the missing *o* in *not*.]

They're going to join us for dinner.
[*They're* is a contraction of *they are*. An apostrophe replaces the missing *a* in *are*.]

John reports that it's a nice day.
[*It's* is a contraction of *it is*. An apostrophe replaces the missing *i* in *is*. Do not use an apostrophe when *its* shows possession: The cat licked *its* paw. In this case *its* is not a contraction of *it is*.]

Use apostrophes with nouns to indicate possession. Add *'s* to singular nouns, whether or not they end in *s*.

This is Martin's jacket.

He received half a day's pay.

The waitress's hours are long.

Add only an apostrophe to plural nouns that end in *s*.

All students' grades are posted in the office.

The secretaries' luncheon was held at the Biltmore Hotel.

Add *'s* to plural nouns that do not end in *s*, such as *men*, *women*, and *children*.

This is the men's restroom.

The children's lockers are just down the hall.

Do not add apostrophes to possessive pronouns: *its, mine, his, hers, ours, yours, theirs, whose.*

Incorrect: The new car in the parking lot is her's.

Correct: The new car in the parking lot is hers.

Incorrect: The rabbit returned to it's burrow.

Correct: The rabbit returned to its burrow.

PROBLEM-SOLVING
Practice 15   Circle the correct form in parentheses.

1. According to most (expert's, experts') opinions, Old English, or Anglo-Saxon, (did'nt, didn't) exist in the time of the ancient Greeks.

2. Old English, in any case, (could'nt, couldn't) really be called English as we speak it.

3. Many influences altered the way English was spoken over the centuries, but English (has'nt, hasn't) lost (its, it's) basic structure.

4. After the Norman Conquest in A.D. 1066, the biggest change in English came from the French (aristocrats', aristocrat's) speech.

5. Consequently, most languages (can't, cann't) compete with English for richness of vocabulary.

6. Even (childrens', children's) books contain a wide variety of words.

7. People in (Shakespeares', Shakespeare's) time probably (wouldnt, would'nt, wouldn't) have believed how widespread their language would become.

Problem-solving for Apostrophes
Edit the following paragraph by inserting apostrophes where necessary.

> Eleteuterio Damo is my grandfather, who passed away in 1996. He was very special to me. I consider him a father figure. He raised me ever since I was a child. My grandfather taught me things I didn't know like how to work a lawnmower. He raised me with great discipline and taught me whats right and whats wrong. In this picture, were at my cousins house. It was Christmas Eve and my whole family got together. One can tell he's a loving person from the way my sisters laying her head on his shoulders. I remember he took good care of me when I had a high fever. Most of the time he would just stay beside me and watch for me to get better. He was a very big guy with broad shoulders and a large belly. He always stayed relaxed and tried to avoid stress. Most of the time I would see him lying down or sitting on a couch like he is in the picture. My grandfather loved to eat. We used to call him the "moon" because of his large stomach and the good thing was that he never got offended when people called him names. My grandfathers smile makes him look like a snob who thinks he's better than everybody, which is kind of true. He was an individual who liked competition. I remember he entered a contest with three contestants to see who had the nicest, cleanest house. He came in second and he refused to admit that someone else had won first place. My grandfather was a person who wanted to be "on top" all the time.
>
> —Charles Singson, *student*   ❏

Quotation Marks

Use quotation marks to set off someone's exact words. (For rules regarding capitalization of quoted material, see pages 467–468 of this handbook. For comma use with quotations, see page 454.)

Incorrect: He said please pass the butter.

Correct: He said, "Please pass the butter."

Do not use quotation marks if the person's words are quoted indirectly—if the person's *exact* words are not used.

Incorrect: Susan reported that "she was feeling much better this morning."

Correct: Susan reported that she was feeling much better this morning.

Use quotation marks for titles of essays, articles, short poems, short stories, songs, chapter titles, and episodes of television programs.

Felippe said that "Sonny's Blues" by James Baldwin was one of the best short stories he had ever read.

They danced cheek to cheek to the music of "Unchained Melody."

Do not put quotation marks around the title of your own essay, either on the first page of your paper or on the title page.

PROBLEM-SOLVING
Practice 16

Insert quotation marks where necessary in the following sentences. Some sentences require commas with quotation marks.

1. How many times have you read the short story The Shawl, by Cynthia Ozick?
2. Taylor replied You have the same opinion I do.
3. The chapter is entitled Getting to Know Your Pet Tarantula.
4. Did Naima say that she wanted to return to the park today?
5. I just listened to an old recording of Smoke Gets in Your Eyes.
6. You may do aerobics the doctor said only if you wear this knee brace.
7. The essay A Case of Mistaken Identities: The Human Body describes Rafael Campo's self-discoveries as a medical student.

Problem-solving for Quotation Marks
Edit the following paragraph for correct use of quotation marks. Be sure to insert commas where needed.

In the final section of the novel *Montana 1948* by Larry Watson, David tells his wife of the images he has of the summer of 1948. He confides that he finds these memories more vivid and lasting than any others of his boyhood. Betsy finds the whole story stunning and fascinating. On Thanksgiving, she brings up the subject of Montana to David's parents by saying, David told me about what happened when you lived in Montana. That sure was the wild West, wasn't it? David's father just explodes at Betsy's question. He screams, Don't blame Montana. Don't ever blame Montana! Then David's father leaves the room and never returns to the meal again.

—Ravinder Degun, *student* ❏

Italics

Italicize the titles of books, plays, movies, works of art, complete record albums, television programs (not the titles of separate episodes), magazines, newspapers, periodicals, and electronic publications such as tapes, disks,

ITAL

computer programs, CD-ROMs, and online databases. Italics is shown by underlining when an italics font is not available.

The novel *For Whom the Bell Tolls* was written by Ernest Hemingway.

Every Sunday, they sit in a sunny café and read the *New York Times.*

Janika was disappointed to discover that the *Mona Lisa* is behind glass.

When you have time, try to access the *Los Angeles Times Online.*

PROBLEM-SOLVING
Practice 17

Correct each sentence by underlining the words to be italicized.

1. Vincent van Gogh's painting Starry Night took my breath away.

2. Every time Victor goes to the dentist's office, he catches up on his reading of People magazine.

3. Have you read the book Always Running, by Luis Rodriguez?

4. She watched so many episodes of Saturday Night Live that she felt she had seen them all.

5. The Readers' Guide to Periodical Literature can help you find articles for your research paper.

Problem-solving for Italics

Edit the following paragraph by underlining any words that should be italicized.

As a child, the only reading I did was sight-reading. I was not taught to read out of a book like most children. I read what I saw on public signs, or around the house. My mother did not read bedtime story books to me, but she did make up her own stories and I used my imagination as she spoke to me. I learned to read in school as I got older, but I found no relation to me or the things I did. My school's storybooks such as Where the Wild Things Are or The Cat in the Hat talked about what weird animals did, the world, or make-believe characters, which was just fiction to me. I was twelve years in the summer of 1992 when my reading history took a turn. I was looking for a book in my godfather's bookshelf and I found A Wrinkle in Time. It was a short novel and I enjoyed the book so much that I read another one—The Outsiders. These were books about teenagers and the things they face in life like peer pressure, boys, friends, and families. I read so many books that summer that I noticed a change at school.

—Leilani Bryant, *student*   ❏

Hyphens

Use a hyphen to connect a compound adjective that appears before a noun. (A compound adjective is two or more descriptive words used as one word.)

This is a *well-constructed* house.

Refer to these *up-to-date* reports.

The *13-year-old* girl was excited to be in the house alone.

Unless the dictionary indicates that the compound adjective is always hyphenated, do not use a hyphen when the words appear after a form of the verb *to be*.

This house is *well constructed*.

These reports are up-to-date.
[Dictionary shows that *up-to-date* is always hyphenated.]

The girl was 13 years old.

Do not use a hyphen if one of the words used to describe the noun ends in *-ly*. The *-ly* usually indicates an adverb rather than an adjective.

Incorrect: The *neatly-made* bed was proof of his domestic skills.

Correct: The *neatly made* bed was proof of his domestic skills.

Incorrect: We walked into a *beautifully-decorated* office.

Correct: We walked into a *beautifully decorated* office.

Use a hyphen in the following compound nouns and words with prefixes. Check your dictionary when you are not sure how to punctuate a compound noun. Some compounds are closed (makeup), some are open (cross section), and some use hyphens (mass-produced).

My *sister-in-law* will arrive on Tuesday.

Your *self-confidence* will soar upon completion of the course.

Use a hyphen to divide a word at the end of a line. Divide words only on syllable breaks. Never divide a one-syllable word. Check a dictionary if you are not sure of a word's syllable breaks.

Incorrect: The instructor began the class with a discussion of the many obvious hall-marks of success.

Correct: The instructor began the class with a discussion of the many obvious hall-marks of success.

Incorrect: She wondered why the bus was late when it never had been late before.

Correct: She wondered why the bus was late when it never had been late before.

Dashes

Use a dash to show a sudden break in thought.

Incorrect: I was sure I saw him wait here he comes!

Correct: I was sure I saw him—wait, here he comes!

Incorrect: That's not what she asked you to do, it's the complete opposite.

Correct: That's not what she asked you to do—it's the complete opposite.

Use dashes to set off information that is less important than the rest of the sentence but too important to enclose in parentheses.

Certain dishes—none of them very complicated or exotic—have made the restaurant quite popular.

Edgar's latest tutor—the one with the small gold earring and the spiked hair—is about to give up on him.

Use a dash before a statement that is a summary or an explanation of the first part of the sentence.

She had everything she needed for the trip—her new boyfriend and the plane tickets.

Motivation, intelligence, perseverance—these are the ingredients for a successful career.

Parentheses

Use parentheses to set off comments that are less important than the rest of the sentence or that provide additional information, such as phone numbers and dates.

Heather's date of birth (June 14, 1980) had been lovingly embroidered on a pillow by her grandmother.

Please call me (310-576-3471) if you have any additional questions about this worthy candidate.

Remember to clean out your locker by the end of this week. (Items left in lockers will be disposed of on March 15.)

Periods go inside the closing parenthesis if a complete sentence is enclosed in the parentheses.

Incorrect: Remember to bring your own Coleman lanterns. (The campsite has no extras available).

Correct: Remember to bring your own Coleman lanterns. (The campsite has no extras available.)

Periods go outside the closing parenthesis if you have enclosed less than a complete sentence in parentheses.

Incorrect: Please enclose the materials we discussed earlier (résumé and reference letters.)

Correct: Please enclose the materials we discussed earlier (résumé and reference letters).

Question marks and exclamation points go inside the closing parenthesis if they belong with the material in parentheses.

Incorrect: Twentieth-century writer Richard Wright (died 1960)? Was greatly influenced by Nathaniel Hawthorne.

Correct: Twentieth-century writer Richard Wright (died 1960?) was greatly influenced by Nathaniel Hawthorne.

Question marks and exclamation points go outside the closing parenthesis if they go with the rest of the sentence.

Incorrect: Can you believe she asked me for money (ten dollars?)

Correct: Can you believe she asked me for money (ten dollars)?

Commas go outside the closing parenthesis.

> **Incorrect:** When you arrive, (aim for twelve noon,) we'll eat lunch.

> **Correct:** When you arrive (aim for twelve noon), we'll eat lunch.

PROBLEM-SOLVING
Practice 18

Correct the following sentences by inserting hyphens, dashes, and parentheses where appropriate.

1. The dealer placed the old fashioned china piece on top of the cupboard a place that she felt would be safe from juvenile fingers.

2. The coach surprised them by saying, "It's not how you play the game it's whether we beat our rival!"

3. The gentleman at the post office carefully printed his address 435 South Maple in beautiful handwriting in the middle of the envelope.

4. My mother in law will visit us for two weeks can you come to meet her?

5. He chose three roses were they tea roses? and placed them in tissue.

6. The instructor remarked that Paul had submitted a well organized essay.

7. These running shoes Nike, Adidas, Brooks are available in many different sizes.

Problem-solving for Hyphens, Dashes and Parentheses
Correct the following paragraph by inserting hyphens, dashes, or parentheses where appropriate.

> Woodblock prints are made with wood, paper, and ink. The preferred wood is cherry wood it is soft enough for detailed pictures, yet sturdy enough to be used many times for printing. Many specialty and construction stores Home Depot for example have a wide variety of softwood and the sales associate can pre cut the wood pieces you desire. Paper from the mulberry tree is ideal if you want to create a woodblock print. Mulberry tree paper is thick, almost cloth like, and has great absorption qualities. The ink used in woodblock prints has to be thick that way it won't run on the paper. Ideal inks are made from a rice paste, and the color can be added to them later. Both paper and ink can be found at a local art supply store for instance, Michael's or Aaron Brothers.
>
> —Vanessa Rivas, *student*   ❑

Brackets

Use brackets to enclose explanatory comments within a direct quotation.

> The commentator reported, "He [the President] adamantly denies all charges and vows to fight them."

Use brackets with the word *sic* to indicate a grammatical or spelling error that was made by the speaker in a direct quotation. This way your reader will know that the person you are quoting, and not you, made the mistake.

> Al wrote, "I'm not use [sic] to missing a day of work—I'm very conscientious."

Ellipsis Points

Use **ellipsis points** enclosed by brackets—three periods with a space before and after each period—to indicate that words have been omitted from quoted material.

> Latisha wrote the following in describing her mother: "The first film about American history she ever saw was [. . .] *Gone with the Wind*."
> [The writer has omitted the words *the well-known movie classic*.]

If you omit words at the end of a quoted sentence, or if you omit a sentence ending within a quoted passage, use four periods instead of three. The fourth period indicates the ending of a sentence.

> Janet says, "I usually like films about history and biography. One I didn't like was . . . *Birth of a Nation* [. . .]."
> [Some of Janet's words within the sentence and at the end of the sentence have been omitted.]

For non-quoted material, use ellipsis marks without brackets to show a thought that is interrupted or incomplete.

> Cuong works extremely hard in the class; his brother, on the other hand . . . well, that's a different story.

Problem-solving in Essay Editing

Edit the following student essay by discovering and correcting as many "surface errors" as you can—these will include any errors in punctuation: commas, semicolons, colons, end punctuation, apostrophes, quotation marks, italics, hyphens, dashes, parentheses, brackets, and ellipsis marks (refer to pages 452–466 in your handbook for examples).

THE GREAT EXPANSION OF THE WEST

Preston Hollister

1   In Ji-Yeon Mary Yufill's essay Lets Tell the Story of All Americas Cultures, she mentions a few historical people that made the United States what it is today. One of the historical people mentioned in her essay is Daniel Boone. This man played a major part in the exploration and settlement of Kentucky.

2   On November 2 1734 Daniel Boone was born near the town of Reading Pennsylvania. In 1753 Boone and his family settled in Yadkin River in what is now North Carolina. Boone became a skillful hunter and trapper with only a little schooling he received in this primitive settlement. In 1767 Boone explored and

settled in the wilderness around the Kentucky River, making one of his many trips in this region.

3   On his most important expedition, he and five companions followed a trail through the Cumberland Gap in eastern Kentucky between 1769 and 1771. In 1775 Boone established a road by which colonists could reach Kentucky. He built a stockade and a fort at the front of Boonesborough where the colonists had settled. Later, the settlers called the road the Wilderness Road. During the American Revolution, that small community suffered repeated attacks by Native Americans. During one of these attacks, Boone was captured by Native American raiders.

4   In the beginning of the 1780s, Boone was forced to abandon his claims and territory around Boonesborough because of invalid titles and he was forced to move to Boones Station Kentucky. Later Boone left Kentucky and lived near Point Pleasant Virginia now West Virginia from 1788 to 1798. In 1799, Boone steered near St. Louis in present day Missouri, where he remained until his death on September 26 1820 at the age of 86.

5   In conclusion Daniel Boone played a huge part in colonists expanding the West and in finding new ways to live. This man was extremely important in the early years of the United States of America.   ○

SOLVING MECHANICS PROBLEMS

Mechanics refers to correct use of capitalization, abbreviation, numbers, and overall manuscript format.

Capitalization

CAP

Capitalize the first word of every sentence.

> The tape is missing.

Capitalize the first word of every quoted sentence. If what is quoted is not a complete sentence, do not capitalize the first word.

> Kyle's coworker replied, "You can take your lunch break whenever you like."

> The narrator describes Enrico as "tall, dark, and ruggedly handsome."

Capitalize all proper nouns: names of people, places, and products.

> After Chihiro Gonsho sent in her name and address on the back of a Cheerios box top, she won a trip to Paris, France, to view the Eiffel Tower.

Capitalize adjectives formed from proper nouns.

> Natalie has a strange but endearing habit of dipping French fries into Russian dressing.

Capitalize days of the week, months, and holidays. Do not capitalize the seasons: spring, summer, fall, or winter.

> The first day of spring, March 21, falls on a Tuesday this year.

Capitalize all main words in the titles of short stories, poems, novels, articles, chapters, speeches, plays, films, songs, works of art, and television shows. Do not capitalize small or insignificant words such as *a, an,* and *the,* or prepositions and conjunctions unless they begin or end the title.

> Sandra Cisneros wrote a wonderful book called *The House on Mango Street.*

Capitalize the specific names of companies, organizations, religions, schools, colleges, and courses. Do not capitalize these general words if they stand alone.

> The Ford Motor Company hired Vikram to speak about the company to local colleges and high schools.

> Francesca transferred from History 101 to a mathematics class.

Capitalize titles when they are used along with a person's name. Do not capitalize titles used after a person's name.

> She told the group that Vice-President Johnson would submit the proposal.

> Give the note to Vincent Ramirez, president of the company.

Capitalize the directions *north, south, east,* and *west* when these words refer to particular sections of the country or of a region but not when they simply refer to a direction.

> This new company manager hails from the South.

> Maria decided to drive west.

PROBLEM-SOLVING
Practice 19   Capitalize any words in the following sentences that need capitalizing.

1. The chapter entitled "raising hamsters for fun and profit" drew many laughs from the audience.

2. The sing family, newly arrived in new york from canada, had never celebrated presidents' day before.

3. Attending the meeting were president Boscone, vice-president Wilson, and Jonas Slovadnich, the secretary of the sloan center for genetic research.

4. Shonte entered the house, opened the refrigerator, took out wonder bread, kraft mayonnaise, and bumble bee tuna, and made herself a sandwich.

5. Last summer we flew on a Wednesday to the grand canyon in arizona.

Problem-solving for Capitalization

Edit the following paragraph by capitalizing all words that should be capitalized.

> More than a century ago, most people had to look after their own health because the health authorities at that time were not knowledgeable enough and also they were not properly equipped to treat a number of illnesses. Then the revolution followed that has led to modern medicine. Physician Donald vickery described three stages of health in the united states that occurred over the last one hundred years: the age of environment, the age of medicine, and the age of lifestyles—better living habits. Current research conducted by u s surgeon general Everett koop has concluded that a great many Americans are suffering from one or more illnesses. Chronic illness that has a longer duration compared to an acute illness includes crippling or incapacitating diseases ranging from alcoholism to Alzheimer's.

> —Ravinder Degun, *student*   ❏

Abbreviations

ABR

Abbreviate standard titles when they come immediately before or after names.

Ms. Susan Winters and Mr. Eduardo Lopez will officiate.

Silvana Olea, M.D., will perform the operation.

Use time-related abbreviations: A.M., P.M., A.D., B.C. (A.M. and P.M. often appear in small capital letters, like this.)

Many people look forward to New Year festivities to occur at 12 A.M. of the year 2008.

Abbreviate the names of well-known organizations, schools, and groups if you have first introduced the full name for the reader.

Jovan had worked for the Central Intelligence Agency for three years, and he considered himself a CIA asset.

Numbers

NUM

Use numerals rather than words for dates, page numbers, street numbers, telephone numbers, measurements, and hours of the day or night when used with A.M. or P.M.

At 2 A.M. on October 4, 2006, Celene completed page 290 of her great American novel.

Use numerals rather than words for numbers of three or more words.

After stacking 349 tangerines on his stomach, Fenton decided to call the *Guinness Book of Records*.

Use numerals rather than words if a sentence contains several numbers, even if some or all of the numbers are small.

> **Incorrect:** The manager told Jerome to order thirty-five reams of paper, forty-eight felt-tip pens, two new computer mousepads, and fifty-five legal pads.

> **Correct:** The manager told Jerome to order 35 reams of paper, 48 felt-tip pens, 2 new computer mousepads, and 55 legal pads.

Use a word rather than a numeral if a sentence begins with a number. This rule applies regardless of the size of the number.

> **Incorrect:** 453 excited participants and 325 well-wishers crowded the hall.

> **Correct:** Four hundred fifty-three excited participants and 325 well-wishers crowded the hall.

PROBLEM-SOLVING
Practice 20

Circle any numbers used incorrectly in the following sentences. Write the correct form in the space to the left.

1. _____ 15 senators addressed the convention and asked those in attendance to vote before five P.M.

2. _____ We test-drove three Hondas, two Accords, and four Fords— I never want to see another car dealership as long as I live.

3. _____ She told the class to turn to page twenty nine and begin to read the essay.

4. _____ Johann resides at twenty four Blanche Street, and he has 2 cats.

5. _____ She is hoping to be tall, at least five feet, eight inches.

Problem-solving for Numbers
Edit the following paragraph to correct any errors you find in number usage.

> White Elephant is a game played during Christmas parties. This game starts with a draw. For example, if there are 8 players, there will be 8 pieces of paper numbered accordingly from one to 8. One of these little pieces of paper is selected at random by each player, with each player holding onto his or her selected number. All players then form a circle and place all wrapped presents brought to the party by each player into the middle of the circle. The game then proceeds with the person who picked number 1. This player number one is given the privilege to pick any of the gifts that are in the middle of the circle. He or she opens the gift so that everyone can see what it is. Then the player who has picked the number 2 has a little advantage because he or she can choose to take the gift that the first player opened or open another gift. The game continues until the last player of White Elephant has the biggest advantage: he or she can choose any of the previously opened gifts.

> —Victoria Castaneda, *student*   ❏

MS

Manuscript Format

Always check with your instructor concerning preferred manuscript format. If your instructor has no special requirements, follow these guidelines:

For handwritten essays, use smooth-edged, lined, white notebook paper and write with blue or black ink only, using appropriate margins.

For typed essays, use good quality 8½-by-11-inch, unlined, white paper. Use a normal, legible font (12-point type if possible), double-space all text, and use approximately 1-inch margins on the top, bottom, and sides of your paper.

For all essays, whether typed or handwritten, indent for paragraphs and write on one side of the paper only. Make sure that your essay has your name, date, class, and the instructor's name in the upper right-hand corner. Unless your instructor has specified a title page, center your title near the top of the first page above the text of your essay. Finally, proofread your paper carefully for any errors. If you need to make one or two last-minute insertions, deletions, or corrections, make them neatly in black or blue ink.

Problem-solving in Essay Editing

Edit the following student essay by discovering and correcting as many "surface errors" as you can—these will include any errors in capitalization, abbreviations, numbers, and manuscript format (refer to pages 467–471 in your handbook for examples).

UNKNOWN TREASURES

Sandra Lee

1 South korea is a mountainous peninsula just South from the northeast corner of china. If one takes a trip to South korea, one can experience the unknown and explore the vast treasures of this country's history and people.

2 Taking a plane trip is the only logical way to get to this country. The price of a round-trip ticket would be about 1481 dollars for adults and 1181 dollars for children ages 8 and younger. The price of tickets may vary each month, so one should be sure to check prices on the Internet. A helpful website called asia travel mart gives quotes for upcoming flights. This site also gives the departure and arrival times.

3 When arriving in korea, one will be tired because of the trip as well as the time difference. Hotel bills can vary, depending upon one's choice in selecting a casual setting or an elegant room. hotel reservations are a must, just as they are

in the U.S. After a good rest, one can go sightseeing. One can visit the famous temples, such as the nakan temple in nakansa. This is a temple that contains some of Korea's finest statues and paintings of battles and great warriors. The temple is surrounded by bonsai trees and small as well as large ponds with lilies, turtles, and frogs. Koreans believe that turtles symbolize long life. There are also National Parks that have many waterfalls and scenic hiking routes. The admission for these parks and temples is free. There are tours that visit temples, parks, dams, and festive areas. These tours range in cost from twenty $ to 40 $ including meals.

4   Besides touring and sightseeing, there are many things to do in Korea without traveling far. There are numerous restaurants that serve wonderful food. *Pojangmachis* are tents set up anywhere the owner feels there will be good business. Customers come in and sit at little tables and pick out what they would like to eat. The foods that are served in *pojangmachis* are traditional finger foods. There are also formal restaurants that serve elegant and delicate food. But for the homesick american traveler, there are also mcdonalds, taco bell, pizza hut, and other western franchises.

5   At night, there are clubs in Korea where people can dance the night away. But for underage people, there are clubs without alcoholic beverages. There are also coffee cafes and tea shops where customers can sit down and enjoy their tea or coffee for as long as they wish. Usually these drinks cost 3 $ per serving.

6   While in South Korea, there are huge malls to visit and early morning outdoor stores in which to shop for bargains. To get the best deals on clothes, shoes, and accessories, learning the technique of bargaining would be useful.

7   After taking a trip to South Korea, one can realize how much he or she has learned about a very different culture. Visiting this beautiful country can be a learning experience as well as a trip one cannot forget.   ○

SOLVING SPELLING PROBLEMS

Spelling Rules

Even though there are exceptions to almost every spelling rule, the following guidelines can help you improve your spelling.

> **Rule 1:** *i* before *e*, except after *c*, or when the combination sounds like *a* in *neighbor* and *weigh.*
>
> ach*ie*ve, fr*ie*nd, f*ie*nd, p*ie*ce, conc*ei*ted, dec*ei*ve, *ei*ght, v*ei*n, w*ei*ght
>
> **Exceptions:** financ*ie*r, soc*ie*ty, spec*ie*s, *ei*ther, l*ei*sure, n*ei*ther, s*ei*ze, w*ei*rd
>
> **Rule 2:** Words that end in *e* keep the *e* if the new ending starts with a consonant.
>
> arrange+ment=arrangement; hope+ful=hopeful; nine+ty=ninety
>
> **Rule 3:** Words that end in *e* drop the *e* if the new ending starts with a vowel.
>
> give+ing=giving; have+ing=having; guide+ance=guidance
>
> **Exceptions:** manageable, serviceable
>
> **Rule 4:** Double the consonants for words that end in a single consonant after a single vowel and have the accent on the last syllable.
>
> begin=beginning; commit=committing; occur=occurring; control=controlling

Words Frequently Misspelled

The following 100 frequently used words are often misspelled by writers. Mastering this list may substantially improve your spelling.

ONE HUNDRED FREQUENTLY MISSPELLED WORDS

academically	behavior	desirable
accessible	beneficial	devise
accidentally	calculation	dilemma
accommodation	catastrophe	discrimination
accompaniment	changeable	dissatisfied
acknowledge	comparative	efficiency
acquaintance	competition	emphasize
adequately	conscientious	endeavor
adolescent	consciousness	enthusiastically
advantageous	controlling	environment
apparent	deceitful	exhibition
attendance	descendant	familiarize

forfeit
fulfill
fundamentally
incidentally
independent
indispensable
inevitable
initiative
institution
interference
license
maintenance
manageable
miniature
misspelled
necessity
noticeable
nuisance
obedience
occasionally
occurrence
opportunity

outrageous
pamphlet
perceive
permanent
permissible
persistent
phenomenon
physician
playwright
politician
privilege
procedure
prove
pursue
quietly
receive
recommendation
reference
rehearsal
relieve
remittance
resources

responsibility
seize
separation
significance
statistics
succeed
suppress
surroundings
symbolic
temperature
tendency
tolerance
tomorrow
tragedy
transparent
universal
unnecessary
variation
vehicle
yield

Using the Wrong Word

The following list contains words that are often confused with each other because they look or sound alike. To use this list effectively, compare the words in the left and right columns, as well as their definitions. Then select the word that best meets your needs.

CHOOSING THE RIGHT WORD

accept = (verb) to receive
except = (preposition) excluding

advice = (noun) suggestion
advise = (verb) to recommend or suggest

affect = (verb) to influence
effect = (noun) result or outcome

already = (adverb) previously
all ready = (adverb) completely ready

brake = (noun) device for stopping
break = (verb) to shatter

conscience = (noun) moral sense
conscious = (adjective) awake, aware

coarse = (adjective) rough, not refined

course = (noun) series of studies; a path

lead = (noun) a heavy metal

lead = (verb) to go first (past tense is *led*)

loose = (adjective) not tight, free

lose = (verb) to suffer loss

passed = (verb) approved, proceeded ahead of

past = (noun) an earlier time; (preposition) having already occurred; beyond

personal = (adjective) private

personnel = (noun) employees

principal = (noun) head of a school; (adjective) important

principle = (noun) a rule or law

quiet = (adjective) still, silent

quite = (adverb) completely, wholly

cite = (verb) to give an example or quote an authority

sight = (noun) ability to see

site = (noun) location

their = (pronoun) belonging to them

there = (adverb) place

they're = (contraction) they are

thorough = (adjective) complete

threw = (verb) past tense of *throw*

through = (preposition) inside

to = (preposition) toward; (infinitive verb form) *to run*

too = (adverb) in addition, very

two = (adjective) a number

whose = (pronoun) belonging to who

who's = (contraction) who is

COMMON PREPOSITIONS

Some of the most common prepositions are listed below:

about	between	on
above	by	onto
across	for	over
along	from	past
among	in	through
at	into	to
before	like	toward
behind	next to	under
beneath	of	with
beside	off	

COMMON SUBORDINATING CONJUNCTIONS

after	because	until
although	before	when
as	if	where
as if	since	while

OTHER IRREGULAR VERBS

Present	Past	Present	Past
become	became	make	made
begin	began	meet	met
bring	brought	pay	paid
buy	bought	put	put
choose	chose	quit	quit
cost	cost	rise	rose
cut	cut	seek	sought
do	did	sell	sold
feel	felt	send	sent
fly	flew	shine	shone
get	got	sing	sang
give	gave	spend	spent
go	went	stand	stood
have	had	steal	stole
hear	heard	swim	swam
keep	kept	take	took
know	knew	teach	taught
lay	laid	tear	tore
lead	led	think	thought
lie	lay	throw	threw
lose	lost	write	wrote

Problem-solving in Essay Editing

Edit the following student essay by discovering and correcting as many "surface errors" as you can. Although this student's essay is perceptive and fairly clear in content, it does have, as do many preliminary drafts, a variety of grammatical, punctuation, word usage, and spelling problems that can be addressed and eliminated if you use your best editing skills.

GEN-X

Dax Mears

1   My generation—how to describe us? We're a group of teenagers we all have different goals and interests in life. All though there are many stereotyped "groups",

no two people are the same. Everyone is unique and special in this Generation X, if others can see past our outer appearance and open themselves up to meeting these one-of-a-kind people. As Forest Gump asserts, "life is like a box of choclates."

2   Myself, I grew up in Indianna until 7th grade. That's when I moved to California. When I moved there I was scared because I saw so many different "groups" I didn't know where to fit in. I quickly learned that there is more to people then the eye can see. For instance, punk rockers, they look like homeless nobodies, but Ive had many punk friends that are geniuses. Another example a group that gets stereotyped based on appearance is the gangsters, they come off as mean and unrelenting, "always looking for a fight kids. I've known gangsters that I have loved as brothers. They are smart and very persistant when it comes to life.

3   I myself fall into the "beach bum alcoholic" group. I admit that I drink occasionally, but underneath that surface there is a lot more to me than the eye can see. In my few years on this earth I have come to accept people regardless of what they look like. I search for what is underneath. Just because I like going to the beach and haning out there with some of the "bro's," I am not a bum.

4   I myself used to stereotype but not any more. I constantly see people on the streets who move over when they see me and my friends walk by. Why? Because of the way I look. There are many negatives about stereotyping. When I had to find a job, it was difficult because people saw me with a shaved head and said, "no way— he can't work for me!" But eventually I found a job working for a guy who saw past my looks and got to know me. Since then, I've been promoted 3 times. Also my generation has been labeled as a bunch of slackers who constantly skip school. Teachers and administrators are right—there are a few Generation X-ers who don't care about their futures, but isn't that true of people of every generation? School because difficult because teachers give up before they even begin, they figure their classes are divided into those who already know the subject and those who doesn't care.

But I proved to myself that I am more than I appear to be, I passed high school with a 2.0 average and now I'm in college and on my way to a bright future.

5   There are some positives to my generation's being stereotyped; we are allowed a lot of space and leeway to mess around we can pull tricks and get caught for child-ish acts but we don't get in trouble because we were expected to screw up. My fa-vorite positive is that I constantly get to prove people wrong. I've had many teachers blow me off and say I'm an "F" student. Then I work my butt off and get a "C" or even a "B" grade their chin hits their chest. This makes me happy because I get to show someone there is personality and wisdom underneath My Gen-X appearance.

6   In closing, my generation may be seen as the shaved-head, baggie-clothes-wearing, druggie generation, but that is completely wrong. This stereotyping is ridiculous, yes, we like to be different, where our clothes baggie, shave our heads and downright party. That doesn't make us bad, the stereotyping of a particular generation has opened my eyes especially when I get older I will accept people for who they are and not for who they appear to be. I just hope that when I go back to my twenty-fifth high school reunion, at least one person will say ya know that Dax kid? I was wrong about him!" ○

SOLVING ESL PROBLEMS

If you were not born in an English-speaking country, you may be having trou-ble with what most native speakers of English take for granted. This could be because English is possessed of a certain lunacy. The following anonymous es-say explores the bizarre nature of the English language:

ENGLISH LUNACY

Let's face it: English is not an easy language. There is no egg in the eggplant, no ham in the hamburger, and neither pine nor apple in the pineapple. English muffins were not invented in England; French fries were not invented in France. We sometimes take English for granted, but if we examine its paradoxes we find that quicksand takes you down slowly, boxing rings are square, and a guinea pig is neither from Guinea nor is it a pig. If writers write, how come fingers don't fing? If the plural of tooth is teeth, shouldn't the plural of phone booth be phone beeth?

If the teacher taught, why didn't the preacher praught? If a vegetarian eats vegetables, what the heck does a humanitarian eat? Why do people recite at a play yet play at a recital? Park on driveways and drive on parkways? How can the weather be as hot as hell on one day and as cold as hell on another? You have to marvel at the unique lunacy of a language where a house can burn up as it burns down and in which you fill in a form by filling it out. A bell is only heard once it goes! English was invented by people, not computers, and it reflects the creativity of the human race (which of course isn't a race at all). That is why when the stars are out, they are visible, but when the lights are out, they are invisible. And why is it that when I wind up my watch, it starts, but when I wind up this essay, it ends? ○

Troubleshooting for ESL Concerns

English must be spoken and written in a way that can be readily understood by listeners as well as readers. The following brief section will be useful for speakers of English as a second language (ESL). As you read, if you are in doubt about any parts of speech or other term referred to, consult the appropriate earlier sections of this handbook.

Articles

There are three *articles* in English: *a*, *an*, and *the*. One of these words will come before all nouns unless what comes directly before a noun is an adjective. You will want to use the article *the* with nouns that refer to specific things. On the other hand, *a* or *an* are used to refer to a generalized item:

> He had his hand on *the* lid of *the* cookie jar.
> (The writer refers to a specific lid of a specific cookie jar.)

> She went to the department store to find *a* cookie jar for her friend.
> (Any cookie jar may do—there is not a particular one in mind.)

Use *an* in place of *a* if it comes before a word beginning with a vowel sound (*a, e, i, o, u*):

> an orange   an egg   an opportunity

Prepositions

Prepositions always begin a prepositional phrase, which is a group of words that includes a preposition and an object. *At, in*, and *on* are the most common prepositions. You can use these three prepositions correctly by memorizing specific uses. Use *at* to show specific time, location, or address. Use *on* to indicate on top of or to indicate a specific day of the week or date. Use *in* to show inclusion within an enclosed area or to indicate a specific time.

> *At* noon the bell rang *in* our classroom and the teacher wrote *on* the board.

> *In* June we arrived *on* time *at* the hotel *in* Canada.

Adjectives

In English, adjectives almost always come before the noun.

> The *concerned* doctor addressed the *young* man wearing a *gray* suit.

Verbs

Present tense verbs show action or a state of being that is happening at the time or that occurs regularly.

John *is washing* the car and Maria *is talking* to him.

Simple past tense verbs show action or a state of being that began and ended in the past.

When the chairman *was presenting* his speech, he *stepped* to the podium.

Future tense verbs show action or a state of being that will or will probably take place.

We *will be visiting* New York City, where *we are going to go* sightseeing with the group.

Present perfect tense shows action or a state of being that occurred over time and is now finished.

The train *has left* the station and Sam *has missed* it again.

Past perfect tense shows action or a state of being occurring in the past before another time in the past.

They *had turned* the corner before they *encountered* the police.

Present progressive tense shows continual action or state of being.

Right now, Fernando *is talking* on the phone.

Past progressive tense shows continual action or state of being that occurred in the past and is now completed.

At the barbecue last night, Jackson *was acting* like a jerk.

Future progressive tense shows continual action or state of being in the general future or at a specific time in the future.

You *will be receiving* your check in the mail some time next week.

Two-part Verbs

The English language uses some verbs that are made up of two words. Some of these are the following:

get along	break down
call up	ask out
clean up	drop in
make up	wake up
help out	play around
leave out	shut up
keep up	put together
give up	pick up

Glossary

abstract subject A subject possessing no physical properties but still existing as an idea, concept, or principle.

academic research Exploration of sources completed formally and according to an accepted format for a collegiate audience. Such research requires the acknowledgment of sources.

active reading Reading in which the reader remains engaged with the text, constantly questioning and responding to the material.

ad hominem A logical fallacy that refers to an attack on specific people associated with an issue; from the Latin phrase meaning "to the man."

alliteration Repetition of consonant or vowel sounds at the beginning of words.

analyze To break each idea in a text down into separate parts in order to consider each part individually.

annotate To mark up, highlight, or take notes in a text.

antonyms Words with opposing meanings.

argument A writing strategy that involves persuading an audience to agree with the writer on a controversial issue.

assonance The use of similar vowel sounds in adjacent or nearby words.

audience The people who read a writer's words on paper or on a computer screen.

autobiographical Having to do with people, places, or events connected to the writer's own life.

begging the question A logical fallacy in which the writer repeats a claim rather than offering any real proof to support it.

beliefs Ideas that are held as true by an individual but can't be proved to others.

blank verse Unrhymed lines of iambic pentameter (unstressed followed by stressed syllables).

body paragraphs Paragraphs that form the middle of the essay and develop the writer's thesis through the use of details, examples, and evidence.

brackets ([ ]) Punctuation marks that permit a writer to insert additional information within a direct quote.

brainstorming A group prewriting activity in which participants call out ideas and comments on a subject while one person records them.

branching A prewriting technique in which the writer takes a subject and breaks it into three or four main areas or subdivisions, using a "tree" with a main trunk for the subject and separate branches for major ideas.

cause/effect A writing strategy that explores why something happens or inquires into the results or consequences of an occurrence.

cause/effect map A prewriting sheet designed for cause/effect essay planning.

character The person or people in the story.

chronological order An arrangement of material based on the time order in which events occur.

circular definition A statement that renames the subject to be defined rather than offering a meaningful explanation.

citing sources (also referred to as **documentation**) The writer's indication in an accepted format that he or she has used words, ideas, or information from a source or sources.

claim An assertion that forms the thesis statement for an essay using argument as a writing strategy.

classification A writing strategy that brings several separate items together under the same category so that distinguishing characteristics can be closely examined.

clustering A prewriting technique for randomly discovering information in a visual rather than a linear way.

comparison A writing strategy that explores the similarities or likenesses between two subjects.

composing process The various stages involved in taking an idea from its beginning to its final written presentation to a reading audience. The composing process includes discovering, drafting, revising, and polishing.

concept map A list of possible subjects for a speech.

concession A clear admission of the opposing side of a writer's argument.

conclusion The closing paragraph or paragraphs at the end of an essay emphasizing the author's thesis, offering closure, and tying the contents of the essay together.

concrete subject A subject possessing physical properties.

connotative meaning The particular emotional associations of a word in the reader's mind.

context The grasp of a word's meaning that results from careful reading of the words, phrases, and sentences directly before and after the word in question.

contrast A writing strategy that explores the differences between two subjects.

controlling idea The writer's opinion about the subject or limitation placed on the subject. Each thesis statement within an essay needs a controlling idea, as does each topic sentence in a paragraph.

coordination Two independent clauses are joined with a comma followed by a coordinating conjunction.

critical thinking The kind of thinking college students engage in when they examine a reading. Critical thinking involves analysis, summary, and evaluation of a text.

crosscutting (film term) A film editing technique. Pieces from two separately shot scenes are intermixed, creating a sequence that moves back and forth between them.

cue words (also called **transitions**) Words or phrases that allow readers to anticipate what is to come in the essay and to move smoothly from one idea to the next.

current evidence Support material from sources that have shared information within the last few years.

definition A statement of the exact nature of a subject, establishing boundaries for what the subject is and is not.

denotative meaning The standard dictionary definition of a word, conveying information in the reader's mind rather than emotional associations.

description A writing strategy that depicts an observable subject with vivid sensory detail.

dialogue Words or sentences spoken by people and set off from the rest of the text by quotation marks or indentation.

direct quote (see **dialogue**) The exact words of a source, without omissions, changes, or additions, and set off from the rest of the text by quotation marks or indentation.

directives Instructive words, usually verbs, that tell what is expected of a student in a timed writing.

discovering (also called **prewriting**) The first stage of the composing process, which involves exploring and gathering ideas and information, and selecting and grouping this material.

division A writing strategy that breaks the subject down into smaller parts and analyzes these parts in relation to the whole.

documentation (see **citing sources**)

draft A rough sketch or early version of an essay.

drafting The second stage of the composing process. The writer gets thoughts on paper in the form of sequenced sentences, paragraphs, and sections.

editing (film term) Transitions between scenes.

ellipsis points (. . .) Punctuation marks within brackets that permit a writer to signal the reader that words have been omitted from a direct quote.

emotional appeals A writer's calls for help from an audience based on persuasive and often emotionally laden word choice.

end-text citations A writer's listing at the end of an essay of the sources he or she has used for ideas or information.

equivocation A logical fallacy in which the writer uses vague or unclear words to mislead the reader.

essay A writing comprising a number of paragraphs that develop and support a single idea, impression, or point.

ethical appeals A writer's calls for support of an opinion or a thesis based on the audience's sense of fairness or moral values.

evaluate To judge the ideas in, and work of, a text.

evaluation portfolio A collection of writing limited to a writer's best writing samples and compiled for the primary purpose of assessment.

evidence Support material for an essay. Evidence may consist of facts, statistics, expert testimony, examples, personal interviews, firsthand experience, or observations.

exemplification A writing strategy in which illustrations are used to develop the main idea.

exposition The basic information the reader or viewer needs at the beginning of a story or film.

extended definition Statements describing the exact nature of a subject and involving many sentences, paragraphs, or an entire essay.

facts Data that are regarded as true rather than controversial.

false dilemma A logical fallacy in which the writer presents only two sides of a complex issue; also referred to as the "either/or fallacy."

final draft The draft of an essay that is shared with the reading audience as a finished piece of writing.

first person A writer's point of view that utilizes the words *I, me, my,* or *us, we, our, ours.*

flashback An interruption in the forward chronological movement of a narrative that returns to some prior time in the sequence of events.

focus A writer's choice of subject and the main point being made about that subject.

follow-up questions Questions that spontaneously arise in an interviewer's mind as a result of the interview subject's answers to an original, predetermined set of questions.

formal outline A list of the main points and subpoints in an essay presented according to certain rules for numbering, lettering, and general format.

frame The borders of the image within which the subject is exposed.

free verse Poetry that relies more on rhythm than on regular meter for its effectiveness.

freewriting Writing on a given topic that proceeds nonstop for a fixed length of time.

future tense A verb tense used to describe actions that have not yet occurred.

hasty generalization A logical fallacy in which the writer jumps to a conclusion without considering all evidence.

illustration A writing strategy that uses examples to support a thesis.

immediate connections Those connections that have occurred recently and that are fairly obvious.

implied topic sentence A topic sentence that only hints at the main idea of a paragraph.

impossibilities Proposals not feasible in the real world and that should be avoided as subjects for argumentative essays.

indexes to periodicals Lists of articles organized by subject and author and available online and in local and college libraries. (The writer can also find indexes to books by subject and author.)

informal outline A rough list of the main points the writer wants to develop in an essay.

in-text citations A writer's indication within the essay that he or she has used words, ideas, or information from a source or sources.

introduction The beginning part of an essay that approaches the subject and captures the interest of the audience.

journal writing Written responses to readings, events, or specific questions in a notebook or binder.

journalists' questions A prewriting technique in which the writer asks a set of standard questions about a subject: *Who? What? When? Where? How? Why?*

listing A prewriting technique in which the writer makes a random list of everything related to a subject.

logical appeals A writer's calls for help based on the audience's sound reasoning and good common sense.

logical fallacies Errors or flaws in reasoning or logical thinking.

logical order An arrangement of material that proceeds in a rational order dictated by the subject. Logical order might be cause/effect or comparison/contrast, for instance.

main point The most important idea in a reading, essay, or any other written work.

manuscript format The layout of a final piece of writing with title, margins, and page numbers. A specific manuscript format may be requested by the instructor.

material The content of a piece of writing, including details, facts, and all supporting evidence.

metaphor A direct comparison of one thing with another.

meter A rhythmic pattern in a poem (created by alternating stressed and unstressed syllables).

microfilm A film on which printed sources are copied in a much smaller size for easier storage.

mood The emotional content of a scene, usually described in terms of feeling.

motif A pattern of identical or similar images recurring throughout a work of literature or film.

narration A writing strategy that involves recounting an event or series of events, usually in chronological order, with close attention to specific details related to the place and people connected to the event.

obituary A description of a deceased person's life and accomplishments, usually published in a newspaper.

objective Having to do with facts rather than feelings or impressions about a subject.

off-topic A situation that occurs when a writer's supporting details no longer clearly relate to the thesis of the essay or the topic sentence of the paragraph.

opinions Issues of public concern about which a person feels strongly.

oversimplification Attributing only one cause or one effect to a situation.

paragraph Several sentences that together develop one thought or main point.

parallel sentence structures Similar sentence structures that are repeated for dramatic effect.

paraphrase A piece of information taken from a source and then put in the writer's own words.

parenthetical citations (see **in-text citations**)

passive voice A voice in writing in which the subject does not perform any action but is acted on by an outside agent.

past tense A verb tense used to describe actions that have already occurred.

peer editing (also called **peer response**) Sharing a draft with another class member or members who provide feedback on the draft.

personal interview A prearranged meeting with a person in which particular questions are asked in order to gather information for a writing assignment.

personification Giving nonhuman things human characteristics or attitudes.

plagiarism The act of stealing someone's words, ideas, or facts without crediting the source.

plan of development In some thesis statements, a group of words that breaks the subject into separate parts.

planning file A file on computer or in a notebook in which a writer records and saves plans for a particular essay or writing assignment.

plot An arrangement in a certain order of events or episodes that occur in a story or film.

point of view The writer's attitude about the subject under consideration.

points The ideas to be discussed equally for each of the two subjects in a comparison/contrast essay.

polishing The fourth and last stage of the composing process. The writer refines language for effect, proofreads for correctness, and checks for correct manuscript format.

portfolio A collection of writing in a folder, notebook, or binder.

post hoc fallacy A false assumption that just because one event precedes another, the first event caused the second event to happen. From the Latin phrase *post hoc, ergo propter hoc,* which means "after this, therefore because of this."

preface An introduction or statement that briefly reveals the plan or purpose of a longer work.

preferences Personal likes and dislikes shaped not by reason, but by background and emotions.

preliminary draft The first draft of an essay.

premise A specific piece of evidence, often used to begin an argumentative essay.

present tense A verb tense used to describe actions that are currently occurring.

preview To examine the chapter headings, background information on the author, and title, length, and complexity of the text.

prewriting (see **discovering**)

private writing Writing that is for the writer's eyes only and not meant to be shared with a reading audience. Examples of private writing include journals, diaries, and personal notes.

process A writing strategy that explains how to do something or how something works.

process portfolio A collection of writing that may include essays, essay drafts, in-class writings, journal writings, and possibly poems and short stories.

proofread To read over and make corrections before presenting a piece of writing to its intended audience.

public writing Writing meant to be read by a specific audience. Examples of public writing include college essays, memos, reports, business letters, and résumés.

purpose A writer's primary goal in writing—to express, inform, or persuade the reader.

range The extent of the subject or the boundaries placed on the subject.

reading log A type of journal in which the writer sets up two columns on each page: the left column contains important direct quotations from the text, along with their page numbers; the right column contains the writer's personal reactions to these quotations.

recursive Capable of being returned to and repeated, as is the case for all the stages of the composing process.

reliable evidence Support material that comes from qualified sources.

remote connections Those connections that are not obvious or that might have come about much earlier.

research To delve into a subject further by going beyond what the writer already knows to explore various sources.

responding An important and recurring part of the composing process; involves reacting to, and interacting with, a writer's draft, either as a shared or as an individual activity.

revising The third stage of the composing process. The writer reflects on a draft and re-sees it to examine the effectiveness of the whole paper in terms of the ideas presented and the ordering of those ideas.

rhyme Words on adjacent lines of poetry that sound the same or almost the same.

rhythm The regular repetition of stressed syllables.

scratch outline A brief, quickly written outline of main points; can be useful in preparing for a timed writing.

second person A writer's point of view that utilizes the words *you, your,* and *yours.*

sensory detail Specific fine points related to the senses.

service learning A kind of participation in community service that includes public writing.

setting The time and place in which the story occurs.

shot A continuously exposed and unedited image made up of a number of frames.

simile A direct comparison of one thing with another using *like* or *as.*

simple definition A brief statement describing the exact nature of a subject in one or two sentences.

spatial order An arrangement of material proceeding left to right, top to bottom, front to back, and so forth.

speaker Person or object that appears to be speaking in a poem.

specific language Words or groups of words that paint a strong, clear, precise picture for the reader.

stanza A part of a poem separated from the next part by extra spacing.

stereotypes Preconceived notions that place someone or something into a group.

structure A writer's arrangement of the material to support the main point clearly and completely.

style The way a writer puts words together to form sentences and then groups of sentences to form longer passages; the grammatical correctness of a piece of writing; the proper appearance of a finished piece of writing as far as acceptable format.

subject The topic on which the writer focuses.

subjective Stressing feelings and impressions rather than factual information about a subject.

subordination A complex sentence is formed by joining two independent clauses with a subordinating conjunction that makes one clause dependent on the other.

subplot A minor complication that relates to the main plot but is not the main focus of the film or work of literature.

summary A statement of the main points of a text, written in the writer's own words.

symbol Something that suggests or stands for an idea, quality, or concept.

synonyms Words with similar meaning.

theme The central or main idea conveyed by the story.

thesaurus A book that contains an alphabetical list of words along with their synomyms and antonyms.

thesis A statement, usually a sentence, that contains the main point, idea, or opinion the writer wants to convey about a subject along with his or her attitude toward the subject.

third person A writer's point of view that utilizes the words *he, him, his; she, her, hers;* or *they, their, theirs.*

tone The writer's attitude; proper tone would be an attitude appropriate for the subject and audience.

topic sentence The sentence that states the overall idea or point the writer is trying to make in a paragraph.

transitions (see **cue words**)

truisms Statements that, while true, are overly obvious or general.

types Kinds or groups.

unabridged dictionary A book that contains thousands of alphabetically listed words along with their part of speech, definition, origin, and history of usage.

unifying principle A basis for breaking down and sorting a subject in a division/classification essay development.

voice The writer's personality and the way this personality is communicated in a piece of writing.

working draft A draft that is in progress.

writer/audience response A part of the composing process in which the writer's work is shared with one or more people who react to the work, offering feedback for the writer to evaluate.

Credits

American Psychological Association Online. "Single Parenting and Today's Family" from **http://www.apahelpcenter.org/articles/article.php?id=16/**. Copyright © 2004 by the American Psychological Association. Reprinted by permission.

Anson, Chris and Robert A. Schwegler. Illustration based on "Know Your Audience and Purpose" from *The Longman Handbook* by Chris Anson and Robert A. Schwegler. (Longman, 2003). Reprinted by permission of Pearson Education, Inc.

Ashe, Arthur. "A Black Athlete Looks at Education" by Arthur Ashe from the *New York Times*, February 6, 1977. Copyright © 1977 Arthur Ashe Inc. licensed by CMG Worldwide, **http://www.CMGWorldwide.com**.

Brown, Margaret R. "Whose Eyes Are These, Whose Nose?" by Margaret R. Brown from *Newsweek*, March 7, 1994. Copyright © 1994 Newsweek, Inc. All rights reserved. Reprinted by permission.

Carson, Ed. Excerpt from "Purging Bingeing" by Ed Carson from the December 1995 issue of *Reason* Magazine. Copyright © 1995, Reason Foundation, **http://www.reason.com**. Reprinted with permission.

Chiat, Jay. "Illusions Are Forever" by Jay Chiat from *Forbes ASAP*, October 2, 2000. Reprinted by permission of *Forbes ASAP Magazine*. Copyright © 2005 Forbes Inc.

Cowan, Elizabeth and Annie Dillard. Excerpt from an interview with Annie Dillard in *Readings for Writing* by Elizabeth Cowan (Scott Foresman and Company, 1983). Used by permission of Elizabeth Harper Neeld, Ph.D., **http://www.elizabethharperneeld.com**.

Cruickshank, Douglas. "Crazy for Dysfunction" by Douglas Cruickshank first appeared in Salon.com, May 3, 2002, at **http://www.Salon.com**. An online version remains in the Salon.com archives. Reprinted with permission.

Daum, Meghan. "We're Lying: Safe Sex and White Lies in the Time of AIDS" by Meghan Daum. Copyright © 1995 by Meghan Daum. Reprinted by permission of International Creative Management, Inc.

Davenport, Guy. From *The Geography of the Imagination* by Guy Davenport. Reprinted by permission of David. R. Godine, Publisher, Inc. Copyright © 1981 by Guy Davenport.

Ehrenreich, Barbara. "Zipped Lips" by Barbara Ehrenreich, *Time*, February 5, 1996. Copyright © 1996 Time Inc. Reprinted by permission.

Goldberg, Natalie. "A List of Topics for Writing Practice" from *Writing Down the Bones* by Natalie Goldberg, © 1986. Reprinted by arrangement with Shambhala Publications, Inc., Boston, **http://www.shambhala.com**

Heilbroner, Robert. From "Don't Let Stereotypes Warp Your Judgments" by Robert Heilbroner from *Reader's Digest*, January 1962, originally appeared in *Think*, June 1961. Reprint courtesy of International Business Machines Corporation. Copyright 1961, © International Business Machines Corporation.

Hoagland, Edward. "Stuttering Time" from *The Tugman's Passage* by Edward Hoagland. Published by The Lyons Press. Copyright © 1979, 1982, 1995 by Edward Hoagland. Reprinted by permission of Lescher & Lescher, Ltd. All rights reserved.

Humphry, Derek. "Offering Euthanasia Can Be an Act of Love" from *Dying with Dignity: Understanding Euthanasia* by Derek Humphry.

Johnson, Beth. Excerpt from "Our Drug Problem" by Beth Johnson. Reprinted by permission of the author.

King, Jr., Martin Luther. From "Letter from Birmingham Jail – April 16, 1963" by Martin Luther King, Jr. Copyright © 1963 Martin Luther King, Jr., renewed 1991 Coretta Scott King. Reprinted by arrangement with the Estate of Martin Luther King, Jr., c/o Writers House as agent for the proprietor, New York, NY.

Kwon, Im Jung. "Facing Down Abusers" by Im Jung Kwon from *Newsweek*, August 10, 1998. Copyright © 1998 Newsweek Inc. All rights reserved. Reprinted by permission.

Lee, Chang-rae. From "Mute in an English-Only World" by Chang-rae Lee from the *New York Times*, April 18, 1996. Copyright © 1996, The New York Times. Reprinted by permission.

Leovy, Jill. "The Path of Books and Bootstraps" by Jill Leovy from *Los Angeles Times*, June 25, 1999. Copyright © 1999 by the Los Angeles Times. Reprinted with permission.

Morrison, Toni. Excerpt from "A Slow Walk of Trees" by Toni Morrison, originally published in the *New York Times*, July 4, 1976. Copyright © 1976 by Toni Morrison. Reprinted by permission of International Creative Management, Inc.

Mueller, Lisel. "Monet Refuses the Operation" from *Alive Together*. Reprinted by permission of Louisiana State

University Press from *Alive Together: New and Selected Poems* by Lisel Mueller. Copyright © 1996 by Lisel Mueller.

Naylor, Gloria. "The Meanings of a Word," originally titled "Mommy, What Does 'Nigger' Mean? A Question of Language" by Gloria Naylor from *The New York Times Magazine*, February 20, 1986. Copyright © 1986 by Gloria Naylor. Reprinted by permission of SLL/Sterling Lord Literistic, Inc.

Nizer, Louis. From "How About Low-Cost Drugs for Addicts?" by Louis Nizer, the *New York Times*, June 8, 1996. Copyright © 1996, The New York Times. Reprinted by permission.

Oates, Joyce Carol. "To Invigorate the Literary Mind, Start Moving Literary Feet" by Joyce Carol Oates. Copyright © 1999, Ontario Review. Reprinted by permission of John Hawkins & Associates, Inc.

O'Connor, Patricia T. and Stewart Kellerman. "Welcome to the E-mail Combat Zone" by Patricia T. O'Connor and Stewart Kellerman, *The New York Times Magazine*, August 11, 2002. Copyright © 2002, The New York Times. Reprinted by permission.

Orwell, George. "A Hanging" from *Shooting an Elephant and Other Essays* by George Orwell. Copyright © by George Orwell 1950. Renewed 1978 by Sonia Pitt-Rivers. Reprinted by permission of Harcourt, Inc., and Bill Hamilton as the Literary Executor of the Estate of the late Sonia Brownell Orwell and Secker & Warburg Ltd.

Randall, Kay. "Generation 9/11" from the University of Texas at Austin website **http://www.utexas.edu/ features.2005/generation**. Reprinted by permission.

Rodriguez, Richard. "The Salsa Zone" by Richard Rodriguez. Copyright © by Richard Rodriguez. Reprinted by permission of George Borchardt, Inc., on behalf of the author.

Russell, Bertrand. "What I Have Lived For" from *Autobiography of Bertrand Russell* by Bertrand Russell. Copyright © 1967 The Bertrand Russell Peace Foundation Ltd. Reproduced by permission of Taylor & Francis Books UK.

Sundeen, Mark. *Car Camping: The Book of Desert Adventures.* New York, NY: HarperCollins, 2000.

Watson, Larry. Excerpt from *Montana, 1948* by Larry Watson (Minneapolis: Milkweed Editions, 1993). Copyright © 1993 by Larry Watson. Reprinted by permission of Milkweed Editions.

Webster's New World Dictionary. Definition of "rose" from *Agnes/Webster's New World® College Dictionary, Third Edition*, 1996. Reprinted with permission of John Wiley & Sons, Inc.

Williams, Bryan and Sharon Knight. From *Healthy for Life: Wellness and the Art of Living*, first edition, by Williams/Knight, 1994. Reprinted with permission of Brooks/Cole, a division of Thomson Learning: **http://www.thomsonrights.com**, fax 800-730-2215.

Yolen, Jane. "Grant Wood: American Gothic" Copyright © 2001 by Jane Yolen. First appeared in *Heart to Heart*, published by Harry N. Abrams, Inc. Reprinted by permission of Curtis Brown, Ltd.

Zevin, Dan. "Roomatism" from *Rolling Stone*, October 20, 1994. Copyright © Rolling Stone LLC 1994. All rights reserved. Reprinted by permission.

Photo Credits

Page 1:	no credit necessary
Page 161:	©Susan Van Etten/PhotoEdit
Page 183:	no credit necessary
Page 299:	©Advertising Archives, UK
Page 305:	©Steven Hunt/Getty Images
Page 318:	Londres, le Parlement; reflets sur la Tamise, 1899–1901, by Monet ©Erich Lessing/Art Resource
Page 333:	©Shaffer-Smith/Index Stock Imagery
Page 337:	©Reuters/Corbis
Page 401:	©The New Yorker Collection, 1998, Marisa Acocella from cartoonbank.com. All rights reserved.
Page 403:	©Jaqui Hurst/Alamy

Index